A Guide to Con...
1993 Edition

A Guide to Company Giving
1993 Edition

Edited by
Michael Eastwood

Compiled by
David Casson
Paul Brown

Additional research by
Daren Felgate

Statistical information supplied by
Extel Financial Ltd

With contributions from:
David Hemsworth, Action Resource Centre
Jerry Marston, Allied Dunbar Assurance plc
The Charities Aid Foundation
Community Links
Keith Bantick, Promotional Campaigns Ltd

A Directory of Social Change publication

A Guide to Company Giving
1993 Edition

Edited by Michael Eastwood

Copyright © 1992 The Directory of Social Change

No part of this book may be stored in a retrieval system or reproduced in any form whatsoever without prior permission in writing from the publisher. The Directory of Social Change is a registered charity.

5th edition. First published 1984.

The Directory of Social Change, Radius Works, Back Lane, London NW3 1HL from whom copies may be obtained.

ISBN 0 907164 96 X

British Library Cataloguing in Publication Data

A catalogue record for this book is available from the British Library.

Printed and bound in Britain by Page Brothers.

Contents

Warning to all readers	6
Introduction	7
Facts and figures	9
Tax and company giving	13
How to make an appeal	18
The top 300 corporate donors	23
Alphabetical listing of companies	**28**
Radio stations	**221**
Per cent giving and the Per Cent Club	246
Company trusts	250
Secondment of staff	252
Employee volunteering	254
Sponsorship	256
Arts sponsorship	260
Member companies of the Association for Business Sponsorship of the Arts	262
Social sponsorship	264
Joint promotions	268
Business in the community	270
Member companies of Business in the Community and Scottish Business in the Community	272
Local enterprise agencies: list of locations	275
Payroll giving	276
Useful contacts	280
Useful publications	284

Warning to all readers

Fictitious entry

The 1993 edition of *A Guide to Company Giving* includes, for the first time, an **entirely fictitious entry**. The address given in this bogus entry is of an existing limited company. All other details (ie. company activity, officers, financial information and donations policy) are fictional.

We have included this entry for monitoring purposes. Many companies have complained to us that despite clearly stated preferences in their donations policy (such as "Support is given only to local charities in areas where the company operates"), the company still is inundated with ill-conceived and wholly inappropriate applications. As a result, the company is often reluctant to give information for this Guide.

We are aware that many of these inappropriate applications are from sources other than this Guide. We are equally aware that the vast majority of the users of this Guide only send letters with a realistic chance of success. However, we do need to establish how many inappropriate applications a typical company will receive. A bogus entry is the most effective way of achieving this.

We are sorry for any inconvenience this will cause to those using this Guide properly. Our concern is to root out those who send circular mailshots indiscriminately to a large number of companies, which serves only to bring their own charity - and voluntary organisations in general - into disrepute.

The fictitious company will reply to all letters received. Therefore, one letter or one telephone call should be the only inconvenience to groups using this Guide properly. We trust that you will understand our reasons.

Basic don'ts when writing to companies

Don't write indiscriminate "Dear Sir/Madam" circular letters to any company you come across. They are always unsuccessful and waste both the charity's and the company's valuable time and money.

Don't use this Guide as a simple mailing list. Select carefully those companies most likely to want to support you.

Don't write to a company which specifically says it does not support your kind of work or your client group.

Don't write to a company unless **at least one of the following applies:**

(a) The company has a declared policy indicating a specific interest in your charity's area of work.

(b) The company operates in the same geographical area as your charity.

(c) You have a strong personal link with a senior officer in the company.

(d) A member of the company's staff is actively involved in your charity.

(e) There is a clear product link between your need and the company's supplies (even here there should usually be a close geographical link).

(f) There is some other good reason to write to that particular company. The fact that the company makes a profit and your charity needs money is not a sufficiently strong link.

Do read carefully the article "How to make an appeal" on page 18 of this Guide.

Introduction

This is the fifth edition of **A Guide to Company Giving**. Whereas previous editions have given information on the top 1,300 donors, this edition describes the charitable activities of the top 1,430 companies by turnover and/or charitable donation. We have therefore deleted over 200 of the smaller companies in 1991 Edition. We believe this gives a clearer picture of the current state of corporate philanthropy in Britain, not least because some members of the Times 1,000 give little or nothing to charity.

A consequence of publishing information on and contacts for company giving is that, inevitably, companies receive many more unsolicited appeals. Marks & Spencer receive over 20,000 letters a year and 25,000 phone calls requesting advice, information and support. They give about 1,500 cash donations. Similarly, Kelloggs receive over 3,000 appeals a year; they support about 400. Howard Hurd, from the Department of Geography at Southampton University, recently surveyed the policy and motivations for charitable giving by 43 of the top 300 corporate donors. He concluded that most of these companies gave between 200 and 600 grants a year (although the actual range was under 40 to over 3,500). Clearly, the vast majority of applications to companies are unsuccessful.

The volume of appeals received can become an administrative nightmare for a company that wants to support charities, but which has limited funds and even less time to consider applications. Indeed, we have been concerned about the number of companies who have complained vehemently about being deluged by inappropriate applications and have consequently insisted that their company name be deleted from the Guide. In almost all cases we have refused this request. Most of the companies concerned had no donations policy in the previous edition so charities in one sense had no publicly stated reason not to write to them. We have particularly encouraged these companies and others which give over £15,000 a year to describe in reasonable detail the kinds of help they prefer to give and the organisations they exclude from support. We have always argued that charities respect such policies.

However, for monitoring purposes we have also included for the first time a completely fictitious entry. We are aware that many of these inappropriate applications are from sources other than this Guide and that the vast majority of the users of this Guide only send letters with a realistic chance of success. However, we do need to establish how many inappropriate applications a typical company will receive. A bogus entry is the most effective way of achieving this. The fictitious company will reply to all letters received so one letter or one telephone call should be the only inconvenience to groups using this Guide properly. We are sorry for any inconvenience but trust that you will understand our reasons.

This book covers the top 1,430 companies in Britain. We give a contact for each company, checked by questionnaire and telephone, who as at August 1992 was the appropriate person to send charity appeals to. We have also tried to establish what the company prefers to support, what it definitely will not support, whether it prefers to give to local or national causes, or charities in which a member of staff is involved. This, together with the information on the basic business of the company, should be sufficient detail on all but the largest companies to enable charities to decide whether or not they can make a relevant application. The top 400 corporate donors are covered in more detail in the companion **The Major Companies Guide**.

For some companies it is effectively impossible to obtain useful information about their giving. One company, with a turnover in 1990/91 of £1,177,000,000 and a pre-tax profit of £31,873,000 said simply: "The company has no budget for charitable donations at present". Another smaller company's policy is: "To give £25-£50 to any requests received with no particular preferences or exclusions".

Since the last edition of the Guide, there seems to have been a movement away from cash giving to other forms of support (eg. advice and expertise). The employee volunteering initiative is one such example. Indeed, one major corporate donor wrote to say that "Your title of 'Company Giving' is at odds with current trends towards mutual concepts of business-community partnerships, social investment and mutual benefit". Similarly, Jeremy Lunn of the Per Cent Club recently pointed out that the Club is encouraging such long-term involvement, especially in providing expertise, and actual cash donations are likely to form a declining proportion of companies' community involvement. "This decade has seen a tremendous growth in management and employee involvement, and, if anything, this trend will accelerate over the next decade. The value of a company's total contribution can be anything up to ten times the value of reported donations." It will be interesting to see whether more companies declare a separate community contributions

Introduction

figure (in addition to the legally required charitable donations figure) as a consequence.

It is pleasing to report once again the increased openness on the part of many companies. We now have donations policies for over 75% of the companies in the Guide (this includes over 300 companies included for the first time). In the introduction to the 1991 Edition, for which about 55% of companies gave a donations policy, we wrote: "Some companies are still reluctant to disclose anything but the minimum reporting requirements of the Companies Act, and show only the total they give to charity. They feel that any information will inevitably lead to more applications and to more disappointment. These companies are in a minority however. We believe their fears are unfounded, that it is the lack of clear information about what the company will and will not consider that leads to so many applications being made. If charities have no reason not to apply, and they need money urgently for their work, most will decide at least to have a try. We hope that by the time of the next edition, all the larger companies and most of the others we include will feel they can disclose what they are doing." We are well on the way to achieving this.

We have also included for the first time a section on BBC and Independent radio stations. (Television companies are included in the main alphabetical listing.) Some stations give cash donations to charity, either from their own resources or through an associated charitable trust. More commonly they are immensely valuable opportunities for publicising charity events and activities, for campaigning and for fundraising over the airwaves. The variety of activities and opportunities is impressive, ranging from BBC Radio Cumbria's lamb bank to Capital Radio's massive Help a London Child.

We would like to thank all the companies who have helped compile this Guide. Although drafts of all the entries were sent to the companies concerned and corrections noted and incorporated, the text, and any mistakes within it, remains ours rather than theirs.

Indeed, although the research for this book has been done as fully and carefully as we are able, we may have missed out some important givers. Certainly, some of the information is incomplete or will become out-of-date, especially contacts for charitable donations and where companies merge or are taken over. We regret such imperfections. If any reader comes across omissions or mistakes in this Guide, please let us know so that future editions can rectify them. A telephone call to the Research Department of the Directory of Social Change Northern Office (051-708 0149) is all that is needed.

Finally, there is a tendency to get company giving somewhat out of proportion. Simply because a company makes large profits does not mean to say that it will be a large giver. For example, one supermarket chain had a turnover of £1,785,000,000 and pre-tax profits of £102,000,000 in 1990/91; charitable donations for the year totalled £63,000 or 0.06% of pre-tax profits. Company donations to charity represent probably no more than 5% of the total fundraised income of the voluntary sector (this includes central and local government grants, money given by the public and grant-making trusts). Indeed, the general public probably give about 10 times as much to charity as companies. However, companies are still an important source of money and help for charities. We hope that the information in this Guide will once again spawn some exciting partnerships between industry and the voluntary sector.

Facts and figures

How much do companies give?

In theory it should be an easy task to work out how much companies give to charity. If a company gives £200 or more in any one year in charitable or political contributions it is legally required to disclose the total of such donations in its annual report and accounts. The information is usually found in the Directors' Report within the company's annual report.

However, there are over 1.1 million companies registered in the UK. It is certainly beyond the scope of the Directory of Social Change to survey all these companies. Furthermore, not all declare donations figures as required; surprisingly this includes some members of the Per Cent Club.

However, this Guide includes all the major companies in Britain by turnover and/or charitable donations. Unless there are glaring omissions in our research, we believe that we have covered all the actual and potential large-scale donors.

The continued growth in company giving

In the 1991 Edition of this Guide, we covered 1,355 companies giving charitable donations totalling £134 million, a marked increase (over 50%) from the 1989 Edition. This edition covers about 1,430 companies whose charitable donations total £169 million. This represents a real terms increase in donations of about 15% since 1990.

There is a temptation to attribute this growth to the increased coverage of the book. However, it is due mainly to the increased donations of the major givers.

On page 23 we list the top 300 corporate donors. Their donations total £151 million or 89% of the donations in this Guide. They also give 97% of the declared community contributions. In the 1991 Edition, the top 300 companies gave a total of £115 million. This represents a real terms increase of 19%. Put another way, the average donation of the top 300 companies has risen from £383,000 to £503,000 per company.

The total amount given

Many companies argue that the charitable donations figure does not reflect the real value of the company's support for charity. Companies such as Barclays and National Westminster Bank give a community contributions figure as well as a charitable donations figure to bridge this gap. In their cases, the difference is substantial (£2 million donations and £9 million community contributions for Barclays, and £2.3 million donations and £11.8 million contributions for Nat West). However,

Top 25 by community contribution

		This edition (1991-92)	Last time (1989-90)
1	British Telecommunications (1)	£14,500,000	£12,000,000
2	British Petroleum (4)	£14,100,000	£9,000,000
3	National Westminster Bank (2)	£11,746,907	£11,348,000
4	British Gas (5)	£10,000,000	£6,000,000
5	Barclays (3)	£9,000,000	£10,000,000
6	Glaxo Holdings (7)	£8,000,000	£4,734,000
7	Shell UK (6)	£6,352,000	£5,975,000
8	Grand Metropolitan (-)	£6,000,000	£1,386,450
9	TSB Group (15)	£5,519,000	£3,500,000
10	Marks & Spencer (9)	£5,500,000	£4,630,000
11	Heron International (19)	£5,329,475	£2,230,000
12	Imperial Chemical Industries (13)	£5,200,000	£3,600,000
13	Unilever (-)	£5,000,000	n/a
14	Lloyds Bank (12)	£4,950,000	£3,687,000
15	Tesco (10)	£4,600,000	£4,600,000
16	Barings (18)	£4,202,000	£2,391,000
17	Thorn EMI (-)	£4,000,000	n/a
18	Cadbury Schweppes (-)	£3,714,000	n/a
19	Midland Group (8)	£3,416,000	£4,631,000
20	Esso UK (14)	£3,200,000	£3,500,000
21	IBM (11)	£3,191,000	£4,100,000
22	Digital (-)	£2,800,000	n/a
23	BAT Industries (16)	£2,700,000	£3,200,000
24	Guinness (-)	£2,662,000	n/a
25	RTZ (21)	£2,542,000	£1,900,000

Note: This list only includes those companies which declare a community contributions figure. The figures for Barings, BAT Industries, Digital, Guinness and Heron International are the declared donations figures only as no separate figure for community contributions was available. Heron International, Barings and TSB give mainly to the Ronson, Baring and TSB Foundations respectively. Particularly the first two foundations operate largely independently of the company (see *A Guide to the Major Trusts*). The comparable figure for our last compilation is also given. Most of these comparisons are over a two-year period. The number in brackets is the company's position in the same table in the 1991 Edition.

Facts and figures

fewer than 100 companies gave us a separate community contributions figure. Those that did not include over two thirds of the Per Cent Club.

The total community contributions declared are £98 million, of which the top 300 companies give £94.5 million. It is impossible to compare community contributions with the 1991 Edition because fewer companies declared them last time.

Community contributions usually includes some or all of the following: non-commercial sponsorship (mainly of the arts and charity events); secondment of company staff to charities; provision of professional services to charities; support for enterprise agencies; non-commercial advertising in charity brochures, annual reports etc.; provision of facilities; loans; administration costs of the donations programme, and gifts in kind. The Per Cent Club's *Reporting Community Involvement*, published in 1991, is a very welcome move to standardise this kind of reporting and we recommend **all** companies to follow its guidelines.

We can no longer estimate the value of the different kinds of community contributions. These are the only figures we have obtained: £57 million in arts sponsorship in 1990/91, of which £14.7 million was corporate membership of arts organisations (ABSA); £25 million in secondments in salary terms (ARC); £12 million in sponsorship of education, environment and other non-arts voluntary organisations in 1991 (Mintel).

There are over 1 million UK companies **not** included in this guide. We have included the largest companies by turnover (the total turnover for the companies in this Guide is over £800 billion) and charitable donations. Of these, over 200 either do not give to charities or do not publish a donations figure, although we know that some are large-scale donors. Over 90% of the giving is done by the 300 largest givers (the mass of small-scale, informal giving to charity by local companies is beyond the scope of this Guide).

The charitable donations and community contributions in this Guide total £267 million. From the figures we obtained, a company's average community contributions figure is 1.65 times higher than its charitable donations figure. If we add an average donations figure (£137,000) for the 200 companies who do not have one and multiply this new total (£196 million) by 1.65, it may be that the actual value of all forms of support of all the companies in the Guide could be as high as £324 million. It will be interesting to see whether, as a result of the Per Cent Club's guidelines, the difference between donations and contributions increases.

Donations as a percentage of profit

A final word on general statistics. In previous editions of this Guide (and its companion **The Major Companies Guide**) we analysed how much the top 400 companies give as a proportion of their pre-tax profits. Until 1990/91, this had always been at or about 0.2% of pre-tax profits. In the 1991 Edition of The Major Companies Guide, we noted that it had risen to 0.25% of pre-tax profits. The average for the 1,200 companies in this Guide who gave us a donations figure is 0.26%, seemingly a much higher figure than previously, but so much depends on the size of the fall of total profits during the current recession. Companies seem generally to have maintained or increased their level of donations despite falling profits. This makes donations appear as a higher proportion of profits. It is unlikely that this high proportion would be retained when profits grow again. Therefore, we have concentrated on the growth of gross charitable donations for the basis of our assertion that total company donations have so far more than survived the ravages of the current economic recession.

Volatility in company giving

On an individual level, company giving is still fairly volatile. 201 companies in the book have increased their donations by 100% or more since the previous edition. We have listed those now giving £50,000 or more. Interestingly, 12 of the 95 companies listed appeared in the equivalent list in the previous edition, so their donations pattern has been one of steady increase. For example, British Coal's donations have risen from £25,000 in 1987 to £82,000 in 1989 to £268,000 in 1991. Marc Rich's donations have risen from £12,000 in 1986 to £80,000 in 1988 to £170,000 in 1991.

Top 25 by charitable donation

		This edition (1991-92)	Last time (1989-90)
1	British Petroleum (1)	£8,500,000	£5,300,000
2	British Telecom (5)	£5,500,000	£2,980,000
3	Heron International (9)	£5,329,475	£2,230,000
4	Barings (8)	£4,202,000	£2,391,000
5	Grand Metropolitan (-)	£4,036,000	£867,000
6	Glaxo Holdings (6)	£3,700,000	£2,848,000
7	Marks & Spencer (3)	£3,425,000	£3,288,000
8	TSB Group (2)	£3,352,000	£3,383,712
9	Imperial Chemical Industries (7)	£3,200,000	£2,700,000
10	Unilever (21)	£3,000,000	£1,000,000
11	BAT Industries (4)	£2,700,000	£3,200,000
12	Guinness (-)	£2,662,000	£813,000
13	National Westminster Bank (12)	£2,328,205	£1,675,175
14	Allied Dunbar (-)	£2,100,000	£1,300,000
15	Shell UK (11)	£2,090,000	£1,769,000
16	IBM (15)	£2,048,000	£1,600,000
17	Barclays (10)	£2,000,000	£2,085,000
18	News International (-)	£1,972,092	£484,337
19	British Gas (14)	£1,900,000	£1,616,000
20	Esso UK (13)	£1,583,748	£1,636,000
21	Seagram Distillers (16)	£1,483,000	£1,416,000
22	BOC Group (-)	£1,450,000	n/a
23	J Sainsbury (23)	£1,400,000	£900,000
24	British Aerospace (-)	£1,310,000	£514,000
25	SmithKline Beecham (-)	£1,247,000	£700,000

Note: These figures only include the statutorily declared figure for charitable donations. As discussed in the text, this greatly understates community contributions, particularly for the largest companies. The comparable figure for our last compilation is also given. Most of these comparisons are over a two-year period. The number in brackets is the company's position in the same table in the 1991 Edition.

Facts and figures

Conversely, other companies' donations have fluctuated violently. Of the 32 companies who were previously giving over £50,000 but whose donations have since at least halved, 11 were in the previous edition as companies who had at least doubled their giving. For example, Gestetner Holdings gave £15,000 in 1987, £101,000 in 1989 and £2,000 in 1991. On a larger scale, Pilkingtons gave £195,000 in 1988, £781,000 in 1989 and £281,000 in 1992. This may reflect economic realities; it may be that they consciously gave substantial support to a special appeal for one year before reverting to their previous levels of giving; it may be due to a PR problem etc.. It certainly warns readers not to assume that a company will automatically maintain or steadily increase its level of donations.

Constancy of the major givers

Notwithstanding the above, it is striking that 18 of the top 20 community contributors in the 1991 Edition feature in the table for the top 25 contributors this time. Of those who have dropped out of the top 25, Reed International have increased their community contributions, but not by enough to remain in the table; Royal Bank of Scotland and the Prudential Corporation are giving about £1.5 million each; General Electric and Hanson Corporation did not give a separate community contributions figure but both give over £750,000 in donations, and British Rail did not give us a figure at all.

Similarly, the top 16 by charitable donations last time all reappear in this edition's top 25 donors. Of the seven companies who have dropped out, Lloyds Bank, the Post Office Group and United Newspapers have all increased their giving at least by the rate of inflation; Hanson and General Electric are mentioned above; Whitbread has

---

Companies *increasing* their declared charitable donations by around 100% or more

201 companies in this book have increased their giving by 100% or more since the previous edition. This list features only those who are now giving £50,000 or more.

Company	Previous figure	Latest figure	Company	Previous figure	Latest figure
Abbey National	194,000 (Dec 89)	600,000 (Dec 91)	Macmillan	12,051 (Dec 88)	118,250 (Dec 90)
Alliance & Leicester	34,658 (Dec 89)	244,825 (Dec 91)	Marshall of Cambridge	85,043 (Aug 86)	267,081 (Dec 90)
Allied London	28,380 (Dec 87)	240,000 (Jun 91)	Bernard Matthews	37,433 (Dec 89)	85,123 (Dec 91)
ANZ Grindlays	17,000 (Sept 87)	88,000 (Sept 91)	Midlands Electricity	4,811 (Mar 90)	113,655 (Mar 92)
APV	51,233 (Dec 87)	134,000 (Dec 91)	Morgan Crucible	35,092 (Jan 89)	85,883 (Jan 92)
Argyll Group	231,000 (Apr 89)	490,000 (Mar 92)	Wm Morrison	48,000 (Feb 90)	137,204 (Feb 92)
Asprey	31,587 (Mar 89)	76,277 (Mar 92)	National Grid	15,670 (Mar 90)	108,792 (Mar 92)
Associated British Food	100,000 (Mar 87)	200,000 (Sept 91)	National Power	78,000 (Mar 90)	323,098 (Mar 92)
Avon Cosmetics	7,958 (Dec 89)	84,657 (Dec 92)	News International	484,337 (Jun 90)	1,972,092 (Jun 92)
BAA Group	157,000 (Mar 90)	378,000 (Mar 92)	NFC	335,500 (Sept 89)	1,300,000 (Sept 91)
Scott Bader	45,058 (Dec 89)	125,132 (Jan 92)	Nuclear Electric	62,000 (Mar 90)	247,785 (Mar 92)
Bank of England	143,000 (Feb 87)	331,000 (Feb 92)	Pearson	340,000 (Dec 89)	917,000 (Dec 91)
Bayer UK	9,222 (Dec 89)	51,162 (Dec 91)	Peugeot	71,611 (Dec 88)	181,000 (Dec 91)
BOC Group	n/a	1,450,000 (Sept 91)	Portals	19,000 (Dec 89)	66,000 (Dec 91)
Bristol & West	8,720 (Dec 89)	105,000 (Dec 91)	Portsmouth & Sunderland	19,994 (Mar 90)	56,046 (Mar 92)
British Aerospace	514,000 (Dec 89)	1,310,000 (Dec 91)	PowerGen	£24,303 (Mar 90)	191,825 (Mar 92)
British Alcan	88,000 (Dec 89)	206,000 (Dec 91)	Queens Moat Houses	14,560 (Dec 88)	57,146 (Dec 91)
British Coal	82,000 (Mar 90)	268,000 (Mar 91)	Ranx Xerox	90,000 (Oct 89)	400,000 (Oct 91)
Bulmer	31,000 (Apr 89)	76,000 (Apr 92)	Ratners	127,000 (Feb 90)	455,000 (Feb 92)
Cadbury Schweppes	175,000 (Dec 90)	550,000 (Dec 91)	Marc Rich	79,783 (Dec 88)	170,000 (Dec 91)
Cape	22,000 (Mar 90)	58,700 (Mar 92)	Rolls Royce	153,000 (Dec 89)	307,000 (Dec 91)
CEF Holdings	31,050 (Apr 88)	196,409 (Apr 90)	Royal Bank of Scotland	508,607 (Sept 89)	1,059,644 (Sept 91)
Charter Consolidated	90,000 (Mar 90)	427,000 (Mar 91)	Scottish Amicable	5,758 (Dec 87)	140,685 (Dec 91)
Cheltenham & Gloucester	13,000 (Dec 89)	60,000 (Dec 91)	Scottish Widows	17,683 (Dec 87)	53,554 (Dec 91)
Coutts & Co	78,714 (Dec 89)	359,000 (Dec 91)	Seeboard	31,973 (Mar 90)	107,000 (Mar 92)
Dawson International	38,373 (Mar 90)	77,000 (Mar 92)	Severn Trent	20,034 (Mar 90)	145,853 (Mar 92)
Eastern Electricity	9,832 (Mar 90)	58,025 (Mar 92)	Shandwick	49,950 (Jul 89)	141,000 (Oct 91)
Enterprise Oil	89,905 (Dec 89)	198,444 (Dec 91)	Shepherd Building	70,000 (Jun 89)	140,000 (Jun 91)
Fine Art Development	58,364 (Mar 89)	127,902 (Mar 92)	Silentnight Holdings	14,075 (Jan 89)	70,381 (Feb 92)
Albert Fisher	30,000 (Aug 89)	61,000 (Aug 91)	South West Electricity	17,000 (Mar 90)	67,000 (Mar 92)
Geest	18,380 (Dec 89)	53,000 (Dec 91)	Telegraph	65,181 (Dec 89)	202,720 (Dec 91)
Granada Group	100,000 (Sept 89)	400,000 (Sept 91)	Texaco	26,294 (Dec 88)	63,771 (Dec 90)
Grand Metropolitan	867,000 (Sept 89)	4,036,000 (Sept 91)	Thomson Corporation	100,000 (Dec 89)	200,000 (Dec 90)
Guinness	813,000 (Dec 89)	2,662,000 (Dec 91)	Thorn EMI	192,000 (Mar 89)	1,052,000 (Mar 92)
Halifax Building Society	242,470 (Jan 90)	592,815 (Jan 92)	Thorntons	20,000 (Jun 89)	62,000 (Jun 91)
C E Heath	23,157 (Mar 89)	80,300 (Mar 92)	Tiphook	16,732 (Apr 89)	132,417 (Apr 92)
Heron International	2,230,000 (Mar 90)	5,329,475 (Mar 91)	Tomkins	24,262 (Apr 90)	106,157 (May 91)
Honeywell	16,600 (Dec 89)	259,480 (Dec 91)	Unilever	1,000,000 (Dec 89)	3,000,000 (Dec 91)
HTV	78,000 (Dec 89)	184,000 (Dec 91)	Union International	25,000 (Dec 89)	57,000 (Dec 91)
Johnson Matthey	121,000 (Mar 89)	246,000 (Mar 92)	Unisys	5,052 (Mar 87)	85,552 (Dec 91)
Kingfisher	383,000 (Feb 90)	910,200 (Feb 92)	Van Leer	621,000 (Dec 88)	1,300,000 (Dec 91)
Kwik Save	30,000 (Aug 90)	62,693 (Aug 91)	Vaux Group	41,000 (Sept 89)	143,000 (Sept 91)
LASMO	50,546 (Dec 89)	104,900 (Dec 91)	VSEL	30,000 (Mar 89)	116,210 (Mar 92)
Littlewoods	91,283 (Dec 88)	292,780 (Dec 90)	Weetabix	9,418 (Jul 89)	325,000 (Jul 91)
London Electricity	30,000 (Mar 90)	116,000 (Mar 92)	John Wood Group	29,269 (May 90)	60,442 (May 91)
Lonrho	157,987 (Sept 89)	345,404 (Sept 91)	WPP Group	49,767 (Dec 88)	167,000 (Dec 91)
McCain	33,638 (Jun 86)	96,027 (Jun 92)	Yorkshire Electricity	47,085 (Mar 90)	114,791 (Mar 92)

Note: Most of these figures cover a 2-year period.

Facts and figures

fallen from £880,000 to £640,000 and TVS lost its ITV franchise and no longer appears in this Guide.

Heron International substantially increased their donations between 1988 and 1991; they have been followed by Guinness whose charitable donations have risen from £813,000 in 1989 to £2,662,000 in 1991. Grand Metropolitan's donations have also risen considerably from £867,000 in 1989 to £4,036,000 in 1991, as have News International's (£484,000 in 1989/90 to £1,972,000 in 1991/92). Other new arrivals in the tables are Thorn EMI, Cadbury Schweppes, Digital, Allied Dunbar (previously we had excluded them from tables as a subsidiary of BAT), BOC Group, British Aerospace and SmithKline Beecham.

Privatisation

As noted in previous editions, privatisation of former nationalised industries has led to a growth in their charitable giving. Most prominently, British Telecom's and British Gas's combined community contributions have grown from £1 million in 1988 to nearly £25 million in 1991.

As we predicted in the last edition of The Major Companies Guide, the water and electricity companies have gradually increased their giving. Some are ahead of the field. Northumbrian Water are now giving £383,000 in charitable donations and £636,000 in community contributions (this has grown from £89,000 in 1989/90) and Northern Electric is a member of the Per Cent Club (current community contributions are £650,000).

Afterword

It will be interesting to monitor the progress of the employee volunteering initiative (see separate article) and how this affects company giving. Already many companies in the Guide state that they prefer to give to charities in which a member of company staff is involved. Some may even move to a position of only giving support for the voluntary activities of their staff. It may be that voluntary organisations look to recruit staff members from different companies onto their management or sub-committees so as to exploit this trend. Will increased voluntary efforts by company staff lead to increased company giving?

Furthermore, companies may seek to develop a stronger business case for their community involvement and tie it in ever more closely with their business objectives. This may be through support for employee volunteering as above; it may be that they move towards more sponsorships and fewer donations. It will be worth keeping an eye on the trends.

It would also be good to see government incentives for companies to sponsor non-arts activity. The Business Sponsorship Incentive Scheme has worked very well for arts organisations (see article on Arts sponsorship). Why is there no equivalent scheme for social sponsorship? Such a scheme would tie in with our recommendations that voluntary organisations should be seeking more from less, that is they should be looking to build committed and larger-scale support from a few companies rather than annually trying to raise two or three figure sums from 500 companies or more.

In general it seems that company giving has more than kept pace with inflation. Charity is seen as a much better business proposition than it was say a decade ago when company giving totalled under £50 million. Also, although company giving constitutes about 5% of grant and fundraised income within the voluntary sector, it is clearly a very marginal area of company expenditure. It seems a fairly cheap way of buying good PR and if it can actually grow through the current recession then it must be deemed valuable. However, the future for company profits is extremely uncertain. Consequently, the future of corporate support for the voluntary sector cannot be guaranteed, although so far it has held up much better than many predicted.

Companies *reducing* their declared charitable donations by at least 50%

103 companies in this book have decreased their giving by 50% or more since the previous edition. This list features only those who were then giving £50,000 or more.

	Previous figure		Latest figure	
AB Electronics	52,000	(Jun 90)	17,000	(Jun 91)
Laura Ashley	144,465	(Jan 89)	10,000	(Jan 92)
Attwoods	72,000	(Jul 89)	27,000	(Jul 92)
Berisford	682,000	(Sept 89)	31,000	(Sept 91)
BICC	600,000	(Dec 89)	200,000	(Dec 91)
Citibank	650,000	(Dec 90)	309,500	(Dec 92)
De La Rue	113,000	(Mar 89)	32,000	(Mar 91)
ECC Group	266,000	(Sept 89)	28,500	(Dec 91)
Esso UK	3,500,000	(Dec 89)	1,583,748	(Dec 91)
Ferranti International	61,171	(Mar 90)	9,000	(Mar 92)
Fiat Auto	70,000	(Dec 88)	26,593	(Dec 90)
Gestetner	101,000	(Oct 89)	2,000	(Oct 91)
Heidelberg Graphic	56,225	(Mar 89)	11,902	(Mar 91)
Higgs & Hill	86,000	(Dec 89)	39,500	(Dec 91)
ITT Industries	446,000	(Dec 89)	4,000	(Dec 90)
Lovell	86,622	(Sept 89)	30,698	(Sept 91)
Lowe Group	129,000	(Dec 89)	47,293	(Dec 90)
LWT Holdings	£319,000	(Dec 89)	35,000	(Dec 91)
Mobil Oil	58,603	(Dec 86)	23,000	(Dec 90)
Next	119,262	(Jan 90)	42,000	(Jan 92)
NORWEB	162,042	(Mar 90)	76,340	(Mar 92)
Pentland	145,000	(Dec 89)	61,000	(Dec 91)
Pilkington	781,000	(Mar 89)	281,000	(Mar 92)
Pirelli	98,826	(Dec 89)	39,836	(Dec 90)
Reed Executive	71,220	(Mar 90)	20,000	(Dec 91)
Rutland Trust	93,800	(Dec 89)	26,200	(Dec 91)
Simon Engineering	52,463	(Dec 89)	23,000	(Dec 91)
Speyhawk	76,000	(Sept 89)	23,000	(Sept 91)
Stakis	80,000	(Oct 89)	26,000	(Sept 91)
Taylor Woodrow	307,706	(Dec 89)	126,911	(Dec 91)
Union Texas	521,652	(Dec 88)	55,778	(Dec 90)
Wolverhampton & Dudley	60,168	(Oct 89)	10,430	(Oct 91)

Tax and company giving

Companies can and do make charitable donations in a number of different ways. Some methods are tax-effective, that is they can be offset against the company's pre-tax profits when calculating the company's Corporation Tax liability. Others are not, and have to be paid out of the company's after-tax income. The 1986 and 1990 Finance Acts introduced a package of measures designed to encourage company giving. It is now far easier for companies to give tax-effectively.

Charities should understand the basic principles of tax-effective giving before they approach companies. With smaller companies, it may be possible to advise them on how to make donations tax-effectively. This will be particularly helpful for private companies (such as companies on local trading estates, dealers and distributors, service companies and local retailers). These companies may never have made charitable donations from company funds, or if they have they may have had these payments disallowed for tax.

The different ways companies give are:

1. A direct payment

A company can donate money to charity simply by writing a cheque for the amount it wishes to give. But such a payment is not an allowable business expense in calculating the company's Corporation Tax liability, and it has to be paid out of the company's after-tax income. Where the company is not paying UK Corporation Tax, this makes no difference. But most UK companies pay Corporation Tax and, by choosing a tax-effective way to organise their giving, they can substantially reduce the cost of their donations.

2. A payment to an Enterprise Agency

Although Enterprise Agencies are not charities as such (the promotion of enterprise is not held to be a charitable purpose), many companies give substantial amounts in cash and kind to Enterprise Agencies. In recognition of the importance of this contribution, under Section 79 of the 1988 Taxes Act payments to approved local Enterprise Agencies are tax-deductible.

3. A single payment under deduction of tax

The scheme for companies to make single payments to charity tax-effectively is known as Gift Aid. It was first introduced in the 1986 Finance Act for Open Companies. It was extended in the 1990 Finance Act to all companies.

An Open Company is a company that is not a Close Company. A Close Company is a company that is controlled by five or fewer persons ('participators'). Where 35% or more of the voting power is in the hands of the public and the company's shares are quoted on a recognised stock exchange, then the company will be deemed to be an Open Company. Most large public companies are Open Companies. Most smaller private companies are Close Companies.

There are different rules for the Gift Aid scheme for Open Companies and Close Companies:

(a) Gift Aid for Open Companies

A single payment by an Open Company to a charity will qualify for Gift Aid relief if the following conditions are met:

- The payment is a payment of money to a UK charity.

- The payment is made under deduction of Income Tax at the Basic Rate. This tax has to be accounted for subsequently to the Inland Revenue. For every £100 that the company wishes to donate, it has to deduct £25 in Income Tax and pay this to the Inland Revenue. The balance of £75 is paid directly to the charity. Alternatively, for every £100 paid to the charity, the company has to account for £33 in Income Tax to the Inland Revenue.

- The company signs a Form R240(SD) to confirm that the tax has been or will be deducted and accounted for, and that the conditions of the Gift Aid scheme are met. This form can be obtained from the Inland Revenue Claims Branch. Many charities keep a stock of these forms for their donors' use.

There is no minimum sum for a donation by an Open Company for the payment to qualify for Gift Aid relief. There is no restriction on the amount that the company can give in any year. There are no specific restrictions on the level of benefit that an Open Company can receive in return for the donation.

(b) Gift Aid for Close Companies

A single payment by a Close Company to a charity will qualify for Gift Aid relief if the following conditions are met:

- The payment is a payment of money to a UK charity.

- The payment is made under deduction of Income Tax as for an Open Company.

- The payment is for a minimum of £400. This is the amount actually paid by the company to the charity (net of Income Tax). The cost to the company of this minimum is £533 including the tax deducted and accounted for to the Inland Revenue. Each payment must be at least £400. Two separate payments of £200 would not qualify. There is no maximum amount that can be paid in any year under the Gift Aid scheme.

- The benefit received by the company in return must not exceed 2.5% of the sum paid to the charity (that is the net amount after deduction of tax) or £250 in total in respect of all benefits received on donations made to that charity in any company year, whichever amount is the smaller. If the benefits exceed this minimum, then the payment will not qualify for Gift Aid relief. For example, if a company gives a donation of £400 towards a theatre production, the company cannot receive in return complementary tickets with a value of more than £10.

Tax and giving

Tax advantages of giving under a Gross Deed of Covenant

Corporation Tax rate	Cost to company of £100 payment (not deductible)	Cost to company of £100 GROSS covenant payment (deductible)	Benefit of giving tax-effectively to the company	Benefit of giving tax-effectively to the charity
35%	£154	£100	£54	Nil
33%	£149	£100	£49	Nil
25%	£133	£100	£33	Nil
Nil	£100	£100	Nil	Nil

Tax advantages of giving under a Net Deed of Covenant

Corporation Tax rate	Cost to company of £100 payment (not deductible)	Cost to company of £100 NET covenant payment (deductible)	Benefit of giving tax-effectively to the company	Benefit of giving tax-effectively to the charity
35%	£154	£133	£21	£33
33%	£149	£133	£16	£33
25%	£133	£133	Nil	£33
Nil	£100	£133	-£33	£33

These tables show the tax advantage for a company organising its giving tax effectively at different prevailing tax rates. For 1992-93, Corporation Tax is payable at 33% for companies earning more than £1,250,000 in pre-tax profits (full rate), or at 25% for companies earning less than £250,000 (small company rate). For companies earning between £250,000 and £1,250,000, the marginal rate of tax that is payable on profits between these two levels is 35%.

- The payment should not be part of an arrangement involving the transfer of an asset to the charity.

Single payment donations have the advantage that a company can make a charitable payment in one year without committing itself to further charitable payments in subsequent years.

Tax has to be deducted when the payment is made. This tax has to be accounted for to the Inland Revenue within 14 days of the end of the quarter in which the tax was deducted. If a company is ignorant of the procedure for tax relief on single donations and simply sends a cheque for the amount it wishes to give, what then? If the charity simply banks the payment, it will not be allowed as a deductible item of expenditure when assessing the company's Corporation Tax Liability. If the charity sends the company Form R40 (SD) the company can then sign this and account for the income tax to the Inland Revenue provided that this is done within the required time limit. It will then treat the donation already made as a NET donation from which tax has been deducted. If it has given £400, this represents a GROSS donation of £533 (33.3% more) for which tax at 25% (£133 in this example) has been deducted. The charity ends up receiving a third more. Provided that the company pays UK Corporation Tax, this procedure allows it to save at least as much Corporation Tax as it has to out in Income Tax. If the company pays Corporation Tax at the Full Rate (33% - see table above), it will save £16 for every £100 donated.

The single payments can be made direct to charities (when the individual charity has to reclaim the Income Tax deducted) or to a half-way house trust (when the trust reclaims the tax and distributes the money to the charity gross - *see paragraph 5*). Using a half-way house charity means that the charity beneficiary does not have to reclaim tax from the Inland Revenue.

4. Payments under Deed of Covenant

Up until 1986, the only way that a company's charitable donations could be made tax-effectively was if the payments were made under a Deed of Covenant.

With the introduction of single payment giving, most donations will probably now be made using the single payment method. However, covenant giving will still continue where companies wish to make a longer term commitment, where Close Companies wish to make donations of less than £400, or where companies are unaware that the single payment scheme exists.

There are two types of covenant that can be used. The **gross covenant**, is normally used. This commits the company to paying over a certain sum *less* Income Tax deducted at the basic rate. The amount stated in the Deed is the amount paid directly to the charity AND the amount of tax deducted which is paid to the Inland Revenue and reclaimed by the charity. The total cost of the donation to the company is the amount stated in the Deed, so the charity ends up with exactly the amount the company wishes to give, and the cost of the donation to the company is reduced because it is tax-deductible.

For example, a company decides to covenant £100 a year for four years to a charity by means of a Gross Covenant. The Deed will describe the payment as "£100 less income tax at the basic rate". The company then deducts income tax at the basic rate (currently 25%, so the company will deduct £25 from the £100 gross amount) and pays it to the Inland Revenue. It pays the remaining £75 to the charity, and the charity then reclaims the £25 from the Inland Revenue. Therefore the company makes a donation of £100 and the charity receives a total of £100.

Using a **net covenant**, the company pays an amount which after deduction of Income Tax at the basic rate equals a certain sum. So the amount stated in the Deed is the amount paid direct to the charity. The company pays this amount to the charity as a payment net of Income Tax at the basic rate (currently 25%); it also has to account to the Inland Revenue for the Income Tax that has been deducted. The charity then reclaims the Income Tax from the Inland Revenue. In all cases the cost of the donation will not exceed the amount that it would have cost the

Tax and giving

company had it been paid as a single non tax-effective donation, and the charity will benefit from the amount of the reclaimed Income Tax.

For example, a company gives a charity a donation of £100 a year for four years under a net covenant. The Deed describes the donation as "a sum of money when after deduction of Income Tax at the basic rate will amount to £100". The charity then reclaims the Income Tax that the company has paid on this £100 (at current rates this amounts to £33.33, so the gross value to the charity is £133.33 from a £100 donation).

A net covenant is normally used by individual donors. There is an advantage to the charity (at the expense of the company) in persuading companies to enter into net covenants. Whichever form of covenant is used, charities are responsible for reclaiming the tax from the Inland Revenue.

5. Payments via a half-way house trust

The problem with using a Deed of Covenant is that it commits the company to making regular payments to the same charity over a number of years. It also means that every time the company wishes to make a charitable donation it must use a properly prepared legal document, deducting tax from the donation and accounting for this tax to the Inland Revenue. Where the Gift Aid procedure is used, the donation has to be made net to the charity, which then has to reclaim tax from the Inland Revenue. Using these schemes involves considerable administration of Income Tax payments and claims both by the company and the recipient charity. To get round these problems there is quite a simple procedure that many companies adopt. They set up their own charitable trust to which they pay over the whole of their charitable budget using one or more Deeds of Covenant or Gift Aid payments. This trust reclaims the Income Tax deducted by the company, which it adds to the amount it has received direct from the company, and makes charitable payments to the charities the company wishes to benefit.

When making payments to their own charitable trust through a Deed of Covenant the company commits itself to making charitable payments for the duration of the covenant, but it does not commit itself to supporting any particular charity. Using the procedure for covenant or Gift Aid payments also simplifies the accounting for the company, which only has to make one payment and complete one Certificate of Deduction of Tax. The recipient charities benefit too, as they receive their donations 'gross' and do not have to go to the bother of reclaiming tax.

About one-third of the top 200 companies have now established their own charitable trusts as a vehicle for their charitable giving. It has been an increasing trend in recent years as companies have come to realise that this offers a flexible, simple and tax-effective method of distributing their charitable donations.

A further advantage of a company trust is that it can be used for making gifts in kind. The trust can purchase the items the company wishes to donate (using funds donated by the company). The trust will then hand over the gift to the charity. This would not be possible for Close Companies making a Gift Aid payment to the trust, as Gift Aid payments must not be associated with the purchase of the asset.

A half-way house charitable trust is simple to establish. It will be controlled by trustees nominated by the company (this provides a ready-made structure for a donations committee). Its income will consist of the charitable payments received from the company plus any interest received on its undistributed cash. For further information, see article on Company trusts.

6. Using the Charities Aid Foundation

The Charities Aid Foundation is itself a half-way house trust established as a service to individual and corporate donors. If a company does not want to go to the bother of setting up its own half-way house trust, it can pay or covenant its donations budget to the Charities Aid Foundation, and then direct the Charities Aid Foundation as to how this sum should be distributed. A small levy is made for this service in the form of a compulsory donation to the Charities Aid Foundation's founder, the National Council for Voluntary Organisations. Details of this service can be obtained from CAF (see address at the end of this article).

7. Establishing a trust with its own resources

A company, or its founders, can decide to establish a charitable trust which has its own capital, which it invests to produce an income. This capital sum can be provided through a transfer of shares in the company (as happened with the **Laura Ashley Foundation** when the company was publicly floated). It is also possible for money to be provided directly by the company (as happened with the **Yorkshire Bank** which transferred £250,000 of its shareholders' funds into a new trust).

The advantage of setting up this form of trust is that a single transfer of capital is made at the outset, rather than an annual transfer out of income. The company has organised its charitable giving for all time, and the charitable donations are then made not out of the company's own funds (which belong to the shareholders), but out of the trust's investment income (which will normally consist of dividends paid by the company). Although the trust is a legally separate entity with its own resources, it sits beside the company and operates in tandem with it. The donations made by the trust do not have to be reported by the company in its annual accounts.

These then are the different tax-effective ways in which companies can donate money to charity. Most larger companies in fact make their donations in a number of these ways. The directors may control a small (or not so small) endowed trust. The company may have set up its own half-way house trust, or use the services of the Charities Aid Foundation for the bulk of its annual charitable donations budget. For the larger, prestigious appeals such as the St Paul's Cathedral restoration fund or the Wishing Well Appeal, the company may have decided to take out a separate Deed of Covenant for that particular appeal. And many companies will now be using one of the single payment procedures making one-off payments to individual charities out of after-tax income either directly or via a half-way house trust.

Inevitably there will be some companies that will not be making tax-deductible donations. They will either be ignorant of the procedures or not want to go to the bother of using them.

Tax and other forms of giving

Companies support charities in a variety of other ways than making a cash donation. This includes secondments, gifts in kind, advertising and sponsorship. The tax situation for these is as follows:

1. Secondments

Until 1983 a company could not offset the cost it incurred in relation to any employee seconded to work for a charity on a temporary (or even a longer term) basis. This arose from the general rule that a company can deduct for tax purposes only the expenditure incurred **wholly and exclusively** for the purpose of its business. The salary costs of a seconded employee does not

Tax and giving

satisfy this business purpose test. Under the terms of the 1983 Finance Act, the salary costs of an employee seconded to a charity can be deducted from liability to Corporation Tax during the period of the secondment if the secondment is (i) on a basis which is expressed (ii) intended to be of a temporary nature. What is temporary is not precisely defined, but most secondments to charity (which are rarely for more than 2 years, and often for a year or less) would qualify.

2. Gifts in kind

If a company makes a gift of stock or equipment there are various ways in which this can be handled, each with different tax implications. If only occasional and relatively insubstantial gifts are made, then these can be "taken off the shelf", "lost" or somehow be given without the transaction appearing in the company's books. An alternative is that the transfer of the gift can be recorded in the company's books, but the value of the gift can be written off before it is donated. If a company chooses either of these methods, VAT is not chargeable in respect of the gift, and the company is able to bear the whole of the cost of the gift out of its pre-tax profits.

Where gifts of real value are made on a regular basis, the procedures described above will be inadequate. If the gift is made directly, it will not be an allowable expense for tax purposes except where it is in furtherance of the trade of the company. Section 577(9) of the 1988 Taxes Act provides that gifts for charity are allowable where made wholly and exclusively for the purposes of the trade of the company, or where they can be justified as so being made; and small gifts to local bodies which are not charities are similarly allowable under Extra Statutory Concession B7.

However, most gifts are not made in furtherance of trade, but as a philanthropic donation. Here, if the value of the gift cannot be written off, the best way is for the company to sell the gift to the charity at cost and then, using some tax-effective method of giving, donate the funds the charity needs to purchase the gift. (Note, though, that a Close Company cannot make a Gift Aid single payment specifically against the purchase of an asset.) The easiest method is to make the gift to a half-way house company charitable trust for onward donation to the recipient charity. IBM has used this method for giving computers by selling them to the **IBM (UK) Trust** for onward donation. The funds for doing this will have been donated by the company to the trust tax-effectively.

The 1991 Finance Act introduced a special concession for gifts of equipment made by companies to schools, universities, and further and higher education establishments. Where the gift is to a qualifying institution, the company can write off its book value when calculating its Corporation Tax liability. This incentive for making gifts in kind tax-effectively may be extended to a wider range of qualifying beneficiaries in the future.

Where an item of value is transferred either as a gift or sold against funds donated by the company, then VAT will normally be payable (as long as it is a taxable supply and not a zero-rated item). The VAT payable will be calculated on the book value of the item (or the sale price if that is higher).

An alternative procedure, adopted by companies such as **Hewlett-Packard**, is for the company to loan the item to the charity or organisation. This can be for some business purpose (eg. research, marketing, product development or testing) and involves no transfer of ownership, so no tax is involved.

3. Advertising

A common way for companies to support charities is through taking paid advertising in a brochure, year-book or diary. Such expenditure will normally be deemed to be an allowable business expenditure, provided that the payments are not outrageous in relation to the advertising space taken. Where a charity is registered for VAT it will have to charge VAT on the advertisement except where the publication meets the following conditions: (a) the advertisements are clearly not of a commercial character; and (b) the brochure contains a significant proportion of non-business advertisements from private individuals. If both these conditions are met, the charge for the advertisement will be outside the scope of VAT.

Many small companies have been happy to pay for advertising as an alternative to making a donation, because it is simple and tax-effective and does not necessitate entering into a Deed of Covenant. However, the Gift Aid procedure for companies will now allow any company to make donations without entering into a long-term commitment, although for a Close Company the minimum donation is £533. This is a step forward because with a donation all the money will go to the charity (whereas if the company pays for advertising space in a charity brochure, part of the value of the payment is swallowed up in printing costs). However, many charities and their agents will continue to solicit advertising for brochure and similar publications and many companies will continue to pay for goodwill advertising. Companies (and the donee charity) should realise that although taking advertising is tax-effective, it does involve a substantial cost in printing which reduces the value of the donation.

4. Sponsorship

If sponsorship (of the arts, sports, events or charitable activities) is a bona fide business expense then it will normally be allowable for tax purposes. However, there have been several problem areas regarding making sponsorship payments tax-effectively. The first has been that sponsorship of capital expenditure has not normally been allowable (although charitable gifts for the purchase of capital items have been allowable if they are made tax-effectively). Secondly much sponsorship cannot be justified **wholly and exclusively** as a business expense; it may be something more than a publicised donation, but the business advantage has not been commensurate with the cost. The Inland Revenue has been disallowing certain "dual purpose" sponsorship on that basis. The third problem area is that relating to payment for entertainment facilities as part of a sponsorship deal, since most entertainment is not an allowable business expense. In such cases, the recommended procedure has been to separate out the entertainment element and for the sponsored organisation to invoice for this separately.

Open Companies can use the Gift Aid to avoid tax problems with their sponsorship. The sponsorship payment should be made as if it were a donation. As such under Section 339 (1-5) of the 1988 Taxes Act it will be allowable as a donation, or if deemed to be otherwise the charity will still be able to reclaim the Income Tax deducted by the company and the company will then be able to treat the item as a business expenditure. To avoid VAT problems, if the recipient organisation is VAT-registered it should invoice the company for the VAT due in respect of the whole of the sponsorship payment. The company itself (if VAT registered) will be able to offset the VAT against its VAT inputs, so this will not result in any additional costs. For a Close Company, where there are limitations on the benefit receivable on a Gift Aid donation for it to qualify for tax relief, it is best to split the payment into two parts, one for the sponsorship element (for which the charity supplies an invoice, including any VAT that may be payable) and the other as a completely separate transaction for the donation (paid tax-effectively). This procedure can also be used by an Open Company.

The tax implications for a charity receiving sponsorship income is a problem area. If the level of sponsorship income is *substantial* the Inland Revenue might consider it trading income on which a profit is being made, and tax that profit. This means that a charity might wish to take professional advice on the best way of receiving sponsorship income.

5. Other business expenditure

There are many other ways in which charities may be able to provide services to companies of a business nature other than through sponsorship. Providing a counselling or advice service to company staff (on issues such as AIDS, alcoholism, bereavement, relationship difficulties, credit card debts, relocation) or providing facilities for training or for staff Christmas parties are methods of income generation which are likely to increase in the more competitive fundraising market of the 1990s. As an expenditure wholly and exclusively for business purposes, such payments will be deductible. As competition for grants increases, some charities are now at least beginning to think about ways in which they can work with companies on some business basis.

6. Payroll giving

Payroll giving is not company giving, but it is closely related. Most large companies are inevitably involved in introducing and administering payroll giving schemes. Until April 1987, payroll giving could be made either under Deed of Covenant by individual employees, or via a simplified covenant procedure agreed with the Inland Revenue. Alternatively payments could be made out of the donor's taxed income (which costs more). The scheme introduced in the 1986 Finance Act allows employees to make charitable payments from their pre-tax income of up to £600 a year. This scheme is described in a separate section.

These briefly are the ground rules for taxation as it relates to corporate philanthropy. For partnerships, the situation is different.

Partnerships

Donations made by a partnership would be allocated pro rata to the individual partners. This may mean that if a partnership makes a single payment, it may not be sufficient to qualify for Gift Aid relief. They may need to take professional advice on the best way of handling its charitable giving.

Tax and giving

Further information

For fuller information see the following publications, all of which are published by:

The Directory of Social Change
Radius Works, Back Lane, London NW3 1HL (071-435 8171):

Tax-Effective Giving: a practical guide (1992 edition), £9.95.

A Guide to Gift Aid (1992), £7.95.

Tax and Giving Subscription Service which includes model documents, sample explanatory leaflets and updates on the latest information and changes in the law or practice, £25.00.

For details of the Charities Aid Foundation service to corporate donors, contact:

Charities Aid Foundation
48 Pembury Road, Tonbridge TN9 2JD (0732-771333).

The tax rates used in this article are those prevailing for 1992-93.

How to make an appeal

Why firms give

Before you make an appeal to industry you must have a basic understanding of why firms give. This enables you to feed them with good reasons why they should support your work. The main reasons why companies give can broadly be categorised as follows:

- Companies give to **create goodwill.** They like to be seen as good citizens. A company may tie its level of donations to that of similar companies, not liking to be thought less generous than its peers.

- Some companies like to **be associated with certain causes;** this helps their image. For example, pet food manufacturers support animal charities, so they are seen as pet lovers, not just profit lovers.

- Companies want to **be seen as good neighbours,** so they support local charities. Company donations to local charities form a large proportion of the total number of gifts by companies, though in actual value it is probably less than one quarter.

- Some companies like to **create good relations with employees** through their charitable giving programme. One way of doing this is to support charities for which the staff are raising money or for whom staff members do volunteer work in their spare time. Some companies have schemes to donate funds to such charities; others may give some preference (though not necessarily an automatic donation) to charitable appeals proposed by employees.

- Some companies give because they realise that giving is good for them, that it has real benefit to the company. A publicised donation or a more high-profile sponsorship can generate some PR benefit, better staff relations or better local community relations in the area from which the company draws its employees. Many of the larger companies recognise this and give out of **enlightened self-interest.**

- There are companies that give because **it is expected of them.** They receive appeals, and they know that other companies also receive appeals and give their support. They will want to support trade charities such as a benevolent fund or an industry research organisation; beyond that they will probably pitch their level of giving more or less at that of their rivals.

- Much giving is on a **knock-for-knock** basis, with company directors soliciting donations for their pet charities (or those of their partners) from their business contacts (these include their friends and colleagues in other companies, and their customers and suppliers). If they receive support for their cause when they request it, they will be obliged to give reciprocal support when they are asked.

- Much giving, particularly by smaller companies, is **decided by the Chairman or Managing Director.** Obviously the causes they are personally interested in will stand a better chance of support. Some large companies have well-established criteria for giving, but even then if you can get a friend of the Managing Director to ask on behalf of your cause, you are more likely to get a donation, even when it does not fit exactly into those criteria. It always helps to have access to the Managing Director or Chairman of a company.

- That brings in the **director's special interest,** where the Managing Director, Chairman or other director uses the company's charitable budget as an extension of a personal account to fulfil their own charitable commitment. The Americans call this the "incorporated pocketbook". There is a thin line between an individual using his or her concerns to influence company decisions and where they use company funds to further their interests.

- Some companies give **because they have always given.** They never review their policies and they believe that they can enjoy a traditional relationship with charities. They see their donations more as an annual subscription and they will keep a list of the charities they wish to support each year. Your aim, therefore, should be to get your charity's name on to such a list where it exists.

- Sometimes firms give **because the charity persists** in approaching them, and they do not like to keep refusing worthwhile causes. Persistence can pay, so unless you know the company won't give to your particular cause (and if you can afford the postage), keep trying. A medical charity once secured a substantial donation from a company after more than 10 years of trying. Most charities would not want to try that long without some indication that the company might be prepared to give its support. If you are turned down you should consider whether you can improve your application or approach.

Howard Hurd's survey, mentioned in our introduction, has some interesting answers from companies as to the motivations behind their company's charitable involvement:

"We do recognise that we are in the community and we do have some sort of social responsibility ... Companies these days have to replace the patrons of old."

"We recognise that our continued business success depends largely upon the economic and social well-being of the communities in which we operate."

"Companies are part of the community. Any company has interest in increasing the health of this community."

"It would be dishonest to pretend we don't want a payback."

"To be seen to be acting as a responsible corporate body."

"We are expected to, therefore it is bad policy not to."

How to make an appeal

"People aren't going to tolerate a company of this size which doesn't put something tangible back into society."

Generally it is worth emphasising the sheer chaos of company giving. Few companies have any real policy for their charitable giving. Mostly they cover a wide range of good causes or attempt to deal with each appeal on its merits. Much company giving is done on the 'old boy network', which is often referred to as 'peer group' giving. Companies do not admit they give in this way, but if you were giving away your shareholders' money you would also dress up what you were doing, perhaps claiming that you gave according to well-defined criteria.

What firms give

Many charities are completely unrealistic about what they might obtain from companies. The business of companies is business; charitable giving is only a sideline. Even for the bigger companies, the sums that are given to individual charities are quite modest, and long-term commitments are seldom made.

A generous donation might be only £1,000; large companies rarely give over £2,500; smaller companies give proportionately less, and local branch outlets may be unable to give over £25. Obviously there are exceptions, where the appeal is particularly relevant or beneficial to the company. Cash donations appear to be a falling percentage of the larger corporate donors' total giving; with the smaller donors, cash support will probably remain their most common form of support for charities.

However, much company support lies outside the field of cash donations:

- **Advertising in brochures** or newsletters. Smaller companies are often prepared to give in this way, if asked, although advertising support is never as valuable as a cash donation. Many companies dislike being approached for advertising by a third party who would also receive a share of the donation.

- **Sponsoring the charity's annual report.** You have to produce this anyway and it provides an opportunity to raise money and acknowledge the support. Some large companies will even print the report in-house. This is particularly useful if you are producing a rather more lavish report than usual, which you can then use to promote your organisation and develop your fundraising. It will also highlight the fact that you are actually doing something to raise money.

- **Sponsoring an event** or activity either locally or nationally. This can range from something which is little more than a publicised donation to a bona fide sponsorship when the sponsor's return is crucial. Some companies handle their sponsorship through their community affairs or charity donations department; in others the marketing department decides. The Managing Director will decide both sponsorship and donations in smaller companies. There are separate sections of this book devoted to arts and social sponsorship.

- **Gifts in kind.** Companies give their products (anything from paint to packaged holidays), raw materials, offcuts and waste, damaged stock or ends of lines, used equipment, furniture or furnishings. Such gifts are often of little cost to the company but immense value to the charity. You need to contact individual companies who might help. For smaller companies, use the telephone and go straight to the top. Another approach is to write a shopping list of items you require - anything from a set of law books for a legal advice centre to furnishings for a day centre or your office, and to circulate this with a personally addressed covering letter to likely companies. Many high street companies will also be happy to provide raffle prizes if you contact the local store manager.

- **Advice and help.** Anything from a formal, full-time secondment to advice given over the telephone on a one-off basis. If there is something you particularly need that you think a company can give you, then it is worth asking. More and more companies see such advice as a formal part of their charitable giving.

- **Other services.** Companies have been known to donate all kinds of services from printing leaflets, using photocopiers, making places available on training courses, lending a room for a reception, use of a JCB excavator and so on. Again this can be done at little or no cost to the company.

- **Contacts.** The support of senior company people can be very helpful in fundraising from the business community. It can also help in your dealings with your local authority and in bringing a more businesslike approach to the planning of what you are doing. Some charities have found it extremely beneficial to recruit senior local or head office business people as committee members or trustees.

- **Employee support.** Some companies undertake fundraising drives for particular charities. A more recent initiative is that of employee volunteering (see separate article). Another aspect of employee support is payroll giving (again see separate article).

It pays to be clear about what you want **before** you approach companies. There is a great deal more they can give than just cash.

Personal contact

Personal contact if you already have it or if you can develop it is extremely important. This has traditionally been the best means of approach. Today, even where the company has a well-defined donations policy, a personal approach to the Chairman, Managing Director or some senior director will not go amiss. This applies both for a national charity approaching large national companies and local charities approaching firms in their local area. One large national charity claims that it only ever approaches companies through personal contact; where it has not got or cannot find any point of contact it does not even bother sending a written appeal. This is obviously extreme and many charities can and do run successful postal appeals.

However, when planning an appeal, an important first step is to find which of your committee members, trustees, patrons and vice-presidents (or whatever device you have for getting the great and good associated with your charity) have influence or know people who have. If you can find a board member on the main board of the company for them to write a personal letter to, that will prove useful. It will also help if you can discover some of the particular interests of one or other of the directors. If you are working in the field of physical or mental handicap, for example, it may be that one of the directors of the company you are approaching has a disabled child and would therefore be more likely to support your cause.

Generally an appeal through a personal contact will work the best. But if you haven't got a contact and can see no way of developing one, then you will have to make do without. You will need to discover the person in the company responsible for handling charity appeals. For smaller companies it will be the Chairman or Managing Director. Larger companies may have a corporate affairs department (if they are a co-ordinated giver). Alternatively, the public affairs or human resources sections or the company secretary's office are common contacts. If you are

How to make an appeal

unable to find out a specific person responsible for charitable donations, get the name of the managing director or company secretary and write personally to him or her.

Some companies will take decisions at a special appeals committee; in others it may come up at a main board meeting. A personally addressed letter greatly improves your chances of success. In fact, many companies will not read appeal letters which are not addressed personally. Paradoxically, the smaller the company the more important it will be to adopt a personal approach.

When sending a written appeal, it can be helpful to get someone who is a 'name' to sign your appeal letter. If you have a prominent supporter who is known in the field of industry or commerce, and not just someone who is known in your own field of good works, try to associate this person with your appeal. Companies will feel that if so-and-so is closely involved then your charity must be worth supporting. It is a means of building bridges between the two very different worlds of industry and charity, of obtaining an endorsement from someone whose opinion is respected.

Developing points of personal contact and improving your knowledge about companies is something you have to build up over the years. Keep a card index of companies who you think may support you, update it each year and use it to record any significant bits of information that will help you in your future fundraising.

Be specific in your approach

Rather than send out a circular mailing to 100 or 1,000 companies, you will be more successful if you select a few companies that you believe will be particularly interested in your project, and approach them with a specific application. In the past, many charities have done circular, mailshot appeals. Today such is the volume of company appeal mail and the competition for funds that charities should only ever send appeals to those companies where they feel they stand a reasonable chance of getting support. Indeed, most companies state that they will not consider circular appeals.

Where you think that a company might be particularly interested in your work, approach that company specifically with an individual appeal. Find a good reason why you believe the company should support you and include this prominently in your letter. You may be able to relate what you are doing as a charity to companies which have some relevance to your work; for example, a children's charity can appeal to companies making children's products; a housing charity to construction companies, building products manufacturers, building societies, etc.. You should be equally specific in your approach to local companies (including small companies based in your area, and large companies with their head office or a major branch or factory locally). Any relationship, however tenuous, creates a point of contact on which you can build a good case for obtaining the company's support. If there is no relationship, should you be approaching that company at all?

There may be occasions where a charity will not want to accept money from a company in a related industry. A health education charity may not want to accept money from a tobacco or brewery company or from the confectionery industry as it might feel that as a result of doing so it would be seen to be compromised. Each charity has to judge where it draws the line.

Be clear about why you need the money

You must be clear about the objectives of the work you are raising money for, particularly its time-scale and how it relates to your overall programme of work. Try to think in project terms rather than seeking money to cover basic administration costs. This can be difficult, because most people spend most of their money on administration in one form or another, so you need to try to conjure up projects out of your current activities to present to potential donors. If you relate what you are doing to a specific time-scale, this again makes what you are applying for appear more of a project than a contribution to your year-on-year core costs.

It is also important how you 'sell' your work to industry. You need crisp and clear applications. Read through them carefully to see both that they make sense and that they are jargon-free. Government bodies (both central and local) and, to a certain extent, grant-making trusts, are bureaucratic machines able to digest descriptive analysis of what you are doing and what you hope to achieve. Industry is much less of a paper machine, so you should confine what you put in your application to the essence of what you are doing. If you are long-winded, hazy or unclear, it will not help you.

Be persistent

Do not underestimate the persistence factor. If you do not receive a donation in the first year, do not assume that the company will never support you. Go back a second and even a third time. If you are going back, mention the fact that you have applied to them previously, perhaps saying that you are now presenting them with something different which may be (you hope) of more interest to them.

If they give you reasons why they are refusing you use them to help you put in more appropriate applications in the future. If they said that they do not give to your particular type of activity then you know that it is absolutely no use your going back. If they said their funds were fully committed, you can try to find out when would be a better time to apply (although it might only have been a convenient excuse because they did not want to give to you).

Note the response to your appeal on a card index and use any information you can glean to improve your chances the next time. People respect persistence, so it really is important to go back again and again.

How to find out which firms to approach

The firms to approach must depend on what sort of organisation you are. If you are a national organisation then an appeal to the country's leading companies is appropriate. Local groups should approach local firms and local branches of national companies which have a presence in their area. All organisations can approach companies in allied fields; for example, theatres can appeal to fabric companies.

You will find the names and addresses of companies, sometimes with the names of the Managing Director and other details, in a whole series of useful directories. The top 1,450 companies are listed in this book. The top 400 donors are listed in **The Major Companies Guide,** which is a companion to this book and gives a detailed breakdown on each company's business as well as detailed information on its charitable giving.

The top 1,000 companies in the UK, plus leading companies in other sectors and overseas, are listed in **The Times 1,000.** The **Kompass Register of British Industry and Commerce** lists members of the CBI and is available in regional sections as well as alphabetically. The **Guide to Key British Enterprises** is a huge directory of leading firms, as is the **Stock Exchange Official Year Book** which lists companies quoted on the Stock Exchange. **The Directory of Directors** and **Who's Who** are useful for finding out more about company directors. These and other publications may well be available in your local reference library. For local companies, you should use a combination of this book, the appropriate regional section

How to make an appeal

of **Kompass** and lists of firms from the local Chamber of Commerce. **The Yellow Pages** is a useful supplement to your local knowledge.

If you want gifts in kind, you should find likely suppliers of what you need. Trade associations will often provide a list of its member companies. Another idea is trade exhibition catalogues which give details of all exhibitors.

Directories and lists are often out of date. If you have time and think it worth expending the effort, telephone the companies and ask if the details you have are correct, for example the Managing Director's name.

One big problem is the ownership of seemingly independent companies. Many companies are in fact a part of a much larger concern. In recent years there has been a substantial number of mergers and take-overs, plus the buying and selling of business between corporations. A useful source is the directory **Who Owns Whom**. Another is **The Major Companies Guide**. You can also use company annual reports, which (for most companies) can be obtained on request. These reports provide good background information on the company, and occasionally information on the company's corporate support programme. Some private (and occasionally public) companies will not send out its annual reports except to shareholders; in such cases you can go to Companies House to get hold of a copy.

Finally there are national and local newspapers which can provide useful information and ideas about who to approach. If a company is about to start up or to close down in an area it may provide opportunities for giving support locally. **Ford of Britain**, for example, has given substantial support to a community and recreational centre in Speke, and **Levi Strauss** has had a planned programme of support in closure areas. Equally a new business initiative can provide a peg for a donation. For example some years ago War on Want wrote to the chairman of a large civil engineering company, which had just won a contract for work on the port at Mombasa; they congratulated the company on its good fortune and pointed out that War on Want had a project close by which was doing excellent work and which the company might want to support. It did want to, and made a substantial donation with the cheque being handed over locally with publicity in the local papers.

Raising money locally

A local charity should adopt a different strategy in its approach to industry than a national charity. An appeal to the larger national companies will only usually have a chance of success if there is some **product link** (where what the charity does is linked to what the company does), or a **geographical link** (perhaps a company's head office, a large factory or a subsidiary company is in your area). There are also other opportunities:

1. Local branches of national companies

Some very large donors, including the high street banks and some multiple stores, give through their local branches. The amounts that can be given without having to be submitted to Head Office for approval are usually much smaller than for national donations; often they are very small, but the money is there. Some companies like to support charities which their staff are involved in. So if you have a volunteer who works for a high street bank, say, then ask him or her whether you can apply to his/her Regional Office for a donation. Some very large donors which have no branch structure make smallish amounts of money available to local charities in areas where they have a presence through their local subsidiaries or plants.

2. Large donors who give locally

Some companies have become predominantly local givers. For example **Allied Dunbar** gives substantially in the Swindon area where it is based. The independent television companies tend to give substantially in their franchise area, as will water and electricity companies. Research into the donations policies of large companies in your area. If you find that none are giving locally at the moment, then perhaps you should think about persuading them to change their policy.

3. Local companies

There are a myriad of companies that make up the local business community. Although these may be a power in your local community, they may not be quoted on the Stock Exchange or have any national presence. These vary from companies employing a few hundred to those employing just a few. The local business community will have its own networks including the **Chamber of Commerce**, the **Rotary Club** and the **Masonic Lodge**. You should think carefully about how to reach these firms and who you might enlist to help you to do so. You can find out who to approach from some of the sources we have already listed, or from your own local knowledge. You could even go door-to-door down the local high street or trading estate, particularly if you are seeking gifts in kind.

4. Companies you have existing contact with

If you have or can create personal contacts, then those companies will be worth approaching. Alternatively, appeal to your suppliers; this will include your bank, solicitors, accountants and those companies that supply you with goods. Always mention the fact that you are a valued customer. If you are a local charity you would appeal to your bank via its Regional Office. Your accountants or solicitors may also be able to provide useful contacts; some charities even appoint advisers with good business connections which they can then bring in when they need to raise money.

Many local firms may find it easier to make you a gift in kind or pay for advertising space in a brochure. Indeed a whole industry of telephone selling of advertising space in diaries and brochures on commission now seems to have grown. Don't just think in terms of cash donations; decide what you want and what these companies might be persuaded to give you. Even make a shopping list of your needs and then think about who to approach for what.

Remember that if you have a strong belief in the importance of what you are doing, then nobody is too small to approach. It is a matter of time, patience and persuasion - and of getting the right person to do the persuading. If you can get some publicity in the local press then this too can be an incentive in persuading local companies to give.

Some key factors

Lastly some points which are important for you to consider when you are constructing your appeal letter:

- Try to think up a project or aspect of your work that the **business sector** might like to support. Generally do not appeal for administration costs or a contribution to an endowment fund (although there will be cases where this approach will succeed). Recognise that companies are likely to be interested in some things and not others. For example a drugs charity would be more likely to get money for education than rehabilitation. An appreciation of the kind of things that companies like to support will be very helpful to you.

- Your letter should be as short as possible. Try to get it all on one side of A4. You can always supply further information as attachments to the appeal letter. Company people are busy. You can help them by making your appeal letter short and to the point. It should be written clearly and concisely and be free

How to make an appeal

from jargon. Someone not acquainted with what you are doing should be able to read and understand it and be persuaded to act on it. Perhaps give your letter in draft to someone outside your charity to read and to comment on before finalising it and sending it out.

- You should state why you need the money and exactly how it will be spent. The letter itself should be straightforward. It should include the following information (not necessarily in this order): what the organisation does, and some background on how it was set up; whom the organisation serves; why the organisation needs funds; how the donation would be spent if it were to be forthcoming, and why you think the company might be interested in supporting you.

- You should attempt to communicate the urgency of your appeal. Fundraising is an intensively competitive business; there is a limited amount of money to give away, and you have to ensure that some of it comes your way. If it appears that although you would like the money now it would not matter terribly much if you got it next year, this will put people off. You should also try to show that your charity is well-run, efficient and cost-effective in how it operates.

- You should mention why you think the company should support your cause. This could range from rather generalised notions of corporate responsibility and the creation of goodwill in the local community to much more specific advantages such as preventing children painting graffiti on their factory walls or the good publicity companies will get from supporting your cause. If the firm's generosity is to be made public, for example through advertising or any publicity arising from the gift, then emphasise the goodwill which will accrue to the company. Most companies would say that they do not require any public acknowledgement for the contributions they make, but most will appreciate and welcome this.

- Ask for something specific. It is all too easy to make a good case and then to mumble something about needing money. Many companies, having been persuaded to give, are not sure how much to give. You can ask them to give a donation of a specific amount (matched to what you believe their ability to contribute to be), or to contribute the cost of a particular item. You can suggest a figure by mentioning what other companies are giving. You can mention a total and say how many donations you will need to achieve this. Don't be unreasonable in your expectations. Just because a company is large and rich, that doesn't mean that it makes big grants. If you have information on the company's grant range, that will be helpful. If not, look at the companies annual total donations figure and make a reasonable inference.

- If you can demonstrate some form of 'leverage' this will be an added attraction. Company donations on the whole are quite modest, but companies like to feel they are having a substantial impact with the money they spend. If you can show that a small amount of money will enable a much larger project to go ahead, or will release further funds say on a matching basis from another source, this will definitely be an advantage.

- Having written a very short appeal letter, you can append some background support literature. This should not be a fifty-page treatise outlining your latest policies, but like your letter it should be crisp and to the point, a record of your achievements, your latest annual report or even a specially produced brochure to accompany your appeal.

- Make sure that the letter is addressed to the correct person at the correct address. It pays to do this background research. Use the various trade directories, business information services or Yellow Pages as appropriate and use the telephone to find out or confirm who to send your letter to. Keep all the information on file as it will make your job much easier next time.

How companies reply to you

Many companies will not even reply to your appeal. A few may acknowledge receipt of your letter, and occasionally you will get thanked for your request and be told that it is being considered and you will only hear the outcome if you are successful.

Up to half of the companies you approach will write back. The exact percentage depends on the spread of the companies you approach. The larger companies have a system for dealing with charity mail, and most will see it as good PR to give a reply. Smaller companies which are not giving much charitable support will not have the time or the resources to do anything but scan the mail and throw most of it in the bin.

What sort of reply should you expect? You will hope to get some donations. If you do an extensive appeal, you will inevitably get a lot of refusals. These will normally be in the form of a pre-printed or word-processed letter or a postcard. Occasionally you will get an individually typed letter of reply. If they say yes, you will get a cheque or a Charities Aid Foundation voucher. But more often they will say no.

How do companies phrase their refusal, and should you take what they say at face value? Some companies have a series of reasons for saying no. In an Oxfam survey on refusals to an appeal they made to industry, they concluded that most replies were phrased in the following terms:

- Funds fully committed (23%).
- Unable to give support (29%).
- Not now/not at this time/not at present (35%).

Other reasons given included: no funds because of a merger or reorganisation; no funds because the company is in financial difficulties; no charitable budget (ie. the company does not make any charitable donations); budget used up or exhausted (there is the implication here that if you had got your appeal in earlier, you might have been more successful, but this is surmise); try later; no we don't want to (a surprisingly rare statement).

The company may not mean what it says. Funds may still be available for those appeals the company wishes to support; the company may be able to give support and just not want to; or it may not want to now or in the future. You should try to read between the lines. Companies in trying to be polite may in fact be misleading you if you take what they say at face value.

If you are successful, remember to say thank you; this is an elementary courtesy which is too often forgotten. If the company gives you any substantial amount of money, then you should probably try to keep them in touch with the achievements related to their donation (such as a brief progress report or copies of your annual report or latest publications).

If you do not succeed, go back again next year (unless they say that it is not their policy to support your type of organisation or to give to charity at all). Persistence pays. If you have received a donation, go back again next year too. The company has demonstrated that it is interested in what you are doing and in supporting you.

The top 300 corporate donors

The following is a list of the top 300 corporate donors in terms of the donations figure they are legally required to declare in their annual report. We have listed the companies alphabetically rather than in order of donations amount because the figures are not really comparable as between one company and another. Firstly, not all the figures are from the same year. Secondly, the way in which a company chooses to report its charitable giving can have a significant impact on any ranking we may attempt. The published figure may include all or only some of the following:

- Cash donations made by head office.
- Cash donations made by branches and plants.
- Cash donations made by subsidiary companies.
- Gifts in kind (at written down value, at cost or at market value).
- Secondments at actual cost to the company.
- Sponsorship of arts activity, events, projects.
- Contributions to enterprise projects (such as enterprise agencies) which are not charities.
- Cost of administering the charitable budget.

For the larger companies (where it is available) we publish a figure for the total community contributions of the company. This is usually the total of all the items listed above (possibly with the exception of administrative costs) which have been spent for the benefit of UK charities. In addition, the company may be making contributions overseas through its overseas subsidiaries or parent company which it will not be obliged to declare.

A company is caught in a dilemma when deciding how much to declare of its charitable contributions. It can report only its cash contributions made directly; at the other extreme it can include all the forms of support it gives. Since it is the shareholders' funds that are being spent, some companies are reluctant to declare more than the legal minimum, ie. their cash donations. Others, particularly the leaders in the field of corporate support, are proud of what they are doing and are keen to declare the total value of what they give.

The Per Cent Club is encouraging companies to spend at least 0.5% (and a full 1% in the longer term) of their UK pre-tax profits on charitable and community support. The target figure will include non-cash as well as cash support. The Per Cent Club has recently published guidelines for its members on how to cost out their overall community support (see article on the Per cent giving and the Per Cent Club).

All companies on this list give donations of £76,300 or more (in the previous edition the cut-off point for the top 300 donors was £61,850; in the 1989 edition it was £35,250). We also specify the members of the Per Cent Club.

Please note that Amersham International, East Midlands Electricity, LWT Holdings, MANWEB, Texaco and Toyota (GB) all make community contributions of £100,000 or more, but their declared cash donations are under £76,000 so they do not appear on this list. There will be other companies who are substantial community contributors but whose relatively small cash donations exclude them from this list.

The top 300 corporate donors

Company	Donations / Contributions	% Club
Abbey National	£600,000 / £1,000,000	-
Alliance & Leicester	£244,825	-
Allied Dunbar Assurance	£2,100,000	% Club
Allied London	£240,000	% Club
Allied Lyons	£840,000	-
AMEC	£150,000	% Club
Anglia Television Group	£195,000	% Club
ANZ Grindlays Bank	£88,000	-
APV	£134,000	-
Argyll Group	£490,000	-
Artix	£162,880	-
ASDA Group	£200,000 / £700,000	% Club
Associated British Foods	£200,000	% Club
Associated British Ports	£87,539	-
Avon Cosmetics	£84,657	% Club
BAA	£378,000	-
Scott Bader	£125,132	-
J C Bamford	£152,000	-
Bank of England	£331,000 / £1,270,000	-
Bank of Scotland	£420,000	% Club
Barclays	£2,000,000 / £9,000,000	% Club
Barings	£4,202,000	% Club
Bass	£975,277	-
BAT Industries	£2,700,000	% Club
BBA Group	£85,000	-
Bestway	£250,000	% Club
BET	£126,000	% Club
BICC	£200,000	-
Biwater	£90,900	-
Blue Circle Industries	£324,000	% Club
BMW	£78,366	-
BOC	£1,450,000	-
Body Shop International	£313,613	-
Booker	£81,000	-
Boots Company	£1,213,016 / £2,356,167	-
C T Bowring	£400,000	% Club
Brent Walker Group	£220,000	-
Bristol & West	£105,000	-
British Aerospace	£1,310,000	% Club
British Airways	£461,000	-
British Alcan	£206,000	-
British Coal	£268,000	-
British Gas	£1,900,000 / £10,000,000	% Club
British Nuclear Fuels	£204,000 / £250,000	% Club
British Petroleum	£8,500,000 / £14,100,000	-
British Steel	£353,000	-
British Sugar	£100,000	-
British Telecom	£5,500,000 / £14,500,000	% Club
BTR	£234,000	-
Bunzl	£205,000	% Club
Burmah Castrol	£172,000	% Club
Burton Group	£300,371	% Club
C & A Stores	£205,000	-
Cable & Wireless	£646,000 / £1,600,000	% Club
Cadbury Schweppes	£550,000 / £3,714,000	% Club
Capital Radio	£81,000	-
Carlton Communications	£237,500	% Club
CEF Holdings	£196,409	-
Central Independant TV	£338,758	% Club
Charter Consolidated	£427,000	-
Charterhouse	£133,672	-
Christies International	£349,000	% Club
Ciba-Geigy	£178,990	% Club
Citibank	£309,500	% Club
Clydesdale Bank	£97,000	-
Coats Viyella	£233,000	% Club
Coca-cola	£102,250	-
Commercial Union	£157,307	-
Conder Group	£84,518	% Club
Conoco UK	£340,000	-
Control Securities	£255,000	% Club
Co-operative Bank	£76,347	-
Cookson Group	£121,000	-
Costain Group	£83,340	-
Courage Group	£170,000 / £900,000	-
Courtaulds	£196,646	-
Coutts & Co	£359,000	-
Daily Mail & General Trust	£253,000	-
Dalgety	£200,082	-
Dawson International	£77,000	-
Digital	£230,000	% Club
Dixons Group	£507,000	% Club
Dow Chemical Co	£77,658	% Club
Duchy of Cornwall	£122,294	% Club
Edmundson Electrical	£98,000	-
Enterprise Oil	£198,444	-
Esso UK	£1,583,748 / £3,200,000	-

The top 300 corporate donors

Company	Donations Contributions	% Club
Express Newspapers	£989,990	-
Fine Art Development	£127,902	% Club
First National Finance	£79,000	-
Fisons	£110,000	% Club
Robert Fleming	£161,817	-
Ford Motor Company	£224,000	-
Forte	£542,000	-
GKN	£128,315	% Club
Gallaher	£426,943	-
Gateway	£127,000	-
General Accident	£389,055 £1,351,055	-
General Electric	£784,000	% Club
S R Gent	£97,071	% Club
Girobank	£212,000	% Club
Glaxo Holdings	£3,700,000 £8,000,000	% Club
Glynwed International	£121,851	% Club
Granada Group	£400,000	-
Grand Metropolitan	£4,036,000 £6,000,000	% Club
Greycoat	£89,282	% Club
Guardian & Manchester Evening News	£346,000	-
Guardian Royal Exchange	£266,649	% Club
Guinness	£2,662,000	% Club
Halifax Building Society	£592,815 £1,048,815	-
Hambros	£232,000	-
Hanson	£786,000	-
Harrisons & Crosfield	£174,286	-
Hawker Siddeley	£171,300	-
C E Heath	£80,300	-
H J Heinz	£131,000	-
Heron International	£5,329,475	% Club
Hewlett-Packard	£87,000	-
Highland Distilleries	£80,000	% Club
Hillsdown Holdings	£355,000	% Club
Honeywell	£259,480	-
House of Fraser	£185,892	-
HTV Group	£184,000	-
IBM	£2,048,000 £3,191,000	% Club
Iceland Frozen Foods	£254,000	% Club
ICI	£3,200,000 £5,200,000	-
ICL	£257,000	-
IMI	£206,000 £282,000	-

Company	Donations Contributions	% Club
Inchcape	£201,000	-
Jaguar Cars	£208,250	% Club
JIB Group	£144,000	-
Johnson Matthey	£246,000	-
Johnson Wax Ltd	£223,193	% Club
Kellogg Co	£410,189 £650,000	% Club
Kingfisher	£910,200 £1,094,000	-
Kleinwort Benson	£269,000	% Club
Kodak Ltd	£410,000	-
Kwik-Fit	£164,000	-
Ladbroke Group	£224,000 £1,000,000	% Club
John Laing	£91,576	% Club
Land Securities	£124,700	-
Laporte	£68,000	-
LASMO	£104,900	-
Lazard Brothers	£205,000	-
Legal & General	£364,700	% Club
Levi Strauss	£149,242	-
John Lewis	£785,000	-
Lex Service	£200,000	% Club
Lilly Industries	£95,000	-
Littlewoods	£239,000	% Club
Lloyds Bank	£1,149,000 £4,950,000	% Club
London & Edinburgh Trust	£198,000	% Club
London Electricity	£116,000 £450,000	-
Lonrho	£345,404	-
Lucas Industries	£325,000	-
McCain	£96,027	-
MacMillan	£118,250	-
Manpower	£140,269	-
Marks & Spencer	£3,425,000 £5,500,000	% Club
Marlowe Holdings	£83,000	-
Mars GB	£208,496	-
Marshall of Cambridge	£267,081	-
Matheson	£130,000	-
Bernard Matthews	£85,123	% Club
John Menzies	£83,000	% Club
MEPC Group	£414,000	-
Merck Sharp & Dohme	£311,586	% Club
MFI	£107,402	-
Midland Bank	£488,397 £3,416,000	% Club

The top 300 corporate donors

Company	Donations / Contributions	% Club
Miller Group	£144,000	% Club
Minet Holdings	$193,000	-
Morgan Crucible	£85,883	-
Morgan Grenfell	£128,000 / £186,000	% Club
Wm Morrison	£137,204	-
National Grid	£108,792	-
National Power	£323,098	-
National Westminster Bank	£2,328,205 / £11,746,907	% Club
Nationwide Anglia	£349,011	-
Nestle Holdings	£447,982	% Club
Newarthill	£85,000	-
News International	£1,972,092	-
NFC	£1,300,000	% Club
Northern Electric	£148,716 / £650,000	% Club
Northern Foods	£440,967	-
Northern Telecom	£236,000	-
Northumbrian Water	£383,000 / £636,000	-
NORWEB	£76,340	-
Norwich Union	£307,000	% Club
Nuclear Electric	£247,785	-
P & O Steam Navigation	£431,000	-
Pearl Group	£310,942	% Club
Pearson	£917,000	% Club
Peugeot Talbot	£181,000	% Club
Pilkington	£281,000	% Club
PMG Investments	£212,000	-
Polypipe	£83,331	-
Post Office Group	£1,200,000 / £1,800,000	-
PowerGen	£191,825	-
PPP	£270,000	-
Price-Waterhouse	£150,000	-
Provincial Group	£108,073	-
Prudential Corporation	£1,049,000 / £1,300,000	% Club
Racal Electronics	£213,000	-
Rank Organisation	£199,988 / £315,000	-
Rank Xerox	£400,000	% Club
Ranks Hovis McDougall	£252,000	% Club
Ratners	£455,000	-
Readers Digest	£106,000	% Club
Reckitt & Colman	£308,000	-
Redland	£129,000	-
Reed International	£417,000 / £2,000,000	% Club
Reuters Holdings	£600,000	% Club
Marc Rich	£170,000	% Club
RMC Group	£136,000	-
Rolls Royce	£307,000	-
Rosehaugh	£204,000	% Club
Rothmans International	£385,163	% Club
N M Rothschild	£510,000	% Club
Royal Bank of Scotland	£1,059,644 / £1,466,723	% Club
Royal Insurance	£498,312	% Club
Royal London Mutual Insurance	£95,800	-
RTZ Corporation	£987,000 / £2,542,000	% Club
Saatchi & Saatchi	£221,000	% Club
J Sainsbury	£1,400,000	% Club
St James's Place	£125,000	% Club
St Martin's Holdings	£103,837	-
Schroders	£281,000	% Club
Scottish Amicable	£140,685	-
Scottish & Newcastle	£343,000	-
Scottish Television	£127,007	% Club
Seagram Distillers	£1,483,000	-
Sealink Stena	£125,737	-
Sears	£317,000	-
Securicor Group	£149,300	% Club
Sedgwick Group	£194,000	% Club
Seeboard	£107,000 / £300,000	-
Severn Trent	£145,853	-
Shandwick	£141,000	-
Shell UK	£2,090,000 / £6,352,000	-
Shepherd Building Group	£140,000	-
Simons Group	£105,782	-
Slough Estates	£222,200	% Club
Smith & Nephew	£467,000	-
W H Smith	£285,000 / £1,300,000	% Club
SmithKline Beecham	£1,247,000	-
Smiths Industries	£288,000	% Club
Standard Chartered	£234,583	-
Sterling Winthrop	£81,924	-
Storehouse	£313,000	-
Sun Alliance	£299,000	-
Sun Life Assurance	£299,741	% Club
John Swire & Sons	£1,625,000	-

The top 300 corporate donors

Company	Donations / Contributions	% Club
TI Group	£173,500	% Club
T & N	£104,552	-
TSB Group	£3,352,000 / £5,519,000	% Club
TV AM	£125,000	-
Tarmac	£271,000	% Club
Tate & Lyle	£260,000 / £315,000	% Club
Taylor Woodrow	£126,911	% Club
Telegraph	£202,720	-
Tesco	£260,000 / £4,600,000	% Club
Thames Water	£106,000	-
Thomson Corporation	£200,000	-
Thorn EMI	£1,052,000 / £4,000,000	% Club
3i Group	£250,000	% Club
3M UK	£219,000	% Club
Tiphook	£132,417	% Club
Tioxide Group	£270,000 / £370,000	-
Tomkins	£106,157	-
Tozer Kemsley & Millbourn	£113,000	-
Trafalgar House	£108,000	-
TSW	£90,545	-
Tyne Tees Television	£118,000 / £192,000	% Club
Unigate	£158,000	-
Unilever	£3,000,000 / £5,000,000	% Club
Unisys	£85,552	-
United Biscuits	£631,000 / £1,470,000	% Club
United Newspapers	£1,168,000	% Club
Van Leer	£1,300,000	-
Vaux Group	£143,000	% Club
Vauxhall Motors	£446,582	-
Vickers	£160,941	% Club
VSEL	£116,210	-
S G Warburg	£685,000	% Club
Weetabix	£325,000	-
Wellcome Foundation	£719,000 / £867,000	% Club
Western United	£122,000	-
Westland Group	£83,294	-
Whitbread	£640,613	% Club
Wickes	£134,000	% Club
Williams Holdings	£136,000	-
Willis Corroon	£481,000	% Club
George Wimpey	£100,000	-
Rudolf Wolff & Co	£122,448	% Club
Woolwich Building Society	£300,000 / £1,500,000	% Club
WPP Group	£167,000	-
Yorkshire Bank	£106,000	-
Yorkshire Electricity	£114,791	-
Yorkshire Television	£108,000	-
Yorkshire Water	£79,200	-

Alphabetical listing

This section gives information on about 1,430 companies. The list includes all Times 1,000 industrial companies; leading companies in banking and finance; insurance companies and building societies; property companies and some nationalised industries. The information was supplied by Extel Financial Ltd and supplemented by our own research.

The following information is given on each company:

1. Name of company

The full name of the company is given. The company may be:

- A public limited company, which is designated plc. This will normally be a company with shares quoted on the Stock Exchange.
- A privately owned company.
- A company taken over and now owned by another company. In such cases the company listed will still have retained its own identity for charitable donations (eg. Allied Dunbar) or where it was recently acquired and the information relates to the pre-takeover period.
- A British subsidiary of an overseas-based company.

The company name may be unfamiliar but it may hide a more familiar branch name or operating subsidiary. Through a continuous process of acquisitions and mergers, companies may now be owned by a holding company, a conglomerate, or a transnational company. We only give the name of the holding company, and you may have to do your own research to link companies and plants you may wish to approach with the head office that operates them and may have ultimate control over their donations. For about 400 of these companies this information is in **The Major Companies Guide** which is the companion volume to this book. Another useful source of information is the company **annual report** which is usually available free on request. This lists subsidiary and associate (less than 50% owned) companies and will usually report on the business activity of the company during the year. Another ready source of information is in the **Who Owns Whom** directory which lists the subsidiary companies of the larger UK companies.

Some companies 'hide' behind initials such as **BAA** (formerly the British Airports Authority), **ECC** (English China Clays) and **NFC** (National Freight Consortium).

Where a company has been taken over (and inevitably more will have been since this Guide went to press), it may continue to operate its own donations activity or the donations may be transferred immediately to the new owner. Although the purchased company may still be making donations under Deeds of Covenant which have yet to run out, the decision making on this function may be retained or transferred to the new owner. This is something you need to find out. As companies move from Deeds of Covenant to single tax-effective payments, it becomes more likely that donations will be centralised and adjusted to the new owner's priorities and interests that much more quickly.

The companies are listed in alphabetical order.

2. Address and telephone

We give the address to which appeals should be sent. Most of the companies listed deal with donations at head office. Some larger companies also decide on donations at regional or plant level. If you are applying to a major subsidiary of a large company, you can either send your appeal to the head office listed in this book or find out first if appeals are considered at regional or plant level.

The telephone number of the company is also given. Appeals should be submitted **in writing** but a telephone number is useful if you wish to ask for details of the company's appeals procedure, request a copy of the latest annual report, or check that the people you are writing to still work for the company or are still the contact for charitable donations. Information goes out of date quite quickly and it can be counterproductive to write to someone who no longer works for the company.

3. Nature of company business

The main area of the company's activity is given. This is useful if you are looking for a product link with your cause, but remember that many of the larger companies span several areas of activity and you may want to supplement the information given here with your personal knowledge or further research.

4. Officers of the company

The names of the chairman and managing director are usually given. There is not room to list all the members of the company's main board. Much company giving, especially for the smaller and medium-sized companies, is conducted on the basis of personal contacts or of support for causes known to the company's senior officers. If you have a contact, use it! Where you have no contact, we give the name and job title of the person responsible for handling charitable donations. This information was checked by telephone.

5. Year end

The date of the company's year end is given. The precise date may in fact vary by a day or two from year to year. Normally a co-ordinated company donor will budget for a certain sum for its charitable donations and stick within this amount. The fact that companies have in the past paid most of this via a Deed of Covenant in order to obtain the available tax advantages has acted as a further incentive to keep within budget. The procedure for making single donations tax-effectively introduced in 1986 has not really affected this.

Some companies allocate all their budget at an annual meeting; others spread donations throughout the year. Some give to causes they wish to support until the budget is used up and then stop; others continue to give even after the budget is spent if an appeal takes their fancy. If they reply to your appeal, many will write to say that their budget is "fully committed". Often this is simply a polite way of refusing support.

The year end is important in that if you get your appeal in soon afterwards the company will not have spent its charitable budget for the coming year. However, if a company allocates its budget evenly throughout the year and receives a flood of applications at the start of its new financial year, some which would have been supported later in the year now miss out. There is no fail-safe answer to this problem. If you need the money, send off an application unless you know that the company will not support you (for whatever reason). However, your chances of success are usually improved by sending the application earlier rather than later in the company's financial year.

6. Financial statistics

The turnover, pre-tax profit and total donated to charity are given. Most relate to 1991/92. These figures give an indication of the scale of the company's giving relative to its size. Where a profit figure appears in brackets, this denotes a loss for the year.

The figure for charitable donations is the figure published by the company and usually relates only to cash donations. It will not include gifts in kind, secondments, advertising or sponsorship. Furthermore a company's present level of donations does not necessarily indicate its future commitments. Sending your appeal to the less generous companies may even persuade them to increase their charitable donations, although in general if a company is only giving a little your chances of success are reduced. Certainly if they never receive appeals there will be no outside pressure on them to change their policy.

For some companies, no donations figure is available. Usually this is because we have been unable to obtain a copy of the company's annual report, although sometimes it means that the company is giving under £200 in charitable and political donations so it does not have to declare a figure.

Some companies do not give any money to charity. Where we know this to be the case, we have stated this in the donations policy.

7. Contact for appeals

Only the very large corporate donors have specialist staff dealing with appeals. For smaller companies the appeals will be sifted through by the company secretary, the marketing or personnel department, or even the chairman or managing director. The contact person is listed on the individual entry, but it may be worth checking that this person has not changed before you send out your appeal. Sending it to a named person and getting that name correct at least gets you off on the right footing.

8. % Club, BitC, ABSA

We list whether the company is a member of the Per Cent Club (% Club), Business in the Community (BitC) or the Association for Business Sponsorship of the Arts (ABSA). Per Cent Club members make a public commitment to contribute at least 0.5% of its UK profits to the community (in the form of charitable donations, gifts in kind, non-commercial sponsorship and other support). Membership of either Business in the Community or the Association for Business Sponsorship of the Arts involves no such formal commitment but indicates at least a sympathy with the aims of the organisations. There is a separate article on each of these organisations later in the Guide.

9. Employees

We state the company's total employees (a worldwide figure) and their UK employees. This gives an indication of the size of the company, the extent of its UK presence which may be helpful both in building employee contacts and in the context of payroll giving.

10. Donations policy in brief

Over 75% of the companies in the book have information on their donations policies. This states their preferences in grant-giving, what they tend to exclude, their typical grant range and any other basic information available on the company's community contributions. We hope applicants will continue to use the information to make more relevant applications.

Those who did not reply fall into one of four categories: some want to keep a low profile and are not prepared to divulge what they do; some give so little that they do not need a policy; some give according to the chairman's whim but do not want to say so; some never got round to replying. This is a shame because the applicant charity has little enough to go on and such companies may well receive more appeals rather than fewer compounding their problem. The best advice to applicants is that they should consider whether there is a particular reason why the company might want to support them before sending off an application (*see article on How to make an appeal*).

How to interpret the donations policy

1. The company does not support charitable appeals of any kind.

Almost always this statement means what it says. Unless you know a senior officer of the company who tells you that exceptions are made for projects recommended by senior personnel, do **not** write to these companies.

2. No response to circular appeals.

This means that "Dear Sir/Madam" letters, whether they are hand-signed or use photocopied signatures, are probably not even read, let alone replied to.

3. Preference for local charities in the areas where the company operates.

This means that appeals by local charities outside areas of company presence (ie. head office, plant, major location, branch) are almost never supported. Local charities in areas of company presence should check whether applications can be made locally or must be sent up to head office.

4. Preference for appeals relevant to company business.

This would include trade charities and charities where there is some kind of product link (eg. Boots giving to medical research and treatment projects). However it may simply mean that only appeals known to the chairman will be supported.

5. Preference for charities where a member of company staff is involved.

If this is the case, either mention the staff connection in your letter of application or arrange for the appeal to be submitted by the relevant member of staff.

6. Preferred areas of support

We asked companies to tick preferred areas for support: children/youth, social welfare, medical, education, recreation, environment/heritage, arts, overseas aid/development, enterprise/training, other (eg. forces welfare, trade charities etc.). This provides a good indication of the sort of appeals most likely to interest the company.

Alphabetical listing

7. Exclusions ("No grants for ...")

Fundraising events/advertising in charity brochures: Many companies prefer to give **direct** support for charitable work.

Appeals from individuals: Companies are approached by individuals in need or going on expeditions or for charity sponsorship. Most companies turn down such requests unless there is a good business reason for giving support.

Denominational (religious) appeals: Few companies support purely denominational appeals, but appeals from churches/synagogues/mosques for projects involving wider needs (especially social welfare) will not necessarily be excluded.

Large national appeals: Some companies have decided that they can make no impact in supporting such appeals. National charities would then be advised to submit appeals for smaller, interesting projects.

Overseas projects: Many companies give low priority to famine relief or appeals for overseas aid or development projects. They argue (a) the charity can easily raise money from the public, or (b) this is a matter for their staff. If a company has an overseas presence in the particular area, it is worth pointing this out or directing the appeal to the overseas subsidiary.

Political and campaigning activity: Almost every company will avoid these appeals as they will either be out of sympathy with the cause or they will not want to step into controversy.

Bricks and mortar: Some companies prefer to support people's efforts rather than buildings. Others may feel that at least with bricks and mortar there will be something to show for their contributions.

8. No information given

For over 20% of the companies, no information is given at all. In such cases, look at the donations figure first. If it is small or where no figure is given, any general appeal is not likely to succeed. Personal contact, local presence or another tie-in are usually crucial. More companies are publishing brief information on their policies, but any additional pressure that potential applicants can bring to encourage companies to be more open would be welcomed. This is in the company's interest as well as the applicant's. Any company which publishes no guidelines may well find itself inundated with appeals they cannot support; this is in nobody's interest.

Abbreviations	
Ch	Chairman
MD	Managing Director
CE	Chief Executive
n/a	Information not available or applicable
Profit	Pre-tax profit (a figure in brackets denotes a loss)
% Club	Member of the Per Cent Club
BitC	Member of Business in the Community
ABSA	Member of the Association for Business Sponsorship of the Arts

Please read page 6 | Alphabetical listing •

Name/Address	Officers	Financial Information	Other Information

☐ AA Brothers Ltd
Wholesale cash & carry

525 Crown Street,
Glasgow G5 9XR
041-429 6188

Ch: Y Ali
Contact: J G Milne
Managing Director

Year Ends: 30 Apr '91
Donations: n/a
Profit: £1,409,000
Turnover: £100,136,000

UK employees: n/a
Total employees: 463

☐ AAF Industries plc
Industrial management

7 Queen Street,
London W1X 9PH
071-408 0345

Ch: J M Liebesman
Contact: H H Schlosberg
Deputy Chairman

Year Ends: 31 Dec '91
Donations: n/a
Profit: £3,683,000
Turnover: £64,463,000

UK employees: n/a
Total employees: 1,100

Donations Policy: Preference for local charities in areas where the company operates and charities in which a member of company staff is involved. Preference for social welfare; medical; education. Grants up to £1,000. Subsidiaries make their own decisions.
No support for circular appeals; appeals from individuals; purely denominational (religious) appeals; large national appeals; overseas projects.

☐ AAH Holdings plc
Pharmaceutical supplies

76 South Park,
Lincoln LN5 8ES
0522-546577

Ch: W M Pybus
MD: A W Revell
Contact: F J Murphy
Company Secretary

Year Ends: 31 Mar '92
Donations: £17,735
Profit: £32,200,000
Turnover: £1,316,900,000

UK employees: n/a
Total employees: 7,667

Donations Policy: Preference for local charities in areas where the company operates.

☐ AB Electronic Products Group plc
Electronic components & systems manufacture

Abercynon,
Mountain Ash,
Mid Glamorgan CF25 4SF
0443-740331

Ch: Sir Peter Phillips
MD: P J Ryder
Contact: Paul Oakley
Group Personnel Director

Year Ends: 30 Jun '91
Donations: £17,000
Profit: £6,273,000
Turnover: £213,370,000

UK employees: n/a
Total employees: 5,265

BitC

Donations Policy: Company policy is: (1) the appeal should have significance for the AB group; (2) the appeal benefits an area of company presence; (3) the applicant is known to a member of the company. Preferred areas are children/youth, education, the arts, environment and heritage, enterprise/training. Grants range between £50 for a small grant made locally up to £30,000 for a large scale sponsorship.
Generally no support for advertising in charity brochures, fundraising events, large national appeals, denominational appeals, individuals.

☐ ABB Kent (Holdings) plc
Industrial instrument makers

Lea Road,
Luton,
Bedfordshire LU1 3AE
0582-31255

Ch: S Carlsson
MD: J P W Notley
Contact: W C Oldhams
Company Secretary

Year Ends: 31 Dec '90
Donations: £2,000
Profit: £7,793,000
Turnover: £175,887,000

UK employees: n/a
Total employees: 3,810

☐ ABB Transportation Ltd
Railway rolling stock construction

St Peter's House,
Gower Street,
Derby DE1 1AH
0332-383850

Ch: J O R Darby
CE: B F A Sodersten
Contact: Karen Wilds
Head of Public Affairs

Year Ends: 30 Sep '91
Donations: n/a
Profit: £41,300,000
Turnover: £299,500,000

UK employees: n/a
Total employees: 8,287

☐ Abbey Life Assurance Company Ltd
Assurance, investments, unit trusts, pensions

100 Holdenhurst Road,
Bournemouth BH8 8AL
0202-292373

Ch: Stephen Moran
MD: Alan Frost
Contact: Anne Osborne
Public Relations Assistant

Year Ends: 31 Dec '91
Donations: £9,000
Profit: £104,000,000
Turnover: n/a

UK employees: 1,980
Total employees: 1,980

Donations Policy: Preference for local charities in areas where the company operates and appeals relevant to company business. Preferred areas of support are social welfare, children and youth, medical, environment and heritage, and the arts. Grants from £25 to £3,000.
No support for circular appeals, fundraising events, advertising in charity brochures, purely denominational (religious) appeals and overseas projects. The company does not advertise or sponsor any charitable events.

☐ Abbey National plc
Financial services

Abbey House,
Baker Street,
London NW1 6XL
071-486 5555

Ch: Sir Christopher Tugendhat
CE: Peter Birch
Contact: K J Taylor (address below)
Secretary, Abbey National
Charitable Trust Ltd

Year Ends: 31 Dec '91
Donations: £600,000
Profit: £618,000,000
Turnover: n/a

UK employees: n/a
Total employees: 18,153

BitC, ABSA

Donations Policy: Support for particular charities concerned with housing, homelessness, disabled people, social welfare, children and youth, and equal opportunities. Donations in response to unsolicited appeals are usually small. A few large donations are made every year to organisations selected by the trustees. Grants range between £100 and £500. The address for the contact is: Genesis House, Midsummer Boulevard, Milton Keynes MK9 2EN. Sponsorship proposals should be addressed to the corporate affairs department at head office. Total community contributions in 1991 were £1 million, including secondments and other staff involvement, sponsorships, youth training and employment and enterprise initiatives.
No response to circular appeals. No support for fundraising events, advertising in charity brochures, appeals from individuals, purely denominational (religious) appeals, overseas projects.

● **Alphabetical listing**   Please read page 6

Name/Address   *Officers*   *Financial Information*   *Other Information*

☐ Abbot Laboratories Ltd
Pharmaceutical & chemical manufacture

Queenborough,   *Ch:* D Gibbons   *Year Ends:* 30 Nov '91   *UK employees:* n/a
Kent ME11 5EL   *Contact:* Mrs Maureen Edward *Donations:* £59,000   *Total employees:* 779
0795-580099   c/o Donations Fund   *Profit:* £33,323,000
                                                      Turnover: £123,334,000

Donations Policy: Preference for local charities in areas of company operation (ie. the Sheerness and Maidenhead areas), appeals related to the company business and charities in which a member of staff is involved. Preferred areas of support are education and local services. The company prefers to give directly rather than through advertising.

☐ Abbott Mead Vickers plc
Advertising agency

191 Old Marylebone Road, *Ch:* D J Abbott   *Year Ends:* 31 Dec '91   *UK employees:* 375
London NW1 5DW   *MD:* P W Mead   *Donations:* £49,389   *Total employees:* 375
071-402 4100   *Contact:* J F McDanell   *Profit:* £5,022,000
                          Finance Director   *Turnover:* £158,920,000   % Club

Donations Policy: Preference is given to appeals relevant to company business. The main beneficiary is the National Advertising Benevolent Society (NABS).

☐ Acatos & Hutcheson plc
Traders of oil & fat products

30 Orchard Place,   *Ch:* I S Hutcheson   *Year Ends:* 29 Sep '91   *UK employees:* n/a
London E14 0JH   *MD:* J G Durban   *Donations:* £11,065   *Total employees:* 1,106
071-987 2066   *Contact:* Peter Watson   *Profit:* £6,678,000
                          Company Secretary   *Turnover:* £228,495,000   % Club

☐ Acco-Rexel Group Holdings plc
Office furniture & computer installations

Gatehouse Road,   *Ch:* F A P Hall   *Year Ends:* 30 Nov '90   *UK employees:* n/a
Aylesbury,   *Contact:* Mrs Philips   *Donations:* n/a   *Total employees:* 3,750
Bucks HP19 3DT   Personal Assistant to the   *Profit:* £17,656,000
0296-81421   Managing Director   *Turnover:* £232,663,000

☐ Acorn Computers Ltd
Design, marketing & distribution of micro computers

Fulbourn Road,   *Ch:* A Uboldi de Capei   *Year Ends:* 31 Dec '89   *UK employees:* n/a
Cherry Hinton,   *MD:* S A Wauchope   *Donations:* £23,000   *Total employees:* 221
Cambridge CB1 4JN   *Contact:* B Salter   *Profit:* £2,525,000
0223-245200   Corporate Affairs Manager   *Turnover:* £44,903,000

Donations Policy: Preference for appeals relevant to company business and to charities in which a member of staff is involved. Preferred areas of support are children and youth, education. Grants to national organisations from £50 to £1,000. Grants to local organisations from £25 to £100. Total community contributions for 1989 were £50,000. "We sometimes offer to match fund purchases of our equipment if there is a particular reason why we should - inadequacy of funding is NOT a reason. Innovative use and/or appeals may help an application to the top of a large pile!"
Generally no support for circular appeals, fundraising events, advertising in charity brochures, appeals from individuals, purely denominational (religious) appeals, local appeals not in areas of company presence, and large national appeals.
The company states it is "inundated with requests". We have not been able to update the policy from the last edition of the Guide.

☐ ACT Group plc
Computer software & services

ACT House,   *Ch:* R K Foster   *Year Ends:* 31 Mar '92   *UK employees:* n/a
111 Hagley Road,   *MD:* M J Hart   *Donations:* £7,680   *Total employees:* 1,609
Edgbaston,   *Contact:* Joan MacGregor   *Profit:* £17,020,000
Birmingham B16 8LB   Personal Assistant to the   *Turnover:* £119,447,000
021-456 1234   Chairman

☒ Adia Meridian Holdings Ltd
Computer equipment dealers

Pyramid House,   *Ch:* P Courbey   *Year Ends:* 31 Dec '89   *UK employees:* n/a
Frimley Business Park,   *Donations:* n/a   *Total employees:* 204
Frimley,   *Profit:* £26,471,000
Camberley GU16 5SG   *Turnover:* £123,249,000
0276-692888

Donations Policy: The company states "we make no charitable donations".

☐ Adwest Group plc
Engineers

Woodley,   *Ch:* F Grant   *Year Ends:* 30 Jun '91   *UK employees:* n/a
Reading,   *MD:* G R Menzies   *Donations:* £15,098 (1992)   *Total employees:* 2,842
Berkshire RG5 4SN   *Contact:* A G Confavreux   *Profit:* £7,104,000
0734-697171   *Turnover:* £122,359,000

Donations Policy: Preference for local charities in areas where the company operates and charities in which a member of company staff is involved. Grants to national and local organisations range between £50 and £1,000.

Please read page 6   Alphabetical listing ●

Name/Address	Officers	Financial Information	Other Information

☐ Agfa-Gevaert Ltd

Marketing of sensitised materials

27 Great West Road,
Brentford,
Middlesex TW8 9AX
081-560 2131

Ch: K Gerlach
Contact: P I Miller
Corporate Relations Manager

Year Ends: 31 Dec '91
Donations: £4,000 (1992)
Profit: (£2,785,000)
Turnover: £173,759,000

UK employees: 860
Total employees: 28,600

Donations Policy: Preference for local appeals in areas of company presence and those relevant to the business. Preference for children and youth; social welfare; medical; education; environment/heritage; arts. Grants to national organisations from £500 to £15,000. Grants to local organisations from £50 to £1,000.
No response to circular appeals. No support for advertising in charity brochures; appeals from individuals; purely denominational (religious) appeals; local appeals not in areas of company presence; large national appeals; overseas projects.
Total community contributions in 1992 were £20,000. Help is usually given in the form of sponsorship for specific projects and is more often in the form of materials or access to company facilities or expertise.

☐ Agip (UK) Ltd

Oil & gas exploration

105 Victoria Street,
London SW1E 6QS
071-630 1400

Ch: A Angelucci
MD: A Muzzin
Contact: J L Stretch
Assistant Managing Director

Year Ends: 31 Dec '85
Donations: n/a
Profit: £63,409,000
Turnover: £128,834,000

UK employees: n/a
Total employees: 52

☐ Agricultural Mortgage Corporation plc

Loans on security of agriculture

AMC House,
Chantry Street,
Andover,
Hampshire SP10 1DD
0264-334344

Contact: R D F Bagley
Solicitor & Company Secretary

Year Ends: 31 Mar '92
Donations: £7,818
Profit: £5,490,000
Turnover: £113,447,000

UK employees: n/a
Total employees: 114

Donations Policy: "The corporation is owned by the Bank of England and the Clearing Banks. The board of directors confines itself to supporting those appeals with a specifically UK agricultural background and leave it to the AMC shareholders to make donations to a wider field. Therefore only charities specifically connected with agriculture in the UK will be considered."

☐ AIM Group plc

Aviation & engineering, property

16 Carlton Crescent,
Southampton SO1 2ES
0703-335111

Ch: J C Smith
Contact: Nick Fenn
Company Secretary

Year Ends: 30 Apr '91
Donations: £3,550
Profit: £3,108,000
Turnover: £58,007,000

UK employees: n/a
Total employees: 939

Donations Policy: Preference for local charities in areas where the company operates. Preference for children and youth; social welfare; medical. Grants to national and local organisations range between £25 and £300.

☐ Air Products plc

Industrial gases & equipment manufacture

Hersham Place,
Moseley Road,
Walton-on-Thames,
Surrey KT12 4RZ
0932-249273

Ch: B F Street
Contact: S Lipscombe
Public Affairs

Year Ends: 30 Sep '92
Donations: £49,000 (1990)
Profit: £2,628,000
Turnover: £208,043,000

UK employees: 2,421
Total employees: n/a

Donations Policy: Support for (a) higher education institutions, where there is some relevance to the company's broad areas of interest; (b) organisations in the localities of its operations concerned with health and welfare, local community investment, art, environment and training. Grants to national organisations from £250 to £6,000. Grants to local organisations from £50 to £5,000.
Generally no support for circular appeals, fundraising events, advertising in charity brochures, appeals from individuals, purely denominational (religious) appeals, local appeals not in areas of company presence, large national appeals, political parties/organisations and overseas projects.

☐ Airedale Holdings plc

Building industry & home products

Royd Ings Avenue,
Keighley,
West Yorkshire BD21 4BY
0535-661133

Ch: P L M Sherwood
CE: J H Foulkes
Contact: Jane Hall
Marketing Controller

Year Ends: 28 Mar '92
Donations: n/a
Profit: (£125,100,000)
Turnover: £186,900,000

UK employees: n/a
Total employees: 3,260

☐ Airflow Streamlines plc

Vehicle dealers & component manufacturers

Main Road,
Far Cotton,
Northampton NN4 9ES
0604-762261

Ch: A Westkey
MD: W Cowley
Contact: D Carpenter
Personnel Officer

Year Ends: 28 Feb '89
Donations: £3,000
Profit: £87,000
Turnover: £61,070,000

UK employees: n/a
Total employees: 828

☐ Airlines of Britain Holdings plc

Air transportation

Donnington Hall,
Castle Donnington,
Derby DE7 2SB
0332-810741

Ch: Sir Michael Bishop
Contact: Tim Healey
Publicity Officer

Year Ends: 31 Dec '91
Donations: £8,960
Profit: £2,111,000
Turnover: £342,266,000

UK employees: n/a
Total employees: 3,905

● **Alphabetical listing**   Please read page 6

Name/Address	Officers	Financial Information	Other Information

☐ Airtours plc
Tour operator

Wavell House,
Holcombe Road,
Helmshore,
Rossendale BB4 4NB
0706-240033

Ch: D Crossland
MD: H H Collinson
Contact: Mrs Jill Scholes
Personal Assistant to the Director
of Group Sales

Year Ends: 30 Sep '91
Donations: £14,600
Profit: £27,514,000
Turnover: £289,538,000

UK employees: n/a
Total employees: 854

Donations Policy: Most of the company's donations are made to the Boothall Children's Hospital. The company donate cash, and occasionally holidays, including Florida holidays, for some of the children from the hospital.

☒ Akzo Chemical Ltd
Chemical manufacturers

Pier Road,
Gillingham,
Kent ME7 1RL
0634-280888

MD: Dr R E Hutton
Contact: Secretary to the Managing
Director

Year Ends: 31 Dec '88
Donations: £9,140
Profit: £34,000
Turnover: £86,106,000

UK employees: n/a
Total employees: 451

Donations Policy: Akzo Chemical has three sites in the UK. Each location has its own budget and appeals should be directed to the appropriate site (Gillingham, Hersham in Surrey, Littleborough in Lancashire). The office at Hersham deals with national appeals.

☒ Akzo Coatings plc
Distribution of paints & wood finishes

135 Milton Park,
Abingdon,
Oxon OX14 4SB
0235-862226

Contact: Martin Wright
Human Resources Manager

Year Ends: 31 Dec '87
Donations: £4,789
Profit: £2,422,000
Turnover: £73,768,000

UK employees: n/a
Total employees: 697

Donations Policy: Supports local charities in areas of company presence and charities in which a member of staff is involved.

☐ Alba plc
Electronic components

Harvard House,
14-16 Thames Road,
Barking IG11 0HX
081-594 5533

Ch: J E Harris
Contact: David Fenton
Marketing Manager

Year Ends: 31 Mar '91
Donations: £30,687
Profit: £4,215,000
Turnover: £111,221,000

UK employees: n/a
Total employees: 280

Donations Policy: All proceeds are given to The Helene Harris Memorial Trust. This trust was founded by the chairman, J E Harris, following the death of his wife. The trust is concerned with the detection, prevention and treatment of Ovarian cancer. The company does not consider other appeals.

☐ Albright & Wilson Ltd
Manufacture of chemical & allied products

PO Box 3,
210-222 Hagley Road West,
Oldbury,
Warley, West Midlands
B68 0NN
071-409 3900

Ch: A T McInnes
MD: R C Paul
Contact: Assistant Company Secretary

Year Ends: 29 Dec '91
Donations: n/a
Profit: (£34,300,000)
Turnover: £589,300,000

UK employees: 3,000
Total employees: 6,200

% Club

Donations Policy: Most support is given in areas of company presence, including assisting local community groups, education and environmental initiatives.

☐ Alexander Stenhouse Ltd
Insurance brokers

10 Devonshire Square,
London EC2M 4LE
071-621 9990

Ch: J B Devine
MD: K J Davis
Contact: John Trayhern
Public Relations Officer

Year Ends: 31 Dec '90
Donations: £4,000
Profit: n/a
Turnover: n/a

UK employees: n/a
Total employees: 1,200

Donations Policy: Donations to insurance orientated charities. Preferred areas are children/youth, social welfare and medical. No brochure advertising, support for denominational appeals or overseas projects.

☐ Alexandra Workwear plc
Clothing

Alexandra House,
Britannia Road,
Patchway,
Bristol BS12 5TP
0272-690808

Ch: Gerald Dennis
CE: John Prior
Contact: Michelle Light
Sales & Marketing Department

Year Ends: 31 Mar '92
Donations: £8,803
Profit: (£490,000)
Turnover: £57,221,000

UK employees: 1,426
Total employees: 1,426

Donations Policy: The company is currently unable to extend the number of charities which it already supports. It does not support the same charity/appeal twice (or more) in one year. Preference for local charities in areas where the company operates, appeals relevant to company business and charities in which a member of company staff is involved. Preference for children and youth; social welfare; medical. No response to circular appeals. No grants for appeals from individuals; purely denominational (religious) appeals; local appeals not in areas of company presence; large national appeals; overseas projects.

☐ Alexon Group plc
Ladies clothing & handbag manufacture

Westminster House,
11 Portland Street,
Manchester M60 1HY
061-237 5229

Ch: L S Snyder
CE: R M Henderson
Contact: David Cohen
Chief Financial Officer

Year Ends: 25 Jan '92
Donations: £3,000
Profit: £11,292,000
Turnover: £114,224,000

UK employees: n/a
Total employees: 3,977

Please read page 6 | Alphabetical listing •

Name/Address	Officers	Financial Information	Other Information

☐ Alfa Laval Company Ltd

Centrifugal & agricultural engineer

Great West Road,
Brentford,
Middlesex TW8 9BT
081-560 1221

Ch: L V Kylberg
MD: U U Brasen
Contact: G Meredith
Company Secretary

Year Ends: 31 Dec '90
Donations: £2,900
Profit: £8,450,000
Turnover: £126,753,000

UK employees: n/a
Total employees: 1,653

Donations Policy: Preference for appeals relevant to company business, charities where members of staff are involved or local appeals in areas of company presence. Support for children/youth, social welfare and medical.
No support for appeals from individuals, denominational appeals, overseas projects or large national appeals.

☐ Allders Ltd

Department store & duty free retailing

Royal London House,
Christchurch Road,
Bournemouth BH1 3LT
0202-298289

Ch: Lord Prior
CE: H B Lipsith
Contact: Miss Sitko
Secretary to the Chairman

Year Ends: 30 Sep '90
Donations: £28,297
Profit: £3,822,000
Turnover: £581,689,000

UK employees: n/a
Total employees: 6,004

Donations Policy: The company has no set policy. Local stores tend to donate products to charities local to their sites.

☐ Alliance & Leicester Building Society

Building society

Hove Administration,
Hove Park,
Hove,
East Sussex BN3 7AZ
0273-775454

Ch: F Crawley
MD: P R White
Contact: J P Day
Assistant General Manager
(Marketing)

Year Ends: 31 Dec '91
Donations: £244,825
Profit: £99,500,000
Turnover: n/a

UK employees: 12,316
Total employees: 12,316

Donations Policy: Preference for local charities in the areas of company presence and national appeals relevant to company business. Preferred areas of support are children and youth, and medical. Grants to national organisations from £100 to £5,000. Grants to local organisations from £25 to £500.
Generally no support for circular appeals, fundraising events, advertising in charity brochures, appeals from individuals, purely denominational (religious) appeals, local appeals not in areas of company presence, and overseas projects.
Sponsorship is seen as a marketing activity, not patronage or a charitable donation, and therefore must have direct relevance to the company's business plan and objectives. Ideally it should give a return to the society equal to that produced by conventional advertising.

☐ Allied Colloids Group plc

Industrial chemicals

PO Box 38,
Cleckheaton Road,
Low Moor,
Bradford BD12 0JZ
0274-671267

Ch: Sir Trevor Holdsworth
MD: P Flesher
Contact: G S Senior
Finance Director

Year Ends: 31 Mar '92
Donations: £52,785
Profit: £42,085,000
Turnover: £254,481,000

UK employees: 1,871
Total employees: 2,642

Donations Policy: Supports only local children's charities in areas of company presence. No national charities.

☐ Allied Dunbar Assurance plc

Insurance

Allied Dunbar Centre,
Swindon SN1 1EL
0793-514514

Ch: G Gleener
MD: A P Leitch
Contact: Des Palmer
Head of Community Affairs

Year Ends: 31 Dec '91
Donations: £2,100,000
Profit: £105,000,000
Turnover: n/a

UK employees: n/a
Total employees: 4,071

% Club, BitC

Donations Policy: Grants are made to a large number of organisations locally, nationally and overseas. Major policies include support for carers and money advice. Various strategic initiatives are continuing to help improve the effectiveness of charities management. Allied Dunbar is a subsidiary of BAT; however it has its own community affairs department and is responsible for administering three staff charities. These funds focus on a limited number of policies, usually from 3 to 5 years. Generally only practical initiatives that help people in need are funded. Annual reports are available.
No response to circular appeals. No grants for fundraising events; advertising in charity brochures; appeals from individuals; purely denominational (religious) appeals.

☐ Allied Irish Banks plc

Banking

Bankcentre-Britain,
Belmont Road,
Uxbridge,
Middlesex UB8 1SA
0895-813759

Contact: Michelle Hastings
Secretary, Charities & Appeals
Committee

Year Ends: 31 Dec '91
Donations: n/a
Profit: £173,200,000
Turnover: n/a

UK employees: 1,000
Total employees: 15,000

% Club, ABSA

Donations Policy: Preference for local charities in areas of company presence and charities in which a member of staff is involved. Preferred areas of support: children and youth; social welfare; medical; recreation; environment and heritage; enterprise/training.
Generally no support for advertising in charity brochures or appeals from individuals. Support for registered charities only.

☐ Allied London Properties plc

Property investors

Allied House,
26 Manchester Square,
London W1A 2HU
071-486 6080

Ch: Sir Geoffrey Leigh
MD: H T Stanton
Contact: J H Nixon
Company Secretary

Year Ends: 30 Jun '91
Donations: £240,000
Profit: (£4,758,000)
Turnover: n/a

UK employees: 97
Total employees: 97

% Club, BitC

Donations Policy: Support is given to a wide range of charitable organisations, especially in the fields of education, health and community affairs. Also preference for children and youth, social welfare, environment and heritage, and the arts. Grants to national organisations from £100 to £10,000. Grants to local organisations from £50 to £500.
No support for appeals from individuals or overseas projects.

• **Alphabetical listing**   Please read page 6

Name/Address   *Officers*   *Financial Information*   *Other Information*

☐ Allied Textile Companies plc   Textiles

    Highburton,   *Ch:* J P Honeysett   *Year Ends:* 30 Sep '91   *UK employees:* n/a
    Huddersfield,   *Contact:* J R Corrin   *Donations:* £4,293   *Total employees:* 2,423
    West Yorkshire HD8 0QJ   Chief Executive   *Profit:* £13,160,000
    0484-604301   *Turnover:* £112,156,000   ABSA

☐ Allied-Lyons plc   Brewers, vintners, food manufacturers

    24 Portland Place,   *Ch:* M C J Jackaman   *Year Ends:* 7 Mar '92   *UK employees:* 63,625
    London W1N 4BB   *CE:* A J Hales   *Donations:* £840,000   *Total employees:* 78,743
    071-323 9000   *Contact:* Clive Burns   *Profit:* £610,000,000
                                          Secretary, Allied-Lyons *Turnover:* £5,360,000,000   BitC
                                          Charitable Trust

Donations Policy: Supports registered charities in the fields of education and science, medical care, social welfare, the arts, urban and rural environment. Preference for local charities in areas where the company operates and appeals relevant to company business. All subsidiary companies have their own charitable budgets and are encouraged to become involved with local organisations. It may often be better to approach a subsidiary company especially if there is a local connection.
Sponsorship proposals should be addressed to Michael Crofts, Corporate Communications Manager, although most sponsorship is undertaken at a local level by subsidiary companies.
The donations figure includes £600,000 given to the Allied-Lyons Charitable Trust, which itself gave £625,000. Overseas donations to charities totalled a further £511,000.

☐ Alusuisse-Lonza (UK) Ltd   Aluminium related products & chemicals

    Imperial House,   *MD:* E I Graham   *Year Ends:* 31 Dec '90   *UK employees:* n/a
    Lypiatt Road,   *Contact:* Richard Rogers   *Donations:* n/a   *Total employees:* 886
    Cheltenham GL50 2QJ   Group Company Secretary *Profit:* £2,696,000
    0242-510511   *Turnover:* £94,627,000

Donations Policy: The company makes three donations of £50 each at Christmas, to the Salvation Army, the Baby Care Unit at St Paul's and a local branch of a cancer charity.

☐ Alvis plc   Electro-optical equipment design, aerospace equipment

    United Scientific House,   *Ch:* J D Robertshaw   *Year Ends:* 30 Sep '91   *UK employees:* n/a
    215 Vauxhall Bridge Road,   *CE:* N M Prest   *Donations:* £26,000   *Total employees:* 2,506
    London SW1V 1EN   *Contact:* John Matthews   *Profit:* £6,028,000
    071-821 8080   Company Secretary   *Turnover:* £114,152,000

Donations Policy: We were unable to obtain a donations policy for this company.

☐ AM International (Holdings) Ltd   Office machinery manufacturers

    Marylands Avenue,   *Ch:* T F E Lane   *Year Ends:* 31 Jul '89   *UK employees:* n/a
    Hemel Hempstead,   *Contact:* Human Resources Department *Donations:* £2,835   *Total employees:* 1,131
    Herts HP2 7ET   *Profit:* £532,000
    0442-242251   *Turnover:* £81,897,000

Donations Policy: The company is currently making no donations, but this situation may change in the future.

☐ Amalgamated Metal Corporation plc   Metal & ores

    Adelaide House,   *Ch:* Dr M H Frenzel   *Year Ends:* 30 Sep '91   *UK employees:* n/a
    London Bridge,   *CE:* V H Sher   *Donations:* £1,000   *Total employees:* 2,208
    London EC4R 9DT   *Contact:* Company Secretary   *Profit:* £4,767,000
    071-626 4521   *Turnover:* £1,778,486,000

Donations Policy: The charity budget is very limited and is confined to certain pre-determined City charities. Unsolicited appeals are not welcomed.

☐ Amber Day Holdings plc   Retail menswear & clothing import

    Noland House,   *Contact:* Philip Green   *Year Ends:* 3 Aug '91   *UK employees:* n/a
    13 Poland Street,   Chairman   *Donations:* £16,000   *Total employees:* 1,913
    London W1V 3DE   *Profit:* £10,140,000
    071-224 2526   *Turnover:* £103,155,000

Donations Policy: We have been unable to obtain a donations policy.

☐ Amdahl (UK) Ltd   Computer systems

    Viking House,   *Ch:* P V Williams   *Year Ends:* 28 Dec '90   *UK employees:* n/a
    29-31 Lampton Road,   *Contact:* Alan Goodale   *Donations:* £27,435   *Total employees:* 342
    Hounslow,   Human Resources Director *Profit:* £7,467,000
    Middlesex TW3 1JD   *Turnover:* £176,759,000
    081-572 7383

Donations Policy: Support is given to local charities and organisations in the Hounslow area.

Please read page 6 | Alphabetical listing •

Name/Address	Officers	Financial Information	Other Information

☐ AMEC plc

Civil engineering & building contractors

Sandiway House,
Hartford,
Northwich,
Cheshire CW8 2YA
0606-883885

Ch: Sir Alan Cockshaw
CE: J S Bateson
Contact: C L Fidler
AMEC Charitable Trust Trustees

Year Ends: 31 Dec '91
Donations: £150,000
Profit: (£9,900,000)
Turnover: £2,338,200,000

UK employees: n/a
Total employees: 30,056

% Club, BitC

Donations Policy: In addition to the £150,000 a further £57,500 was given by the Charitable Trust. National charities of all types will be considered by the trustees of the Trust. Non-charitable grants cannot be considered. Local charities may be supported by individual group companies. Grants to national organisations range from £500 to £2,500. Grants to local organisations range from £50 to £500.

☐ Amerada Hess Ltd

Oil industry

2 Stephen Street,
London W1P 1PL
071-636 7766

Ch: L Hess
MD: W S H Laidlaw
Contact: Charities Committee

Year Ends: 31 Dec '91
Donations: £44,000
Profit: £18,924,000
Turnover: £349,830,000

UK employees: 578
Total employees: 578

BitC

Donations Policy: Preference for local charities in the areas of company presence and appeals relevant to company business. The company prefers to support specific projects and encourages employee involvement. Preferred areas of support are children and youth, social welfare, medical, disabled people and education. Grants can be up to £10,000.
Head office (London) supports mainly charities working in London, and the Aberdeen office deals with appeals relevant to that region (Aberdeen office: Scott House, Hareness Road, Altens, Aberdeen AB1 4LE).
Generally no support for advertising in charity brochures, purely denominational (religious) appeals, local appeals not in areas of company presence, overseas projects and political appeals.

☐ American Express Company

Travel & financial services

Portland House,
Stag Place,
London SW1E 5BZ
071-834 5555

Contact: Public Affairs Department

Year Ends: 31 Dec '89
Donations: n/a
Profit: n/a
Turnover: n/a

UK employees: n/a
Total employees: 107,542

% Club, BitC, ABSA

Donations Policy: Preference for local charities in the areas of company presence and appeals relevant to company business. Preferred areas of support: the arts; education and training of young people in projects related to company business; social welfare particularly child care and elderly people; environment and heritage.
No support for circular appeals, brochure advertising, fundraising events, appeals from individuals, purely denominational (religious) appeals, local appeals not in areas of company presence, large national appeals or overseas projects.

☐ Amersham International plc

Healthcare & life-science products

Amersham Place,
Little Chalfont,
Buckinghamshire HP7 9NA
0494-544000

Ch: Sir Edwin Nixon
MD: W M Castell
Contact: Mrs Sharon Christians
Director, Corporate Communications

Year Ends: 31 Mar '92
Donations: £67,985
Profit: £20,700,000
Turnover: £273,500,000

UK employees: n/a
Total employees: 3,357

% Club, BitC, ABSA

Donations Policy: Support is directed to (a) professional bodies, medical and research establishments and educational institutions, and (b) industrial and commercial causes especially involving training for disabled people. Specific projects rather than general running costs are supported. Preference for appeals relevant to company business and local charities in the areas of company presence especially involving young, elderly and disabled people and the arts. Grants to national organisations from £500 to £5,000. Grants to local organisations (from subsidiary companies which have their own budgets) from £50 to £2,000.
No support for individuals, advertising in brochures, purely denominational (religious) appeals, circular appeals, fundraising events or larger national appeals.
Total community contributions in 1991/92 were £120,000.

☐ AMI Healthcare Group plc

Health care services

4 Cornwall Terrace,
Regents Park,
London NW1 4QP
071-486 1266

Contact: Gloria Marshall
Personal Assistant to the Managing Director

Year Ends: 31 Dec '90
Donations: £18,430 (1991)
Profit: £25,605,000
Turnover: £201,788,000

UK employees: n/a
Total employees: 4,261

Donations Policy: The company has long established links with the NSPCC which receives most of its support. In addition, individual hospitals within the group support local charitable appeals. Preference for children and youth; medical.
No grants for advertising in charity brochures; appeals from individuals; purely denominational (religious) appeals; local appeals not in areas of company presence; large national appeals; overseas projects.

☐ AMP of Great Britain Ltd

Manufacture of electrical interconnection

Merrion Avenue,
Stanmore,
Middlesex HA7 4RS
081-954 2356

MD: R H Kaleida (General Manager)
Contact: Richard Fereday
Personnel & Administration Director

Year Ends: 31 Dec '90
Donations: £3,000
Profit: £9,750,000
Turnover: £99,519,000

UK employees: 730
Total employees: 730

Donations Policy: Employee councils are allocated a limited amount of money and choose which charities to support. All written requests pass through the councils. The councils consider requests for financial donations only. Grants to local organisations from £50 to £200.
No requests to buy raffle or function tickets or general appeals. No grants to national organisations.

• **Alphabetical listing** Please read page 6

Name/Address	Officers	Financial Information	Other Information

☐ Amstrad plc
Electronic audio equipment manufacture & distrib.

Michael Joyce Consultants,
19 Garrick Street,
London WC2E 9BB
071-836 6801

Ch: A M Sugar
Contact: Nick Hewer
Public Relations Manager

Year Ends: 30 Jun '91
Donations: £7,500
Profit: £20,159,000
Turnover: £528,414,000

UK employees: n/a
Total employees: 1,017

BitC

Donations Policy: The company has supported local charities, but prefers to make products available at a charity discount.

☐ Anchor Foods Ltd
Dairy produce

PO Box 82,
Frankland Road,
Blagrove,
Swindon SN5 8YZ
0793-532181

Ch: P J Robertson
MD: E Verschueren
Contact: Mike Otter
Marketing Director

Year Ends: 26 May '91
Donations: £2,810
Profit: £2,636,000
Turnover: £176,024,000

UK employees: n/a
Total employees: 395

Donations Policy: Preference for local charities in areas where the company operates. Donations are usually of Anchor products for raffle/draw prizes. No grants for appeals from individuals; local appeals not in areas of company presence; large national appeals.

☐ Arthur Andersen & Co
Accountants

1 Surrey Street,
London WC2R 2PS
071-438 3000

Contact: Ian Simpson
Company Secretary

Year Ends:
Donations: n/a
Profit: n/a
Turnover: n/a

UK employees: n/a
Total employees: n/a

% Club, BitC, ABSA

Donations Policy: The firm supports a number of enterprise organisations. It also supports the arts, hospices, education, community action and disabled groups' charities.

☐ Gavin Anderson & Co
Financial corporate communications

32 Grosvenor Gardens,
London SW1W 0DH
071-730 3456

Ch: A J Maitland
CE: Howard Lee
Contact: Fiona Harrison
Personnel Director

Year Ends: 30 Sep '89
Donations: £12,000
Profit: £6,487,000
Turnover: £53,665,000

UK employees: n/a
Total employees: 472

ABSA

☐ Anglesey Aluminium Metal Ltd
Aluminium reduction

Penrhos Works,
Holyhead,
Gwynedd LL65 2UJ
0407-763333

Ch: L Davis
MD: B D Farmer
Contact: D A Frost
Personnel Superintendent

Year Ends: 31 Dec '91
Donations: £10,000
Profit: n/a
Turnover: £95,000,000

UK employees: n/a
Total employees: 650

Donations Policy: Only supports charities in North West Wales, with preference for the county of Gwynedd. Preference for children and youth, medical, environment and heritage, and the arts. Grants from £30 to £100.
No grants for fundraising events; advertising in charity brochures; appeals from individuals; purely denominational (religious) appeals; local appeals not in areas of company presence; large national appeals; overseas projects.
The company is a subsidiary of RTZ see separate entry.

☐ Anglia Television Group plc
Television broadcasting equipment

Anglia House,
Norwich NR1 3JG
0603-615151

Ch: Sir Peter Gibbings
CE: D S McCall
Contact: Gina Boltwood
Secretary to Grants Committee

Year Ends: 31 Dec '91
Donations: £195,000
Profit: £8,726,000
Turnover: £153,368,000

UK employees: n/a
Total employees: 738

% Club

Donations Policy: Tends to support charities operating in its franchise area and appeals relevant to company business. Preferred areas of support: education, environment and heritage, the arts and enterprise/training. Grants to local organisations from £250 to £5,000.
No support for appeals from individuals, purely denominational (religious) appeals, large national appeals, overseas projects or advertising in charity brochures.

☐ Anglian Water plc
Water & sewerage services

Anglian House,
Ambury Road,
Huntingdon,
Cambridgeshire PE18 6NZ
0480-433433

Ch: Bernard Henderson
MD: Alan Smith
Contact: Fiona MacNeil
Head of Public Relations

Year Ends: 31 Mar '92
Donations: £53,000
Profit: £171,300,000
Turnover: £523,100,000

UK employees: n/a
Total employees: 5,224

Donations Policy: Preference for charities in the company's area of operation and charities related to company business. Donations include £37,000 to WaterAid, a charity established to bring safe water and basic sanitation to poor communities in the developing world.

☐ Anglo United plc
Coal & liquid fuel distribution

Newgate House,
Broombank Road,
Chesterfield,
Derbyshire S41 9QJ
0246-454583

Ch: D P McErlain
MD: J H Gainham
Contact: H S Muirhead
Company Secretary

Year Ends: 31 Mar '92
Donations: £63,488
Profit: £8,330,000
Turnover: £555,959,000

UK employees: n/a
Total employees: 3,650

Donations Policy: All applications are considered on their merits. Grants range from £50 to £2,000.
No support for advertising in charity brochures.

Please read page 6 | Alphabetical listing •

Name/Address	Officers	Financial Information	Other Information

☐ Henry Ansbacher Holdings plc
Banking

One Mitre Square,
London EC3A 5AN
071-283 2500

Ch: Richard Fenhalls
Contact: Mrs Catherine Fisher
Secretary to the Charities Committee

Year Ends: 31 Dec '91
Donations: £63,710
Profit: (£8,231,000)
Turnover: n/a

UK employees: 113
Total employees: n/a

Donations Policy: Preference for children, youth and social welfare.
No grants for fundraising events; advertising in charity brochures; appeals from individuals; purely denominational (religious) appeals; local appeals not in areas of company presence; large national appeals; overseas projects. No response to circular appeals.

☐ ANZ Grindlays Bank plc
Banking

Minerva House,
PO Box 7,
Montague Close,
London SE1 9DH
071-378 2121

Ch: Sir Brian Shaw
MD: B P Ranford
Contact: Francis Parsons
Regional Co-ordinator for Publicity

Year Ends: 30 Sep '91
Donations: £88,000
Profit: £98,253,000
Turnover: n/a

UK employees: 383
Total employees: n/a

Donations Policy: The bank supports Southwark based charities. No support for larger national charities.

☐ API Group plc
Paper manufacturers

Silk House,
Park Green,
Macclesfield SK11 7NU
0625-610334

Ch: P R Armitage
MD: E Holroyd
Contact: A Sentance,
Company Secretary

Year Ends: 30 Sep '91
Donations: £3,019
Profit: £703,000
Turnover: £62,471,000

UK employees: n/a
Total employees: 830

☐ Appleyard Group plc
Vehicle distribution

Windsor House,
Cornwall Road,
Harrogate HG1 2PW
0423-531999

Contact: M Williamson
Chairman

Year Ends: 31 Dec '91
Donations: £10,000
Profit: £1,806,000
Turnover: £389,581,000

UK employees: n/a
Total employees: 2,347

Donations Policy: Preference for local charities in areas of company presence and appeals relevant to the business. No support for large national appeals, circular appeals, denominational appeals, appeals from individuals, brochure advertising or fundraising events.

☐ APV plc
Process engineers & plant manufacturers

1 Lygon Place,
London SW1W 0JR
071-730 7244

Ch: Sir Peter Cazelet
Contact: P Williams
Appeals Secretary

Year Ends: 31 Dec '91
Donations: £134,000
Profit: £30,800,000
Turnover: £874,400,000

UK employees: 4,173
Total employees: 12,980

Donations Policy: To support charities whose aims would be of benefit to the company, its shareholders or its employees or to the standing of group companies in the community. It therefore prefers to support appeals in areas of company presence and appeals in which a member of staff is involved. Within these guidelines it supports heritage and the environment, social welfare, medical, the arts and education, trade benevolent funds and other miscellaneous organisations. Locally grants range from £40 to £200 and nationally from £100 to £11,500.
No support for individuals, advertising in brochures, circular appeals, fundraising events, non-charities, local appeals not in areas of company presence, political organisations or religious appeals (other than the restoration of national monuments).

☐ Aquascutum Group plc
High grade clothing manufacture & distribution

100 Regent Street,
London W1A 2AQ
071-734 6090

Contact: P Bennett
Chairman

Year Ends: 31 Jan '89
Donations: £7,990
Profit: £2,546,000
Turnover: £49,819,000

UK employees: n/a
Total employees: 1,780

Donations Policy: Preference for local appeals relevant to the business. Preferred areas are children/youth, education and medical.
No support for circular appeals, appeals from individuals or denominational appeals.

☐ ARA Services plc
Service management

Honey End Lane,
Tilehurst,
Reading RG3 4QL
0734-596761

MD: W S D McCall
Contact: Debbie Covington
Secretary to the Managing Director

Year Ends: 30 Sep '91
Donations: £9,000
Profit: £4,000,000
Turnover: £85,000,000

UK employees: 6,500
Total employees: 6,500

Donations Policy: The company provides support and/or sponsorship for members of staff and, if appropriate, client companies engaged in charitable work.
Generally no support for circular appeals, fundraising events, advertising in charity brochures, appeals from individuals, purely denominational (religious) appeals, local appeals not in areas of company presence, large national appeals or overseas projects.

☐ Archer Daniels Midland International Ltd
Foodstuffs, animal feed & bakery equipment manufacture

1 & 2 Callender Cottages,
Church Manorway,
Erith,
Kent DA8 1DL
081-312 3620

Contact: D McGill
Managing Director

Year Ends: 31 Dec '90
Donations: n/a
Profit: £385,000
Turnover: £137,625,000

UK employees: n/a
Total employees: 642

Donations Policy: The company states "we make no charitable donations".

● **Alphabetical listing**   Please read page 6

Name/Address	Officers	Financial Information	Other Information

☐ **Argos plc**   Catalogue stores

489-499 Avebury Boulevard,   Ch: D L Donne   Year Ends: 28 Dec '91   UK employees: n/a
Saxon Gate West,   CE: M J Smith   Donations: £44,094   Total employees: 12,152
Central Milton Keynes   Contact: Mrs Penny Brown   Profit: £62,090,000
MK9 2NW   Charity Appeals Administrator   Turnover: £926,649,000
0908-690333

Donations Policy: Preference for local charities in areas where the company operates, especially around Milton Keynes, and charities that have company staff involved. Preference for children and youth; social welfare; medical; enterprise/training; charities working with disabled people. Donations are usually £25 gift vouchers or particular items requested from the stores. Grants to national organisations from £25 to £1,300. Grants to local organisations from £20 to £6,000.
No response to circular appeals. No grants for advertising in charity brochures; local appeals not in areas of company presence; large national appeals. Overseas projects are not usually supported.

☐ **Argus Press Ltd**   Printers

Somerset House,   Ch: G E Fowkes   Year Ends: 31 Mar '90   UK employees: n/a
London Road,   Contact: M J McKenna   Donations: £5,068   Total employees: 2,378
Redhill,   Company Secretary   Profit: £2,738,000
Surrey RH1 1LU   Turnover: £124,024,000
0737-768611

☐ **Argyll Group plc**   Retailers of food & drink

6 Millington Road,   Ch: M A Grant   Year Ends: 30 Mar '92   UK employees: n/a
Hayes,   Contact: Sheila Underwood   Donations: £490,000   Total employees: 65,635
Middlesex UB3 4AY   Community Affairs Manager   Profit: £364,500,000
081-848 8744   Turnover: £5,093,300,000

Donations Policy: The group has supported enterprise, education and environmental initiatives. Support for small local appeals is usually decided by district managers. Local managers can give small support to local charities in the form of raffle prizes and such like.

☐ **Arjo Wiggins Appleton plc**   Papers & pulp manufacture

Gateway House,   Ch: A W P Stenham   Year Ends: 31 Dec '91   UK employees: n/a
Basing View,   CE: S R Walls   Donations: £74,602   Total employees: 18,911
Basingstoke RG21 2EE   Contact: P Billinghurst   Profit: £231,500,000
0256-842020   Gateway House Manager   Turnover: £2,486,700,000   BitC

Donations Policy: The company is currently formulating a donations policy.

☐ **Arkady Feed (UK) Ltd**   Animal feed stuffs & grain

Congress House,   MD: K Jansa   Year Ends: 30 Nov '90   UK employees: n/a
Lyon Road,   Contact: Claudia Hunt   Donations: n/a   Total employees: n/a
Harrow,   Secretary to the Managing   Profit: £325,000
Middlesex HA1 2HY   Director   Turnover: £121,417,000
081-424 9111

☐ **Armitage Shanks Group Ltd**   Building materials & bathroom fittings

Armitage,   Ch: Kenneth L Shanks   Year Ends: UK employees: n/a
Nr Rugeley,   MD: Leonard Clarke   Donations: n/a   Total employees: n/a
Staffordshire WS15 4BT   Contact: Peter Carruthers   Profit: n/a
0543-490253   Company Secretary   Turnover: n/a

Donations Policy: The company is a subsidiary of Blue Circle Industries plc (see separate entry), but has its own donations budget.

☐ **Armour Trust plc**   Industrial holding company

Centre Point,   Contact: Chairman   Year Ends: 30 Apr '92   UK employees: 500
New Oxford Street,   Donations: £1,000   Total employees: 500
London WC1A 1DU   Profit: £1,400,000
071-497 0000   Turnover: £22,000,000   % Club

Donations Policy: Supports a variety of charitable activities. No grants for fundraising events; advertising in charity brochures; appeals from individuals; purely denominational (religious) appeals; local appeals not in areas of company presence; large national appeals; overseas projects.

☐ **Armstrong World Industries Ltd**   Manufacture of flooring, suspended ceilings & insulation

Armstrong House,   Ch: R Kemp   Year Ends: 31 Dec '90   UK employees: n/a
38 Market Square,   Contact: John Champion   Donations: £12,724   Total employees: 1,000
Uxbridge,   Personnel Manager   Profit: £10,874,000
Middlesex UB8 1NG   Turnover: £126,210,000
0895-251122

Donations Policy: Preference for local charities in areas where the company operates. Preference for social welfare; environment/heritage; enterprise/training.
No response to circular appeals. No grants for fundraising events; advertising in charity brochures; appeals from individuals; purely denominational (religious) appeals; local appeals not in areas of company presence; large national appeals or overseas projects.

Please read page 6 | Alphabetical listing ●

Name/Address | *Officers* | *Financial Information* | *Other Information*

☐ Artix Ltd
Civil engineering & power driven equipment

North West Industrial Estate,
Peterlee,
County Durham SR8 2HX
091-586 3333

Ch: D J B Brown
Contact: P J Clapham
Personnel Manager

Year Ends: 30 Sep '90
Donations: £162,880
Profit: £3,261,000
Turnover: £107,077,000

UK employees: n/a
Total employees: 1,125

Donations Policy: Preference for charities in which a member of company staff is involved. Donations are made to the best appeals from local charities.

☐ ASDA Group plc
Superstore operators

ASDA House,
Southbank,
Great Wilson Street,
Leeds LS11 5AD
0532-435435

Ch: P Gillam
CE: A Norman
Contact: Public Relations Department

Year Ends: 2 May '92
Donations: £200,000
Profit: (£364,800,000)
Turnover: £4,529,000,000

UK employees: n/a
Total employees: 65,799

% Club, BitC

Donations Policy: Charities local to ASDA stores should direct applications to the general store manager. At head office level the company tends to concentrate on one or two national charities each year. Charitable status is a requirement for applicants. Preference for local organisations in areas of company presence, those connected with company business, and those concerned with children, youth and families. Grants to national organisations from £250 to £60,000. Grants to local organisations from £10 to £2,000.
Total community contributions in 1991/92 were £700,000, but this is likely to decrease in the coming year.
No grants for advertising in charity brochures; appeals from individuals; purely denominational (religious) appeals; local appeals not in areas of company presence; large national appeals; overseas projects.

☐ Ashley Group plc
Food & window blinds distribution

22 Grosvenor Square,
London W1X 9LF
071-409 7595

Ch: J White
MD: A Thomas
Contact: Jane M Stables
Company Secretary

Year Ends: 31 Aug '91
Donations: n/a
Profit: £13,659,000
Turnover: £389,933,000

UK employees: n/a
Total employees: 3,696

Donations Policy: No figure for charitable donations is given in the annual report.

☐ Laura Ashley Holdings plc
Manufacturers of ladies garments, retailing

Laura Ashley Charities
Committee,
Carno,
Powys,
Mid-Wales SY17 5LQ
0686-624050

Ch: Sir Bernard Ashley
MD: Jim Maxmin
Contact: Janet C Holdsworth
Secretary to the Charity
Committee

Year Ends: 25 Jan '92
Donations: £10,000
Profit: £2,690,000
Turnover: £260,747,000

UK employees: n/a
Total employees: 6,168

% Club

Donations Policy: The company supports a variety of charities with preference for charities concerned with children and youth, medical, education and elderly people. Preference for charities in which a member of staff is involved and local appeals in areas of company presence, but charities from elsewhere are not excluded. Grants to national organisations from £100 to £500. Grants to local organisations from £25 to £100.
Direct support, rather than eg. advertising in brochures, is preferred. No support for overseas projects.

☐ Asprey plc
Goldsmiths, silversmiths

165-169 New Bond Street,
London W1Y 0AR
071-493 6767

Ch: J R Asprey
Contact: R J Philpott
Director

Year Ends: 31 Mar '92
Donations: £76,277
Profit: £19,355,000
Turnover: £107,197,000

UK employees: n/a
Total employees: 896

Donations Policy: Each year the directors select one charity to which a large donation is made. Very little money is available for unsolicited appeals.

☐ Assi Packaging (UK) Ltd
Corrugated fireboard containers manufacture

Arpley,
Warrington,
Cheshire WA1 1LP
0925-36622

Contact: P Quirk
Personnel Manager

Year Ends: 31 Dec '90
Donations: n/a
Profit: £726,000
Turnover: £125,164,000

UK employees: n/a
Total employees: 1,952

Donations Policy: The company and staff nominate a local charity for which to raise funds. In 1992, the main support was for the local hospital's Scanner Appeal.

☐ Associated British Foods Group
Food products

Bowater House,
Weston Centre,
68 Knightsbridge,
London SW1X 7LR
071-589 6363

Ch: Garry H Weston
Contact: Secretary to the Garfield Weston Foundation

Year Ends: 14 Sep '91
Donations: £200,000
Profit: £332,400,000
Turnover: £3,510,400,000

UK employees: n/a
Total employees: 53,975

% Club, BitC

Donations Policy: Subsidiaries control a large part of the group's donations programme, and policies are therefore determined largely at a local level. All applicants must have charitable status.
No sponsorship is undertaken.

● **Alphabetical listing** Please read page 6

Name/Address *Officers* *Financial Information* *Other Information*

☐ Associated British Ports Holdings plc
Port operators & property developers

150 Holborn, *Ch:* Sir Keith Stuart *Year Ends:* 31 Dec '91 *UK employees:* n/a
London EC1N 2LR *Contact:* Ms H C Rees *Donations:* £87,539 *Total employees:* 2,759
071-430 1177 Assistant Company Secretary *Profit:* £31,000,000
  Turnover: £310,300,000

Donations Policy: Support for (a) charities related to port industry, (b) those which have been of direct assistance to employees and their families, and (c) major national medical charities. Locally, port managers have small budgets for donations to local charities. Grants to national organisations from £750 to £2,500. Grants to local organisations from £100 to £1,000.
No support for circular appeals, fundraising events, appeals from individuals, purely denominational (religious) appeals, local appeals not in areas of company presence or overseas projects. Advertising in charity brochures is rare, the company prefers to make a direct donation. Sponsorship proposals should be addressed to Mrs M Collins, Press & Publicity Manager.

☐ Associated Fisheries plc
Trawling, engineering, food & cold storage

The Gatehouse, *Ch:* H K FitzGerald *Year Ends:* 31 Dec '91 *UK employees:* n/a
16 Arlington Street, *MD:* D Bowley *Donations:* £7,715 *Total employees:* 762
London SW1A 4RD *Contact:* J R J Lucas *Profit:* £1,016,000
071-491 3655 Company Secretary *Turnover:* £83,592,000

☐ Associated Fresh Foods Ltd
Dairy & food products manufacture

Craven House, *MD:* F G B Blake *Year Ends:* 28 Apr '90 *UK employees:* n/a
87 Kirkstall Road, *Contact:* Lucia White *Donations:* £1,435 *Total employees:* 1,814
Leeds LS3 1JE Marketing Secretary *Profit:* £3,584,000
0532-440141   *Turnover:* £164,362,000

☐ Associated Octel Company Ltd
Manufacture & sale of anti-knock compounds

PO Box 17, *MD:* Dr J S Little *Year Ends:* 31 Dec '86 *UK employees:* 2,271
Oil Sites Road, *Contact:* G Leathes *Donations:* n/a *Total employees:* n/a
Ellesmere Port, Company Secretary *Profit:* £16,936,000
Wirral L65 4HF   *Turnover:* £85,520,000
051-355 3611

Donations Policy: The company supports local and national causes on a selective basis, but does not duplicate the support given to causes by its international shareholding companies.

☐ ASTEC (BSR) plc
Power conversion & electronic products

High Street, *Ch:* B H E Christopher *Year Ends:* 31 Dec '91 *UK employees:* n/a
Wollaston, *CE:* G W Tamke *Donations:* £4,704 *Total employees:* 11,711
Stourbridge, *Contact:* Anne Smallwood *Profit:* £4,810,000
West Midlands DY8 4PG   *Turnover:* £273,021,000
0384-440044

☐ ASW Holdings plc
Steel-making & re-rolling

PO Box 207, *Ch:* G Duncan *Year Ends:* 31 Dec '91 *UK employees:* n/a
St Mellons, *MD:* A G Cox *Donations:* £8,631 *Total employees:* 3,063
Cardiff CF3 0YJ *Contact:* Eira Purves *Profit:* £2,300,000
0222-471333 Public Relations Administrator *Turnover:* £390,700,000 BitC, ABSA

☐ W S Atkins Ltd
Engineering, planning, management consultancy

Woodcote Grove, *Ch:* C T Wyatt *Year Ends:* 31 Mar '91 *UK employees:* n/a
Ashley Road, *Contact:* Paul Jowers *Donations:* £22,463 *Total employees:* 2,518
Epsom, Public Relations *Profit:* £8,813,000
Surrey KT18 5BW   *Turnover:* £111,246,000
0372-726140

Donations Policy: Preference for local charities in areas where the company operates.

☐ Atlas Copco UK Holdings Ltd
Compressors & power tools

Swallowdale Lane, *Ch:* C H Sporborg *Year Ends:* 31 Dec '91 *UK employees:* n/a
Hemel Hempstead, *MD:* C H Mitchell *Donations:* n/a *Total employees:* 1,317
Herts HP2 7HA *Contact:* John Forman *Profit:* £5,177,000
0442-61201 Communications Department *Turnover:* £127,573,000

☐ Attock Oil Ltd
Crude oil & gas exploration

38 Grosvenor Gardens, *Ch:* Dr G R Pharaon *Year Ends:* 31 Dec '90 *UK employees:* n/a
London SW1W 0EB *MD:* M A Baqi *Donations:* n/a *Total employees:* 2,883
071-730 5888   *Profit:* £11,613,000
  Turnover: £113,801,000

Donations Policy: The company supports selected Pakistani charities. Unsolicited appeals will therefore not be supported.

Please read page 6   Alphabetical listing ●

Name/Address	Officers	Financial Information	Other Information

Attwoods plc
Mineral extractors, waste disposal

Stoke Common Road,
Fulmer,
Buckinghamshire SL3 6HA
0753-662700

Ch: M K Foreman
Contact: T J Penfold
 Executive Director

Year Ends: 31 Jul '92
Donations: £27,000
Profit: £5,400,000
Turnover: £44,400,000

UK employees: 1,194
Total employees: 4,643

% Club, BitC

Donations Policy: Preference for local charities in areas of company presence, charities where a member of staff is involved and organisations concerned with children/youth. Grants range between £25 and £1,000.
No response to circular appeals. No support for purely denominational (religious) appeals; local appeals not in areas of company presence; overseas projects.

Aurora plc
Precision metallurgical engineers

Aurora House,
PO Box 644,
Meadowhall Road,
Sheffield S9 1JD
0742-610011

MD: E A Brightmove
Contact: P W F Wilson
 Director

Year Ends: 30 Jun '91
Donations: £1,000
Profit: n/a
Turnover: n/a

UK employees: 1,000
Total employees: 1,050

Donations Policy: Preference for children and youth and medical charities. Grants are about £25.
No grants for fundraising events; advertising in charity brochures; appeals from individuals; purely denominational (religious) appeals or local appeals not in areas of company presence.

Austin Reed Group plc
Menswear retailers & manufacturers

103-113 Regent Street,
London W1A 2AJ
071-734 6789

Ch: B A Reed
MD: N H L Fitton
Contact: Alison Johns
 Marketing Department

Year Ends: 31 Jan '92
Donations: £10,232
Profit: £3,234,000
Turnover: £75,093,000

UK employees: n/a
Total employees: 1,589

Automated Security (Holdings) plc
Rental of security alarm systems

25-26 Hampstead High Street,
London NW3 1QA
071-435 7161

Ch: T V Buffett
Contact: Paul Strudwick
 Company Secretary

Year Ends: 30 Nov '91
Donations: £18,000
Profit: £23,201,000
Turnover: £193,694,000

UK employees: n/a
Total employees: 4,451

Donations Policy: Principally national appeals in the areas of children and youth and social welfare. Grants to national organisations from £100 to £5,000. Grants to local organisations from £50 to £250.
No support for appeals from individuals, purely denominational (religious) appeals or local appeals not in areas of company presence.

Automotive Products plc
Vehicle & aircraft equipment

Tachbrook Road,
Leamington Spa,
Warwickshire CV31 3ER
0926-470000

Ch: P F Crawford
Contact: F R Chandley
 Group Publicity Manager

Year Ends: 31 Dec '91
Donations: £34,000
Profit: £5,700,000
Turnover: £269,200,000

UK employees: n/a
Total employees: 5,076

Donations Policy: We have not been able to obtain a donations policy. The company is a subsidiary of the BBA group plc (see separate entry).

Avis Europe Ltd
Vehicle rental

Park Road,
Bracknell,
Berkshire RG12 1HZ
0344-426644

Ch: W A Cathcart
Contact: Lesley Collier
 Personnel Director

Year Ends: 28 Feb '89
Donations: £4,300
Profit: £71,991,000
Turnover: £623,293,000

UK employees: n/a
Total employees: 6,306

Avon Cosmetics Ltd
Manufacturers of cosmetics

Nunn Mills Road,
Northampton NN1 5PA
0604-232425

Ch: J E Preston
Contact: Vicky Smith
 Public Relations Officer

Year Ends: 31 Dec '90
Donations: £84,657 (1992)
Profit: £3,725,000
Turnover: £155,341,000

UK employees: n/a
Total employees: 2,110

% Club, BitC

Donations Policy: Preference for national organisations actively involved in the community, throughout the UK, with particular emphasis on family issues, women's healthcare and social welfare. At a local level, preference for activities in areas of company presence, appeals relevant to company business and charities in which employees are involved. Support is also given through product donations and use of in-house company services. The company encourages and supports employee participation in fundraising events of local and national charities.
Generally no grants for circular appeals, advertising in charity brochures; appeals from individuals; purely denominational (religious) appeals; local appeals not in areas of company presence; overseas projects or sporting events.

• **Alphabetical listing** Please read page 6

Name/Address	Officers	Financial Information	Other Information

☐ Avon Rubber plc
Manufacture of rubber products

Bath Road,
Melksham,
Wiltshire SN12 8AA
0225-703101

Ch: Rt Hon Lord Farnham
MD: A K Mitchard
Contact: Gordon Morris
Group Publicity Manager

Year Ends: 30 Sep '91
Donations: £27,000
Profit: £965,000
Turnover: £227,184,000

UK employees: n/a
Total employees: 5,120

Donations Policy: Preference for local charities in areas of company presence. Applications in writing, not by telephone. No support for circular appeals, overseas projects, appeals from individuals, local appeals not in areas of company presence or large national appeals.

☐ BAA plc
Airport operators

130 Wilton Road,
London SW1V 1LQ
071-834 9449

Ch: Dr N Brian Smith
CE: Sir John Egan
Contact: J Grice
Company Secretary

Year Ends: 31 Mar '92
Donations: £378,000
Profit: £192,000,000
Turnover: £810,000,000

UK employees: 8,816
Total employees: 8,816

ABSA

Donations Policy: Most giving is through subsidiary companies. Support is given to charities on the basis that they should benefit the company, its staff or airport passengers. Preference for: education, medical, the arts, social/environment and general. Grants to national organisations from £500 to £10,000. Grants to local organisations from £100 to £2,500. Local appeals should be directed to the local airports.
Generally no support for circular appeals, fundraising events, appeals from individuals, purely denominational (religious) appeals, local appeals not in areas of company presence, overseas projects or advertising in charity brochures.
The company sponsors the arts and education. The contact is T D Morgan, Director Corporate Communications, at Head Office.

☐ Babcock International Group plc
Engineers & contractors

The Lodge,
Badminton Court,
Church Street,
Amersham, Buckinghamshire
HP7 0DD
0494-727296

Ch: Rt Hon Lord King of Wartnaby
MD: G O Whitehead
Contact: John Allen
Group Company Secretary

Year Ends: 31 Mar '92
Donations: £10,242
Profit: £50,062,000
Turnover: £830,223,000

UK employees: 10,278
Total employees: 15,398

Donations Policy: Preference for local charities in areas of company presence and appeals relevant to company business. Preferred areas of support: children and youth, social welfare, medical, education, recreation, overseas aid/development and enterprise/training.
No support for circular appeals, appeals from individuals, purely denominational (religious) appeals, local appeals not in areas of company presence or large national appeals.

☐ Scott Bader Company Ltd
Chemical intermediates & synthetic resins

Wollaston,
Wellingborough,
Northants NN9 7RL
0933-663100

Ch: James O'Brien
MD: Ian Henderson
Contact: Michael J Jones
Commonwealth Secretary

Year Ends: 3 Jan '92
Donations: £125,132
Profit: £4,147,000
Turnover: £69,136,000

UK employees: 410
Total employees: 470

Donations Policy: "To seek out and support charitable work that will contribute to the development of a genuinely just and peaceful industrial and social order." Preference for charities in which a member of staff is involved. Preferred areas of support are children and youth, social welfare, medical, overseas aid/development, pump priming and newer charities. Grants to national organisations range from £50 to £10,000, and to local organisations, from £25 to £10,000. A further £60,000 was given to projects in southern Africa, with grants ranging from £100 to £15,000.
Generally no support for "bricks and mortar" appeals, purely denominational (religious) appeals, appeals from individuals, animal charities, large national appeals, circular appeals, fundraising events, advertising in charity brochures.

☐ N G Bailey Organisation Ltd
Electrical, mechanical & instrumentation engineering

Denton Hall,
Denton,
Ilkley LS29 0HH
0943-601933

Ch: N S Bailey
CE: B Cooper
Contact: M Rogowski
Company Secretary

Year Ends: 1 Mar '91
Donations: n/a
Profit: £2,480,000
Turnover: £192,741,000

UK employees: n/a
Total employees: 3,710

☐ William Baird plc
Textiles, industrials, investments

79 Mount Street,
London W1Y 5HJ
071-409 1785

Ch: T D Parr
Contact: Mrs P M Allsop
Company Secretary

Year Ends: 31 Dec '91
Donations: £50,801
Profit: £25,072,000
Turnover: £532,807,000

UK employees: n/a
Total employees: 16,188

Donations Policy: The company will consider any charitable requests, but regards those for the relief of suffering, poverty and illness most favourably. Applications should be in writing only.
Generally no support for circular appeals, fundraising events, advertising in charity brochures, appeals from individuals, purely denominational (religious) appeals, local appeals not in areas of company presence and overseas projects.

☐ F W Baker Ltd
Farming & meat wholesaling

The Abbatoir,
Crick,
Northampton NN6 7TZ
0788-823711

Contact: G W Baker
Managing Director

Year Ends: 31 Jul '90
Donations: n/a
Profit: £3,368,000
Turnover: £103,638,000

UK employees: n/a
Total employees: 643

Donations Policy: The company supports only local charities. The company states "about nine out of ten local charities usually receive a donation of cash or products".

Please read page 6   Alphabetical listing ●

Name/Address	Officers	Financial Information	Other Information

☐ Baker Hughes Ltd — Oil & mining equipment

2nd Floor,
Hammersley House,
5-8 Warwick Street,
London W1R 5RA
071-287 6585

Contact: Peter Woolley
Managing Director

Year Ends: 30 Sep '91
Donations: £16,377
Profit: £4,805,000
Turnover: n/a

UK employees: n/a
Total employees: 2,290

Donations Policy: Preference for local charities in areas where the company operates, appeals relevant to company business and charities in which a member of company staff is involved.

☐ J C Bamford Excavators Ltd — Earth moving equipment manufacturers

Rocester,
Uttoxeter,
Staffordshire ST14 5JP
0889-590312

Ch: A P Bamford
Contact: L Mitchell
Administrator, Bamford Charity
Foundation

Year Ends: 31 Dec '89
Donations: £152,000 (1991)
Profit: £25,260,000
Turnover: £328,552,000

UK employees: n/a
Total employees: 1,513

Donations Policy: Support is given to projects in the areas of community service, health and medicine, education, science and religion. The Bamford Foundation only supports appeals originating from within 25 miles of head office. Grants to local organisations from £50 to £1,000.
Generally no support for circular appeals, advertising in charity brochures, local appeals not in areas of company presence, large national appeals and overseas projects. Proposals for arts sponsorship are not welcomed.

☐ Bank of America — Banking

1 Alie Street,
London E1 8DE
071-634 4000

Contact: Public Relations Department

Year Ends: 28 Feb '87
Donations: £15,000
Profit: n/a
Turnover: n/a

UK employees: n/a
Total employees: n/a

Donations Policy: The bank supports recognised charities in its areas of operation, ie. Hackney, Croydon and Bromley. It supports local business centres and makes small donations of up to £100 to very local appeals. The bank prefers to spread its small budget thinly. Staff raise money by organising events.

☐ Bank of England — Banking

Threadneedle Street,
London EC2R 8AH
071-601 4444

Contact: Secretary
Charitable Appeals Committee

Year Ends: 28 Feb '92
Donations: £331,000
Profit: £98,514,000
Turnover: n/a

UK employees: 4,500
Total employees: n/a

BitC

Donations Policy: Support is given largely to registered charities both national and local. Preferred areas of support: organisations working with young, elderly, underprivileged or disabled people; medical and environmental charities. Grants to national organisations from £250 to £2,000. Grants to local organisations from £100 to £500.
No response to circular appeals. No support for personal appeals, sponsorship requests, fundraising events, advertising in charity brochures, purely denominational (religious) appeals, local appeals not in areas of company presence, overseas projects or animal charities. Total community contributions were £1,270,000.

☐ Bank of Scotland — Banking

PO Box No.5,
The Mound,
Edinburgh EH1 1YZ
031-243 5451

Contact: G J Gerrard
Executive Assistant

Year Ends: 28 Feb '92
Donations: £420,000
Profit: £134,100,000
Turnover: n/a

UK employees: n/a
Total employees: 16,100

% Club, ABSA

Donations Policy: There are no specific activities which the bank prefers to support, although preference is given to local charities in the areas of company presence. Grants range between £100 and £40,000.
No support for circular appeals, fundraising events, appeals from individuals, purely denominational (religious) appeals, local appeals not in areas of company presence or political appeals.
Sponsorship proposals to R E Scott, Sponsorship Manager, Bank of Scotland, 61 Grassmarket, Edinburgh EH1 2JF.

☐ Sidney C Banks plc — Grain & agricultural specialists

29 St Neots Road,
Sandy,
Bedfordshire SG19 1LD
0767-680351

Ch: J P U Burr
MD: M C Banks, R L Banks
Contact: C N Thomson
Company Secretary

Year Ends: 30 Apr '91
Donations: £1,150
Profit: £2,205,000
Turnover: £195,229,000

UK employees: n/a
Total employees: 389

☐ Banque Nationale de Paris plc — Banking

8-13 King William Street,
London EC4P 4HS
071-895 7070

Ch: Lord Hunt of Tamworth
MD: Mr Amzallat
Contact: Mrs Dougan
Public Relations Officer

Year Ends: 31 Dec '87
Donations: £20,000
Profit: £16,954,000
Turnover: n/a

UK employees: n/a
Total employees: n/a

Donations Policy: Preference for local charities in areas where the company operates, appeals relevant to company business and those with a City or Anglo-French connection. Preference for medical, children and youth.
No response to circular appeals. No grants for appeals from individuals; purely denominational (religious) appeals; local appeals not in areas of company presence; overseas projects. Occasionally support is given to fundraising events and large national appeals.

● **Alphabetical listing**   Please read page 6

Name/Address	Officers	Financial Information	Other Information

☐ Barclays plc
Banking

Fleetway House,
25 Farringdon Street,
London EC4A 4LP
071-489 1995

Ch: A R F Buxton
Contact: B J Blair
Deputy Head, Barclays
Community Enterprise

Year Ends: 31 Dec '91
Donations: £2,000,000
Profit: £533,000,000
Turnover: n/a

UK employees: 82,857
Total employees: 111,400

% Club, BitC, ABSA

Donations Policy: Support is normally restricted to registered charities whose aim is to improve the quality of lives of young, elderly, disadvantaged and disabled people. Support also for environment, education (if relevant to banking) and medical research (through members of the Association of Medical Research Charities). Grants to national organisations from £500 to £5,000. Grants to local organisations from £100 to £1,000.
Local appeals are assessed by the bank's network of regional offices, each of which has its own donations budget. Overseas support is given largely through the group's operations in the countries concerned. There is a limited budget in the UK for selected large overseas development and welfare charities.
Other support: The bank is interested in charitable sponsorships which give it and the charity good value. In addition the bank supports many enterprise and training initiatives. The Barclays Youth Action Scheme is due to end in 1992, after 7 years and is expected to be replaced by new schemes encouraging groups of young and elderly people and community groups to support their communities. The bank also undertakes arts and youth sports sponsorship (contact: Miss R I Frost, Sponsorship Manager, Public Relations Department). Environmental sponsorships should be addressed to B Carr.
No support for circular appeals, fundraising events, appeals from individuals, purely denominational (religious) appeals, local appeals not in areas of company presence, dangerous activities, or intermediate fundraising bodies.
Total community contributions were over £9,000,000.

☐ Barings plc
Banking

8 Bishopsgate,
London EC2N 4AE
071-280 1000

Ch: P Baring
Contact: Rosemary Hawkins
Trust Administrator, The Baring Foundation

Year Ends: 31 Dec '91
Donations: £4,202,000
Profit: £42,481,000
Turnover: n/a

UK employees: 1,541
Total employees: 3,000

% Club, BitC

Donations Policy: All the annual ordinary dividend and virtually all the donations made by Barings plc are paid to the Baring Foundation which deals with charitable appeals received by the company. The Foundation is a grant making charity which made 1,092 grants totalling £8,269,670 in 1991. Details of the policy and procedure of the Foundation can be found in the Guide to the Major Trusts.

☐ Charles Barker Ltd
Advertising practitioners

Senator House,
85 Queen Victoria Street,
London EC4V 4AB
071-628 1866

Contact: Sue Welland
Account Executive

Year Ends: 31 Dec '86
Donations: £7,433
Profit: £3,430,000
Turnover: £277,788,000

UK employees: n/a
Total employees: 6,720

ABSA

☐ Barr & Stroud Ltd
Engineers

15 Caxton Street,
Anniesland,
Glasgow G13 1HZ
041-954 9601

Ch: Trefor G Jones
MD: Tom O'Neill
Contact: Lynn Forrest
Assistant Company Secretary

Year Ends: 31 Mar '92
Donations: £6,500
Profit: n/a
Turnover: £57,000,000

UK employees: 950
Total employees: n/a

Donations Policy: Preference for local appeals in areas of company presence and appeals relevant to company business. Preference for children and youth; social welfare; medical; recreation. Grants for local and national organisations range between £100 and £500.
No grants for appeals from individuals; purely denominational (religious) appeals; local appeals not in areas of company presence; overseas projects.

☐ Barr & Wallace Arnold Trust plc
Holidays, travel & motor dealers

21 The Calls,
Leeds LS2 7ER
0532-499322

Ch: J M Barr
Contact: P A Spetch
Financial Director

Year Ends: 31 Dec '91
Donations: £5,461
Profit: £4,306,000
Turnover: £229,496,000

UK employees: n/a
Total employees: 1,522

☐ A G Barr plc
Soft drink manufacturers

North Road,
Atherton,
Manchester M29 0RA
0942-882691

Ch: W R G Barr
Contact: Mrs Cunningham
Marketing Department

Year Ends: 26 Oct '91
Donations: n/a
Profit: £4,753,000
Turnover: £89,957,000

UK employees: n/a
Total employees: 1,382

Donations Policy: Unsolicited appeals are not welcomed as the budget is too limited.

☐ Barratt Developments plc
Builders, estate developers

Wingrove House,
Ponteland Road,
Newcastle-upon-Tyne
NE5 3DP
091-286 6811

Ch: Sir Lawrie Barratt
CE: F Eaton
Contact: F Brown
Company Secretary

Year Ends: 30 Jun '91
Donations: £16,691
Profit: (£105,900,000)
Turnover: £465,900,000

UK employees: n/a
Total employees: 3,000

BitC

Donations Policy: The company does not publish its donations policy.

Please read page 6   **Alphabetical listing** ●

Name/Address	Officers	Financial Information	Other Information

☐ Barratts & Baird (Holdings) Ltd

Abbatoir operators, food manufacturers

PO Box 7,
Harvills Hawthorn,
West Bromwich,
West Midlands B70 0TG
021-556 1277

Ch: R J Barratt
Contact: A R Pugh
        Company Secretary

Year Ends: 1 Mar '91
Donations: n/a
Profit: £178,000
Turnover: £117,411,000

UK employees: n/a
Total employees: 1,074

☐ Henry Barrett Group plc

Steel building & services

Barrett House,
Cutler Heights Lane,
Dudley Hill,
Bradford BD4 9HU
0274-682281

Ch: D Parvin
MD: J S Barrett

Year Ends: 31 Aug '91
Donations: n/a
Profit: £442,000
Turnover: £115,274,000

UK employees: n/a
Total employees: 1,350

Donations Policy: The company only sponsors the Henry Barrett Group Charitable Trust which alleviates financial hardship amongst employees, former employees and their families, at the discretion of the trustees.

☐ BASF plc

Chemical & audio video products

151 Wembley Park Drive,
Wembley,
Middlesex HA9 8JG
081-908 3188

Ch: Dr A Eckell
MD: B Rigby
Contact: H C Pattinson
        Manager of External Affairs

Year Ends: 31 Dec '91
Donations: £50,000
Profit: n/a
Turnover: £1,064,000,000

UK employees: 2,200
Total employees: 120,000

          ABSA

Donations Policy: Preference for local charities in areas where the company operates. The company sponsors the Halle Concerts Society as a corporate member.
No grants for purely denominational (religious) appeals; local appeals not in areas of company presence.

☐ Bass plc

Brewers, drinks, pub retailing

66 Chiltern Street,
London W1M 1PR
071-486 4440

Ch: Ian Prosser
Contact: Mrs Hilary Prewer
        Secretary to the Bass Charitable
        Trust

Year Ends: 30 Sep '92
Donations: £975,277
Profit: £508,000,000
Turnover: £4,383,000,000

UK employees: n/a
Total employees: 90,104

          BitC, ABSA

Donations Policy: Special consideration to appeals (a) originating in areas where the company has a substantial presence; (b) with which an employee has a close and active association; (c) which are "action projects". Many donations are given in response to appeals initially made to Bass operating companies. Local appeals should be addressed to the public relations manager at the appropriate regional office. Grants to national organisations range from £1,000 to £20,000. Grants to local organisations from £250 to £3,000. Established charities should always send up-to-date audited accounts with any appeal. Preference for children and youth; medical; environment/heritage; arts; and elderly people.
No support for: individuals; expeditions; advertising in souvenir brochures, diaries, etc. (including charity support advertising in newspapers); appeals from organisations acting as an intermediary between recipient and donor; organisations concerned with alcohol abuse (this is supported at national level); overseas projects.
Corporate sponsorship proposals to Ben Hanbury, Director of Corporate Affairs.

☐ BAT Industries plc

Tobacco, retails, paper, financial services

Windsor House,
50 Victoria Street,
London SW1H 0NL
071-222 7979

Ch: Sir Patrick Sheehy
Contact: Secretary to the Appeals
        Committee

Year Ends: 31 Dec '91
Donations: £2,700,000
Profit: £1,050,000,000
Turnover: £16,480,000,000

UK employees: 15,499
Total employees: 212,316

      % Club, BitC, ABSA

Donations Policy: Donations include payments to various trusts concerned with management education, research, student welfare and the arts. Money is also given to business-related youth projects and to national heritage and social welfare organisations. The group's operating companies act autonomously in their community support.
Generally no support for circular appeals, appeals from individuals, purely denominational (religious) appeals, local appeals not in areas of company presence or large national appeals.
Corporate sponsorship appeals should be addressed to Miss S Fisher.

☐ Batleys plc

Cash & carry wholesalers

977 Leeds Road,
Huddersfield,
West Yorkshire HD2 1UP
0484-544211

Ch: L Batley
Contact: B Firth
        Managing Director

Year Ends: 27 Apr '91
Donations: £14,307
Profit: £7,002,000
Turnover: £426,466,000

UK employees: n/a
Total employees: 1,328

☐ Baxi Partnership Ltd

Domestic heating appliance manufacture

Brownedge Road,
Bamber Bridge,
Preston,
Lancashire PR5 6SN
0772-36201

MD: D W Dry
Contact: Tony Dilworth
        Donations Manager

Year Ends: 28 Mar '90
Donations: n/a
Profit: £8,487,000
Turnover: £72,486,000

UK employees: n/a
Total employees: 1,253

Donations Policy: Preference for local charities in areas where the company operates.

● **Alphabetical listing**   Please read page 6

Name/Address   *Officers*   *Financial Information*   *Other Information*

☐ Baxter Healthcare Ltd
                                                                                           Hospital equipment manufacturers

Caxton Way,   *MD:* J F Adey   *Year Ends:* 30 Nov '90   *UK employees:* n/a
Thetford,   *Contact:* Miss Pippa Hooker   *Donations:* £27,297   *Total employees:* 1,792
Norfolk IP24 3SE   *Profit:* £4,854,000
0842-754581   *Turnover:* £130,917,000

Donations Policy: Strong preference for local charities in the areas of company operation and appeals relevant to company business.

☐ Bayer plc
                                                                                           Marketing of products of Bayer AG

Bayer House,   *Ch:* J V Webb   *Year Ends:* 31 Dec '91   *UK employees:* n/a
Strawberry Hill,   *MD:* L Aaberg   *Donations:* £51,162   *Total employees:* 1,410
Newbury,   *Contact:* Colin Freedman   *Profit:* £3,051,000
Berkshire RG13 1JA   *Turnover:* £360,958,000   % Club
0635-39000

Donations Policy: The company supports local charities and events in areas of company presence. Preference for charities in which a member of staff is involved and for children/youth, education, arts, medical and environment and heritage.
No support for advertising in charity brochures, circular appeals or local appeals not in areas of company presence.

☐ BBA Group plc
                                                                                           Automotive & engineering products

Whitechapel Road,   *Ch:* V E Treves   *Year Ends:* 31 Dec '91   *UK employees:* 8,360
Cleckheaton,   *MD:* Dr J G White   *Donations:* £85,000   *Total employees:* 22,856
West Yorkshire BD19 6HP   *Contact:* P A Smith   *Profit:* £49,400,000
0274-874444   Company Secretary   *Turnover:* £1,252,100,000

Donations Policy: Preferred areas of support: children and youth, education, environment and heritage, and the arts. Grants to national organisations from £250 to £3,000. Grants to local organisations from £100 to £1,000.
Generally no support for advertising in charity brochures.

☐ BBC Enterprises Ltd
                                                                                           TV programme licensing & sale of related products

Woodland,   *Ch:* I Phillips   *Year Ends:* 31 Mar '91   *UK employees:* n/a
80 Wood Lane,   *CE:* C J Arnold-Baker   *Donations:* n/a   *Total employees:* 993
London W12 0TT   *Contact:* Tim O'Neil   *Profit:* £6,055,000
081-752 5252   Sponsorship Director   *Turnover:* £197,622,000   ABSA

☐ BDO Binder Hamlyn
                                                                                           Chartered accountants, management consultant

20 Old Bailey,   *Contact:* Sally Brunning   *Year Ends:* 30 Apr '92   *UK employees:* n/a
London EC4M 7BH   Public Relations Manager   *Donations:* n/a   *Total employees:* n/a
071-489 9000   *Profit:* n/a
                                                              Turnover: n/a

Donations Policy: The company has a policy of not supporting any charity on a corporate basis. Donation decisions are made by individual partners and there is no overall figure available.

☐ James Beattie plc
                                                                                           Retail department stores

71-78 Victoria Street,   *Ch:* Sir Eric Pountain   *Year Ends:* 31 Mar '92   *UK employees:* n/a
Wolverhampton,   *MD:* G T Lowndes, C M S Jones *Donations:* £11,235   *Total employees:* 1,900
West Midlands WV1 3PQ   *Contact:* Mrs Beeby   *Profit:* £7,727000
0902-22311   Deputy Assistant to General   *Turnover:* £78,733,000
                              Manager

☐ Bell & Howell Ltd
                                                                                           Scientific equipment manufacturers

33-35 Woodthorpe Road,   *Ch:* W J Donaldson   *Year Ends:* 2 Jan '89   *UK employees:* 500
Ashford,   *Contact:* Jennifer Heap   *Donations:* £2,459   *Total employees:* n/a
Middlesex TW15 2RZ   Human Resources Director   *Profit:* £316,000
0784-251234   *Turnover:* £55,102,000

Donations Policy: Support only to local charities in areas where the company operates. Preference for appeals relevant to company business and charities in which a member of company staff is involved. Preferred areas of support: children and youth and medical causes.
No grants for advertising in charity brochures; appeals from individuals; purely denominational (religious) appeals; local appeals not in areas of company presence; overseas projects. Sponsorship is not available.

☐ Bellway plc
                                                                                           Housebuilding

Horsley House,   *Ch:* K Bell   *Year Ends:* 31 Jul '91   *UK employees:* n/a
Regent Centre,   *MD:* H C Dawe   *Donations:* £19,652   *Total employees:* 589
Gosforth,   *Contact:* G W O'Connell   *Profit:* £9,313,000
Newcastle-upon-Tyne   Marketing Manager   *Turnover:* £108,243,000
NE3 3LU
091-285 0121

Donations Policy: We have been unable to obtain a donations policy.

Please read page 6 | Alphabetical listing •

Name/Address	Officers	Financial Information	Other Information

☐ Bemrose UK Ltd

Specialist printing & packaging

PO Box 52,
Wayzgoose Drive,
Derby DE2 6XP
0332-31242

Ch: D C Wigglesworth
MD: S R G Booth
Contact: G Bennington

Year Ends: 31 Dec '91
Donations: £5,270
Profit: £3,285,000
Turnover: £48,638,000

UK employees: 1,150
Total employees: 1,150

Donations Policy: Preference for local charities in areas of company presence. Each project will be viewed on its merits.

☐ Ben Line Group Ltd

Transport & freight

33 St Mary's Street,
Edinburgh EH1 1TN
031-557 2323

Ch: W R E Thompson
Contact: Gavin Strachan
Marketing Manager

Year Ends: 31 Mar '91
Donations: n/a
Profit: £1,238,000
Turnover: £143,806,000

UK employees: n/a
Total employees: 1,304

Donations Policy: The company gives almost exclusively to seafarer's charities.

☐ Bennett & Fountain Ltd

Wholesale & retail of electrical goods

40 Warton Road,
Stratford,
London E15 2ND
081-555 9999

Ch: P Aginsky
Contact: Alan Siddons
Managing Director

Year Ends: 30 Jun '90
Donations: £3,720 (1989)
Profit: (£3,939,000)
Turnover: £88,144,000

UK employees: n/a
Total employees: 1,603

Donations Policy: No support for circular appeals or charitable appeals of any kind.

☐ Bensons Crisps plc

Food manufacture & distribution

Freckleton Road,
Kirkham,
Preston,
Lancashire PR4 3RB
0772-683383

Ch: M Jones
Contact: Joanne Taylor
Charity Co-ordinator

Year Ends: 25 Nov '91
Donations: £11,603
Profit: £1,002,000
Turnover: £26,267,000

UK employees: n/a
Total employees: 753

Donations Policy: Preference for local charities in areas where the company operates, in the fields of children and youth, social welfare and medical.
No grants for purely denominational (religious) appeals; large national appeals; overseas projects.

☐ Bentalls plc

Department stores

Anstee House,
Wood Street,
Kingston-upon-Thames,
Surrey KT1 1TS
081-546 2002

Ch: L Edward Bentall
MD: G Peacock, J Ryan
Contact: L Edward Bentall
Chairman

Year Ends: 1 Feb '92
Donations: £25,223
Profit: £1,429,000
Turnover: £70,997,000

UK employees: 1,194
Total employees: 1,194

% Club

Donations Policy: To support local charities or branches of national charities in the south of England near the towns where the company trades, usually by giving gift tokens. Preference for children/youth, social welfare, education and medical causes. Grants to national organisations from £100 to £2,000. Grants to local organisations from £5 to £1,000.
No support for large national appeals, overseas projects, appeals from individuals or advertising in charity brochures.

☐ Berisford International plc

Merchanting & commodity trading

One Prescot Street,
London E1 8AY
071-481 9144

Ch: J R Sclater
MD: A J Bowkett
Contact: Company Secretary's Department

Year Ends: 30 Sep '91
Donations: £31,000
Profit: (£20,500,000)
Turnover: £694,000,000

UK employees: n/a
Total employees: 1,000

% Club

Donations Policy: Berisford states that it will not be making any charitable donations in the foreseeable future.

☐ Berkeley Group plc

Housebuilding

Langton Priory,
Portsmouth Road,
Guildford,
Surrey GU2 5EH
0483-65666

Ch: G J Roper
MD: A W Pidgley
Contact: Tony Moul
Company Secretary

Year Ends: 30 Apr '91
Donations: £14,000
Profit: £165,000
Turnover: £100,287,000

UK employees: n/a
Total employees: 237

Donations Policy: Preference for local charities in areas of company presence and children's charities.

☐ Bernstein Group plc

Furniture manufacturers

PO Box 33,
Manchester Old Road,
Middleton,
Manchester M24 1AR
061-653 9191

Contact: Pat Lomas
Secretary to the Chairman

Year Ends: 31 Oct '91
Donations: £30,755
Profit: £3,248,000
Turnover: £59,211,000

UK employees: 643
Total employees: 643

% Club

Donations Policy: Preference for children and youth; medical; education; recreation; arts; enterprise/training. Preference for local charities in areas where the company operates.

● **Alphabetical listing**　　　　　　　　　　　　　　　　　　　　　　　　　　　　　　　　　　　Please read page 6

Name/Address　　　　　　　　　*Officers*　　　　　　　　*Financial Information*　　　　　*Other Information*

☐ Berry Brothers & Rudd Ltd
Wine & spirit merchants

3 St James' Street, London SW1A 1EG 071-396 9600	*Ch:* J R Rudd *MD:* F C D Berry Green *Contact:* C J Roberts 　　Finance Director	*Year Ends:* 31 Dec '91 *Donations:* £6,100 *Profit:* £3,350,000 *Turnover:* £63,088,000	UK employees: n/a Total employees: 150

Donations Policy: Charitable donations are limited to trade charities and requests from customers of the company. The figure quoted for donations does not include sponsorship. The company contributes approximately £120,000 a year in this way. General and circular appeals will not be considered.

☐ Best Travel Ltd
Tour operators

31 Topsfield Parade, Crouchend, London N8 8PT 081-348 9241	*MD:* M Shacalis *Contact:* Miss Alex Kleathous 　　Company Secretary	*Year Ends:* 31 Oct '90 *Donations:* £555 *Profit:* £1,101,000 *Turnover:* £107,718,000	UK employees: n/a Total employees: 86

☐ Bestway (Holdings) Ltd
Cash & carry warehouses

Abbey Road, Park Royal, London NW10 7BW 081-453 1234	*Ch:* M A Pervez *Contact:* Zia Khan 　　Trustee of the Bestway Foundation	*Year Ends:* 30 Jun '90 *Donations:* £250,000 (1991) *Profit:* £9,132,000 *Turnover:* £377,716,000	UK employees: n/a Total employees: 721 % Club

Donations Policy: The company seeks to assist disadvantaged individuals by means of bursaries for higher education, health care provision and social work support.

☐ BET plc
Industrial holding company

Stratton House, Piccadilly, London W1X 6AS 071-629 8886	*Ch:* Sir Christopher Harding *MD:* John Clark *Contact:* J R Parry 　　Company Secretary	*Year Ends:* 1 Apr '92 *Donations:* £126,000 *Profit:* £18,500,000 *Turnover:* £2,344,800,000	UK employees: 75,879 Total employees: 104,019 % Club, BitC, ABSA

Donations Policy: Operating subsidiaries donate to appeals in their local areas.
Generally no support for circular appeals, fundraising events or appeals from individuals.

☐ J Bibby & Sons plc
Industrial & agricultural group

16 Stratford Place, London W1N 9AF 071-629 6243	*Ch:* R M Mansell Jones *Contact:* Carolyn Price-White 　　Secretary to the Charities 　　Committee	*Year Ends:* 28 Sep '91 *Donations:* £73,000 *Profit:* £35,308,000 *Turnover:* £547,290,000	UK employees: 4,103 Total employees: 5,973

Donations Policy: Support is given only to traditional charities, such as those concerned with elderly, young, sick and disabled people. Preference also for the arts, environment and heritage, social welfare, medical and education. Preference is given to projects in areas of company presence and to appeals in which a member of staff is involved. Grants to national organisations from £250 to £2,000. Grants to local organisations from £250 to £1,000.
No support for non-charities, advertising in charity brochures or fundraising events.

☐ BICC plc
Cable manufacturers, electrical engineers

Devonshire House, Mayfair Place, London W1X 5FH 071-629 6622	*Ch:* R A Biggam *Contact:* Stuart Murray 　　Company Secretary	*Year Ends:* 31 Dec '91 *Donations:* £200,000 *Profit:* £81,000,000 *Turnover:* £3,790,000,000	UK employees: n/a Total employees: 42,000 BitC

Donations Policy: The company only supports charities of direct relevance to the group's operations where the person making the appeal is known to the company. The company states "Please do what you can to discourage the many no-hopers who continue to write to us. It is such a waste of money for all concerned".
No support for fundraising events, advertising in charity brochures, sponsorship, circular appeals or appeals from individuals.

☐ Edward Billington & Son Ltd
Food merchants

4th Floor, Cunard Building, Liverpool L3 1EL 051-236 5371	*Contact:* E J Billington 　　Chairman	*Year Ends:* 30 Apr '91 *Donations:* £4,974 *Profit:* £1,735,000 *Turnover:* £111,725,000	UK employees: n/a Total employees: 484

Donations Policy: Local charities in areas of company presence are preferred.

☐ Percy Bilton plc
Property investment, civil engineering

Bilton House, Uxbridge Road, Ealing, London W5 2TL 081-567 7777	*Ch:* W K Kennedy *CE:* R W A Groom *Contact:* W K Kennedy 　　Chairman	*Year Ends:* 31 Dec '91 *Donations:* £2,844 *Profit:* £17,426,000 *Turnover:* n/a	UK employees: n/a Total employees: 241

Donations Policy: The company does not welcome unsolicited appeals from charities as its charitable budget is very limited.

Please read page 6 | | | | Alphabetical listing ●

Name/Address	Officers	Financial Information	Other Information

☐ Bird Group of Companies

Scrap metal processing

Longmarston,
Stratford-upon-Avon
CV37 8AQ
0789-720431

Contact: W T Bird
Chairman

Year Ends: 30 Oct '88
Donations: £15,055
Profit: £2,313,000
Turnover: £62,060,000

UK employees: n/a
Total employees: 349

Donations Policy: We have been unable to obtain a donations policy.

☐ Birmingham Midshires Building Society

Building society

PO Box 81,
35-49 Lichfield Street,
Wolverhampton WV1 1EL
0902-710710

Ch: C J James
MD: M Jackson
Contact: Tony McGarahan
Head of Corporate
Communications

Year Ends: 31 Dec '91
Donations: £4,143
Profit: £9,500,000
Turnover: n/a

UK employees: n/a
Total employees: 2070

Donations Policy: Preference for charities in areas where the society has a presence. Preferred areas of support are children and youth, education, enterprise/training.
No response to circular appeals. No support for advertising in charity brochures, appeals from individuals, purely denominational (religious) appeals, local appeals not in areas of company presence, large national appeals, overseas projects, building restoration or political purposes.

☐ Biro BIC Ltd

Manufacturers of ball point pens

Whitby Avenue,
Park Royal,
London NW10 7SG
081-965 4060

Ch: F W G Bolt
Contact: D K Hartridge
Managing Director

Year Ends: 31 Dec '88
Donations: £2,024
Profit: £8,624,000
Turnover: £53,450,000

UK employees: n/a
Total employees: 767

☐ Birse Group plc

Building & civil engineering, telecommunications

Humber Road,
Barton-on-Humber,
South Humberside DN18 5BW
0652-33222

Contact: P M Birse
Chairman

Year Ends: 30 Apr '92
Donations: n/a
Profit: (£13,200,000)
Turnover: £356,100,000

UK employees: n/a
Total employees: 1,823

☐ BIS Group Ltd

Information & marketing services

Seaco House,
20 Upper Ground,
London SE1 9PN
071-633 0866

Ch: G M R Graham
Contact: Mrs June A Hicks
Director of Human Resources

Year Ends: 31 Dec '90
Donations: £10,000
Profit: £4,981,000
Turnover: £115,403,000

UK employees: n/a
Total employees: 2,218

Donations Policy: Preference for local charities in areas where the company operates and for appeals relevant to company business.
No grants for advertising in charity brochures; appeals from individuals; purely denominational (religious) appeals; local appeals not in areas of company presence; overseas projects and political appeals.

☐ Bishopgate Insurance Ltd

Insurance

Bishopgate House,
Tollgate,
Eastleigh,
Hampshire SO5 3YA
0703-644455

Ch: P N O Robinson
Contact: Phil Barter
Chairman of the Sports & Social
Committee

Year Ends: 31 Dec '91
Donations: £10,530
Profit: (£4,121,000)
Turnover: n/a

UK employees: n/a
Total employees: 313

☐ Bison Floors Ltd

Civil engineering, precast concrete

Thorney Lane,
Iver,
Buckinghamshire SL0 9HQ
0753-652909

Contact: Gordon Wright
Finance Director

Year Ends: 31 Dec '85
Donations: £27,800
Profit: £8,061,000
Turnover: £123,609,000

UK employees: 2,022
Total employees: n/a

Donations Policy: Preference for local charities in areas of company presence.
No response to circular appeals.

☐ Biwater Ltd

Water treatment, civil engineering

Biwater House,
Station Approach,
Dorking,
Surrey RH4 1TZ
0306-740740

Ch: A E White
Contact: C R J Goscomb
Finance Director & Company
Secretary

Year Ends: 31 Dec '90
Donations: £90,900
Profit: £10,500,000
Turnover: £283,500,000

UK employees: n/a
Total employees: 3,421

Donations Policy: Preference for local charities in areas of company presence, especially organisations involved with children/youth, education, enterprise/training.
No sponsorship and no support for advertising in charity brochures, overseas appeals, purely denominational (religious) appeals or appeals from individuals.

● **Alphabetical listing**   Please read page 6

Name/Address	Officers	Financial Information	Other Information

☐ Black & Decker Ltd
                                                                                                                                              Power tool manufacturers

Westpoint,
The Grove,
Slough SL1 1QQ
0753-511234

Ch: C B Powell-Smith
Contact: John Lea
  Personnel Director

Year Ends: 25 Sep '90
Donations: £8,211
Profit: £79,548,000
Turnover: £413,498,000

UK employees: n/a
Total employees: 5,199

☐ Peter Black Holdings plc
                                                                                                                                              Footwear & luggage manufacture

Lawkholme Lane,
Keighley,
West Yorkshire BD21 3JQ
0535-661177

Ch: T S S Black
MD: R G Leivers
Contact: Mrs A M Hooley
  Personnel Manager

Year Ends: 1 Jun '91
Donations: £20,819
Profit: £7,235,000
Turnover: £126,041,000

UK employees: n/a
Total employees: 3,526

Donations Policy: Preference for local charities in areas where the company operates. Preference for children and youth; education; arts.

☐ R H Blackwell Ltd
                                                                                                                                              Retail booksellers

50 Broad Street,
Oxford OX1 3BQ
0865-792792

Ch: R M Blackwell
MD: T D Collins
Contact: David Taylor
  Marketing Manager

Year Ends: 2 Sep '90
Donations: £8,850
Profit: £7,426,000
Turnover: £190,802,000

UK employees: n/a
Total employees: 1,816

☐ Blagden Industries plc
                                                                                                                                              Steel drum manufacturers & reconditioners

Tonman House,
63-77 Victoria Street,
St Albans,
Hertfordshire AL1 3LR
0727-40907

Ch: D T Wilkinson
MD: G C Smith
Contact: G R Cohen
  Group Personnel Manager

Year Ends: 31 Dec '91
Donations: £10,140
Profit: £11,059,000
Turnover: £218,308,000

UK employees: n/a
Total employees: 2,704

Donations Policy: Preference for local charities in areas of company presence and appeals relevant to company business. Preferred areas of support: children and youth, medical, education, environment and heritage, enterprise/training.
No support for circular appeals, advertising in charity brochures, local appeals not in areas of company presence or overseas projects.

☐ A F Blakemore & Son Ltd
                                                                                                                                              Wholesale distribution

Long Acres Industrial Estate,
Rosehill,
Willenhall,
West Midlands WV13 2JP
0902-366066

Ch: G M Blakemore
Contact: G Patterson
  Cash & Carry Manager

Year Ends: 30 Apr '91
Donations: n/a
Profit: £3,546,000
Turnover: £222,066,000

UK employees: n/a
Total employees: 940

Donations Policy: Preference for local charities in areas where the company operates and charities in which a member of company staff is involved. The company supports Barnardos, the Blind Institute and a local hospice. The company, because of staff involvement, has also been involved in sending products to Romanian orphanages.

☐ Blenheim Group plc
                                                                                                                                              Exhibition & conference management, trade publications

Blenheim House,
630 Chiswick High Road,
London W4 5BG
081-742 2828

Ch: N D Buch
CE: P Soar
Contact: M Fletcher
  UK Managing Director

Year Ends: 31 Aug '91
Donations: £11,000
Profit: £28,300,000
Turnover: £122,200,000

UK employees: n/a
Total employees: 548

Donations Policy: The company concentrates its support on a small number of charities which it supports for a period of time. In the UK, the Cottage Homes Charity has been supported for several years and support is now also being given to Hammersmith Hospital's "Help Hammer Cancer Appeal". Significant sums are raised for these charities by customers and employees as well as direct donations from the company. No response to circular appeals and no support for individuals.

☐ Bloor Holdings Ltd
                                                                                                                                              Builders

Ashby Road,
Measham,
Burton-on-Trent,
Staffordshire DE12 7JP
0530-270100

Ch: J S Bloor
Contact: D Mehta
  Financial Director

Year Ends: 31 Mar '91
Donations: £28,250
Profit: £8,796,000
Turnover: £105,030,000

UK employees: n/a
Total employees: 493

Donations Policy: We have been unable to obtain a donations policy.

☐ Blue Circle Industries plc
                                                                                                                                              Cement & allied products

84 Eccleston Square,
London SW1V 1PX
071-828 3456

Ch: Sir Peter Walters
MD: J W McColgan
Contact: Mrs Margaret Nunn

Year Ends: 31 Dec '91
Donations: £324,000
Profit: £124,200,000
Turnover: £1,113,800,000

UK employees: n/a
Total employees: 18,253

  % Club, BitC

Donations Policy: Preference for local charities in areas of company presence, appeals relevant to company business and charities in which a member of staff is involved. Preferred areas of support are education, environment and heritage, and the arts. National grants from £50 to £1,000 and local grants from £25 to £100.
No support for individuals, advertising in charity brochures, purely denominational appeals, local appeals not in areas of company presence, animal charities or prisoners' welfare charities.
Sponsorship proposals to Mrs Miranda Evans. Local appeals to the relevant regional office.

Please read page 6 — Alphabetical listing

Name/Address	Officers	Financial Information	Other Information

☐ BM Group plc
Mechanical engineers

BM House,
Avon Reach,
Chippenham,
Wiltshire   SN15 1EE
0249-656263

Ch: M Thorne
MD: H Sutton

Year Ends: 30 Jun '91
Donations: nil
Profit: £34,069,000
Turnover: £396,351,000

UK employees: n/a
Total employees: 5,209

Donations Policy: The company has a policy of making no charitable donations.

☐ BMP DDB Needham Worldwide Ltd
Advertising

12 Bishopsbridge Road,
London   W2 6AA
071-258 3979

Contact: Shirley Watson
Financial Director

Year Ends: 31 Dec '91
Donations: £41,617
Profit: £2,800,000
Turnover: £208,000,000

UK employees: 325
Total employees: n/a

% Club

Donations Policy: The company has six deeds of covenant worth £26,000 in total. Two nominated charities (voted for by staff) receive £5,000. The balance is spent usually in connection with events involving staff. Preference for children and youth; medical; education and the arts.
No grants for appeals from individuals; purely denominational (religious) appeals; local appeals not in areas of company presence; large national appeals; overseas projects. No response to circular appeals.

☐ BMW (GB) Ltd
Distributors for BMW products

Ellesfield Avenue,
Bracknell,
Berkshire   RG12 4TA
0344-426565

Ch: H Heitmann
Contact: Rosemary Davies
Public Relations Executive

Year Ends: 31 Dec '90
Donations: £78,366
Profit: £60,624,000
Turnover: £800,526,000

UK employees: n/a
Total employees: 411

ABSA

Donations Policy: Major donations are given to two or three national charities, preferably related to the motor industry, children or a charity in which a member of staff has a particular interest. Smaller donations are also made to local charities. The company has a separate arts sponsorship and education programme. Grants to national organisations from £250 to £5,000. Grants to local organisations from £50 to £1,000.
No response to circular appeals.

☐ BNB Resources Group Ltd
Human advertising practitioners

30 Farringdon Street,
London   EC4A 4EA
071-634 1200

Ch: D Norman
Contact: Paul Kendall
Group Company Secretary

Year Ends: 31 Dec '89
Donations: £6,457
Profit: £4,448,000
Turnover: £102,555,000

UK employees: n/a
Total employees: 370

Donations Policy: Preference for local charities in the areas of company presence, appeals relevant to company business and charities in which a member of staff is involved. Preferred areas of support are children and youth, medical, and environment and heritage. Grants range from £50 to £2,000.
No support for circular appeals, fundraising events, advertising in charity brochures.

☐ BOC Group plc
Industrial gases, health care products & services

Chertsey Road,
Windlesham,
Surrey   GU20 6HJ
0276-77222

Ch: P Rich
Contact: Mrs Sandie Pearce
Assistant Manager, Corporate Relations

Year Ends: 30 Sep '91
Donations: £1,450,000
Profit: £310,100,000
Turnover: £2,718,500,000

UK employees: n/a
Total employees: 40,088

% Club, BitC, ABSA

Donations Policy: Main categories of support: (a) Environment projects, funded through the BOC Foundation for the Environment (an independent body); (b) Donations to charities supported by company employees through a matched giving scheme; (c) Donations to charities with a clear business link to BOC, mostly in some quite narrowly defined areas of medical research, to which the company is committed for several years. These are generally funded through, or in collaboration with, BOC's various business divisions. Grants to national organisations range from £500 to £25,000 and to local organisations from £50 to £1,000.
Local appeals should be directed to the group's regional offices. Overseas support is given by subsidiaries in their countries of operation.
No support for appeals from individuals, fundraising events, circular appeals, political or religious organisations.

☐ Boddington Group plc
Brewers

Queens Court,
Wilmslow Road,
Alderley Edge,
Cheshire   SK9 7RR
0625-586656

Ch: D P Cassidy
MD: H V Reid
Contact: E A Englefield
Company Secretary

Year Ends: 31 Dec '91
Donations: £36,000
Profit: £20,315,000
Turnover: £185,043,000

UK employees: n/a
Total employees: 4,628

Donations Policy: Preference for local charities in areas where the company operates and appeals relevant to company business. Preference for children and youth; social welfare; medical; education; the arts. Grants to national organisations from £100 to £1,000. Grants to local organisations from £50 to £500.
No response to circular appeals. No support for appeals from individuals; local appeals not in areas of company presence; large national appeals; overseas projects.

● **Alphabetical listing**   Please read page 6

Name/Address   *Officers*   *Financial Information*   *Other Information*

☐ Body Shop International plc
                                                                                                    Skin & hair care products

Hawthorn Road,   *Ch:* Gordon Roddick   *Year Ends:* 28 Feb '92   *UK employees:* n/a
Wick,   *MD:* Anita Roddick   *Donations:* £313,613   *Total employees:* 1,926
Littlehampton,   *Contact:* Leoni Frean   *Profit:* £25,203,000
West Sussex   BN17 7LR   Foundation Manager   *Turnover:* £147,441,000
0903-731500

Donations Policy: The Body Shop Foundation has been set up to administer Body Shop International's charitable budget as from 1990/91. Budget is allocated to projects selected by the foundation's trustees. Preference for environment, overseas aid/development, human rights, enterprise/training, homelessness and local charities in the areas of company presence for product donations. Grants to national organisations from £1,000 to £25,000. Grants to local organisations from £100 to £1,000.
Unsolicited appeals are not generally considered. Generally no support for circular appeals, advertising in charity brochures, appeals from individuals, purely denominational (religious) appeals and local appeals not in areas of company presence.

☐ Bodycote International plc
                                                                                      Metallurgical services, thermal processors

140 Kingsway,   *Ch:* J C Dwek   *Year Ends:* 31 Dec '91   *UK employees:* 1,504
Manchester   M19 1BA   *MD:* J Chesworth   *Donations:* £14,000   *Total employees:* 2,057
061-257 2345   *Contact:* J C Dwek   *Profit:* £11,511,000
                                  Chairman   *Turnover:* £66,481,000   % Club

Donations Policy: Preference for local charities in areas where the company operates and appeals relevant to company business. Preference for children and youth; social welfare; medical; education. Total community contributions in 1991 were £55,000.
No support for appeals from individuals.

☐ Booker plc
                                                                                                               Food distribution

Portland House,   *Ch:* Sir Michael Caine   *Year Ends:* 31 Dec '92   *UK employees:* n/a
Stag Place,   *CE:* J F Taylor   *Donations:* £81,000   *Total employees:* 25,574
London   SW1E 5AY   *Contact:* Maggie van Reenen *Profit:* £103,900,000
071-828 9850   *Turnover:* £3,289,100,000   ABSA

Donations Policy: Booker plc has a charities committee which meets twice a year to consider appeals. A record of all donations is kept; from this the aim is to give to as wide a range of charities as possible. Operating companies are responsible for their own donations to a large extent. Preference for appeals relevant to company business and charities in which a member of company staff is involved. Grants to national organisations from £100 to £2,500. Grants to local organisations from £100 to £500. The company operates a scheme to match employee contributions £ for £.
Generally no support for fundraising events or advertising in charity brochures.

☐ Boosey & Hawkes plc
                                                                                               Sheet music & musical instruments

295 Regent Street,   *Ch:* W F Connor   *Year Ends:* 31 Dec '91   *UK employees:* n/a
London   W1R 8JH   *CE:* R Holland   *Donations:* £2,090   *Total employees:* 1,147
071-580 2060   *Contact:* R A Fell   *Profit:* £4,012,000
                                  Managing Director   *Turnover:* £53,715,000

☐ Henry Boot & Sons plc
                                                                                                       Construction engineers

Bannercross Hall,   *Ch:* D H Boot   *Year Ends:* 31 Dec '91   *UK employees:* 2,101
Eccleshall Road,   *Contact:* E J Boot   *Donations:* £11,412   *Total employees:* n/a
Sheffield   S11 9PD   Managing Director   *Profit:* £6,766,000
0742-555444   *Turnover:* £129,903,000

☐ Boots Company plc
                                                                                              Pharmaceuticals & consumer products

Nottingham   NG2 3AA   *Ch:* Sir Christopher Benson *Year Ends:* 31 Mar '92   *UK employees:* 79,036
0602-493068   *CE:* Sir James Blyth   *Donations:* £1,213,016   *Total employees:* n/a
                                  Contact: Mrs S A Bickley   *Profit:* £374,200,000
                                  Secretary, Boots Charitable Trust *Turnover:* £3,655,700,000   BitC

Donations Policy: The funding priorities are set out below. Appeals from both national and local charities within these categories will be considered. Local charities are more likely to be successful if they are located in an area where the company is substantially represented. (a) healthcare; (b) education; (c) economic development. Appeals are also considered from the headquarters of NATIONAL charities working within the following charitable categories: (a) family, maternity and child welfare; (b) animal welfare. Overseas aid is given by group companies in the countries where they operate. In the UK all financial support for overseas aid goes to the Save the Children Fund. The company also considers appeals from any charity which benefits Nottingham or Nottinghamshire.
Grants to national organisations from £750 to £2,500. Grants to local organisations from £50 to £1,000.
Appeals from individuals, private fundraising groups, and organisations which are not registered with the Charity Commission, are ineligible for consideration. Fundraising events are rarely supported and support is not given to overseas projects.
Total community contributions in 1991/92 were £2,356,167.

☐ Borden (UK) Ltd
                                                                                                        Resins, plastic packing

Thomas Road,   *Contact:* Mike Chilcott   *Year Ends:* 31 Dec '90   *UK employees:* n/a
North Baddesley,   Divisional Purchasing Director *Donations:* n/a   *Total employees:* n/a
Southampton   SO52 9ZB   *Profit:* £8,662,000
0703-732131   *Turnover:* £215,061,000

Donations Policy: Support only to very local charities in areas where the company operates. Grants from £20 to £300. Total community contributions are up to £5,000.
No grants for advertising in charity brochures; appeals from individuals; purely denominational (religious) appeals; local appeals not in areas of company presence; large national appeals; overseas projects.

54

Please read page 6 | | | Alphabetical listing

Name/Address	Officers	Financial Information	Other Information

☐ Border Television plc
Television programme contractor

The Television Centre,
Carlisle CA1 3NT
0228-25101

Ch: Melvyn Bragg
MD: James Graham
Contact: Peter Brownlow
Company Secretary

Year Ends: 30 Apr '92
Donations: £13,841
Profit: £1,216,000
Turnover: £10,093,000

UK employees: n/a
Total employees: 144

☐ Robert Bosch Ltd
Electrical product distributors

PO Box 98, Broadwater Park,
North Orbital Road,
Denham,
Uxbridge UB9 5HJ
0895-834466

Ch: A K Stewart-Roberts
MD: Dr K Liedtke
Contact: Rod Harman
Publicity Manager

Year Ends: 31 Dec '91
Donations: £21,835
Profit: £5,109,000
Turnover: n/a

UK employees: 847
Total employees: n/a

Donations Policy: The parent company, Robert Bosch GmbH, is 90% owned by a charitable trust and therefore most dividends are used for charitable purposes. For this reason the group policy is to restrict charitable giving by its subsidiaries. The figures given refer only to Robert Bosch Ltd in Denham.

☐ Boustead plc
Manufacturing & distribution

14-15 Conduit Street,
London W1R 9TG
071-491 7674

Ch: Sir Thomas MacPherson
CE: R J Barton
Contact: Mrs Sandra Nash
Secretary to the Chief Executive

Year Ends: 31 Dec '91
Donations: £5,000
Profit: £5,138,000
Turnover: £87,916,000

UK employees: n/a
Total employees: 882

Donations Policy: The board select four main charities to support. Other appeals are therefore unlikely to be successful. Sponsorship is not undertaken.

☐ Bow Valley Petroleum (UK) Ltd
Hydrocarbon exploration

Fanum House,
48 Leicester Square,
London WC2H 7LT
071-839 8744

Ch: Lord Michael Fitzalan Howard
Contact: Mrs J Logan
Personnel Administrator

Year Ends: 31 Dec '85
Donations: n/a
Profit: £27,890,000
Turnover: £103,892,000

UK employees: n/a
Total employees: n/a

☐ Bowater plc
Packaging & print

Bowater House,
Knightsbridge,
London SW1X 7NN
071-584 7070

Ch: N C Ireland
MD: J D R Lyon
Contact: Bob Bird
Director, Group Public Relations

Year Ends: 31 Dec '91
Donations: £40,000
Profit: £112,700,000
Turnover: £1,206,100,000

UK employees: n/a
Total employees: 18,800

Donations Policy: The company supports youth and anti-drugs projects, social welfare, medical, and a range of general charities. Grants range from £500 to £2,000.
No support for renovation of buildings, secondment, local appeals not in areas of company presence, advertising in brochures.

☐ C T Bowring & Company Ltd
Insurance brokers

The Bowring Building,
PO Box 145,
Tower Place,
London EC3P 3BE
071-357 1000

Ch: P L Wroughton
Contact: Roy Rutter, Executive Director
C T Bowring (Charities Fund) Ltd

Year Ends: 31 Dec '91
Donations: £400,000
Profit: £38,000,000
Turnover: £120,000,000

UK employees: n/a
Total employees: 3,588
% Club, ABSA

Donations Policy: Recipient organisations must be registered charities. Preference for local charities in areas where the company operates, appeals relevant to company business and charities in which a member of company staff is involved. Preferred areas of support: youth, social welfare, medicine and the arts. It has also supported charities connected with conservation. Grants typically £250 to £1,000.
No support for individuals, schools or expeditions, circular appeals, advertising in charity brochures, purely denominational appeals, large national appeals or local appeals not in areas of company presence.
Sponsorship proposals should be addressed to Mrs Carole Bowring, Public Relations.

☐ Bowthorpe plc
Electrical engineers

Gatwick Road,
Crawley,
West Sussex RH10 2RZ
0293-528888

Ch: R A Parsons
MD: J M Westhead
Contact: M Arnaouti
Company Secretary

Year Ends: 31 Dec '91
Donations: £5,866
Profit: £40,323,000
Turnover: £220,549,000

UK employees: n/a
Total employees: 4,494

Donations Policy: Preference for local charities in areas of company presence and appeals relevant to the business. Direct support preferred.
No support for overseas projects, denominational appeals, appeals from individuals, circular appeals.

☐ BPB Industries plc
Gypsum, building materials, paper & engineering

Langley Park House,
Uxbridge Road,
Slough SL3 6DU
0753-573273

Ch: A G Turner
MD: A Brooks, C J Bushell
Contact: Clare Carpenter
Assistant Company Secretary

Year Ends: 31 Mar '92
Donations: £47,000
Profit: £37,800,000
Turnover: £1,021,000,000

UK employees: n/a
Total employees: 12,581

Donations Policy: The company only gives to registered charities and mainly to charities which benefit the shareholders, employees, local community or group as a whole. Grants range from £100 to £1,000.
Generally no support for local appeals not in areas of company presence or overseas aid/development. No sponsorship is undertaken.

Alphabetical listing

Please read page 6

Name/Address	Officers	Financial Information	Other Information

☐ BPCC Ltd

Printers

111 Park Road,
London NW8 7JL
071-262 3223

Ch: M C Stoddart
CE: P J Holloran
Contact: Geoff Garwood
Personnel Director

Year Ends: 31 Dec '90
Donations: £32,900
Profit: £9,437,000
Turnover: £308,677,000

UK employees: n/a
Total employees: 6,098

BitC

Donations Policy: We were unable to obtain a donations policy from the company.

☐ Bradford & Bingley Building Society

Building society

PO Box No 88,
Crossflatts,
Bingley,
West Yorkshire BD16 2UA
0274-555555

Ch: Donald Hanson
CE: Geoffrey Lister
Contact: K Cromar
Controller, Secretarial Services

Year Ends: 31 Dec '91
Donations: £38,644
Profit: £103,234,000
Turnover: n/a

UK employees: n/a
Total employees: 3,419

BitC

☐ Bradford & Sons Ltd

Building & timber merchants

98 Hendford Hill,
Yeovil,
Somerset BA20 2QR
0935-23311

Ch: P S Bradford
Contact: M David
Company Secretary

Year Ends: 30 Apr '92
Donations: £3,100
Profit: £277,000
Turnover: £33,770,000

UK employees: n/a
Total employees: 472

Donations Policy: Preference for local charities in areas where the company operates, appeals relevant to company business and charities in which a member of company staff is involved. Preference for children and youth; social welfare; medical. Grants to national organisations from £50 to £250. Grants to local organisations from £50 to £1,000.
No response to circular appeals. No grants for advertising in charity brochures; appeals from individuals; purely denominational (religious) appeals; overseas projects.

☐ Brake Brothers plc

Frozen food suppliers

Godinton Road,
Ashford,
Kent TN23 1ED
0233-637370

Ch: W T Brake
MD: F R Brake
Contact: Sales Director

Year Ends: 31 Dec '91
Donations: £23,013
Profit: £15,398,000
Turnover: £223,038,000

UK employees: n/a
Total employees: 2,261

Donations Policy: Preference for local charities and appeals relevant to company business.
No support for brochure advertising, circular appeals, national appeals, overseas projects, appeals from individuals.

☐ Brammer plc

Transmission belting, bearing distribution

1 Tabley Court,
Victoria Street,
Altrincham,
Cheshire WA14 1EZ
061-928 3363

Ch: H M Lang
MD: R G Ffoulkes-Jones
Contact: D Nicholson
Company Secretary

Year Ends: 31 Dec '91
Donations: £8,451
Profit: £9,162,000
Turnover: £111,509,000

UK employees: n/a
Total employees: 1,134

☐ Brent Chemicals International plc

Industrial chemicals manufacturers

Ridgeway,
Iver,
Buckinghamshire SL0 9JJ
0753-651812

Ch: Lord Lane of Horsell
MD: S C Cuthbert
Contact: J G Lawrence
Company Secretary

Year Ends: 31 Dec '91
Donations: £3,532
Profit: £5,242,000
Turnover: £99,965,000

UK employees: 1,151
Total employees: n/a

☐ Brent Walker Group plc

Hotels, catering, leisure

Brent Walker House,
19 Rupert Street,
London W1V 7FS
071-465 0111

Ch: G A Walker
Contact: Miss Sadie McKinlay
Group Communications Officer

Year Ends: 31 Dec '90
Donations: £220,000
Profit: £117,613,000
Turnover: £1,763,389,000

UK employees: n/a
Total employees: 14,490

Donations Policy: The company states that due to restructuring it no longer has a budget for sponsorship or charity donations.

☐ Bricom Group Ltd

Transport & aviation services

Milton Heath House,
Westcolt Road,
Dorking,
Surrey RH4 3NB
0306-740445

Ch: N C Ireland
MD: J F K Lee
Contact: Miss L Evans
Personnel Department

Year Ends: 31 Dec '89
Donations: £8,000 (1988)
Profit: £48,070,000
Turnover: £492,235,000

UK employees: n/a
Total employees: 13,603

☐ Bridgewater Paper Co Ltd

Newsprint production, waste paper recycling

North Road,
Ellesmere Port,
Wirral L65 1AF
051-355 7272

Ch: A M J van Hattum
Contact: Dr Jarvis
Employee Relations Manager

Year Ends: 31 Dec '90
Donations: n/a
Profit: £8,729,000
Turnover: £127,608,000

UK employees: n/a
Total employees: 628

Please read page 6 — Alphabetical listing

Name/Address	Officers	Financial Information	Other Information

☐ Bridon plc
Wire, rope & fibres

Carr Hill,
Doncaster,
South Yorkshire DN4 8DG
0302-344010

Ch: J J West
MD: D J Allday
Contact: Ian Doig
Assistant Company Secretary

Year Ends: 31 Dec '91
Donations: £50,000
Profit: £3,600,000
Turnover: £319,300,000

UK employees: n/a
Total employees: 5,152

% Club

Donations Policy: Preference for local charities in the areas of company presence. Preferred areas of support are children and youth, social welfare, medical, education and enterprise/training.
Generally no support for advertising in charity brochures, appeals from individuals, purely denominational (religious) appeals, local appeals not in areas of company presence and overseas aid/development. A response is only made to written applications.

☐ Bridport-Gundry plc
Net & specialist textile

The Court,
West Street,
Bridport DT6 3QU
0308-56666

Ch: P N Darley
MD: B M Cowley
Contact: G MacSporran
Company Secretary

Year Ends: 31 Jul '91
Donations: £8,000
Profit: £818,000
Turnover: £32,372,000

UK employees: n/a
Total employees: 823

Donations Policy: Preference for local charities in areas of company presence and appeals relevant to the business. Support goes mainly to children/youth, social welfare, medical, education, environment and heritage. Grants to local organisations from £25 to £250.
No support for circular appeals, fundraising events, advertising in charity brochures, appeals from individuals, purely denominational (religious) appeals, local appeals not in areas of company presence, large national appeals and overseas projects.

☐ Brintons Ltd
Woven carpet manufacturers

Exchange Street,
Kidderminster DY10 1AG
0562-820000

Ch: C T C Brinton
MD: H F Lowe
Contact: Mrs Barbara Turner
Welfare Officer

Year Ends: 2 Jul '88
Donations: £30,690 (1991)
Profit: £7,351,000
Turnover: £68,449,000

UK employees: n/a
Total employees: 2,098

% Club

Donations Policy: Preference for local charities in areas where the company operates.
No grants for appeals from individuals; purely denominational (religious) appeals; local appeals not in areas of company presence. No sponsorship is undertaken. Total community contributions in 1990/91 were about £50,000.

☐ Bristol & West Building Society
Building society

Bristol & West Building,
PO Box 27,
Broad Quay,
Bristol BS99 7AX
0272-294271

Ch: Sir John Wills
CE: P A FitzSimons
Contact: Doreen Hill
Secretary to the Charity Committee

Year Ends: 31 Dec '91
Donations: £105,000
Profit: £67,388,000
Turnover: n/a

UK employees: n/a
Total employees: 2,143

BitC

Donations Policy: Most donations are made through the Bristol & West Charitable Trust. Preferred areas of support: children and youth, education, the arts and enterprise/training. Preference also to charities in which a member of staff is involved.
No support for advertising in charity brochures, appeals from individuals, purely denominational (religious) appeals and overseas projects.

☐ Bristol Myers Squibb Holdings Ltd
Manufacturers of pharmaceuticals

Swakeleys House,
Milton Road,
Ickenham,
Uxbridge UB10 8NS
0895-639911

Ch: B L Kane
Contact: Julie Anne Kennett

Year Ends: 31 Dec '90
Donations: £47,551
Profit: £6,803,000
Turnover: £283,861,000

UK employees: n/a
Total employees: 2,571

Donations Policy: Only supports local charities in areas of company presence and appeals related to company business.
No support for denominational (religious) appeals, appeals from individuals or circular appeals.

☐ Bristol United Press Ltd
Newspaper proprietors

Temple Way,
Bristol BS99 7HD
0272-260080

Ch: S G G Clarke
Contact: Miss A Cottrell
Secretary to Managing Director

Year Ends: 31 Mar '92
Donations: £6,617
Profit: £4,064,000
Turnover: £61,375,000

UK employees: n/a
Total employees: 1,341

Donations Policy: Preference for appeals relevant to company business and local charities in the areas of company presence. The company does give to local branches of national charities. Preferred areas of support: children and youth, social welfare and medical. Grants range from £50 to £200. Sponsorship proposals should be addressed to J N Bilton, Marketing Manager at the above address.
Generally no support for circular appeals, fundraising events, advertising in charity brochures, purely denominational (religious) appeals, local appeals not in areas of company presence, large national appeals and overseas projects.

☐ Bristol Water plc
Water company

PO Box 218,
Bridgwater Road,
Bristol BS99 7AU
0272-665881

Ch: Sir John Vernon Wills
MD: John Richard Browning
Contact: Company Secretary

Year Ends: 31 Mar '92
Donations: £8,563
Profit: £4,547,000
Turnover: £47,881,000

UK employees: n/a
Total employees: 623

Donations Policy: Each application is considered on merit by the directors at their monthly meeting. They receive many requests and support both local and national organisations. Preference for local charities in areas of company presence and appeals relevant to company business. Preferred areas of support are children and youth, environment and heritage, enterprise/training, and overseas aid/development (WaterAid). Grants range from £10 to £350. Consumers are also encouraged to donate to WaterAid by 'rounding-up' their bills.
No support for circular appeals, fundraising events, advertising in charity brochures, appeals from individuals, purely denominational (religious) appeals and local appeals not in areas of company presence.

● **Alphabetical listing** Please read page 6

Name/Address   *Officers*   *Financial Information*   *Other Information*

☐ Britannia Building Society
Building society

PO Box 20,   *Ch:* John L Hill   *Year Ends:* 31 Dec '91   *UK employees:* n/a
Newton House,   *MD:* F Michael Shaw   *Donations:* £20,016   *Total employees:* 2,894
Leek,   *Contact:* Tonya Green   *Profit:* £64,040,000
Staffordshire ST13 5RG   Public Relations Manager   *Turnover:* n/a
0538-399399

Donations Policy: Preference for local charities in the areas of company presence and charities in which a member of staff is involved. Preferred areas of support are children and youth, social welfare, environment and heritage and enterprise/training. Grants to national organisations from £100 to £1,000. Grants to local organisations from £25 to £50.
Generally no support for circular appeals, advertising in charity brochures, appeals from individuals, purely denominational (religious) appeals, local appeals not in areas of company presence, overseas projects. No donations are made for political purposes.

☐ Britannia plc
Disperse equipment manufacturing

Emerson Court,   *Ch:* A B Morrall   *Year Ends:* 31 Aug '89   *UK employees:* n/a
Alderley Road,   *MD:* C J Shaw   *Donations:* £8,153   *Total employees:* 1,293
Wilmslow,   *Contact:* J M Yates   *Profit:* £1,241,000
Cheshire SK9 1NX   Company Secretary   *Turnover:* £56,728,000
0625-535353

Donations Policy: Preference for local charities in the areas of company presence. Preferred areas of support are children and youth, social welfare, medical and education.
Generally no support for advertising in charity brochures, appeals from individuals, purely denominational (religious) appeals, and large national appeals.

☐ Britannic Assurance plc
Insurance

Moor Green Lane,   *Ch:* M A H Willett   *Year Ends:* 31 Dec '91   *UK employees:* n/a
Moseley,   *MD:* J A Jefferson   *Donations:* £29,713   *Total employees:* 4,636
Birmingham B13 8QF   *Contact:* D Potter   *Profit:* £24,692,000
021-449 4444   Administration Manger   *Turnover:* n/a

Donations Policy: Preference for children and youth; social welfare and recreation.
No grants for fundraising events; advertising in charity brochures; appeals from individuals; purely denominational (religious) appeals; local appeals not in areas of company presence; large national appeals; overseas projects. No response to circular appeals.

☐ British Aerospace plc
Manufacture of aircraft, communications

11 The Strand,   *Ch:* J C Cahill   *Year Ends:* 31 Dec '91   *UK employees:* n/a
London WC2N 5JT   *CE:* R H Evans   *Donations:* £1,310,000   *Total employees:* 123,200
071-930 1020   *Contact:* Miss Sue Windridge   *Profit:* £81,000,000
   Company Secretary   *Turnover:* £10,562,000,000   % Club, BitC

Donations Policy: The company is particularly sympathetic to service/ex-service charities and children's causes. Support is also given to medical, education and enterprise/training projects and the company is a keen supporter of local conservation projects. The company prefers to give directly, but does support advertising in charity brochures and fundraising events on certain occasions. Grants to national organisations from £100 to £20,000. Grants to local organisations from £50 to £20,000.
The group sponsors education, sports and arts events for young people and is involved in a wide range of projects to promote better understanding between industry and education at both national and local level. Sponsorship proposals should be addressed to J M Wooding, Director of Public Affairs.
Generally no support for circular appeals, appeals from individuals, purely denominational (religious) appeals, local appeals not in areas of company presence and overseas projects.

☐ British Airways plc
Air transportation

PO Box 10,   *Ch:* Lord King of Wartnaby   *Year Ends:* 31 Mar '92   *UK employees:* n/a
Heathrow Airport,   *MD:* Sir Colin Marshall   *Donations:* £461,000   *Total employees:* 50,209
Hounslow,   *Contact:* Jacqueline Ive   *Profit:* £285,000,000
Middlesex TW6 2JA   Charities & External Affairs   *Turnover:* £5,224,000,000   BitC
081-759 5511   Administrator

Donations Policy: In 1991/92, the largest grants were given to Age Concern England and the Cancer Relief MacMillan Fund. No further information available.

☐ British Alcan Aluminium plc
Aluminium & associated products

Chalfont Park,   *Ch:* D M Ritchie   *Year Ends:* 31 Dec '91   *UK employees:* n/a
Gerrards Cross,   *Contact:* Secretary to the Charitable Trust   *Donations:* £206,000   *Total employees:* 9,511
Buckinghamshire SL9 0QB   *Profit:* (£45,600,000)
0753-887373   *Turnover:* £730,800,000   BitC

Donations Policy: Priority to charities in need of funds rather than very well supported charities. The company also supports charities close to company locations. Preferred areas of support are children and youth, social welfare, medical, environment and heritage, elderly people, homelessness and disabled people.
Grants to national organisations from £250 to £500. Grants to local organisations from £50 to £300.
No support for non-charities, advertising in charity brochures, fundraising events, circular appeals, appeals from individuals, purely denominational (religious) appeals, local appeals not in areas of company presence, overseas projects, large national appeals and animal charities.
Sponsorship proposals should be addressed to R J Gaunt, Corporate Relations Manager.

Please read page 6 | | | Alphabetical listing •

Name/Address	Officers	Financial Information	Other Information

☐ British Arkady Co Ltd
Flour millers, yeast foods

Skerton Road,
Old Trafford,
Manchester M16 0NJ
061-872 7161

MD: J R Mahlich
Contact: G Garton
Company Secretary

Year Ends: 31 Dec '88
Donations: £4,061
Profit: £5,559,000
Turnover: £102,545,000

UK employees: n/a
Total employees: 674

Donations Policy: Preference for local charities and especially for very local events and appeals relevant to the business. Appeals that do not meet these criteria are unlikely to succeed.

☐ British Coal Corporation
Coalmining

Hobart House,
Grosvenor Place,
London SW1X 7AE
071-235 2020

Ch: J N Clarke
Contact: T A Thomas
Economics Department

Year Ends: 25 Mar '91
Donations: £268,000
Profit: £78,000,000
Turnover: £3,950,000,000

UK employees: n/a
Total employees: 79,100

Donations Policy: Charitable donations are only made by the Corporation to charities very closely associated to coal-mining. Support is mainly given to the Coal Trade Benevolent Association. The donations figure given above also includes enterprise and environmental initiatives carried on by British Coal in the regions where it operates.
British Coal Enterprise is a member of Business in the Community.

☐ British Fuels Group Ltd
Solid fuel & fuel oils distribution

Cawood House,
Otley Road,
Harrogate,
North Yorkshire HG3 1RF
0423-568068

Ch: M J Edwards
Contact: Stephanie Oates
Secretary to the Chief Executive

Year Ends: 29 Sep '90
Donations: n/a
Profit: £2,241,000
Turnover: £503,993,000

UK employees: n/a
Total employees: 2,084

☐ British Gas plc
Gas suppliers

Rivermill House,
152 Grosvenor Road,
London SW1V 3JL
071-821 1444

Ch: R Evans
Contact: Colin Campbell
Head of Community Relations

Year Ends: 31 Dec '91
Donations: £1,900,000
Profit: £1,469,000,000
Turnover: £10,485,000,000

UK employees: 80,443
Total employees: 84,540

% Club, BitC, ABSA

Donations Policy: Particular preference for organisations concerned with disabled and disadvantaged people. The company also helps youth and community based arts and sports, and programmes helping to overcome the problems of disadvantaged groups, especially in inner cities. Generally no support for circular appeals, appeals from individuals, purely denominational (religious) appeals, large national appeals, political appeals, bricks and mortar appeals and animal organisations.
Total community contributions were £10,000,000.

☐ British Land Company plc
Property investment

10 Cornwall Terrace,
Regents Park,
London NW1 4QP
071-486 4466

Contact: John Ritblat
Chairman

Year Ends: 31 Dec '91
Donations: £41,955
Profit: n/a
Turnover: n/a

UK employees: n/a
Total employees: 479

% Club, BitC

Donations Policy: Particular support is given to charities involving young people especially in activity based projects. Support is also given to environmental projects.
No grants for fundraising events, appeals from individuals, local appeals not in areas of company presence.

☐ British Nuclear Fuels plc
Nuclear fuel services

Risley,
Warrington,
Cheshire WA3 6AS
0925-832000

Ch: J R S Guinness
MD: N Chamberlain
Contact: Mrs C Rankin
Community Fund Officer

Year Ends: 31 Mar '92
Donations: £204,000
Profit: £161,000,000
Turnover: £1,082,000,000

UK employees: n/a
Total employees: 15,783

% Club, BitC

Donations Policy: Mainly support for schemes and charities in the North-West (including national appeals based in the North West). Preference given to organisations concerned with children and youth and elderly people "where the organisation has taken measures to help themselves". Support is also given to sport, health, education, environment, arts and museums. Typical national grants range from £100 to £15,000. Local grants range from £25 to £1,000.
No support for circular appeals, large national appeals (except North West based), small purely local appeals not in areas of company presence, fundraising events, advertising in charity brochures, purely denominational (religious) appeals, or overseas projects.
Total community contributions in 1991/92 were £250,000, not including other forms of sponsorship eg. Cumbria Development Fund.

☐ British Petroleum Company plc
Oil industry

BP House,
Breakspear Way,
Hemel Hempstead,
Hertfordshire HP2 4UL
0442-232323

Ch: Lord Ashburton
MD: D A G Simon
Contact: Chris Marsden
Head of Community & Educational Relations

Year Ends: 31 Dec '91
Donations: £8,500,000
Profit: £1,203,000,000
Turnover: £32,613,000,000

UK employees: n/a
Total employees: 115,250

ABSA, BitC

Donations Policy: "Expenditure on community and educational programmes is made on the basis of mutual benefit to BP and our many community partners. There are no fixed areas of support but broad priorities are education, environment and enterprise. Activities are closely tied to business objectives and emphasise employee involvement. Programmes, therefore, tend to be relevant to BP site activities and the personal as well as business expertise which BP employees can contribute."
No support for political appeals, religious/sectarian causes, bricks and mortar appeals, capital endowments, investment funds, bursaries and individuals.

● **Alphabetical listing**   Please read page 6

Name/Address	Officers	Financial Information	Other Information

☐ British Polythene Industries plc
Polythene packaging

96 Port Glasgow Road,
Greenock PA15 2RP
0475-745432

Ch: C McLatchie
Contact: A N Macdonald
Finance Director

Year Ends: 31 Dec '91
Donations: £18,000
Profit: £10,250,000
Turnover: £156,070,000

UK employees: n/a
Total employees: 1,774

Donations Policy: We have been unable to obtain a charitable donations policy.

☐ British Railways Board
Passenger railway services

Euston House,
24 Eversholt Street,
London NW1 1DZ
071-928 5151

Ch: Sir Bob Reid
Contact: James Crowe
BR Community Unit (Manager)

Year Ends: 31 Mar '91
Donations: n/a
Profit: £93,100,000
Turnover: £3,076,900,000

UK employees: n/a
Total employees: 135,597

% Club, BitC, ABSA

Donations Policy: The company does not make charitable donations as such, all support being business related and covering a wide range of national and local organisations. Support given ranges from £1,000 to £60,000 (national) and from £100 to £5,000 (local).

☐ British Shoe Corporation Holdings plc
Footwear & fashion retailing

Sunningdale Road,
Leicester LE3 1UR
0533-320202

Ch: G Maitland Smith
Contact: S Mounfield
Company Secretary

Year Ends: 31 Jan '92
Donations: £68,000
Profit: £68,700,000
Turnover: £876,800,000

UK employees: n/a
Total employees: 23,184

Donations Policy: Decisions are made on criteria such as the location/area, amount requested and the type of charity. Preferred areas of support are children and youth, education and the arts. Grants to local organisations from £20 to £5,000.
Generally no support for circular appeals, advertising in charity brochures, purely denominational (religious) appeals, local appeals not in areas of company presence, large national appeals and overseas projects.

☐ British Steel plc
Manufacture & sale of steel

9 Albert Embankment,
London SE1 7SN
071-735 7654

Ch: Sir Robert Scholey
MD: Brian Moffat
Contact: R J Reeves
Company Secretary

Year Ends: 28 Mar '92
Donations: £353,000
Profit: (£55,000,000)
Turnover: £4,598,000,000

UK employees: n/a
Total employees: 49,100

BitC, ABSA

Donations Policy: The company makes grants centrally, mainly to national appeals. Preference also for local charities in the areas of company presence, appeals relevant to company business and charities in which a member of staff is involved. It also supports the arts, environmental projects and educational activities. Grants to national organisations from £250 to £10,000. Grants to local organisations from £1,000 to £5,000.
Grants to appeals in the steel industry areas are made either by the local works or through the Julian Melchett Trust. This trust gave grants totalling £123,800 in 1990/91 (of which £100,000 was donated by British Steel). The trust supports a wide range of projects and aims to encourage community development and self-help initiatives, stimulate voluntary service and promote partnership between the statutory and voluntary bodies engaged in community care in current and former mining areas.
Generally no support for appeals from individuals, purely denominational (religious) appeals, local appeals not in areas of company presence or overseas projects.

☐ British Sugar plc
Sugar & animal food manufacturers

PO Box 26,
Oundle Road,
Peterborough,
Cambridgeshire PE2 9QU
0733-63171

Ch: G H Weston
MD: P J Jackson
Contact: John Smith
Public Relations Manager

Year Ends: 15 Sep '91
Donations: £100,000
Profit: £128,500,000
Turnover: £694,300,000

UK employees: n/a
Total employees: 3,241

Donations Policy: Support is focused on projects of particular benefit to the communities in which the company operates and in which employees live and work, especially health and health care, education, environment and enterprise. Projects where a member of staff is involved are given special attention. Grants range from £20 to £500.
General appeals are not normally supported. No support for circular appeals, appeals from individuals, advertising in charity brochures, large national appeals, local appeals not in areas of company presence, overseas projects or purely denominational (religious) appeals.
British Sugar is a wholly owned subsidiary of Associated British Foods Group (see separate entry).

☐ British Telecommunications plc
Telecommunications services

BT Community Affairs,
B3001,
81 Newgate Street,
London EC1A 7AJ
071-356 4995

Ch: Iain Vallance
MD: M L Hepher
Contact: Miss Cathy McGuinness

Year Ends: 31 Mar '92
Donations: £5,500,000
Profit: £3,073,000,000
Turnover: £13,337,000,000

UK employees: n/a
Total employees: 219,000

% Club, BitC, ABSA

Donations Policy: British Telecom supports a wide range of charities, both local and national, in response to written appeals. The Charities Programme selects a theme for each year to provide a focus for donations. In 1991/92 this was caring in the community. A set of accounts must be included with applications. Preference for children and youth; social welfare; medical; education; environment/heritage; arts; enterprise/training and disabled people. Grants to national organisations from £250 to over £100,000. Grants to local organisations from £50 to over £50,000.
No denominational appeals, political appeals, appeals from individuals, brochure advertising, circular appeals or overseas projects.
Total community contributions were £14,500,000.
Sponsorship appeals should be addressed to Rodger Broad, Sponsorship Manager, Room A301.

Please read page 6   **Alphabetical listing** ●

Name/Address	Officers	Financial Information	Other Information

☐ **British Tissues Ltd**   Paper manufacturers & converters

43-51 Lowlands Road,
Harrow,
Middlesex HA1 2BW
081-864 5411

MD: C J Hayes
Contact: Helen Pooley
Personnel Manager

Year Ends: 31 Dec '88
Donations: £3,688
Profit: £12,813,000
Turnover: £118,228,000

UK employees: n/a
Total employees: 1,650

Donations Policy: Preference to local charities and appeals relevant to the business. Preferred areas of support: children/youth and medical. No support for overseas projects, appeals from individuals, denominational appeals, brochure advertising.

☐ **British Vita plc**   Manufacture of polymeric products

Soudan Street,
Middleton,
Manchester M24 2DB
061-643 1133

Ch: R McGee
CE: R H Sellars
Contact: Alan Teague
Company Secretary

Year Ends: 31 Dec '91
Donations: £49,000
Profit: £50,356,000
Turnover: £694,276,000

UK employees: 4,030
Total employees: 9,658

Donations Policy: Preference for local appeals in areas of company presence and appeals relevant to the business. Priority to children/youth, education, enterprise/training. No support for large national appeals, denominational appeals, overseas projects or brochure advertising.

☐ **Brixton Estate plc**   Property investment

22-24 Ely Place,
London EC1N 6TQ
071-242 6898

Ch: H S Axton
MD: D F Gardner
Contact: Mrs Tina Ford
Secretary, Charity Committee

Year Ends: 31 Dec '91
Donations: £50,000
Profit: £20,867,000
Turnover: £57,200,000

UK employees: n/a
Total employees: 105

Donations Policy: Priority to charities in areas of company presence and national charities. Grants range from £100 to £1,000. Support for registered charities only. No support for individuals, students, fundraising events, local appeals not in areas of company presence, local branches of national charities and charities whose main aim is to support other charities.

☐ **Bromsgrove Industries plc**   Specialist engineering

Neville House,
42-46 Hagley Road,
Birmingham B16 8PZ
021-456 1088

Ch: B M Sedghi
CE: S G Mills
Contact: Mrs Pam Evans
Secretary to the Chairman

Year Ends: 31 Mar '92
Donations: £30,000
Profit: £7,090,000
Turnover: £90,054,000

UK employees: n/a
Total employees: 1,870

Donations Policy: The donations figure stated includes a commitment to donate £25,000 a year to The Prince's Youth Business Trust.

☐ **Brother International Europe Ltd**   Electrical distributors

1 Tame Street,
Audenshaw,
Manchester M34 5JE
061-330 6531

Ch: K Tazaki
Contact: J P Kelly
Advertising Manager

Year Ends: 30 Sep '90
Donations: £9,859
Profit: £560,000
Turnover: £137,027,000

UK employees: n/a
Total employees: 80

☐ **Brown & Jackson plc**   Commodity trading

Battle Bridge House,
300 Gray's Inn Road,
London WC1X 8DX
071-278 9635

Ch: J B H Jackson
CE: I Gray
Contact: Secretary to the Chairman

Year Ends: 30 Sep '91
Donations: nil
Profit: £14,853,000
Turnover: £127,308,000

UK employees: n/a
Total employees: 4,605

Donations Policy: Company policy is to make no charitable donations.

☐ **Brown & Tawse Group plc**   Steel & tube stockholders & engineers

PO Box 159,
Imperial Street,
Bromley-by-Bow,
London E3 3JQ
081-980 4466

Ch: G Black
MD: D K Rae
Contact: P Forster
Publicity Department

Year Ends: 31 Mar '91
Donations: £4,292
Profit: £1,170,000
Turnover: £166,073,000

UK employees: n/a
Total employees: 1,594

☐ **David Brown Investments Ltd**   Engineering products

Park Works,
Park Road,
Huddersfield HD4 5DD
0484-422180

Ch: Mrs A B Abecassis
Contact: Bob Holroyd
Corporate Director

Year Ends: 31 Oct '87
Donations: £1,966
Profit: £4,450,000
Turnover: £79,459,000

UK employees: n/a
Total employees: 2,596

☐ **Matthew Brown plc**   Brewers

Edinburgh House,
Cowling Brow,
Chorley,
Lancashire
0257-265544

Ch: G Reed
MD: G Hildrew
Contact: Mrs Sally Sykes
Public Relations

Year Ends: 27 Sep '86
Donations: £5,708
Profit: £10,132,000
Turnover: £56,636,000

UK employees: n/a
Total employees: 2,100

Donations Policy: Preference for local charities and appeals relevant to the business. No large national appeals, circular appeals, overseas projects or denominational appeals.

• **Alphabetical listing**   Please read page 6

Name/Address   *Officers*   *Financial Information*   *Other Information*

☐ N Brown Group plc
                                                                                                         Direct mail order business
53 Dale Street,   *Ch:* Sir David Alliance   *Year Ends:* 29 Feb '92   *UK employees:* n/a
Manchester M60 6ES   *MD:* J Martin   *Donations:* £11,542   *Total employees:* 1,320
061-236 8256   *Contact:* Mrs Gill Brierley   *Profit:* £15,686,000
                                      Secretary to the Financial Director   *Turnover:* £152,616,000

☐ Brown Shipley Holdings plc
                                                                                              Merchant banking, financial services
10 Fosters Lane,   *Ch:* W J A Dacombe   *Year Ends:* 31 Mar '92   *UK employees:* 845
London EC2V 6HH   *Contact:* Jill Holt   *Donations:* £20,000   *Total employees:* n/a
071-726 4058   Personnel Department   *Profit:* (£27,143,000)
                                                                            Turnover: n/a   % Club

Donations Policy: Please note that donations are not being made at present, and the situation is unlikely to change in the coming year.

☐ Bryant Group plc
                                                                                         Building, developing & property investment
Cranmore House,   *Ch:* A C Bryant   *Year Ends:* 31 May '92   *UK employees:* n/a
Cranmore Boulevard,   *MD:* A MacKenzie   *Donations:* £42,948   *Total employees:* 831
Shirley,   *Contact:* Kathy Harding   *Profit:* £20,300,000
Solihull,   Secretary to the Chairman   *Turnover:* £322,900,000   % Club
West Midlands B90 4SD
021-711 1212

Donations Policy: Preference for local charities in areas of company presence.
No response to circular appeals. No grants for local appeals not in areas of company presence; large national appeals; overseas projects;
political appeals. Support is rarely given for advertising in charity brochures or purely denominational (religious) appeals.

☐ BSE-Genex Co Ltd
                                                                                        Tour operators & motor vehicle distributors
Heddon House,   *Ch:* A Dozet   *Year Ends:* 31 Dec '90   *UK employees:* n/a
149-151 Regent Street,   *Donations:* n/a   *Total employees:* 266
London W1R 8HP   *Profit:* £3,545,000
071-437 0206   *Turnover:* £551,166,000

Donations Policy: We were unable to obtain any more information from this company.

☐ BSG International plc
                                                                                             Vehicle distribution, servicing, leasing
Burgess House,   *Ch:* H A Whittall   *Year Ends:* 31 Dec '91   *UK employees:* n/a
1270 Coventry Road,   *MD:* T C Cannon   *Donations:* £4,500   *Total employees:* 6,207
Yardley,   *Contact:* Reg Smith   *Profit:* £11,118,000
Birmingham B25 8BB   Assistant Company Treasurer   *Turnover:* £569,775,000
021-706 6155

☐ BSS Group plc
                                                                                   Heating, plumbing & pipeline equipment suppliers
Fleet House,   *Ch:* I H Philips   *Year Ends:* 31 Mar '92   *UK employees:* n/a
Lee Circle,   *CE:* P Cooper   *Donations:* £6,734   *Total employees:* 1,501
Leicester LE1 3QQ   *Contact:* David Johns   *Profit:* £10,018,000
0533-623232   Company Secretary   *Turnover:* £209,190,000

☐ BTP plc
                                                                                              Chemicals, biocides & industrial
Hayes Road,   *Ch:* F W Buckley   *Year Ends:* 31 Mar '92   *UK employees:* n/a
Cadishead,   *Contact:* A D Pollitt   *Donations:* £3,746   *Total employees:* 1,964
Manchester M30 5BX   Managing Director   *Profit:* £18,229,000
061-775 3945   *Turnover:* £175,233,000

Donations Policy: Preference for local charities in areas where the company operates. There are 30 companies in the group, each company
manager is able to make donations, but in practice few do. Appeals should be addressed to the relevant company/branch manager.

☐ BTR plc
                                                                                              Construction, energy & electrical
Silvertown House,   *Ch:* Sir Owen Green   *Year Ends:* 31 Dec '91   *UK employees:* 34,359
Vincent Square,   *MD:* A R Jackson   *Donations:* £234,000   *Total employees:* 140,000
London SW1P 2PL   *Contact:* S K Williams   *Profit:* £917,000,000
071-834 3848   Company Secretary   *Turnover:* £6,742,000,000

Donations Policy: Preference for national appeals, charities which have an affinity to industries in which the company is involved and
projects in which a member of staff is involved. Preferred areas of support are social welfare, health and medical, environment and heritage,
and education and science. Local appeals are only considered if they are close to company locations, and should be directed to the local
subsidiary. Grants to national organisations from £500 to £3,000. Grants to local organisations from £250 to £2,000.
No response to circular appeals. No grants for fundraising events; advertising in charity brochures; appeals from individuals; overseas
projects.

Please read page 6 **Alphabetical listing** ●

Name/Address	Officers	Financial Information	Other Information

☐ Bucknall Group plc
Surveyors & construction industry consultants

5 Scotland Street,
Birmingham B1 2RR
021-200 2282

Ch: D J Bucknall
Contact: Alison Thompson
Administrator

Year Ends: 30 Apr '92
Donations: £17,000
Profit: (£1,918,000)
Turnover: £17,262,000

UK employees: n/a
Total employees: 443

% Club

Donations Policy: The company select three charities to receive support rather than responding to unsolicited appeals.

☐ A F Budge Ltd
Civil engineering contractors

West Carr Road,
Retford,
Nottinghamshire DN22 7SW
0777-706789

Ch: A F Budge
Contact: Mrs Pat Walker
Secretary to the Chairman

Year Ends: 31 Dec '90
Donations: £34,265
Profit: £12,182,000
Turnover: £250,965,000

UK employees: n/a
Total employees: 2,384

Donations Policy: Preference for local charities in areas of company presence, appeals relevant to the business and where a member of staff is involved. Within these categories, preference for children/youth, social welfare, medical.
No response to circular appeals. No grants for advertising in charity brochures; appeals from individuals; purely denominational (religious) appeals; local appeals not in areas of company presence.

☐ Budgens plc
Food retailers

PO Box 9,
Stonefield Way,
South Ruislip,
Middlesex HA4 0JR
081-422 9511

Ch: C T Clague
CE: J A von Spreckelsen
Contact: Jan Davies
Marketing Controller

Year Ends: 27 Apr '91
Donations: £30,871
Profit: £14,676,000
Turnover: £272,287,000

UK employees: n/a
Total employees: 3,562

Donations Policy: Most of the company's donations are given to the National Children's Home. The company also supports local charities in areas of company presence on a smaller scale, usually donating vouchers worth about £5 for the company's stores.

☐ Bull Information Systems Ltd
Data processing equipment

Computer House,
Great West Road,
Brentford,
Middlesex TW3 9DH
081-568 9191

Ch: B Long
CE: G J McNeil
Contact: David Youens
Human Resources Director

Year Ends: 31 Dec '90
Donations: £39,000
Profit: £52,677,000
Turnover: £201,423,000

UK employees: n/a
Total employees: 2,506

Donations Policy: We have been unable to obtain a donations policy.

☐ Bullough plc
Engineers, furniture manufacturers

21 The Crescent,
Leatherhead,
Surrey KT22 8DY
0372-379088

Ch: D B Battle
MD: R J Steel
Contact: D B Battle
Chairman

Year Ends: 31 Oct '91
Donations: £6,000
Profit: £20,845,000
Turnover: £292,589,000

UK employees: n/a
Total employees: 5,636

Donations Policy: The company states that its policy is to give no charitable donations.

☐ H P Bulmer Holdings plc
Manufacturers of cider

The Cider Mills,
Plough Lane,
Hereford HR4 0LE
0432-352000

Ch: J E Bulmer
MD: J K Rudgard
Contact: Giles Bulmer
Director

Year Ends: 24 Apr '92
Donations: £76,000
Profit: £17,100,000
Turnover: £221,900,000

UK employees: 1,183
Total employees: 1,479

Donations Policy: Supports only local charities, particularly in Hereford, and specific trade-related national charities.
No response to circular appeals. No grants for advertising in charity brochures; local appeals not in areas of company presence; large national appeals; overseas projects.

☐ Bunge & Co Ltd
Grain, cotton & commodity merchants

Bunge House,
15-25 Artillery Lane,
London E1 7HA
071-247 4444

Ch: B de la Tour D'auvergne
Contact: W Tregoning
Assistant Secretary

Year Ends: 31 Dec '90
Donations: £4,897
Profit: £18,965,000
Turnover: £520,800,000

UK employees: n/a
Total employees: 1,225

☐ Bunzl plc
Paper & paper products

Stoke House,
Stoke Green,
Stoke Poges,
Slough SL2 4JN
0753-693693

Ch: D W Kendall
MD: A Habgood
Contact: Mrs L Savage
Secretary, Planning

Year Ends: 31 Dec '91
Donations: £205,000
Profit: £31,700,000
Turnover: £1,394,700,000

UK employees: n/a
Total employees: 8,903

% Club, BitC

Donations Policy: To fund specific community projects initiated by subsidiary companies where the company is the 'key player'. The company also responds to a limited number of national appeals. Head office prefers to support charities in areas such as the arts, social welfare, health, conservation, animal welfare, education and enterprise. Typical grants are about £1,000. Otherwise preference for local charities in areas of company presence, appeals relevant to company business and charities in which a member of staff is involved. Subsidiaries have their own budgets and should be contacted directly.
No support for advertising in charity brochures, appeals from individuals, political appeals, local appeals not in areas of company presence.

• **Alphabetical listing**　　　　　　　　　　　　　　　　　　　　　　　　　　　　　　　Please read page 6

Name/Address	Officers	Financial Information	Other Information

☐ Frederick H Burgess plc
　　　　　　　　　　　　　　　　　　　　　　　　　　　　　　　Agricultural & fuel oil distributors

The Green,　　　　　　　　　　　　Ch: H F Burgess　　　　Year Ends: 31 Dec '90　　　　UK employees: n/a
Stafford ST17 4BL　　　　　　　　MD: A F Burgess　　　　Donations: £107　　　　　　　Total employees: 1,279
0785-223131　　　　　　　　　　　Contact: W Burgess　　　Profit: £1,754,000
　　　　　　　　　　　　　　　　　　　　　Director　　　　　　Turnover: £106,653,000

☐ Burmah Castrol plc
　　Oil industry

Burmah Castrol House,　　　　　　Ch: L M Urquhart　　　　　Year Ends: 31 Dec '91　　　　UK employees: n/a
Pipers Way,　　　　　　　　　　　MD: J M Fry　　　　　　　Donations: £172,000　　　　　Total employees: 24,230
Swindon,　　　　　　　　　　　　Contact: Secretary to the Appeals　Profit: £165,500,000
Wiltshire SN3 1RE　　　　　　　　　　　Committee　　　　　Turnover: £2,352,400,000　　　% Club, BitC, ABSA
0793-511521

Donations Policy: The firm receives hundreds of requests each year for financial assistance, so support is focused mainly on two areas: firstly smaller charities close to company operations (ie. within 20 miles of one of the company's larger operating units); secondly, to those charities whose work is nationwide. Support is mainly concentrated on health, welfare and educational organisations, particularly those concerned with elderly people and disadvantaged children. Donations have also been given to charities concerned with national heritage and the arts. Grants to national organisations from £500 to £3,500. Grants to local organisations from £50 to £3,000.
Generally no support for individuals, expeditions, exchanges, study tours, advertising in charity brochures, purely denominational (religious) appeals, political organisations, third party organisations acting on behalf of charities, individual schools, playgroups, and mother/toddler groups - except when special schemes are announced.

☐ Burton Group plc
　　　　　　　　　　　　　　　　　　　　　　　　　　　　　Retailers of menswear & womenswear

214 Oxford Street,　　　　　　　　Ch: Sir John Hoskyns　　　Year Ends: 31 Aug '91　　　　UK employees: n/a
London W1N 9DF　　　　　　　　CE: J L Hoerner　　　　　Donations: £300,371　　　　　　Total employees: 27,369
071-636 8040　　　　　　　　　　Contact: E F Gallagher　　Profit: £13,400,000
　　　　　　　　　　　　　　　　　　　Corporate Affairs & Investor　Turnover: £1,661,100,000　　% Club, BitC
　　　　　　　　　　　　　　　　　　　Relations Director

Donations Policy: Please note: due to the current economic situation, the company is not supporting any additional charities. Unsolicited appeals will therefore not be successful.

☐ Burtonwood Brewery plc
　　Brewers

Burtonwood Village,　　　　　　　Ch: J G Dutton-Forshaw　　Year Ends: 31 Mar '92　　　　UK employees: n/a
Nr Warrington,　　　　　　　　　Contact: Ms Elizabeth Lloyd　Donations: £6,492　　　　　　Total employees: 1,130
Cheshire WA5 4PJ　　　　　　　　　　Marketing Manager　　Profit: £4,615,000
0925-225131　　　　　　　　　　　　　　　　　　　　　　　Turnover: £44,675,000

☐ Bush Boake Allen Holdings (UK)
　　　　　　　　　　　　　　　　　　　　　　　　　　Chemicals, flavour, fragrance manufacturers

Blackhorse Lane,　　　　　　　　Ch: J W Boyden　　　　　Year Ends: 25 Mar '91　　　　UK employees: n/a
Walthamstow,　　　　　　　　　Contact: Mrs Norma Venn　Donations: £12,949　　　　　　Total employees: 1,650
London E17 5QP　　　　　　　　　Secretary to Personnel Director　Profit: £3,447,000
081-531 4211　　　　　　　　　　　　　　　　　　　　　Turnover: £135,739,000

☐ Butlin's Ltd
　　　　　　　　　　　　　　　　　　　　　　　　　　　　　　Holiday centres & holiday hotels

Head Office,　　　　　　　　　　MD: J Whittel　　　　　　Year Ends: 31 Oct '91　　　　UK employees: n/a
Bognor Regis,　　　　　　　　　Contact: Jackie Collier　　Donations: n/a　　　　　　　　Total employees: 4,286
West Sussex PO21 1JJ　　　　　　　Secretary to the Managing　Profit: £9,763,000
0243-860068　　　　　　　　　　　Director　　　　　　　　Turnover: £136,535,000

Donations Policy: The company channels all its support to the Variety Club of Great Britain. The company is a subsidiary of the Rank Organisation plc, see separate entry.

☐ C & A Stores
　　Retailers

64 North Row,　　　　　　　　　Contact: The Secretary, C & A Charitable　Year Ends: 31 Dec '90　　UK employees: n/a
London W1A 2AX　　　　　　　　　Trust (address below)　Donations: £205,000　　　　　Total employees: n/a
071-629 1244　　　　　　　　　　　　　　　　　　　　　Profit: n/a
　　　　　　　　　　　　　　　　　　　　　　　　　　　Turnover: n/a

Donations Policy: The C & A Charitable Trust operates primarily through the local C & A stores. Staff take the initiative both in selecting the small number of registered charities to benefit in their area and in helping to raise funds for them. Preferred charities directly benefit children, elderly people or disadvantaged people within the UK.
The trust is therefore unable to respond to unsolicited appeals. Brochure appeals are not supported.
The address for the C & A Charitable Trust is: 20 Old Bailey, London EC4M 7BH.

☐ Cable & Wireless plc
　　　　　　　　　　　　　　　　　　　　　　　　　　　　　　　International telecommunications

Mercury House,　　　　　　　　Ch: Lord Young of Graffham　Year Ends: 31 Mar '92　　　UK employees: n/a
Theobalds Road,　　　　　　　　CE: J H Ross　　　　　　　Donations: £646,000　　　　　Total employees: 38,835
London WC1X 8RX　　　　　　　Contact: Aubrey Davidson　Profit: £643,500,000
071-315 4126　　　　　　　　　　　Community Affairs Manager　Turnover: £3,176,200,000　　% Club, BitC, ABSA

Donations Policy: The policy is currently under review; unsolicited appeals are not welcome.
Total community contributions in 1991/92 were £1.6 million.

Please read page 6   **Alphabetical listing** ●

Name/Address	Officers	Financial Information	Other Information

☐ Cadbury Schweppes plc
Confectionery, soft drinks, food

1-4 Connaught Place,
London W2 2EX
071-262 1212

Ch: Sir Graham Day
MD: N D Cadbury
Contact: Secretary, Cadbury Schweppes Charitable Trust

Year Ends: 28 Dec '91
Donations: £550,000
Profit: £316,400,000
Turnover: £3,232,300,000

UK employees: 16,568
Total employees: 34,982

% Club, BitC

Donations Policy: The trust plans its giving in advance for each year; unsolicited appeals are not encouraged. Preference for charities relevant to company business, in areas of company presence, with company staff involvement and active in the following areas: education; enterprise; environment; equal opportunities. Grants to national organisations from £10,000 to £40,000. Grants to local organisations from £1,000 to £5,000.
No response to circular appeals. No grants for fundraising events; advertising in charity brochures; appeals from individuals; purely denominational (religious) appeals; overseas projects.
Total community contributions in 1991 were £3,714,000.

☐ Caffyns plc
Automobile agents & engineers

Meads Road,
Eastbourne,
East Sussex BN20 7DR
0323-30201

Ch: A M Caffyn
MD: A E F Caffyn, R J M Caffyn
Contact: R J M Caffyn Joint Managing Director

Year Ends: 31 Mar '92
Donations: £2,200
Profit: £63,000
Turnover: £127,824,000

UK employees: n/a
Total employees: 1,076

Donations Policy: Preference for local charities in areas of company presence and charities in which a member of staff is involved.

☐ Cakebread Robey & Co plc
Distribution of building materials

318-326 Southbury Road,
Enfield,
Middlesex EN1 1TT
081-804 8244

Ch: M S Earle
CE: C J Burrowes, P B Langdale
Contact: Miss Beryl Castle Secretary to the Chairman

Year Ends: 31 Dec '91
Donations: £2,656
Profit: (£1,651,000)
Turnover: £22,928,000

UK employees: n/a
Total employees: 315

Donations Policy: To support a wide range of charities, both national and international. Preferred areas of support: children and youth, medical, environment and heritage, overseas aid/development and ex-servicemen's charities. Grants to national organisations from £15 to £25.
Generally no support for circular appeals, fundraising events, advertising in charity brochures, appeals from individuals, purely denominational (religious) appeals, large national appeals.

☐ CALA plc
Housebuilder, property developers

42 Colinton Road,
Edinburgh EH10 5BT
031-346 0194

Ch: G A Ball
MD: R G Hanna, A J Kelley
Contact: Miss L G Glover Secretary to the Chairman

Year Ends: 30 Jun '91
Donations: £28,164
Profit: £6,944,000
Turnover: £93,300,000

UK employees: n/a
Total employees: 335

% Club

Donations Policy: Preference for charities in areas of company presence, particularly Edinburgh.

☐ Caledonia Investments plc
Investment trust

Cayzer House,
1 Thomas More Street,
London E1 9AR
071-481 4343

Ch: Lord Cayzer
CE: Peter N Buckley
Contact: Major M G Wyatt Executive Director

Year Ends: 31 Mar '92
Donations: £43,000
Profit: £34,700,000
Turnover: n/a

UK employees: n/a
Total employees: 1,257

Donations Policy: Preference for appeals relevant to company business and charities in which a member of company staff is involved. Preference for education; environment/heritage; arts; enterprise/training. Grants to national organisations from £200 to £2,000.
No grants for fundraising events; advertising in charity brochures; purely denominational (religious) appeals; local appeals not in areas of company presence; large national appeals; overseas projects; circular appeals.

☐ Calor Group plc
Petroleum gas

Appleton Park,
Riding Court Road,
Datchet,
Slough SL3 9JG
0753-540000

Ch: A M Davies
CE: F Schukken
Contact: Mrs V Gibbs Secretary to the Committee

Year Ends: 31 Dec '91
Donations: £53,964
Profit: £45,000,000
Turnover: £362,200,000

UK employees: n/a
Total employees: 2,979

BitC

Donations Policy: Only consider national registered charities.
No grants for fundraising events; advertising in charity brochures; appeals from individuals; local charities or appeals.

☐ Camellia plc
Fine art dealers, tea & coffee producers, consumer goods

3 Carlos Place,
London W1Y 5AE
071-629 5728

Ch: G Fox
Contact: D M Bacon Managing Director

Year Ends: 31 Dec '91
Donations: £23,445
Profit: £13,131,000
Turnover: £163,946,000

UK employees: n/a
Total employees: 68,566

Donations Policy: Support is limited to organisations supporting children and youth, elderly people and medical. Grants up to £500.
No response to circular appeals. No grants for fundraising events; advertising in charity brochures; appeals from individuals; purely denominational (religious) appeals; large national appeals; overseas projects.

● **Alphabetical listing** Please read page 6

Name/Address	Officers	Financial Information	Other Information

☐ Campbell Grocery Products Ltd

Food manufacturers

Hardwick Road,
King's Lynn,
Norfolk PE30 4HS
0553-692266

MD: J W T Mustoe
Contact: Fred Rainforth
Personnel Manager

Year Ends: 31 Jul '90
Donations: £9,000
Profit: £1,815,000
Turnover: £45,000,000

UK employees: 500
Total employees: n/a

% Club

Donations Policy: Prefer to give to local charities in the King's Lynn area and to charities in which a member of staff is involved. Preferred areas of support: children and youth, social welfare, medical, education and the arts. Grants to local organisations from £20 to £800. No support for circular appeals, denominational appeals, large national appeals, overseas projects, appeals from individuals, brochure advertising or local appeals not in areas of company presence.

☐ Campbell's UK Ltd

Meat & other food manufacture

Heathrow Boulevard,
284 Bath Road,
West Drayton,
Middlesex UB7 0DT
081-564 8686

Contact: Mrs K Penney
Group Management Development
& Training Manager

Year Ends: 29 Jul '90
Donations: n/a
Profit: £23,329,000
Turnover: £201,313,000

UK employees: n/a
Total employees: 3,318

Donations Policy: The company states "we make donations to projects and charities in the towns where our factories are located, but the contacts between the factories and charitable groups are sufficiently good that they do not need advertising".
The subsidiary Campbell Grocery Products Ltd has its own entry (see above).

☐ W Canning plc

Speciality chemicals, electronic component dist.

Canning House,
St Paul's Square,
Birmingham B3 1QR
021-236 8224

Ch: D H Probert
Contact: R A Lewis
Company Secretary

Year Ends: 31 Dec '91
Donations: £17,000
Profit: £5,717,000
Turnover: £117,035,000

UK employees: 400
Total employees: 1,194

Donations Policy: Preference for local charities in the areas of company presence. Grants from £10 to £5,000.
Generally no support for circular appeals, fundraising events, brochure advertising, appeals from individuals or large national appeals.

☐ Cannon Street Investments plc

Investment holding company

New London Bridge House,
25 London Bridge Street,
London SE1 9SG
071-403 4857

Ch: J N Maclean
CE: R P Binks
Contact: Mrs M O'Neil
Office Manager

Year Ends: 31 Dec '91
Donations: nil
Profit: (£34,882,000)
Turnover: £295,018,000

UK employees: n/a
Total employees: 3,186

☐ Canon (UK) Ltd

Marketing of copiers

Canon House,
Manor Road,
Wallington,
Surrey SM6 0AJ
081-773 3173

Contact: G Thorn
Public Relations Manager

Year Ends: 31 Dec '90
Donations: n/a
Profit: £24,551,000
Turnover: £331,537,000

UK employees: n/a
Total employees: 2,377

% Club, BitC

☐ Cantors plc

Furnishing stores

164-170 Queens Road,
Sheffield S2 4DY
0742-766461

Ch: Harold Cantor
MD: Jack Davis
CE: Nicholas Jeffrey
Contact: Barry Rudkin
Personnel Controller

Year Ends: 29 Apr '91
Donations: £11,460
Profit: £3,401,000
Turnover: £57,025,000

UK employees: n/a
Total employees: 798

% Club

Donations Policy: The group is an active supporter of the Furniture Trades Benevolent Association.

☐ Caparo Industries plc

Engineering, industrial services

Caparo House,
103 Baker Street,
London W1M 1FD
071-486 1417

Contact: Dr S Paul
Chairman

Year Ends: 31 Dec '91
Donations: £20,107
Profit: £14,116,000
Turnover: £220,575,000

UK employees: n/a
Total employees: 2,177

% Club, BitC

Donations Policy: Education and medical research are the most favoured areas for support; preference also for children and youth, environment and heritage and enterprise/training. Grants to national organisations from £10 to £1,000. Grants to local organisations from £10 to £500.
No support for circular appeals, fundraising events, brochure advertising, individuals, purely denominational appeals, local appeals not in areas of company presence, large national appeals or overseas projects. Sponsorship is not undertaken.

☐ Cape plc

Building materials

Iver Lane,
Uxbridge,
Middlesex UB8 2JQ
0895-274626

Ch: J W Herbert
MD: M J Farebrother
Contact: M G Pitt-Payne
Company Secretary

Year Ends: 31 Mar '92
Donations: £58,700
Profit: £13,579,000
Turnover: £202,855,000

UK employees: 3,025
Total employees: 4,279

Donations Policy: To support national charities involved in social welfare, training, medical research, third world development and the environment. Donations may be made to special projects in areas of company presence or those related to the business. Donations are only given to registered charities and are made through the Charities Aid Foundation.

Please read page 6 | | | Alphabetical listing ●

Name/Address | *Officers* | *Financial Information* | *Other Information*

☐ Capital & Counties plc
Property development

St Andrew's House,
40 Broadway,
London SW1H 0BU
071-222 7878

Ch: D Gordon
MD: B Jolly
Contact: Margaret Harwood
Public Relations Manager

Year Ends: 31 Dec '91
Donations: £72,805
Profit: £29,000,000
Turnover: £55,800,000

UK employees: n/a
Total employees: 897

Donations Policy: Preference for local charities in the areas of company presence and appeals relevant to company business. Other appeals are not likely to be supported. Grants to national organisations from £100 to £5,000. Grants to local organisations from £50 to £500.

☐ Carborundum Abrasives plc
Manufacture of abrasive products

Trafford Park,
Manchester M17 1HP
061-872 2381

Ch: T A Egan
Contact: J C Collins
Personnel Manager

Year Ends: 31 Dec '89
Donations: £4,000
Profit: £4,546,000
Turnover: £66,922,000

UK employees: n/a
Total employees: 1,478

☐ Carclo Engineering Group plc
Card clothing & general engineering

177 Kirkstall Road,
Leeds LS4 2AQ
0532-422880

Ch: J W D Ewart
Contact: W Bates
Assistant Company Secretary

Year Ends: 31 Mar '92
Donations: £2,097
Profit: £5,628,000
Turnover: £78,763,000

UK employees: 1,698
Total employees: 1,841

Donations Policy: A donation is made to the Common Good Trust (based in Huddersfield); no other charitable donations are made. No appeals should be sent to the company.

☐ Cargill plc
Commodity trading agent & principal

Knowle Hill Park,
Fairmile Lane,
Cobham,
Surrey KT11 2PD
0932-861000

Ch: R Murray
Contact: D Nelson Smith
Chairman, Charities Committee

Year Ends: 31 May '92
Donations: £56,000
Profit: £10,395,000
Turnover: £1,301,094,000

UK employees: 4,722
Total employees: 6,020

% Club

Donations Policy: Preference for local charities in areas where the company operates, appeals relevant to company business and charities in which a member of company staff is involved. Preference for children and youth; social welfare; medical; arts; sport. Grants to national organisations from £50 to £5,000. Grants to local organisations from £50 to £3,000.
No grants for advertising in charity brochures; appeals from individuals; local appeals not in areas of company presence; overseas projects.

☐ Carlsberg Brewery Ltd
Brewers

Bridge Street,
Northampton NN1 1PZ
0604-234333

Ch: P J Svanholm
MD: M S Macdonald
Contact: David Edwards
Sponsorship Manager

Year Ends: 30 Sep '91
Donations: n/a
Profit: £48,051,000
Turnover: £144,508,000

UK employees: n/a
Total employees: 798

☐ Carlton Communications plc
TV & photographic production

15 St George Street,
Hanover Square,
London W1R 9DE
071-499 8050

Ch: Michael Green
MD: Keith Edelman
Contact: Beverley Matthews

Year Ends: 30 Sep '91
Donations: £237,500
Profit: £88,833,000
Turnover: £537,967,000

UK employees: n/a
Total employees: 4,443

% Club, BitC, ABSA

Donations Policy: Support for education/training (special interest in media fields; in general preference for educational establishments rather than individuals' programmes); the community (disadvantaged young people and homeless people); the arts (theatres and television/film related); health (medical research; victims of disease, illness and people with physical/mental disabilities). Preference for local charities in areas where the company operates, appeals relevant to company business and charities in which a member of company staff is involved. Grants range from £200 to £5,000.
No response to circular appeals. No grants for appeals from individuals; local appeals not in areas of company presence; overseas projects; appeals for building or general administrative costs; political appeals.

☐ Carnell Motor Group Ltd
New & used motor vehicles sale & repair

Marshgate,
Doncaster,
South Yorkshire DN5 8AF
0302-321383

Contact: Gill Sobczuk
Secretary to the Managing Director

Year Ends: 28 Apr '91
Donations: £1,121
Profit: £32,000
Turnover: £96,331,000

UK employees: n/a
Total employees: 572

☐ Carr's Milling Industries plc
Flour millers, bakers

Old Croft,
Stanwix,
Carlisle CA3 9BA
0228-28291

Ch: I C Carr
Contact: D B Armstrong
Managing Director

Year Ends: 31 Aug '91
Donations: £3,291
Profit: £543,000
Turnover: £68,962,000

UK employees: n/a
Total employees: 965

Donations Policy: Grants to local charities only, especially where relevant to the business or where a member of staff is involved. Preferred areas of support: children and youth, social welfare and medical.
No support for circular appeals, appeals from individuals, purely denominational appeals, local appeals not in areas of company presence, large national appeals.

Alphabetical listing

Name/Address	Officers	Financial Information	Other Information

☐ R G Carter (Holdings) Ltd — Builders

9 High Road,
Drayton,
Norwich   NR8 6AH
0603-867355

Ch: R G Carter
MD: S H Tuddenham
Contact: G Furness
Company Secretary

Year Ends: 31 Dec '90
Donations: £25,100
Profit: £7,996,000
Turnover: £115,005,000

UK employees: n/a
Total employees: 1,792

Donations Policy: The company has no particular preferences.

☐ Casket plc — Clothing manufacturers

Gorse Mill,
Gorse Street,
Chadderton,
Oldham   OL9 9RJ
0532-591434

Ch: N R Balfour
CE: J Smith
Contact: Charity Committee

Year Ends: 30 Jun '92
Donations: £1,954
Profit: £2,062,000
Turnover: £71,930,000

UK employees: n/a
Total employees: 786

☐ Cater Allen Holdings plc — Banking & discounting

20 Birchin Lane,
London   EC3V 9DJ
071-623 2070

Ch: James C Barclay
Contact: John Pound
Company Secretary

Year Ends: 30 Apr '92
Donations: £26,885
Profit: £8,130,000
Turnover: n/a

UK employees: n/a
Total employees: 301

Donations Policy: Preference for local charities in areas of company presence and large national charities.

☐ Caterpillar (UK) Ltd — Earthmoving equipment manufacture

Peckleton Lane,
Desford,
Leicestershire   LE9 9JT
0455-822441

Ch: R E Fischbach
Contact: S Pitt
Personnel Manager

Year Ends: 30 Nov '90
Donations: £8,640
Profit: £6,780,000
Turnover: £310,402,000

UK employees: n/a
Total employees: 1,220

☐ Cattles (Holdings) plc — Holding company

Haltemprice Court,
38 Springfield Way,
Anlaby,
Hull   HU10 6RR
0482-564422

Ch: Roy Waudby
CE: J Edward Cran
Contact: P H Prescott
Group Company Secretary

Year Ends: 31 Dec '91
Donations: £647
Profit: £9,800,000
Turnover: £244,677,000

UK employees: n/a
Total employees: 3,146

☐ CDP UK Advertising Ltd — Advertising agents

110 Euston Road,
London   NW1 2DQ
071-388 2424

Ch: John Salmon
Contact: D J D Pullen
Company Secretary

Year Ends: 31 Dec '90
Donations: £25,420
Profit: £791,000
Turnover: £213,402,000

UK employees: n/a
Total employees: 489

Donations Policy: Preference for appeals relevant to company business, but no donations are being made at present.

☐ CEF Holdings Ltd — Electrical wholesalers & manufacturers

1 Station Road,
Kenilworth,
Warwicks   CV8 1JJ
0926-58126

Ch: R H Thorn
Contact: N C Constable
Company Secretary

Year Ends: 30 Apr '90
Donations: £196,409
Profit: £22,827,000
Turnover: £370,669,000

UK employees: n/a
Total employees: 3,614

Donations Policy: The company makes donations through its charitable trust, and presumably can only make donations to organisations/projects deemed by law to be charitable.

☐ Central Independent Television plc — Independent TV programme contractor

Central House,
Broad Street,
Birmingham   B1 2JP
021-643 9898

Ch: L F Hill
Contact: Elaine Mitchell
Corporate Affairs

Year Ends: 31 Dec '91
Donations: £338,758
Profit: £24,449,000
Turnover: £306,531,000

UK employees: n/a
Total employees: 1,203
% Club, BitC, ABSA

Donations Policy: Support is given to charities, voluntary groups and arts organisations based in the Central region. Central administers grant-aid and sponsorship direct to the charity. Preferred areas of support: youth, people with special needs, people with disabilities, the arts, inner city initiatives, enterprise/training, environment and heritage, and recreation. Grants to local organisations from £50 to £2,000. No support for circulars; fundraising events; advertising in charity brochures; individuals; purely denominational (religious) appeals; local appeals not in areas of company presence; large national appeals; overseas projects; revenue funding; vehicles; capital building projects; political causes.

Please read page 6   Alphabetical listing •

Name/Address	Officers	Financial Information	Other Information

☐ Ceres (UK) Ltd
Grain merchants

Warren House,
Bell Lane,
Thame,
Oxon OX9 3AL
0844-261261

Contact: G R Webb
Managing Director

Year Ends: 31 Dec '90
Donations: n/a
Profit: £849,000
Turnover: £327,782,000

UK employees: n/a
Total employees: 64

☐ Channel Four Television Co Ltd
TV programmes transmissions

60 Charlotte Street,
London W1P 2AX
071-927 8635

Ch: Sir Richard Attenborough
MD: J Dukes
Contact: Marketing Department

Year Ends: 31 Mar '87
Donations: nil
Profit: £7,030,000
Turnover: £135,870,000

UK employees: n/a
Total employees: 267

ABSA

Donations Policy: Company policy is to make no cash donations to charity.

☐ Charnos plc
Textile manufacturers

Corporation Road,
Ilkeston,
Derbyshire DE7 4BP
0602-322191

Contact: R Noskwith
Chairman

Year Ends: 31 Dec '91
Donations: £50,088
Profit: £3,605,449
Turnover: £58,462,000

UK employees: n/a
Total employees: 2,276

% Club

Donations Policy: Preference for local charities in the areas of company presence and appeals relevant to company business. Preferred areas of support: children and youth, medical, environment and heritage and the arts. Grants to national organisations from £50 to £2,000. Grants to local organisations from £10 to £100.
Generally no support for circular appeals, purely denominational (religious) appeals, large national appeals or overseas projects.

☐ Charter Consolidated plc
Manufacturing, building products & services

7 Hobart Place,
London SW1W 0HH
071-838 7000

Ch: Sir Michael Edwardes
CE: J W Herbert
Contact: Jill Sherratt
Public Affairs Manager

Year Ends: 31 Mar '91
Donations: £427,000
Profit: £77,500,000
Turnover: £450,100,000

UK employees: n/a
Total employees: 8,084

BitC

Donations Policy: The company supports charities which comply with their strict guidelines and has little money free to allocate to unsolicited appeals, which are not welcome. Preference for local charities in the areas of company presence and appeals relevant to company business. Funds are allocated annually and thereafter all requests are turned down.
Generally no support for circular appeals, fundraising events, brochure advertising, appeals from individuals, purely denominational appeals, local appeals not in areas of company presence or overseas projects.

☐ Charterhouse plc
Banking

1 Paternoster Row,
St Paul's,
London EC4M 7DH
071-248 4000

Ch: M V Blank
MD: D W Parish
Contact: Miss S P Coatman
Secretary, Charterhouse
Charitable Trust

Year Ends: 30 Sep '91
Donations: £133,672
Profit: £21,200,000
Turnover: n/a

UK employees: n/a
Total employees: 777

BitC

Donations Policy: The Charterhouse Charitable Trust makes donations to registered charities only, mainly nationwide charities or charities local to areas of company presence (ie. Edinburgh, Glasgow, Liverpool and London). Preference is also given to charities in which a member of staff is involved. Applications must be in writing.
No support for appeals from individuals, political groups, advertising in charity brochures or sponsorship.

☐ Cheltenham & Gloucester Building Society
Building society

Chief Office,
Barnett Way,
Gloucester GL4 7RL
0452-372372

Ch: John Bays
CE: Andrew Longhurst
Contact: Lisa Oversby
Marketing Services Manager

Year Ends: 31 Dec '91
Donations: £60,000
Profit: £183,800,000
Turnover: n/a

UK employees: n/a
Total employees: 2,821

Donations Policy: Preference for local charities in areas where the company operates. Preference for medical; education; enterprise/training. Grants to national organisations from £100 to £200. Grants to local organisations from £100 to £20,000.
No response to circular appeals. No grants for advertising in charity brochures; appeals from individuals; purely denominational (religious) appeals; local appeals not in areas of company presence; overseas projects.

☐ Chevron (UK) Ltd
Distribution of petroleum products

2 Portman Street,
London W1H 0AN
071-487 8100

MD: C M Smith
Contact: C Lavington
Public Affairs Manager

Year Ends: 31 Dec '90
Donations: n/a
Profit: £252,988,000
Turnover: £1,104,044,000

UK employees: n/a
Total employees: 751

ABSA

Donations Policy: Charities should note that the majority of causes supported are predetermined and that the company is therefore able to respond to few additional requests for assistance. Donations and sponsorship are spread across the arts, education, environment and social welfare, largely in north-east Scotland.

• **Alphabetical listing**   **Please read page 6**

Name/Address	Officers	Financial Information	Other Information

☐ Chloride Group plc
Power supply, battery & related systems manufacture

15 Wilton Road,
London SW1V 1LT
071-834 5500

Ch: R Horrocks
CE: K Hodgkinson
Contact: D J Wright
Company Secretary

Year Ends: 31 Mar '91
Donations: £745
Profit: £5,100,000
Turnover: £215,600,000

UK employees: n/a
Total employees: 7,809

Donations Policy: Currently restricted to existing commitments. No unsolicited appeals.

☐ Christie Group plc
Sale & valuation of businesses

2 York Street,
London W1A 1BP
071-224 6860

Contact: David B Rugg
Managing Director

Year Ends: 31 Mar '92
Donations: £6,000
Profit: (£889,000)
Turnover: £17,303,000

UK employees: n/a
Total employees: 450

Donations Policy: Preference for appeals relevant to company business, trade charities and charities in which a member of staff is involved. Grants to national organisations from £100 to £2,000. Grants to local organisations from £5 to £100.
No support for circular appeals, fundraising events, advertising in charity brochures, appeals from individuals, purely denominational appeals, local appeals not in areas of company presence, large national appeals or overseas projects.

☐ Christies International plc
Auctioneers

8 King Street,
St James',
London SW1Y 6QT
071-839 9060

Ch: Lord Carrington
MD: C M Davidge
Contact: Mrs Robin Hambro
Charities Department

Year Ends: 31 Dec '91
Donations: £349,000
Profit: £6,363,000
Turnover: £102,664,000

UK employees: n/a
Total employees: 1,442

% Club, ABSA

Donations Policy: Preference for charities working in the fields of heritage, arts, conservation, health and child care, education and the environment. Also a preference for specifically London charities (rather than those that happen to be based in London), for appeals relevant to company business and charities in which a member of staff is involved. Regional offices of the company do have a limited budget which they can use as they wish. Grants to national organisations from £200 to £5,000. Grants to local organisations from £100 to £500.
No support for circular appeals, appeals from individuals or purely denominational (religious) appeals.

☐ Chrysalis Group plc
Records & publishing

The Chrysalis Building,
Bramley Road,
London W10 6SP
071-221 2213

Ch: C N Wright
Contact: Nick Watkins
Deputy Group Managing Director

Year Ends: 31 Aug '91
Donations: £2,698
Profit: £11,519,000
Turnover: £95,590,000

UK employees: n/a
Total employees: 942

☐ Church & Co Ltd
Manufacturers & retailers of footwear

St James,
Northampton NN5 5JB
0604-751251

Ch: I B Church
MD: J G Church
Contact: R Plowman
Personnel Manager

Year Ends: 31 Dec '89
Donations: £4,887
Profit: £4,023,000
Turnover: £69,102,000

UK employees: 1,768
Total employees: 2,166

☐ Charles Church Holdings plc
Housebuilding

Charles Church House,
Knoll Road,
Camberley,
Surrey GU15 3TQ
0276-62299

Ch: S B Church
MD: N King
Contact: N King
Group Managing Director

Year Ends: 31 Aug '90
Donations: £2,850
Profit: £56,439,000
Turnover: £97,073,000

UK employees: n/a
Total employees: 270

Donations Policy: To support certain local charities and causes of benefit to the local community.

☐ CI Group plc
Steel re-rollers, engineers, builders

Showell Road,
Wolverhampton,
West Midlands WV10 9NL
0902-772022

Ch: A E Hargreaves
Contact: R W F Yates
Chief Executive

Year Ends: 31 Jan '91
Donations: £5,254
Profit: £4,830,000
Turnover: £93,700,000

UK employees: n/a
Total employees: 1,561

☐ CIA Group plc
Advertising consultancy

1 Paris Garden,
London SE1 8NU
071-633 9999

Ch: C J Ingram
Contact: Julie Ticehurst
Personal Assistant to the Chairman

Year Ends: 31 Dec '91
Donations: £25,000
Profit: £2,829,000
Turnover: £172,416,000

UK employees: n/a
Total employees: 150

Donations Policy: The company's charity committee meets quarterly. Preference for children and youth; medical; education; environment and heritage; enterprise/training. Grants range from £25 to £5,000.
No response to circular appeals. No grants for advertising in charity brochures; purely denominational (religious) appeals; local appeals not in areas of company presence; overseas projects.

Please read page 6 | | | Alphabetical listing ●

Name/Address	Officers	Financial Information	Other Information

☐ **Ciba-Geigy plc** Speciality chemicals, pharmaceuticals

Hulley Road,
Macclesfield,
Cheshire SK10 2NX
0625-421933

Ch: J S Fraser
Contact: Mrs D Anderson
Secretary to the Charities Committee

Year Ends: 31 Dec '91
Donations: £178,990
Profit: £11,582,000
Turnover: £691,679,000

UK employees: 5,676
Total employees: 5,676

% Club, BitC, ABSA

Donations Policy: Preference for national charities concerned with mentally and physically disabled people and to local charities where the company has a business presence. Grants range from £50 to £500.
Generally no support for non-charities, campaigning work by charities, appeals from individuals, advertising in charity brochures, fundraising events, circular appeals, denominational or political appeals, local appeals not in areas of company presence and overseas projects.
Sponsorship proposals to K V Turpie, Public Relations Manager.

☐ **Circle K (UK) Ltd** Retail convenience stores

Fareham Point,
Wycombe Road,
Fareham,
Hampshire PO16 7BU
0329-822666

Contact: Jill Petchey
Director of Human Resources

Year Ends: 28 Mar '90
Donations: n/a
Profit: £17,416,000
Turnover: £115,748,000

UK employees: n/a
Total employees: 3,265

☐ **Citibank** Banking

PO Box 78,
Citibank House,
336 Strand,
London WC2R 1HB
071-240 1222

Ch: John McFarlane
Contact: Kathryn Carassalini
Corporate Affairs Director

Year Ends: 31 Dec '92
Donations: £309,500
Profit: n/a
Turnover: n/a

UK employees: 4,000
Total employees: 92,000

% Club, BitC, ABSA

Donations Policy: The bank usually seeks out projects it wants to support rather than responding to appeals. Preference for projects and organisations which may have difficulty in raising funds from the private sector, and are based near the bank's main offices. The bank supports a relatively small number of projects, usually over a four year period. Current main areas supported are education and training, the arts, and the environment. No new commitments will be considered until 1994.
Generally no support for non-charities, circular appeals, fundraising events, advertising in charity brochures, appeals from individuals, purely denominational (religious) appeals, local appeals not in areas of company presence, large national appeals, overseas projects, campaigning work by charities or political appeals.

☐ **Citroen UK Ltd** Vehicle importers & distributors

221 Bath Road,
Slough SL1 4BA
0753-822100

Ch: X Karcher
MD: P Boisjoly
Contact: Public Affairs Director

Year Ends: 31 Dec '90
Donations: £10,965
Profit: £4,287,000
Turnover: £477,340,000

UK employees: n/a
Total employees: 423

☐ **City Centre Restaurants plc** Restaurants

122 Victoria Street,
London SW1E 5LG
071-834 0585

Ch: B W M Johnston
CE: P Kaye
Contact: Miss Lesley Jones
Corporate Administrator

Year Ends: 31 Dec '91
Donations: nil
Profit: £9,101,000
Turnover: £79,821,000

UK employees: 3,360
Total employees: 3,378

☐ **Citygrove Leisure plc** Subsidiaries engaged in retail, leisure

Chelsea Garden Market,
Chelsea Harbour,
London SW10 0XE
071-352 8750

Contact: D Woolf
Chairman

Year Ends: 30 Nov '88
Donations: £2,807
Profit: £5,545,000
Turnover: £63,107,000

UK employees: n/a
Total employees: 26

☐ **Civil Aviation Authority** Regulatory body

CAA House,
45-59 Kingsway,
London WC2B 6TE
071-379 7311

Ch: C J Chataway
MD: T Murphy

Year Ends: 31 Mar '92
Donations: n/a
Profit: £13,749,000
Turnover: £199,241,000

UK employees: n/a
Total employees: 7,375

Donations Policy: The authority rarely supports charitable appeals, when it does they are related to aviation.

☐ **Arnold Clark Automobiles Ltd** Motor vehicles

St George's House,
St George's Road,
Glasgow G3 6LB
041-332 2626

Contact: Arnold Clark
Managing Director

Year Ends: 31 Dec '90
Donations: n/a
Profit: £3,042,000
Turnover: £211,108,000

UK employees: n/a
Total employees: 1,442

• **Alphabetical listing**   **Please read page 6**

Name/Address	Officers	Financial Information	Other Information

☐ C & J Clark Ltd
Shoe makers

40 High Street,
Street,
Somerset BA16 0YA
0458-43131

Ch: L V D Tindale
MD: J C Clothier
Contact: Ian Ritchie
Public Relations Manager

Year Ends: 31 Jan '92
Donations: £60,000
Profit: £20,389,000
Turnover: £594,223,000

UK employees: n/a
Total employees: 19,550

ABSA

Donations Policy: The company supports charities close to its head office (address above) or its factories. No grants to national charities or appeals from outside these areas. Preference for charities in which a member of staff is involved. Preferred areas of support: children and youth, education, recreation, environment and heritage and the arts. Grants from £50 to £500.
Generally no support for circular appeals, brochure advertising, purely denominational appeals, local appeals not in areas of company presence, large national appeals or overseas projects.

☐ Matthew Clark plc
Wine & spirit distributors

183-185 Central Street,
London EC1V 8DR
071-253 7646

Ch: F W Gordon-Clark
MD: P Aikens
Contact: C S Gordon-Clark
Director

Year Ends: 30 Apr '91
Donations: £4,145
Profit: £5,619,000
Turnover: £69,976,000

UK employees: n/a
Total employees: 386

Donations Policy: Priority to the major medical charities with further emphasis on alcohol and children/youth related charities, local appeals in areas of company presence, appeals relevant to company business and charities in which a member of staff is involved. Donations are usually a four year covenant of £500.

☐ T Clarke plc
Electrical engineers & contractors

Stanhope House,
116-118 Walworth Road,
London SE17 1JL
071-252 7676

Ch: P E Stanborough
Contact: B Moss
Company Secretary

Year Ends: 31 Dec '91
Donations: £4,900
Profit: £1,887,000
Turnover: £59,239,000

UK employees: n/a
Total employees: 979

☐ Horace Clarkson plc
Shipbroking, insurance broking, shipowning

12 Camomile Street,
London EC3A 7BP
071-283 8955

Ch: H L C Greig
Contact: Marion Warwicker
Secretary to the Managing Director

Year Ends: 31 Dec '91
Donations: £36,222
Profit: £5,532,000
Turnover: £42,000,000

UK employees: 440
Total employees: 551

Donations Policy: Preference for appeals relevant to company business and charities in which a member of company staff is involved. The company prefers to give direct to charities rather than eg. advertising in charity brochures.
Generally no support for individuals.

☐ Claverley Company Ltd
Newspaper publishers & newsagents

51-53 Queen Street,
Wolverhampton,
West Midlands WV1 3BU
0902-313131

Contact: M G D Graham
Chairman

Year Ends: 30 Dec '90
Donations: £18,827
Profit: £11,764,000
Turnover: £128,092,000

UK employees: n/a
Total employees: 1,975

Donations Policy: "We believe we can best help charities through the publicity we give them. However we are sympathetic to appeals and to certain causes." Preference for local charities in areas of company presence, especially children/youth, education, medical, enterprise/training and environment/heritage.
No support for brochure advertising, appeals from individuals, denominational appeals, local appeals not in areas of company presence or overseas projects.

☐ Clayform Properties plc
Property dealers & developers

24 Bruton Street,
Mayfair,
London W1X 7DA
071-491 8400

Ch: M D Wigley
MD: R T E Ware
Contact: Mrs V Chatterjee
Personal Assistant to the Managing Director

Year Ends: 31 Dec '91
Donations: nil
Profit: (£20,635,000)
Turnover: £91,539,000

UK employees: n/a
Total employees: 2,054

Donations Policy: No donations are being given at present.

☐ Clerical Medical Investment Group
Insurance

Narrow Plain,
Bristol BS2 0JH
0272-290566

Ch: Sir Douglas S Morpeth
MD: R D Corley
Contact: John Slann
Marketing Services Manager

Year Ends: 31 Dec '90
Donations: £43,945
Profit: n/a
Turnover: n/a

UK employees: 2,000
Total employees: 2,100

BitC, ABSA

Donations Policy: The group has a small budget for donations as it is a mutual society owned by its members. Each case is considered on its merits, but the group would seek to add value to enterprises that are viable without its help. Grants to national organisations from £50 to £5,000. Grants to local organisations from £25 to £5,000.
No grants for advertising in charity brochures; appeals from individuals; large national appeals.

Please read page 6 | | | Alphabetical listing •

Name/Address	Officers	Financial Information	Other Information

☐ **Clifford Foods plc**   Manufacture & distribution of food & drinks

Western Road,
Bracknell,
Berkshire RG12 1QA
0344-425741

Ch: J Clifford
MD: M B Bunting
Contact: W G Hague
Assistant Company Secretary

Year Ends: 31 Dec '91
Donations: £61,000
Profit: £5,296,000
Turnover: £140,576,000

UK employees: 1,523
Total employees: 1,523

% Club

Donations Policy: One-off donations to organisations with general charitable objectives in areas where the company has a presence and to UK, international and third world charities. Preferred areas of support: children and youth, social welfare, medical and overseas aid/development. Grants to national organisations from £300 to £2,000. Grants to local organisations from £5 to £500. UK, international and third world charity requests to W G Hague at Head Office. Other requests to local offices as appropriate.
Generally no support for circular appeals, fundraising events, brochure advertising, appeals from individuals, purely denominational appeals or local appeals not in areas of company presence.

☐ **Cluff Resources plc**   Oil & minerals exploration, development

58 St James' Street,
London SW1A 1LD
071-493 8272

Ch: J G Cluff
Contact: Miss Alison Cowan
Personal Assistant to the Chairman

Year Ends: 31 Dec '90
Donations: £19,000
Profit: £2,506,000
Turnover: £16,721,000

UK employees: n/a
Total employees: 398

Donations Policy: The company has no particular preferences and is willing to consider all appeals. Donations are decided by the chairman.

☐ **Clugston Ltd**   Construction, contractors, plant & tool hire

St Vincent House,
Normanby Road,
Scunthorpe DN15 8QT
0724-843491

Ch: J W A Clugston
CE: D E Burgess
Contact: R L Hurst
Company Secretary

Year Ends: 26 Jan '91
Donations: £11,897
Profit: £1,249,000
Turnover: £105,731,000

UK employees: n/a
Total employees: 906

Donations Policy: Support for a few charities through local connections as and when appropriate.

☐ **Clyde Petroleum plc**   Oil & gas exploration & production

Coddington Court,
Coddington,
Ledbury,
Hereford HR8 1JL
0531-640811

Ch: Dr C B Phipps
MD: J M Gourlay
Contact: P S J Zatz
Finance Director

Year Ends: 31 Dec '91
Donations: £20,770
Profit: £3,043,000
Turnover: £87,241,000

UK employees: 85
Total employees: 150

Donations Policy: Preference for local charities in areas of company presence, charities where a member of staff is involved or appeals relevant to the business. Grants to national organisations from £100 to £300. Grants to local organisations from £50 to £300.
No grants for individuals; local appeals not in areas of company presence; denominational or large national appeals; overseas projects.

☐ **Clydesdale Bank plc**   Banking

150 Buchanan Street,
Glasgow G1 2HL
041-248 7070

Ch: Sir David Nickson
CE: A R Cole-Hamilton
Contact: Alan Sloan
Manager, Community Relations

Year Ends: 30 Sep '91
Donations: £97,000
Profit: £64,019,000
Turnover: n/a

UK employees: 7,522
Total employees: n/a

ABSA

Donations Policy: The bank prefers to support Scottish organisations concerned with medicine and social welfare, education and youth, environment and local natural disasters (ie. in Scotland). National grants range from £100 to £10,000. Local grants range from £50 to £500.
No response to circular appeals. No grants for fundraising events; advertising in charity brochures; individuals; purely denominational (religious) appeals; local appeals not in areas of company presence; large national appeals; overseas projects; political appeals.

☐ **CMB Foodcan plc**   Packaging containers & central heating

Woodside,
Perry Wood Walk,
Worcester WR5 1EQ
0905-762000

Contact: Miss P Axtell
Secretary, Subscriptions & Donations Committee

Year Ends: 31 Dec '90
Donations: £11,000
Profit: £36,507,000
Turnover: £336,513,000

UK employees: n/a
Total employees: 2,460

☐ **CMG (Computer Management Group) Ltd**   Management & computer consultancy services

Carrier House,
1-9 Warwick Row,
London SW1E 5ER
071-630 7833

Year Ends: 31 Dec '90
Donations: nil
Profit: £7,016,000
Turnover: £96,231,000

UK employees: n/a
Total employees: 1,575

☐ **Coates Brothers plc**   Printing inks & industrial surface coatings

16 Palace Street,
London SW1E 5BQ
071-630 5777

Ch: D J Youngman
Contact: A E Lascelles
Company Secretary

Year Ends: 31 Dec '88
Donations: £7,578
Profit: £34,317,000
Turnover: £345,020,000

UK employees: n/a
Total employees: 5,360

Donations Policy: Preference for local charities in the areas of company presence, appeals relevant to company business and charities in which a member of staff is involved. Preferred areas of support: children and youth, social welfare, education, environment and heritage. Grants to national organisations from £100 to £500. Grants to local organisations from £25 to £75.
Generally no support for fundraising events, advertising in charity brochures, purely denominational (religious) appeals or local appeals not in areas of company presence.

● **Alphabetical listing** Please read page 6

Name/Address	Officers	Financial Information	Other Information

☐ **Coats Viyella plc** Textiles

A
28 Savile Row, *Ch:* Sir David Alliance *Year Ends:* 31 Dec '91 *UK employees:* n/a
London W1X 2DD *Contact:* S Dow *Donations:* £233,000 *Total employees:* 61,055
071-734 5321   Group Secretary *Profit:* £111,400,000
   Turnover: £1,947,500,000 % Club, BitC, ABSA

Donations Policy: Charities which the Appeals Committee ordinarily support come under the following headings: education; community; arts, medical research and health care; the environment. Beneficiaries are almost invariably closely associated with the company and its associates. Grants to national organisations from £2,000 to £10,000. Grants to local organisations from £1,000 to £10,000. Generally no support for circular appeals or local appeals not in areas of company presence.

☐ **Coca-Cola Holdings (UK) Ltd** Soft drink manufacturers

B
Pemberton House, *Contact:* Ian Muir *Year Ends:* 31 Dec '90 *UK employees:* n/a
Wrights Lane,   Manager of External Affairs *Donations:* £102,250 *Total employees:* 537
London W8 5SN   *Profit:* £14,545,000
071-938 2131   *Turnover:* £134,451,000 BitC

Donations Policy: Supports a limited number of major national charities principally involved with children and environmental initiatives.

☐ **Colefax & Fowler Group plc** Design & selling of furnishing fabrics

A
39 Brook Street, *Ch:* T Parr *Year Ends:* 30 Apr '89 *UK employees:* n/a
London W1Y 2JE *CE:* D Green *Donations:* £9,623 (1991) *Total employees:* 206
071-493 2231 *Contact:* Trudy Ballard *Profit:* £2,709,000
   Press Officer *Turnover:* £19,037,000

Donations Policy: Preference for children; medical; arts.
No grants for appeals from individuals; purely denominational (religious) appeals.

☐ **Colgate Palmolive Ltd** Household & personal care products

B
Guildford Business Park, *Ch:* J T Reid *Year Ends:* 31 Dec '90 *UK employees:* 702
Middleton Road, *Contact:* Linda Wallace *Donations:* £52,799 *Total employees:* n/a
Guildford,   Group Communications Manager *Profit:* £4,126,000
Surrey GU2 5LZ   *Turnover:* £102,741,000
0483-302222

Donations Policy: Prefers to support as many local causes (organisations and individuals where appropriate) as possible. Preference for appeals relevant to company business and charities in which a member of staff is involved, especially children/youth, medical, education. No advertising in charity brochures/souvenir programmes. No deeds of covenant for large amounts; exceptional requests would be considered, but are unlikely to be supported. No circular appeals, purely denominational (religious) appeals, overseas projects, political appeals.

☐ **Colorvision plc** Sale of televisions, video recorders, satellite systems

Perdio House, *Ch:* Neville Michaelson *Year Ends:* 31 Mar '92 *UK employees:* n/a
Woodend Avenue, *MD:* Stuart Tingler *Donations:* £6,000 *Total employees:* 728
Speke, *Contact:* Marketing Department *Profit:* £2,026,000
Liverpool L24 9WF   *Turnover:* £88,463,000
051-448 1515

☐ **Colt Car Co Ltd** Vehicle distributors

Watermoor, *Contact:* David Miles *Year Ends:* 31 Mar '91 *UK employees:* n/a
Cirencester,   Public Affairs Manager *Donations:* £13,999 *Total employees:* 306
Gloucestershire GL7 1LF   *Profit:* £15,626,000
0285-655777   *Turnover:* £175,752,000

Donations Policy: Budget strictly limited through government-imposed import restrictions. Preference for local charities or where a member of staff is involved, especially children/youth and medical.
No support for large national appeals, circulars, overseas appeals, brochure advertising, denominational appeals, individuals.

☐ **Colt International Ltd** Heating & ventilation equipment

B
New Lane, *Ch:* J O Hea *Year Ends:* 31 Dec '88 *UK employees:* n/a
Havant, *Contact:* P O'Hey *Donations:* £5,808 *Total employees:* 1,142
Hampshire PO9 2LY   Managing Director *Profit:* £2,335,000
0705-451111   *Turnover:* £62,617,000

Donations Policy: Preference for local charities, especially children/youth, social welfare and medical.
Generally no support for circular appeals, fundraising events, advertising in charity brochures, appeals from individuals, purely denominational (religious) appeals or overseas projects.

☐ **Commercial Union plc** Insurance & life assurance

A
Commercial Union House, *Ch:* N H Baring *Year Ends:* 31 Dec '91 *UK employees:* 9,503
69 Park Lane, *CE:* A L Brend *Donations:* £157,307 *Total employees:* n/a
Croydon CR9 1BG *Contact:* Senior Executive Assistant *Profit:* (£68,600,000)
071-283 7500   *Turnover:* n/a BitC, ABSA

Donations Policy: Main areas of support are social welfare, medical care, education, young people, environment and heritage. National grants range from £100 to £10,000. Local grants range from £100 to £1,000.

Please read page 6 | Alphabetical listing •

Name/Address	Officers	Financial Information	Other Information

☐ **Commodore Business Machines (UK) Ltd** — Marketing microcomputer products

Commodore House, The Switchback, Gardner Road, Maidenhead SL6 7XA
0628-770088

Ch: I Gould
Contact: Marketing Department

Year Ends: 30 Jun '91
Donations: nil
Profit: £3,602,000
Turnover: £94,836,000

UK employees: n/a
Total employees: 72

☐ **Compaq Computer Ltd** — Microcomputer manufacture

Brookfield House, 44 Davies Street, London W1Y 2BL

Contact: Julie-Ann Hadley, Charities Co-ordinator

Year Ends: 31 Dec '90
Donations: £12,000
Profit: £12,978,000
Turnover: £285,492,000

UK employees: n/a
Total employees: 208

Donations Policy: Recipient organisations should be registered charities (although exceptions may be made), must be able to demonstrate project/programme sustainability and allow Compaq to publicise positive results. Eligible projects are: health and social services; arts and culture (including environmental preservation); community (including rehabilitation schemes, energy conservation, local community improvement, and special events). Donations are also given to an on going local charity of the committees choice (reviewed annually). Grants range from £20 to £1,000.
No support for organisations who have some form of political bias, discriminatory organisations, organisations that promote religious faith, individuals, sport teams, films or movies, advertising/promotional events or advertising space in brochures or programmes, chain letters.

☐ **Compass Group plc** — Catering Services

Queen's Wharf, Queen Caroline Street, London W6 9RJ
081-741 1541

Ch: Dr A I Lenton
CE: F H Mackay
Contact: Cathi Fisher, Marketing Director

Year Ends: 29 Sep '91
Donations: £7,475
Profit: £32,000,000
Turnover: £320,900,000

UK employees: n/a
Total employees: 20,285

☐ **Computacenter Ltd** — Computer design & supply

Computacenter House, 93-101 Blackfriars Road, London SE1 8HW
071-620 2222

Ch: P J Ogden
MD: P W Hulme
Contact: Jim Atherton, Marketing Manager

Year Ends: 31 Dec '90
Donations: £629
Profit: £7,001,000
Turnover: £200,993,000

UK employees: n/a
Total employees: 682

☐ **Computervision Ltd** — Computer equipment distribution

Innovation Court, New Street, Basingstoke, Hampshire RG21 1DP
0256-58133

MD: J E Hayden
Contact: Peter Russell, Director

Year Ends: 31 Dec '90
Donations: n/a
Profit: £3,421,000
Turnover: £116,800,000

UK employees: n/a
Total employees: 937

☐ **Concentric plc** — Controls & assemblies for industry

Coleshill Road, Sutton Coldfield, West Midlands B75 7AZ
021-378 4229

Ch: A C Firth
Contact: R F Miles, Company Secretary

Year Ends: 30 Sep '91
Donations: £20,169
Profit: £4,223,000
Turnover: £112,884,000

UK employees: n/a
Total employees: 2,011

Donations Policy: Preference for local charities in areas where the company operates.

☐ **Conder Group plc** — Steel-framed building construction

Moorside Road, Winnall, Winchester, Hampshire SO23 7SJ
0962-882222

Ch: Dr R A Paine
CE: A C Lovell
Contact: Liz Atkinson, Group Public Relations Manager

Year Ends: 31 Dec '90
Donations: £84,518
Profit: £19,287,000
Turnover: £287,370,000

UK employees: n/a
Total employees: 2,952
% Club

Donations Policy: The company is particularly concerned with environmental conservation which it supports through the Conder Charitable Trust. This supports "charitable organisations having as an object the control of the human population (provided this shall contribute to the relief of poverty, hardship or distress) and charitable organisations for the conservation of wildlife". Funds are allocated annually normally in September/October. Preference for local charities in areas where the company operates and appeals relevant to company business. Support is also given to children and youth, social welfare, medical and enterprise/training.
No response to circular appeals. No grants for advertising in charity brochures; appeals from individuals; purely denominational (religious) appeals; political organisations.

☐ **Conoco (UK) Ltd** — Petroleum products

Park House, 116 Park Street, London W1Y 4NN
071-408 6000

Ch: J M Stinson
Contact: Jan Newland, Secretary of UK Contributions Committee

Year Ends: 31 Dec '90
Donations: £340,000
Profit: £377,300,000
Turnover: £2,483,700,000

UK employees: n/a
Total employees: 7,312
BitC

Donations Policy: No support for political organisations, religious organisations or sporting events.

• **Alphabetical listing**   Please read page 6

Name/Address	Officers	Financial Information	Other Information

☐ Constantine Holdings Ltd   Property

10 Grafton Street,
London W1X 3LA
071-493 9484

Ch: J H F Simson
Contact: E Magee
Finance Director

Year Ends: 31 Dec '88
Donations: £5,500
Profit: £1,901,000
Turnover: £28,422,000

UK employees: n/a
Total employees: 425

Donations Policy: Donations to selected charities subject to annual review. Preference for children/youth, medical, National Trust. No response to unsolicited or circular appeals.

☐ Continental Microwave (Holdings) plc   Engineering & manufacture of telecommunications

1 Crawley Green Road,
Luton,
Bedfordshire LU1 3LB
0582-424233

MD: J Clifford
Contact: J Choi
Group Director of Finance & Administration

Year Ends: 31 Dec '91
Donations: £5,000
Profit: £1,100,000
Turnover: £24,400,000

UK employees: n/a
Total employees: 369

Donations Policy: Preference for local charities in areas where the company operates. Preference for children and youth; medical. No grants for advertising in charity brochures; purely denominational (religious) appeals.

☐ Continental Tyres Ltd   Tyre manufacturers

4-8 High Street,
Yiewsley,
West Drayton,
Middlesex UB7 7DJ
0895-445678

MD: D Connell
Contact: Ms Moira Model
Personnel Officer

Year Ends: 31 Dec '90
Donations: n/a
Profit: £181,000
Turnover: £131,563,000

UK employees: n/a
Total employees: 1,305

☐ Continental UK Ltd   Grains, oilseeds & oils traders

Southside,
105 Victoria Street,
London SW1E 6QT
071-828 7868

MD: L A Barrett
Contact: Mrs Jenny Ball
Personnel Manager

Year Ends: 31 Mar '91
Donations: n/a
Profit: £2,122,000
Turnover: £149,262,000

UK employees: n/a
Total employees: 94

☐ Contract Papers (Holdings) Ltd   Paper merchanting

Sovereign House,
Rhosili Road,
Brackmills,
Northampton NN4 0JE
0604-706060

Contact: Vince Collins
Advertising & Marketing Manager

Year Ends: 31 Dec '90
Donations: n/a
Profit: £3,311,000
Turnover: £103,460,000

UK employees: n/a
Total employees: 229

☐ Control Data Ltd   Computer systems

3 Roundwood Avenue,
Stockley Park,
Uxbridge,
Middlesex UB11 1AG
081-848 1919

Contact: Personnel Department

Year Ends: 30 Nov '86
Donations: n/a
Profit: £3,410,000
Turnover: £71,269,000

UK employees: n/a
Total employees: 493

☐ Control Securities plc   Property & property related leisure

3A Southwark Bridge Office Village,
London SE1 9HW
071-815 0805

Contact: Sydney Robin
Chairman

Year Ends: 30 Sep '91
Donations: £255,000
Profit: £44,425,000
Turnover: £130,554,000

UK employees: n/a
Total employees: n/a
% Club

Donations Policy: Preference for children and youth; social welfare; medical; arts; enterprise/training. An important aspect of the company's policy is the, "integration and bridge building between mainstream British society and the minority communities". No response to circular appeals.

☐ D C Cook Holdings plc   Motor vehicle retailers

73 Sheffield Road,
Rotherham,
South Yorkshire S60 1DA
0709-373688

Ch: D C Cook
Contact: B Singleton
Managing Director

Year Ends: 30 Apr '91
Donations: £2,000
Profit: £1,483,000
Turnover: £122,671,000

UK employees: n/a
Total employees: 834

☐ William Cook plc   Manufacture of steel castings

Parkway Avenue,
Sheffield S9 4WA
0742-730121

Ch: A Cook
Contact: Carol Gladwin
Secretary to the Directors

Year Ends: 30 Mar '91
Donations: £18,386
Profit: £12,178,000
Turnover: £133,220,000

UK employees: n/a
Total employees: 1,689

Donations Policy: A lump sum is given to the South Yorkshire Foundation and they deal with all requests.

Please read page 6 — Alphabetical listing

Name/Address	Officers	Financial Information	Other Information

☐ Cookson Group plc
Metal refining & smelting, paints

130 Wood Street,
London EC2V 6EQ
071-606 4400

Ch: R Malpas
MD: R Oster
Contact: Mrs Dowton
Secretary to the Appeals Committee

Year Ends: 31 Dec '91
Donations: £121,000
Profit: £34,400,000
Turnover: £1,198,500,000

UK employees: n/a
Total employees: 13,862

Donations Policy: Supports a conservation campaign through World Wide Fund for Nature and British Trust for Conservation Volunteers. No further information available.

☐ Coombe Farm Foods Holdings Ltd
Dairy products marketing

St Olaves,
19 Woolley Street,
Bradford-on-Avon,
Wiltshire BA15 1AD
02216-3939

Ch: S M D Oliver
Contact: D Gerhardt
Managing Director

Year Ends: 31 Mar '91
Donations: n/a
Profit: £817,000
Turnover: £106,780,000

UK employees: n/a
Total employees: 379

☐ Cooper (GB) Ltd
Engineering - aerospace & petroleum industries

Houston Road,
Livingstone,
West Lothian EH54 5BZ
0506-31122

Contact: L MacMillan
Director of Employee Relations

Year Ends: 30 Jun '90
Donations: £8,303
Profit: £1,548,000
Turnover: £129,206,000

UK employees: n/a
Total employees: 2,450

☐ Co-operative Bank plc
Banking

1 Balloon Street,
Manchester M60 4EP
061-832 3456

Ch: T Agar
MD: T J Thomas
Contact: Peter Walker
Head of Business Development & Public Relations

Year Ends: 13 Jan '91
Donations: £76,347
Profit: £14,872,000
Turnover: n/a

UK employees: 4,437
Total employees: n/a

BitC

Donations Policy: The bank makes only small charitable donations. Preference for local charities in the areas of company presence and appeals relevant to company business. Preferred areas of support: children and youth, social welfare, environment and heritage and enterprise/training.
Generally no support for circular appeals, advertising in charity brochures, purely denominational (religious) appeals, local appeals not in areas of company presence, large national appeals or overseas projects.

☐ Co-operative Insurance Society Ltd
Insurance

Miller Street,
Manchester M60 0AL
061-837 4043

Ch: D J Wise
MD: A D Sneddon
Contact: R G Taylor
Assistant Secretary

Year Ends: 31 Dec '92
Donations: n/a
Profit: n/a
Turnover: n/a

UK employees: 11,000
Total employees: 11,000

Donations Policy: No donations figure is declared in the annual report, but the society uses the Charities Aid Foundation for its charitable giving. Preferred areas of support: medical research, children, environment and social welfare. Grants to national organisations from £1,000 to £2,000. Grants to local organisations from £50 to £200.
Generally no support for fundraising events, advertising in charity brochures, appeals from individuals, purely denominational (religious) appeals or local appeals not in areas of company presence.

☐ Co-operative Wholesale Society Ltd
Supplier to Co-operative stores & banks

PO Box 53,
New Century House,
Corporation Street,
Manchester M60 4ES
061-834 1212

Ch: G L Fyfe
CE: David Skinner
Contact: Geoff Simpson
Public Affairs Manager

Year Ends: 12 Jan '92
Donations: n/a
Profit: £47,100,000
Turnover: £3,141,300,000

UK employees: 40,000
Total employees: 40,000

Donations Policy: The company wholly owns the Co-operative Bank plc, see separate entry.

☐ Coopers Holdings Ltd
Industrial holding company

Bridge House,
Gipsy Lane,
Swindon SN2 6DZ
0793-532111

Ch: R Cooper
MD: S A Hill
Contact: D Connors
Personal Assistant to the Managing Director

Year Ends: 31 Dec '90
Donations: £1,849
Profit: £141,000
Turnover: £142,457,000

UK employees: n/a
Total employees: 530

☐ Coopers & Lybrand Deloitte
Accountants

Plumtree Court,
London EC4A 4HT
071-583 5000

Ch: C Brandon Gough
Contact: J Tedder
Partner

Year Ends: 31 Dec '88
Donations: £22,081
Profit: £9,039,000
Turnover: £524,697,000

UK employees: n/a
Total employees: 5,428

% Club, BitC, ABSA

Donations Policy: The firm provides direct financial support and business advisory services to a number of charitable bodies.

• **Alphabetical listing**   Please read page 6

Name/Address   *Officers*   *Financial Information*   *Other Information*

☐ Corah
Knitted clothing & fabric manufacture

St John Street,   *Ch:* G N Corah   *Year Ends:* 31 Dec '87   *UK employees:* n/a
Off Burleys Way,   *CE:* J Foulkes   *Donations:* £12,400   *Total employees:* 5,594
Leicester LE1 9BB   *Contact:* I Hamilton   *Profit:* £1,745,000
0533-620811   Company Secretary   *Turnover:* £96,013,000

☐ Cornhill Insurance plc
Insurance

57 Ladymead,   *Ch:* C G Burrows   *Year Ends:* 31 Dec '91   *UK employees:* n/a
Guildford,   *Contact:* J Darby   *Donations:* £22,914   *Total employees:* 3,014
Surrey GU1 1DB   Company Secretary   *Profit:* (£39,500,000)
0483-68161   *Turnover:* n/a

Donations Policy: Preference for local charities in areas where the company operates and charities concerned with children, disabled people and people with special needs. Most donations are made through the Charities Aid Foundation to registered charities.
No grants for advertising in charity brochures; appeals from individuals; political appeals; and rarely to overseas projects.

☐ Corning Consumer Ltd
Glass manufacturers

Wear Glass Works,   *Ch:* D W Swindells   *Year Ends:* 4 Dec '88   *UK employees:* n/a
Sunderland,   *MD:* J A Brown   *Donations:* £11,114   *Total employees:* 1,094
Tyne & Wear SR4 6EJ   *Contact:* I G Strother   *Profit:* £8,504,000
091-567 6222   Company Secretary   *Turnover:* £62,653,000

Donations Policy: Preference for local charities in the areas of company presence. Preferred areas of support are children and youth, social welfare, medical, education and enterprise/training.
Generally no support for telephone appeals, circular appeals, local appeals not in areas of company presence or overseas projects.

☐ Cornwell Parker plc
Furniture manufacturers, textile wholesalers

PO Box 22,   *Ch:* M H T Jourdan   *Year Ends:* 31 Jul '91   *UK employees:* n/a
The Courtyard,   *Contact:* Clive Hallett   *Donations:* £23,985   *Total employees:* 1,751
Frogmoor,   Head of Human Resources   *Profit:* £8,048,000
High Wycombe,   *Turnover:* £92,785,000
Bucks HP13 5DJ
0494-521144

Donations Policy: Preference for local charities in areas of company presence (High Wycombe, Chipping Norton, Edmonton, Padiham, Bournemouth) and appeals relevant to company business. Grants to national organisations from £50 to £500. Grants to local organisations from £5 to £100.
Generally no support for circular appeals, brochure advertising, purely denominational appeals, local appeals not in areas of company presence, large national appeals and overseas projects.

☐ Cosalt Caravans Ltd
Ships chandlery, caravan manufacture

Convamore Road,   *Ch:* E A Brian   *Year Ends:* 3 Sep '91   *UK employees:* n/a
Grimsby,   *Contact:* M Brown   *Donations:* £4,274   *Total employees:* 1,723
South Humberside DN32 9JL   Marketing Manager   *Profit:* £2,465,000
0472-358931   *Turnover:* £80,331,000

☐ Costain Group plc
Construction & development

111 Westminster Bridge Road,   *Ch:* P B Sawdy   *Year Ends:* 31 Dec '91   *UK employees:* n/a
London SE1 7UE   *CE:* P J Costain   *Donations:* £83,340   *Total employees:* 14,276
071-928 4977   *Contact:* G Langham   *Profit:* £69,200,000
                                  Company Secretary   *Turnover:* £1,315,700,000   BitC

Donations Policy: The donations committee decides on 10 to 20 charities to support at the beginning of each year, generally establishing long-term deeds of covenant. The arts, education and the environment are all supported. Preference for local charities in the areas where the company operates and appeals relevant to company business.
Local appeals should be addressed to an office in the vicinity.
No support for circular appeals or advertising in charity brochures.

☐ Countryside Properties plc
Property developers

Countryside House,   *Ch:* A H Cherry   *Year Ends:* 30 Sep '91   *UK employees:* n/a
The Warley Hill Business Park,   *Contact:* C Crook   *Donations:* £5,833   *Total employees:* 345
The Drive,   Sales & Marketing Director   *Profit:* £3,049,000
Brentwood,   *Turnover:* £87,120,000
Essex CM13 3AT
0277-260000

Donations Policy: Preference for local charities in areas of company presence and appeals relevant to the business.
No support for circular appeals, large national appeals, overseas appeals or purely denominational (religious) appeals.

Please read page 6 | Alphabetical listing •

Name/Address | *Officers* | *Financial Information* | *Other Information*

☐ Courage Group Ltd
Brewers

Ashby House,
1 Bridge Street,
Staines,
Middlesex TW18 4TP
0784-466199

Ch: M Foster
Contact: Bernard Ryan
Trustee, Courage Charitable Trust

Year Ends: 30 Jun '91
Donations: £170,000
Profit: £204,596,000
Turnover: £844,834,000

UK employees: n/a
Total employees: 8,520

BitC

Donations Policy: The company supports a wide range of charities particularly those linked to the licensed trade. Preference also for local charities in areas where the company operates, appeals relevant to company business and charities in which a member of company staff is involved. Preference for medical; education; recreation; environment/heritage; arts; enterprise/training. Grants to national organisations from £1,000 to £17,000. Grants to local organisations from £50 to £5,000.
No response to circular appeals. No grants for fundraising events; advertising in charity brochures; appeals from individuals; local appeals not in areas of company presence; overseas projects.
Total community contributions were over £900,000.

☐ Courtaulds plc
Coatings, performance materials, chemicals

50 George Street,
London W1A 2BB
071-612 1000

Ch: Sir Christopher Hogg
MD: Sipko Huismans
Contact: D A Stevens
Deputy Company Secretary

Year Ends: 31 Mar '92
Donations: £196,646
Profit: £201,400,000
Turnover: £1,942,600,000

UK employees: 11,000
Total employees: 23,000

Donations Policy: Preferably registered charities. Main areas of support are charities that have a link with the company in some way or have direct relevance to its business. Local factories and offices have small amounts to give away.
Generally no support for advertising in charity brochures, appeals from individuals, purely denominational appeals, political appeals, or local appeals not in areas of company presence.

☐ Courtaulds Textiles plc
Clothing manufacture

13-14 Margaret Street,
London W1A 3DA
071-331 4500

Ch: I Rae
MD: J Connor, A P Walker

Year Ends: 31 Dec '91
Donations: £32,000
Profit: £13,163,000
Turnover: £419,230,000

UK employees: 19,569
Total employees: 20,181

Donations Policy: Most of the company's donations are made through individual businesses in order to concentrate support on charities considered to be of most relevance to company employees and their communities. Preference for children and youth; social welfare; medical; education; environment/heritage; enterprise/training. Appeals should be addressed to individual businesses within the group.
No grants for appeals from individuals; purely denominational (religious) appeals; local appeals not in areas of company presence; overseas projects.

☐ Courts (Furnishers) plc
Retailers of house furniture

The Grange,
1 Central Road,
Morden,
Surrey SM4 5RX
081-640 3322

Ch: P C Cohen
MD: B J R Cohen
Contact: Edwin N Cohen
Director

Year Ends: 31 Mar '92
Donations: £14,000
Profit: £9,049,000
Turnover: £175,048,000

UK employees: n/a
Total employees: 3,184

Donations Policy: Preference for local charities in areas where the company operates and appeals relevant to company business. Preference for children and youth; social welfare; medical; recreation.
No grants for fundraising events; advertising in charity brochures; appeals from individuals; purely denominational (religious) appeals; local appeals not in areas of company presence; large national appeals.

☐ Coutts & Co
Banking

440 Strand,
London WC2R 0QS
071-379 6262

Ch: D B Money-Coutts
MD: A J Robarts
Contact: T J Lewis
Administrator, The Coutts
Charitable Trust

Year Ends: 31 Dec '91
Donations: £359,000
Profit: (£15,166,000)
Turnover: n/a

UK employees: 2,090
Total employees: n/a

BitC

Donations Policy: The trustees consider all appeals individually on their merits and do not have any specific policy as to those which they will support other than that they must be UK registered charities.
Generally no support for brochure advertising, appeals from individuals or overseas projects.
Sponsorship proposals to Head of Business Development, address as above.

☐ Coventry Building Society
Building society

Economic House,
PO Box 9,
High Street,
Coventry CV1 5QN
0203-555255

Ch: I N Smith
CE: M H Ritchley
Contact: Keith Railton
Marketing Controller

Year Ends: 31 Dec '91
Donations: £1,583
Profit: £21,300,000
Turnover: £54,878,000

UK employees: n/a
Total employees: 881

Donations Policy: Preference for local charities in areas of company presence, particularly those concerned with children and youth, and social welfare. Coventry Building Society rules do not allow for direct donations to charity. Any support is provided through advertising programmes etc. or, in special local cases, by having items printed.
No circular appeals, local appeals/fundraising events outside areas of company presence, brochure advertising, appeals from individuals, large national appeals, purely denominational (religious) appeals or overseas projects.
Applications should be sent to the contact at PO Box 105, 1st Floor, West Orchard House, 28 Corporation Street, Coventry CV1 1QR.

● **Alphabetical listing**   Please read page 6

Name/Address	Officers	Financial Information	Other Information

Cow & Gate Ltd
Manufacture & marketing of babyfoods

White Horse Business Park,
Trowbridge,
Wiltshire BA14 0XQ
0225-768381

Ch: B G Pendle
Contact: Communications Department

Year Ends: 31 Dec '88
Donations: £14,161 (1991)
Profit: £1,827,000
Turnover: £66,202,000

UK employees: n/a
Total employees: 382

Donations Policy: Support only for appeals relevant to company business ie. infant feeding (0-1 years). Grants to national organisations from £15 to £2,000. Grants to local organisations from £15 to £1,000. In addition to charitable donations the company has made other community contributions totalling £2,090.
No response to circular appeals. No grants for fundraising events; purely denominational (religious) appeals; local appeals not in areas of company presence; overseas projects.

T Cowie plc
Motor vehicle dealers

Millfield House,
Hylton Road,
Sunderland SR4 7BA
091-514 4122

Ch: T Cowie
Contact: Robert Blower
Corporate Communications Manager

Year Ends: 31 Dec '91
Donations: £21,846
Profit: £18,207,000
Turnover: £564,851,000

UK employees: n/a
Total employees: 2,266

Donations Policy: The company supports a select number of projects helping disadvantaged people in the communities where the company has a major presence (the North East, West Midlands and East Anglia).
No grants for sport, arts, science research or heritage appeals.
Total community contributions were about £30,000.

CPC (UK) Ltd
Food, glucose syrups, starches

Claygate House,
Littleworth Road,
Esher,
Surrey KT10 9PN
0372-462181

Ch: R K Moss
MD: P W Phillips
Contact: Miss P Ingold
Senior Personnel Officer

Year Ends: 30 Sep '90
Donations: £8,885
Profit: £5,297,000
Turnover: £182,341,000

UK employees: n/a
Total employees: 2,000

Donations Policy: Preference for local appeals, but this does not preclude other appeals. Preferred areas of support: children and youth, social welfare, education, environment and heritage and enterprise/training.
Generally no support for circular appeals, advertising in charity brochures, purely denominational appeals, local appeals not in areas of company presence, large national appeals or overseas projects.

Crane Ltd
Fluid control equipment

Nacton Road,
Ipswich,
Suffolk IP3 9QH

Ch: R S Evans
MD: R Young
Contact: John Barbrook

Year Ends: 31 Dec '88
Donations: £2,084 (1991)
Profit: £2,872,000
Turnover: £55,360,000

UK employees: n/a
Total employees: 1,726

Donations Policy: The company makes a number of smaller donations rather than a few large donations, preferring to support local appeals/initiatives, where the company has a local interest. Preference for children and youth; medical; education; environment/heritage; enterprise/training. Grants range from £25 to £100.
No grants for advertising in charity brochures; purely denominational (religious) appeals; local appeals not in areas of company presence; overseas projects.

Cray Electronics Holdings plc
Telecommunications, software systems

2 West Mills,
Newbury,
Berkshire RG14 5HG
0635-521321

Ch: Sir Peter Michael
MD: J M Richards
Contact: D P C Tidsall
Company Secretary

Year Ends: 30 Apr '92
Donations: £8,020
Profit: £4,787,000
Turnover: £84,786,000

UK employees: n/a
Total employees: 1,726

Crest Nicholson plc
Housing, leisure & engineering

Crest House,
39 Thames Street,
Weybridge,
Surrey KT13 8JG
0932-847272

Ch: J St Lawrence
CE: J Callcutt
Contact: M J Cutler
Group Secretary

Year Ends: 31 Oct '91
Donations: £9,000
Profit: £59,385,000
Turnover: £324,162,000

UK employees: n/a
Total employees: 1,595

Donations Policy: Preference for local charitable organisations in the areas of company presence and charities in which a member of staff is involved. The company prefers to make one substantial sum to a national charity once every four/five years, especially in the areas of children and youth, social welfare and medical, and prefers this donation to be connected with the provision of a permanent benefit eg. hospital bed, equipment etc. Grants to local organisations from £50 to £150.
Generally no support for advertising in charity brochures, appeals from individuals, purely denominational (religious) appeals, local appeals not in areas of company presence or overseas projects.

Cresvale Ltd
Eurobond dealers

4 Battlebridge Lane,
London SE1 2JB
071-357 6400

Contact: Anne Ochshorn
Administration Manager

Year Ends:
Donations: n/a
Profit: n/a
Turnover: n/a

UK employees: n/a
Total employees: n/a

% Club

Donations Policy: We have been unable to obtain a policy for this company.

Please read page 6 | Alphabetical listing ●

Name/Address	Officers	Financial Information	Other Information

☐ Croda International plc
Chemical manufacturers

Cowick Hall,
Snaith,
Goole,
North Humberside DN14 9AA
0405-860551

Ch: M R Valentine
CE: K G G Hopkins
Contact: G E Bates
Company Secretary

Year Ends: 31 Dec '91
Donations: £13,367
Profit: £21,300,000
Turnover: £352,500,000

UK employees: 3,700
Total employees: 5,136

Donations Policy: All appeals are considered by a committee. Preference for local charities in the areas of company presence. Preferred areas of support: social welfare, medical and education. Grants to local organisations from £100 to £250.
Generally no support for circular appeals, fundraising events, brochure advertising, appeals from individuals, purely denominational appeals, large national appeals or overseas projects.

☐ James Cropper plc
Paper & board manufacturers

Burnside Mills,
Kendal,
Cumbria LA9 6PZ
0539-722002

Ch: J A Cropper
MD: N W Willink
Contact: O G D Acland
Personnel Director & Company Secretary

Year Ends: 31 Mar '92
Donations: £15,257
Profit: £1,060,000
Turnover: £40,297,000

UK employees: 439
Total employees: 439

% Club

Donations Policy: Preference for local charities in areas where the company operates and appeals relevant to company business. Preference for social welfare; education; recreation; environment/heritage; arts; enterprise/training.

☐ Croudace Holdings Ltd
Property development

Croudace House,
Godstone Road,
Caterham,
Surrey CR3 6XQ
0883-346464

Ch: J B Ratcliffe
MD: C A Henley
Contact: Mrs R Jex
Secretary to the Chairman

Year Ends: 30 Sep '90
Donations: £4,219
Profit: £2,135,000
Turnover: £115,379,000

UK employees: n/a
Total employees: 647

☐ Crown House Engineering plc
Electrical & mechanical engineering & tableware

320 Purley Way,
Croydon CR9 2DE
081-686 2411

Ch: P Edge-Partington
Contact: K Escott
Managing Director

Year Ends: 31 Mar '89
Donations: £4,149
Profit: £3,567,000
Turnover: £154,049,000

UK employees: n/a
Total employees: 2,864

☐ Crystal Motor Group
Motor dealers

71 Holderness Road,
Hull HU8 7NJ
0482-25732

Ch: P B Oughtred
MD: Robin D Waite
Contact: Les Cooper
Dealer Principal

Year Ends: 31 Dec '90
Donations: £3,834
Profit: £1,415,000
Turnover: £94,755,000

UK employees: n/a
Total employees: 629

Donations Policy: The Group includes Crystal of Hull, Harrogate and Scarborough. Most of the charitable budget is given to BEN (the motor trade benevolent charity). The remainder is always given to causes local to areas of company presence. Preferred areas of support: children and youth and education.
No support for circular appeals, fundraising events, appeals from individuals, local appeals not in areas of company presence, large national appeals, overseas appeals, denominational appeals or brochure advertising.

☐ Cummins Engine Company Ltd
Diesel engines & component manufacturers

Yarm Road,
Darlington,
Co Durham DL1 4PW
0325-460606

Ch: J Patrick
MD: J C Macfarlane
Contact: Susan Chilton
Secretary to the Trustees

Year Ends: 31 Dec '90
Donations: £42,621 (1991)
Profit: £9,771,000
Turnover: £393,403,000

UK employees: n/a
Total employees: 4,628

Donations Policy: The company supports projects local to the company's manufacturing plants and offices, with particular emphasis on education/experience for young people. Also preference for charities in which a member of staff is involved. Grants to national organisations from £100 to £500. Grants to local organisations from £25 to £2,000.
No support for non-charities, circular appeals, fundraising events, advertising in charity brochures, purely denominational (religious) appeals or local appeals not in areas of company presence.

☐ Curfin Investments Ltd
Motor vehicle dealers

161 Chertsey Road,
Twickenham,
Middlesex TW1 1EP
081-891 1313

Ch: A Jaffe
MD: J Jaffe
Contact: Mrs J Langford
Secretary to the Managing Director

Year Ends: 30 Apr '91
Donations: £30,907
Profit: £1,974,000
Turnover: £131,971,000

UK employees: n/a
Total employees: 946

Donations Policy: Preference for local charities in areas where the company operates. The company prefers to give donations in kind where this is possible, eg. helping with transport, providing old engines etc..
Generally no grants for advertising in charity brochures; appeals from individuals; local appeals not in areas of company presence; overseas projects.

● **Alphabetical listing** Please read page 6

Name/Address *Officers* *Financial Information* *Other Information*

☐ Cyanamid of Great Britain Ltd
Medical & agricultural products

Cyanamid House,
Fareham Road,
Gosport,
Hampshire PO13 0AS
0329-224000

MD: M J Wilson
Contact: Michael Gates
Public Relations Manager

Year Ends: 30 Nov '91
Donations: £35,000
Profit: £7,700,000
Turnover: £194,800,000

UK employees: 2,106
Total employees: 2,106

Donations Policy: Preference for appeals on behalf of disabled and disadvantaged people especially in areas local to company presence and where the company has a professional interest. Greatest emphasis is on charities in which company employees are involved. A significant portion of company support goes to a pre-selected charity/need each year. Grants to national organisations from £100 to £2,500. Grants to local organisations from £50 to £500.
No support for sporting, political or religious organisations, or circular appeals, and usually no support for the cost of brochures or other printing matters.

☐ Daejan Holdings plc
Property investment

Freshwater House,
158-162 Shaftesbury Avenue,
London WC2H 8HR
071-836 1555

Ch: B S E Freshwater
Contact: C C Morse
Company Secretary

Year Ends: 31 Mar '91
Donations: £60,000
Profit: £16,356,000
Turnover: £22,719,000

UK employees: n/a
Total employees: 159

Donations Policy: Mainly supports orthodox Jewish charities, especially in the medical and educational fields in the USA, UK and Israel. Support is also given to organisations concerned with the relief of poverty.
Organisations dealing with professional fundraisers, large overhead expenses and expensive fundraising campaigns are avoided. No support for the arts, enterprise or conservation.

☐ Daewoo UK Ltd
General merchants

Templar House,
82 Northolt Road,
Harrow HA2 0YL
081-423 7200

MD: B H Kang
Contact: Mrs D Mark
Personnel Officer

Year Ends: 31 Dec '90
Donations: nil
Profit: £389,000
Turnover: £191,715,000

UK employees: n/a
Total employees: 74

☐ Dagenham Motors Group plc
Ford car & van & Iveco Ford commercial dealerships

Ford House,
New Road,
Dagenham RM9 6EX
081-592 6655

Contact: D Philip
Chairman

Year Ends: 31 Dec '91
Donations: n/a
Profit: £2,112,000
Turnover: £127,002,000

UK employees: n/a
Total employees: 829

☐ Daily Mail & General Trust plc
Newspaper publishers

Northcliffe House,
2 Derry Street,
London W8 5TT
071-938 6000

Ch: Viscount Rothermere
MD: C J F Sinclair
Contact: V Harmsworth
Director of Corporate Affairs

Year Ends: 30 Sep '91
Donations: £253,000
Profit: £47,700,000
Turnover: £644,100,000

UK employees: n/a
Total employees: 9,677

ABSA

Donations Policy: Preference for charities connected with the printing industry and charities local to the company and its subsidiaries.
No support for circular appeals, fundraising events, advertising in charity brochures, appeals from individuals, purely denominational (religious) appeals, local appeals not in areas of company presence, large national appeals or overseas projects.

☐ Dairy Crest Ltd
Milk & dairy products manufacture

Dairy Crest House,
Portsmouth Road,
Surbiton,
Surrey KT6 5QL
081-398 4155

Ch: G R John
CE: G Bar
Contact: Sue Twidle
Communications Department

Year Ends: 31 Mar '91
Donations: n/a
Profit: £31,873,000
Turnover: £1,177,000,000

UK employees: n/a
Total employees: 11,937

Donations Policy: The company has no budget for charitable donations at present.

☐ Daiwa Europe Bank plc
Banking

City Tower,
40 Basinghall Street,
London EC2V 5DE
071-315 3900

Ch: G W Taylor
CE: K Rembutsu
Contact: Janice Webb
Personnel Department

Year Ends: 31 Mar '92
Donations: £2,620
Profit: £2,755,000
Turnover: n/a

UK employees: n/a
Total employees: n/a

BitC

☐ DAKS Simpson Group plc
Tailors & clothiers

34 Jermyn Street,
London SW1 6HS
071-439 8781

Ch: J P N Mengers
MD: J C R Franks
Contact: L C F Parker
Administrator, Charity Committee

Year Ends: 31 Jul '90
Donations: £50,000
Profit: £4,163,000
Turnover: £69,618,000

UK employees: n/a
Total employees: 2,217

% Club

Donations Policy: Support for children's charities; equipment for children's wards in hospitals; equestrian charities; charities in which a director or member of staff is involved; trade charities. Grants to national organisations from £200 to £12,500. Grants to local organisations from £200 to £2,500.
Generally no support for circular appeals, fundraising events, appeals from individuals or overseas projects.

Please read page 6 — Alphabetical listing

Name/Address	Officers	Financial Information	Other Information

Dale Electric International plc
Electricity generating sets

Electricity Buildings,
Filey,
Yorkshire YO14 9PJ
0723-514141

Ch: T McDonald
CE: I L Dale
Contact: J Armistead
Company Secretary

Year Ends: 29 Apr '90
Donations: £2,187 (1991)
Profit: £232,860
Turnover: £59,286,296

UK employees: n/a
Total employees: 1,051

Donations Policy: Support only for local charities in the areas of company presence and preference for charities in which a member of staff is involved. Preferred areas of support: children and youth, social welfare, medical, education, recreation. Grants to local organisations from £25 to £250.
Generally no support for circular appeals, advertising in charity brochures, appeals from individuals, purely denominational (religious) appeals, local appeals not in areas of company presence, large national appeals or overseas projects.

Dalepak Foods plc
Manufacture of frozen food products

Dale House,
Leeming Bar,
Northallerton,
North Yorkshire DL7 9DQ
0677-424111

Ch: M D Abrahams
CE: C R Ivory
Contact: P Holley
Financial Director

Year Ends: 30 Apr '92
Donations: £30,615
Profit: £3,926,000
Turnover: £40,612,000

UK employees: n/a
Total employees: 632

Donations Policy: The company's Charity Committee considers all applications in December/January. The company has a preference for national charities, including overseas charities, and organisations local to Northallerton. Grants to national organisations £200 to £400 paid in CAF vouchers. Grants to local organisations £20 to £200 paid in cheques or product vouchers.
The company does not usually support appeals from individuals or local appeals not in areas of company presence.

Dalgety plc
International merchants

100 George Street
London W1H 5RH
071-486 0200

Ch: J J West
CE: M E Warren
Contact: B E Gandy
Group Secretary

Year Ends: 30 Jun '92
Donations: £200,082
Profit: £116,800,000
Turnover: £3,982,400,000

UK employees: n/a
Total employees: 16,073

Donations Policy: Preference for local charities in areas where the company operates, appeals relevant to company business and charities in which a member of company staff is involved. Grants to national organisations from £500 to £2,500. Grants to local organisations from £500 to £1,000.
No response to circular appeals. No grants for fundraising events; advertising in charity brochures; appeals from individuals; local appeals not in areas of company presence; overseas projects.

Dana Ltd
Automotive component manufacture & distribution

Great Eastern House,
Greenbridge Road,
Stratton St Margaret,
Swindon SN3 3LB
0793-513315

CE: Southwood J Morcott
Contact: Keith Brooks
Personnel Director

Year Ends: 31 Oct '90
Donations: £10,468
Profit: £5,157,000
Turnover: £211,465,000

UK employees: n/a
Total employees: 2,982

Donations Policy: Supports two chosen charities only: BEN (the Motor and Allied Trade Benevolent Fund) and the local Thamesdown Community Trust which co-ordinates requests and channels support as appropriate. Unsolicited appeals are therefore not supported.

Danka Business Systems plc
Supply of business equipment in USA

40 George Street,
London W1H 5RE
071-935 4650

Ch: M A Vaughan-Lee
MD: D M Doyle
Contact: P G Dumond
Company Secretary

Year Ends: 31 Mar '92
Donations: £25,000
Profit: £11,677,000
Turnover: £115,023,000

UK employees: n/a
Total employees: 1,801

Donations Policy: Preference for local charities in areas where the company operates.

Data General Ltd
Marketing computers

Hounslow House,
724-734 London Road,
Hounslow,
Middlesex TW3 1PD
081-758 6000

Contact: David Smythe
Financial Director

Year Ends: 28 Sep '91
Donations: £9,448
Profit: (£11,537,000)
Turnover: £66,007,000

UK employees: n/a
Total employees: 491

Davenport Vernon plc
Motor vehicle dealers & hirers

London Road,
High Wycombe,
Buckinghamshire HP11 7EU
0494-530021

Contact: D J Baker
Chairman

Year Ends: 30 Sep '91
Donations: £6,027
Profit: £1,433,000
Turnover: £99,519,000

UK employees: n/a
Total employees: 582

Davis Service Group plc
Ford main dealers

34 Francis Grove,
Wimbledon,
London SW19 4DY
081-543 6644

Ch: N W Benson
CE: J C Ivey

Year Ends: 31 Dec '91
Donations: £2,413
Profit: £16,667,000
Turnover: £309,230,000

UK employees: n/a
Total employees: 14,874

Donations Policy: The company is currently making no charitable donations.

● **Alphabetical listing**   Please read page 6

Name/Address *Officers* *Financial Information* *Other Information*

☐ Dawson International plc
Textiles, clothing, knitting

9 Charlotte Square, *Ch:* R A B Miller *Year Ends:* 31 Mar '92 *UK employees:* 6,000
Edinburgh EH2 4DR *Contact:* Mrs R G Glynne-Percy *Donations:* £77,000 *Total employees:* 12,000
031-220 1919 Corporate Affairs Executive *Profit:* £30,090,000
 Turnover: £414,958,000 ABSA

Donations Policy: Preference for local charities in the areas of company presence and appeals relevant to company business. Preferred areas of support: children and youth, medical, education, the arts and enterprise/training.
Generally no support for local appeals not in areas of company presence, large national appeals or overseas projects.

☐ De Beers Consolidated Mines Ltd
Diamond mining & marketing

40 Holborn Viaduct, *Contact:* J J I Hawkins *Year Ends:* 31 Dec '89 *UK employees:* n/a
London EC1P 1AJ See address below *Donations:* n/a *Total employees:* n/a
071-353 1545 *Profit:* £922,320,000
 Turnover: n/a

Donations Policy: In 1989, the Oppenheimer Trust's income was £108,000. This appears to be a donation from the company. In general the trust supports causes local to areas of company presence, particularly in the fields of health, education and welfare. Only registered charities are supported. Most grants are between £100 and £500. Appeals should be addressed to J J I Hawkins, Oppenheimer Charitable Trust, 17 Charterhouse Street, London EC1N 6RA.

☐ De La Rue plc
Security printers

6 Agar Street, *Ch:* P F Orchard *Year Ends:* 31 Mar '91 *UK employees:* 5,266
London WC2N 4DE *MD:* J J S Marshall *Donations:* £32,000 *Total employees:* 8,734
071-836 8383 *Contact:* Miss A M Bullen *Profit:* £58,935,000
 Appeals Secretary to the De La Rue *Turnover:* £369,627,000
 Jubilee Trust

Donations Policy: The Trust supports a very limited number of registered charities which have already been selected.
Generally no support for circular appeals, fundraising events, brochure advertising, individuals, purely denominational appeals, local appeals not in areas of company presence or large national appeals.

☐ Debenham Tewson & Chinnocks Holdings plc
Property advisers

44 Brook Street, *Ch:* R N Lay *Year Ends:* 30 Apr '92 *UK employees:* n/a
London W1A 4AG *MD:* G A T Turnbull *Donations:* £6,515 *Total employees:* 657
071-408 1161 *Contact:* Mrs Ann Newton *Profit:* £1,590,000
 Secretary to the Chairman *Turnover:* £34,831,000

Donations Policy: No response to circular appeals.

☐ Del Monte Foods International Ltd
Food distributors

Del Monte House, *Ch:* L R Allen *Year Ends:* 30 Nov '90 *UK employees:* n/a
240 London Road, *Contact:* Helen Guttridge *Donations:* n/a *Total employees:* 5,602
Staines TW18 4JD Secretary to the Managing *Profit:* £11,378,000
0784-461555 Director *Turnover:* £158,232,000

☐ Delta plc
Electronic equipment, metals

Greets Green Road, *Ch:* G H Wilson *Year Ends:* 28 Dec '91 *UK employees:* 9,993
West Bromwich, *CE:* R A Easton *Donations:* £35,863 *Total employees:* 14,115
West Midlands B70 9ER *Contact:* Mrs T P Randall *Profit:* £65,830,000
021-500 6188 Secretary, Appeals Committee *Turnover:* £774,040,000

Donations Policy: Supports UK organisations on a very planned broad sectional basis covering medical, disabled people, youth, children's welfare, community, historical/environmental, service/ex-service, arts and education. Grants to national organisations from £100 to £800. Grants to local organisations from £25 to £100.
Generally no support for circular appeals, fundraising events, advertising in charity brochures, appeals from individuals, purely denominational (religious) appeals, local appeals not in areas of company presence and overseas projects.

☐ Deminex UK Oil & Gas Ltd
Oil & gas exploration

Bowater House, *Ch:* D Lehning *Year Ends:* 31 Dec '90 *UK employees:* n/a
68 Knightsbridge, *Contact:* S J Ashford *Donations:* £1,100 *Total employees:* 72
London SW1X 7LD Company Secretary *Profit:* £87,376,000
071-589 7033 *Turnover:* £246,989,000

☐ Desmond & Sons Ltd
Manufacture of garments

Drumahoe, *Ch:* D F Desmond *Year Ends:* 31 Dec '88 *UK employees:* n/a
Londonderry BT47 3SD *Contact:* A Hamilton *Donations:* £31,719 *Total employees:* 2,815
0504-44901 Personnel Manager *Profit:* £3,013,000
 Turnover: £61,424,000

Donations Policy: Preference for local charities in the areas of company presence and charities in which a member of staff is involved. Preferred areas of support: children and youth, medical and overseas aid/development.
Generally no support for circular appeals, advertising in charity brochures, purely denominational (religious) appeals, local appeals not in areas of company presence, large national appeals or overseas projects.

Please read page 6 — Alphabetical listing

Name/Address	Officers	Financial Information	Other Information

J A Devenish plc
Public houses, wine bars & restaurants

15 Trinity Street,
Weymouth,
Dorset DT4 8TP
0305-761111

Ch: M R Cannon
CE: J W Clark
Contact: Peter Dawes
Company Secretary

Year Ends: 30 Sep '91
Donations: £11,774
Profit: £11,466,000
Turnover: £87,278,000

UK employees: n/a
Total employees: 2,583

Donations Policy: Mainly local charities in areas of company presence. Preferred areas of support are children and youth, social welfare, medical and education.
No support for circular appeals, appeals from individuals, purely denominational (religious) appeals or local appeals not in areas of company presence.

Dewhirst Group plc
Clothing

Dewhirst House,
Westgate,
Driffield,
North Humberside YO25 7TH
0377-42561

Ch: H A Vice
Contact: T C Dewhirst
Managing Director

Year Ends: 17 Jan '92
Donations: £8,359
Profit: £4,127,000
Turnover: £130,466,000

UK employees: n/a
Total employees: 5,393

Dexion Group plc
Storage & materials handling equipment

Maylands Avenue,
Hemel Hempstead,
Hertfordshire HP2 7EW
0442-242261

Ch: S Hinchliff
Contact: Martin Webster
Company Executive

Year Ends: 30 Dec '90
Donations: £2,350 (1991)
Profit: £8,767,000
Turnover: £139,720,000

UK employees: n/a
Total employees: 1,795

Donations Policy: Preference for local charities in areas where the company operates. Preference for children and youth; medical; education; environment/heritage; enterprise/training. Grants range from £25 to £35.
No grants for advertising in charity brochures; appeals from individuals; purely denominational (religious) appeals; large national appeals; overseas projects.

DHL International Ltd
Transport services

Orbital Park,
Great South West,
Hounslow,
Middlesex TW4 6JS
081-890 9393

Contact: Lynn Humphries
Corporate Affairs Manager

Year Ends:
Donations: n/a
Profit: n/a
Turnover: n/a

UK employees: n/a
Total employees: n/a

% Club, BitC

Donations Policy: Preference for children and youth; social welfare; medical; overseas aid/development.
No grants for fundraising events; advertising in charity brochures; appeals from individuals; purely denominational (religious) appeals; local appeals not in areas of company presence; large national appeals; overseas projects.

Digger Ltd
Coal production

1 Pascall Close,
St Mellons,
Cardiff CF3 0LW
0222-777222

Ch: G H Waddell
CE: C J Hotson
Contact: Mrs Nash
Office Administrator

Year Ends: 31 Dec '90
Donations: n/a
Profit: £10,828,000
Turnover: £125,038,000

UK employees: n/a
Total employees: 1,418

Digital Equipment Co Ltd
Distributors of digital computers

Worton Grange,
Imperial Way,
Reading,
Berkshire RG2 0TR
0734-868711

Ch: G S Shingles
Contact: Contributions Specialist

Year Ends: 1 Jun '90
Donations: £230,000
Profit: n/a
Turnover: £936,000,000

UK employees: 7,000
Total employees: n/a

% club, BitC, ABSA

Donations Policy: Most support is given in kind. Cash donations tend to be at a local community level only. Support is given to education and research, health care and research, organisations concerned with disabled people, social and cultural projects, including environmental, community and arts organisations. Organisations must be registered charities. Local grants range from £250 to £1,000. National grants from £8,000 to £150,000.
Generally no support for appeals from individuals, purely denominational (religious) appeals or overseas projects.
In the year ending 1990, worldwide charitable contributions totalled £2,800,000; no separate figure for the UK was available.

Digital Equipment Scotland Ltd
Manufacture of computers

Mosshill Industrial Estate,
Ayr KA6 6BE
0292-266955

MD: D Lawrence
Contact: Jim Manderson
Corporate Communications Manager

Year Ends: 30 Jun '90
Donations: £30,532
Profit: £18,460,000
Turnover: £576,021,000

UK employees: n/a
Total employees: 1,737

Donations Policy: The company only supports local charities in the areas of company presence. Preference for charities in which a member of staff is involved. Major support for disabled organisations; preference also for children and youth, social welfare, medical, education, the arts and enterprise/training. Grants to local organisations from £200 to £500.
No support for circular appeals, fundraising events, brochure advertising, purely denominational appeals, local appeals not in areas of company presence or national appeals.

● **Alphabetical listing** Please read page 6

Name/Address	Officers	Financial Information	Other Information

☐ **Diploma plc** Manufacturing & engineering, industrial

20 Bunhill Row,
London EC1Y 8LP
071-638 0934

Ch: A J C Thomas
Contact: A M R Parkinson
Company Secretary

Year Ends: 30 Sep '91
Donations: £9,000
Profit: £14,500,000
Turnover: £141,900,000

UK employees: n/a
Total employees: 1,612

☐ **Dixons Group plc** Retailers of electrical goods

29 Farm Street,
London W1X 3RD
071-499 3494

Ch: S Kalms
Contact: Corporate Affairs Department

Year Ends: 2 May '92
Donations: £507,000
Profit: £70,300,000
Turnover: £1,862,700,000

UK employees: 10,311
Total employees: 14,446

% Club, BitC, ABSA

Donations Policy: Preference for medical; education; environment/heritage; arts; enterprise/training. Requests from national charities are administered by the Dixons Charitable Trust Committee. Local requests are forwarded to head office by local branches.
No response to circular appeals. No support for appeals from individuals, overseas projects, single expeditions or secondment.

☐ **DMB & B Holdings Ltd** Advertising agency

2 St James's Square,
London SW1Y 4JN
071-839 3422

CE: Graham Hinton, Tony Douglas
Contact: A C C Cook
Financial Director

Year Ends: 31 Dec '90
Donations: £16,269
Profit: £382,000
Turnover: £247,182,000

UK employees: n/a
Total employees: 694

% Club

☐ **Dobson Park Industries plc** Mining machinery, engineering & power tools

Dobson Park House,
Manchester Road,
Ince,
Wigan WN2 2DX
0942-31421

Ch: A Kaye
CE: O J Chapple
Contact: E C Townsend
Financial Director

Year Ends: 28 Sep '91
Donations: £11,681
Profit: £13,085,000
Turnover: £233,653,000

UK employees: n/a
Total employees: 4,314

Donations Policy: Preference for local charities in the areas of company presence and charities that have relevance to the various operating companies in the UK. Preferred areas of support are social welfare and medical.
No support for circular appeals, purely denominational appeals, local appeals not in areas of company presence or overseas projects.

☐ **Domino Printing Sciences plc** Jet printing systems manufacturing

Saxon Way,
Bar Hill,
Cambridge CB3 8TU
0954-781888

Ch: G Dennis
MD: H Whitesmith
Contact: Mrs Meg Wilson
Executive Secretary

Year Ends: 29 Oct '91
Donations: £16,778
Profit: £9,000,000
Turnover: £60,400,000

UK employees: n/a
Total employees: 719

Donations Policy: Preference for local charities in areas of company presence and charities in which a member of staff is involved. Preference for social welfare, medical, education, recreation, environment and heritage and the arts. Grants to local organisations from £20 to £1,000.
Generally no support for circular appeals, advertising in charity brochures, appeals from individuals, local appeals not in areas of company presence, large national appeals or overseas projects.

☐ **R R Donnelley Ltd** Colour printing, telephone directory production

The Printing Works,
Boroughbridge Road,
York YO2 5SS
0904-798241

MD: C H Renton
Contact: Peter Kiveal
Personnel Director

Year Ends: 31 Dec '90
Donations: n/a
Profit: £6,111,000
Turnover: £111,565,000

UK employees: n/a
Total employees: 1,083

☐ **Dow Chemical Company Ltd** Chemicals & plastics, agricultural

Lakeside House,
Stockley Park,
Uxbridge,
Middlesex UB11 1BE
081-848 8688

Ch: H G Nicklin
Contact: Jane C Mackey
Public Affairs

Year Ends: 31 Dec '90
Donations: £77,658
Profit: £6,621,000
Turnover: £362,650,000

UK employees: n/a
Total employees: 699

% Club

Donations Policy: Preference for local charities in areas of company presence, particularly children/youth, education, medical and the arts. Grants to national organisations from £100 to £1,500. Grants to local organisations from £25 to £5,000.
No support for circular appeals, brochure advertising or overseas projects.
Note: Financial data may be inaccurate as reported costs are for whole group excluding USA.

☐ **Dow Corning Ltd** Silicone products manufacturing

Barry Plant,
Cardiff Road,
Barry,
South Glamorgan CF6 7YL
0446-732350

Contact: Mrs J Sanders
Secretary to the Training Manager

Year Ends: 31 Dec '91
Donations: n/a
Profit: £16,957,000
Turnover: £157,180,000

UK employees: 569
Total employees: 569

Please read page 6 | | | Alphabetical listing •

Name/Address	Officers	Financial Information	Other Information

☐ Dresser (Holdings) Ltd
Petrochemical plants & petroleum products

197 Knightsbridge,
London   SW7 1RJ
071-584 7065

Contact: J G F Tostee
Managing Director

Year Ends: 31 Oct '90
Donations: £4,800
Profit: £19,726,000
Turnover: £245,432,000

UK employees: n/a
Total employees: 3,272

Donations Policy: The company only supports charities with which company employees are connected.

☐ Louis Dreyfus & Co Ltd
Merchants & shippers

162 Queen Victoria Street,
London   EC4V 4BS
071-489 9489

Contact: R E Cornwell
Chairman

Year Ends: 31 Dec '90
Donations: £1,074
Profit: £4,937,000
Turnover: £786,651,000

UK employees: n/a
Total employees: 142

☐ Drilton Ltd
Builders & civil engineers

Hiview House,
Highgate Road,
London   NW5 1TN
071-267 4366

Ch: J Murphy
Contact: G Coffey
Administration Manager

Year Ends: 31 Dec '90
Donations: £24,842
Profit: £9,388,000
Turnover: £127,210,000

UK employees: n/a
Total employees: 2,026

☐ Druck Ltd
Manufacture electronic pressure measuring devices

Fir Tree Lane,
Groby,
Leicester   LE6 0FH
0533-314314

Ch: J Salmon
Contact: Jane Hough
Company Secretary

Year Ends: 31 Mar '92
Donations: £6,000
Profit: £2,326,000
Turnover: £18,711,000

UK employees: 419
Total employees: n/a

Donations Policy: Preference for local charities in areas of company presence. Donations will be given to larger charities which the company believes to be worthwhile. Preferred areas of support: children and youth, social welfare and medical.
Generally no advertising in charity brochures, purely denominational appeals or local charities not in areas of company presence.

☐ Du Pont (UK) Ltd
Chemical manufacturers

Wedgwood Way,
Stevenage,
Hertfordshire   SG1 4QN
0438-734000

Ch: P H McKie
Contact: D S Billett
Managing Director

Year Ends: 14 Dec '91
Donations: n/a
Profit: £27,134,000
Turnover: £548,699,000

UK employees: n/a
Total employees: 2,434

% Club

☐ Duchy of Cornwall
Agricultural estates, woodland, property

10 Buckingham Gate,
London   SW1E 6LA
071-834 7346

Ch: Prince of Wales
Contact: Company Secretary

Year Ends: 31 Dec '87
Donations: £122,294 (1991)
Profit: £1,940,691
Turnover: n/a

UK employees: n/a
Total employees: n/a

% Club, BitC

Donations Policy: Support is mainly provided for Duke of Cornwall's Benevolent Fund and for bodies with whom the Duchy is in some way involved. Preference for local charities in areas where the company operates. Grants from £200 to £1,000.
No grants for advertising in charity brochures; purely denominational (religious) appeals; local appeals not in areas of company presence; overseas projects.

☐ Dunhill Holdings plc
Luxury consumer products, tobacco

30 Duke Street,
St James's,
London   SW1Y 6DL
071-499 9566

Ch: Edmund C Skepper
MD: Sior Pendle
Contact: Stephen Jessey
Corporate Marketing Manager

Year Ends: 31 Mar '92
Donations: £57,000
Profit: £76,014,000
Turnover: £254,562,000

UK employees: n/a
Total employees: 2,016

% Club

Donations Policy: Preferred areas of support are children and youth and people with disabilities.
No support for circular appeals, advertising in charity brochures, individuals, purely denominational appeals and overseas projects.

☐ Dunkeld Group plc
Design & manufacture of clothing

24-30 Great Titchfield Street,
London   W1P 7AD
071-580 2266

Ch: Harry Rogers
Contact: Richard Lawson
Managing Director

Year Ends: 30 Nov '89
Donations: £11,592
Profit: £552,000
Turnover: £37,656,000

UK employees: n/a
Total employees: 1,295

☐ Duracell Batteries Ltd
Dry battery manufacturers

Mallory House,
Hazelwick Avenue,
Three Bridges,
Crawley   RH10 1FQ
0293-611666

Ch: P Schatz
Contact: Miss A C Naish
Human Resource Department

Year Ends: 30 Jun '90
Donations: £2,318 (1992)
Profit: £1,975,000
Turnover: £143,089,000

UK employees: n/a
Total employees: 893

Donations Policy: Preference for local charities in areas of company presence. Preferred areas of support: children and youth; education; environment and heritage. Large national appeals and advertising in charity brochures are only occasionally supported.
No support for appeals from individuals, purely denominational appeals, local appeals not in areas of company presence, overseas projects.

● **Alphabetical listing** Please read page 6

Name/Address	Officers	Financial Information	Other Information

☐ East Midlands Electricity plc
Electricity supply

PO Box 4, North PDO,
398 Coppice Road,
Nottingham NG5 7HX
0602-269711

Ch: John Harris
MD: Norman Askew
Contact: Gillian Garratt
Corporate Relations Executive

Year Ends: 31 Mar '92
Donations: £62,000
Profit: £150,000,000
Turnover: £1,583,800,000

UK employees: n/a
Total employees: 8,243

BitC, ABSA

Donations Policy: Support is given to organisations and projects within the areas in which the company operates. The focus is on partnerships with support in kind for real effect, rather than cash donations. Preference is given to the following areas in relation to company businesses: employee involvement, elderly people, the environment, energy efficiency, young people, cultural life, enterprise and education. Grants to local organisations range from £25 to £5,000. Total community contributions in 1991/92 were £572,000.
No response to circular appeals. Generally no involvement in advertising in charity publications, appeals from individuals, purely denominational (religious) appeals, large national appeals, overseas projects, animal and medical research charities, and political groups.

☐ Eastern Counties Newspapers Group Ltd
Newspaper publishing

Prospect House,
Rowen Road,
Norwich NR1 1RE
0603-628311

Ch: T J A Coleman
CE: G H C Copeman
Contact: Douglas Bird
Managing Director

Year Ends: 31 Dec '90
Donations: £24,000
Profit: £8,192,000
Turnover: £104,594,000

UK employees: n/a
Total employees: 2,022

Donations Policy: Preference for local charities in areas where the company operates.

☐ Eastern Electricity plc
Electricity supply

PO Box 40,
Wherstead,
Ipswich IP9 2AQ
0473-688688

Ch: Dr J C Smith
MD: J Devaney
Contact: W N Moss
Company Secretary

Year Ends: 31 Mar '92
Donations: £58,025
Profit: £143,100,000
Turnover: £1,878,100,000

UK employees: n/a
Total employees: 9,754

BitC, ABSA

Donations Policy: Supports charities in the company's region or national charities which will direct the money to the region. Preference for children and youth; social welfare; medical; enterprise/training. Grants to national organisations from £50 to £33,000. Grants to local organisations from £30 to £4,000.
No grants for local appeals not in areas of company presence.

☐ Eaton Ltd
Engineers

Eaton House,
Staines Road,
Hounslow TW4 5DX
081-572 7313

Ch: D Dawson
MD: G Vieten
Contact: Alan Kekwick
Corporate Affairs Director

Year Ends: 31 Dec '90
Donations: £19,894
Profit: £3,002,000
Turnover: £112,774,000

UK employees: n/a
Total employees: 2,072

Donations Policy: Mainly national charities dealing with education and medical research and social groups.

☐ EBC Group plc
Construction industry

Cranmere Court,
Lustleigh Close,
Exeter EX2 8RD
0392-52272

Ch: H Cockcroft
Contact: Julian Turnbull
Group Secretary

Year Ends: 31 Dec '91
Donations: £11,045
Profit: £2,037,000
Turnover: £60,000,000

UK employees: 516
Total employees: 516

Donations Policy: Preference for local charities (including local branches of national charities) in areas where the company operates, namely Devon, Cornwall, Somerset, Avon and Dorset, and charities in which a member of company staff is involved. Preference for children and youth; social welfare; medical; environment/heritage; enterprise/training. Grants range from £50 to £500.
No grants for fundraising events; advertising in charity brochures; purely denominational (religious) appeals; local appeals not in areas of company presence; overseas projects; political organisations.

☐ ECC International Ltd
Production & sale of industrial minerals

John Keay House,
St Austell,
Cornwall PL25 4DJ
0726-74482

Ch: Lord Chilver
MD: G R W Lovering, A L Shearer
Contact: A G Hawken
Divisional Company Secretary

Year Ends: 31 Dec '91
Donations: £28,500
Profit: £115,400,000
Turnover: £1,011,900,000

UK employees: n/a
Total employees: 11,843

Donations Policy: The majority of grants are given locally, specifically to conservation and environmental groups in Cornwall and Devon. Preference is given where a member of staff is involved. Local grants range from £25 to £2,000.
Generally no support for circular appeals, fundraising events, brochure advertising, appeals from individuals, local appeals not in areas of company presence, large national appeals or overseas projects.
Sponsorship proposals to C P Dart, Advertising Manager (commercial sponsorship); A G Hawken (remaining sponsorship appeals).

☐ Economist Newspaper Ltd
Newspaper publishers

25 St James's Street,
London SW1A 1HA
071-839 7000

Ch: Sir John Harvey-Jones
CE: D S Gordon
Contact: Jean Simkins, Chairwoman
Group Charities Committee

Year Ends: 31 Mar '92
Donations: £48,000
Profit: £11,376,000
Turnover: £103,990,000

UK employees: n/a
Total employees: 740

% Club

Donations Policy: Prefers to give direct support to small bodies or specific projects, where relatively small sums will have a real effect. Typical grants range from £50 to £250. Donations are given to four main areas: (a) local/staff/business connections; (b) welfare and (usually medical) research; (c) education (including personal development, voluntary service and some public education); (d) arts, carefully directed to grass-roots and special projects.
No large or sectarian or single service (among forces) charities. Gala events with heavy costs and popular appeals with royal or show-business backing are avoided. No support for non-charities, circulars, advertising in charity brochures, individuals, purely denominational (religious) appeals, large national appeals, church restoration appeals, politically sensitive causes or ordinary educational establishments.

Please read page 6 — Alphabetical listing

Name/Address	Officers	Financial Information	Other Information

☐ Edmundson Electrical Ltd
Wholesale distributors of electrical products

Tatton Street,
Knutsford,
Cheshire WA16 6AY
0565-633811

Contact: D T McNair
Managing Director

Year Ends: 31 Dec '88
Donations: £98,000
Profit: £17,570,000
Turnover: £342,650,000

UK employees: n/a
Total employees: 2,586

Donations Policy: The company supports the relevant trade charity. Unsolicited appeals are not supported.

☐ Edrington Holdings Ltd
Whisky & food products

106 West Nile Street,
Glasgow G1 2QX
041-332 6525

Ch: J A R Macphail
Contact: Company Secretary

Year Ends: 31 Dec '90
Donations: £22,750
Profit: £29,979,000
Turnover: £94,329,000

UK employees: n/a
Total employees: 914

Donations Policy: We have been unable to obtain a donations policy for this company.

☐ EDS-Scicon UK Ltd
Computer consultancy

4 Roundwood Avenue,
Stockley Park,
Uxbridge,
Middlesex UB11 1BQ
081-848 8989

CE: P E Swinstead
Contact: Sue O'Kane
Marketing & Community Action Group

Year Ends: 31 Dec '89
Donations: £35,000
Profit: £7,232,000
Turnover: £283,304,000

UK employees: n/a
Total employees: 5,368

Donations Policy: The company supports local schools, hospitals, hospices' and appeals and events that could benefit employees or their families. Preference for charities in which a member of company staff is involved. Donations of old computers and office machinery are also made.
The company does not advertise in charity brochures.

☐ EIS Group plc
Engineering

6 Sloane Square,
London SW1W 8EE
071-730 9187

Ch: M Q Walters
Contact: P J K Haslehurst
Chief Executive

Year Ends: 31 Dec '91
Donations: £1,577
Profit: £14,423,000
Turnover: £189,940,000

UK employees: n/a
Total employees: 4,005

☐ Eldridge, Pope & Co plc
Brewers

The Dorchester Brewery,
Dorchester DT1 1QT
0305-251251

Ch: C Pope
MD: J Pope
Contact: Peter Hyde
Advertising Manager

Year Ends: 30 Sep '91
Donations: £3,736
Profit: £1,101,000
Turnover: £42,168,000

UK employees: n/a
Total employees: 1,365

Donations Policy: Preference for local charities in the areas of company presence and appeals relevant to the business. Preferred areas of support: children and youth, education, environment and heritage, the arts and enterprise/training.
Generally no support for circular appeals, advertising in charity brochures, purely denominational appeals, local appeals not in areas of company presence, overseas projects and political appeals.

☐ Eleco Holdings plc
Property development & investment

Belcon House,
Essex Road,
Hoddesdon,
Hertfordshire EN11 0DR
0992-467141

Ch: F L J Walton
MD: M J Webster
Contact: Mrs S A Rolfe
Secretary to the Chief Executive

Year Ends: 30 Jun '92
Donations: £4,568
Profit: £3,351,000
Turnover: £56,810,000

UK employees: n/a
Total employees: 650

Donations Policy: Preference for local charities in areas where the company operates and children's charities. Support also for social welfare and medical charities. Grants range from £50 to £100.
No grants for advertising in charity brochures; purely denominational (religious) appeals; local appeals not in areas of company presence.

☐ Electrocomponents plc
Electronic component manufacturers & distribution

21 Knightsbridge,
London SW1X 7LY
071-245 1277

Ch: Sir Keith Bright
CE: Robert Lawson
Contact: Robert Tomkinson
Group Finance Director

Year Ends: 31 Mar '92
Donations: £45,941
Profit: £49,900,000
Turnover: £395,100,000

UK employees: n/a
Total employees: 2,997

Donations Policy: Preference for local charities in areas where the company operates and appeals relevant to company business. Grants to national organisations from £100 to £6,000. Grants to local organisations from £100 to £500.
No grants for appeals from individuals; purely denominational (religious) appeals; local appeals not in areas of company presence.

☐ Electrolux Holdings Ltd
Domestic appliances

Oakley Road,
Luton,
Bedfordshire LU4 9QQ
0582-491234

Ch: G P H James
CE: Dr R S Baxter
Contact: G P H James
Chairman

Year Ends: 31 Dec '89
Donations: n/a
Profit: £10,586,000
Turnover: £373,976,000

UK employees: n/a
Total employees: 5,816

Alphabetical listing

Please read page 6

Name/Address	Officers	Financial Information	Other Information

☐ Electron House plc
Computer equipment, electronic components

17 Birkheads Road,
Reigate,
Surrey RH2 0AU
0737-242464

Ch: R S Leigh
MD: B B J Charles
Contact: R S Leigh,
Chairman

Year Ends: 31 May '91
Donations: £1,000
Profit: £968,000
Turnover: £126,861,000

UK employees: n/a
Total employees: 546

Donations Policy: The chairman nominates two charities that the company supports.

☐ Elf Atochem UK Holdings Ltd
Plastics & chemicals

Colthrop Way,
Thatcham,
Newbury,
Berkshire RG13 4NR
0635-870000

MD: J M C Puckridge
Contact: P Hutchinson
Company Secretary

Year Ends: 31 Dec '90
Donations: n/a
Profit: £563,000
Turnover: £275,897,000

UK employees: n/a
Total employees: 422

☐ Elf Petroleum UK plc
Gas & condensate producer, oil & gas exploration

Knightsbridge House,
197 Knightsbridge,
London SW7 1RZ
071-589 4588

Ch: F Isoard
MD: J Bouchard
Contact: Keith Jameson
Company Secretary

Year Ends: 31 Dec '91
Donations: £42,945
Profit: £292,300,000
Turnover: £1,629,300,000

UK employees: n/a
Total employees: n/a

ABSA

Donations Policy: No particular area of support. Donations usually given through the Charities Aid Foundation, occasionally directly.

☐ B Elliott plc
Electrical, specialist & mechanical engineering

Elliott House,
Victoria Road,
North Acton,
London NW10 6NY
081-961 7333

Ch: S B Gibbs
CE: M J E Frye
Contact: R S Johnson
Company Secretary

Year Ends: 31 Mar '91
Donations: £6,600
Profit: £6,517,000
Turnover: £136,126,000

UK employees: n/a
Total employees: 2,449

BitC

Donations Policy: Preference for local charities in areas where the company operates. Preference for children and youth; social welfare; education; overseas aid/development; enterprise/training. Grants to local and national organisations range from £250 to £500. No response to circular appeals. No grants for advertising in charity brochures; appeals from individuals; purely denominational (religious) appeals.

☐ Ellis & Everard plc
Distributors of industrial chemicals

46 Peckover Street,
Bradford BD1 5BD
0274-308052

Ch: S Everard
MD: P S Wood
Contact: Robert Welburn
Company Secretary

Year Ends: 30 Apr '92
Donations: £30,000
Profit: £12,600,000
Turnover: £383,400,000

UK employees: n/a
Total employees: 2,156

BitC

Donations Policy: Charitable donations are handled by the Charities Aid Foundation. Preference for children and youth; medical. No response to circular appeals. No grants for appeals from individuals or local appeals not in areas of company presence.

☐ EMAP plc
Printing & publishing

1 Lincoln Court,
Lincoln Road,
Peterborough,
Cambridgeshire PE1 2RF
0733-68900

Ch: G R Russell
CE: R W Miller
Contact: Penny Hooson
Administration Manager

Year Ends: 28 Mar '92
Donations: £38,000
Profit: £27,114,000
Turnover: £269,445,000

UK employees: n/a
Total employees: 4,124

Donations Policy: Major donations are selected by staff ballot. In addition many charitable appeals are supported by the Group's newspapers, magazines and radio stations.

☐ Emerson Electric UK Ltd
Electrical tools & equipment manufacture

39 Portman Square,
London W1H 9FH
071-486 2755

Contact: O Delage
Managing Director

Year Ends: 30 Sep '90
Donations: n/a
Profit: £9,126,000
Turnover: £122,903,000

UK employees: n/a
Total employees: 1,830

☐ Emess plc
Lighting & electrical products

20 St James's Street,
London SW1A 1HA
071-321 0127

Ch: M Meyer
Contact: V Cobb
Company Secretary

Year Ends: 31 Dec '91
Donations: £20,333
Profit: £4,200,000
Turnover: £160,200,000

UK employees: n/a
Total employees: 3,121

Donations Policy: Preference for local charities in areas of company presence. Preferred areas of support are social welfare, medical, enterprise/training, the arts.
No support for circular appeals, fundraising events, purely denominational (religious) appeals, appeals from individuals or local appeals not in areas of company presence.

Please read page 6   Alphabetical listing •

Name/Address	Officers	Financial Information	Other Information

☐ **Emhart International Ltd**   Holding company

Lyn House,   *Ch:* P Gustafson   *Year Ends:* 31 Dec '88   *UK employees:* n/a
39 The Parade,   *Contact:* J W Randall   *Donations:* £17,618   *Total employees:* 44
Oadby,   Managing Director   *Profit:* £7,912,000
Leicester LE2 5BB   *Turnover:* n/a
0533-717241

Donations Policy: From a small budget support is given to as wide a range of charities as possible, with preference for children and youth, social welfare, medical, education and overseas aid/development. Grants from £100 to £500. In 1991, donations were about £4,000.
No support for fundraising events, advertising in charity brochures, appeals from individuals, purely denominational (religious) appeals.

☐ **Empire Stores Group plc**   Mail order retailing

18 Canal Road,   *Ch:* R M Mays-Smith   *Year Ends:* 27 Apr '91   *UK employees:* n/a
Bradford BD99 4XB   *Contact:* Mrs Kathleen Clark   *Donations:* £14,728   *Total employees:* 2,376
0274-729544   Secretary to the Managing   *Profit:* £4,872,000
                                   Director   *Turnover:* £231,065,000

Donations Policy: Support for charities local to the head office (Bradford) and the major warehouse (Wakefield). The company tries to spread support over a variety of causes bearing in mind the need and the ability of the charity to solicit other funds. Education and the arts are a low priority. Direct support preferred.
Large national appeals, overseas projects, denominational appeals, appeals from individuals are not supported.

☐ **Energy & Technical Services Group plc**   Heating & air conditioning equipment

8 Headfort Place,   *Ch:* Lord Ezra   *Year Ends:* 30 Mar '91   *UK employees:* n/a
London SW1X 7BH   *CE:* D G S Waterstone   *Donations:* £2,860   *Total employees:* 1,607
071-823 2288   *Contact:* Peter Holloway   *Profit:* £17,024,000
                                 Marketing Manager   *Turnover:* £93,100,000

Donations Policy: Restricts charitable contributions to cases which are "clearly relevant".

☐ **Engelhard Ltd**   Traders in precious metals

Chancery House,   *Ch:* J Biondo   *Year Ends:* 31 Dec '90   *UK employees:* n/a
St Nicholas Way,   *Contact:* J D Ollard   *Donations:* £1,830   *Total employees:* 679
Sutton,   European Sales & Marketing   *Profit:* £7,174,000
Surrey SM1 1SB   Director   *Turnover:* £5,628,135,000
081-397 5292

☐ **Enichem UK Ltd**   Manufacture of synthetic rubber

Charleston Road,   *Ch:* E Albonico   *Year Ends:* 31 Dec '90   *UK employees:* 102
Hardley,   *MD:* E T Phelan   *Donations:* £1,817   *Total employees:* n/a
Hythe,   *Contact:* C Rinieri   *Profit:* £219,000
Southampton SO4 6YY   Human Resources Manager   *Turnover:* £155,140,000
0703-894919

☐ **Enterprise Oil plc**   Oil & gas exploration

Grand Buildings,   *Ch:* G J Hearne   *Year Ends:* 31 Dec '91   *UK employees:* n/a
Trafalgar Square,   *Contact:* Mrs Jane Stevenson   *Donations:* £198,444   *Total employees:* n/a
London WC2N 5EJ   Secretary, Donations Committee   *Profit:* £114,400,000
071-925 4000   *Turnover:* £487,600,000

Donations Policy: Donations given from head office only. Preference for projects in areas where the company operates and appeals where a member of staff is involved. Large national appeals are supported, particularly social welfare, medical, children and youth, education and organisations concerned with physically and mentally disabled people.
No support for advertising in charity brochures or appeals from individuals.

☐ **Epson (UK) Ltd**   Data processing equipment

Campus 100,   *Contact:* D Pinchbeck   *Year Ends:* 31 Mar '91   *UK employees:* n/a
Maylands Avenue,   Managing Director   *Donations:* £675   *Total employees:* 197
Hemel Hempstead,   *Profit:* £11,983,000
Herts HP2 7EZ   *Turnover:* £95,171,000
0442-61144

☐ **Equity & Law plc**   Insurance investments

Equity & Law Charitable Trust,   *Ch:* Sir Douglas Wass   *Year Ends:* 31 Dec '91   *UK employees:* 2,247
Amersham Road,   *CE:* C J Brockson   *Donations:* £23,554   *Total employees:* n/a
High Wycombe HP13 5AL   *Contact:* W M Brown   *Profit:* £23,300,000
0494-463463   Company Secretary   *Turnover:* n/a   BitC

Donations Policy: About 50% of the trust's income is used to match contributions made by employees under the Give As You Earn scheme. 40% is for annual donations to existing beneficiaries (with a few changes from year to year) including medical research, relief of suffering, welfare including rehabilitation, youth, elderly people, education and the arts. The remainder is used for single donations for special appeals which might be of a capital nature or for a special need, (such as coping with a disaster) not as a substitute for regular or routine contributions.
No support for individuals or individual projects, nor for charities operating on a regional, local or international basis.

● **Alphabetical listing**   Please read page 6

Name/Address	Officers	Financial Information	Other Information

Era Group plc
                                                                                                                    Specialist retailing & wholesaling

Enterprise House,   *Ch:* A W Fay   *Year Ends:* 31 Dec '91   UK employees: n/a
Maxted Road,   *Contact:* Nick Evans   *Donations:* nil   Total employees: 722
Hemel Hempstead,   Financial Director   *Profit:* £2,167,000
Hertfordshire HP2 7BT   *Turnover:* £71,126,000
0442-61721

ERF (Holdings) plc
                                                                                                        Commercial vehicles & plastic manufacture

Sun Works,   *Ch:* E P Foden   *Year Ends:* 30 Mar '91   UK employees: n/a
Sandbach,   *Contact:* Mrs Margaret Pickford   *Donations:* £10,000   Total employees: 1,153
Cheshire CW11 9DN   Secretary to the Chairman *Profit:* £4,471,000
0270-763223   *Turnover:* £102,548,000

Donations Policy: Preference for local charities in the areas of company presence.

Ericsson Ltd
                                                                                                                    Telecommunications equipment

Public Systems,   *Contact:* Mrs C Powell   *Year Ends:* 31 Dec '90   UK employees: n/a
Telecommunications Centre,   *Donations:* £28,039   Total employees: 2,354
Charles Avenue,   *Profit:* £20,736,000
Burgess Hill,   *Turnover:* £315,808,000
West Sussex RH15 9UB
0444-234567

Donations Policy: Preference for appeals relevant to company business and charities in which a member of company staff is involved. Preferred area of support is education.
No response to circular appeals. No grants for advertising in charity brochures; appeals from individuals; purely denominational (religious) appeals; large national appeals; overseas projects.

Erith plc
                                                                                                                            Builders merchants

32 Bridge Street,   *Ch:* G P Davies   *Year Ends:* 31 Dec '91   UK employees: n/a
Hitchin,   *CE:* A B Castledine   *Donations:* £2,800   Total employees: 671
Hertfordshire SG5 2DF   *Contact:* Mrs McMahon   *Profit:* £24,000
0462-437535   Secretary to the Directors *Turnover:* £67,464,000

Donations Policy: All donations are made through the Charities Aid Foundation. Preference for local charities in areas of company presence. No support for brochure advertising, appeals from individuals, purely denominational appeals, local appeals not in areas of company presence or overseas projects.

Ernst & Young
                                                                                                                                     Accountants

Beckett House,   *Contact:* Ms Catherine McCormack *Year Ends:*   UK employees: n/a
Lambeth Palace Road,   Secretary   *Donations:* n/a   Total employees: n/a
London SE1 7EU   *Profit:* n/a
071-928 2000   *Turnover:* n/a   % Club, BitC, ABSA

Donations Policy: Many charitable organisations are supported through the regional offices.

Erskine House Group plc
                                                                                                        Distribution & service of office equipment

Erskine House,   *Ch:* B McGillivray   *Year Ends:* 30 Mar '92   UK employees: n/a
Oak Hill Road,   *Contact:* S Westcott   *Donations:* £1,595   Total employees: 2,893
Sevenoaks,   Marketing Director   *Profit:* £12,729,000
Kent TN13 1NW   *Turnover:* £178,917,000
0732-460044

Esselte Letraset Ltd
                                                                                                                Office & retail stores supplies

Esselte House,   *Contact:* Sue Stevens   *Year Ends:* 31 Dec '88   UK employees: 1,576
4 Buckingham Gate,   Executive Secretary   *Donations:* £27,692   Total employees: 20,066
London SW1E 6JR   *Profit:* £3,628,000
071-973 5200   *Turnover:* £77,569,000

Donations Policy: The company is currently having to cut back on its charitable donations, and is only able to support a small number of charities to which regular donations have been made in the past.

Esso UK plc
                                                                                                                                    Oil industry

Esso House,   *Ch:* Sir Archibald Forster   *Year Ends:* 31 Dec '91   UK employees: n/a
Victoria Street,   *MD:* D Clayman, K H Taylor   *Donations:* £1,583,748   Total employees: 4,000
London SW1E 5JW   *Contact:* P J Troesdale   *Profit:* £313,000,000
071-834 6677   Community Affairs Co-ordinator *Turnover:* £6,223,000,000   BitC, ABSA

Donations Policy: Priority to projects involved with education (particularly environmental and scientific), the environment, and health and safety. Almost all funds are committed at the beginning of the year, therefore unsolicited requests are rarely supported.
No grants for fundraising events; advertising in charity brochures; appeals from individuals; purely denominational (religious) appeals; local appeals not in areas of company presence; large national appeals; overseas projects.
Total community contributions in 1991 were £3.2 million.

Please read page 6 | Alphabetical listing •

Name/Address	Officers	Financial Information	Other Information

☐ **Etam plc** — Ladies fashionwear retailers

213 Oxford Street,
London W1R 2AH
071-437 4806

Ch: Sir John Nott
MD: R C J East
Contact: Helen Lewis
Public Relations Controller

Year Ends: 1 Feb '92
Donations: £15,700
Profit: £11,820,000
Turnover: £212,596,000

UK employees: n/a
Total employees: 3,853

B

Donations Policy: Preference for major national charities concerned with health. Donations are made through the Charities Aid Foundation. All giving is done at national level; local branches do not make donations and no support is given to individuals.

☐ **Eternit UK Ltd** — Manufacture & sale of building materials

Whaddon Road,
Meldreth,
Nr Royston,
Hertfordshire SG8 5RL
0763-260421

Ch: J Beeckman
Contact: W A Burgess
Managing Director

Year Ends: 31 Dec '90
Donations: £275 (1991)
Profit: £943,000
Turnover: £104,053,000

UK employees: n/a
Total employees: 996

Donations Policy: Preference for local charities in areas where the company operates, appeals relevant to company business and charities in which a member of company staff is involved. Preference for social welfare; medical; education.
Grants to local organisations from £25 to £100.
No grants for purely denominational (religious) appeals; local appeals not in areas of company presence; large national appeals; overseas projects. No response to circular appeals.

☐ **European Grain & Shipping Ltd** — Grain, animal feeds, edible nuts & seeds merchants

Borough House,
88 Borough High Street,
London SE1 1LP
071-403 0766

MD: J D Marsdale
Contact: Personnel Officer

Year Ends: 31 Dec '90
Donations: n/a
Profit: £497,000
Turnover: £148,515,000

UK employees: n/a
Total employees: 69

☐ **Eurotherm plc** — Electronic equipment design & manufacture

Leonardslee,
Brighton Road,
Lower Beeding,
Horsham,
West Sussex RH13 6PP
0403-891665

Ch: Dr J L Leonard
MD: C A Hultman
Contact: Debbie Hinks
Secretary to the Chairman

Year Ends: 31 Oct '91
Donations: £13,403
Profit: £7,149,000
Turnover: £157,725,000

UK employees: n/a
Total employees: 2,714

% Club

Donations Policy: Preference for local charities in areas where the company operates and charities in which a member of company staff is involved. Preference for children and youth; education; enterprise/training.

☐ **Eurotunnel plc** — Tunnel construction

Victoria Plaza,
111 Buckingham Palace Road,
London SW1W 0ST
071-834 7575

Contact: Tony Gueterbock
Public Affairs Manager

Year Ends:
Donations: n/a
Profit: n/a
Turnover: n/a

UK employees: n/a
Total employees: n/a

% Club, BitC, ABSA

Donations Policy: Preference for local charities in areas where the company operates and for appeals relevant to company business.
No response to circular appeals. No grants for fundraising events; advertising in charity brochures; appeals from individuals; purely denominational (religious) appeals; local appeals not in areas of company presence; large national appeals; overseas projects.

☐ **Evans Halshaw Holdings plc** — Motor vehicle dealers

4 Highland Court,
Cranmore Avenue,
Shirley,
Solihull,
West Midlands B90 4LE
021-711 4888

Ch: A G Dale
Contact: Jenny Ashmore
Secretary to the Chairman

Year Ends: 31 Dec '91
Donations: £6,723
Profit: £3,860,000
Turnover: £339,688,000

UK employees: n/a
Total employees: 2,164

Donations Policy: Support is divided between three causes: BEN (the motor trades benevolent fund), a children's hospital and a hospice. No unsolicited appeals.

☐ **Eve Group plc** — Civil engineering & property development

Minster House,
Plough Lane,
London SW17 0AZ
081-946 3085

Ch: R G Ames
MD: G M Hough
Contact: J Woolhead
Company Secretary

Year Ends: 31 Mar '92
Donations: £4,272
Profit: £3,263,000
Turnover: £39,078,000

UK employees: n/a
Total employees: 528

Donations Policy: Preference for appeals relevant to company business and charities in which a member of staff is involved. Preferred areas of support: youth, medical, education, environment and heritage and enterprise/training.
Generally no support for circular appeals, brochure advertising, appeals from individuals, local appeals not in areas of company presence or overseas projects.

● **Alphabetical listing** Please read page 6

Name/Address *Officers* *Financial Information* *Other Information*

☐ Everards Brewery Ltd
Brewers

Castle Acres,
Narborough,
Leicester LE9 5BY
0533-630900

Ch: R Everard
MD: N Lloyd
Contact: R A S Everard
The Everard Foundation

Year Ends: 30 Sep '89
Donations: £874 (1991)
Profit: £3,472,000
Turnover: £23,526,000

UK employees: n/a
Total employees: 1,190

Donations Policy: In 1991, donations totalling £19,094 were also made from the Everard Foundation (a family charity). Support is given to a range of local charities in areas where the company operates.
No grants for advertising in charity brochures; appeals from individuals; purely denominational (religious) appeals; local appeals not in areas of company presence; large national appeals; overseas projects.

☐ Evered Bardon plc
Industrial products, metal forming

Radcliffe House,
Blenheim Court,
Lode Lane,
Solihull,
West Midlands B91 2AA
021-711 1717

Ch: Sir Peter Parker
CE: P W G Tom
Contact: Mrs K J Willis
Company Secretarial Assistant

Year Ends: 31 Dec '91
Donations: £52,857
Profit: £26,900,000
Turnover: £334,000,000

UK employees: n/a
Total employees: 4,114

BitC

Donations Policy: "The company is currently fulfilling its commitments on charity covenants already in place and has reluctantly decided that no further donations will be possible in the near future." Preference for social welfare; medical; education; environment/heritage; enterprise/training. Grants to national organisations from £500 to £4,000. Grants to local organisations from £10 to £250.
No grants for local appeals not in areas of company presence; overseas projects.

☐ Evode Group plc
Manufacture of adhesives, jointing compounds

Common Road,
Stafford ST16 3EH
0785-57755

Ch: A H Simon
CE: D S Winterbottom
Contact: Mrs June Ryan
Marketing Services Executive

Year Ends: 28 Sep '91
Donations: £34,000
Profit: £7,300,000
Turnover: £279,000,000

UK employees: n/a
Total employees: 3,675

Donations Policy: Preference for local charities in areas of company presence. Preferred areas of support: children and youth, and medical.
No grants for purely denominational (religious) appeals; local appeals not in areas of company presence; overseas projects.

☐ Expamet International plc
Expanded metal products

Clifton House,
83-89 Uxbridge Road,
Ealing,
London W5 5TA
081-840 5070

Ch: J G Beasley
MD: A W Orr
Contact: Mrs Ann Parkin
Pensions Trustee

Year Ends: 31 Dec '91
Donations: £3,500
Profit: £7,258,000
Turnover: £141,013,000

UK employees: n/a
Total employees: 2,467

Donations Policy: Only one charity is currently supported; the Stars Organisation for Spastics. The company is involved in a project to raise £90,000 over 15 months to build a bungalow for four disabled people in Manchester. Beyond this there is a preference for children and youth.
No support for large national appeals, denominational appeals, overseas projects.

☐ Express Newspapers plc
Newspapers & periodicals

Ludgate House,
245 Blackfriars Road,
London SE1 9UX
071-928 8000

Ch: Lord Stevens
MD: Andrew Cameron
Contact: David Tough
Chief Accountant

Year Ends: 28 Dec '91
Donations: £989,990
Profit: £25,009,000
Turnover: £280,963,000

UK employees: n/a
Total employees: 1,545

Donations Policy: Support is given mainly to national charities, although local charities are considered. Preferred areas of support: children and youth, social welfare, medical, education, environment and heritage, the arts and enterprise/training. Grants to national organisations from £50 to £250. Grants to local organisations from £25 to £100. The company also runs the Helicopter Emergency Medical Service.
No support for advertising in charity brochures, appeals from individuals or overseas projects.

☐ Extel Financial Ltd
News services, printing, advertising

23-27 Tudor Street,
London EC4Y 0HR
071-353 1080

Contact: Martin Brook
Managing Director

Year Ends: 31 Dec '88
Donations: £2,520
Profit: £10,014,000
Turnover: £85,361,000

UK employees: n/a
Total employees: 1,871

☐ Exxon Chemical Ltd
Production & sale of chemicals

4600 Parkway,
Fareham,
Hants PO15 7AP
0489-884400

Ch: J G Holloway
Contact: Mrs A Pretty (address below)

Year Ends: 31 Dec '91
Donations: £28,325
Profit: £11,860,000
Turnover: £424,890,000

UK employees: n/a
Total employees: 1,764

Donations Policy: Preference for local charities in areas of company presence (with preference for charities in which a member of staff is involved, especially children and youth, social welfare, medical, education, environment and heritage and the arts) and to other voluntary bodies whose work directly benefits disabled or disadvantaged people of all ages. Only direct support for charitable work. Grants to local organisations from £100 to £2,000.
No national appeals, circular appeals, advertising in charity brochures, appeals from individuals, purely denominational (religious) appeals, overseas projects, political appeals or sports clubs.
The contact is Mrs A Pretty, Exxon Chemical Ltd, Cadland Road, Hythe, Southampton SO4 6NP (0703-893822).

Please read page 6   **Alphabetical listing** •

Name/Address	Officers	Financial Information	Other Information

☐ Faber Prest plc
Transport, slag reduction & car retailing

3 Riverside House,
Mill Lane,
Newbury,
Berkshire RG14 5RE
0635-582211

Ch: R J Prest
CE: R S D Feaviour
Contact: K Anthony
Group Personnel Manager

Year Ends: 30 Sep '91
Donations: £26,329
Profit: £3,135,000
Turnover: £76,728,000

UK employees: n/a
Total employees: 1,187

Donations Policy: The company usually gives to local charities based in the Sheffield area, where its main operations are situated, or to local branches of national charities in the same area.

☐ Faccenda Holdings Ltd
Poultry processors

Willow Road,
Brackley,
Northants NN13 5HB
0280-703641

Ch: R M Faccenda
MD: Mrs S Faccenda
Contact: Mrs Clampin
Personal Assistant to the Chairman

Year Ends: 30 Apr '90
Donations: n/a
Profit: £699,000
Turnover: £96,330,000

UK employees: n/a
Total employees: 920

☐ Fairey Group plc
Electronics, aerospace & defence equipment

Station Road,
Egham,
Surrey TW20 9NP
0784-470470

Ch: D J Kingsbury
CE: J W Poulter
Contact: Mrs Wendy Jacobs
Personal Assistant to the Chief Executive

Year Ends: 31 Dec '91
Donations: £9,000
Profit: £14,501,000
Turnover: £88,805,000

UK employees: n/a
Total employees: 1,884

☐ Farnell Investments Ltd
Electronic components & equipment manufacture

Sandbeck Way,
Wetherby,
West Yorkshire LS22 4DN
0937-581961

Ch: R Kidd
MD: J B Smith
Contact: S Collyer
Administration Manager

Year Ends: 2 Feb '92
Donations: £10,000
Profit: £32,713,000
Turnover: £204,933,000

UK employees: n/a
Total employees: 3,044

☐ Favor Parker Ltd
Animal feed manufacturers

The Halls,
Stoke Ferry,
King's Lynn,
Norfolk PE33 9SE
0366-500911

Ch: M J B Parker
Contact: Stephen Curd
Assistant Company Secretary

Year Ends: 2 Feb '91
Donations: £4,778
Profit: £949,000
Turnover: £109,675,000

UK employees: n/a
Total employees: 2,043

Donations Policy: Preference for local charities in the areas of company presence. Grants of up to £200.

☐ FCB Advertising Ltd
Advertising agency

110 St Martin's Lane,
London WC2N 4DY
071-240 7100

Ch: T Dalton
Contact: P Perry
Company Secretary

Year Ends: 31 Dec '87
Donations: £10,620
Profit: £699,000
Turnover: £56,850,000

UK employees: n/a
Total employees: 349

Donations Policy: Support for charities concerned with children and appeals relevant to company business.

☐ Fenner plc
Power transmission engineers

Welton Hall,
Welton,
Brough,
Humberside HU15 1PQ
0482-668098

Ch: P W Barker
MD: T H P Brown
Contact: R L Galloway
Company Secretary

Year Ends: 31 Aug '91
Donations: £11,000
Profit: £7,437,000
Turnover: £203,732,000

UK employees: n/a
Total employees: 4,477

☐ Fenwick Ltd
Departmental stores

39 Northumberland Street,
Newcastle-upon-Tyne
NE99 1AR
091-232 5100

Ch: J J Fenwick
Contact: Mrs J Moles
Secretary to the Company Secretary

Year Ends: 25 Jan '92
Donations: £59,554
Profit: £19,847,000
Turnover: £155,833,000

UK employees: n/a
Total employees: 1,952

Donations Policy: Support for projects in regions where the company operates or in which employees are involved. No support for circular appeals or small purely local appeals not in areas of company presence.

☐ Ferguson International Holdings plc
Printing, packing & plastics

Appleby Castle,
Appleby,
Cumbria CA16 6XH
07683-51402

Ch: D P Cassidy
Contact: M B Saint
Group Managing Director

Year Ends: 29 Feb '92
Donations: £10,667
Profit: £6,630,000
Turnover: £121,295,000

UK employees: n/a
Total employees: 2,137

% Club, ABSA

Donations Policy: Most giving is at a local level, aimed at causes relevant to the local community or employees.

● **Alphabetical listing** Please read page 6

Name/Address　　　*Officers*　　　*Financial Information*　　　*Other Information*

☐ **Ferguson Ltd**　　　　　　　　　　　　　　Colour televisions, video & satellite products

Cambridge House,　　*Contact:* A C Dickens　　*Year Ends:* 31 Dec '90　　*UK employees:* n/a
270 Great Cambridge Road,　　Company Secretary　　*Donations:* n/a　　*Total employees:* 2,152
Enfield,　　　　　　　　　　　　*Profit:* £43,130,000
Middlesex EN1 1ND　　　　　　*Turnover:* £217,688,000
081-344 4444

☐ **Ferranti International plc**　　　　　　　　　Electrical & electronic engineers

Bridge House,　　*Ch:* C E Anderson　　*Year Ends:* 31 Mar '92　　*UK employees:* 4,708
Park Road,　　*Contact:* A R Cooper　　*Donations:* £9,000　　*Total employees:* 7,311
Gatley,　　　　Company Secretary　　*Profit:* (£39,600,000)
Cheadle,　　　　　　　　　　　　*Turnover:* £362,200,000　　% Club
Cheshire SK8 4HZ
061-428 3644

Donations Policy: Most giving is at a local level, aimed at causes relevant to the local community or employees.

☐ **Ferruzzi Trading (UK) Ltd**　　　　　　　　　Food commodities dealer

103 Mount Street,　　*Ch:* Sir Richard Butler　　*Year Ends:* 31 Dec '90　　*UK employees:* n/a
London W1Y 5HE　　*MD:* M R Engelbach　　*Donations:* n/a　　*Total employees:* n/a
071-493 1005　　*Contact:* Carol Watling　　*Profit:* £1,908,000
　　　　　　　　Office Manager　　*Turnover:* £178,633,000

☐ **Fiat Auto (UK) Ltd**　　　　　　　　　　　　Fiat & Lancia car distributors

Fiat House,　　*MD:* M Massara　　*Year Ends:* 31 Dec '90　　*UK employees:* n/a
266 Bath Road,　　*Contact:* Peter Newton　　*Donations:* £26,593　　*Total employees:* 457
Slough,　　　　Public Relations Director　　*Profit:* £5,882,000
Berkshire SL1 4HJ　　　　　　*Turnover:* £309,858,000　　ABSA
0753-511431

Donations Policy: Preference for organisations working with children and youth.
Generally no support for circular appeals, appeals from individuals, purely denominational appeals, local appeals not in areas of company presence or overseas projects.

☐ **Fife Indmar plc**　　　　　　　　　　　　　　Light & general engineering

115 Hanover Street,　　*Ch:* G A H Hepburn　　*Year Ends:* 31 Dec '91　　*UK employees:* n/a
Edinburgh EH2 1DG　　*MD:* A J Ritchie　　*Donations:* £6,953　　*Total employees:* 679
031-220 3388　　*Contact:* G Hepburn　　*Profit:* £906,000
　　　　　　　　Chairman　　*Turnover:* £31,805,000

Donations Policy: Preference for local charities in areas of company presence and charities in which a member of staff is involved. Preferred areas of support: children and youth, social welfare, medical, the arts and enterprise/training. Budget is allocated at discretion of chairman and managing director. Grants to national organisations from £50 to £5,000. Grants to local organisations from £25 to £1,000. Generally no support for local appeals not in areas of company presence.

☐ **Fii Group plc**　　　　　　　　　　　　　　　Footwear manufacturers

48 George Street,　　*Ch:* M Sumray　　*Year Ends:* 31 May '91　　*UK employees:* n/a
London W1H 5PG　　*Contact:* Richard Sumray　　*Donations:* £7,963　　*Total employees:* 2,348
071-935 8463　　Group Business Administrator　　*Profit:* £7,150,000
　　　　　　　　　　　　　　Turnover: £80,340,000

Donations Policy: The company states "We generally support organisations we have known for some time. There is little scope for donating to new charities and it is generally not worth them contacting us". Preference for appeals relevant to company business and charities in which a member of company staff is involved. Grants range from £50 to £500.
No response to circular appeals. No grants for appeals from individuals; purely denominational (religious) appeals; local appeals not in areas of company presence; large national appeals; overseas projects.

☐ **Fina plc**　　　　　　　　　　　　　　　　　Crude oil & gas refinery & exploration

Fina House,　　*Ch:* Sir Peter M Horden　　*Year Ends:* 31 Dec '91　　*UK employees:* n/a
Ashley Avenue,　　*CE:* E Demeure de Lespaul　　*Donations:* £28,506　　*Total employees:* 1,954
Epsom,　　*Contact:* N C P Vandervell　　*Profit:* £5,530,000
Surrey KT18 5AD　　Company Secretary　　*Turnover:* £1,135,993,000　　ABSA
0372-726226

Donations Policy: The company donate about £10,000 to one national charity. The balance is given in grants of £50 to £500 to local charities in areas where the company operates. Preference for appeals relevant to company business and charities in which a member of company staff is involved. Preference for children and youth; medical; environment/heritage; arts. Charity fundraising by staff is matched by the company pound for pound.
No grants for fundraising events; advertising in charity brochures; appeals from individuals; purely denominational (religious) appeals; local appeals not in areas of company presence; overseas projects.
The donations figure stated above includes sponsorship payments. The contact for sponsorship is K B Parfitt, Corporate & External Affairs Manager.

Please read page 6 | Alphabetical listing ●

Name/Address — *Officers* — *Financial Information* — *Other Information*

☐ Fine Art Developments plc

Greeting card manufacture, mail order

Dawson Lane,
Dudley Hill,
Bradford BD4 6HW
0274-651188

Ch: K Chapman
Contact: D Hale
Company Secretary

Year Ends: 31 Mar '92
Donations: £127,902
Profit: £29,719,000
Turnover: £287,303,000

UK employees: n/a
Total employees: 4,675

% Club

A.

Donations Policy: Donations are spread over 200 organisations with particular emphasis on those working with children and disabled people, including many less well-known charities.

☐ James Finlay plc

International traders & financiers

Finlay House,
10-14 West Nile Street,
Glasgow G1 2PP
041-204 1321

Ch: R J K Muir
Contact: R W McCracken
Company Secretary

Year Ends: 31 Dec '91
Donations: £18,633
Profit: £10,882,000
Turnover: £143,686,000

UK employees: n/a
Total employees: 32,354

B

Donations Policy: Preference for local charities in the areas of company presence, especially in the fields of children and youth, social welfare, medical (not professional bodies), education, environment/heritage and overseas aid/development. Donations are made by overseas branches direct to local charities in the countries where they operate. Grants to national organisations from £25 to £500. Grants to local organisations from £25 to £2,000.
Generally no support for circular appeals, fundraising events, advertising in charity brochures, appeals from individuals, purely denominational (religious) appeals, local appeals not in areas of company presence or overseas projects. No sponsorship of gala programmes, TV charity appeals, charity dinners etc..

☐ Finning Holdings Ltd

Suppliers of earthmoving equipment

Watling Street,
Cannock,
Staffordshire WS11 3LL
0543-462551

Ch: D Lord
MD: N B Lloyd
Contact: G Smith
Personnel Manager

Year Ends: 31 Dec '91
Donations: £4,844
Profit: £987,000
Turnover: £126,242,000

UK employees: n/a
Total employees: 1,122

B.

Donations Policy: Preference for local charities in areas where the company operates and appeals relevant to company business. Preference for children and youth; medical; education; environment/heritage. Grants to local organisations from £25 to £50.
No support for circular appeals, advertising in charity brochures; appeals from individuals; purely denominational (religious) appeals; local appeals not in areas of company presence; large national appeals; overseas projects.

☐ First Leisure Corporation plc

Entertainments

7 Soho Street,
Soho Square,
London W1V 5FA
071-437 9727

Ch: Lord Delfont
CE: J O Conlan
Contact: D W Wright
Company Secretary

Year Ends: 31 Oct '91
Donations: £3,807
Profit: £30,367,000
Turnover: £108,739,000

UK employees: n/a
Total employees: 3,242

B.

Donations Policy: Preference for local charities in areas of company presence, appeals relevant to company business and charities where a member of staff is involved. Preferred areas of support: children and youth, medical. Grants to national organisations from £25 to £500. Grants to local organisations from £10 to £100.
Generally no support for circular appeals, fundraising events, purely denominational appeals, local appeals not in areas of company presence, large national appeals and overseas projects.

☐ First National Finance Corp plc

Bankers

PO Box 505,
St Alphage House,
Fore Street,
London EC2P 2HJ
071-638 2855

Ch: R M Mays-Smith
CE: T J B Wrigley
Contact: S J Clayman
Director

Year Ends: 31 Oct '91
Donations: £79,000
Profit: (£31,904,000)
Turnover: n/a

UK employees: n/a
Total employees: 1,579

Donations Policy: Donations are covenanted to about 12 major national charities, mainly medical. It is therefore very unlikely that unsolicited appeals will be successful.

☐ Albert Fisher Group plc

Food distribution & services

Fisher House,
61 Thames Street,
Windsor SL4 7QW
0753-857111

Ch: S R Walls
Contact: G Shillinglaw
Group Company Secretary

Year Ends: 31 Aug '91
Donations: £61,000
Profit: £89,032,000
Turnover: £1,095,556,000

UK employees: n/a
Total employees: 6,629

BitC

B.

Donations Policy: To support charities involved with the food industry (eg. nutritional research) and certain local causes. Grants to national organisations from £1,000 to £25,000. Grants to local organisations up to £2,500.
Generally no support for appeals from individuals, purely denominational appeals or local appeals not in areas of company presence.

☐ Fisons plc

Chemical fertilisers

Fison House,
Princes Street,
Ipswich IP1 1QH
0473-232525

Ch: P V M Egan
CE: C A Scroggs
Contact: J M Bailey
Company Secretary

Year Ends: 31 Dec '91
Donations: £110,000
Profit: £190,500,000
Turnover: £1,225,300,000

UK employees: n/a
Total employees: 14,336

% Club, BitC

A.

Donations Policy: The company has a charitable trust (correspondent as above). In 1989, the trust had an income of £105,095 and gave grants totalling £56,504. The trust supports general charitable purposes; it will not support individuals.

• **Alphabetical listing**   Please read page 6

Name/Address   *Officers*   *Financial Information*   *Other Information*

☐ **Fitch-RS plc**   Design

Porters House,   *Ch*: R A Fitch   *Year Ends*: 31 Dec '91   *UK employees*: n/a
4 Crinan Street,   *CE*: M J Beck   *Donations*: £26,700   *Total employees*: 519
London N1 9UE   *Contact*: Katherine Crompton-Jenkinson   *Profit*: (£416,900)
071-278 7200   Personal Assistant to the   *Turnover*: £18,107,100
                                Chairman

Donations Policy: We have been unable to obtain a donations policy.

☐ **FKI plc**   Electrical & specialist engineering

West House,   *Ch*: J Whalley   *Year Ends*: 31 Mar '92   *UK employees*: n/a
Kings Cross Road,   *MD*: R Beeston   *Donations*: nil   *Total employees*: 13,545
Halifax,   *Contact*: Clare Wickham   *Profit*: £30,517,000
West Yorkshire HX1 1EB   Secretary to the Chief Executive *Turnover*: £739,094,000
0422-330267

Donations Policy: Company policy is to make no charitable donations.

☐ **Robert Fleming Holdings Ltd**   Merchant banking

25 Copthall Avenue,   *Ch*: R Fleming   *Year Ends*: 31 Mar '92   *UK employees*: 2,379
London EC2R 7DR   *CE*: J Manser   *Donations*: £161,817   *Total employees*: n/a
071-638 5858   *Contact*: D Pocknee   *Profit*: £76,621,000
                                Secretary, Charity Committee   *Turnover*: n/a

Donations Policy: Each appeal is considered on its merits. Preference for local charities in the areas of company presence and charities in which a member of company staff is involved. Grants to national organisations from £200 to £500. Grants to local organisations from £100 to £300.
Generally no support for circular appeals, fundraising events, brochure advertising, appeals from individuals or local appeals not in areas of company presence.

☐ **FLT & Metals Ltd**   Traders in metals & bearings

1-5 Long Lane,   *MD*: A Dujezynski   *Year Ends*: 31 Dec '90   *UK employees*: n/a
London EC1A 9HA   *Contact*: Office Manager   *Donations*: £56,650   *Total employees*: 24
071-606 1272   *Profit*: £1,311,000
                                                               Turnover: £164,357,000

Donations Policy: The company is Polish. No information is available on the donations policy of the company and we were unable to confirm the above figures.

☐ **Folkes Group plc**   Industrial property & engineering, merchanting

Forge House,   *Contact*: C J Folkes   *Year Ends*: 31 Dec '90   *UK employees*: n/a
Old Forge Trading Estate,   Chairman   *Donations*: £1,823 (1991)   *Total employees*: 828
Dudley Road,   *Profit*: £4,025,000
Lye,   *Turnover*: £47,714,000
Stourbridge DY9 8EL
0384-424242

Donations Policy: No donation will exceed £10. Preference for appeals relevant to company business and local appeals in areas of company presence, particularly children and youth, and medical causes.
No support for large national appeals, overseas projects, purely denominational (religious) appeals, advertising in charity brochure or fundraising events.

☐ **Food Brokers (Holdings) Ltd**   Food product services & distribution

Food Broker House,   *Ch*: D S Cracknell   *Year Ends*: 31 Dec '89   *UK employees*: n/a
Northarbour Road,   *MD*: R Hudson   *Donations*: £2,210 (1988)   *Total employees*: 367
North Harbour,   *Contact*: Elaine Howieson   *Profit*: £481,000
Portsmouth,   Secretary to the Personnel   *Turnover*: £80,749,000
Hampshire PO6 3TD   Director
0705-219900

☐ **Forbo CP Ltd**   Floor & wall coverings, industrial PVC sheetings

Station Road,   *MD*: J T Ions   *Year Ends*: 31 Dec '90   *UK employees*: n/a
Cramlington,   *Contact*: Alan Rakison   *Donations*: n/a   *Total employees*: 1,744
Northumberland NE23 8AQ   Personnel Manager   *Profit*: £8,507,000
0670-718222   *Turnover*: £105,706,000

Name/Address	Officers	Financial Information	Other Information

☐ Ford Motor Company Ltd

Motor vehicle manufacturers

Eagle Way,
Brentwood,
Essex CM13 3BW
0277-253000

Ch: I G McAllister
Contact: Maurice K Hurrell
Administrator, Ford of Britain
Trust

Year Ends: 31 Dec '91
Donations: £224,000
Profit: (£935,000,000)
Turnover: £6,191,000,000

UK employees: 50,700
Total employees: 51,800

BitC

Donations Policy: In addition to the donations figure above, the company has a four-year covenant with the Ford of Britain Trust, a charitable organisation wholly supported by company contributions, providing the trust with an income of £250,000 a year for each of the years 1990-93 inclusive.
Support preferably to registered charities. Majority of donations are one-off grants to local charities in areas of company presence and charities in which a member of staff is involved. Within these guidelines preference is given to organisations concerned with children and youth, social welfare, medical (but not research), education, recreation, environment and the arts. Grants to national organisations from £500 to £5,000. Grants to local organisations from £50 to £5,000.
National charities are rarely supported, except in respect of specific local projects in Ford areas. Generally no support for circular appeals, fundraising events, brochure advertising, appeals from individuals, purely denominational appeals, local appeals not in areas of company presence or overseas projects.

☐ Forte plc

Hotels, catering & leisure

166 High Holborn,
London WC1V 6TT
071-836 7744

Ch: Lord Forte
MD: R Forte
Contact: T Russell
Group Company Secretary

Year Ends: 31 Jan '92
Donations: £542,000
Profit: £73,000,000
Turnover: £2,662,000,000

UK employees: n/a
Total employees: 89,500

BitC

Donations Policy: The group states that all applications are considered on their merits and that no specific areas of work are given priority. However in recent years, main areas of support have included organisations concerned with medical care and disabled people. The company is also involved in education and environmental initiatives.
No support for appeals from individuals.

☐ Forward Technology Industries Ltd

Electronics, specialised machinery

2 Pont Street,
London SW1X 9EL
071-235 9196

Ch: H Prevezer
MD: K Cobley
Contact: Mark Bolger
Company Secretary

Year Ends: 31 Dec '89
Donations: £5,000
Profit: £2,270,000
Turnover: £42,847,000

UK employees: 254
Total employees: n/a

Donations Policy: The company donates about £5,000 a year (5 donations of £1,000 each) in the late autumn. Preferred areas of support: children and youth, social welfare and medical.
No support for circular appeals, fundraising events, advertising in charity brochures, appeals from individuals or purely denominational appeals.

☐ Foster Wheeler Ltd

Industrial services, equipment

Foster Wheeler House,
Station Road,
Reading,
Berkshire RG1 1LX
0734-585211

Ch: W C Chatman
Contact: John Ramsden
Personnel Director

Year Ends: 31 Dec '90
Donations: £33,657 (1991)
Profit: £4,122,000
Turnover: £202,933,000

UK employees: n/a
Total employees: 1,890

% Club

Donations Policy: Support only to local charities in areas where the company operates. Preference for appeals relevant to company business and charities in which a member of company staff is involved. Preference for children and youth; social welfare; medical; education; environment/heritage; arts; enterprise/training. Grants to national organisations from £100 to £15,000. Grants to local organisations from £25 to £1,000.
No response to circular appeals. No grants for fundraising events; advertising in charity brochures; appeals from individuals; purely denominational (religious) appeals; local appeals not in areas of company presence; large national appeals; overseas projects.
Total community contributions in 1991 were £63,000.

☐ Foster Yeoman Ltd

Limestone quarry owners

Marston House,
Marston Bigot,
Frome,
Somerset BA11 5DU
0373-451001

MD: D Tidmarsh
Contact: Peter Chapman
Public Relations Manager

Year Ends: 31 May '87
Donations: £7,415
Profit: £3,074,000
Turnover: £53,635,000

UK employees: n/a
Total employees: n/a

Donations Policy: The company is currently making no charitable donations.

☐ FR Group plc

Design, manufacture & sale of defence equipment

Brook Road,
Wimborne,
Dorset BH21 2BJ
0202-882121

Ch: M J Cobham
CE: G F Page
Contact: Brian Moore
Financial Director

Year Ends: 31 Dec '91
Donations: £39,603
Profit: £21,400,000
Turnover: £168,400,000

UK employees: n/a
Total employees: 3,658

Donations Policy: The company restricts its support to local appeals in areas of company presence and appeals relevant to company business. Preference for enterprise and training, children and youth.
No support for circular appeals, large national appeals, overseas projects, purely denominational appeals.

● **Alphabetical listing**   Please read page 6

Name/Address	Officers	Financial Information	Other Information

☐ Freemans plc
Mail order business

139 Clapham Road,
London SW99 0HR
071-735 7644

Ch: J M Pickard
MD: M L Hawker
Contact: J J Pearmund
Financial Director

Year Ends: 3 Feb '90
Donations: £70,000
Profit: £23,869,000
Turnover: £484,300,000

UK employees: n/a
Total employees: 5,165

Donations Policy: Support for local organisations in areas of company presence, or national organisations working in the communities where there are company establishments. In particular this includes South London, Peterborough and Sheffield. Preferred areas of support: children and youth (including summer playschemes), social welfare, medical and enterprise/training. Grants from £25 to £500.
No support for circular appeals, fundraising events, advertising in charity brochures, appeals from individuals, purely denominational (religious) appeals, political appeals, sport or arts sponsorship, campaigning work by charities, local appeals not in areas of company presence, large national appeals and overseas projects.

☐ Thomas French & Sons plc
Curtain styling product manufacturers

Sharston Road,
Wythenshawe,
Manchester M22 4TN
061-998 1811

Ch: T J French
MD: H R J Griffith
Contact: A E Lister
Chairman of Charity Committee

Year Ends: 30 Sep '91
Donations: £2,000
Profit: £753,000
Turnover: £13,693,000

UK employees: 280
Total employees: 315

Donations Policy: Preference for local charities in areas where the company operates, appeals relevant to company business and charities in which a member of company staff is involved. Preference for children and youth; social welfare; medical. Grants to national organisations from £20 to £30. Grants to local organisations from £20 to £100.
No response to circular appeals. No grants for fundraising events; advertising in charity brochures; purely denominational (religious) appeals; local appeals not in areas of company presence; large national appeals; overseas projects.

☐ Friends' Provident Life Office
Long-term insurance

Pixham End,
Dorking,
Surrey RH4 1QA
0306-740123

Ch: Lord Jenkin of Roding
MD: F G Cotton
Contact: J S Murdoch
Publicity & Communications
Manager (address below)

Year Ends: 31 Dec '91
Donations: £60,250
Profit: £517,000,000
Turnover: n/a

UK employees: 2,791
Total employees: n/a

ABSA

Donations Policy: The company does not normally respond reactively to appeals, but channels its funds into the establishment of a Friends Provident Research Fellowship to be administered by the British Heart Foundation. Any additional support would be to charities in medical research, preferring preventative medicine to aftercare. Preference may also be given to local charities in the areas of company presence and organisations concerned with children and youth. Grants to national organisations from £500 to £5,000. Grants to local organisations from £50 to £300. Appeals to: UK House, Castle Street, Salisbury, Wiltshire SP1 3SH.
No response to circular appeals. No support for overseas projects, local charities outside areas of company presence, denominational appeals (except Quaker), appeals from individuals.

☐ Frizzell Financial Services Ltd
Insurance brokers

Frizzell House,
County Gates,
Bournemouth BH1 2NF
071-247 6595

Contact: Colin Taylor
Director of Public Affairs

Year Ends:
Donations: n/a
Profit: n/a
Turnover: n/a

UK employees: n/a
Total employees: n/a

% Club

Donations Policy: Preference for social welfare; medical and environment/heritage.
No response to circular appeals. No grants for fundraising events; advertising in charity brochures; appeals from individuals; purely denominational (religious) appeals; local appeals not in areas of company presence; large national appeals; overseas projects.

☐ Frogmore Estates plc
Property development

8 Manchester Square,
London W1A 2JZ
071-224 4343

Ch: D J Cope
MD: P G Davies
Contact: Trevor Birchmore
Company Secretary

Year Ends: 30 Jun '91
Donations: £10,862
Profit: £7,106,000
Turnover: £47,558,000

UK employees: n/a
Total employees: 91

Donations Policy: No support for circulars, appeals from individuals, purely denominational (religious) appeals or overseas projects.

☐ Frontline Distribution Ltd
Microcomputer equipment

Intec-1,
Wade Road,
Basingstoke,
Hampshire RG24 0NE
0256-463344

MD: M C Mulford

Year Ends: 31 Mar '90
Donations: n/a
Profit: £204,000
Turnover: £103,446,000

UK employees: n/a
Total employees: 305

☐ Fruehauf Ltd
Sale & manufacture of semi-trailers

Rash's Green,
Toftwood,
Dereham,
Norfolk NR19 1JF
0362-695353

Contact: G Thomson
Corporate & Public Affairs
Manager

Year Ends: 31 Dec '88
Donations: £10,554
Profit: £4,570,000
Turnover: £92,587,000

UK employees: n/a
Total employees: 1,196

Donations Policy: To support people and events specifically involved in the industry (not racing), or to support local group activities with educational or youth development aims. Grants (to local organisations) from £25 to £250.
Generally no support for circular appeals, advertising in charity brochures, purely denominational (religious) appeals or large national appeals.

Please read page 6 | Alphabetical listing •

Name/Address	Officers	Financial Information	Other Information

☐ Fuji Photo Film (UK)

Photographic goods manufacturers

125 Finchley Road,
Swiss Cottage,
London NW3 6JH
071-586 5900

Ch: M Ohrinshi
Contact: Adrian Clark
Corporate Business Manager

Year Ends: 31 Aug '89
Donations: £8,947
Profit: £1,099,000
Turnover: £61,465,000

UK employees: 144
Total employees: n/a

☐ Fujitsu Europe Ltd

Marketing of electronic appliances

2 Longwalk Road,
Stockley Park,
Uxbridge UB11 1AB
081-573 4444

MD: A Iwakata
Contact: Mrs A Peinke
Administration Manager

Year Ends: 31 Mar '90
Donations: £7,954
Profit: £4,813,000
Turnover: £207,237,000

UK employees: n/a
Total employees: 452

Donations Policy: Preference for local charities in the areas of company presence especially children and youth, social welfare, medical and education. Grants to local organisations from £50 to £250.
Generally no support for circular appeals, fundraising events, advertising in charity brochures, appeals from individuals, purely denominational (religious) appeals, local appeals not in areas of company presence, large national appeals or overseas projects.

☐ Fuller Smith & Turner plc

Brewers

Griffin Brewery,
Chiswick Lane South,
London W4 2QB
081-994 3691

Ch: A G F Fuller
MD: M J Turner
Contact: Ian Turner

Year Ends: 31 Mar '92
Donations: £20,000
Profit: £7,803,000
Turnover: £76,234,000

UK employees: n/a
Total employees: 1,327

☐ Furness-Withy (Shipping) Ltd

Shipowners

53 Brighton Road,
Redhill,
Surrey RH1 6YL
0737-771122

Contact: W E Kirkbride
General Manager

Year Ends: 31 Dec '88
Donations: £21,000
Profit: £13,728,000
Turnover: £280,478,000

UK employees: n/a
Total employees: 1,234

Donations Policy: The company only makes donations to marine associated charities and small donations local to company sites.

☐ Fyffes Group Ltd

Fruit importers

12 York Gate,
Regents Park,
London NW1 4QJ
071-487 4472

Ch: A J Ellis
Contact: Anne Ross
Publicity Department

Year Ends: 31 Oct '90
Donations: £15,000
Profit: £9,083,000
Turnover: £361,121,000

UK employees: n/a
Total employees: 2,571

Donations Policy: Applications are dealt with on an ad hoc basis. Preference for appeals relevant to company business. Local charities are considered by local branches of the group.

☐ Gallaher Ltd

Tobacco, optical, housewares, distilled spirits, retail dist.

Members Hill,
Brooklands Road,
Weybridge KT13 0QU
0932-859777

Ch: A D Househam
Contact: Mrs S A Sear
Secretary, Charities Committee

Year Ends: 31 Dec '91
Donations: £426,943
Profit: £295,400,000
Turnover: £4,678,300,000

UK employees: n/a
Total employees: 26,294

BitC, ABSA

Donations Policy: Support mainly for large national charities and smaller organisations in regions where the company operates. Preferred areas of support: social welfare, enterprise/training, disabled people and charities where a member of staff is involved. Grants to national organisations from £500 to £1,000. Grants to local organisations from £100 to £500. Local branches are given guidelines and a budget for making their own donations.
Generally no support for circular appeals, telephone appeals, fundraising events, brochure advertising, appeals from individuals, purely denominational appeals or local appeals not in areas of company presence.

☐ Galliford plc

Civil engineering, building & development

Wolvey Grange,
Wolvey,
Hinkley,
Leicestershire LE10 3JD
0455-220533

Ch: P Galliford
MD: G R Marsh
Contact: Mrs R Shannon
Corporate Affairs Executive

Year Ends: 30 Jun '91
Donations: £15,122
Profit: £6,385,000
Turnover: £225,122,000

UK employees: n/a
Total employees: 1,798

Donations Policy: The company prefers to give charitable contributions/sponsorships to charities who aim to help local people in need and organisations seeking to help young people achieve personal success, particularly with some affinity to its own industry. Preference also for charities in which a member of staff is involved. Policy is determined by the company's main board of directors. Preferred areas of support: children and youth, medical, education, the arts and enterprise/training. Grants to national organisations from £25 to £500. Grants to local organisations from £25 to £100.
No support for circular appeals, advertising in charity brochures, purely denominational appeals, local appeals not in areas of company presence or overseas projects.

☐ Gan Minster Insurance Group

Insurance

Minster House,
Arthur Street,
London EC4R 9BJ
071-623 5280

Ch: A P D Lancaster
MD: B J M Bellenguier
Contact: Company Secretary

Year Ends: 31 Dec '91
Donations: n/a
Profit: (£14,300,000)
Turnover: n/a

UK employees: n/a
Total employees: 704

● **Alphabetical listing**   **Please read page 6**

Name/Address	Officers	Financial Information	Other Information

☐ F G Gates plc
Motor traders

140 High Road,
South Woodford,
London E18 2QS
081-504 4466

Ch: E F Gates
MD: J Coleman
Contact: B R Gates
Deputy Chairman

Year Ends: 31 Dec '91
Donations: £2,339
Profit: £1,319,000
Turnover: £56,349,000

UK employees: n/a
Total employees: 460

Donations Policy: Preference for local charities in the areas of company presence. Preferred areas of support: children and youth, social welfare. Grants to local organisations from £100 to £200.
Generally no support for circular appeals, brochure advertising, appeals from individuals, purely denominational appeals, local appeals not in areas of company presence, large national appeals or overseas projects.

☐ Gates Rubber Company Ltd
Rubber products

Edinburgh Road,
Heathhall,
Dumfries DG1 1QA
0387-53111

Ch: D E Miller
Contact: A N Watt
General Manager, Footwear

Year Ends: 29 Dec '92
Donations: n/a
Profit: £921,000
Turnover: £90,896,000

UK employees: n/a
Total employees: 1,199

Donations Policy: Preference for local charities in areas where the company operates and charities in which a member of company staff is involved. Preference for children and youth and elderly people; social welfare; education; recreation; enterprise/training. Grants up to £300.

☐ Gateway Corporation plc
Food retailing

Stockley House,
Wilton Road,
London SW1V 1LU
071-233 5353

Ch: Ernest H Sharp
CE: David D Smith
Contact: Michael Brown
Secretary to the Charitable Trust

Year Ends: 25 Apr '92
Donations: £127,000
Profit: £18,000,000
Turnover: £3,024,200,000

UK employees: n/a
Total employees: 46,988

BitC

Donations Policy: Main areas of support are social welfare, community services, education and scientific research. It runs a "Help a Local Child" programme, giving grants to children in the community surrounding its stores to relieve problems or promote ambitions. National grants range from £500 to £2,000. Local grants range from £100 to £500.
No support for advertising in charity brochures, appeals from individuals, purely denominational (religious) appeals, local appeals not in areas of company presence or fundraising events.

☐ Geest plc
Fresh fruit & vegetable suppliers

White House Chambers,
Spalding,
Lincolnshire PE11 2AL
0775-761111

Ch: L W van Geest
CE: D A Sugden
Contact: Mrs Rachel Dixon
Public Relations Assistant

Year Ends: 28 Dec '91
Donations: £53,000
Profit: £26,204,000
Turnover: £626,318,000

UK employees: n/a
Total employees: 6,740

% Club

Donations Policy: Support for local charities in areas of company presence and those relevant to company business. Preferred area of support: children and youth. Grants to local organisations from £50 to £200.
No response to circular appeals. No support for brochure advertising, appeals from individuals, purely denominational appeals, local appeals not in areas of company presence, large national appeals or overseas projects.

☐ General Accident plc
Insurance

Pitheavlis,
Perth PH2 0NH
0738-21202

Ch: Earl of Airlie
CE: W N Robertson
Contact: D J McPherson
Assistant Secretary

Year Ends: 31 Dec '91
Donations: £389,055
Profit: (£171,600,000)
Turnover: n/a

UK employees: 14,725
Total employees: n/a

Donations Policy: Support for mainly national charities covering the fields of education, medical research and health care, children and elderly people, and social welfare. Local charities are dealt with by local branches; many appeals are then referred to head office. Total community contributions in 1991 were £1,351,055.
No support for circular appeals, advertising in charity brochures, fundraising events or appeals from individuals.

☐ General Electric Company plc
Electrical engineers

1 Stanhope Gate,
London W1A 1EH
071-493 8484

Ch: Lord Prior
MD: Lord Weinstock
Contact: The Hon Mrs Sara Morrison
Director

Year Ends: 31 Mar '92
Donations: £784,000
Profit: £829,000,000
Turnover: £5,774,000,000

UK employees: 75,430
Total employees: 104,995

BitC, ABSA

Donations Policy: Preference for local charities in the areas of company presence. Main areas of support are children and youth, social welfare, education and training. Direct support preferred. Applications for local support should be made in writing to the local operating unit. Grants to national organisations from £1,000 to £5,000. Grants to local organisations from £500 to £2,000.
No support for circular appeals, fundraising events, advertising in charity brochures, appeals from individuals, purely denominational (religious) appeals, building appeals or local appeals not in areas of company presence.

☐ General Utilities plc
Water industry investors

14 Headfort Place,
London SW1X 7DH
071-259 5244

Ch: Sir William S Dugdale
Contact: Warren Newman
Head of Public Relations

Year Ends: 31 Mar '92
Donations: £16,535
Profit: £32,243,000
Turnover: £132,280,000

UK employees: n/a
Total employees: 1,461

Donations Policy: Preference for local charities in areas where the company operates. Preference for environment/heritage and the arts (via sponsorship).
No grants for advertising in charity brochures; appeals from individuals; purely denominational (religious) appeals; local appeals not in areas of company presence; large national appeals; overseas projects.

Please read page 6 — Alphabetical listing •

Name/Address	Officers	Financial Information	Other Information

☐ S R Gent plc
Clothing manufacturers

8 Harewood Row,
London NW1 6SE
071-723 4243

Ch: P M Wolff
CE: P Wetzel
Contact: John H Whitmore
 Personnel Director

Year Ends: 30 Jun '92
Donations: £97,071
Profit: £2,285,000
Turnover: £127,987,000

UK employees: 3,566
Total employees: 3,798

% Club

Donations Policy: Emphasis on industry related training including involvement in the Clothing & Allied Products Industry Training Board.

☐ Gerald Ltd
Metal merchants

Europe House,
World Trade Centre,
St Katharine by the Tower,
London E1 9AA
071-867 9400

Ch: G L Lennard
MD: R Kestenbaum, P J Burgess
Contact: Derek Over
 Financial Director

Year Ends: 5 Apr '87
Donations: n/a
Profit: n/a
Turnover: £1,377,116,000

UK employees: n/a
Total employees: 70

☐ Gerber Foods International
Processed foods

Northway House,
1379 High Road,
Whetstone,
London N20 9LP
081-446 1424

Contact: Carol Harris
 Secretary to the Chairman

Year Ends: 27 Dec '86
Donations: n/a
Profit: £5,304,000
Turnover: £91,972,000

UK employees: n/a
Total employees: 636

☐ Gerrard & National Holdings plc
Interest market investments

33 Lombard Street,
London EC3V 9BQ
071-623 9981

Ch: R B Williamson
Contact: Earl Of Eglinton & Winton

Year Ends: 5 Apr '92
Donations: £55,735
Profit: £11,113,000
Turnover: n/a

UK employees: 589
Total employees: n/a

% Club, BitC

Donations Policy: Preference for children and youth; social welfare; medical; education; environment/heritage; arts; enterprise/training. Selected charities are supported for a four year period, after which they are reviewed. Appeals are therefore not welcome.

☐ Michael Gerson Ltd
Finance & leasing

Downland Close,
Whetstone,
London N20 9LB
081-446 1300

Contact: Michael Gerson
 Chairman

Year Ends:
Donations: n/a
Profit: n/a
Turnover: n/a

UK employees: n/a
Total employees: n/a

% Club

Donations Policy: We have been unable to obtain a donations policy for this company.

☐ Gestetner Holdings plc
Reprographic equipment manufacturer

66 Chiltern Street,
London W1M 2AP
071-465 1000

Ch: B A Sellers
Contact: Roger Headey
 Personnel Co-ordinator

Year Ends: 31 Oct '91
Donations: £2,000
Profit: £22,500,000
Turnover: £898,300,000

UK employees: n/a
Total employees: 11,211

Donations Policy: Preference for local charities in areas of company presence, appeals relevant to the business and charities in which a member of staff is involved.
No appeals from individuals, purely denominational appeals or local appeals not in areas of company presence.

☐ Gillette UK Ltd
Razor & blade manufacturers

Gillette Corner,
Great West Road,
Isleworth,
Middlesex TW7 5NP
081-560 1234

Ch: P Mohlar
Contact: Richard Bryce
 Human Resources Manager

Year Ends: 30 Nov '91
Donations: £60,000
Profit: £11,992,000
Turnover: £179,440,000

UK employees: n/a
Total employees: 1,500

% Club, BitC

Donations Policy: The company's policy is to set aside about 1% of pre-tax profits each year in order to contribute to the educational, cultural and social services activities of the communities in which it's operations are based. In the UK donations are concentrated in the Hounslow, Brentford, Ealing area and the Reading area. Support is also given to local branches of national organisations. Grants to local organisations from £100 to £10,000.
No grants for appeals from individuals; purely denominational (religious) appeals; local appeals not in areas of company presence; large national appeals (see above); overseas projects. Advertising in charity brochures is rarely undertaken.

☐ Girobank plc
Banking

10 Milk Street,
London EC2V 8JH
071-600 6020

Ch: F W Crawley
MD: Lewis Evans
Contact: Philip Bryant (address below)
 Head of Group Public Relations

Year Ends: 31 Dec '91
Donations: £212,000
Profit: £48,800,000
Turnover: n/a

UK employees: 5,684
Total employees: 5,684

% Club, BitC

Donations Policy: The bank only gives donations to registered charities. Preference for local charities in areas where the company operates. It aims to support a wide range of activities with preference for children and youth, social welfare, medical, environment and heritage and enterprise/training. Grants to national organisations from £50 to £100. Grants to local organisations from £50 to £75.
No response to circular appeals. No grants for fundraising events; advertising in charity brochures; appeals from individuals; purely denominational (religious) appeals.

● **Alphabetical listing**   Please read page 6

Name/Address   *Officers*   *Financial Information*   *Other Information*

☐ GKN plc
                                                                                                   Automotive, defence & industrial services
Ipsley House,   *Ch*: Sir David Lees   *Year Ends*: 31 Dec '91   *UK employees*: 12,000
PO Box 55,   *Contact*: A F George   *Donations*: £128,315   *Total employees*: 30,000
Redditch,   Company Secretary   *Profit*: £95,000,000
Hereford & Worcester   *Turnover*: £1,925,400,000   % Club, BitC
B98 0TL
0527-517715

Donations Policy: GKN, a strong supporter of Business in the Community, supports mainly initiatives in education, the community and health and welfare. Companies are linked with local schools in integrated activities of secondment of teachers and employees, work experience and young enterprise. Subsidiaries have developed strong employee charitable involvement in their localities and some preference is given to appeals from organisations in areas where the company has a branch. Local appeals should be addressed to local branches.
No support for circular appeals, fundraising events, brochure advertising, appeals from individuals or local appeals not in areas of company presence.

☐ Glass Glover Group plc
                                                                                                                      Contract distribution
Loversall Hall,   *Ch*: E Walters   *Year Ends*: 30 Sep '90   *UK employees*: n/a
Loversall,   *CE*: D Metcalf   *Donations*: £14,000   *Total employees*: 3,131
Doncaster,   *Contact*: C Ferris   *Profit*: £2,272,000
South Yorkshire   DN11 9OD   Company Secretary   *Turnover*: £103,284,000
0302-850999

Donations Policy: Preference for local charities in the areas of company presence and appeals relevant to company business. Preferred areas of support: children and youth, medical and environment and heritage.
Generally no support for advertising in charity brochures, purely denominational (religious) appeals, local appeals not in areas of company presence or overseas projects.

☐ Glaxo Holdings plc
                                                                                                                   Pharmaceutical manufacturers
Lansdowne House,   *Ch*: Sir Paul Girolami   *Year Ends*: 30 Jun '92   *UK employees*: n/a
Berkeley Square,   *CE*: Dr E Mario   *Donations*: £3,700,000   *Total employees*: 37,083
London   W1X 6BP   *Contact*: S M Bicknell   *Profit*: £1,427,000,000
071-493 4060   Manager, Charity/Community   *Turnover*: £4,096,000,000   % Club, BitC, ABSA
                           Contributions

Donations Policy: Grants are made by Group Appeals Committee in the following categories: (a) advancement of science and healthcare (particular emphasis is given to this category), (b) relief of suffering and poverty, (c) preservation of national heritage and culture, (d) international appeals.
No support for appeals from individuals, fundraising events, advertising in charity brochures or purely denominational (religious) appeals. Arts sponsorship proposals should be sent to Mrs E Browne, Associate Manager, Community Relations. Glaxo companies also help support a wide range of community projects intended to improve education and its relationship to business, to promote employment and to improve the environment. Organisations seeking support for local community projects within the region of Glaxo sites should apply to the appropriate regional contact.
Total community contributions in 1991/92 were £8 million, equivalent to 5.2% UK pre-tax profit.

☐ M J Gleeson Group plc
                                                                                                            Civil engineers & building contractors
London Road,   *Ch*: J P Gleeson   *Year Ends*: 30 Jun '91   *UK employees*: n/a
North Cheam,   *MD*: D J Gleeson   *Donations*: £12,600   *Total employees*: 1,852
Sutton,   *Contact*: John McCartney   *Profit*: £11,849,000
Surrey   SM3 9BS   Group Marketing Controller   *Turnover*: £199,309,000
081-644 4321

Donations Policy: The company has no fixed policy and supports a variety of local and national appeals. Evidence that a charity is receiving the donation, without significant fundraiser's costs being deducted, is appreciated. Preferred areas of support: children and youth, social welfare and medical. Grants from £25 to £2,500.

☐ Glunz (UK) plc
                                                                                                                      Holding company
Station Road,   *Ch*: L Aaronson   *Year Ends*: 30 Sep '89   *UK employees*: n/a
Cowie,   *Contact*: Mrs Crossman   *Donations*: £7,000   *Total employees*: 875
Sterlingshire   FK7 7BQ   Secretary to the Managing   *Profit*: £2,119,000
0786-812921   Director   *Turnover*: £84,067,000

Donations Policy: The company makes small donations to local charities in areas of company presence. It does not sponsor/support individuals (except employees).

☐ Glynwed International plc
                                                                                                       Engineering & building products, steel
Headland House,   *Ch*: G Davies   *Year Ends*: 30 Dec '91   *UK employees*: n/a
New Coventry Road,   *Contact*: J C Blakeley   *Donations*: £121,851   *Total employees*: 12,613
Sheldon,   Glynwed Charitable Trust   *Profit*: £25,500,000
Birmingham   B26 3AZ   *Turnover*: £949,900,000   % Club
021-742 2366

Donations Policy: The Glynwed Charitable Trust only supports projects/organisations deemed by law as charitable.

Please read page 6 — Alphabetical listing

Name/Address	Officers	Financial Information	Other Information

☐ Gold Greenlees Trott plc
Advertising agency

82 Dean Street,
London W1V 5AB
071-437 0434

Ch: M D Gold, M E Greeenlees
Contact: Simone Simmons
Personal Assistant to the
Financial Director

Year Ends: 30 Apr '91
Donations: £41,000
Profit: £5,022,000
Turnover: £266,601,000

UK employees: n/a
Total employees: 855

Donations Policy: The company is currently trying to concentrate its support on charities associated with children.

☐ Goode Durrant plc
Industrial holding company

22 Buckingham Street,
London WC2N 6PU
071-782 0010

Ch: D J Kingsbury
Contact: D Henderson
Company Secretary

Year Ends: 30 Apr '92
Donations: £17,000
Profit: £5,139,000
Turnover: £178,560,000

UK employees: 1,338
Total employees: 1,338

Donations Policy: Head office budget is used mainly to support national charities. Subsidiary companies support charities local to their particular areas of operation. Preferred areas of support: children and youth, social welfare, medical and environment and heritage. Grants from £50 to £500.
Generally no support for fundraising events, brochure advertising, appeals from individuals, purely denominational appeals, local appeals not in areas of company presence or overseas projects.

☐ Goodhead Group plc
Printing & publishing

Launton Road,
Bicester,
Oxon OX6 7QZ
0869-253322

Ch: C R Rosser
Contact: Maureen Clegg
Secretary to the Chairman

Year Ends: 31 May '90
Donations: £19,000
Profit: £4,019,000
Turnover: £78,441,000

UK employees: n/.a
Total employees: 1,231

Donations Policy: Preference for local charities in the areas of company presence, but this does not exclude other charities/causes being considered.
Generally no support for circular appeals, fundraising events, purely denominational appeals or overseas projects.

☐ Gooding Investments
Investment holding company

27 Park Place,
Cardiff CF1 3BA
0222-390191

Ch: A J Gooding
Contact: Mrs W Robinson
Executive Assistant

Year Ends: 31 Dec '88
Donations: £21,000
Profit: £1,848,000
Turnover: £42,165,000

UK employees: n/a
Total employees: 552

Donations Policy: Preference for Welsh-based charities.

☐ Goodyear Great Britain Ltd
Tyres & rubber products

Stafford Road,
Bushbury,
Wolverhampton,
West Midlands WV10 6DH
0902-22321

Ch: J W Richardson
Contact: David Clayton
Public Relations Manager

Year Ends: 31 Dec '90
Donations: £4,175
Profit: £7,833,000
Turnover: £380,887,000

UK employees: n/a
Total employees: 5,660

Donations Policy: Preference for local charities in the areas of company presence. Preferred areas of support: children and youth, social welfare, education, environment and heritage.
Generally no support for circular appeals, fundraising events, brochure advertising, appeals from individuals or purely denominational appeals.

☐ Gordon Meats (Smithfield) Ltd
Meat wholesalers

230 Central Meat Markets,
Smithfield,
London EC1A 9LH
071-236 6286

MD: P F Jackson
Contact: Gordon Hogg

Year Ends: 5 Apr '90
Donations: n/a
Profit: £1,855,000
Turnover: £105,077,000

UK employees: n/a
Total employees: 563

☐ GR (Holdings) plc
Fur processing, garments

5th Floor,
54 Jermyn Street,
London SW1Y 6LX
071-408 1747

Ch: A D Stalbow
Contact: Simon Reiss
Director

Year Ends: 30 Jun '91
Donations: £29,462
Profit: £1,619,000
Turnover: £6,187,000

UK employees: n/a
Total employees: 265

Donations Policy: The company supports individuals and organisations concerned with sick, elderly, disabled and disadvantaged people.

☐ W R Grace Ltd
Manufacture of chemical products

Northdale House,
North Circular Road,
London NW10 7UH
081-965 0611

Ch: P R Johnston
Contact: R E Green
Chief Financial Officer

Year Ends: 31 Dec '90
Donations: £10,263
Profit: £7,530,000
Turnover: £161,698,000

UK employees: n/a
Total employees: 1,682

● **Alphabetical listing** Please read page 6

Name/Address	Officers	Financial Information	Other Information

☐ Grampian Country Food Group Ltd
Farming & rearing poultry

White Myers,
Mastrick,
Aberdeen AB2 6HT
0224-662040

Ch: A J Duncan
Contact: John Flett
General Manager

Year Ends: 31 May '90
Donations: £4,135
Profit: £8,058,000
Turnover: £105,616,000

UK employees: n/a
Total employees: 1,489

☐ Grampian Holdings plc
Transport, retail, sports goods, pharmaceuticals

Stag House,
Castlebank Street,
Glasgow G11 6DY
041-357 2000

Ch: W Y Hughes
Contact: W B G Roy
Company Secretary

Year Ends: 31 Dec '91
Donations: £44,000
Profit: £11,154,000
Turnover: £142,832,000

UK employees: n/a
Total employees: 2,692

% Club

Donations Policy: Preference for local charities in the areas of company presence and charities in which a member of staff is involved. Preferred areas of support: children and youth, social welfare, medical, education, recreation, and enterprise/training. Grants to national organisations from £250 to £5,000. Grants to local organisations from £100 to £2,000.
No grants for fundraising events; advertising in charity brochures; purely denominational (religious) appeals.

☐ Grampian Television plc
Television programme contractors

Queen's Cross,
Aberdeen AB9 2XJ
0224-646464

Ch: Douglas Hardie
CE: Donald H Waters
Contact: Graham Good
Director of Finance & Company Secretary

Year Ends: 29 Feb '92
Donations: £45,212
Profit: £3,180,000
Turnover: £20,411,000

UK employees: n/a
Total employees: 190

Donations Policy: To support organisations and individuals within the north of Scotland transmission area. Preference is given to the arts and areas relating to the broadcasting industry. Preference also for children and youth, environment and heritage and enterprise/training. Grants from £50 to £100. Donations include £36,393 to the arts and sciences and £8,819 to other charities.
Generally no support for circular appeals, brochure advertising, purely denominational appeals, local appeals not in areas of company presence, political appeals, large national appeals or overseas projects.

☐ Granada Group plc
Entertainments

36 Golden Square,
London W1R 4AH
071-734 8080

Ch: A Bernstein
CE: G Robinson
Contact: G Parrott
Group Secretary

Year Ends: 30 Sep '91
Donations: £400,000
Profit: £56,900,000
Turnover: £1,392,300,000

UK employees: n/a
Total employees: 21,097

ABSA

Donations Policy: Operating companies are encouraged to budget for contributions to charities relevant either to their own operations or the geographical areas in which they operate. Preferred areas of support: children and youth, medical, education, environment and heritage and the arts.
At group level the major initiative for 1991 was the Granada Wheel Appeal, which raised £1.4 million for a number of charities. In addition, the 1990 ITV Telethon included a major contribution of staff time and resources raising over £1.7 million in the Granada region for north west charities.
Generally no support for circular appeals, fundraising events, advertising in charity brochures, appeals from individuals, purely denominational (religious) appeals, local appeals not in areas of company presence or overseas projects.

☐ Grand Metropolitan plc
Food, drink, retailing

20 St James's Square,
London SW1Y 4RR
071-321 6000

Ch: Sir Allen Sheppard
MD: I Martin
Contact: T J Coleman
Trustee & Secretary, Grand Metropolitan Charitable Trust

Year Ends: 30 Sep '91
Donations: £4,036,000
Profit: £963,000,000
Turnover: £8,748,000,000

UK employees: n/a
Total employees: 98,181

% Club, BitC, ABSA

Donations Policy: The trustees review annually the core charitable areas on behalf of the Group. Support is focussed currently in three areas: education and training, special needs, and inner city regeneration. Favourable consideration is also given to local charities in the areas of company presence, appeals relevant to company business and charities connected with important contacts for the Group (eg. customers, suppliers). Support is also given to training or education programmes of particular benefit to industry and provision of positive help in areas such as unemployment. Grants to national organisations from £1,000 to £100,000. Grants to local organisations from £100 to £5,000.
Appeals should be addressed to the contact at 64-65 North Road, Brighton BN1 1YD.
Total UK contributions in 1991 were £6,000,000 and world-wide donations were £18,000,000.
No response to circular appeals.

☐ William Grant & Sons Ltd
Distillers of scotch whisky

Glenfiddich Distillery,
Dufftown,
Keith,
Banffshire AB55 4DH
0340-20373

Ch: A G Gordon
Contact: Karen Ambrose
Public Relations Manager

Year Ends: 27 Dec '90
Donations: £14,025
Profit: £28,000,000
Turnover: £160,313,000

UK employees: n/a
Total employees: 962

Donations Policy: Preference for local charities across a broad spectrum of causes.
Large national appeals and brochure advertising not generally supported. Glossy brochures not favourably regarded.

Please read page 6 — Alphabetical listing

Name/Address	Officers	Financial Information	Other Information

Graseby plc
Precision instruments, medical electronics

Lynton House,
7-12 Tavistock Square,
London WC1H 9LT
071-383 3060

Ch: J B H Jackson
CE: P J Lester
Contact: S Glick
Company Secretary

Year Ends: 31 Dec '91
Donations: £3,000
Profit: £10,314,000
Turnover: £107,273,000

UK employees: n/a
Total employees: 1,903

Donations Policy: Preference for local charities in areas where the company operates and appeals relevant to company business. Preference for children and youth; medical; education; environment/heritage; enterprise/training. Grants from £50 to £250.
No grants for fundraising events; advertising in charity brochures; appeals from individuals; purely denominational (religious) appeals; local appeals not in areas of company presence; large national appeals; overseas projects.

Great Portland Estates plc
Property development & investment

Knighton House,
56 Mortimer Street,
London W1N 8BD
071-580 3040

Ch: Richard Peskin
Contact: Sally Maclaren
Secretary to the Chairman

Year Ends: 31 Mar '92
Donations: £59,914
Profit: £33,910,000
Turnover: n/a

UK employees: n/a
Total employees: 10

Donations Policy: Support for 'deserving causes'. No real preferences, apart from housing/homelessness (eg. support for Shelter), which is appropriate for a property company. All donations are made through the Charities Aid Foundation.

Great Southern Group plc
Funeral services

Farringdon House,
East Grinstead,
Sussex RH19 1EW
0342-327755

Contact: E N Spencer
Chief Executive

Year Ends: 31 Dec '91
Donations: £6,650
Profit: £4,676,000
Turnover: £27,733,000

UK employees: n/a
Total employees: 989

Donations Policy: Preference for local charities in areas where the company operates, appeals relevant to company business and charities in which a member of company staff is involved. Preference for children and youth; medical; education; arts. Grants to national organisations from £25 to £100. Grants to local organisations from £25 to £500.
No grants for advertising in charity brochures; appeals from individuals; local appeals not in areas of company presence; overseas projects.
Total giving in 1992 is likely to exceed £50,000 due to "underwritten" efforts by staff and gifts from associated funds.

Great Universal Stores plc
Stores & mail order

18-22 The Haymarket,
London SW1Y 4DQ
071-636 4080

Ch: Lord Wolfson of Marylebone
Contact: Dr Barbara Rashbass
Director of Wolfson Foundation

Year Ends: 31 Mar '91
Donations: £53,000
Profit: £431,300,000
Turnover: £2,522,900,000

UK employees: n/a
Total employees: 27,753

Donations Policy: By far the major part of the company's charitable donations are made through the Wolfson Foundation (see Guide to the Major Trusts). Preferred areas of support: children and youth, medical, education and the arts.
Generally no support for circular appeals, fundraising events, advertising in charity brochures, appeals from individuals, purely denominational appeals.

Greenalls Group plc
Owners & managers of public houses, hotels & off-licences

Wilderspool Brewery,
Warrington,
Cheshire WA4 6RH
0925-51234

Ch: C J B Hatton
MD: A G Thomas
Contact: A W A Spiegelberg
Company Secretary

Year Ends: 27 Sep '91
Donations: £51,713
Profit: £64,141,000
Turnover: £471,453,000

UK employees: n/a
Total employees: 16,874

Donations Policy: The company seeks to serve the community in the main areas where its employees live and work, particularly in the North West.

Greene King plc
Brewers, maltsters, wine & spirit merchants

Westgate Brewery,
Bury St Edmunds,
Suffolk IP33 1QT
0284-763222

Ch: S J B Redman
MD: T J W Bridge
Contact: Mark Hunt
Public Relations Manager

Year Ends: 5 May '91
Donations: £19,867
Profit: £22,057,000
Turnover: £126,259,000

UK employees: n/a
Total employees: 1,337

Donations Policy: We have been unable to obtain a donations policy.

Greggs plc
Bakers

1 Lambton Road,
Jesmond,
Newcastle-upon-Tyne
NE2 4RX
091-281 7721

Ch: I D Gregg
MD: M J Darrington
Contact: Felicity Gregg
Charity Administrator

Year Ends: 30 Dec '91
Donations: £44,808
Profit: £6,074,000
Turnover: £95,540,000

UK employees: n/a
Total employees: 5,639

Donations Policy: The company has recently set up a charitable trust, through which the company's donations are made. Support is given only to causes in the Tyne & Wear area. Larger grants are made twice a year, smaller grants can be considered at other times. The separate divisions of the company have their own charity committees supporting causes local to their area of operation.
In addition to the figure given above, the company donated £28,350 to the Keep Sunday Special campaign.
No sponsorship is undertaken.

● **Alphabetical listing** Please read page 6

Name/Address	Officers	Financial Information	Other Information

☐ Grey Communications Group Ltd
Advertising, property management & travel agents

215-227 Great Portland Street, London W1N 5HD
071-636 3399

Contact: Lynne Robertson, Personal Assistant to the Managing Director

Year Ends: 30 Sep '90
Donations: £36,065
Profit: £262,000
Turnover: £163,242,000

UK employees: n/a
Total employees: 573

Donations Policy: No particular preferences, but the company does not support the same charity two years running. Grants range from £200 to £1,500.

☐ Greycoat plc
Property investment & development

Leconfield House, Curzon Street, London W1Y 8AS
071-491 8688

Ch: Geoffrey Wilson
MD: R Spinney, P Thornton
Contact: Norman Brown, Company Secretary

Year Ends: 31 Mar '91
Donations: £89,282
Profit: (£38,504,000)
Turnover: £34,354,000

UK employees: n/a
Total employees: 69

% Club

Donations Policy: Preference for children and youth; social welfare; environment/heritage.
No grants for fundraising events; advertising in charity brochures; appeals from individuals; purely denominational (religious) appeals; local appeals not in areas of company presence; large national appeals; overseas projects. No response to circular appeals.

☐ Grosvenor Grain & Feed Co Ltd
Animal feed products

Grosvenor House, Station Approach, Meols, Wirral L47 8XA
051-632 5951

Ch: G H Alcock
MD: P Harris
Contact: R Jones, Director

Year Ends: 31 Mar '91
Donations: n/a
Profit: £550,000
Turnover: £95,822,000

UK employees: n/a
Total employees: n/a

☐ Guardian & Manchester Evening News plc
Newspaper & magazine publishers

164 Deansgate, Manchester M60 2RR
061-832 7200

Ch: H J Roche
Contact: A V Townsend, Company Secretary

Year Ends: 30 Mar '92
Donations: £346,000
Profit: £19,203,000
Turnover: £184,875,000

UK employees: n/a
Total employees: 3,088

Donations Policy: The company covenants its donations to a number of charities. Smaller appeals are considered every six months, when about 10 appeals receive donations of £50 to £200.
No support for political appeals.
Appeals sent directly to individual papers are dealt with separately.

☐ Guardian Royal Exchange plc
Insurance

Royal Exchange, London EC3V 3LS
071-283 7101

Ch: C E A Hambro
MD: S A Hopkins
Contact: A Wilkins, Appeals Secretary

Year Ends: 31 Dec '91
Donations: £266,649
Profit: (£210,000,000)
Turnover: n/a

UK employees: 8,697
Total employees: n/a

% Club, BitC, ABSA

Donations Policy: The main areas of charitable support are social welfare, community services and health, medical care and the arts.
Preference is given to national organisations with appeals from local organisations only considered where the company has a major presence (ie. London, Ipswich, Lytham, Edinburgh). All applications should be made to head office.
Typically grants range from £500 to £1,000.
No support for circular appeals, fundraising events, appeals from individuals, purely denominational (religious) appeals, local appeals not in areas of company presence or overseas projects.

☐ Guinness Mahon Holdings plc
Banking

32 St Mary at Hill, London EC3P 3AJ
071-623 9333

Ch: Geoffrey Bell
Contact: Mrs Sue Watson, Charitable Officer

Year Ends: 30 Sep '90
Donations: £27,338
Profit: (£3,900,000)
Turnover: n/a

UK employees: 500
Total employees: n/a

Donations Policy: Preference for local charities in London and the South East.

☐ Guinness plc
Brewers & distillers

39 Portman Square, London W1H 9HB
071-486 0288

Ch: Sir Anthony Tennant
MD: A A Greener
Contact: Chris Davidson, Public Affairs Director

Year Ends: 31 Dec '91
Donations: £2,662,000
Profit: £956,000,000
Turnover: £4,067,000,000

UK employees: n/a
Total employees: 23,027

% Club, BitC, ABSA

Donations Policy: Support is given to registered charities only. Preference for charities for which employees raise money. The company operates two "employee matching" schemes. Preference for children and youth; social welfare; medical; education; environment/heritage; arts; enterprise/training.
No grants for appeals from individuals or local appeals not in areas of company presence.

Please read page 6 — Alphabetical listing

Name/Address	Officers	Financial Information	Other Information

Gulf Oil (Great Britain) Ltd
Refining & distribution of petroleum products

The Quadrangle,
Imperial Square,
Cheltenham GL50 1TF
0242-225225

MD: D L Setchell
Contact: G M Wareing
Public Affairs Manager

Year Ends: 31 Dec '90
Donations: n/a
Profit: £79,000,000
Turnover: £720,705,000

UK employees: 942
Total employees: n/a

Donations Policy: Limited budget available, used to support local charities in the Cheltenham area. Employees can request donations for charities in which they are involved. Preference for children and youth, medical, environment and heritage. Grants from £50 to £100. Generally no support for circular appeals, fundraising events, brochure advertising, appeals from individuals, purely denominational appeals, local appeals not in areas of company presence, large national appeals or overseas projects.

Haden MacLellan Holdings plc
Manufacture, distribution & automated systems

Haleworth House,
Tite Hill,
Egham,
Surrey TW20 0LT
0784-439791

Ch: H Cottam
CE: M Hawley
Contact: Rob Durrant
Assistant Company Secretary

Year Ends: 31 Dec '91
Donations: £13,212
Profit: £14,619,000
Turnover: £352,176,000

UK employees: n/a
Total employees: 5,323

Donations Policy: Charitable donations are undertaken by the company's numerous UK and overseas subsidiaries. The company does not wish to receive any requests at head office.

Halifax Building Society
Building society

Trinity Road,
Halifax,
West Yorkshire HX1 2RG
0422-333333

Ch: Jon Foulds
CE: Jim Birrell
Contact: Manager
Group Community Affairs

Year Ends: 31 Jan '92
Donations: £592,815
Profit: £628,000,000
Turnover: n/a

UK employees: n/a
Total employees: 18,021

BitC

Donations Policy: Donations are made mainly on a local basis in areas of company presence and to charities in which a member of staff is involved. Typical grants range from £500 to £5,000. Support is given to children and youth, social welfare, medical, education, environment, enterprise/training, homelessness, elderly and disabled people.
Total community contributions in 1991 were £1,048,815.
No support for circular appeals, fundraising events, brochure advertising, individuals, purely denominational appeals, political appeals, military appeals, animal welfare, academic research, sporting appeals, large national appeals or overseas projects.

Hall & Woodhouse Ltd
Brewers

The Brewery,
Blandford St Mary,
Dorset DT11 9LS
0258-452141

Ch: J M Woodhouse
MD: T D M Hart
Contact: B Miller
Public Relations Manager

Year Ends: 31 Jan '88
Donations: £7,057
Profit: £4,276,000
Turnover: £56,912,000

UK employees: n/a
Total employees: 1,022

Donations Policy: The company prefers to give to local charities in areas of company presence and to appeals relevant to its business. No response to circular appeals. No grants for advertising in charity brochures; appeals from individuals; purely denominational (religious) appeals; local appeals not in areas of company presence; large national appeals.

Hall Engineering (Holdings) plc
General engineering

Harlescott Lane,
Shrewsbury SY1 3AS
0743-235541

Ch: R N C Hall
MD: B E W Hinkins
Contact: M A Youens
Assistant Group Secretary

Year Ends: 31 Dec '91
Donations: £4,000
Profit: £5,066,000
Turnover: £147,420,000

UK employees: n/a
Total employees: 1,903

Donations Policy: Preference for local charities in the areas of company presence and appeals relevant to company business. Preferred areas of support: medical, environment and heritage.
Generally no support for circular appeals, brochure advertising, purely denominational appeals, local appeals not in areas of company presence or overseas projects.

James Hall & Co (Holdings) Ltd
Wholesale grocers & provision merchants

89-91 Blackpool Road,
Riddleton,
Preston PR2 6DY
0772-705555

Ch: W S Hall
MD: I S W Hall, A N Hall
Contact: Financial Director

Year Ends: 21 Mar '91
Donations: n/a
Profit: £3,772,000
Turnover: £102,627,000

UK employees: n/a
Total employees: 349

Halliburton Holdings Ltd
Construction, oil & gas services

Halliburton House,
3 Putney Bridge Approach,
London SW6 3JD
071-371 5500

Contact: Bob Pollock
Regional Manager

Year Ends: 31 Dec '90
Donations: £48,375
Profit: £9,432,000
Turnover: £413,720,000

UK employees: n/a
Total employees: 5,819

Donations Policy: Head office in US decides all company donations. No unsolicited appeals.

Hallmark Cards (Holdings) Ltd
Manufacture & sale of greetings cards

Station Road,
Henley-on-Thames,
Oxon RG9 1LQ
0491-578383

Ch: K F Wheal
Contact: Moira MacKechnie
Personnel Manager

Year Ends: 31 Dec '88
Donations: £5,297
Profit: £7,296,000
Turnover: £81,335,000

UK employees: n/a
Total employees: 1,555

● **Alphabetical listing**   Please read page 6

Name/Address	Officers	Financial Information	Other Information

☐ Hambro Countrywide plc
Estate agencies & financial services

Queensgate,
1 Myrtle Road,
Brentwood,
Essex CM14 5EG
0277-264466

Ch: C H Sporborg
MD: J M May, H D Hill
Contact: Mrs Lock
Group Public Relations Manager

Year Ends: 31 Dec '91
Donations: £5,000
Profit: £6,489,000
Turnover: £93,233,000

UK employees: n/a
Total employees: 4,075

☐ Hambros plc
Banking & finance

41 Tower Hill,
London EC3N 4HA
071-480 5000

Ch: C E A Hambro
Contact: P L Patrick
Company Secretary

Year Ends: 31 Mar '91
Donations: £232,000 (1992)
Profit: £80,411,000
Turnover: n/a

UK employees: 5,950
Total employees: 7,137

BitC

Donations Policy: Most donations are made by head office. Preference for children and youth, health and medical care, education, environment/heritage and the arts. Preference also for local charities in areas of company presence and projects in which a member of staff is involved. Grants to national organisations from £500 to £5,000. Grants to local organisations from £50 to £500. Local appeals should be sent to the appropriate regional office.
Corporate sponsorship proposals to Mrs L Orman, Corporate Communications Manager.
No support for circular appeals, appeals from individuals, purely denominational (religious) appeals or local appeals not in areas of company presence.

☐ Hammerson Property Investment & Development
Property investment

100 Park Lane,
London W1Y 4AR
071-629 9494

Ch: Sydney Mason
MD: John Parry
Contact: Christopher Smith
Head of Corporate Public Relations

Year Ends: 31 Dec '91
Donations: £58,714
Profit: £55,500,000
Turnover: n/a

UK employees: n/a
Total employees: 378

ABSA

Donations Policy: Preference for appeals in some way related to company employees, customers or clients. Each application is considered on its merits, but about 95% of applications will be unsuccessful.

☐ Hampson Industries plc
Engineering & manufacturing

Hampson Court,
77 Birmingham Road,
West Bromwich,
West Midlands B70 6PY
021-553 4681

Ch: J M Wardle
MD: I R Walker
Contact: C J Clayton
Financial Director

Year Ends: 31 Mar '92
Donations: £9,380
Profit: £4,056,000
Turnover: £73,159,000

UK employees: n/a
Total employees: 2,421

☐ Hanson plc
Consumer products

1 Grosvenor Place,
London SW1X 7JH
071-245 1245

Ch: Lord Hanson
CE: D C Bonham
Contact: Miss Nicola J Blyth
Benefits Manager

Year Ends: 30 Sep '91
Donations: £786,000
Profit: £1,319,000,000
Turnover: £7,691,000,000

UK employees: n/a
Total employees: 70,000

BitC, ABSA

Donations Policy: Support is concentrated on major educational and medical projects; very little money is available for general appeals. Generally no support for circular appeals, fundraising events, brochure advertising or appeals from individuals.

☐ Harmondsworth Investments Ltd
Construction, management & interior contracting

Manor Court,
High Street,
Harmondsworth,
Middlesex UB7 0AQ
081-759 3331

Ch: A M Davies
Contact: J C Watts
Chief Executive

Year Ends: 31 Dec '90
Donations: £9,293
Profit: £1,255,000
Turnover: £253,248,000

UK employees: n/a
Total employees: 1,703

☐ Harmony Leisure Group plc
Management of restaurants, public houses, hotels

24 Craven Terrace,
Lancaster Gate,
London W2 2QH
071-258 3836

Ch: Sir Stanley Grinstead
Contact: Stanley Lever
Managing Director

Year Ends: 31 Mar '89
Donations: £8,936
Profit: £128,000
Turnover: £8,172,000

UK employees: n/a
Total employees: 337

☐ Harper Collins Publishers
Publishers

PO Box 1,
Glasgow G4 0NB
041-772 3200

Ch: F I Chapman
MD: G Craig
Contact: D Sloman

Year Ends: 27 Dec '87
Donations: £28,000
Profit: £24,082,000
Turnover: £162,680,000

UK employees: n/a
Total employees: 3,083

Donations Policy: Preference for local appeals and those in which member of staff is involved.
No support for non-charities, advertising in charity brochures, fundraising events, appeals from individuals, local appeals not in areas of company presence or overseas projects.
Total community contributions in 1987 were £33,085.

Please read page 6 — Alphabetical listing

Name/Address	Officers	Financial Information	Other Information

☐ Philip Harris Holdings Ltd

Lynn Lane,
Shenstone,
Staffordshire WS14 0EE
0543-480077

Ch: B J F Haller
MD: D C Macey, D Linney
Contact: Bob Young
Administration & Personnel Manager

Year Ends: 31 Mar '89
Donations: £3,356
Profit: £911,000
Turnover: £65,531,000

Education & medical equipment suppliers

UK employees: n/a
Total employees: 589

Donations Policy: "Limited resources are given to what are considered the most deserving cases". A preference for local charities and education.

☐ T C Harrison Group Ltd

53-67 London Road,
Sheffield S2 4LD
0742-751515

Ch: E Harrison
MD: M Muscroft
Contact: See policy

Year Ends: 31 Dec '90
Donations: £15,305
Profit: £1,689,000
Turnover: £151,100,000

Ford main dealers

UK employees: n/a
Total employees: 1,103

Donations Policy: All charitable donations are made through the South Yorkshire Foundation.
Direct appeals to the company should not be made.

☐ Harrisons & Crosfield plc

One Great Tower Street,
London EC3R 5AH
071-711 1400

Ch: J N Maltby
CE: G W Paul
Contact: Company Secretary

Year Ends: 31 Dec '91
Donations: £174,286
Profit: £71,200,000
Turnover: £1,825,000,000

Eastern merchants, exporters & importers

UK employees: n/a
Total employees: 33,047

BitC

Donations Policy: Donations are channelled through the Harrisons & Crosfield Charitable Trust. The trust's policy is to support charities assisting disadvantaged people. Grants are mostly one-off or recurrent for up to four years. There are also some annual donations. Preference is given to charities in which a member of staff is involved.
Applications are not invited from charities and not considered from individuals. Local appeals and requests for advertising in souvenir brochures are rarely considered. Telephone or written requests from professional fundraisers are discouraged.

☐ Hartons Group plc

Snaithing Grange,
Snaithing Lane,
Sheffield S10 3LF
0742-306500

Ch: C P Astin
Contact: Mrs Watson
Marketing Department

Year Ends: 31 Dec '91
Donations: n/a
Profit: (£5,359,000)
Turnover: £92,871,000

Plastics, consumer products

UK employees: n/a
Total employees: 668

Donations Policy: Preference for local charities in the areas of company presence and appeals relevant to company business. Preferred areas of support: children and youth, social welfare and medical. Grants to national organisations from £50 to £250. Grants to local organisations from £25 to £100. Charitable donations in 1989 were £11,565 which included an exceptional donation of £10,000 to the Hillsborough disaster fund.
Generally no support for appeals from individuals, purely denominational appeals, local appeals not in areas of company presence or overseas projects.

☐ Hartstone Group plc

1 St Andrew's Court,
Wellington Street,
Thame,
Oxfordshire OX9 3GG
0844-261544

Ch: S P Barker
Contact: J Cronk
Group Company Secretary

Year Ends: 31 Mar '92
Donations: £24,712
Profit: £22,064,000
Turnover: £237,790,000

Clothing, handbags, leathergoods

UK employees: 1,000
Total employees: 4,500

Donations Policy: Most donations are made on a specific planned basis. This is supplemented by small ad hoc donations, particularly to charities in areas where the company operates and appeals relevant to company business.
Normally no response to circular appeals.

☐ Hartwell plc

Seacourt Tower,
West Way,
Oxford OX2 0JG
0865-204300

Contact: J Y Wei
Chief Executive

Year Ends: 30 Nov '90
Donations: £16,046 (1991)
Profit: £8,896,000
Turnover: £547,718,000

Vehicle distribution sales & service

UK employees: n/a
Total employees: 3,578

Donations Policy: Preference for organisations supporting underprivileged children, senior citizens, physically disabled people and deserving medical research. Preference also given to charities in which members of staff are involved, in particular, locally and relevant to business.
Generally no support for appeals from individuals, as well as the arts and promotions.

☐ Haslemere Estates plc

4 Carlos Place,
Mayfair,
London W1Y 5AE
071-629 1105

MD: P R van Romunde
Contact: Miss H Bostock
Office Manageress

Year Ends: 31 Dec '91
Donations: £25,000
Profit: n/a
Turnover: n/a

Property development

UK employees: 28
Total employees: 28

Donations Policy: The company supports children in need in Central London. Grants to local and national organisations range from £5,000 to £10,000.
No response to circular appeals. No grants for fundraising events; advertising in charity brochures; appeals from individuals; purely denominational (religious) appeals; local appeals not in areas of company presence; large national appeals; overseas projects.

• **Alphabetical listing**   Please read page 6

Name/Address   *Officers*   *Financial Information*   *Other Information*

☐ Haverhill Meat Products Ltd
                                                                                                    Bacon curing

Little Wratting,   *Ch:* Sir Roy Griffiths   *Year Ends:* 17 Feb '91   *UK employees:* n/a
Haverhill,   *MD:* Paul Collins   *Donations:* £13,814   *Total employees:* 1,855
Suffolk   CB9 7TD   *Contact:* Don Everitt   *Profit:* £13,042,000
0440-704444   Company Secretary   *Turnover:* £112,557,000

Donations Policy: Preference for local charities in the areas of company presence. Grants to local organisations from £25 to £1,000. Generally no support for circular appeals, fundraising events, purely denominational (religious) appeals, local appeals not in areas of company presence, large national appeals or overseas projects.

☐ Hawker Siddeley Group plc
                                                            Mechanical & electrical engineering & metals

18 St James's Square,   *Ch:* Sir Peter Baxendell   *Year Ends:* 31 Dec '90   *UK employees:* 21,800
London   SW1Y 4LJ   *CE:* A K Watkins   *Donations:* £171,300   *Total employees:* 44,600
071-627 7685   *Contact:* R J Stone   *Profit:* £140,400,000
                                    Secretary to the Charities *Turnover:* £2,178,000,000
                                    Committee

Donations Policy: Direct giving preferred rather than support for fundraising events. There is a local bias but national appeals are also supported. Preference is given to projects in which a member of staff is involved.

☐ Haymills Holdings Ltd
                                                            Building, civil engineering, property development

Empire House,   *Ch:* J Woodhouse   *Year Ends:* 31 Mar '91   *UK employees:* n/a
Hanger Green,   *Contact:* I Ferris   *Donations:* £3,185   *Total employees:* 882
London   W5 3BD   Financial Director   *Profit:* £3,034,000
081-997 5602   *Turnover:* £100,060,000

☐ Hays plc
                                                                                    Business & transport services

Hays House,   *Ch:* R E Frost   *Year Ends:* 30 Jun '91   *UK employees:* n/a
Millmead,   *Contact:* John Sapwell   *Donations:* £24,000   *Total employees:* 5,193
Guildford,   Assistant Company Secretary *Profit:* £56,825,000
Surrey   GU2 5HJ   *Turnover:* £668,481,000
0483-302203

Donations Policy: Generally supports small local charities which have no access to national funds. Particular emphasis is given to charities which provide for the elderly and the very young, particularly disability charities. National support is given to the arts. Grants to national organisations, where given, ranges from £250 to £2,500. Grants to local organisations from £50 to £500.
Generally no support for circular appeals, advertising in charity brochures, purely denominational (religious) appeals, local appeals not in areas of company presence, large national appeals or overseas projects.

☐ Hazlewood Foods plc
                                                                                Manufacture of sauces & condiments

Empire Works,   *Ch:* P E Barr   *Year Ends:* 31 Mar '92   *UK employees:* n/a
Rowditch,   *CE:* C J Ball   *Donations:* £38,884   *Total employees:* 7,898
Derby   DE1 1NB   *Contact:* K Higginson   *Profit:* £51,300,000
0332-295295   Company Secretary   *Turnover:* £632,400,000

☐ Healds Foods Ltd
                                                                                    Wholesale & retail dairymen

2 Broadway,   *MD:* A D Swallow   *Year Ends:* 1 Oct '88   *UK employees:* n/a
Hyde,   *Contact:* Mrs Alison Price   *Donations:* £1,802   *Total employees:* 958
Cheshire   SK14 4QQ   Sales & Marketing Co-ordinator *Profit:* £3,749,000
061-368 1332   *Turnover:* £93,929,000

☐ Healey & Baker
                                                                            Surveyors, auctioneers & estate agents

29 St George Street,   *Contact:* Paul Orchard-Lisle *Year Ends:* 30 Apr '92   *UK employees:* 400
London   W1A 3BG   Senior Partner   *Donations:* £30,000   *Total employees:* 500
071 629 9292   *Profit:* n/a
                                                              Turnover: n/a   % Club, BitC

Donations Policy: The company's charitable trust supports a wide variety of causes both local and national, but generally where there is some link to the firm's work or its Partners' particular interests.
On going commitments are not generally entertained. No response to circular appeals.

☐ Heart of England Building Society
                                                                                                Building society

Olympus Avenue,   *Ch:* E R Jeynes   *Year Ends:* 29 Feb '92   *UK employees:* n/a
Tachbrook Park,   *CE:* M O Travis   *Donations:* n/a   *Total employees:* 468
Warwick   CV34 6NQ   *Contact:* Mrs N Curwood   *Profit:* £2,300,000
0926-496111   Public Relations Manager *Turnover:* n/a

Donations Policy: The Society's policy is not to make charitable or political donations.
The society does however, participate in and support a large number of local and regional fundraising activities.

Please read page 6 — Alphabetical listing

Name/Address	Officers	Financial Information	Other Information

☐ C E Heath plc

Insurance brokers, underwriting agents

133 Houndsditch,
London EC3A 7AH
071-234 4000

Ch: M H Kier
CE: P E Presland
Contact: N Rowe
Company Secretary

Year Ends: 31 Mar '92
Donations: £80,300
Profit: £19,106,000
Turnover: £140,756,000

UK employees: n/a
Total employees: 3,905

Donations Policy: Preference for capital and medical research projects aimed at the relief of human suffering. Grants range from £1,000 to £2,000.
No grants for appeals from individuals; purely denominational (religious) appeals; local appeals not in areas of company presence.

☐ Hecht, Heyworth & Alcan Ltd

Rubber, cocoa & edible nuts dealers

Myrtil House,
70 Clifton Street,
London EC2A 4SP
071-377 8773

MD: A M Porter
Contact: Finance Director

Year Ends: 31 Dec '90
Donations: £760
Profit: £3,176,000
Turnover: £102,865,000

UK employees: n/a
Total employees: 53

☐ Heidelberg Graphic Equipment Ltd

Sale of printing machinery

69-76 High Street,
Brentford,
Middlesex TW8 0AA
081-560 4100

Ch: W P Zimmermann
Contact: V R Cooper
Company Secretary

Year Ends: 31 Mar '91
Donations: £11,902
Profit: £1,220,000
Turnover: £94,115,000

UK employees: n/a
Total employees: 432

% Club

Donations Policy: Due to a significant fall in profits, the company has changed the formula of its charitable contributions from 0.5% to 1.5% of post-tax profits. The company also loans printing equipment to colleges and charities on a "peppercorn" rent basis.

☐ H J Heinz Company Ltd

Food manufacturers

Hayes Park,
Hayes,
Middlesex UB4 8AL
081-573 7757

Ch: A J F O'Reilly
MD: J F Hinch
Contact: Mrs Ann Banks
Donations Co-ordinator

Year Ends: 27 Apr '91
Donations: £131,000
Profit: £43,432,000
Turnover: £484,843,000

UK employees: n/a
Total employees: 4,117

BitC

Donations Policy: Donations are made by the Heinz Company Ltd Charitable Trust which confines its giving to purposes accepted in law as charitable. It gives priority to (a) projects in the local communities in which it operates; (b) support for medical aspects of nutrition and health, with particular emphasis on paediatrics; (c) projects connected with the food manufacturing industry. Grants to national organisations from £1,000 to £5,000. Grants to local organisations from £250 to £2,500.
Generally no support for circular appeals, advertising in charity brochures, purely denominational (religious) appeals, political causes, individuals undertaking educational/vocational studies or individuals/groups for sponsored events. No commercial sponsorship is undertaken.

☐ Henderson Administration Group plc

Investment advisory & management services

3 Finsbury Avenue,
London EC2M 2PA
071-638 5757

Ch: D M Backhouse
CE: B H B Wrey
Contact: Sue Ford
Secretary

Year Ends: 31 Mar '92
Donations: £61,000
Profit: £17,000,000
Turnover: n/a

UK employees: n/a
Total employees: 448

Donations Policy: Preference for local charities in the areas of company presence and charities in which a member of staff is involved. Support for charities concerned with people is preferred (ie. children and youth, social welfare, medical, education), though not to the exclusion of other causes. Grants to national and local organisations range from £100 to £1,000.
No circular appeals.

☐ Henderson Security Ltd

Sliding door gear manufacture, engineering

Unit 4,
Tannery Road,
High Wycombe,
Buckinghamshire HP13 7EQ
0494-450211

MD: W A Clark, T W Dodd
Contact: Audrey Payne
Secretary to the Managing Director

Year Ends: 28 Feb '87
Donations: £5,382
Profit: £4,424,000
Turnover: £86,908,000

UK employees: n/a
Total employees: 2,271

☐ Henlys Group plc

Motor vehicle manufacture & distribution

Henly House,
53 Theobold Street,
Borehamwood,
Hertfordshire WD6 4RT
081-207 3664

Ch: D H Matthews
MD: R W Wood
Contact: Mrs S L Sutton
Communications Officer (address below)

Year Ends: 31 Dec '91
Donations: £10,460
Profit: (£6,808,000)
Turnover: £334,380,000

UK employees: n/a
Total employees: 13,959

Donations Policy: The company encourages fundraising and sponsorship for charitable events largely through support given to its own employees engaged in activities targeted at local and national concerns. Preferred areas of support are social welfare, medical appeals, education and enterprise/training. Grants to national organisations range from £30 to £200, and to local organisations from £20 to £2,000.
No support for circular appeals, purely denominational appeals, brochure advertising, local appeals not in areas of company presence or overseas projects.
Appeals should be addressed to the contact at: Henlys Group plc, Cayton Low Road, Eastfield, Scarborough YO11 3BY.

● **Alphabetical listing**   Please read page 6

Name/Address   *Officers*   *Financial Information*   *Other Information*

☐ Hepworth plc
                                                                                 Manufacture of vitrified clay pipes

Tapton Park Road,   *Ch:* Professor R Smith   *Year Ends:* 31 Dec '91   *UK employees:* n/a
Sheffield S10 3FS   *CE:* J D Carter   *Donations:* £71,000   *Total employees:* 10,067
0742-306599   *Contact:* Company Secretary   *Profit:* £70,400,000
                                                                 Turnover: £661,300,000

Donations Policy: Support is concentrated on local charities and a very restricted number of selected projects of special interest to the company, especially children and youth, social welfare and education. Grants range from £50 to £100.
No response to circular appeals. No grants for fundraising events; advertising in charity brochures; appeals from individuals; purely denominational (religious) appeals; local appeals not in areas of company presence; large national appeals; overseas projects.

☐ Heron International plc
                                                                                 Garage operators, insurance, property

Heron House,   *Ch:* G M Ronson   *Year Ends:* 31 Mar '91   *UK employees:* n/a
19 Marylebone Road,   *Contact:* Morton Creeger   *Donations:* £5,329,475   *Total employees:* 2,271
London NW1 5JL   Executive Director, The Ronson   *Profit:* £17,500,000
071-486 4477   Foundation   *Turnover:* £537,500,000   % Club, BitC

Donations Policy: With the exception of advertising in charity brochures (£45,000) and secondment (£10,000), all donations are made through the Ronson Foundation. Through this, support is directed to charitable organisations which help people who are disadvantaged through environmental, social, mental or physical disability. Additionally, it offers some support in the areas of education and the arts.
Grants to national organisations from £25 to £375,000. Grants to local organisations from £10 to £1,000.
No support for individuals, funding deficits, expeditions or general appeals.
Please note: the charitable funds of both Heron International and the Ronson Foundations are fully committed. Directors of Heron and trustees of the foundation will not consider further applications during 1993 or 1994, following which the situation will be reviewed.

☐ Herring Baker Harris plc
                                                                                 Commercial estate agents, property advisers

26-28 Sackville Street,   *MD:* Peter E T Farrington   *Year Ends:* 30 Apr '88   *UK employees:* n/a
London W1X 2QL   *Contact:* Tony Mummery   *Donations:* £2,779   *Total employees:* n/a
071-734 8155   Company Secretary   *Profit:* n/a
                                                                 Turnover: n/a   ABSA

☐ Hertz (UK) Ltd
                                                                                                            Car hirers

Radnor House,   *Ch:* J G Astrand   *Year Ends:* 31 Dec '90   *UK employees:* n/a
1272 London Road,   *Contact:* Stephen Jones   *Donations:* n/a   *Total employees:* 1,236
Norbury,   Marketing Director   *Profit:* £648,000
London SW16 4DQ   *Turnover:* £125,110,000
081-679 1777

Donations Policy: To support a small number of charities which are selected annually. No other appeals are considered.

☐ Hewden Stuart plc
                                                                                                Plant hirers & sellers

135 Buchanan Street,   *Ch:* Sir Matthew Goodwin   *Year Ends:* 29 Jan '92   *UK employees:* n/a
Glasgow G1 2JA   *MD:* A F Findlay   *Donations:* £23,660   *Total employees:* 3,559
041-221 7331   *Contact:* Sir Matthew Goodwin   *Profit:* £15,047,000
                               Chairman   *Turnover:* £170,935,000   % Club

Donations Policy: Support for national charities and those which benefit employees (eg. health and welfare).

☐ Hewlett-Packard Ltd
                                                                                 Electronic apparatus manufacturers

Cain Road,   *Ch:* D A Baldwin   *Year Ends:* 31 Oct '90   *UK employees:* n/a
Bracknell,   *MD:* J T Golding   *Donations:* £87,000   *Total employees:* 4,339
Berkshire RG12 1HN   *Contact:* Lyn Worsfold   *Profit:* £8,969,000
0344-773100   *Turnover:* £650,459,000

Donations Policy: Charitable contributions are made to a wide range of organisations, with the main areas of support being local community-based charities (within a 25-mile radius of the company's factories) and selected national charities. Preference for charitable organisations in which staff are involved. Preferred areas of support: children and youth, social welfare, education, environment and heritage and enterprise/training.
Generally no support for advertising in charity brochures, appeals from individuals, purely denominational (religious) appeals, political appeals, or overseas projects.

☐ Heygate & Sons Ltd
                                                                                                Flour & provender milling

Bugbrooke Mills,   *Contact:* Robert Heygate   *Year Ends:* 26 Mar '88   *UK employees:* n/a
Northampton NN7 3UH   Chairman   *Donations:* £2,152   *Total employees:* 62
0604-830381   *Profit:* £1,000,000
                                                                 Turnover: £11,033,000   % Club

☐ Heywood Williams Group plc
                                                                                 Manufacture of building materials

Waverley,   *Ch:* R E Hinchliffe   *Year Ends:* 31 Dec '91   *UK employees:* n/a
Edgerton Road,   *Contact:* Mrs P White   *Donations:* £10,700   *Total employees:* 6,603
Huddersfield HD3 3AR   Secretary to the Chairman   *Profit:* £19,216,000
0484-435477   *Turnover:* £347,434,000

Donations Policy: The company has an annual covenant with the Huddersfield Common Good Trust in support of local charities.

Please read page 6 | Alphabetical listing ●

Name/Address	Officers	Financial Information	Other Information

☐ Hi-Tec Sports plc
Sports & leisure footwear

Aviation Way,
Southend-on-Sea,
Essex SS2 6GH
0702-541741

Ch: F van Wezel
MD: S Rogers
Contact: Colin Woolridge
Marketing Manager

Year Ends: 2 Feb '92
Donations: n/a
Profit: £9,061,000
Turnover: £127,826,000

UK employees: n/a
Total employees: 461

Donations Policy: No charitable donations figure is given in the company annual report.

☐ Hickson International plc
Chemical products manufacture

Weldon Road,
Castleford,
West Yorkshire WF10 2JT
0977-556565

Ch: Sir Gordon Jones
Contact: Beverley Walker
Personnel Administrator

Year Ends: 31 Dec '91
Donations: £38,000
Profit: £23,737,000
Turnover: £367,437,000

UK employees: n/a
Total employees: 3,516

Donations Policy: The company supports local charities associated with human suffering or occasionally the arts if directly relevant to company business.
No support for circular appeals, large national appeals, purely denominational (religious) appeals, fundraising events, brochure advertising, overseas projects, appeals from individuals.

☐ Higgs & Hill plc
Construction, property development

Crown House,
Kingston Road,
New Malden,
Surrey KT3 3ST
081-942 8921

Ch: Sir Brian Hill
CE: J A Theakston
Contact: Joy Balory
Assistant Group Secretary

Year Ends: 31 Dec '91
Donations: £39,500
Profit: £16,700,000
Turnover: £345,167,000

UK employees: n/a
Total employees: 1,830

Donations Policy: Donations are channelled to causes close to the company's business locations, appeals relevant to company business and charities in which a member of staff is involved. Preferred areas of support: social welfare, education and enterprise/training. Grants to national organisations from £50 to £1,000. Grants to local organisations from £50 to £250.
No support for circular appeals, fundraising events, appeals from individuals, purely denominational (religious) appeals or overseas projects.

☐ Highcroft Investment Trust plc
Financial trust

Lamarsh Road,
Botley Road,
Oxford OX2 0HZ
0865-791700

Contact: J C Kingerlee
Company Secretary

Year Ends: 31 Dec '88
Donations: £2,000 (1991)
Profit: £612,000
Turnover: n/a

UK employees: n/a
Total employees: 12

Donations Policy: The charities to be supported are selected at the Board meeting in May.
No direct approaches to the company are considered.

☐ Highland Distilleries Co plc
Malt whisky distillers

106 West Nile Street,
Glasgow G1 2QY
041-332 7511

Ch: J M Goodwin
MD: B G Ivory
Contact: Personnel & Administration
Manager

Year Ends: 31 Aug '91
Donations: £80,000
Profit: £28,164,000
Turnover: £163,368,000

UK employees: n/a
Total employees: 370

% Club

Donations Policy: The company supports a range of local charity and community activities particularly in the more remote areas where its distilleries are located. Support also for the arts, job creation, education opportunities for young people, inner city projects and research into alcohol abuse.

☐ Hillier Parker May & Rowden Ltd
Auctioneers & surveyors

77 Grosvenor Street,
London W1A 2BT
071-629 7666

Contact: John Swain
Partnership Secretary

Year Ends:
Donations: n/a
Profit: n/a
Turnover: n/a

UK employees: n/a
Total employees: n/a

% Club, BitC

Donations Policy: Donations to registered charities only which must meet one (or both) of two criteria: (a) the charitable initiatives are promoted by, involve, or are particularly related to the Firm's clients, partners and/or staff; (b) the charitable initiatives have a particular relevance to property and/or the environment. Individual donations are normally £250 although larger sums will be considered in special circumstances.

☐ Hillsdown Holdings plc
General traders

Hillsdown House,
32 Hampstead High Street,
London NW3 1QD
071-794 0677

Contact: Sir Harry Solomon
Chairman

Year Ends: 31 Dec '91
Donations: £355,000
Profit: £186,800,000
Turnover: £4,656,600,000

UK employees: n/a
Total employees: 48,652

% Club, ABSA

Donations Policy: Support is concentrated on medical research. Donations are made at the chairman's discretion. Subsidiaries have their own donations budgets.

● **Alphabetical listing**   Please read page 6

Name/Address	Officers	Financial Information	Other Information

☐ HiLo Manufacturing Ltd

Manufacture of pallet racking

Elmington Works,　　　　　　*Contact:* David Davies　　　　　*Year Ends:*　　　　　　　　　UK employees: n/a
130 Nathan Way,　　　　　　　　　　　　Managing Director　　*Donations:* n/a　　　　　　　Total employees: n/a
London SE28 0AU　　　　　　　　　　　　　　　　　　　　　　*Profit:* n/a
081-855 6000　　　　　　　　　　　　　　　　　　　　　　　　*Turnover:* n/a　　　　　　　　　　　　　　　　% Club

Donations Policy: Preference for charities in which a member of company staff is involved and local charities in areas where the company operates. The company gives about 5% of its pre-tax profit to the HiLo Community Trust. The trust is administered by a committee elected from the company's staff. Preference for children and youth; social welfare and education.
No grants for fundraising events; advertising in charity brochures; appeals from individuals; purely denominational (religious) appeals; local appeals not in areas of company presence; large national appeals; overseas projects. No response to circular appeals.

☐ Hitachi Consumer Products (UK) Ltd

Television manufacture

Hirwaun Industrial Estate,　　*Contact:* Christine Powell　　*Year Ends:* 31 Mar '91　　UK employees: n/a
Aberdare,　　　　　　　　　　　　　　Senior Personnel Manager　*Donations:* nil　　　　　　Total employees: 954
Mid-Glamorgan CF44 9UY　　　　　　　　　　　　　　　　　　*Profit:* £330,000
0685-811451　　　　　　　　　　　　　　　　　　　　　　　　*Turnover:* £102,390,000

☐ Hitachi Europe Ltd

Import & sale of electronic equipment

Whitebrook,　　　　　　　　　*Contact:* Kathleen Pritchard　　*Year Ends:* 31 Mar '91　　UK employees: n/a
Lower Cookham Road,　　　　　　　　Community Liaison Manager　*Donations:* £9,795　　　　Total employees: 583
Maidenhead SL6 8YA　　　　　　　　　　　　　　　　　　　　*Profit:* £3,256,000
0628-585000　　　　　　　　　　　　　　　　　　　　　　　　*Turnover:* £505,481,000

☐ Hitachi Sales (UK) Ltd

Electrical goods distribution & manufacture

Hitachi House,　　　　　　　　*MD:* T Nakayama　　　　　　　*Year Ends:* 31 Mar '91　　UK employees: n/a
Station Road,　　　　　　　　*Contact:* Jane Brownlie　　　*Donations:* £12,379　　　Total employees: 213
Hayes,　　　　　　　　　　　　　　Secretary to the Deputy Managing　*Profit:* £632,000
Middlesex UB3 4DR　　　　　　　　Director　　　　　　　　　　*Turnover:* £149,584,000
081-848 8787

Donations Policy: At the start of each year the company specifically identifies three charities: one local, one national, and one industry-related. These charities are supported through the following 12 months. Unsolicited appeals will not be supported.

☐ Hodder & Stoughton Holdings Ltd

Publishers

Mill Road,　　　　　　　　　　*Ch:* P Attenborough　　　　*Year Ends:* 31 Mar '89　　UK employees: n/a
Dunton Green,　　　　　　　　*Contact:* A M Brown　　　　　*Donations:* £16,500　　　Total employees: 855
Sevenoaks,　　　　　　　　　　　　　　　　　　　　　　　　　*Profit:* £1,449,000
Kent TN13 2YA　　　　　　　　　　　　　　　　　　　　　　*Turnover:* £57,627,000
0732-450111

Donations Policy: Preference for local charities in areas where the company operates, appeals relevant to company business and charities in which a member of company staff is involved. Preference for children and youth; social welfare; education; environment/heritage; arts; enterprise/training.
No response to circular appeals. No grants for fundraising events; advertising in charity brochures; purely denominational (religious) appeals; local appeals not in areas of company presence; large national appeals; overseas projects.

☐ Hoechst UK Ltd

Chemicals, pharmaceuticals, dyestuffs, paints

Hoechst House,　　　　　　　*Ch:* A L Baltzer　　　　　　*Year Ends:* 31 Dec '91　　UK employees: n/a
Salisbury Road,　　　　　　　*Contact:* W R Davies　　　　*Donations:* £45,000　　　Total employees: 2,314
Hounslow,　　　　　　　　　　　　Company Secretary　　　　*Profit:* £17,299,000
Middlesex TW4 6JH　　　　　　　　　　　　　　　　　　　　*Turnover:* £414,041,000　　　　ABSA
081-570 7712

Donations Policy: Preference for appeals in regions where company has a presence. Typical grants range from £50 to £5,000.
No support for appeals from individuals, local appeals not in areas of company presence or overseas projects.

☐ Hogg Group plc

Insurers & Lloyds brokers

Lloyds Chambers,　　　　　　*Ch:* J H Vaughn　　　　　　　*Year Ends:* 31 Dec '91　　UK employees: n/a
1 Portsoken Street,　　　　　*MD:* A H Jackson　　　　　　　*Donations:* £30,857　　　Total employees: 2,750
London E1 8DF　　　　　　　*Contact:* Karen Gibbons　　　*Profit:* £16,804,000
071-480 4000　　　　　　　　　　Public Relations Executive　*Turnover:* £112,960,000

Donations Policy: We have not been able to obtain a donations policy.

☐ Hogg Robinson plc

Travel, property & financial services

Select House,　　　　　　　　*Ch:* B R Perry　　　　　　　*Year Ends:* 31 Mar '92　　UK employees: n/a
15 Victoria Way,　　　　　　*Contact:* Leisure, Marketing　*Donations:* £3,724　　　　Total employees: 3,781
Woking GU21 1DD　　　　　　　　　　　　　　　　　　　　　*Profit:* £15,160,000
0483-756923　　　　　　　　　　　　　　　　　　　　　　　*Turnover:* £102,528,000

Donations Policy: Support for Save The Children Fund and local/staff involved charities. Preferred area of support: children and youth.
Grants to national organisations up to £1,000. Grants to local organisations up to £500.
Generally no support for circular appeals, brochure advertising or appeals from individuals.

Please read page 6 | | | Alphabetical listing •

Name/Address	Officers	Financial Information	Other Information

☐ **Hollandsche Beton Groep (UK)** — Civil engineers

St James House,
Knoll Road,
Camberley,
Surrey GU15 3XW
0276-63484

MD: J R Grice
Contact: G Medcroft
Human Resources Manager

Year Ends: 31 Dec '88
Donations: £3,126
Profit: £3,934,000
Turnover: £166,083,000

UK employees: n/a
Total employees: 1,519

☐ **Holmes & Marchant Group plc** — Marketing consultants

Brands House,
Kingshill Road,
High Wycombe HP13 5BB
0494-711225

Ch: J F Holmes
Contact: Marion Randolph
Personal Assistant to the Chairman

Year Ends: 30 Sep '91
Donations: £675
Profit: £2,104,000
Turnover: £46,211,000

UK employees: n/a
Total employees: 300

Donations Policy: Preference for local charities in areas where the company operates, appeals relevant to company business and charities in which a member of company staff is involved. Preferred area of support: children and youth. Grants from £50 to £100.
No grants for fundraising events; appeals from individuals; purely denominational (religious) appeals; local appeals not in areas of company presence; large national appeals; overseas projects; political, racist or sexist organisations.

☐ **Honda Motor Europe Ltd** — Vehicle importers

Caversham,
Bridge House,
Waterman Place,
Reading RG1 8DN
0734-566399

Ch: H Ikari
Contact: John Page
Human Resources Manager

Year Ends: 31 Mar '90
Donations: n/a
Profit: £9,599,000
Turnover: £370,422,000

UK employees: n/a
Total employees: 749

☐ **Honeywell Ltd** — Control & information systems

Honeywell House,
Charles Square,
Bracknell RG12 1EB
0344-424555

Ch: D A Kennedy
Contact: Chris Clark
Marketing Promotions Manager

Year Ends: 31 Dec '91
Donations: £259,480
Profit: £20,336,000
Turnover: £201,306,000

UK employees: n/a
Total employees: 2,658

BitC, ABSA

Donations Policy: Priority areas of support: (a) the relief of suffering and promotion of medical research in the UK; (b) social welfare; (c) educational projects (not research grants); (d) programmes initiated or supported by Honeywell employees; (e) deserving charitable projects local to a Honeywell site; (f) charitable requests connected with any area of Honeywell business.
No donations to: programmes/organisations which are neither truly national nor have a positive impact on communities around Honeywell sites; organisations of a political, racist or sexist nature; solely denominational projects. Generally will not donate to third parties, allow representatives of charities onto its premises, accept charity raffle tickets for sale inside the company or support individuals.

☐ **Hong Kong & Shanghai Banking Corporation** — Banking

99 Bishopsgate,
London EC2P 2LA
071-638 2300

Ch: T W O'Brien (Executive Director)
Contact: Mrs A K Cheeseman
Public Affairs Department

Year Ends: 31 Dec '91
Donations: £45,000
Profit: £245,000,000
Turnover: n/a

UK employees: 1,100
Total employees: n/a

BitC

Donations Policy: Total donations in 1991 were £2.6 million, but there is only a relatively small budget for giving in the UK. Preference for local charities in areas where the company operates. Preference for education; environment/heritage; enterprise/training; homelessness.
No response to circular appeals. No grants for appeals from individuals; purely denominational (religious) appeals; local appeals not in areas of company presence.

☐ **Hoover Ltd** — Household appliance manufacturers

Dragonparc,
Abercanid,
Merthyr Tydfil,
Mid-Glamorgan CF48 1PQ
0685-721000

Ch: M R Rawson
MD: W R Foust, A E Williamson
Contact: Ms Caroline Knight
Manager, Marketing & Media Relations

Year Ends: 30 Nov '90
Donations: n/a
Profit: £16,485,000
Turnover: £212,237,000

UK employees: 5,130
Total employees: n/a

Donations Policy: Preference for local charities in areas of company presence and charities in which a member of staff is involved. Generally no support for circular appeals or purely denominational (religious) appeals.

☐ **Robert Horne Paper Company Ltd** — Paper merchants

Huntsman House,
Mansion Close,
Moulton Park,
Northampton NN3 1LA
0604-495333

Ch: M T Bairstow
MD: J S Mason
Contact: Personnel Department

Year Ends: 31 Dec '90
Donations: £35,000
Profit: n/a
Turnover: £227,000,000

UK employees: n/a
Total employees: 747

Donations Policy: Support for local charities in areas where company operates. Grants of £10 to £50.

☐ **Horserace Totaliser Board** — Racecourse totalisers, off-course cash & credit offices

Tote House,
74 Upper Richmond Road,
London SW15 2SU
081-874 6411

Ch: Lord Wyatt of Weeford
CE: B M McDonnell
Contact: G Webster
Publicity Department

Year Ends: 31 Mar '91
Donations: n/a
Profit: £3,124,000
Turnover: £212,596,000

UK employees: n/a
Total employees: 1,186

● **Alphabetical listing** Please read page 6

Name/Address — *Officers* — *Financial Information* — *Other Information*

☐ Hoskyns Group plc
Computer systems & consultants

Hoskyn House,
130 Shaftesbury Avenue,
London W1V 7DN
071-434 2171

- *Ch:* E G Unwin
- *MD:* A C E Robinson, A F Fisher
- *Contact:* Gill Boughton

- *Year Ends:* 31 Oct '91
- *Donations:* £25,989
- *Profit:* £14,299,000
- *Turnover:* £200,663,000

- UK employees: n/a
- Total employees: 3,297

Donations Policy: The company chooses a single charity to make contributions to every year through internal fund-raising etc..
No brochure advertising at corporate level.

☐ House of Fraser plc
Department store operators

1 Howick Place,
London SW1P 1BH
071-834 1515

- *Ch:* A Fayed
- *Contact:* J R P Davies
  Company Secretary

- *Year Ends:* 29 Apr '91
- *Donations:* £185,892
- *Profit:* £52,600,000
- *Turnover:* £1,113,200,000

- UK employees: n/a
- Total employees: 19,859
- BitC

Donations Policy: Donations mainly reserved for associations related to the retail trade. Support is also given in the fields of children and youth, social welfare, medical, environment and heritage and the arts.
Generally no support for circular appeals, appeals from individuals, purely denominational appeals, local appeals not in areas of company presence or overseas projects.

☐ How Group plc
Building installation & maintenance

Intersection House,
110 Birmingham Road,
West Bromwich,
West Midlands B70 6RX
021-500 5000

- *Ch:* P C How
- *CE:* D Summerfield
- *Contact:* Jeff Hall
  Financial Director

- *Year Ends:* 31 Dec '91
- *Donations:* £9,000
- *Profit:* £1,295,000
- *Turnover:* £223,887,000

- UK employees: n/a
- Total employees: 3,105

☐ Howden Group plc
Engineers, gas & air handling plant

Old Govan Road,
Renfrew,
Strathclyde PA4 0XJ
041-886 6711

- *Ch:* J Jackson
- *CE:* J Johnsen
- *Contact:* A G Maclachlan
  Company Secretary

- *Year Ends:* 30 Apr '91
- *Donations:* £23,617
- *Profit:* £2,990,000
- *Turnover:* £330,563,000

- UK employees: n/a
- Total employees: 5,006

Donations Policy: The company has no set policy.

☐ HTV Group plc
Television programme contractors

Culverhouse Cross,
Cardiff CF5 6XJ
0222-590590

- *Ch:* P L M Sherwood
- *CE:* C D Romaine
- *Contact:* P M Forster
  Deputy Secretary

- *Year Ends:* 31 Dec '91
- *Donations:* £184,000
- *Profit:* £441,000
- *Turnover:* £171,699,000

- UK employees: 1,226
- Total employees: 1,226
- ABSA

Donations Policy: Only supports organisations within the HTV transmission area, donations being divided equally between the two regions (Wales and West of England). Typical grants range from £50 to £5,000.
The group also contribute to the ITV Association Television Fund.
Sponsorship requests to Mansel Jones at head office or Peter Sanderson, The Television Centre, Bath Road, Bristol BS4 3HG.

☐ Hunter Saphir plc
Food producers

Eurocentre,
Whitstable Road,
Faversham,
Kent ME13 8BQ
0795-532264

- *Ch:* N P G Saphir
- *Contact:* Peter Austin
  Managing Director

- *Year Ends:* 29 Feb '92
- *Donations:* £5,000
- *Profit:* £2,510,000
- *Turnover:* £181,469,000

- UK employees: n/a
- Total employees: 1,580

Donations Policy: Preference for local charities in areas of company presence, appeals relevant to the company business and charities where a member of staff is involved.

☐ Hunterprint Group plc
Commercial colour printing

15 Saxon Way East,
Oakley Hay Industrial Park,
Corby,
Northants NN18 9EX
0536-747474

- *Ch:* Sir Ian MacGregor
- *MD:* Tony Caplin
- *Contact:* David Dalton
  Managing Director, Operations

- *Year Ends:* 29 Sep '91
- *Donations:* £163
- *Profit:* £6,318,000
- *Turnover:* £49,576,000

- UK employees: n/a
- Total employees: 626

☐ Hunting Gate Group Ltd
House building & development

4 Hunting Gate,
Hitchin,
Hertfordshire SG4 0TB
0462-434444

- *Ch:* C J Baker
- *MD:* J A B Redgrave
- *Contact:* David Taylor
  Group Financial Director

- *Year Ends:* 30 Sep '88
- *Donations:* £9,000
- *Profit:* £7,187,000
- *Turnover:* £100,986,000

- UK employees: n/a
- Total employees: 338

Donations Policy: The company states that it will be making no donations for the foreseeable future.

Please read page 6 — Alphabetical listing

Name/Address	Officers	Financial Information	Other Information

Hunting plc
Industrial holding company

3 Cockspur Street,
London SW1Y 5BQ
071-321 0123

- Ch: R H Hunting
- CE: K W Miller
- Contact: Mrs Joan Sayers
  Secretary to the Chairman

- Year Ends: 31 Dec '91
- Donations: £39,000
- Profit: £21,052,000
- Turnover: £749,670,000

- UK employees: n/a
- Total employees: 7,302
- % Club

Donations Policy: The company is a very active supporter of the arts, sponsoring the Hunting/Observer Art prizes. Subsidiaries have their own sponsorship budgets.

Huntingdon International Holdings plc
Engineering/environmental research

Research Centre,
PO Box 2,
Huntingdon,
Cambs PE18 6ES
0480-890431

- MD: P Dawes
- Contact: Marketing Director

- Year Ends: 30 Sep '91
- Donations: n/a
- Profit: £16,908,000
- Turnover: £123,051,000

- UK employees: n/a
- Total employees: 3,363

Charles Hurst Holdings Ltd
Vehicle distribution & service

Boucher Road,
Belfast BT12 6LR
0232-381721

- Ch: K H Cheevers
- MD: F Maguire
- Contact: G Scott
  Financial Director

- Year Ends: 31 Dec '85
- Donations: £7,000
- Profit: £1,033,000
- Turnover: £78,643,000

- UK employees: n/a
- Total employees: 644
- % Club

Donations Policy: The company tends to support local organisations in areas of company presence and local branches of national charities.

IBC Vehicles Ltd
Manufacturer of vehicles & spare parts

PO Box 163,
Kimpton Road,
Luton,
Bedfordshire LU2 0TY
0582-422266

- Ch: J F Smith
- Contact: Charity Committee
  Personnel Department

- Year Ends: 31 Dec '90
- Donations: £6,195
- Profit: £26,000,000
- Turnover: £142,559,000

- UK employees: n/a
- Total employees: 1,775

IBM United Kingdom Holdings Ltd
Information handling equipment manufacture

PO Box 41,
North Harbour,
Portsmouth PO6 3AU
0705-321212

- Ch: Sir Anthony Cleaver
- CE: N J Temple
- Contact: E J N Hart
  Trust Administrator (address below)

- Year Ends: 31 Dec '91
- Donations: £2,048,000
- Profit: (£124,000,000)
- Turnover: n/a

- UK employees: n/a
- Total employees: 15,665
- % Club, BitC, ABSA

Donations Policy: IBM provides support through the donation of resources in the following areas: education, the environment, information technology for people with disabilities and the empowerment of the voluntary sector. This support may be as cash, equipment, secondment of staff, employee time, use of facilities, training and management assistance. Preference for local charities in areas where the company operates and charities in which a member of company staff is involved.
Generally, support will be one-off donations. Grants from £25 to £80,000. Support is not committed to projects over an extended period for operational expenses. Total community contributions in 1991 were £3,191,000.
No response to circular appeals. No grants for building projects, political, religious or sectarian organisations, overseas activities or expeditions, recreational and sports clubs, individuals, nor to appeals by third parties on behalf of a charity.
There is no formal application process. All requests to be in writing and to include the aims of the organisation as well as details of what assistance is required. Address for the trust: IBM Southbank, 76 Upper Ground, London SE1 9PZ (071-928 1777).
Sponsorship proposals to Marketing Communications, IBM Basingstoke, PO Box 117, Mountbatten House, Basing View, Basingstoke RG21 1EJ.

Ibstock Johnsen plc
Brick manufacture & wood pulp agents

Lutterworth,
Leicester LE17 4PS
0455-553071

- Ch: P C Hyde-Thomson
- MD: I D Maclellan
- Contact: A H Taylor
  Company Secretary

- Year Ends: 31 Dec '91
- Donations: £37,153
- Profit: £10,577,000
- Turnover: £285,344,000

- UK employees: 1,616
- Total employees: 4,550

Donations Policy: Some priority is given to appeals from Leicestershire, particularly in the field of education and other matters of general social concern.

Iceland Frozen Foods Holdings plc
Frozen food retailers

Second Avenue,
Deeside Industrial Park,
Deeside,
Clwyd CH5 2NW
0244-830100

- Ch: M C Walker
- MD: R S Kirk
- Contact: Barbara Crampton
  Customer Services Manager

- Year Ends: 31 Dec '91
- Donations: £254,000
- Profit: £46,318,000
- Turnover: £889,064,000

- UK employees: n/a
- Total employees: 7,879
- % Club, BitC

Donations Policy: The company has a major on-going commitment to support its "adopted" charity. It also makes numerous small donations to fundraising appeals in areas of company presence. Preference for charities in which a member of company staff is involved. Preference for children and youth; social welfare; medical; education; environment/heritage. Grants to national organisations range from £10 to £100,000, and to local organisations from £10 to £500.
No support for appeals from non-charities, circular appeals, advertising in charity brochures (with rare exceptions), local appeals not in areas of company presence. No sponsorship is undertaken.

• **Alphabetical listing** Please read page 6

Name/Address	Officers	Financial Information	Other Information

☐ ICL plc

Computer & telecommunication systems

ICL House,
1 High Street,
Putney,
London SW15 1SW
081-788 7272

Ch: C L Bonfield
Contact: Rod Scott
Company Secretary

Year Ends: 31 Dec '91
Donations: £257,000
Profit: £78,200,000
Turnover: £1,875,700,000

UK employees: n/a
Total employees: 26,760

Donations Policy: In recent years the company has supported the Kensington Computer Museum with grants of £60,000 a year. The company expects to continue this support. University professorships are supported as are educational charities and charities recommended by members of staff. No other appeals will be considered.

☐ Illingworth Morris & Woolcombers Ltd

Manufacturers of wool textiles

Fairweather Green,
Thornton Road,
Bradford,
West Yorkshire BD8 0HZ
0274-542255

Ch: A J Lewis
Contact: M Bradley
Company Secretary

Year Ends: 31 Mar '90
Donations: £7,000
Profit: £9,043,000
Turnover: £68,389,000

UK employees: n/a
Total employees: 3,269

Donations Policy: No particular areas of preference, although the arts and overseas development receive low priority.

☐ IM Group

Car & spare part concessionaires

Ryder Street,
West Bromwich,
West Midlands B70 0EJ
021-522 2000

Ch: R N Edmiston
Contact: T J O'Neill
Promotions Manager

Year Ends: 31 Dec '90
Donations: £2,147
Profit: £15,704,000
Turnover: £146,890,000

UK employees: n/a
Total employees: 249

☐ IMI plc

Drinks dispense, fluid power, building products, engineering

PO Box 216,
Witton,
Birmingham B6 7BA
021-356 4848

Ch: Sir Eric Pountain
CE: G J Allen
Contact: Secretary, IMI Charitable Appeals Committee

Year Ends: 31 Dec '91
Donations: £206,000
Profit: £73,300,000
Turnover: £968,000,000

UK employees: 10,733
Total employees: 18,493

Donations Policy: Most donations are distributed by head office through the Charities Aid Foundation. The balance is distributed by main subsidiaries which have separate budgets for donations. National grants range from £250 to £5,000 and local grants from £25 to £5,000. Preference for charities of direct or indirect benefit to the business, those which benefit or are likely to benefit employees (present, past and potential) and charities located and working in areas where the company has its major interests. Preferred areas of support are the arts and culture, social welfare, health and medical care, education, religion and sport.
Total community contributions in 1991 were £282,000.
The company gives direct to charities and not to organisations which are themselves collecting for charity. No support for circular appeals, fundraising events, advertising in charity brochures, appeals from individuals, local appeals not in areas of company presence, large national appeals or overseas projects.

☐ Imperial Chemical Industries plc

Petrochemicals, pharmaceuticals

Imperial Chemical House,
9 Millbank,
London SW1P 3JF
071-834 4444

Ch: D H Henderson
Contact: G H R Musker
Appeals Secretary

Year Ends: 31 Dec '91
Donations: £3,200,000
Profit: £843,000,000
Turnover: £12,488,000,000

UK employees: n/a
Total employees: 128,600

BitC, ABSA

Donations Policy: Direct support is preferred. Donations are made through the ICI Charitable Trust and Appeals Committee. National charities are supported from head office with grants ranging from £500 to £5,000. Much support is at a local level, with support for local grassroots charities, grants ranging from £50 to £1,000. Preferred areas of support: education, enterprise and training, medical charities, youth organisations, conservation groups and organisations working with mentally and physically disabled people, and elderly people. Total community contributions in 1991 were £5.2 million. Sponsorship proposals should be addressed to Miss S Shackleton, Public Affairs Department. Overseas projects are supported by ICI businesses in the places where they are located.
No response to circular appeals. No grants for fundraising events; advertising in charity brochures; appeals from individuals; purely denominational (religious) appeals; local appeals not in areas of company presence; overseas projects; building appeals.

☐ Imry Holdings Ltd

Property developer

19 St James's Square,
London SW1Y 4JT
071-321 0266

Ch: M Myers
Contact: Debbie Hibbs
Administration Department

Year Ends: 31 Mar '89
Donations: £2,750
Profit: n/a
Turnover: n/a

UK employees: n/a
Total employees: n/a

☐ Inchcape plc

International services & marketing

St James's House,
23 King Street,
London SW1Y 6QY
071-321 0110

Ch: Sir David Plastow
CE: C D Mackay
Contact: J Duncan
Secretary to the Inchcape Charitable Trust

Year Ends: 31 Dec '91
Donations: £201,000
Profit: £185,200,000
Turnover: £3,635,800,000

UK employees: n/a
Total employees: 38,000

BitC, ABSA

Donations Policy: Support for major UK national charities and UK registered charities active in countries where the Group operates. Total world-wide donations were £547,000. Main areas of support, on a very selective basis, are the arts, social welfare, community services, health and medical care, conservation and the environment, animal welfare and education. Grants from £500 to £10,000. About half the groups charitable giving is done from headquarters and group companies also have their own budgets for donations.
No response to circular appeals. No support for non-registered charities, advertising in charity brochures, appeals from individuals, purely denominational (religious) appeals, local appeals not in areas of company presence or regional appeals from national charities.

Please read page 6 — Alphabetical listing

Name/Address	Officers	Financial Information	Other Information

☐ Inco Europe Ltd
Nickel refiners

1-3 Grosvenor Place,
London SW1X 7EA
071-235 2040

Contact: Miss S A James
Assistant Company Secretary

Year Ends: 31 Dec '90
Donations: £27,000 (1991)
Profit: £25,086,000
Turnover: £700,203,000

UK employees: n/a
Total employees: 3,696

Donations Policy: Donations are made through the International Nickel Donations Fund Limited. Preference for local charities in the areas of company presence, appeals relevant to company business and charities in which a member of staff is involved. Preferred areas of support: children and youth, social welfare, medical and education. Grants from £100 to £1,000.
No support for circular appeals, fundraising events, advertising in charity brochures, appeals from individuals, purely denominational (religious) appeals, local appeals not in areas of company presence, large national appeals and overseas projects.

☐ Independent Television News Ltd
Television news programming

200 Grays Inn Road,
London WC1X 8XZ
071-833 3000

Ch: Richard Dunn
CE: Robert Phillis
Contact: Press Office

Year Ends: 29 Jul '90
Donations: n/a
Profit: £2,260,000
Turnover: £101,260,000

UK employees: n/a
Total employees: 750

Donations Policy: The organisation say they are not allowed to make donations to charities. Even with appeals such as the Appeal For Africa the Disasters & Emergencies Committee had to obtain air time and ITN just provided the facilities to make the broadcast.

☐ Independent TV Publications Ltd
Publishing magazines & books

247 Tottenham Court Road,
London W1P 0AU
071-323 3222

Ch: G A Cooper
Contact: Geoffrey Kalman
Company Secretary

Year Ends: 29 Jul '88
Donations: £1,767
Profit: £7,838,000
Turnover: £83,599,000

UK employees: n/a
Total employees: 295

☐ Indespension Ltd
Trailer/trailer equipment

Belmont Road,
Bolton,
Lancashire BL1 7AQ
0204-309797

Contact: Mrs Graham
Marketing Director

Year Ends:
Donations: n/a
Profit: n/a
Turnover: n/a

UK employees: n/a
Total employees: n/a

% Club

Donations Policy: Preference for children and youth; social welfare; medical and education.
No grants for fundraising events; advertising in charity brochures; appeals from individuals; purely denominational (religious) appeals; local appeals not in areas of company presence; large national appeals; overseas projects.

☐ Ingersoll-Rand Holdings Ltd
Engineers

PO Box 2,
Chorley New Road,
Horwich,
Bolton,
Lancashire BL6 6JN
0204-690690

Ch: R D Wendeborn
Contact: Mrs Barbara Clueit
Personnel Manager

Year Ends: 31 Dec '91
Donations: £2,812
Profit: £15,597,000
Turnover: £179,445,000

UK employees: n/a
Total employees: 2,311

Donations Policy: Support for medical, children and youth. Preference for charities in which a member of staff is involved.
No support for circular appeals, advertising in charity brochures, purely denominational (religious) appeals, local appeals not in company areas.

☐ Intel Corporation Ltd
Integrated circuits & systems

Pipers Way,
Swindon,
Wiltshire SN3 1RJ
0793-696000

Ch: K Chapple
Contact: Jo O'Boyle
Senior Administration Specialist

Year Ends: 29 Dec '90
Donations: £16,297
Profit: £10,204,000
Turnover: £153,360,000

UK employees: n/a
Total employees: 438

Donations Policy: We were unable to obtain a policy from this company.

☐ Interlink Express plc
Parcel collection & delivery service

Brunswick Court,
Brunswick Square,
Bristol BS2 8PE
0272-426900

Ch: R Gabriel
Contact: Peter Gent
Commercial Director

Year Ends: 30 Jun '91
Donations: £18,113
Profit: £6,932,000
Turnover: £51,388,000

UK employees: n/a
Total employees: 525

Donations Policy: Appeals are initially considered on a local level by regional depots and should not be made to the head office.

☐ International Corn Co (UK) Ltd
Commodity brokers

Orwell Terminal,
Duke Street,
Ipswich,
Suffolk IP3 0AG
0473-219691

Ch: D Moreland
Contact: Paul Bateson
Manager

Year Ends: 31 Dec '90
Donations: n/a
Profit: £300,000
Turnover: £103,596,000

UK employees: n/a
Total employees: 9

● **Alphabetical listing** Please read page 6

Name/Address	Officers	Financial Information	Other Information

☐ **International General Electric (USA) Ltd** — Holding company

3 Shortlands,
Hammersmith,
London W6 8BX
081-741 9900

Contact: Jacqueline Byrne

Year Ends: 31 Dec '90
Donations: £3,750
Profit: £3,842,000
Turnover: £216,752,000

UK employees: n/a
Total employees: 866

☐ **Interpublic Ltd** — Advertising agency

4 Golden Square,
London W1R 3AE
071-734 7116

Ch: E P Beard
Contact: Linda Ellis
Director & Company Secretary

Year Ends: 31 Dec '90
Donations: £50,000
Profit: £2,301,000
Turnover: £432,644,000

UK employees: n/a
Total employees: 1,222

Donations Policy: Appeals should be made to subsidiaries, not to the Group. Applicants to Lintas, 84 Eccleston Square, London (071-822 8888); or to McCann-Erickson Advertising Ltd, 36 Howland Street, London W1A 1AT (071-580 6690).

☐ **Invergordon Distillers Group plc** — Prod. & marketing of scotch whisky, gin, vodka & liqueur

9-21 Salamander Place,
Leith,
Edinburgh EH6 7JL
031-554 4404

Ch: J L Millar
MD: C G Greig
Contact: Miss Valerie Baird
Marketing Manager

Year Ends: 31 Dec '91
Donations: £14,052
Profit: £32,200,000
Turnover: £92,400,000

UK employees: n/a
Total employees: 507

☐ **INVESCO Mim plc** — Banking & finance

11 Devonshire Square,
London EC2M 4YR
071-626 3434

Ch: Lord Stevens of Ludgate
Contact: Elinor Ball
Secretary to the Charity
Committee

Year Ends: 31 Dec '91
Donations: £51,640
Profit: £14,534,000
Turnover: n/a

UK employees: n/a
Total employees: 1,075

Donations Policy: Preference for local charities in the areas of company presence and charities in which a member of staff is involved. Preferred areas of support are organisations concerned with disabled children, homelessness, the arts, cancer appeals and London-based teaching hospitals. National grants from £250 to £2,500. Local grants from £200 to £5,000.
Generally no support for fundraising events, advertising in charity brochures, appeals from individuals, purely denominational (religious) appeals, local appeals not in areas of company presence or overseas projects.

☐ **Iron Trades Insurance Company Ltd** — Insurance

Iron Trades House,
21-24 Grosvenor Place,
London SW1X 7JA
071-235 6033

Ch: G H Sambrook
Contact: R Philipps
Company Secretary

Year Ends: 31 Dec '91
Donations: £15,327
Profit: n/a
Turnover: n/a

UK employees: n/a
Total employees: n/a

Donations Policy: The company stated "management review annually all donations to prioritise within a budgeted target". Preference for children and youth; social welfare; medical; education; recreation; environment/heritage and appeals relevant to company business. Grants to national organisations from £100 to £2,500. Grants to local organisations from £100 to £2,000.
No grants for fundraising events; advertising in charity brochures; appeals from individuals. No response to circular appeals.

☐ **Isis Group plc** — Construction engineers

Stratton Road,
Marshgate,
Swindon,
Wiltshire SN1 2PT

Ch: L A B Park
MD: J Arbuckle
Contact: Mrs Joan Bevan
Secretary to the Chairman

Year Ends: 31 Mar '89
Donations: £8,558
Profit: £2,276,000
Turnover: £82,119,000

UK employees: n/a
Total employees: 573

Donations Policy: The company supports one main charity, therefore unsolicited appeals are not supported.

☐ **Istel Group Ltd** — Computer & communications products

PO Box 5,
Grosvenor House,
Prospect Hill,
Redditch,
Hereford & Worcester B97 4DQ
0527-64274

Ch: J P Leighfield
MD: J A C MacFarlane
Contact: Mrs Nicky Morgan
Personnel Manager

Year Ends: 31 Dec '90
Donations: n/a
Profit: £40,015,000
Turnover: £130,056,000

UK employees: n/a
Total employees: 2,154

☐ **C Itoh (UK) plc** — Trading company

76 Shoe Lane,
London EC4A 3JB
071-822 0822

MD: I Tsuchida
Contact: A Butler
Personnel Manager

Year Ends: 31 Mar '92
Donations: £10,000
Profit: £1,225,000
Turnover: £750,000,000

UK employees: 90
Total employees: 125

BitC

Donations Policy: The company makes an annual donation of £10,000 to the Charities Aid Foundation, who allocate this to charities at their discretion.
No response to circular appeals.

Please read page 6   **Alphabetical listing** •

Name/Address	Officers	Financial Information	Other Information
☐ **ITT Industries Ltd**			Manufacturers of electronic equipment
Jays Close, Viables Estate, Basingstoke, Hampshire RG22 4BW 0256-473171	Contact: Ron Howard Personnel Director	Year Ends: 31 Dec '90 Donations: £4,000 Profit: £9,350,000 Turnover: £139,763,000	UK employees: n/a Total employees: 2,713
☐ **Iveco Ford Truck Ltd**			Truck manufacturer & importer
Iveco Ford House, Station Road, Watford WD1 1SR 0923-246400	MD: A B Fox Contact: Nigel Emms External Affairs Manager	Year Ends: 31 Dec '91 Donations: n/a Profit: (£38,600,000) Turnover: £139,300,000	UK employees: n/a Total employees: 1,300

Donations Policy: Preference for local charities in areas where the company operates.
No response to circular appeals. No grants for fundraising events; advertising in charity brochures; appeals from individuals; purely denominational (religious) appeals; local appeals not in areas of company presence; large national appeals; overseas projects.

☐ **Ivory & Sime plc**			Investment management
One Charlotte Square, Edinburgh EH2 4DZ 031-225 1357	Ch: David Newbiggin MD: Alan Munro Contact: Gordon Neilly Financial Director	Year Ends: 30 Apr '92 Donations: £7,919 Profit: £4,522,000 Turnover: £13,927,000	UK employees: n/a Total employees: 138
☐ **William Jackson & Son plc**			Bakers, confectioners, meat products
40 Derringham Street, Hull HU3 1EW 0482-224131	Ch: P B Oughtred MD: C M Oughtred Contact: Mrs Argent Secretary	Year Ends: 27 Apr '91 Donations: £11,273 Profit: £2,982,000 Turnover: £207,754,000	UK employees: n/a Total employees: 3,698
☐ **Jacob's Bakery Ltd**			Manufacture & sale of food products
121 Kings Road, Reading, Berkshire RG1 3EF	Ch: P Jaeckin MD: S D Freedman Contact: M Butler Secretary to Personnel Director	Year Ends: 31 Dec '91 Donations: £4,959 Profit: £6,634,000 Turnover: £195,431,000	UK employees: n/a Total employees: 3,432
☐ **Jaguar Cars Ltd**			Car manufacturers
Browns Lane, Allesley, Coventry CV5 9DR 0203-402121	Ch: William Howden Contact: Communications & Public Affairs Department	Year Ends: 31 Dec '90 Donations: £208,250 Profit: n/a Turnover: n/a	UK employees: n/a Total employees: 12,100 % Club, BitC, ABSA

Donations Policy: Support exclusively for local charities in the areas of company presence and charities in which a member of staff is involved, especially children and youth, social welfare and medical. It will support national charities if they have a local branch, or can in some way, benefit the groups' employees and their families.
Generally no support for fundraising events, advertising in charity brochures, purely denominational (religious) appeals, large national appeals or overseas projects.

☐ **Jardine European Motors plc**			Motor vehicle retail
6 Crutched Friars, London EC3V 9AQ 071-480 6633	Contact: J J G Brown Chairman	Year Ends: 31 Dec '90 Donations: n/a Profit: £4,224,000 Turnover: £94,842,000	UK employees: n/a Total employees: 981
☐ **Jarrold & Sons Ltd**			Printing, publishing & retail stores
5 London Street, Norwich NR2 1JF 0603-660661	Ch: J P Jarrold Contact: Richard Jarrold Managing Director	Year Ends: 28 Jan '89 Donations: £4,000 Profit: £5,056,000 Turnover: £62,831,000	UK employees: n/a Total employees: 1,300

Donations Policy: The John Jarrold Trust has an income of around £40,000 a year, and supports general charitable purposes with a particular emphasis on education and research in the natural sciences.
No grants to individuals. Funds are fully committed for the time being.

☐ **Jarvis plc**			Construction & property
57 Great Eastern Street, London EC2A 3QD 071-729 8020	Ch: H P Bard Contact: Keith Young Marketing Manager (address see below)	Year Ends: 31 Dec '91 Donations: £3,683 Profit: £238,000 Turnover: £119,651,000	UK employees: n/a Total employees: 1,042

Donations Policy: The address for the contact is: J Jarvis & Son Ltd, Construction House, Southend Arterial, Romford, Essex RM3 0NU.

● **Alphabetical listing**　　　　　　　　　　　　　　　　　　　　　　　　　　　　　　　　　　Please read page 6

Name/Address　　　　　　　　　*Officers*　　　　　　　　*Financial Information*　　　　*Other Information*

☐ Jenners (Princes St) Edinburgh Ltd　　　　　　　　　　　　　　　　　　　　　　　Departmental stores

48 Princes Street,　　　　　　　　*Ch:*　R D Miller　　　　　　*Year Ends:* 31 Jan '90　　　*UK employees:* n/a
Edinburgh EH2 2YJ　　　　　　*Contact:* Miss Glenda Hale　　　*Donations:* £6,379　　　　　*Total employees:* 673
031-225 2442　　　　　　　　　　　　Secretary to the Chairman　　*Profit:* £2,048,000
　　　　　　　　　　　　　　　　　　　　　　　　　　　　　　　　Turnover: £28,076,000

Donations Policy: Grants to major charities and much smaller sums to charities with which company customers are involved. Support goes mainly to health, education, enterprise/training. Local charities and charities known to members of staff or where staff are involved are also supported.
No support for circular appeals, fundraising events, appeals from individuals or purely denominational (religious) appeals. Unsolicited appeals from unknown sources are not welcomed.
The company states: "We hope charities realise the enormous number of appeals a business exposed to the public gets". Some arts sponsorship is undertaken. In addition, over £4,000 is given in the form of charitable advertising, use of premises by collectors, tombola prizes, loans of equipment, etc..

☐ Jessups plc　　　　　　　　　　　　　　　　　　　　　　　　　　　　　　　　　　　Motor vehicle dealers

140 London Road,　　　　　　　　*Ch:*　A Jessup　　　　　　　*Year Ends:* 31 Aug '89　　　*UK employees:* n/a
Romford,　　　　　　　　　　　*MD:*　J Bacchus　　　　　　　*Donations:* £4,500　　　　　*Total employees:* 496
Essex RM7 9QS　　　　　　　*Contact:* Mrs Mary Steptoe　　　*Profit:* £2,803,000
0708-722311　　　　　　　　　　　　Secretary to the Managing　　*Turnover:* £97,725,000
　　　　　　　　　　　　　　　　　　　　Director

Donations Policy: Appeals relevant to the business are supported.

☐ JIB Group plc　　　　　　　　　　　　　　　　　　　　　　　　　　　　　　　　　　　Insurance broking

Jardine House,　　　　　　　　　*Ch:*　C G R Leach　　　　　　*Year Ends:* 31 Dec '91　　　*UK employees:* n/a
6 Crutched Friars,　　　　　　　*CE:*　R J O Barton　　　　　　*Donations:* £144,000　　　　*Total employees:* 3,532
London EC3N 2HT　　　　　　*Contact:* Stuart Anslow-Wilson　*Profit:* £20,058,000
071-528 4444　　　　　　　　　　　　Deputy Chairman/Chairman　*Turnover:* £168,948,000
　　　　　　　　　　　　　　　　　　　　Charities Committee

Donations Policy: The Charities Committee meets 4 times a year. Most of the company's donations are done through Deeds of Covenant, this is probably a long-term commitment. Other donations are usually £100 to £250 paid in Charities Aid Foundation vouchers.
No grants for fundraising events; advertising in charity brochures; appeals from individuals; large national appeals.

☐ JLI Group plc　　　　　　　　　　　　　　　　　　　　　　　　　　　　　　　Food processing & distribution

PO Box 54,　　　　　　　　　　*Ch:*　J M Alexander　　　　　*Year Ends:* 31 Mar '89　　　*UK employees:* n/a
JLI House,　　　　　　　　　　*CE:*　Y Gottesman　　　　　　*Donations:* £1,809　　　　　*Total employees:* 769
Guildford Street,　　　　　　　*Contact:* Ian Bayer　　　　　　*Profit:* £3,171,000
Chertsey,　　　　　　　　　　　　　　Financial Director　　　　*Turnover:* £84,345,000
Surrey KT16 9ND
0932-569599

☐ Johnson & Firth Brown plc　　　　　　　　　　　　　　　　　　　　　　　　　　　Specialist engineers

Weston House,　　　　　　　　　*Ch:*　J M Clay　　　　　　　*Year Ends:* 30 Sep '91　　　*UK employees:* n/a
Manchester Road,　　　　　　　*MD:*　R G Hardie, D J Hall　　*Donations:* £9,512　　　　　*Total employees:* 2,197
Clifton,　　　　　　　　　　　*Contact:* Tony Edisbury　　　　*Profit:* £9,616,000
Manchester M27 2ND　　　　　　　　Company Secretary　　　　*Turnover:* £118,986,000
061-793 0275

Donations Policy: "We make modest donations from a limited budget, only to national charities which might be of some benefit to our employees or their families at some time." Preferred areas are children and youth, social welfare, medical, environment and heritage, enterprise and training. Grants from £100 to £500.
No support for advertising in charity brochures, overseas projects, individual appeals, denominational appeals or local appeals not in areas of company presence. Direct support preferred.

☐ Johnson & Johnson Ltd　　　　　　　　　　　　　　　　　　　　　　　　　　Healthcare & baby products

Foundation Park,　　　　　　　　*Ch:*　P Dupasquier　　　　　*Year Ends:* 29 Dec '85　　　*UK employees:* n/a
Roxborough Way,　　　　　　　*MD:*　K H Ashwell　　　　　　*Donations:* £51,827　　　　*Total employees:* 2,185
Maidenhead,　　　　　　　　　*Contact:* Miss Kim Brayne　　　*Profit:* £4,651,000
Berkshire SL6 3UG　　　　　　　　Human Resources Administrator　*Turnover:* £99,912,000
0628-822222

Donations Policy: We have been unable to obtain a donations policy.

☐ Johnson Group Cleaners plc　　　　　　　　　　　　　　　　　　　　　　　Dry cleaners & textile rental

Mildmay Road,　　　　　　　　　*Ch:*　T M Greer　　　　　　　*Year Ends:* 28 Dec '91　　　*UK employees:* n/.a
Bootle,　　　　　　　　　　　*MD:*　R G F Zemy, J R Wahl　*Donations:* £12,000　　　　*Total employees:* 6,986
Merseyside L20 5EW　　　　　*Contact:* T M Greer　　　　　　*Profit:* £15,975,000
051-933 6161　　　　　　　　　　　　Chairman　　　　　　　　*Turnover:* £154,531,000

Donations Policy: Johnson Group is a group of autonomous operating subsidiaries. Charitable donations are 99% arranged at local level. Preference for local charities in the areas of company presence in the fields of children and youth, social welfare, environment and heritage. Generally no support for circular appeals, appeals from individuals, purely denominational (religious) appeals, local appeals not in areas of company presence, large national appeals or overseas projects.

Name/Address	Officers	Financial Information	Other Information

☐ Johnson Matthey plc

Gold, silver & platinum refiners

New Garden House,
78 Hatton Garden,
London EC1N 8JP
071-269 8000

Ch: D J Davies
CE: R K A Wakeling
Contact: Company Secretary

Year Ends: 31 Mar '92
Donations: £246,000
Profit: £66,300,000
Turnover: £1,732,900,000

UK employees: n/a
Total employees: 6,468

Donations Policy: Preference for charities which have some connection with the company's activities. Support also for local charities in the areas of company presence and charities in which a member of staff is involved. Direct support preferred rather than advertising in charity brochures etc..

☐ Johnson Wax Ltd

Manu. of polishing, cleaning & hygiene products

Frimley Green
Camberley,
Surrey GU16 6AJ
0276-63456

Ch: S C Johnson
MD: J Molan
Contact: Tony Bracking

Year Ends: 30 Jun '89
Donations: £223,193 (1992)
Profit: £5,473,000
Turnover: £61,978,000

UK employees: 470
Total employees: n/a

% Club, BitC

Donations Policy: The company gives 3%-4% of its pre-tax profits for charitable purposes each year. Preference for local charities in the areas of company presence, mainly in Surrey and Hampshire. Preferred areas of support: children and youth, social welfare, medical, education, the arts and enterprise/training and particularly the environment.
In 1991/92, a total of £91,000 was given to organisations/projects under the heading social endeavour, £93,000 to cultural and educational endeavour, and £39,000 to medical endeavour. Grants to national organisations from £1,000 to £25,000. Grants to local organisations from £25 to £25,000.
Generally no support for fundraising events, appeals from individuals, purely denominational appeals.

☐ Johnston Group plc

Construction & mechanical engineers

Johnston House,
Hatchlands Road,
Redhill,
Surrey RH1 1BG
0737-242466

Ch: W G S Johnston
MD: J M S Johnston
Contact: Mrs J Bennett
Secretary to the Chairman

Year Ends: 31 Dec '91
Donations: £15,600
Profit: £1,087,000
Turnover: £119,904,000

UK employees: n/a
Total employees: 1,618

Donations Policy: Preference for local charities in areas of company presence, appeals relevant to company business and charities in which a member of staff is involved. Preferred areas of support: children and youth, social welfare, medical, education and recreation.
No support for fundraising events, brochure advertising, appeals from individuals, purely denominational appeals, local appeals not in areas of company presence or overseas projects.

☐ Jones & Brother

Distribution of sewing machines

Shepley Street,
Audenshaw,
Manchester M34 5JD
061-330 6531

Ch: K Tazaki
Contact: J P Kelly
Advertising Manager

Year Ends: 30 Sep '87
Donations: £9,221
Profit: £2,197,000
Turnover: £61,745,000

UK employees: n/a
Total employees: 376

☐ Jones Lang Wootton

Chartered surveyors, auctioneers & valuers

22 Hanover Square,
London W1A 2BN
071-493 6040

Ch: Clive Pickford
Contact: John Bassett
Financial Services

Year Ends: 30 Apr '92
Donations: n/a
Profit: n/a
Turnover: n/a

UK employees: 700
Total employees: 3000

% Club, BitC

Donations Policy: Preference for medical, education and the arts. Support is given to all types of charities depending on the relevance to the firm's business and it's clients. Preference for appeals relevant to company business and for charities in which a member of company staff is involved.
No grants for fundraising events; advertising in charity brochures; appeals from individuals; purely denominational (religious) appeals; local appeals not in areas of company presence; large national appeals; overseas projects. No response to circular appeals.

☐ Jones, Stroud (Holdings) plc

Manufacturers of fabrics

New Street,
Long Eaton,
Nottingham NG10 1HF
0602-734421

Ch: P L Jones
MD: D L Jones
Contact: P R Rimmer
Group Secretary

Year Ends: 31 Mar '90
Donations: £3,000
Profit: £6,222,000
Turnover: £60,338,000

UK employees: 1,217
Total employees: 1,515

Donations Policy: Support for local (Long Eaton and district) charities only. Preference for charities in which a member of staff is involved. No response to circular appeals. No grants for fundraising events; advertising in charity brochures; appeals from individuals; purely denominational (religious) appeals; local appeals not in areas of company presence; large national appeals; overseas projects. No sponsorship.

☐ JVC (UK) Ltd

UK distributor of Victor Co products

JVC House,
JVC Business Park,
Priestley Way,
London NW2 7BA
081-450 3282

Contact: Mary Hard
Secretary to the Managing Director

Year Ends: 31 Mar '91
Donations: n/a
Profit: £1,825,000
Turnover: £133,283,000

UK employees: n/a
Total employees: 181

• **Alphabetical listing** Please read page 6

Name/Address *Officers* *Financial Information* *Other Information*

☐ Kalamazoo plc

Business systems & services

Kalamazoo Works,
Northfield,
Birmingham B31 2RW
021-411 2345

Ch: P J Harrop
MD: M Langmore
Contact: P J Peerey
Deputy Company Secretary

Year Ends: 31 Mar '92
Donations: £12,000
Profit: £611,000
Turnover: £38,655,000

UK employees: n/a
Total employees: 1,462

% Club

Donations Policy: The financial information is for an eight month period.

☐ Kalon Group plc

Manufacture of paint, wallcoverings

Huddersfield Road,
Birstall,
Batley,
West Yorkshire WF17 9XA
0924-477201

Ch: R Boissier
Contact: M Hennessy
Group Managing Director

Year Ends: 31 Dec '91
Donations: £33,126
Profit: £9,219,000
Turnover: £98,542,000

UK employees: n/a
Total employees: 1,330

Donations Policy: The company selects one charity a year to receive donations and support from fundraising. Other than this only local appeals or appeals related to company business are considered.

☐ Kellogg Co of Great Britain Ltd

Cereal food manufacturers

The Kellogg Building,
Talbot Road,
Manchester M16 0PU
061-869 2000

Ch: T A Knowlton
Contact: C H Woodcock
Manager, Corporate Affairs

Year Ends: 31 Dec '89
Donations: £410,189 (1991)
Profit: £58,633,000
Turnover: £431,086,0000

UK employees: 2,860
Total employees: 3,006

% Club, BitC

Donations Policy: The company is committed to involvement in the communities in which it operates. It targets resources on welfare, local community regeneration and education of children. Support is also given to a number of health initiatives, local enterprise agencies and environmental initiatives. Two-thirds of total community support is focussed on the North West, the balance being spread nationally. Grants to national organisations from £100 to £20,000. Grants to local organisations from £25 to £20,000. Total community contributions were £650,000.
Generally no support for circular appeals, fundraising events, advertising in charity brochures, appeals from individuals, purely denominational (religious) appeals, local appeals not in areas of company presence or overseas projects. The company does not generally provide funding for the arts.
Each year the company receives about 3,000 applications of which about 400 are successful.

☐ Kemira Coatings Ltd

Surface coatings & urethane polymers

Rookwood Way,
Haverhill,
Suffolk CB9 8PQ
0440-706666

CE: B R Parks
Contact: Ron Hill
Assistant Company Secretary

Year Ends: 31 Dec '90
Donations: £5,406
Profit: £6,695,000
Turnover: £98,897,000

UK employees: n/a
Total employees: 1,428

☐ Kemira Ince Ltd

Inorganic fertiliser manufacture

Ince,
Chester CH2 4LB
051-357 2777

MD: C J Powell
Contact: Mrs L M Mottram
Press & Public Relations Officer

Year Ends: 31 Dec '90
Donations: n/a
Profit: £3,458,000
Turnover: £166,264,000

UK employees: n/a
Total employees: 765

☐ Kerrygold Co Ltd

Marketing, distribution, packaging of food products

Sunnyhills Road,
Leek,
Staffordshire ST13 5SP
0538-399111

Ch: J M Paterson
Contact: D Gwilt
Personnel Department

Year Ends: 31 Dec '90
Donations: £1,557
Profit: £297,000
Turnover: £151,799,000

UK employees: n/a
Total employees: 900

Donations Policy: The company generally only supports local charities for which it has a fixed budget. Preferred areas of support are children and youth and medical. Grants to local organisations from £25 to £250.
Generally no support for circular appeals, purely denominational (religious) appeals, local appeals not in areas of company presence, large national appeals or overseas projects.

☐ Kimberley-Clark Ltd

Cellulose wadding products

Larkfield,
Aylesford,
Kent ME20 7PS
0622-717700

MD: R W Huggins
Contact: Carolyn Burton
Personnel Officer

Year Ends: 31 Dec '90
Donations: £39,192
Profit: £18,092,000
Turnover: £245,598,000

UK employees: n/a
Total employees: 2,900

Donations Policy: Preference for local charities in areas of company presence, in particular those concerned with children and youth, social welfare, education and medical.
No support for circular appeals, appeals from individuals, purely denominational (religious) appeals, large national appeals or overseas projects.

Please read page 6 — Alphabetical listing

Name/Address	Officers	Financial Information	Other Information

☐ Kingfisher plc
General retail merchants

North West House,
119 Marylebone Road,
London NW1 5PX
071-724 7749

Ch: G J Mulcahy
Contact: Tim Clement-Jones
Company Secretary

Year Ends: 3 Feb '92
Donations: £910,200
Profit: £227,700,000
Turnover: £3,388,800,000

UK employees: n/a
Total employees: 37,462

BitC

Donations Policy: The company and its subsidiaries are contributors to a number of community projects, either in cash, in kind or by donation of human resources. The company has supported several organisations concerned with: crime prevention, women's enterprise, and homelessness. Grants to national organisations from £5,000 to £25,000.
Total community contributions (including charitable donations) in 1991 were £1,094,000.
In addition to Kingfisher's support each of its major subsidiaries concentrate on particular charities or projects, and should be contacted directly. Subsidiaries include B&Q, Comet and Woolworths.
Generally no support for circular appeals, brochure advertising, appeals from individuals, purely denominational appeals, local appeals not in areas of company presence, overseas projects or building projects.

☐ Kingsway Group plc
Concrete block manufacturers

Celcon House,
289-293 High Holborn,
London WC1V 7HU
071-242 9766

Ch: H Schmidt-Hansen
MD: B S Prime
Contact: M Spinks
Marketing Manager

Year Ends: 31 Dec '90
Donations: £4,000
Profit: £3,119,000
Turnover: £103,445,000

UK employees: n/a
Total employees: 1,671

☐ Kleinwort Benson Group plc
Banking

20 Fenchurch Street,
London EC3P 3DB
071-623 8000

Ch: D A E R Peake
CE: J G W Agnew
Contact: P J M Prain
Kleinwort Benson Charitable Trust

Year Ends: 31 Dec '91
Donations: £269,000
Profit: £27,900,000
Turnover: n/a

UK employees: 2,363
Total employees: n/a

% Club, BitC, ABSA

Donations Policy: Normally appeals from national charities only are considered. Main areas of support are arts/culture, social welfare, community services, health/medical, conservation/environment and enterprise. Preference for appeals from projects in which a member of staff is involved. Grants to national organisations from £250 to £1,000.
Generally no support for appeals from individuals, purely denominational (religious) appeals, local appeals or overseas projects.
Sponsorship proposals should be addressed to Mrs C F Willis.

☐ Austin Knight Ltd
Advertising practitioners

Knightway House,
20 Soho Square,
London W1A 1DS
071-437 9261

MD: K G Fordham
Contact: Martin Purvis
Company Secretary

Year Ends: 30 Sep '90
Donations: £16,200
Profit: £384,000
Turnover: £127,845,000

UK employees: n/a
Total employees: 677

☐ Knight Frank & Rutley
Property consultants & estate agents

20 Hanover Square,
London W1R 0AH
071-629 8171

Ch: A Shelley, Senior Partner
Contact: Shaun Longsdon

Year Ends:
Donations: n/a
Profit: n/a
Turnover: n/a

UK employees: n/a
Total employees: n/a

% Club, BitC

Donations Policy: Most donations are to medical and disability charities, with a very small proportion going to the arts and education.

☐ Kodak Ltd
Photographic goods manufacturers

PO Box 66,
Kodak House,
Station Road,
Hemel Hempstead,
Herts HP1 1JU
0442-61122

Ch: Erroll Yates
MD: Tony Waterlow
Contact: J G Richardson
Corporate Communications Department

Year Ends: 31 Dec '91
Donations: £410,000
Profit: £81,500,000
Turnover: £946,400,000

UK employees: 8,504
Total employees: n/a

ABSA

Donations Policy: Support for registered charities in areas of company presence, working in the fields of community service, medicine, conservation and the environment, the arts and young people. Preference is given to projects in which a member of staff is involved where the project is consistent with company policy.
Generally no support for circular appeals, brochure advertising, appeals from individuals, local appeals not in areas of company presence, large national appeals or overseas projects.

☐ KPMG Peat Marwick
Chartered accountants

1 Puddle Dock,
London EC4V 3PD
071-236 8000

Contact: Nigel May
Partnership Secretary

Year Ends: 31 Mar '90
Donations: n/a
Profit: n/a
Turnover: £431,000,000

UK employees: 10,700
Total employees: n/a

% Club, BitC, ABSA

Donations Policy: Preference for appeals relevant to the business, local charities or appeals where a member of staff is involved, especially social welfare, medical and the arts.
No support for religious or overseas charities. Appeals must be in writing.

• **Alphabetical listing**   **Please read page 6**

Name/Address   *Officers*   *Financial Information*   *Other Information*

☐ Kraft General Foods Ltd
                                                                                                              Food manufacturers

European Manufacturing   *Ch:* H H Roberts   *Year Ends:* 31 Dec '90   *UK employees:* n/a
Business Unit,   *Contact:* R Bell   *Donations:* £14,352   *Total employees:* 900
Banbury,   Managing Director   *Profit:* £14,437,000
Oxfordshire OX16 7QU   *Turnover:* £180,575,000
0295-264433

Donations Policy: The company does not donate to charities outside Banbury.

☐ Kronospan Ltd
                                                                                                              Manufacture & sale of chipboard

Maesgwyn Farm,   *Ch:* M M Kaindl   *Year Ends:* 30 Sep '88   *UK employees:* n/a
Chirk,   *Contact:* D C Wood   *Donations:* £17,573 (1989)   *Total employees:* 525
Wrexham LL14 5NT   Associate Director   *Profit:* £5,262,000
0691-773361   *Turnover:* £71,036,000

Donations Policy: Preference for local charities in the areas of company presence especially in the areas of children and youth, social welfare, medical, education and recreation. Grants to local organisations from £25 to £1,500.
No support for advertising in charity brochures, local appeals not in areas of company presence, large national appeals or overseas projects.

☐ Kunick plc
                                                                                                              Providers of care & leisure services

Low Lane,   *Ch:* C Burnett   *Year Ends:* 30 Sep '91   *UK employees:* n/a
Horsforth,   *CE:* G Smith   *Donations:* n/a   *Total employees:* 3,162
Leeds LS18 4ER   *Contact:* Miss Sam Ellis   *Profit:* £12,370,000
0532-390001   Secretary to the Managing   *Turnover:* £116,405,000
                                Director

☐ Kuoni Travel Ltd
                                                                                                              Travel agents

Kuoni House,   *Ch:* P Diethelm   *Year Ends:* 31 Dec '90   *UK employees:* n/a
Deepdene Avenue,   *Contact:* Richard Good   *Donations:* £20,000 (1991)   *Total employees:* 239
Dorking,   Personnel Manager   *Profit:* £19,985,000
Surrey RH5 4AZ   *Turnover:* £151,255,000
0306-740888

Donations Policy: Preference for local charities in the areas of company presence (Dorking), appeals relevant to company business and charities in which a member of staff is involved. Preference for children and youth.
No response to circular appeals. No support for purely denominational (religious) appeals, appeals from individuals or local appeals not in areas of company presence.

☐ Kuwait Petroleum (UK Holdings) Ltd
                                                                                                              Petroleum products

80 New Bond Street,   *Ch:* N H Sultan   *Year Ends:* 30 Jun '91   *UK employees:* n/a
London W1Y 9DA   *Contact:* Maureen Daly   *Donations:* £13,000   *Total employees:* 686
071-491 4000   Brands & Communications   *Profit:* £18,318,000
                                Assistant   *Turnover:* £233,870,000

☐ Kwik Save Group plc
                                                                                                              Supermarket operators

Warren Drive,   *Ch:* Sir Timothy Harford   *Year Ends:* 31 Aug '91   *UK employees:* n/a
Prestatyn,   *MD:* G Seabrook   *Donations:* £62,693   *Total employees:* 13,211
Clwyd LL19 7HU   *Contact:* J Smith   *Profit:* £101,668,000
0745-887111   Merchandise Director   *Turnover:* £1,784,500,000

Donations Policy: The company adopts a "charity of the year" (currently the NSPCC) and channels all activities into this. Preference for local charities in the areas of company presence especially social welfare. Tends to offer help in form of shopping vouchers.
No support for circular appeals, advertising in charity brochures, appeals from individuals, purely denominational (religious) appeals, large national appeals or overseas projects.

☐ Kwik-Fit Holdings plc
                                                                                                              Tyre, exhaust & car repair centres

17 Corstorphine Road,   *Ch:* T Farmer   *Year Ends:* 29 Feb '92   *UK employees:* n/a
Edinburgh EH12 6DD   *Contact:* Peter Holmes   *Donations:* £164,000   *Total employees:* 3,216
031-337 9200   Director of Marketing   *Profit:* £32,106,000
                                                               Turnover: £253,782,000

Donations Policy: Preference for local charities in areas where the company operates, particularly those aiming to promote enterprise and initiative amongst young people, and to support moves towards automotive safety.
No response to circular appeals. No grants for advertising in charity brochures or appeals from individuals.

☐ Kyle Stewart Ltd
                                                                                                              Building contractors

Ardshiel House,   *Ch:* R M I Stewart   *Year Ends:* 30 Sep '88   *UK employees:* n/a
Empire Way,   *MD:* J Trussler   *Donations:* £40,302   *Total employees:* 909
Wembley HA9 0NA   *Contact:* R Hickson   *Profit:* £4,139,000
081-902 5321   Financial Director   *Turnover:* £114,839,000

Donations Policy: Mainly supports charities concerned with children.

Please read page 6 | | | Alphabetical listing •

Name/Address — *Officers* — *Financial Information* — *Other Information*

☐ Kymmene UK plc

Paper manufacturers

4 Stratford Place,
London W1N 0HB
071-495 4666

MD: N Davenport
Contact: S P Daykin
Marketing Services Director

Year Ends: 31 Dec '88
Donations: £5,000 (1989)
Profit: £2,655,000
Turnover: £91,058,000

UK employees: 50
Total employees: n/a

Donations Policy: Preference for appeals relevant to company business and charities in which a member of staff is involved. Preferred areas of support: children and youth, education, environment and heritage, the arts and enterprise/training.
Generally no support for purely denominational appeals, large national appeals or overseas projects.

☐ L'Oreal (UK) Ltd

Manufacture & distribution of L'Oreal products

30 Kensington Church Street,
London W8 4HA
071-937 5454

Ch: L Owen-Jones
MD: P Sajot
Contact: Director of Public Relations

Year Ends: 31 Dec '88
Donations: £8,576 (1991)
Profit: £8,599,000
Turnover: £185,184,000

UK employees: n/a
Total employees: 2,021

Donations Policy: Preference for children and youth; medical; education; environment/heritage; arts. The company responds to all requests, and supplies products, where appropriate, for fundraising events. Total community contributions in 1991 were £16,576.
No grants for advertising in charity brochures; appeals from individuals; purely denominational (religious) appeals; overseas projects.

☐ Ladbroke Group plc

Hotel, bookmaking, retail, property

10 Cavendish Place,
London W1M 9DJ
071-323 5000

Ch: C Stein
MD: P M George
Contact: C Stein
Chairman

Year Ends: 31 Dec '91
Donations: £224,000
Profit: £210,400,000
Turnover: £3,785,700,000

UK employees: n/a
Total employees: 53,429

% Club, BitC, ABSA

Donations Policy: No donations policy as such. Grants to national organisations from £10 to £58,000. Grants to local organisations from £10 to £10,000. The company is also involved in various enterprise and education initiatives and sponsors the arts. As a member of the Per Cent Club, the company is presumably making total community contributions in the region of £1 million. Requests for community involvement and arts sponsorship should be sent to Brian Offen, Marketing Services Manager.
No support for advertising in charity brochures, circular appeals, appeals from individuals or local appeals not in areas of company presence.

☐ John Laing plc

Construction engineers

Page Street,
London NW7 2ER
081-959 3636

Ch: J M K Laing
Contact: Secretary to Laing's Charitable Trust

Year Ends: 31 Dec '91
Donations: £91,576
Profit: £65,300,000
Turnover: £1,577,600,000

UK employees: n/a
Total employees: 12,800

% Club, BitC, ABSA

Donations Policy: Preference for charities in areas where the company or a subsidiary has a presence. The bulk of John Laing's giving is carried out by the Laing's Charitable Trust see A Guide to the Major Trusts. The company (not the trust) also supports various enterprise and education initiatives and sponsors the arts.
No support for non-charities, appeals from individuals, advertising in charity brochures, circular appeals, local charities not in areas of company presence.

☐ Laird Group plc

Sealing systems, service industries, transport

3 St James's Square,
London SW1Y 4JU
071-839 6441

Ch: J A Gardiner
Contact: D Hudson
Company Secretary

Year Ends: 31 Dec '91
Donations: £38,000
Profit: £28,375,000
Turnover: £523,789,000

UK employees: n/a
Total employees: 10,575

Donations Policy: Regular annual support to a few selected charities. Grants range from £100 to £5,000. The company also sponsors worthwhile activities on a one-off basis.

☐ Lamont Holdings plc

Textile manufacturing

Purdy's Lane,
Belfast BT8 4AX
0232-491111

Ch: Sir Desmond Lorimer
Contact: M G Lamont
Company Secretary & Group
Financial Controller

Year Ends: 31 Dec '91
Donations: £11,934
Profit: £8,112,000
Turnover: £109,070,000

UK employees: n/a
Total employees: 1,622

% Club

Donations Policy: As a member of the Per Cent Club, the company presumably makes total community contributions of about £40,000.

☐ Lancaster plc

Motor vehicle dealers

Charter Court,
Newcommon Way,
Colchester,
Essex CO4 4TG
0206-751122

Ch: J J G Brown
MD: J M Ritchie
Contact: Sheila Saunders
Personal Assistant to the
Managing Director

Year Ends: 31 Dec '91
Donations: £11,204
Profit: (£1,739,000)
Turnover: £185,563,000

UK employees: n/a
Total employees: 908

Donations Policy: Support for local charities in East Anglia and appeals relevant to company business.

☐ Lancer Boss Group Ltd

Fork-lift truck manufacturers & distributors

Grovebury Road,
Leighton Buzzard,
Bedfordshire LU7 8SR
0525-372031

Ch: Sir Neville Bowman-Shaw
Contact: Anne Duke
Personnel Manager

Year Ends: 31 Mar '91
Donations: £8,011
Profit: £4,411,000
Turnover: £202,894,000

UK employees: n/a
Total employees: 2,381

● **Alphabetical listing**　　　　　　　　　　　　　　　　　　　　　　　　　　　　　　　　　Please read page 6

Name/Address	Officers	Financial Information	Other Information

☐ Land Securities plc
Property development & investment

5 Strand,
London WC2N 5AF
071-413 9000

Ch: P J Hunt
Contact: L A Jones
Company Secretary

Year Ends: 31 Mar '92
Donations: £124,700
Profit: £227,500,000
Turnover: £406,700,000

UK employees: 492
Total employees: n/a

Donations Policy: The company has no set policy, but it is unlikely that appeals from local charities outside areas of company presence will be successful. Preference for children and youth charities. Difficult medical research appeals have been supported and other worthwhile causes are occasionally supported eg. a donation was made to the Hillsborough Disaster Appeal. The company receives 80-90 applications every 6 weeks, when the charity committee meet and choose the most suitable applications.

☐ C J Lang & Son Ltd
Food distribution

332 Clepington Road,
Dundee DD3 8SJ
0382-561100

Ch: C C Lang
CE: A Murdoch
Contact: D C Walker
Marketing Director

Year Ends: 30 Apr '91
Donations: £25,000
Profit: £2,071,000
Turnover: £155,872,000

UK employees: n/a
Total employees: 968

Donations Policy: The company makes donations to the C J Lang Charitable Trust. The trust has a preference for Scottish charities.

☐ Laporte plc
Chemical manufacturers

3 Bedford Square,
London WC1B 3RA
071-580 0223

Ch: R Bexon
MD: K J Minton
Contact: R D Ward
Head of Public Affairs

Year Ends: 31 Dec '91
Donations: £68,000
Profit: £97,200,000
Turnover: £424,200,000

UK employees: n/a
Total employees: 5,498

Donations Policy: Preference for local charities in the areas of company presence, mainly the north of England. The company supports mainly the caring charities as the most practical way of helping those who have to depend on others for support owing to incapacity, disability etc.. The company also supports medical research, youth vocational training and charities linked to the chemical industry. Grants to national organisations from £100 to £5,000. Grants to local organisations from £15 to £500.
The committee does not give twice to any organisation in a twelve month period, however worthy the cause. No support for circular appeals, fundraising events, advertising in charity brochures, appeals from individuals, local appeals not in areas of company presence or overseas projects.

☐ LASMO plc
Oil & gas exploration

100 Liverpool Street,
London EC2M 2BB
071-945 4500

Ch: Lord Rees
CE: W W C Greentree
Contact: Hilary Wilson
Head of Public Affairs

Year Ends: 31 Dec '91
Donations: £104,900
Profit: £28,800,000
Turnover: £280,600,000

UK employees: n/a
Total employees: 1,388

Donations Policy: Preference for national causes or local charities in areas where the company has operations. Grants to national organisations from £250 to £5,000. Grants to local organisations from £100 to £1,000.
Generally no support for circular appeals, advertising in charity brochures, appeals from individuals, purely denominational (religious) appeals or local appeals not in areas of company presence.

☐ Walter Lawrence plc
Building contractors

Lawrence House,
Pishiobury,
Sawbridgeworth,
Hertfordshire CM21 0AF
0279-725001

Ch: B J Prichard
CE: T J C Mawby
Contact: Mrs Crane
Personal Assistant to Chief Executive

Year Ends: 31 Dec '90
Donations: £17,352 (1989)
Profit: £14,411,000
Turnover: £261,556,000

UK employees: n/a
Total employees: 1,478

Donations Policy: Preference for local charities in areas of company presence, particularly children and youth, recreation and enterprise/training. Grants to national organisations from £100 to £500. Grants to local organisations from £25 to £500.
No support for circular appeals, advertising in charity brochures, appeals from individuals, purely denominational (religious) appeals or overseas projects.

☐ Lawrie Group plc
Tea & coffee producers, consumer goods, garden equipment

Wrotham Place,
Wrotham,
Sevenoaks,
Kent TN15 7AE
0732-884488

Ch: H K FitzGerald
Contact: P A Leggatt
Director

Year Ends: 31 Dec '90
Donations: £22,170
Profit: £12,915,000
Turnover: £161,816,000

UK employees: n/a
Total employees: 68,551

Donations Policy: Preference for local charities in areas where the company operates.

☐ Lazard Brothers & Co Ltd
Banking capital markets, corporate finance

21 Moorfields,
London EC2P 2HT
071-588 2721

Ch: D J Verey
Contact: Secretary to the Charities Committee

Year Ends: 31 Dec '89
Donations: £205,000
Profit: £21,000,000
Turnover: n/a

UK employees: 614
Total employees: n/a

Donations Policy: All appeals are considered on their merits, no particular areas of preference.

Please read page 6 | Alphabetical listing ●

Name/Address	Officers	Financial Information	Other Information

☐ Arthur Lee & Sons plc
Steel manufacturing

PO Box 54,
Meadowhall,
Sheffield   S9 1HU
0742-437272

Ch: P W Lee
Contact: David Lee
Marketing Director

Year Ends: 30 Sep '91
Donations: £9,673
Profit: £861,000
Turnover: £105,561,000

UK employees: n/a
Total employees: 1,441

Donations Policy: Preference for local charities in the areas of company presence and charities in which a member of staff is involved. "We prefer to think of our donations as support for worthwhile organisations and not as PR or advertising. We accept on merit, and prefer some knowledge of the appeal subject."

☐ Leeds & Holbeck Building Society
Building society

105 Albion Street,
Leeds   LS1 5AS
0532-459511

CE: Arthur Stone
Contact: Alan Bradey
Mortgage Arrears Manager

Year Ends: 31 Dec '91
Donations: n/a
Profit: £12,307,000
Turnover: n/a

UK employees: n/a
Total employees: 670

☐ Leeds Permanent Building Society
Building society

Permanent House,
1 Lovell Park Road,
Leeds   LS1 1NS
0532-438181

Ch: J M Barr, President
CE: J M Blackburn
Contact: Suzanne Phillips
Public Relations Officer

Year Ends: 30 Sep '91
Donations: £14,364
Profit: £190,200,000
Turnover: n/a

UK employees: n/a
Total employees: 5,200

Donations Policy: Preference for appeals relevant to company business. Preference for children and youth; social welfare; medical; education; environment/heritage; arts; overseas aid/development; enterprise/training. Donations are usually small.
No response to circular appeals. No grants for fundraising events; appeals from individuals; purely denominational (religious) appeals; local appeals not in areas of company presence. A limited amount of advertising in charity brochures is undertaken.
In addition to direct donations, over £3,000,000 has been raised for three British charities through the society's Visa affinity card scheme.

☐ Legal & General plc
Insurance

Temple Court,
11 Queen Victoria Street,
London   EC4N 4TP
071-528 6200

Ch: Sir James Ball
CE: David Prosser
Contact: Julie Vivian
Advertising & Sponsorship Manager

Year Ends: 30 Dec '91
Donations: £364,700
Profit: £11,300,000
Turnover: n/a

UK employees: n/a
Total employees: 8,837

% Club, BitC, ABSA

Donations Policy: The company has an established long-term programme. This is run pro-actively in that the company seeks out organisations which meet its criteria. Unsolicited appeals are not welcome, although information about organisations which work in the relevant areas is always useful. The programme currently covers: (a) quality of life in retirement; (b) medical research and health education for life threatening conditions; (c) housing; (d) crime prevention; (e) enterprise agencies and equal opportunities for women in self employment.
Local programmes fund a range of community activities in areas where employees live and work. Local appeals should be addressed to appropriate regional contacts in Brighton and Hove, Reigate and Banstead, and Enfield.
No support for circular appeals, fundraising events, brochure advertising, appeals from individuals, purely denominational appeals, large national appeals or overseas projects.

☐ Leica Cambridge Ltd
Scientific instrument manufacture

Clifton Road,
Cambridge   CB3 8EL
0223-411411

Ch: T J Gooding
Contact: Nicola Russell
Personnel Department

Year Ends: 31 Mar '89
Donations: £5,587
Profit: £7,701,000
Turnover: £116,518,000

UK employees: 1,062
Total employees: n/a

Donations Policy: The company states that it gives no charitable donations.

☐ Leigh Interests plc
Environmental services

Lindon Road,
Brownhills,
Walsall,
West Midlands   WS8 7BB
0543-452121

Ch: Malcolm Wood
Contact: Mrs Recordon
Publicity Department

Year Ends: 31 Mar '91
Donations: £2,000
Profit: £14,767,000
Turnover: £96,685,000

UK employees: n/a
Total employees: 1,578

% Club

☐ John Lelliot Group plc
Building contractors

80 South Audley Street,
London   W1Y 5TA
071-409 1717

Ch: J H Lelliott
Contact: Tony Hobbs
Public Relations Manager

Year Ends: 30 Jun '90
Donations: £11,000
Profit: £5,091,000
Turnover: £240,405,000

UK employees: n/a
Total employees: 938

☐ Leo Burnett Ltd
Advertising & marketing

48 St Martin's Lane,
London   WC2N 4EJ
071-836 2424

Ch: R Wheatly
Contact: Mary Ogden
Personal Assistant to the Chairman

Year Ends: 31 Dec '90
Donations: £21,629
Profit: £722,000
Turnover: £116,135,000

UK employees: n/a
Total employees: 194

Donations Policy: The donations budget is allocated a long time in advance. Charities must be related to advertising.

• **Alphabetical listing**   Please read page 6

Name/Address	Officers	Financial Information	Other Information

☐ **Leopold Lazarus Ltd**   Metal merchants

    20-34 St Bride Street,   *Ch:* W Griessmann   *Year Ends:* 31 Dec '90   *UK employees:* n/a
    London EC4A 4DL   *Contact:* J Mears   *Donations:* £574   *Total employees:* 36
    071-583 8060   Company Secretary   *Profit:* £257,000
                                                                   Turnover: £154,265,000

☐ **Lep Group plc**   International freight forwarders

    87 East Street,   *Ch:* David N James   *Year Ends:* 31 Dec '91   *UK employees:* 2,778
    Epsom,   *Contact:* Valerie Wagstaffe   *Donations:* n/a   *Total employees:* 12,503
    Surrey KT17 1DT   Personal Assistant to the   *Profit:* (£59,062,000)
    0372-729595   Chairman   *Turnover:* £1,511,000,000

☐ **Levi Strauss & Co**   Manufacturers of clothes

    489 Avenue Louise,   *MD:* Jack Gerrish   *Year Ends:* 30 Nov '90   *UK employees:* n/a
    1050 Brussels,   *Contact:* Alan Christie   *Donations:* £149,242   *Total employees:* 1,238
    Belgium   Community Affairs Manager   *Profit:* £16,341,000
    32-02-641,62,24   *Turnover:* £130,233,000   BitC

Donations Policy: Support is focussed in Northampton, Dundee, Belshill near Glasgow, and Whitburn in West Lothian (the company's main sites). The company supports job creation and community-based development; job training, placement and access strategies; community leadership development; care for Aids/HIV positive sufferers and risk education; childcare; general social welfare. Grants range from £300 to £15,000.
Grants are of two types: (a) Community involvement team grants are employee directed, made by teams of employee volunteers developing projects with local applicant groups. These should be directed to the relevant local plant.
(b) Special emphasis grants are to support creative and innovative projects within the categories outlined above.
No support for circular appeals, fundraising events, advertising in charity brochures, appeals from individuals, purely denominational (religious) appeals, local appeals not in areas of company presence, large national appeals, overseas projects, political appeals, arts or sports sponsorship.

☐ **John Lewis Partnership plc**   Department stores & supermarkets

    171 Victoria Street,   *Ch:* P T Lewis   *Year Ends:* 25 Jan '92   *UK employees:* n/a
    London SW1E 5NN   *Contact:* Secretary, Central Committee for *Donations:* £785,000   *Total employees:* 40,200
    071-828 1000   Claims   *Profit:* £47,100,000
                                                                     Turnover: £2,280,400,000

Donations Policy: Cash contributions to charities and the arts total over 1% of pre-tax profits. The Partnership gives extensively to organisations of charitable status at both national and local level, but prefers to give directly to the organisations concerned.
The chairman is responsible for about half of the charitable giving and gives to organisations which, in broad terms, fall into the categories of the arts, education and the environment. The rest of the donations are made at national and local levels to organisations which are broadly concerned with welfare. These donations are determined by the committees of democratically elected bodies (Central Council and Branch Councils) independent of management. Grants range from £250 to £8,000.
Generally no support for circular appeals, fundraising events, advertising in charity brochures, appeals from individuals, purely denominational (religious) appeals, local appeals not in areas of company presence or overseas projects. No sponsorship is undertaken.

☐ **Lewis Trust Group Ltd**   Clothing retail, property investment, banking, travel

    Chelsea House,   *Contact:* Irene Pettifer   *Year Ends:* 31 Dec '90   *UK employees:* n/a
    West Gate,   Secretary to the Managing   *Donations:* n/a   *Total employees:* 4,349
    London W5 1DR   Director   *Profit:* £3,936,000
    081-998 8822   *Turnover:* £211,193,000

☐ **Lex Services plc**   Car & commercial vehicle distributors

    Lex House,   *Ch:* T E Chinn   *Year Ends:* 31 Dec '91   *UK employees:* n/a
    17 Connaught Place,   *MD:* P Turnbull   *Donations:* £200,000   *Total employees:* 6,000
    London W2 2EL   *Contact:* Charles Murray   *Profit:* £500,000
    071-723 1212   Community Affairs Manager   *Turnover:* £1,320,800,000   % Club, BitC

Donations Policy: The company supports registered charities serving the arts, education, the environment, medicine and social welfare (including children, young and elderly people). Preference for local charities in the areas of company presence, appeals relevant to company business and charities in which a member of staff is involved.
Generally no support for circular appeals, appeals from individuals, purely denominational (religious) appeals, local appeals not in areas of company presence, political appeals, large national appeals or overseas projects.

☐ **Liberty plc**   Dealers in fabrics, carpets

    Regent Street,   *CE:* H Weblin   *Year Ends:* 27 Jan '92   *UK employees:* 937
    London W1R 6AH   *Contact:* Miss K Whitten   *Donations:* £7,817   *Total employees:* 1,196
    071-734 1234   Secretary to the Chairman   *Profit:* £5,661,000
                                                                     Turnover: £84,879,000

Please read page 6 — Alphabetical listing •

Name/Address	Officers	Financial Information	Other Information

☐ Lilley plc
Civil engineering & building contractors

331 Charles Street,
Glasgow G21 2QX
041-552 6565

Ch: Sir Lewis Robertson
CE: R C M Rankin
Contact: Miss Cathy Cullis
Public Relations Officer

Year Ends: 31 Dec '91
Donations: £20,000
Profit: £4,995,000
Turnover: £339,719,000

UK employees: n/a
Total employees: 3,673

Donations Policy: The company does not have a policy as such, each application is considered on its merits. However there is a preference for local charities in areas where the company operates, appeals relevant to company business and charities in which a member of company staff is involved. Preference also for children and youth and the arts. Grants to national organisations from £100 to £6,000. Grants to local organisations from £20 to £7,500. In addition to charitable donations, other community contributions totalled £8,740.

☐ Lilly Industries Ltd
Medical instruments, medicines, agriculture

Dextra Court,
Chapel Hill,
Basingstoke,
Hampshire RG21 2SY
0256-473241

Ch: R A Matricaria
MD: A S Clark
Contact: D G Anthony
Secretary to the Grants Committee

Year Ends: 31 Dec '91
Donations: £95,000
Profit: £4,766,000
Turnover: £213,358,000

UK employees: 2,163
Total employees: 30,800

Donations Policy: Registered charitable status is desirable. Support for medical and social projects (especially those which benefit children) and charities which have a bearing on agriculture. Preference for local charities in areas of company presence and charities in which a member of staff is involved. Grants to national organisations from £100 to £300. Grants to local organisations from £50 to £100. The company is also involved in local enterprise and education initiatives.
No response to circular appeals. No grants for fundraising events; advertising in charity brochures; appeals from individuals; purely denominational (religious) appeals; local appeals not in areas of company presence; large national appeals; overseas projects; bricks and mortar appeals.

☐ Linde Holdings Ltd
Holding company

Kingsclere Road,
Basingstoke,
Hampshire RG21 2XJ
0256-473131

Ch: Sir Emmanuel Kaye
Contact: P Steele
Personnel Director

Year Ends: 30 Apr '88
Donations: £108,000
Profit: £812,000
Turnover: £255,499,000

UK employees: n/a
Total employees: 5,168

Donations Policy: The company states that it is currently making no donations.

☐ Lindsey Holdings Ltd
Grain merchanting & cleaning, bulk cargo handling

Lindsey House,
Hemswell Cliff,
Gainsborough,
Lincs DN21 5TH
0427-668661

Contact: C W Henson
Managing Director

Year Ends: 30 Jun '90
Donations: n/a
Profit: £222,000
Turnover: £100,455,000

UK employees: n/a
Total employees: 66

☐ Lindsey Oil Refinery Ltd
Oil refinery operations

Killingholme,
Grimsby,
South Humberside DN40 3LW
0469-571175

Contact: M Laville
Manager, Personnel & Administration

Year Ends: 31 Dec '88
Donations: £15,000 (1992)
Profit: £277,000
Turnover: £70,258,000

UK employees: n/a
Total employees: 493

Donations Policy: Support only to local charities in areas where the company operates. Preference for charities in which a member of company staff is involved. Preference for children and youth; medical; education; environment/heritage; arts.
Grants to local organisations from £50 to £1,000.
No response to circular appeals. No grants for advertising in charity brochures; purely denominational (religious) appeals; local appeals not in areas of company presence; large national appeals; overseas projects.

☐ Linpac Group Ltd
Packaging manufacturers

1 Charles Street,
Louth,
Lincolnshire LN11 0LA
0507-600700

Ch: M Cornish
Contact: R D Coulam
Sales & Marketing Director

Year Ends: 31 Dec '90
Donations: £39,000
Profit: £35,657,000
Turnover: £504,795,000

UK employees: n/a
Total employees: 6,871

Donations Policy: Direct giving is preferred, advertising in charity brochures is avoided.

☐ Linread plc
Forged & precision components

St Paul's House,
21-23 St Paul's Square,
Birmingham B3 1RB
021-236 8303

Ch: M P Tahany
Contact: Mrs T L Guinivan
Secretary to the Directors

Year Ends: 31 Dec '91
Donations: £7,400
Profit: (£2,101,000)
Turnover: £39,700,000

UK employees: n/a
Total employees: 979

Donations Policy: "We are inundated with appeals and obviously cannot donate to all of them. Therefore we have a policy of donating to charities in the areas in which we operate." Generally, appeals are considered once a year at a main board meeting, although small 'one-offs' are reviewed as appropriate. Preferred areas of support: children and youth, medical, education and enterprise/training. Grants from £25 to £350. In addition to charitable donations other community contributions totalled £4,000.
Generally no support for brochure advertising, purely denominational appeals, local appeals not in areas of company presence, large national appeals or overseas projects. "No phone calls please."

• **Alphabetical listing**   Please read page 6

Name/Address	Officers	Financial Information	Other Information

☐ **Linton Park plc**   Food processing, plantations

    Linton Park,   *Ch:* H K Fitzgerald   *Year Ends:* 31 Dec '91   *UK employees:* n/a
    Linton,   *Contact:* M C Perkins   *Donations:* £9,000   *Total employees:* 11,137
    Nr Maidstone,   Managing Director   *Profit:* £4,420,000
    Kent ME17 4AB   *Turnover:* £124,300,000
    0622-746655

☐ **LIT Holdings plc**   Investment & fund management, financial services

    Dorland House,   *Ch:* John Botts   *Year Ends:* 31 Dec '91   *UK employees:* n/a
    20 Regent Street,   *CE:* C Castleman   *Donations:* nil   *Total employees:* 921
    London SW1Y 4PZ   *Contact:* Paul Guildersleeves   *Profit:* £1,288,000
    071-839 8411   *Turnover:* £81,499,000

☐ **Littlewoods Organisation plc**   Mail order trading & retail stores

    100-110 Old Hall Street,   *Ch:* L W van Geest   *Year Ends:* 31 Dec '91   *UK employees:* n/a
    Liverpool L70 1AB   *CE:* Sir Desmond Pitcher   *Donations:* £239,000   *Total employees:* 21,353
    051-235 2222   *Contact:* M Hogarth   *Profit:* £97,014,000
         Company Secretary   *Turnover:* £2,262,499,000   % Club, BitC

Donations Policy: Support for a number of national projects and a wide range of organisations on Merseyside, particularly involving underprivileged and socially deprived groups of people and equal opportunities.

☐ **Lloyd Thompson Group plc**   Holiday company

    Beaufort House,   *MD:* Peter Lloyd   *Year Ends:* 30 Jun '91   *UK employees:* n/a
    15 St Botolph Street,   *Contact:* George Hilton   *Donations:* £9,557   *Total employees:* 198
    London EC3A 7LT   Company Secretary   *Profit:* £11,262,000
    071-247 2345   *Turnover:* £29,729,000

☐ **Lloyd's of London**   Insurance underwriting market

    One Lime Street,   *Ch:* David Coleridge   *Year Ends:* 31 Dec '89   *UK employees:* n/a
    London EC3M 7HA   *Contact:* M J Crick   *Donations:* £604,000 (1991)   *Total employees:* 2,581
    071-623 7100   Secretary, Lloyd's Charities Trust   *Profit:* £32,098,000
             Turnover: £164,156,000

Donations Policy: Lloyd's Charities Trust is funded mainly by voluntary covenanted subscriptions from members of Lloyds and by interest on its accumulated endowment. Most grants are made either to national charities or to specific appeals. Grants are usually between £250 and £1,000. A proportion of the fund is also used pro-actively for projects relevant to the Lloyd's community and its activities eg. projects for rehabilitation, especially after accidents, safety at sea, and inner city regeneration.
There is also a community initiative programme involving support for enterprise and education initiatives focussed on the Spitalfields ward of Tower Hamlets. This is totally separate from the Charities Trust.

☐ **Lloyds Bank plc**   Banking & finance

    Corporate Communications,   *Ch:* Sir Jeremy Morse   *Year Ends:* 31 Dec '91   *UK employees:* 62,000
    71 Lombard Street,   *Contact:* Andy Finch   *Donations:* £1,149,000   *Total employees:* 71,723
    London EC3P 3BS   Manager, Community Affairs   *Profit:* £645,000,000
    071-626 1500   *Turnover:* n/a   % Club, BitC, ABSA

Donations Policy: The main thrust of support is towards education, employment, environment, health and social welfare.
Generally no support for circular appeals, fundraising events, advertising in charity brochures, appeals from individuals, purely denominational (religious) appeals or overseas projects.
National sponsorships are handled centrally (D M Goldesgeyme, Sponsorship Manager); local or regional sponsorships should be directed to regional executive officers.
Total community contributions were £4,950,000 including donations, sponsorships, secondments and other community related activities.

☐ **Lloyds Chemists plc**   Chemist, drugstore & health food retailer

    Manor House,   *Ch:* A J Lloyd   *Year Ends:* 30 Jun '91   *UK employees:* n/a
    Manor Road,   *Contact:* Peter Lloyd   *Donations:* n/a   *Total employees:* 4,409
    Mancetter,   Director of Retail Operations   *Profit:* £20,760,000
    Atherstone CV9 1QY   *Turnover:* £247,494,000
    0827-260011

Donations Policy: No charitable donations figure is given in the company annual report.

☐ **Logica plc**   Information technology

    68 Newman Street,   *Ch:* P G Bosonnet   *Year Ends:* 30 Jun '91   *UK employees:* n/a
    London W1A 4SE   *CE:* D W Mann   *Donations:* n/a   *Total employees:* 3,439
    071-637 9111   *Contact:* Corporate Relations   *Profit:* £3,676,000
             Turnover: £186,324,000   ABSA

Donations Policy: The company does not make charitable donations at a corporate level, "preferring to leave individual staff to contribute to charities of their choice". It does provide other support including software implementation and consultancy services either free of charge, at cost price or at a discount.
The company sponsors the arts and supports enterprise agencies and education initiatives.

Please read page 6 — Alphabetical listing

Name/Address	Officers	Financial Information	Other Information

Londis (Holdings) Ltd
Sale of groceries to member companies

Eurogroup House,
67-71 High Street,
Hampton Hill,
Middlesex TW12 1LZ
081-941 0344

Ch: P Williams
CE: G S White
Contact: Sue Jennings
Secretary to the Chief Executive

Year Ends: 25 Jan '91
Donations: n/a
Profit: £568,000
Turnover: £170,806,000

UK employees: n/a
Total employees: 480

Donations Policy: The company ploughs profits back into the business and it's structure does not allow for sponsorship or charity donations.

London & Edinburgh Insurance Group
Life & general insurance

The Warren,
Worthing,
West Sussex BN14 9QD
0903-820820

Ch: R A Barberis
Contact: Miss G D Kelly
Director of Group Marketing & Corporate Relations

Year Ends: 31 Dec '90
Donations: £28,097
Profit: (£1,700,000)
Turnover: n/a

UK employees: n/a
Total employees: 1,057

Donations Policy: Support for organisations concerned with elderly, infirm and disabled people, and deprived children, in areas of company presence.
No support for circular appeals, brochure advertising or overseas projects.

London & Edinburgh Trust plc
Property development, financial services

243 Knightsbridge,
London SW7 1DH
071-581 1322

Ch: J L Beckwith
MD: S McDonald, N Sheehan
Contact: R H Wooley
Company Secretary

Year Ends: 31 Dec '91
Donations: £198,000
Profit: (£138,100,000)
Turnover: £271,400,000

UK employees: n/a
Total employees: 3,341

% Club

Donations Policy: Support for a wide variety of local community projects and charities especially in areas of community presence. Donations are directed to human need charities. Typical grants are about £500.

London & Manchester Group plc
Insurance

Winslade Park,
Exeter,
Devon EX5 1DS
0392-52155

Ch: J M Thomson
CE: D A L Jubb
Contact: Helen Bartlett
Personnel Department

Year Ends: 31 Dec '91
Donations: £54,000
Profit: £21,227,000
Turnover: n/a

UK employees: n/a
Total employees: 3,211

% Club

Donations Policy: The group splits its giving into three main categories: (a) local charitable giving in Exeter, where the company is based - the chief executive decides these appeals; (b) local sponsorship in Exeter; (c) support of national charities, which makes up the largest part of donations, decided by the chairman. Donations are made to charities across the board, the largest amount being donated to medical research. Other areas of support include enterprise, education, conservation, the arts, and organisations concerned with elderly, disabled and homeless people. Donations in kind of old equipment are also made to charities.

London & Scandinavian Ltd
Metallurgical & chemical products

45 Wimbledon Hill Road,
London SW19 7LZ
081-947 1221

Ch: E Grunfeld
MD: A D Ewart, J Pearson
Contact: Ms P D Stacey
Administrator

Year Ends: 31 Dec '90
Donations: £20,783
Profit: £1,593,000
Turnover: £95,702,000

UK employees: n/a
Total employees: 474

Donations Policy: Preference for children and youth; medical; education; occasionally environment/heritage; the arts. The company supports many of the same charities from one year to another. Donations range from £50 to £1,000.
No grants for fundraising events; advertising in charity brochures; purely denominational (religious) appeals.

London Clubs International plc
Casino operation

3 Tottenham Court Road,
London W1P 0AD
071-637 5464

Ch: R P Hanson
MD: M M Kingsley
Contact: P Isaacs
President

Year Ends: 31 Mar '91
Donations: n/a
Profit: £12,335,000
Turnover: £145,061,000

UK employees: n/a
Total employees: 2,143

Donations Policy: No charitable donations figure is given in the annual report.

London Electricity plc
Electricity supply

Templar House,
81-87 High Holborn,
London WC1V 6NU
071-242 9050

Ch: John Wilson
MD: Roger Urwin
Contact: Derek Salter

Year Ends: 31 Mar '92
Donations: £116,000
Profit: £142,500,000
Turnover: £1,347,100,000

UK employees: n/a
Total employees: 6,581

BitC, ABSA

Donations Policy: Support is directed to London activities and needs. Aim to have wide appeal and for sponsorships to be participative. Aim to channel donations to a few areas of support. These can change and have included homelessness, drug problems, and deaf charities. Grants range from £100 to £5,000.
No response to circular appeals. No grants for advertising in charity brochures; appeals from individuals; purely denominational (religious) appeals; local appeals not in areas of company presence; large national appeals; overseas projects.
Total community contributions in 1991/92 were about £450,000.

● **Alphabetical listing**   Please read page 6

Name/Address   *Officers*   *Financial Information*   *Other Information*

☐ London International Group plc

Healthcare products, photoprocessing

35 New Bridge Street,
London EC4V 6BJ
071-489 1977

MD: A J Butterworth
CE: A E Woltz
Contact: Alan Marshall
Company Secretary

Year Ends: 31 Mar '92
Donations: £17,350
Profit: £39,400,000
Turnover: £398,100,000

UK employees: n/a
Total employees: 10,153

Donations Policy: The parent company does not deal with charitable donations. The following subsidiaries can be approached: LRC Products Ltd, North Circular Road, London E4 8QA (081-527 2377); ColourCare International Ltd, Riverside House, Avon Approach, Salisbury, Wiltshire SP1 3SJ (0722-412202). Most of the company's donations budget is directed to the combating of AIDS. Donations in other respects are limited, with a preference for local charities in areas of company presence and appeals relevant to company business. Preferred areas of support: children and youth, medical and overseas aid/development. Grants to national organisations from £100 to £1,000. Grants to local organisations from £100 to £250. Awards to AIDS charities totalled £7,500 plus gifts in kind and educational support.
Generally no support for circular appeals, fundraising events, advertising in charity brochures, appeals from individuals, purely denominational (religious) appeals or local appeals not in areas of company presence.

☐ London Regional Transport

Provision of public transport in Greater London

4th Floor,
55 Broadway,
London SW1H 0BD
071-222 5600

Ch: C W Newton
Contact: S Blandford
Public Relations

Year Ends: 31 Mar '92
Donations: n/a
Profit: (£16,200,000)
Turnover: £985,200,000

UK employees: n/a
Total employees: 42,728

☐ James Longley (Holdings) Ltd

Building contractors

East Park,
Crawley,
West Sussex RH10 6AP
0293-561212

Ch: Peter Longley
Contact: Peter Longley
Chairman of Longley Trust

Year Ends: 31 Dec '88
Donations: £43,667 (1991)
Profit: £3,792,000
Turnover: £81,961,000

UK employees: n/a
Total employees: 862

Donations Policy: All requests are passed to the Longley Trust which prefers to give to local charities in Crawley and construction industry charities. Preference also for charities in which a member of staff is involved. Grants to national organisations from £100 to £250. Grants to local organisations from £25 to £5,000.
Generally no support for circular appeals, fundraising events, brochure advertising, appeals from individuals, purely denominational appeals, local appeals not in areas of company presence, large national appeals or overseas projects.

☐ Lonrho plc

Mining, agriculture, textiles, construction

Cheapside House,
138 Cheapside,
London EC2V 6BL
071-606 9898

Ch: M J J Leclezio
MD: R W Rowland
Contact: Sir Peter Youens
Chairman, Appeals Committee

Year Ends: 30 Sep '91
Donations: £345,404
Profit: £207,000,000
Turnover: £2,998,000,000

UK employees: n/a
Total employees: 113,094

Donations Policy: Support for a wide range of national and local charities, with preference for medical charities.
No support for advertising in charity brochures or appeals from individuals and no sponsorship. Appeals for overseas projects should be referred to subsidiaries in the relevant countries.

☐ Lookers plc

Sale & hire of motor vehicles

776 Chester Road,
Manchester M32 0QH
061-865 0041

Ch: W K Martindale
Contact: D J Blakeman
Company Secretary

Year Ends: 30 Sep '91
Donations: £5,700
Profit: £3,209,000
Turnover: £359,636,000

UK employees: n/a
Total employees: 2,477

☐ Lopex plc

Marketing communications group

63 St Martin's Lane,
London WC2N 4BH
071-836 0281

Ch: J R W Castle
Contact: M Deane
Company Secretary

Year Ends: 31 Dec '91
Donations: £30,000
Profit: £398,000
Turnover: £206,627,000

UK employees: n/a
Total employees: 1,584

Donations Policy: The company has no set policy it is generally on a first come first served basis.

☐ Lorne Stewart plc

Construction services

Stewart House,
Kenton Road,
Harrow HA3 9TU
081-204 3464

Ch: W Boulton
CE: R Read
Contact: S A Mallick
Financial Director

Year Ends: 31 Mar '91
Donations: n/a
Profit: £2,149,000
Turnover: £121,998,000

UK employees: n/a
Total employees: 18,907

Donations Policy: Preference for local charities in areas of company presence. The company is a subsidiary of BET plc (see separate entry).

☐ Y T Lovell (Holdings) plc

Building contractors

Marsham House,
Station Road,
Gerrards Cross,
Buckinghamshire SL9 8ER
0753-882211

Ch: A P Hichens
MD: R H Sellier
Contact: Allan Price
Company Secretary

Year Ends: 30 Sep '91
Donations: £30,698
Profit: (£20,307,000)
Turnover: £362,984,000

UK employees: n/a
Total employees: 2,444

Donations Policy: During the difficult economic climate the board has decided to suspend donations to charities, but when making donations the company usually prefers to support children and youth; social welfare; environment/heritage; arts.

Please read page 6   **Alphabetical listing** ●

Name/Address	Officers	Financial Information	Other Information

☐ Low & Bonar plc

Packaging, engineering, textiles, travel

Bonar House,
Faraday Street,
Dundee DD1 9JA
0382-818171

Ch: I MacPherson
MD: R J Jarvis
Contact: Mrs Anne Henry
          Administrative Secretary to the
          Charitable Trust

Year Ends: 30 Nov '91
Donations: £39,478
Profit: £24,282,000
Turnover: £307,652,000

UK employees: 1,780
Total employees: 4,401

% Club

Donations Policy: Relief of human suffering generally; priority for medical and welfare charities, including research, treatment and general welfare. Preference for disabled and elderly people, children and youth, environment and heritage, the arts and overseas aid/development, especially for local charities in the areas of company presence. Grants to national organisations from £200 to £1,000. Grants to local organisations from £100 to £500.
Generally no grants for fundraising events; advertising in charity brochures; appeals from individuals; purely denominational (religious) appeals; local appeals not in areas of company presence.

☐ Wm Low & Company plc

Supermarket & superstore operators

PO Box 73,
Baird Avenue,
Dryburgh Industrial Estate,
Dundee DD1 9NF
0382-814022

Ch: J L Millar
Contact: H L Findlay
          Finance Director

Year Ends: 2 Sep '91
Donations: £9,422
Profit: £23,561,000
Turnover: £383,962,000

UK employees: n/a
Total employees: 5,529

Donations Policy: To support in a minor way as many deserving local charities as possible. Preferred areas of support: children and youth, social welfare, medical and recreation. Grants to local organisations are generally between £15 and £100.
No support for circular appeals, national appeals, overseas projects, brochure advertising, purely denominational (religious) appeals or local appeals not in areas of company presence.

☐ Lowe Group

Advertising agents

Bowater House,
68-114 Knightsbridge,
London SW1X 7LT
071-584 5033

Ch: F L Lowe
MD: D Wheldon
Contact: Lucinda Holmes
          General Manager

Year Ends: 31 Dec '90
Donations: £47,293
Profit: £17,991,000
Turnover: £677,319,000

UK employees: n/a
Total employees: 1,798

Donations Policy: Support for non-charities and charities, advertising in charity brochures, large national appeals and the arts. Preference is given to projects in which a member of staff is involved.
No support for appeals from individuals, circular appeals or small local appeals not in areas of company presence.

☐ Lowndes Lambert Group Holdings Ltd

Holding company for insurance brokers

Lowndes Lambert House,
53 Eastcheap,
London EC3P 3HL
071-283 2000

Ch: R Watts
CE: R J G Shaw
Contact: John Bartington
          Director

Year Ends: 31 Mar '92
Donations: £22,167
Profit: £9,269,000
Turnover: £48,611,000

UK employees: 930
Total employees: 1,209

Donations Policy: Preference for charities in which a member of company staff is involved and children's charities. Grants from £25.

☐ Lucas Industries plc

Vehicle & aircraft accessory manufacturers

Brueton House,
New Road,
Solihull,
West Midlands B91 3TX
021-627 6000

Ch: Sir Anthony Gill
MD: L A Edwards
Contact: Denise Foers
          Secretarial Administrator

Year Ends: 31 Jul '91
Donations: £325,000
Profit: £83,600,000
Turnover: £2,365,000,000

UK employees: n/a
Total employees: 54,942

BitC

Donations Policy: Main areas of support: education, scientific research, welfare, religious organisations and the arts. Particular emphasis on local charities working in areas of company presence and which benefit employees and the community. Donations are distributed by head office and local plants.

☐ LWT (Holdings) plc

Independent TV programme contractors

The London Television Centre,
Upper Ground,
London SE1 9LT
071-620 1620

Ch: C Bland
MD: Greg Dyke
Contact: Suzy Stoyel
          Public Affairs Manager

Year Ends: 31 Dec '91
Donations: £35,000
Profit: £25,218,000
Turnover: £260,461,000

UK employees: 723
Total employees: 723

% Club

Donations Policy: Preference for the arts, social welfare, community services and small local charities based within LWT transmission area. Grants from £100 to £5,000. Total community contributions in 1991 were £187,000.
No support for circular appeals, fundraising events, brochure advertising, appeals from individuals, purely denominational (religious) appeals, local appeals not in areas of company presence, large national appeals or overseas projects. No sponsorship of charity events.

☐ M & G Group plc

Unit & investment trust management

Three Quays,
Tower Hill,
London EC3R 6BQ
071-626 4588

Ch: Sir David Money-Coutts
MD: L E Linaker
Contact: Accounts Manager

Year Ends: 30 Sep '91
Donations: £42,601
Profit: £39,238,000
Turnover: n/a

UK employees: 755
Total employees: 755

Donations Policy: Preference for local charities in areas of company presence, appeals relevant to company business and charities in which a member of staff is involved. Preferred areas of support are children and youth, social welfare, education, environment and heritage and enterprise/training. Grants range from £250 to £2,500.
Generally no support for circular appeals, fundraising events, advertising in charity brochures, appeals from individuals, purely denominational (religious) appeals, large national appeals and overseas projects.

● **Alphabetical listing**   Please read page 6

Name/Address   *Officers*   *Financial Information*   *Other Information*

☐ McAlpine plc
                                                                                          Building, civil engineering

Hooton Road,   *Ch:* Sir John Milne   *Year Ends:* 31 Oct '91   *UK employees:* n/a
South Wirral,   *Contact:* L D R Thompson   *Donations:* £30,000   *Total employees:* 5,269
Cheshire L66 7ND   Administration Manager   *Profit:* £9,311,000
051-339 4141   *Turnover:* £620,815,000   BitC

Donations Policy: Preference for local charities in areas where the company operates and charities in which a member of company staff is involved. Preference for children and youth; education.

☐ McArthur Group Ltd
                                                                                          Steel & iron merchants

Foundry Lane,   *Contact:* A R D McArthur   *Year Ends:* 31 Dec '91   *UK employees:* n/a
Fish Ponds Trading Estate, Chairman   *Donations:* £5,210   *Total employees:* 461
Bristol BS5 7UE   *Profit:* (£224,000)
0272-656242   *Turnover:* £44,596,000

Donations Policy: Preference for local appeals in areas of company operation, appeals relevant to company business and charities in which a member of company staff is involved. Grants to national organisations from £25 to £100. Grants to local organisations from £25 to £1,500. No grants for purely denominational (religious) appeals; local appeals not in areas of company presence; large national appeals; overseas projects.

☐ McCain Foods (GB) Ltd
                                                                                          Freezer foods

Havers Hill,   *Contact:* Mrs L Baker   *Year Ends:* 30 Jun '92   *UK employees:* n/a
Scarborough,   Secretary to the Charities   *Donations:* £96,027   *Total employees:* 1,969
North Yorkshire YO11 3BS   Committee   *Profit:* £22,886,000
0723-584141   *Turnover:* £211,412,000

Donations Policy: Prefer all donations to be made locally, large national charities are only supported through local fundraising events. Preference for appeals relevant to company business. Preferred areas of support: children and youth; medical; education; recreation/sport; environment and heritage; the arts; enterprise/training. Grants to national organisations from £500 to £1,000. Grants to local organisations from £50 to £10,000.
Generally no support for circular appeals; fundraising events; advertising in charity brochures; appeals from individuals; purely denominational (religious) appeals or local appeals not in areas of company presence.
Sponsorship proposals to J S Blackburn, Chairman, Charity Committee.

☐ McCarthy & Stone plc
                                                                                          Sheltered accommodation

26-32 Oxford Road,   *Contact:* J S McCarthy   *Year Ends:* 31 Aug '91   *UK employees:* n/a
Bournemouth,   Chairman   *Donations:* n/a   *Total employees:* 2,002
Dorset BH8 8EZ   *Profit:* (£16,900,000)
0202-292480   *Turnover:* £73,100,000

Donations Policy: It is the policy of McCarthy & Stone to consider "requests for support by registered charities or special events that are directly related to our retired customers and our elderly in need".

☐ McClaughlin & Harvey plc
                                                                                          Contracting & residential developments

15 Trench Road,   *Ch:* C A Denny   *Year Ends:* 31 Dec '91   *UK employees:* n/a
Mallusk,   *MD:* A M Stoddart   *Donations:* £1,480   *Total employees:* 581
Newtownabbey,   *Contact:* S A S Hamill   *Profit:* £5,397,000
County Antrim BT36 8FA   Company Secretary   *Turnover:* £98,364,000
0232-342777

☐ MacDonald Martin Distilleries plc
                                                                                          Scotch whisky

MacDonald House,   *Ch:* D W A MacDonald   *Year Ends:* 31 Mar '92   *UK employees:* n/a
186 Commercial Street,   *MD:* N A H McKerrow   *Donations:* £15,000   *Total employees:* 219
Edinburgh EH6 6NN   *Contact:* D W A MacDonald   *Profit:* £8,567,000
031-554 4477   Chairman   *Turnover:* £31,808,000

Donations Policy: Preference for local charities in areas where the company operates and for appeals relevant to company business. Preference for children and youth, social welfare (including alcohol abuse), medical and elderly people. Grants to national organisations from £50 to £1,000. Grants to local organisations from £25 to £250.
No grants for advertising in charity brochures; appeals from individuals; purely denominational (religious) appeals; local appeals not in areas of company presence; overseas projects.
Sponsorship proposals to Mrs Lesley Young.

☐ McDonald's Restaurants Ltd
                                                                                          Quick service restaurants

11-59 High Road,   *Contact:* Ms E Bensilum   *Year Ends:* 31 Dec '91   *UK employees:* n/a
East Finchley,   Assistant Public Relations   *Donations:* see below   *Total employees:* 26,200
London N2 8AW   Manager   *Profit:* £29,500,000
081-883 6400   *Turnover:* £515,000,000   % Club, BitC

Donations Policy: Preference for children and youth; medical; education; environment/heritage; enterprise/training. The company has organised training and enterprise schemes in Wolverhampton and Nottingham.
£1 million was donated to the Ronald McDonald House at Alder Hey. The Ronald McDonald House programme aims to provide a comfortable family environment for parents and close relatives of children being treated at nearby hospitals. £400,000 was donated to various children's charities via "Ronald McDonald Children's Charities".
Regional and local appeals should be directed to the appropriate marketing department in London, Manchester or Birmingham.
No grants for appeals from individuals; purely denominational (religious) appeals; overseas projects.

Please read page 6 | | | Alphabetical listing •

Name/Address	Officers	Financial Information	Other Information

☐ McDonnell Douglas Information Systems Ltd — Computer design & manufacture

Maylands Park South,
Boundary Way,
Hemel Hempstead,
Herts HP2 7HU
0442-232424

Contact: David Malaperiman
Communications Director

Year Ends: 31 Dec '91
Donations: n/a
Profit: £14,254,000
Turnover: £139,797,000

UK employees: 1,560
Total employees: 2,000

Donations Policy: Supports local charities in areas of company presence through the Hertfordshire Community Trust.

☐ MacFarlane Group (Clansman) plc — Packaging, printing

41 Sutcliffe Road,
Glasgow G13 1AH
041-959 4444

Contact: Sir Norman MacFarlane
Chairman & Managing Director

Year Ends: 31 Dec '91
Donations: £10,000
Profit: £6,850,000
Turnover: £82,656,000

UK employees: n/a
Total employees: 1,709

% Club

Donations Policy: Charitable donations are generally made to Scottish charities through the N S MacFarlane Charitable Trust.

☐ M & W Mack Ltd — Horticultural produce distributors

43 North Street,
Chichester,
West Sussex PO19 1NF
0243-787646

Ch: D Mack
Contact: C P Mack
Executive Chairman

Year Ends: 28 Apr '89
Donations: £4,745
Profit: £1,462,000
Turnover: £90,842,000

UK employees: n/a
Total employees: 360

☐ MacKays Stores Holdings Ltd — Textile manufacture & retail

Caledonia Street,
Paisley PA3 2JR
041-887 9151

Contact: I W McGeogh
Managing Director

Year Ends: 21 Apr '89
Donations: £4,640
Profit: £4,817,000
Turnover: £87,105,000

UK employees: n/a
Total employees: 2,548

☐ McKechnie plc — Metal & plastic building products

Leighswood Road,
Aldridge,
Walsall,
West Midlands WS9 8DS
0922-743887

Ch: Dr J Butler
Contact: Mrs Rita Stokes
Assistant Company Secretary

Year Ends: 31 Jul '91
Donations: £11,525
Profit: £20,500,000
Turnover: £300,104,000

UK employees: n/a
Total employees: 6,582

☐ MacMillan Ltd — Publishers

Houndmills,
Basingstoke,
Hampshire RG21 2XS
0256-29242

Ch: Second Earl of Stockton
Contact: Brian McKenzie
Personnel Manager

Year Ends: 31 Dec '90
Donations: £118,250
Profit: £5,239,000
Turnover: £189,992,000

UK employees: 1,196
Total employees: 1,923

Donations Policy: There is a strong preference for local charities operating in areas of company presence or for appeals relevant to the business. Preferred areas of support are education, children/youth and the arts. Where appropriate MacMillan prefers to donate a selection of books for fundraising purposes.
Generally no support for large national appeals, circular appeals, brochure advertising, appeals from individuals and local appeals not in areas of company presence.

☐ James McNaughton Paper Group Ltd — Paper merchanting

5th Floor,
71 Kingsway,
London WC2B 6ST
071-242 6021

Contact: S K Chakravarty
Managing Director

Year Ends: 31 Dec '91
Donations: n/a
Profit: £2,958,000
Turnover: £118,144,000

UK employees: n/a
Total employees: 469

☐ MacPherson plc — Paints & other surface coatings

9 Rookwood Way,
Haverhill,
Suffolk CB9 8PQ
0440-706666

Ch: C E J Whenham
Contact: Caroline Brown
Recruitment Officer

Year Ends: 31 Dec '86
Donations: £4,888
Profit: £2,167,000
Turnover: £100,883,000

UK employees: n/a
Total employees: 6,354

☐ Macro UK Ltd — Cash & carry merchandising

Charles House,
Albert Street,
Eccles,
Manchester M30 0LJ
061-707 1585

Ch: P Fentener Van Vlissingen
Contact: Mrs Vivienne Cramer
Marketing Manager

Year Ends: 31 Dec '90
Donations: £51,854
Profit: £10,020,000
Turnover: £645,418,000

UK employees: n/a
Total employees: 6,920

Donations Policy: Preference for small charities local to the company's stores. Direct giving is preferred rather than support for advertising in brochures or fundraising events.

• **Alphabetical listing** Please read page 6

Name/Address	Officers	Financial Information	Other Information

☐ **Maersk Co Ltd** Ship owners

10 Cabot Square,
Canary Wharf,
London E14 4QL
071-712 5000

Ch: A B Marshall
MD: N J Iversen
Contact: Mrs Thornton
Company Secretary

Year Ends: 31 Dec '89
Donations: £3,018 (1988)
Profit: £34,798,000
Turnover: £187,870,000

UK employees: n/a
Total employees: 2,761

☐ **MAI plc** Advertising, money broking, printing

8 Montague Close,
London Bridge,
London SE1 9RD
071-407 7624

Ch: Sir Ian Morrow
Contact: C R Hollick
Managing Director

Year Ends: 30 Jun '91
Donations: £26,000
Profit: £66,300,000
Turnover: £361,500,000

UK employees: n/a
Total employees: 4,619

Donations Policy: The companies charity budget is fully allocated to charities that the directors and staff are particularly interested in. Therefore it would be unwise to apply for a donation without the support of a member of staff.

☐ **E D & F Man Ltd** Commodity Brokers

Sugar Quay,
Lower Thames Street,
London EC3R 6DU
071-285 3000

Contact: David Boehm
Charitable Trust

Year Ends:
Donations: n/a
Profit: n/a
Turnover: n/a

UK employees: n/a
Total employees: n/a

% Club, BitC

Donations Policy: Donations are made through the charitable trust. This made grants totalling over £186,000 in 1990/91. Support is given to enterprise initiatives in East London, charities concerned with underprivileged and disabled young people at home and abroad, and in particular charities in which a member of company staff is involved.

☐ **Manchester Airport plc** International airport operation

Manchester M22 5PA
061-489 3000

Ch: Councillor J Flanagan
CE: G W Thompson
Contact: Pam Roberts
Public Relations Administrator

Year Ends: 31 Mar '91
Donations: £72,700
Profit: £32,564,000
Turnover: £127,159,000

UK employees: n/a
Total employees: 2,059

Donations Policy: The company make no cash donations to charities, but most applicants will receive an airport pen and occasionally an atlas for raffles or fundraising.
For charity sponsorship contact Sharon Allen in the Legal Department.

☐ **Manchester Ship Canal Co** Operators of Manchester ship canal

Quay West,
Collier Street,
Runcorn,
Cheshire WA1 1HA
061-872 2411

Ch: R Hough
Contact: A J Dickinson
Company Secretary

Year Ends: 31 Dec '91
Donations: £8,900
Profit: £9,662,000
Turnover: £20,191,000

UK employees: 366
Total employees: 366

Donations Policy: Preference for local charities in areas where the company operates and appeals relevant to company business. Preference for children and youth; social welfare; medical; education; environment/heritage. Grants to national organisations from £75 to £500. Grants to local organisations from £25 to £250.
No grants for fundraising events.

☐ **Manders Holdings plc** Paint & printing ink manufacturers, property

PO Box 186,
Old Heath Road,
Wolverhampton,
West Midlands WV1 2QT
0902-871028

Ch: R Amos
MD: R M Akers
Contact: J Farmer
Company Secretary

Year Ends: 31 Dec '91
Donations: £2,055
Profit: £6,040,000
Turnover: £101,632,000

UK employees: n/a
Total employees: 1,311

☐ **Manganese Bronze Holdings plc** Vehicles, metal components & casting

1 Love Lane,
London EC2Y 7HJ
071-606 0088

Contact: Jamie Barwick
Managing Director

Year Ends: 31 Jul '91
Donations: £2,190
Profit: (£949,000)
Turnover: £69,731,000

UK employees: n/a
Total employees: 1,328

☐ **Mannesmann Demag Ltd** Civil engineering

Beamont Road,
Banbury,
Oxfordshire OX16 7QZ
0295-264555

Ch: V W K Hellman
Contact: J W G Rockall
Personnel Manager

Year Ends: 31 Dec '91
Donations: £13,412 (1990)
Profit: £3,484,000
Turnover: £62,376,000

UK employees: 326
Total employees: n/a

Donations Policy: Support is given only to local charities in areas where the company operates. Preferred areas of support are children and youth, social welfare, enterprise/training and charities in which a member of staff is involved. Grants to local organisations range from £30 to £100.
No support for circular appeals, advertising in charity brochures, appeals from individuals, purely denominational (religious) appeals, local appeals not in areas of company presence, large national appeals or overseas projects.

Please read page 6 — Alphabetical listing

Name/Address	Officers	Financial Information	Other Information

☐ Manpower UK Ltd
Staff recruitment services

International House,
66 Chiltern Street,
London W1M 1PR
071-224 6688

Ch: M S Fromstein
Contact: Ouida Weaver
Human Resources Manager

Year Ends: 31 Oct '90
Donations: £140,269
Profit: £55,720,000
Turnover: £2,009,521,000

UK employees: n/a
Total employees: 7,912

BitC

Donations Policy: Company giving is very focussed with the company giving committed support to a few projects.

☐ R Mansell Ltd
Building contractors

13-27 Grant Road,
Croydon,
Surrey CR9 6BU
081-654 8191

Ch: L Hill
Contact: B Adams
Managing Director

Year Ends: 3 Jan '91
Donations: £4,778
Profit: £1,031,000
Turnover: £126,477,000

UK employees: n/a
Total employees: 1,111

% Club

Donations Policy: Support for medical appeals, youth training and education, community projects. Sponsored DUMP 89, a campaign which collected and disposed of 1.5 tonnes of hazardous medicine and pills.

☐ Mansfield Brewery plc
Brewing, wines, spirits & soft drinks

Littleworth,
Mansfield,
Nottinghamshire NG18 1AB
0623-25691

Ch: G C Kent
MD: W McCosh
Contact: John Hare
Company Secretary

Year Ends: 31 Mar '92
Donations: £4,000
Profit: £10,999,000
Turnover: £114,453,000

UK employees: n/a
Total employees: 3,925

Donations Policy: Preference for local charities in areas where the company operates and for social welfare and medical.
No response to circular appeals. No grants for purely denominational (religious) appeals; local appeals not in areas of company presence or overseas projects.

☐ Manweb plc
Electricity supply

Sealand Road,
Chester CH1 4LR
0244-377111

Ch: Bryan Weston
CE: J E Roberts
Contact: Joy King
Head of Public Relations

Year Ends: 31 Mar '92
Donations: £74,170
Profit: £94,700,000
Turnover: £834,600,000

UK employees: n/a
Total employees: 4,600

% Club, BitC, ABSA

Donations Policy: Priority is given to: projects in the Manweb area; projects to help work creation and new enterprises; support of fundraising efforts of Manweb staff through Manweb plc's Charity Chest; projects to help elderly and disabled people; projects to help encourage electricity-related curriculum and syllabus development in educational establishments. Grants range from £10 to £1,000.
No support for appeals from individuals, national charities (unless fund is used solely for local project), preservation of historic buildings, research, expeditions, political or military organisations, circular appeals, advertising in charity brochures, purely denominational (religious) appeals, local appeals not in areas of company presence or overseas projects.
Sponsorship for sporting events and advertisements in publications etc. will normally only be considered commercially in terms of potential advertising benefits. Sponsorship of the arts will be limited to two or three events a year, planned well in advance.
Total community contributions in 1991/92 were £350,170.

☐ Marks & Spencer plc
International retail company

Michael House,
37-67 Baker Street,
London W1A 1DN
071-935 4422

Ch: Sir Richard Greenbury
MD: C V Silver
Contact: Miss E Callender, Mrs Y Pennicott

Year Ends: 31 Mar '92
Donations: £3,425,000
Profit: £623,500,000
Turnover: £5,793,400,000

UK employees: 55,750
Total employees: 67,894

% Club, BitC, ABSA

Donations Policy: Marks & Spencer's community involvement policy is to support the communities in which the company trades through cash contributions and secondment of staff to a wide range of projects and voluntary organisations. Priorities include people with special needs, elderly people, homeless people, young unemployed people and disadvantaged people particularly in inner cities. Grants range from £25 to £75,000.
No response to circular appeals. No support for capital projects, endowment funds, expeditions, sports (except for people with special needs), fundraising events, appeals from individuals, and animal or overseas charities.
Total community contributions for 1991/92 were £5.5 million including £1.5 million in secondments. Arts, health and care, and heritage and community arts appeals should be addressed to Miss E Callender. Secondment proposals and education and training appeals should be addressed to Miss Y Pennicott. Stores have a small budget for local initiatives, managed by the store's charitable donations committee.

☐ Marley plc
Manufacturer of building trade products

London Road,
Riverhead,
Sevenoaks,
Kent TN13 2DS
0732-455255

Ch: G Russell
CE: J C Castle
Contact: Mrs Margaret Barber
Head Office Administration Manager

Year Ends: 31 Dec '91
Donations: £66,000
Profit: £25,000,000
Turnover: £574,300,000

UK employees: n/a
Total employees: 10,119

Donations Policy: Both national and local appeals are considered.

☐ Marling Industries plc
Manufacturer of industrial textiles

14 Aylmer Parade,
London N2 0PF
081-340 4687

Ch: P E J Held
MD: P Wiseman
Contact: P E J Held
Chairman

Year Ends: 31 Mar '91
Donations: £19,000
Profit: £3,597,000
Turnover: £121,827,000

UK employees: n/a
Total employees: 2,282

Donations Policy: Preference for local charities in areas of company presence, especially children, education and the arts.

• **Alphabetical listing**　　　　　　　　　　　　　　　　　　　　　　　　　　　　　　　　Please read page 6

Name/Address　　　　　　*Officers*　　　　　　*Financial Information*　　　　*Other Information*

☐ Marlowe Holdings Ltd
Distributor of electrical, DIY & garden products

PO Box 1,　　　　　　　　　*MD:* R Y Ballantyne　　　*Year Ends:* 31 Dec '90　　*UK employees:* n/a
Tatton Street,　　　　　　　　　　　　　　　　　　　*Donations:* £83,000　　　*Total employees:* 2,724
Knutsford,　　　　　　　　　　　　　　　　　　　　*Profit:* £22,633,000
Cheshire　　　　　　　　　　　　　　　　　　　　*Turnover:* £418,501,000

Donations Policy: We have been unable to obtain any information on this company, other than to confirm the head office address.

☐ Mars GB Ltd
Food manufacturers

Eskdale Road,　　　　　　*Ch:* M G Pullan　　　　　*Year Ends:* 29 Dec '90　　*UK employees:* n/a
Winnersh Triangle,　　　　*Contact:* Jill Lark　　　　　*Donations:* £208,496　　*Total employees:* 6,834
Wokingham,　　　　　　　　External Relations Co-ordinator　　*Profit:* £53,852,000
Berkshire RG11 5AQ　　　　　　　　　　　　　　　*Turnover:* £1,377,470,000　　　　　ABSA
0734-697700

Donations Policy: Priority for charities concerned with industry and trade, health and safety, education, the environment and youth. Grants to national organisations from £150 to £10,000. Grants to local organisations in areas of company presence from £25 to £10,000.

☐ Marshall Cavendish Ltd
Publishers

119 Wardour Street,　　　　*MD:* C G Lim　　　　　　*Year Ends:* 31 Aug '90　　*UK employees:* 357
London W1V 3PD　　　　*Contact:* Joanna Page　　　*Donations:* £7,653　　　*Total employees:* 420
071-734 6710　　　　　　Office Manager　　　　　　*Profit:* £3,050,000
　　　　　　　　　　　　　　　　　　　　　　　　Turnover: £96,418,000

☐ Marshall Food Group Ltd
Broiler chicken breeders

Newbridge,　　　　　　　　*Ch:* E C Tarr　　　　　　*Year Ends:* 30 Sep '90　　*UK employees:* n/a
Midlothian EH28 8SW　　*CE:* W M Marshall　　　　*Donations:* £977　　　　*Total employees:* 4,010
031-333 3341　　　　　　*Contact:* Miss J Marshall　　*Profit:* £7,653,000
　　　　　　　　　　　　　Commercial Donations　　　*Turnover:* £141,314,000
　　　　　　　　　　　　　Co-ordinator

Donations Policy: Support is given only to local charities in Scotland, especially in areas where the company operates. Preference for appeals relevant to company business and for charities in which a member of company staff is involved. Preference for children and youth; medical; environment/heritage; arts; enterprise/training. Where possible donations are in the form of chicken products.
No response to circular appeals. No grants for advertising in charity brochures; local appeals not in areas of company presence; large national appeals; overseas projects.

☐ Marshall of Cambridge (Holdings) Ltd
Engineering

Airport House,　　　　　　*Ch:* M J Marshall　　　　　*Year Ends:* 31 Dec '90　　*UK employees:* n/a
The Airport,　　　　　　　*MD:* C L Greaves　　　　　*Donations:* £267,081　　*Total employees:* 2,654
Cambridge CB5 8RY　　*Contact:* G Bruce　　　　　*Profit:* £14,760,000
0223-61133　　　　　　　Company Secretary　　　　*Turnover:* £243,606,000

Donations Policy: As a private company, Marshall has always pursued a "low profile" policy for its charitable giving, although the level of giving has remained high. The company therefore believes it inappropriate to publicise the types of projects it supports.

☐ Marshalls Finance Ltd
Moneybroking

Lloyds Chambers,　　　　*Ch:* A D Burton　　　　　*Year Ends:* 30 Apr '92　　*UK employees:* 500
1 Portsoken Street,　　　　*Contact:* P J Bentley　　　　*Donations:* £5,000　　　*Total employees:* 1,234
London E1 8DF　　　　　Group Finance Director　　　*Profit:* £23,927,000
071-481 1511　　　　　　　　　　　　　　　　　　*Turnover:* £140,957,000

☐ Marshalls Halifax plc
Concrete production, rock drilling equipment

Hall Ings,　　　　　　　　*Ch:* D R Marshall　　　　　*Year Ends:* 31 Mar '91　　*UK employees:* n/a
Southowram,　　　　　　　*Contact:* S Marshall　　　　*Donations:* £4,931　　　*Total employees:* 3,022
Halifax,　　　　　　　　　　　　　　　　　　　　　*Profit:* £12,731,000
West Yorkshire HX3 9TW　　　　　　　　　　　　*Turnover:* £184,370,000
0422-264521

☐ Marston's Brewery
Brewers, wine & spirit merchants

PO Box 26,　　　　　　　　*Ch:* M W F Hurdle　　　　*Year Ends:* 28 Mar '92　　*UK employees:* n/a
Shobnall Road,　　　　　　*MD:* D W Gordon　　　　*Donations:* £44,824　　*Total employees:* 3,031
Burton-on-Trent,　　　　　*Contact:* S Dennis　　　　　*Profit:* £15,058,000
Staffordshire DE14 2BW　　Group Trade Marketing Manager　　*Turnover:* £116,001,000
0283-31131

Donations Policy: Support for local and national appeals relevant to company business, trade related appeals and causes in which the company as a brewery is interested (ie. alcohol abuse). Support is also given for social welfare, enterprise and the arts.
No support for appeals from individuals, overseas projects, local appeals not in areas of company presence, large national appeals or overseas projects.

Please read page 6 — Alphabetical listing

Name/Address	Officers	Financial Information	Other Information

☐ Martini & Rossi Ltd

Wine merchants

Yorkshire House,
Grosvenor Crescent,
London SW1W 7EP
071-235 4030

Ch: Duke of Marlborough
Contact: S Goggin
Sponsorship Manager UK

Year Ends: 31 Dec '88
Donations: £28,000 (1991)
Profit: £9,427,000
Turnover: £74,565,000

UK employees: n/a
Total employees: 232

% Club

Donations Policy: Martini are in the process of formulating a new policy. In addition to the £28,000 charitable donations, £20,000 was donated to trade charities such as the Licensed Victuallers and the Wine & Spirit Trade Benevolent Society. Although the company makes small cash donations it spends more than £10,000 on advertising in charity programmes and another £10,000 in giving bottles to tombolas, raffles etc..
No support for circular appeals, purely denominational (religious) appeals, overseas projects or fundraising events.

☐ Marubeni UK plc

Industrial, agricultural & consumer goods traders

120 Moorgate,
London EC2M 6SS
071-826 8600

Contact: Y Terao
General Manager, Administration Department

Year Ends: 31 Mar '91
Donations: £2,384
Profit: £1,775,000
Turnover: £316,195,000

UK employees: n/a
Total employees: 118

☐ MAT Group Ltd

Transport & ancillary services

Arnold House,
36-41 Holywell Lane,
London EC2P 2EQ
071-247 6500

Ch: P A Kunzler
Contact: K M Turner
Marketing Director

Year Ends: 30 Sep '90
Donations: £5,133 (1988)
Profit: (£612,000)
Turnover: £82,568,000

UK employees: n/a
Total employees: 1,113

☐ Matheson & Co Ltd

Insurance broking, car distribution

3 Lombard Street,
London EC3V 9AQ
071-528 4000

Ch: H N L Keswick
Contact: J J G Brown
Director

Year Ends: 31 Dec '90
Donations: £130,000
Profit: £3,077,000
Turnover: £270,988,000

UK employees: n/a
Total employees: 3,523

Donations Policy: Donations are made through the Charities Aid Foundation and include some long-term covenants. Preference for charities in which a member of company staff is involved. The company supports many Hong Kong related charities including the Gurkha Welfare Fund.

☐ Matsushita Electric (UK) Ltd

TV set & microwave manufacture

Wyncliffe Road,
Pentwyn Industrial Estate,
Cardiff CF2 7XB
0222-540011

MD: Y Koyama
Contact: C Johns
Internal Affairs Manager

Year Ends: 31 Mar '91
Donations: n/a
Profit: £3,127,000
Turnover: £195,275,000

UK employees: n/a
Total employees: 1,578

☐ Bernard Matthews plc

Integrated turkey producers

Great Witchingham Hall,
Norwich,
Norfolk NR9 5QD
0603-872611

Ch: B T Matthews
MD: B J Joll
Contact: J G Brown
Company Secretary

Year Ends: 31 Dec '91
Donations: £85,123
Profit: £13,190,000
Turnover: £148,379,000

UK employees: n/a
Total employees: 2,544

Donations Policy: Preference for local charities in areas where the company operates. Preference for children and youth charities, environment and the arts.
No response to circular appeals. No grants for advertising in charity brochures; appeals from individuals; local appeals not in areas of company presence; large national appeals; overseas projects.

☐ Maxell (UK) Ltd

Audio & video tapes, micro batteries, floppy discs

Apley,
Telford,
Shropshire TF6 6DA
0952-251911

Contact: G Bullock
Personnel Manager

Year Ends: 31 Mar '91
Donations: n/a
Profit: £173,000
Turnover: £107,659,000

UK employees: n/a
Total employees: 549

☐ May Gurney & Co Ltd

Civil engineering

Trowse,
Norwich NR14 8SZ
0603-627281

Contact: Jim Holmes
Chairman

Year Ends: 31 Mar '90
Donations: £2,566 (1989)
Profit: £4,571,000
Turnover: £88,547,000

UK employees: n/a
Total employees: 1,017

Donations Policy: Preference for local charities in areas of company presence. Unsolicited appeals not welcome.

☐ Mayne Nickless Europe plc

Security services

Mabel Street,
The Meadows,
Nottingham NG2 3ED
0602-864110

Ch: L A Bytheway
Contact: John Spate
Director of Administration & Finance

Year Ends: 30 Jun '91
Donations: n/a
Profit: £2,804,000
Turnover: £149,035,000

UK employees: n/a
Total employees: 8,352

● **Alphabetical listing** Please read page 6

Name/Address	Officers	Financial Information	Other Information

☐ MB Caradon plc

Caradon House,
24 Queens Road,
Weybridge,
Surrey KT13 9UX
0932-850850

Ch: A P Hichens
CE: P J Jansen
Contact: E Cameron

Year Ends: 31 Dec '91
Donations: £58,849
Profit: £106,400,000
Turnover: £679,200,000

Holding company

UK employees: n/a
Total employees: 11,192

Donations Policy: Preference for local charities in areas where the company operates and appeals relevant to company business.

☐ MCL Group Ltd

77 Mount Ephraim,
Tunbridge Wells,
Kent TN4 8BS
0892-510088

Ch: H Tanka
MD: J E Ebenezer
Contact: Valerie Teal
Group Operations Manager

Year Ends: 31 Dec '90
Donations: £64,000 (1991)
Profit: £14,208,000
Turnover: £264,406,000

Vehicle importers

UK employees: n/a
Total employees: 386

% Club

Donations Policy: The company continues to maintain a policy of concentrating its support upon good causes and appeals within the local community. Nevertheless more than 100 diverse charities many of which are national receive assistance in one form or another from the group during any one year.
Support is given to appeals relevant to company business and preference for charities in which a member of company staff is involved. Preference for children and youth; social welfare; medical; environment/heritage; arts; overseas aid/development. Grants to national organisations from £25 to £10,000. Grants to local organisations from £25 to £3,000.
No grants for purely denominational (religious) appeals; local appeals not in areas of company presence.

☐ MECO International Ltd

11 Walker Street,
Edinburgh EH3 7NE
031-225 4455

Contact: Angus Graham
Office Manager

Year Ends: 31 Dec '90
Donations: £10,000
Profit: £5,859,000
Turnover: £160,057,000

Heavy industrial equipment for mining industry

UK employees: n/a
Total employees: 2,093

☐ Medical & Media Communications

Brigade House,
8 Parsons Green,
London SW6 4TN
071-371 5044

Contact: J Stephenson
Chief Executive

Year Ends:
Donations: n/a
Profit: n/a
Turnover: n/a

PR for medical companies

UK employees: n/a
Total employees: n/a

% Club

Donations Policy: To support the development and good management of charitable organisations through direct contact and executive support. Preference for children and youth; social welfare; medical; education. Preference for charities in which a member of company staff is involved.
No grants for advertising in charity brochures; appeals from individuals; purely denominational (religious) appeals; local appeals not in areas of company presence. No response to circular appeals. The company prefers to work with organisations rather than making direct donations or advertising.

☐ Meggitt plc

Farrs House,
Cowgrove,
Wimborne,
Dorset BH21 4EL
0202-841141

Ch: K H Coates
MD: H N P McCorkell
Contact: M S Shaw
Company Secretary

Year Ends: 31 Dec '91
Donations: £1,000
Profit: £23,460,000
Turnover: £301,919,000

Aviation instruments manufacture

UK employees: n/a
Total employees: 7,768

☐ Melton Medes Ltd

6 Union Road,
Nottingham NG3 1FH
0602-582277

Ch: N R Puri
CE: J E Philpotts
Contact: Miss Lyn Stevens
Personal Assistant to the Chairman

Year Ends: 31 Dec '90
Donations: £7,800
Profit: £6,613,000
Turnover: £162,338,000

Engineering, carpet manufacture, fibres, paper & polymer

UK employees: n/a
Total employees: 3,109

Donations Policy: Melton Medes have their own Charitable Trust called the Puri Foundation. This trust supports: (a) people in need particularly living in Nottinghamshire and past and present employees of the company, and people in need living in the continent of India, in particular citizens of the towns of Mullan Pur near Chandigarh and Ambala; (b) education of children attending schools or colleges by provision of equipment or facilities not normally provided by the Local Authority; (c) provision of facilities for recreation; (d) education and training of young people living in Nottinghamshire who are in need.

☐ MEMEC

17 Thame Park Road,
Thame,
Oxfordshire OX9 3XD
0844-261919

Ch: R T Skipworth
Contact: C Stevens
Finance Director

Year Ends: 31 Dec '89
Donations: £4,667
Profit: £6,697,000
Turnover: £97,373,000

Distribution of electronic components

UK employees: n/a
Total employees: 591

Please read page 6 — Alphabetical listing

Name/Address	Officers	Financial Information	Other Information

☐ **John Menzies plc** — Newsagents, booksellers, stationers

Hanover Buildings,
Rose Street,
Edinburgh EH2 2YQ
031-225 8555

Ch: J M Menzies
MD: Hon F R Noel-Paton
Contact: C A Anderson
Company Secretary

Year Ends: 4 May '92
Donations: £87,000
Profit: £25,400,000
Turnover: £1,081,800,000

UK employees: n/a
Total employees: 12,831

% Club

Donations Policy: Preference for job creation, medical and environmental charities. Particular preference is given to Scottish charities and to giving long-term covenanted support. Community contributions are also made through secondment of managers to voluntary organisations.

☐ **MEPC Group plc** — Property investment, development

12 St James's Square,
London SW1Y 4LB
071-911 5300

Ch: Sir Christopher Benson
MD: J L Tuckley
Contact: Secretary to the Charity Committee

Year Ends: 30 Sep '91
Donations: £414,000
Profit: £143,300,000
Turnover: n/a

UK employees: 1,056
Total employees: n/a

BitC

Donations Policy: The company supports a wide range of charities. The donations figure includes £37,500 paid in connection with archaeological investigations. The group also funds a post-graduate bursary at each of Cambridge, Reading and City Universities in property related subjects.

☐ **Mercedes-Benz UK Ltd** — Motor car distributors

Mercedes-Benz Centre,
Tongwell,
Milton Keynes,
Buckinghamshire MK15 8BA
0908-668899

Ch: W Niefer
MD: H Tauscher
Contact: J Evans
Press & Public Relations Manager

Year Ends: 31 Dec '90
Donations: £28,000
Profit: £737,000
Turnover: £882,683,000

UK employees: n/a
Total employees: 1,189

Donations Policy: The company supports charities that have a connection with the motor industry or with the Milton Keynes area. Grants range from £25 to £2,000.

☐ **Merchant Retail Group plc** — Retailers

6 Old Lodge Place,
St Margarets Road,
Twickenham,
Middlesex TW1 1RQ
081-744 2266

Ch: E Kinder
MD: D Wallis
Contact: M J Jones
Finance Director

Year Ends: 28 Mar '92
Donations: nil
Profit: £1,721,000
Turnover: £155,039,000

UK employees: n/a
Total employees: 2,826

☐ **Merck, Sharpe & Dohme Holdings Ltd** — Manufacturing chemists

Hertford Road,
Hoddesden,
Hertfordshire EN11 9BU
0992-467272

MD: U Lawton
Contact: Public Affairs Department

Year Ends: 31 Dec '90
Donations: £311,586
Profit: £877,000
Turnover: £184,747,000

UK employees: n/a
Total employees: 1,726

% Club, BitC

Donations Policy: The company supports charities enhancing the quality of medical care, medical research, medical education and other educational initiatives. Some preference is given to local charities in areas of company presence and to charities in which a member of staff is involved.

☐ **Merrill Lynch International Ltd** — Financial services

25 Ropemaker Street,
London EC2Y 9LY
071-867 2000

Ch: C R Reeves
Contact: R Spiegelberg
Director of Corporate Communications

Year Ends:
Donations: n/a
Profit: n/a
Turnover: n/a

UK employees: n/a
Total employees: n/a

% Club

☐ **Mersey Docks & Harbour Co** — Operation of port facilities

Port of Liverpool Building,
Pier Head,
Liverpool L3 1BZ
051-200 2020

Ch: W B Slater
MD: P T Furlong
Contact: W J Bowley
Director of Legal Services

Year Ends: 31 Dec '91
Donations: £10,000
Profit: £13,165,000
Turnover: £69,490,000

UK employees: n/a
Total employees: 1,606

Donations Policy: Preference for local charities in the areas of company presence and appeals relevant to company business. Preferred areas of support: children and youth, social welfare and medical.
In addition a limited number of small donations (from £50 to £150) are made on an annual basis to certain local charitable organisations from The Mersey Docks & Harbour Company Charitable Fund which is maintained separately. Grants from the fund totalled £1,875 in 1990/91. No response to circular appeals. No grants for fundraising events; advertising in charity brochures; appeals from individuals; purely denominational (religious) appeals; local appeals not in areas of company presence; large national appeals; overseas projects.

☐ **Metal Closures Group plc** — Metal & plastic packaging

Bromford Lane,
West Bromwich,
West Midlands B70 7HY
021-553 2900

MD: J Cassera
Contact: Pamela Cuthbert
Secretary to the Managing Director

Year Ends: 31 Dec '88
Donations: £8,333
Profit: £7,644,000
Turnover: £114,934,000

UK employees: n/a
Total employees: 2,865

• **Alphabetical listing**   Please read page 6

Name/Address	Officers	Financial Information	Other Information

☐ **Metalchem International Ltd**   Selling metals, chemicals, crystals etc.

79-83 Great Portland Street,   *Contact:* Mrs Joy Chaplin   *Year Ends:* 31 Dec '90   *UK employees:* n/a
London   W1N 5FA   Company Secretary   *Donations:* n/a   *Total employees:* n/a
071-580 3482   *Profit:* £237,000
                                                                                                 Turnover: £136,670,000

☐ **Metalrax plc**   Miscellaneous mechanical engineering

Ardath Road,   *Ch:* J M Wardle   *Year Ends:* 31 Dec '91   *UK employees:* n/a
Kings Norton,   *MD:* E S Moore   *Donations:* £7,618   *Total employees:* 1,446
Birmingham   B38 9PN   *Contact:* T R Jones   *Profit:* £7,213,000
021-433 3444   Financial Director   *Turnover:* £62,912,000

Donations Policy: Preference for local charities in the areas of company presence. Preferred areas of support: children and youth, social welfare, environment and heritage, the arts. Grants to national organisations from £50 to £100; grants to local organisations from £25 to £50. In addition to charitable donations £3,000 was given in other community contributions.
Generally no support for fundraising events, advertising in charity brochures, purely denominational appeals, local appeals not in areas of company presence or overseas projects.

☐ **Meteor Group plc**   Sale of motor vehicles, leasing self-drive vehicles

Warwick House,   *Ch:* David Guest   *Year Ends:* 31 Dec '90   *UK employees:* n/a
35 Spring Road,   *Contact:* Mrs G J Severn   *Donations:* n/a   *Total employees:* 363
Hall Green,   Company Secretary   *Profit:* £533,000
Birmingham   B11 3EA   *Turnover:* £117,247,000
021-702 2455

☐ **Meyer International plc**   Merchanting of building materials & timber

Villiers House,   *Ch:* R W Jewson   *Year Ends:* 31 Mar '92   *UK employees:* 7,199
41-47 Strand,   *MD:* J M Dobby   *Donations:* £52,000   *Total employees:* 9,562
London   WC2N 5JG   *Contact:* C Hildrey   *Profit:* £24,600,000
071-839 7766   Assistant Secretary   *Turnover:* £1,125,800,000   % Club, BitC

Donations Policy: Donations are made through the Charities Aid Foundation. Preference is given to those activities and projects concerned with the protection and preservation of the environment. Grants to national organisations from £50 to £5,000. Grants to local organisations from £50 to £2,000. Total community contributions in 1991/92 were £165,000.
No response to circular appeals.

☐ **MFI Furniture Group plc**   Manufacture & sale of furniture

Southon House,   *Ch:* D S Hunt   *Year Ends:* 25 Apr '92   *UK employees:* n/a
333 The Hyde,   *Contact:* P Cunningham   *Donations:* £107,402   *Total employees:* 7,848
Edgware Road,   Public Relations &   *Profit:* £8,800,0000
Colindale,   Communications Manager *Turnover:* £644,400,000
London   NW9 6TD
081-200 8000

Donations Policy: Most donations are made through the Charities Aid Foundation. Nationwide support is given to the National Children's Home. Where possible the small remaining budget is given to many different causes, but generally in areas of company presence. Preference for children and youth.
No grants for purely denominational (religious) appeals; local appeals not in areas of company presence; overseas projects.

☐ **Michelin Tyre plc**   Tyre manufacturers

Campbell Road,   *Ch:* M J De Logeres   *Year Ends:* 31 Dec '91   *UK employees:* n/a
Stoke-on-Trent,   *MD:* J Callies   *Donations:* £37,000   *Total employees:* 10,002
Staffordshire   ST4 4EY   *Contact:* P Niblett   *Profit:* £46,743,000
0782-402081   Public Relations Manager *Turnover:* £588,017,000
                                                   (Manufacturing)

Donations Policy: Strong preference for local charities in the areas of company presence, appeals relevant to company business and charities in which a member of staff is involved. Preferred areas of support: children/youth, social welfare and enterprise.
No support for overseas projects, purely denominational (religious) appeals, circular appeals or local appeals not in areas of company presence.

☐ **Midland Bank plc**   Banking

Poultry,   *Ch:* Sir Peter Walters   *Year Ends:* 31 Dec '91   *UK employees:* 51,197
London   EC2P 2BX   *CE:* B G Pearse   *Donations:* £488,397   *Total employees:* 57,640
071-260 8000   *Contact:* A A Furniss   *Profit:* £36,000,000
                                                   Sponsorship & Donations *Turnover:* n/a   % Club, BitC, ABSA
                                                   Manager

Donations Policy: Recipient organisations must be registered charities. Grants are given to a wide range of charitable purposes, with emphasis on social and welfare needs, particularly concerning inner cities and young people. A small level of support is also provided for the environment and education.
No response to circular appeals. No grants for fundraising events; advertising in charity brochures; appeals from individuals; overseas projects.
Appeals from local charities are dealt with by regional officers. Community contributions totalled £3,416,000 in 1990.

Name/Address	Officers	Financial Information	Other Information

Midland Shires Farmers Ltd

Inputs to farming trade

County Mills,
Worcester WR1 3NU
0905-25541

Ch: A M Beckett
Contact: Charlotte Moody
Publicity Manager

Year Ends: 31 Oct '90
Donations: n/a
Profit: £345,000
Turnover: £94,826,000

UK employees: n/a
Total employees: 743

Midlands Electricity plc

Electricity supply

Mucklow Hill,
Halesowen,
West Midlands B62 8BP
021-423 2345

Ch: Bryan Townsend
MD: Richard Young
Contact: Mike Dernie
Public Relations Manager

Year Ends: 31 Mar '92
Donations: £113,655
Profit: £142,100,000
Turnover: £1,454,100,000

UK employees: n/a
Total employees: 7,575

BitC

Donations Policy: Preference for local charities in the areas of company presence and charities in which a member of staff is involved. Preferred areas of support: children and youth, social welfare, education, environment, enterprise/training and elderly people. Grants to national organisations from £250 to £5,000. Grants to local organisations from £50 to £5,000.
Generally no support for circular appeals, appeals from individuals, purely denominational (religious) appeals, local appeals not in areas of company presence, large national appeals or overseas projects.

Miller Group Ltd

Building & civil engineering

18 South Groathill Avenue,
Edinburgh EH4 2LW
031-332 2585

Ch: J Miller
CE: D W Cawthra
Contact: Janet Tully
Appeals Administrator

Year Ends: 31 Dec '91
Donations: £144,000
Profit: £537,000
Turnover: £238,790,000

UK employees: n/a
Total employees: 2,197

% Club

Donations Policy: The company prefers to help many causes in a small way, particularly those in the vicinity of the company's main offices.

Minet Holdings plc

Insurance brokers

66 Prescot Street,
London E1 8BU
071-481 0707

Ch: R W Pettitt
Contact: Maxine Hooper
Public Relations Assistant

Year Ends: 30 Sep '90
Donations: $193,000
Profit: $29,849,000
Turnover: $266,003,000

UK employees: n/a
Total employees: 3,645

Donations Policy: Preference for local appeals in areas of company presence and charities involved with children and youth or cancer. Charities supported/recommended by Lloyds will be preferred. Animal charities will not be supported.

Minmetco Ltd

Metals & commodity dealers

80 Cannon Street,
London EC4N 6EJ
071-606 8321

MD: U Bagri
Contact: R J Gatehouse
Director

Year Ends: 30 Sep '90
Donations: n/a
Profit: £6,490,000
Turnover: £279,022,000

UK employees: n/a
Total employees: n/a

Mirror Group Newspapers plc

Newspaper publishing

PO Box 160,
The Mirror Building,
Holborn Circus,
London EC1P 1DQ
071-353 0246

Ch: Sir Robert Clark
CE: V L Horwood
Contact: Bill Berentemsel
Fund Administrator for The Man of
the People Appeal Fund

Year Ends: 29 Dec '91
Donations: £36,000
Profit: £47,300,000
Turnover: £459,900,000

UK employees: n/a
Total employees: 3,873

Donations Policy: The company make donations to groups working with people who are disabled, ill, elderly or young and also to hospices and cancer research. Donations are only given to UK registered charities.
The group also run the Man of the People Appeal Fund in conjunction with news stories and appeals for readers donations. Money is raised towards the end of the year, trustees meet in March and make payments in April. Donations are given to major disaster appeals. Ethiopia and Somalia famine appeals and the Mother Theresa Fund have been major beneficiaries in recent years. In 1992 the Fund paid £318,000 to over 100 successful applicants. There were over 1,000 unsuccessful applicants.
No support is given to social welfare, education, recreation, environment/heritage.

MISYS plc

Supply of computer systems & services

Burleigh House,
Chappel Oak,
Salford Priors Square,
Worcestershire CV37 0NZ
0386-871373

Contact: Mrs Shirley Lynall
Personal Assistant to the
Chairman

Year Ends: 31 May '92
Donations: £2,622
Profit: £9,118,000
Turnover: £68,023,000

UK employees: 1,270
Total employees: n/a

Mitsubishi Corporation (UK) Ltd

Technological, industrial & consumer products

Bow Bells House,
Bread Street,
London EC4M 9BQ
071-822 0022

Contact: S M Whittome
Charities & Donations
Committee

Year Ends: 31 Mar '92
Donations: £8,000
Profit: £4,343,000
Turnover: £4,786,104,000

UK employees: n/a
Total employees: 170

% Club; BitC

Donations Policy: Preference for local charities in areas where the company operates. Preference for social welfare; medical; education; environment; overseas aid/development.
No grants for advertising in charity brochures; appeals from individuals; purely denominational (religious) appeals; local appeals not in areas of company presence; large national appeals.

● **Alphabetical listing**   Please read page 6

Name/Address   *Officers*   *Financial Information*   *Other Information*

☐ Mitsubishi Electric UK Ltd
Manufacture of electronic products

Travellers Lane,
Hatfield,
Hertfordshire AL10 8XB
0707-276100

Ch: Sir Peter Parker
CE: P K Thomlinson
Contact: Josephine Jeka
Communications Officer

Year Ends: 31 Dec '91
Donations: £12,000
Profit: £611,000 (1990)
Turnover: £372,000,000

UK employees: n/a
Total employees: 2,000

Donations Policy: Charitable donations are given to local organisations in the Hatfield area that are nominated by a member of staff. Preference for children and youth; medical; education. Grants to local organisations from £100 to £1,000.
The company's corporate sponsorship involves long-term support of the arts. Community contributions amounted to £24,000 in 1991.
No response to circular appeals. No grants for advertising in charity brochures; appeals from individuals; purely denominational (religious) appeals; local appeals not in areas of company presence; large national appeals; overseas projects.

☐ Mitsui & Co UK plc
Metals, oils, chemicals & textiles etc. traders

20 Old Bailey,
London EC4M 7QQ
071-822 0321

MD: O Fukumuro
CE: S Sano
Contact: D Bagshaw
Personnel Manager

Year Ends: 31 Mar '92
Donations: £3,215
Profit: £5,374,000
Turnover: £6,618,000,000

UK employees: n/a
Total employees: 135

BitC

Donations Policy: Preference for local charities in areas where the company operates. Preference for children and youth; social welfare; medical; education; and events contributing to Anglo-Japanese relations. Grants to national organisations from £100 to £1,000. Grants to local organisations from £100 to £2,000.
No response to circular appeals. No grants for advertising in charity brochures; appeals from individuals; large national appeals.

☐ MK Electric Ltd
Manufacturers of electric plugs & sockets

1 Shrubbery Road,
Edmonton,
London N9 0PB
081-807 5151

Contact: B R Edwards
Personnel Director

Year Ends: 28 Mar '87
Donations: £2,000 (1991)
Profit: £19,600,000
Turnover: £140,900,000

UK employees: n/a
Total employees: 4,978

Donations Policy: Support only to local charities in areas where the company operates. Preference for children and youth; medical; education. Grants range from £10 to £100.
No response to circular appeals. No grants for fundraising events; advertising in charity brochures; purely denominational (religious) appeals; local appeals not in areas of company presence; large national appeals; overseas projects.

☐ ML Holdings plc
Aeronautical engineering

Ajax Avenue,
Slough,
Berkshire SL1 4BQ
0753-523838

Ch: Sir Peter Horsley
MD: P G Pollocks
Contact: Keith Worrall
Employee Relations Manager

Year Ends: 31 Mar '92
Donations: £10,109
Profit: (£2,240,000)
Turnover: £84,300,000

UK employees: n/a
Total employees: 2,159

☐ Mo & Domsjo (UK) Ltd
Timber, pulp, paper & board products

General Wolfe House,
83 High Street,
Westerham,
Kent TN16 1RE
0959-564288

Ch: V R Baylis
MD: G H Gallico
Contact: Company Secretary

Year Ends: 31 Dec '90
Donations: n/a
Profit: £7,330,000
Turnover: £239,965,000

UK employees: n/a
Total employees: 1,567

☐ Mobil Oil Co Ltd
Oil industry

Mobil House,
54-60 Victoria Street,
London SW1E 6QB
071-828 9777

Ch: B M Davis
Contact: D Charlton
Manager, Public Affairs
Programmes

Year Ends: 31 Dec '90
Donations: £23,000
Profit: £55,533,000
Turnover: £1,150,028,000

UK employees: n/a
Total employees: 1,806

% Club, ABSA

Donations Policy: Recipient organisations must be registered charities. The main areas supported are education, medical and social welfare. Priority is given to local branches of national charities in areas of company presence (central London, Merseyside, the North East, South East).
In addition to centrally co-ordinated giving, the Mobil Centenary Trust supports events recommended by employees.

☐ G Modiano Ltd
Importers & exporters in wool

Rodwell House,
100 Middlesex Street,
London E1 7HD
071-377 7550

Contact: G Modiano
Chairman

Year Ends: 31 Mar '90
Donations: £11,501 (1989)
Profit: (£1,677,000)
Turnover: £105,734,000

UK employees: n/a
Total employees: 50

☐ Molins plc
Tobacco, paper & packaging machinery

11 Tanners Drive,
Blakelands,
Milton Keynes MK14 5LU
0908-663666

Ch: J C Orr
MD: P W Greenwood
Contact: A Rist
Director of Personnel

Year Ends: 31 Dec '91
Donations: £7,000
Profit: £11,480,000
Turnover: £154,970,000

UK employees: n/a
Total employees: 2,826

Donations Policy: Preference for local charities in areas where the company operates. Grants to local organisations from £50 to £500.
No grants for local appeals not in areas of company presence.

Please read page 6   Alphabetical listing •

Name/Address	Officers	Financial Information	Other Information

☐ Monarch Airlines Ltd
Airline & tour operators

Luton International Airport, Luton LU2 9NU *0582-400000*	*Contact:* M J Ellingham Company Secretary	*Year Ends:* 30 Nov '90 *Donations:* n/a *Profit:* £5,271,000 *Turnover:* £189,340,000	*UK employees:* n/a *Total employees:* 1,081

☐ Monsanto plc
Chemical & plastic products

Chineham Court, Chineham, Basingstoke, Hampshire RG24 0UL *0256-57288*	*Contact:* N Sumpter Personnel Director	*Year Ends:* 31 Dec '91 *Donations:* £45,000 *Profit:* £3,481,000 *Turnover:* £271,608,000	*UK employees:* n/a *Total employees:* 2,090

Donations Policy: The company supports local charities in areas of company presence and national charities. There is a preference to charities working with disabled people, children and youth and education. The company has supported NSPCC, VSO, Romanian Orphans and tries to help self supporting projects. The company has strong links with schools and education. It matches donations raised for charities by employees. The charity committee meets four times a year and tends to exclude the more well known charities.
No grants for fundraising events; advertising in charity brochures; appeals from individuals; purely denominational (religious) appeals; local appeals not in areas of company presence; large national appeals; animal charities.

☐ Morgan Crucible Company plc
Materials & components for industry

Morgan House, Windsor, Berkshire SL4 1EP *0753-837000*	*Ch:* Sir James Spooner *MD:* E B Farmer *Contact:* D J Coker Company Secretary	*Year Ends:* 5 Jan '92 *Donations:* £85,883 *Profit:* £61,000,000 *Turnover:* £627,800,000	*UK employees:* 4,695 *Total employees:* 11,841

Donations Policy: Mainly support for relatively small charities in the fields of medical care and research. Grants range from £200 to £500. Some limited support for arts in areas of company presence.
No support for larger national appeals, small purely local appeals not in areas of company presence, appeals from individuals or overseas projects.

☐ Morgan Grenfell Group plc
International merchant banking

23 Great Winchester Street, London EC2P 2AX *071-826 6998*	*Ch:* J A Craven *CE:* M W R Dobson *Contact:* R P Elliston	*Year Ends:* 31 Dec '91 *Donations:* £128,600 *Profit:* £51,474,000 *Turnover:* n/a	*UK employees:* 1,304 *Total employees:* 2,229 % Club, BitC

Donations Policy: Recipients must be registered charities. Support is primarily given to national charities but local charities are supported if they are in, or for the benefit of, or have another connection with, the City of London. Grants usually range from £250 to £500.
No support for advertising in brochures, small local appeals not in areas of company presence or appeals from individuals.
Sponsorship proposals to B C Woodford.
In addition to charitable donations, other community contributions totalled £57,400.

☐ Morland & Co plc
Materials & components for industry

The Brewery, PO Box 5, Oak Street, Abingdon, Oxon OX14 5DD *0235-553377*	*Ch:* Sir Humphrey Prideaux *MD:* I M Cutterbuck *Contact:* G Pridmore Marketing Manager	*Year Ends:* 30 Sep '91 *Donations:* £8,000 *Profit:* n/a *Turnover:* £33,694,000	*UK employees:* n/a *Total employees:* 730

Donations Policy: Preference for local charities or local fundraising projects in areas of company presence.
No grants for local appeals not in areas of company presence; large national appeals; overseas projects.

☐ Morrison Construction Group Ltd
Construction industry & related services

Morrison House, 12 Atholl Crescent, Edinburgh EH3 8HA *031-228 4188*	*Ch:* A F Morrison *Contact:* Gill Laird Group Public Relations Manager	*Year Ends:* 31 Mar '92 *Donations:* £29,786 *Profit:* £5,100,000 *Turnover:* £193,200,000	*UK employees:* n/a *Total employees:* 2,174

Donations Policy: Each subsidiary and area head office makes it's own donations and decides it's own policy. Charities should approach a subsidiary or area office, to find out if they have a policy that will support them, before sending in an application. The Scottish area offices appear to have a preference for Scottish charities.

☐ Wm Morrison Supermarkets plc
Supermarket proprietors

Hillmore House, Thornton Road, Bradford, West Yorkshire BD8 9AX *0274-494166*	*Ch:* K D Morrison *Contact:* K Ounsworth Secretary to the Charitable Trust	*Year Ends:* 1 Feb '92 *Donations:* £137,204 *Profit:* £62,649,000 *Turnover:* £1,117,974,000	*UK employees:* n/a *Total employees:* 12,166

Donations Policy: Each year a single charity is nominated (The Imperial Cancer Research Fund in 1992/93), which is supported by the company as well as through fundraising. Other appeals are supported through the Wm Morrison Charitable Trust. Each store also has a small budget for local community causes.

● **Alphabetical listing** Please read page 6

Name/Address	Officers	Financial Information	Other Information

☐ Motherwell Bridge Holdings Ltd
Heavy engineering

PO Box 4,
Logans Road,
Motherwell ML1 3NP
0698-66111

Ch: A R Miller
MD: J C A Crawford
Contact: G Caldwell
Marketing Manager

Year Ends: 31 Dec '90
Donations: £8,200
Profit: £4,528,000
Turnover: £117,694,000

UK employees: n/a
Total employees: 2,590

☐ Mount Charlotte Thistle Hotels
Hotel operators

2 The Calls,
Leeds LS2 7JU
0532-439111

Ch: S C Smith-Cox
MD: R E G Peel
Contact: K V F Pawson
Financial Director

Year Ends: 31 Dec '89
Donations: £17,378 (1991)
Profit: £47,596,000
Turnover: £155,450,000

UK employees: n/a
Total employees: 6,416

Donations Policy: Preference for local charities in areas where the company operates and for appeals relevant to company business. The company prefers to give on going support to existing charities.

☐ Mount Isa Holdings (UK) Ltd
Investments, metallurgy & mining

Botany Road,
Northfleet,
Gravesend,
Kent DA11 9BG
0474-351188

Ch: R H Y Mills
Contact: M Gladwin
Company Secretary

Year Ends: 30 Jun '91
Donations: £9,947
Profit: £2,691,000
Turnover: £146,882,000

UK employees: n/a
Total employees: 459

☐ John Mowlem & Co plc
Construction industry

White Lion Court,
Swan Street,
Isleworth,
Middlesex TW7 6RN
081-568 9111

Ch: Sir Philip Beck
MD: J R Marshall, C Beck
Contact: Arthur Birchall
Company Secretary

Year Ends: 31 Dec '91
Donations: £40,717
Profit: £3,000,000
Turnover: £1,316,000,000

UK employees: n/a
Total employees: 15,800

Donations Policy: The company's charity committee sets the criteria each year for the range of charities they will support. The committee meets twice a year and all applications meeting these criteria are considered. In 1992, this included charities working with elderly people and hospices. Grants range from £250 to £500.
No grants for fundraising events; advertising in charity brochures; appeals from individuals.

☐ MTM plc
Chemicals manufacture

Rudby Hall,
Hutton,
Rudby,
Yarm,
Cleveland TF1 0JN
0642-701078

Contact: Andrea Larkin
Assistant Communications
Manager

Year Ends: 31 Dec '91
Donations: £23,016
Profit: £20,547,000
Turnover: £104,403,000

UK employees: n/a
Total employees: 1,109

Donations Policy: Preference for charities in which a member of company staff is involved. The company matches contributions made by employees, through payroll giving, to their chosen charity. The company prefers to support children and youth; social welfare; medical; education; environment and heritage, overseas aid/development.
No response to circular appeals.

☐ J Murphy & Sons Ltd
Building & civil engineering contractors

Hiview House,
Highgate Road,
London NW5 1TN
071-267 4366

Ch: J Murphy
Contact: Joe O'Connor
Contracts Manager

Year Ends: 31 Dec '90
Donations: £24,842
Profit: £9,389,000
Turnover: £142,709,772

UK employees: n/a
Total employees: n/a

% Club

Donations Policy: Preference for community, health and welfare. Support is mainly directed to ill, homeless and destitute people as well as research into cancer, schizophrenia, drug and alcohol abuse.
No grants for fundraising events; advertising in charity brochures; appeals from individuals; purely denominational (religious) appeals; local appeals not in areas of company presence; large national appeals; overseas projects. No response to circular appeals.

☐ Murphy Petroleum Ltd
Hydrocarbons, crude oil refining, petroleum products

Winston House,
Dollis Park,
Finchley,
London N3 1HZ
081-349 9191

MD: J N Copeland
Contact: Personnel Manager

Year Ends: 31 Dec '90
Donations: n/a
Profit: £41,521,000
Turnover: £214,386,000

UK employees: n/a
Total employees: 165

☐ Murray International Holdings Ltd
Metals, property, contracting, electronics, office supplies

Murray House,
4 Redheughs Rigg,
South Gyle,
Edinburgh EH12 9PQ
031-317 7000

Ch: D E Murray
MD: J MacDonald
Contact: Samantha Foster
Secretary to the Managing Director

Year Ends: 31 Jan '91
Donations: n/a
Profit: £5,496,000
Turnover: £135,571,000

UK employees: n/a
Total employees: 1,508

Please read page 6 — Alphabetical listing

Name/Address	Officers	Financial Information	Other Information

☐ N & B Holdings Ltd
Electrical goods manufacture & supply

Federation House,
Hope Street,
Liverpool L1 9BW
051-708 0136

Ch: A Whitworth
MD: P FitzPatrick
Contact: Margaret Higgins
Human Resources Manager

Year Ends: 31 Dec '91
Donations: £18,400
Profit: £4,561,000
Turnover: £51,584,000

UK employees: n/a
Total employees: 167

Donations Policy: Preference for local charities in areas where the company operates, appeals relevant to company business and charities in which a member of company staff is involved. Preference for children and youth; social welfare; education; environment; arts; overseas aid/development. Grants to national organisations from £100 to £2,500. Grants to local organisations from £25 to £750.
No response to circular appeals. No grants for appeals from individuals; purely denominational (religious) appeals; large national appeals.

☐ Napier Brown Holdings Ltd
Sugar & produce merchants

1 St Katharines Way,
London E1 9UN
071-488 9951

Contact: P G Ridgewell
Managing Director

Year Ends: 31 Mar '91
Donations: £34,667
Profit: £10,105,000
Turnover: £358,063,000

UK employees: n/a
Total employees: 1,073

Donations Policy: The company makes most of it's donations to cancer related charities through Deed of Covenant. This commitment is long-term so the company will not be able to support new appeals.

☐ National & Provincial Building Society
Building society

Provincial House,
Bradford,
West Yorkshire BD1 1NL
0274-733444

Ch: R J Newton
MD: David O'Brien
Contact: Rita Donoghue
Programmes Developer

Year Ends: 31 Dec '91
Donations: £37,500
Profit: £100,400,000
Turnover: n/a

UK employees: n/a
Total employees: 3,521

Donations Policy: Preferred areas of support are children and youth, education, environment and heritage, the arts and enterprise/training. Sponsorship appeals can be addressed either to Rita Donoghue or Bruce Bulgin at the above address.
Generally no support for brochure advertising or overseas projects.

☐ National Car Parks Ltd
Car park managers

21 Bryanston Street,
Marble Arch,
London W1A 4NH
071-499 7050

Ch: R F Hobson, Sir Donald Gosling
MD: G Layton
Contact: Miss A Pell
Sales & Marketing

Year Ends: 31 Mar '91
Donations: £32,282
Profit: £57,238,000
Turnover: £194,910,000

UK employees: n/a
Total employees: 3,892

Donations Policy: The company only gives to charities with which it is already associated.

☐ National Express Holdings Ltd
Coach services

Ensign Court,
4 Vicarage Road,
Edgbaston,
Birmingham B15 3ES
021-456 1122

Ch: J C Myers
Contact: S Render
Press Officer

Year Ends: 31 Dec '90
Donations: n/a
Profit: £4,206,000
Turnover: £122,924,000

UK employees: n/a
Total employees: 2,000

☐ National Farmers Union Mutual Insurance
Insurance

Tiddington Road,
Stratford-upon-Avon
CV37 7BJ
0789-204211

Ch: A Evans
MD: A S Young
Contact: Steve Wood
Marketing Superintendent

Year Ends: 31 Dec '91
Donations: £38,745
Profit: (£8,500,000)
Turnover: n/a

UK employees: n/a
Total employees: 2,256

☐ National Grid Company plc
Electricity supply

National Grid House,
Kirby Corner Road,
Coventry CV4 8JY
0203-537777

Ch: D G Jefferies
CE: W Kerss
Contact: Sue Tyler

Year Ends: 31 Mar '92
Donations: £108,790
Profit: £314,500,000
Turnover: £1,319,900,000

UK employees: n/a
Total employees: 6,217

BitC, ABSA

Donations Policy: Major schemes involve the countryside and environment, and the arts. Support is also given to education and research related to science and business, youth and preventative medicine. Local donations may cover a wider range depending on the needs of the local community. Local appeals should be made to regional offices. Grants to national organisations from £50 to £70,000. Grants to local organisations from £50 to £1,200.
Generally no support for circular appeals, purely denominational (religious) appeals or local appeals not in areas of company presence.

☐ National Home Loans Holdings plc
Mortgage loans

51 Homer Road,
Solihull,
West Midlands B91 3QJ
021-711 3333

Contact: Deborah Bateman
Executive Secretary to the Finance Director

Year Ends: 30 Sep '91
Donations: £7,125 (1990)
Profit: (£17,360,000)
Turnover: n/a

UK employees: n/a
Total employees: 480

BitC

Donations Policy: Preference for local charities in the areas of company presence, social welfare, education and the arts. Grants generally range from £50 to £500.
Generally no support for purely denominational (religious) appeals, local appeals not in areas of company presence or overseas projects.

● **Alphabetical listing** Please read page 6

Name/Address *Officers* *Financial Information* *Other Information*

☐ National Magazine Company Ltd
Publishers

72 Broadwick Street, *Ch:* F A Bennack *Year Ends:* 31 Dec '90 *UK employees:* n/a
London W1V 2BP *MD:* T G Mansfield *Donations:* £19,152 *Total employees:* 665
071-439 5000 *Contact:* Judith O'Sullivan *Profit:* £7,093,000
 Secretary to the Managing *Turnover:* £134,563,000
 Director

Donations Policy: The group has a preference for Action Research. Each magazine takes on a charity to support for one year. The group make donations of a years subscription to it's magazines, advertising in charity brochures and some small cash donations. The company produce Cosmopolitan, Company, Good House Keeping, Country Living, Harpers & Queen, Esquire, House Beautiful, She, Antique Collector, Containerisation International.

☐ National Oilwell (UK) Ltd
Drilling machinery

Bird Hall Lane, *Contact:* Bob Cooke *Year Ends:* 30 Nov '89 *UK employees:* n/a
Cheadle Heath,   Managing Director *Donations:* £2,000 (1991) *Total employees:* 464
Stockport,   *Profit:* (£3,920,000)
Cheshire SK3 0SA   *Turnover:* £33,407,000
061-428 0755

Donations Policy: Donations are mostly to local charities that assist people and medical causes. Preference for children's charities, social welfare, education, recreation, the environment and heritage, enterprise/training. Grants to local and national organisations range from £50 to £500.
No support for appeals from individuals, overseas projects, sponsorships, circular appeals, local appeals not in areas of company presence or large national appeals.

☐ National Power plc
Electricity supply

Sudbury House, *Ch:* Sir Trevor Holdsworth *Year Ends:* 31 Mar '92 *UK employees:* n/a
15-20 Newgate Street, *CE:* John Baker *Donations:* £323,098 *Total employees:* 11,421
London EC1A 7AU *Contact:* Andre Harbart *Profit:* £514,000,000
071-454 9494   Sponsorship Manager *Turnover:* £4,701,000,000 BitC, ABSA

Donations Policy: Donations are made through the National Power Charitable Trust. The trust has chosen Barnardo's as its current major beneficiary. It also matches pound for pound sums raised by staff. The company also supports a range of arts, education and community programmes near its operating sites.

☐ National Semiconductor UK Ltd
Microelectronic components

Kembrey Park, *Ch:* H Rothrah *Year Ends:* 29 May '91 *UK employees:* n/a
Swindon, *Contact:* L Parker *Donations:* £2,800 *Total employees:* 1,695
Wiltshire SW2 6UT   Personnel Manager *Profit:* £5,719,000
0793-614141   *Turnover:* £251,752,000

☐ National Westminster Bank plc
Banking

1st Floor, *Ch:* Lord Alexander of Weedon QC *Year Ends:* 31 Dec '91 *UK employees:* 93,000
1-2 Broadgate, *Contact:* Ms A Jordan *Donations:* £2,328,205 *Total employees:* n/a
London EC2M 2AD   Senior Executive, Community *Profit:* £110,000,000
071-714 4000   Relations *Turnover:* n/a % Club, BitC, ABSA

Donations Policy: Aims to support projects with a particular emphasis on education, environment, equal opportunities, sport, particularly cricket, and the arts. In addition support is given to areas relevant to the bank or its staff. Grants range from £5,000 to £50,000
Sponsorship programmes aim to promote financial effectiveness and enterprise skills for both organisations and individuals. These include the financial literacy programme in schools, money management programme and business skills in minority communities.
No response to circular appeals. No support for individuals, purely denominational appeals, overseas tours, hazardous pursuits, appeals for building fabric or third party giving.
Total community contributions in 1991 were £11,746,907.

☐ Nationwide Anglia Building Society Group
Building society

Chesterfield House, *Ch:* Sir Colin Corness *Year Ends:* 4 Apr '92 *UK employees:* 15,045
Bloomsbury Way, *CE:* Tim Melville-Ross *Donations:* £349,011 *Total employees:* n/a
London WC1V 6PW *Contact:* Nigel Snell *Profit:* £201,900,000
071-242 8822   Public Relations Manager *Turnover:* n/a BitC

Donations Policy: Prefers to support charities relieving human suffering, especially targeting young, elderly and disabled people, through sponsorship and involvement in fundraising events.
No support for appeals from individuals or animal charities.

☐ NCR Ltd
Manufacturers of business systems

206 Marylebone Road, *Ch:* R M Fleet *Year Ends:* 30 Nov '91 *UK employees:* 3,656
London NW1 6LY *Contact:* Pat Stroudley *Donations:* £36,793 *Total employees:* 3,779
071-723 7070   Charities Committee *Profit:* £30,781,000
   Turnover: £312,988,000 ABSA

Donations Policy: "In general we prefer to donate to charities established on a national basis. We do contribute in some measure to locally based charities and to ones in which our members are active." Preference for medical charities. Grants to national organisations from £50 to £500; grants to local organisations from £50 to £100.
No support for appeals from individuals or purely denominational appeals.

Please read page 6 — Alphabetical listing ●

Name/Address	Officers	Financial Information	Other Information

☐ **NEC Technologies (UK) Ltd** — Computer, fax & mobile telephone manufacture

Castlefarm Campus,
Priorslee,
Telford,
Shropshire   TF2 9SA
0952-299000

Contact: D Jones
Personnel Officer

Year Ends: 31 Mar '91
Donations: £9,106
Profit: £1,367,000
Turnover: £130,305,000

UK employees: n/a
Total employees: 730

BitC

☐ **NEC (UK) Ltd** — Marketing of communications & computers

NEC House,
1 Victoria Road,
London   W3 6UL
081-993 8111

MD: K Suzuki
Contact: I Toombs
Assistant General Manager - Personnel

Year Ends: 31 Mar '91
Donations: £16,000
Profit: £545,000
Turnover: £158,876,000

UK employees: 319
Total employees: 319

Donations Policy: The companies donations policy is reviewed annually. Preference for appeals relevant to company business. At present, the company is supporting some activities within "Business in the Community" and "West London Leadership" which are directly relevant to the local area. Grants up to £5,000.
No response to circular appeals. No grants for fundraising events; advertising in charity brochures; appeals from individuals; purely denominational (religious) appeals; local appeals not in areas of company presence; large national appeals; overseas projects.
Sponsorship proposals to Miss T Furuhashi.

☐ **James Neill Holdings Ltd** — Tool manufacturers & general engineers

Handsworth Road,
Handsworth,
Sheffield,
South Yorkshire   S13 9BR
0742-449911

Ch: J H Neill
MD: P B Bullock
Contact: Miss S Henderson
Sales & Marketing Director

Year Ends: 31 Dec '86
Donations: £3,572
Profit: £57,467,000
Turnover: £821,211,000

UK employees: n/a
Total employees: 9,725

☐ **Nestle Holdings (UK) plc** — Food manufacturers & distributors

St George's House,
Croydon,
Surrey   CR9 1NR
081-686 3333

Ch: P H Blackburn
Contact: R F Claydon
Corporate Affairs Manager

Year Ends: 29 Dec '90
Donations: £447,982
Profit: £7,600,000
Turnover: £1,558,400,000

UK employees: n/a
Total employees: 21,165

% Club, BitC, ABSA

Donations Policy: Donations are made through the Nestle Charitable Trust. Special consideration is given to projects in areas of company presence.
The donations made by the subsidiary Rowntree Mackintosh are now incorporated in Nestle's charitable support.

☐ **Nestor-BNA plc** — Healthcare & specialist personnel

20A Church Road,
Welwyn Garden City,
Herts   AL8 6PS
0707-373222

Ch: H J Hann
CE: M G Rogers
Contact: Mrs Baker
Personal Assistant to the Chief Executive

Year Ends: 31 Dec '91
Donations: £2,865
Profit: £5,305,000
Turnover: £100,536,000

UK employees: n/a
Total employees: 1,766

☐ **Neville Russell** — Accountants

246 Bishopsgate,
London   EC2M 4PB
071-377 1000

Contact: Miss Kim West
National Marketing Manager

Year Ends:
Donations: n/a
Profit: n/a
Turnover: n/a

UK employees: n/a
Total employees: n/a

% Club, BitC

Donations Policy: Support is given in the form of time and money to a wide range of locally-based charities concerned with social welfare of children and young people. Resources have also been made available to drug rehabilitation and AIDS care and research.

☐ **Newarthill plc** — Construction, property & investment

Eaton Court,
Mayland Avenue,
Hemel Hempstead,
Herts   HP2 7DR
0442-233444

Ch: Sir John Hedley Greenborough
Contact: Mrs Hendicott
Public Relations Manager

Year Ends: 31 Oct '91
Donations: £85,000
Profit: £42,802,000
Turnover: £463,656,000

UK employees: n/a
Total employees: 3,509

Donations Policy: The company as a matter of policy does not complete questionnaires and we have not been able to obtain any information on it's charitable donations.

☐ **Newman Tonks Group plc** — Metal, hardware manufacturers

Hospital Street,
Birmingham   B19 2YG
021-359 3221

Ch: D E Rogers
Contact: N F Keegan
Group Finance Director

Year Ends: 31 Dec '91
Donations: £11,290
Profit: £15,106,000
Turnover: £221,975,000

UK employees: n/a
Total employees: 4,433

● **Alphabetical listing** Please read page 6

Name/Address	Officers	Financial Information	Other Information

☐ **News International plc** Printing & publishing

PO Box 495,
Virginia Street,
London E1 9XY
071-782 6000

Ch: A S B Knight
MD: A A Fischer
Contact: Andrew Whyte
External Relations Manager

Year Ends: 30 Jun '92
Donations: £1,972,092
Profit: £48,076,000
Turnover: £696,167,000

UK employees: n/a
Total employees: 4,120

Donations Policy: Group policy: Donations to registered charities only. Preference for education, the local community, arts and the environment. National grants range from £500 to £50,000. Individuals and political parties are not supported.
Subsidiary companies: All areas are supported throughout the group, with particular interest towards children, sport, education and the environment. Support is also given to health and hospitals, the arts, inner city enterprises, organisations concerned with mentally and physically disabled people and elderly people. Local grants range from £5 to £10,000.
Appeals to subsidiaries should be directed to managing directors, managing editors or editors.

☐ **Next plc** Multiple tailors

Desford Road,
Enderby,
Leicester LE9 5AT
0533-866411

Ch: Lord Wolfson
CE: D C Jones
Contact: P Bailey
Company Secretary

Year Ends: 31 Jan '92
Donations: £42,000
Profit: £12,300,000
Turnover: £462,000,0000

UK employees: n/a
Total employees: 7,872

Donations Policy: Funds are concentrated on a small number of areas, the main beneficiaries are health related charities. Currently all support is going to the Macmillan Nurses Fund. Preference for charities in which a member of staff is involved. Local charities are supported by branches wherever possible.

☐ **NFC plc** Road haulage & related services

The Merton Centre,
45 St Peters Street,
Bedford MK40 2UB
0234-272222

Ch: J K Watson
CE: J D Mather
Contact: J W C Letchford
Company Secretary

Year Ends: 30 Sep '91
Donations: £1,300,000
Profit: £93,700,000
Turnover: £1,663,700,000

UK employees: n/a
Total employees: 33,861

% Club, BitC

Donations Policy: Priority is usually given to national appeals, though recently this has been broadened to include local charities connected with sport and the environment. Preference for social welfare, community services, health and medicine, charities concerned with children, elderly, sick and disabled people, housing, education, conservation of the environment/heritage and overseas aid. Grants to national organisations from £250 to £40,000; grants to local organisations from £50 to £300.
No support for circular appeals, fundraising events, advertising in charity brochures, appeals from individuals, purely denominational appeals, local appeals not in areas of company presence or political appeals. No sponsorship is undertaken.

☐ **J N Nichols (Vimto) plc** General food manufacturing

Ledson Road,
Wythenshawe,
Manchester M23 9NL
061-998 8801

Ch: G A Adkin
MD: P J Nichols
Contact: C Sefton
Marketing Manager

Year Ends: 31 Dec '91
Donations: £10,150
Profit: £7,700,000
Turnover: £47,025,000

UK employees: n/a
Total employees: 255

Donations Policy: Preference for children and youth.
No response to circular appeals. No grants for advertising in charity brochures; appeals from individuals; purely denominational (religious) appeals; large national appeals.

☐ **Nissan Motor Manufacturing (UK) Ltd** Motor vehicles manufacturer

Washington Road,
Sunderland SR5 3NS
091-415 0000

MD: I Gibson
CE: P Stoddart
Contact: Peter Armstrong
Community Relations

Year Ends: 31 Mar '90
Donations: £29,975
Profit: £46,962,000
Turnover: £361,080,000

UK employees: n/a
Total employees: 2,370

Donations Policy: The company are in the process of formulating a new policy. It is thought that the company will expand their existing area of support to cover a larger area of the North East. The company adopts two local charities and gives them a lot of support, other local charities then receive small donations of up to £250.
No support for individuals or the National Health Service.

☐ **NMC Group plc** Paper & plastic packaging

40 South Audley Street,
London W1Y 5DH
071-491 2880

Ch: D C Marshall
CE: N S Gordon
Contact: Paul Mower
Finance Director

Year Ends: 31 Mar '92
Donations: £26,118
Profit: £5,011,000
Turnover: £93,616,000

UK employees: n/a
Total employees: 1,149

☐ **NNC Ltd** Nuclear power reactors

Booths Hall,
Chelford Road,
Knutsford,
Cheshire WA16 8QZ
0565-633800

Ch: Sir Frank Gibb
MD: C E Pugh
Contact: Kathy Ross
Personnel Officer

Year Ends: 31 Mar '87
Donations: £7,000 (1990)
Profit: £8,291,000
Turnover: £294,883,000

UK employees: n/a
Total employees: 3,055

Donations Policy: Almost all grants to local charities in areas of company presence. Preferred areas of support: children and youth; social welfare; medical; education; environment and heritage. Grants to local organisations from £50 to £500.
Generally no support for circular appeals, advertising in charity brochures, large national appeals, local appeals not in areas of company presence, overseas projects.

Please read page 6 — Alphabetical listing

Name/Address	Officers	Financial Information	Other Information

☐ Nobel Industries Sweden (UK) Ltd
Chemical, dental & paints products manufacture

23 Grosvenor Road,
St Albans,
Herts AL1 3AW
0727-41421

Contact: I L Marshall
Managing Director

Year Ends: 31 Dec '90
Donations: n/a
Profit: £4,130,000
Turnover: £142,778,000

UK employees: n/a
Total employees: 2,352

☐ Norcros plc
Ceramics & building suppliers

Norcros House,
Bagshot Road,
Bracknell RG12 3SW
0344-861878

Ch: J L G Sheffield
CE: M E Doherty
Contact: J M Wilson
Assistant Company Secretary

Year Ends: 31 Mar '92
Donations: £44,000
Profit: £15,591,000
Turnover: £394,012,000

UK employees: 6,463
Total employees: 7,704

Donations Policy: Normally supports only charities that have a geographical or industrial link with the company. Preferred areas of support: children and youth; medical; education. Grants to national organisations £150 to £10,000; grants to local organisations £50 to £1,500. No support for circulars, brochure advertising, campaigning work by charities, individuals, school expeditions, denominational appeals, local appeals not in areas of company presence, large national or overseas appeals, arts sponsorship. Applications must be in writing.

☐ Normans Group plc
Discount food retailers

Station Yard,
Budleigh Salterton,
Devon EX9 6RU
0392-822322

Ch: M H Swan
Contact: C Collis
Office Manager

Year Ends: 1 Apr '89
Donations: £11,000
Profit: £5,026,000
Turnover: £168,641,000

UK employees: 2,766
Total employees: 4,791

☐ Norsk Hydro (UK) Ltd
Manufacturers of chemical fertilisers

69 London Road,
Twickenham,
Middlesex TW1 1EE
081-891 1366

Ch: J M Clay
MD: J G Spiers
Contact: Mrs H Greaves
Personnel Manager

Year Ends: 31 Dec '90
Donations: £6,600 (1991)
Profit: £21,030,000
Turnover: £412,094,000

UK employees: n/a
Total employees: 2,383

Donations Policy: Support for smaller less well known charities, especially in the areas of children, education, medical and enterprise/training. Preference for local charities in the areas of company presence. Grants from £100 to £500. The company has a sponsorship budget directed towards the arts, education and the environment.
No response to circular appeals. No grants for advertising in charity brochures; appeals from individuals; purely denominational (religious) appeals; local appeals not in areas of company presence; large national appeals; overseas projects.

☐ North of England Building Society
Building society

50 Fawcett Street,
Sunderland SR1 1SA
091-565 6272

Ch: R Shiel
CE: R W Linden
Contact: Stan Owram
General Manager, Marketing

Year Ends: 31 Dec '91
Donations: n/a
Profit: £15,430,000
Turnover: n/a

UK employees: n/a
Total employees: 557

Donations Policy: No charitable donations are given, but the society offer a collecting service at branches for disaster funds and national charity appeals where appropriate.

☐ North West Water Group plc
Water & sewerage services

Dawson House,
Liverpool Road,
Great Sankey,
Warrington WA5 3LW
0925-234000

Ch: Dennis Grove
CE: Robert Thian
Contact: Christine Miles
Corporate Communications
Department

Year Ends: 31 Mar '92
Donations: £47,000
Profit: £230,000,000
Turnover: £789,000,000

UK employees: n/a
Total employees: 8,201

Donations Policy: Support, usually in the form of sponsorship, only for organisations related to the company business, particularly organisations and individuals involved in recreation and conservation, especially with young people and disabled people.

☐ Northamber plc
Computer equipment supplier

1 Lion Park Avenue,
Chessington,
Surrey KT9 1ST
081-391 4100

Ch: D M Phillips
Contact: D Mann
Marketing Manager

Year Ends: 30 Apr '92
Donations: £5,000
Profit: (£2,745,000)
Turnover: £93,082,000

UK employees: n/a
Total employees: 264

☐ Northern Electric plc
Electricity distribution & supply

Carliol House,
Market Street,
Newcastle-upon-Tyne NE1 6NE
091-221 2000

Ch: David Morris
MD: Tony Hadfield
Contact: David Faulkner
Director of Corporate Affairs

Year Ends: 31 Mar '92
Donations: £148,716
Profit: £98,200,000
Turnover: £813,700,000

UK employees: n/a
Total employees: 5,500

% Club, BitC, ABSA

Donations Policy: Preference for local charities in the areas of company presence and of perceived value to the community. There is a fair spread throughout the region. The company states that there is the "possibility of high gearing (ie. supporting an event that has a prospect of itself raising cash from the public)", especially if there is good value for money in profile terms for the company. Preferred areas of support: children and youth, social welfare, medical, education, environment and heritage, the arts and enterprise/training. Grants to national organisations from £50 to £1,000. Grants to local organisations from £200 to £25,000.
No response to circular appeals. No grants for appeals from individuals; purely denominational (religious) appeals; local appeals not in areas of company presence; large national appeals; overseas projects. Total community contributions in 1991/2 were £650,000.

● **Alphabetical listing** Please read page 6

Name/Address　　　　　*Officers*　　　　　*Financial Information*　　　　　*Other Information*

☐ Northern Foods plc
Dairymen, food manufacturers

Beverley House,　　　　*Ch:* C R Haskins　　　　*Year Ends:* 31 Mar '92　　　　*UK employees:* n/a
St Stephen's Square,　　*Contact:* Celia Woodward　*Donations:* £440,967　　　*Total employees:* 27,002
Hull HU1 3XG　　　　　　　Charitable Appeals Committee　*Profit:* £126,200,000
0482-25432　　　　　　　　　　　　　　*Turnover:* £1,444,200,000　　　BitC

Donations Policy: Resources are concentrated on relieving deprivation in inner cities (including enterprise and training) and in the third world. Support is given to selective educational projects. Some preference for local charities in the areas of company presence.
The company tends not to support the larger national charities, and does not support circular appeals, fundraising events, advertising in charity brochures, appeals from individuals, purely denominational (religious) appeals.

☐ Northern Ireland Electricity
Electricity supply

PO Box 2,　　　　　　*Contact:* Paul Nicholson　　*Year Ends:* 31 Mar '91　　　*UK employees:* n/a
Damesfort, Crockard,　　　Director of Corporate Affairs　*Donations:* n/a　　　　*Total employees:* 5,735
120 Malone Road,　　　　　　　　　　　　　*Profit:* £87,600,000
Belfast BT9 5HT　　　　　　　　　　　　　*Turnover:* £403,600,000　　　ABSA
0232-661100

Donations Policy: It appears that the company make no donations to charities, but the employees have raised over £60,000

☐ Northern Rock Building Society
Building society

Northern Rock House,　　*Ch:* Viscount Ridley　　*Year Ends:* 31 Dec '91　　*UK employees:* n/a
Gosforth,　　　　　　　*MD:* J C Sharp　　　　　*Donations:* n/a　　　　　*Total employees:* 1,654
Newcastle-upon-Tyne NE3 4PL　*Contact:* David Henderson　*Profit:* £54,560,000
091-285 7191　　　　　Advertising & Public Relations　*Turnover:* £115,752,000
　　　　　　　　　　　　Manager

Donations Policy: The company did not wish to give details of its donations policy, as it is already 2/3 times oversubscribed.

☐ Northern Telecom Europe
Telecommunications & electronics

Stafferton Way,　　　　*Ch:* Lord Keith of Castleacre　*Year Ends:* 31 Dec '89　*UK employees:* n/a
Maidstone,　　　　　　*Contact:* Dr O'Dochartaigh　　*Donations:* £236,000　　*Total employees:* 36,393
Berkshire SL6 1AY　　　Director, External Affairs &　*Profit:* £278,000,000
0628-812000　　　　　Communication　　　　　　*Turnover:* £2,607,400,000

Donations Policy: Support for local charities and those relevant to the company's business. Preference for education, medicine and the arts.

☐ Northumbrian Water Group plc
Water & sewerage services

Northumbria House,　　*Ch:* Sir Michael Straker　*Year Ends:* 31 Mar '92　　*UK employees:* n/a
Regent Centre,　　　　*CE:* David Cranston　　　*Donations:* £383,000　　　*Total employees:* 2,450
Gosforth,　　　　　　*Contact:* Sharron Ashurst　*Profit:* £61,100,000
Newcastle-upon-Tyne NE3 3PX　Corporate Affairs Assistant　*Turnover:* £203,500,000　ABSA
091-284 3151

Donations Policy: Preference for local charities in the areas of company presence and appeals relevant to company business. Preferred areas of support are children and youth, education, enterprise, environment and heritage. The company's sponsorship will lean towards educational projects relevant to the water industry (eg. engineering scholarships). The company supports WaterAid. Grants to national and local organisations from £50 to £10,000.
Total community contributions in 1991 were £636,000.
Generally no support for circular appeals, advertising in charity brochures, local appeals not in areas of company presence, large national appeals, overseas projects.

☐ NORWEB plc
Electricity supply

Talbot Road,　　　　*Ch:* Kenneth Harvey　　*Year Ends:* 31 Mar '92　　*UK employees:* n/a
Manchester M16 0HQ　*Contact:* H F Hurford　　*Donations:* £76,340　　　*Total employees:* 7,814
061-873 8000　　　Head of Administration　*Profit:* £137,900,000
　　　　　　　　　　　　　　　　　　　　Turnover: £1,318,000,000　　BitC

Donations Policy: The company aims to support causes within its operating area. Donations are given for medical research, disabled people, socially disadvantaged people, sporting activities and other worthwhile causes which benefit the community in the North West. Preference for charities in which a member of company staff is involved. Grants range from £250 to £5,000.
No grants for appeals from individuals; purely denominational (religious) appeals; local appeals not in areas of company presence; overseas projects, animal welfare.

☐ Norwest Holst Holdings Ltd
Civil engineering

Toft Hall,　　　　　*Ch:* W C Allan　　　*Year Ends:* 31 Mar '91　　*UK employees:* n/a
Toft Road,　　　　　*MD:* P J Mason　　　*Donations:* £5,000　　　*Total employees:* 3,980
Knutsford,　　　　　*Contact:* Group Personnel Department　*Profit:* £4,960,000
Cheshire WA16 9PD　　(address below)　　*Turnover:* £414,274,000
0565-55365

Donations Policy: Support for registered charities only, principally those involved in health issues (particularly cancer). Preference for local charities in areas where the company operates. Grants to national organisations from £100 to £200; grants to local organisations from £50 to £100.
No response to circular appeals. No grants for fundraising events; advertising in charity brochures; appeals from individuals; purely denominational (religious) appeals; local appeals not in areas of company presence; large national appeals; overseas projects.
Address for appeals: Astral House, Imperial Way, Watford, Herts WD2 4YX (0923-233433).

Please read page 6 | | | Alphabetical listing •

Name/Address	Officers	Financial Information	Other Information

☐ Norwich Union Life Insurance Society
Insurance

Surrey Street,
Norwich NR1 3NG
0603-622200

Ch: M G Falcon
CE: A Bridgewater
Contact: M D Oxbury
Assistant Secretary

Year Ends: 31 Dec '91
Donations: £307,000
Profit: n/a
Turnover: n/a

UK employees: 15,759
Total employees: n/a

% Club, BitC, ABSA

Donations Policy: Varied, but particular consideration when related to business. Preference to prominent charities in the Norwich and Sheffield areas and to charities involved in medical research, environment, education, enterprise/job creation and with disabled people. Donations are usually £100 to £500, but can be a lot more. No donations to individuals.

☐ NSM plc
Mining, oil, property

Mansfield Road,
Hafland,
Chesterfield S41 0JW
0246-558558

Ch: D T Carr
CE: Mr Jermine
Contact: Judy Gascoigne
Secretary to the Chief Executive

Year Ends: 31 Mar '92
Donations: £6,588
Profit: £5,719,000
Turnover: £147,266,000

UK employees: n/a
Total employees: 2,575

☐ Nu-Swift International Ltd
Fire protection equipment & services

Wistons Lane,
Elland,
West Yorkshire HX5 9DS
0422-372852

Ch: I Dorr
Contact: Miss Sharon Wilson
Secretary to the Chairman

Year Ends: 31 Jan '91
Donations: £14,783
Profit: £26,529,000
Turnover: £355,363,000

UK employees: 295
Total employees: 24,052

Donations Policy: Preference for local charities in areas where the company operates or charities in which a member of company staff is involved. The company supports local schools and churches and occasionally students to work abroad. Main areas of support have been cancer research and related charities.

☐ Nuclear Electric plc
Electricity supply

Barnett Way,
Barnwood,
Gloucester GL4 7RS
0452-652222

Ch: J G Collier
Contact: Head of Public Relations

Year Ends: 31 Mar '92
Donations: £247,785
Profit: £62,000,000
Turnover: £2,432,000,000

UK employees: n/a
Total employees: 12,674

BitC

Donations Policy: Company policy is to (a) Give corporately to two or three national charities plus specific appeals related to the company objectives; (b) Delegate local giving to location managers with the emphasis on matching funds raised by staff. Preference for children and youth; social welfare; medical; environment/heritage. Grants to national organisations from £1,000 to £10,000. Grants to local organisations from £10 to £200.
No response to circular appeals. No grants for advertising in charity brochures; appeals from individuals; local appeals not in areas of company presence; overseas projects.

☐ Nurdin & Peacock plc
Cash & carry wholesalers

Bushey Road,
Raynes Park,
London SW20 0JJ
081-946 9111

Ch: W M Peacock
MD: D G Rowley
Contact: Mrs Lloyd
Secretary to the Managing Director

Year Ends: 31 Dec '91
Donations: £46,687
Profit: £27,631,000
Turnover: £1,369,578,000

UK employees: n/a
Total employees: 4,791

Donations Policy: Preference for trade-related charities and those chosen by staff locally.
No support for circular appeals, fundraising events, brochure advertising, individuals, denominational appeals, local appeals not in areas of company presence, large national appeals or overseas projects.

☐ Oakstead Holdings Ltd
Garage proprietors, lubricating oils retailers

The Pinnacles,
Elizabeth Way,
Harlow,
Essex CM19 5AR
0279-443221

Ch: A C Pond
Contact: R D Hillier
Company Secretary

Year Ends: 5 Apr '92
Donations: £10,250
Profit: £1,430,000
Turnover: £120,051,000

UK employees: n/a
Total employees: 62

☐ Occidental International Oil Inc
Oil

123 Buckingham Palace Road,
London SW1W 9SR
071-828 5600

Ch: J E Brading
Contact: A Blake-Milton
Public Relations Manager

Year Ends: 31 Dec '88
Donations: £44,000
Profit: £75,680,000
Turnover: £213,622,000

UK employees: n/a
Total employees: 1,048

Donations Policy: Support is given to health and social concerns, education and the arts.

☐ Ocean Group plc
Freight distribution, marine & environment services

India Buildings,
Water Street,
Liverpool L2 0RB
051-236 9292

Ch: P I Marshall
MD: N C F Barber
Contact: Roger Morris
Secretary, PH Holt Charitable Trust

Year Ends: 31 Dec '91
Donations: n/a
Profit: £51,000,000
Turnover: £1,345,500,000

UK employees: n/a
Total employees: 11,000

% Club, BitC

Donations Policy: Contributes to a number of charities both nationally and on Merseyside.

• **Alphabetical listing**   Please read page 6

Name/Address	Officers	Financial Information	Other Information

☐ OCS Group Ltd
Cleaning & security services

79 Limpsfield Road,
Sanderstead,
Surrey CR2 9LB
081-651 3211

Ch: D H G Goodliffe
Contact: M H George
Treasurer

Year Ends: 31 Mar '89
Donations: £8,173 (1992)
Profit: £7,736,000
Turnover: £153,882,000

UK employees: n/a
Total employees: 30,369

Donations Policy: Preference for appeals relevant to company business or for charities in which a member of company staff is involved. Preference for environment and heritage. Sponsorship and donations are committed for long periods in advance to environmental projects and sports scholarships. Grants range from £100 to £1,000.

☐ Ogilvy & Mather Ltd
Marketing & advertising

Lancaster Place,
London WC2 7EZ
071-712 3000

Ch: P F Warren
Contact: P Selvey
Company Secretary

Year Ends: 31 Dec '87
Donations: £31,069
Profit: £6,686,000
Turnover: £310,051,000

UK employees: n/a
Total employees: 2,124

Donations Policy: Preference for appeals relevant to the business. The main charity supported by the company is the Mudshoot Farm, an inner city farm. The company does the advertising for Save the Children Fund and Romanian Orphanage Trust, it is unclear if this is paid for or part of the companies charitable support.

☐ Oliver Group plc
Multiple footwear retailers

Grove Way,
Castle Acres,
Narborough,
Leicester LE9 5BZ
0533-630444

Ch: I D Oliver
MD: G R Taylor
Contact: Miss J Bradbury
Secretary to Managing Director

Year Ends: 31 Dec '91
Donations: £6,025
Profit: (£10,700,000)
Turnover: £84,920,000

UK employees: n/a
Total employees: 3,556

☐ Olivetti Systems & Networks Ltd
Data processing systems & software

PO Box 89,
86-88 Upper Richmond Road,
Putney,
London SW15 2UR
081-785 6666

Contact: Rosanna Inzani

Year Ends: 31 Dec '90
Donations: n/a
Profit: £3,143,000
Turnover: £155,673,000

UK employees: n/a
Total employees: 1,453

ABSA

☐ Omega (UK) Holdings Ltd
Motor vehicles repair & distribution

Trevelyan House,
7 Church Road,
Welwyn Garden City,
Herts AL8 6NT
0707-373330

Ch: A M Megerisi
Contact: Debbie Phillips
Personnel Manager

Year Ends: 31 Dec '90
Donations: £979
Profit: £14,000
Turnover: £106,185,000

UK employees: n/a
Total employees: 777

☐ Omnicom UK plc
Advertising & marketing services

12 Bishopsbridge Road,
London W2 6AA
071-258 3979

Ch: M Boase
Contact: Isabel McKay
Group Payroll Personnel Manager

Year Ends: 31 Dec '90
Donations: £66,297
Profit: £5,624,000
Turnover: £284,143,000

UK employees: n/a
Total employees: 1,462

Donations Policy: The staff nominate charities for support which are voted on and the most successful charities receive donations of about £5,000. The company supports the Multiple Sclerosis Society and the National Advertising Benevolent Society. Preference for appeals relevant to company business. All donations are paid in Charities Aid Foundation vouchers.

☐ A Oppenheimer & Co Ltd
Export merchants & agents

20 Vanguard Way,
Shoeburyness,
Southend-on-Sea,
Essex SS3 9RA
0702-297785

Ch: John J Adler
Contact: D B Mitchell
Company Secretary

Year Ends: 31 Dec '90
Donations: £265
Profit: £5,026,000
Turnover: £106,181,000

UK employees: 120
Total employees: 1,753

Donations Policy: Support is mainly overseas; negligible in the UK. Preference for local charities in the areas of company presence.

☐ Orion Insurance Company plc
Insurance

Orion House,
Bouverie Road West,
Folkestone,
Kent CT20 2RW
0303-850303

Ch: Norman H Smith
MD: Albert Luan Koert
Contact: Madeleine Cordes
Assistant Company Secretary

Year Ends: 31 Dec '91
Donations: £6,000
Profit: (£35,294,000)
Turnover: n/a

UK employees: 577
Total employees: 577

Donations Policy: In general the company supports charities associated with Orion or the insurance industry. It rarely responds to unsolicited appeals outside this policy. Preference for local charities in the areas of company presence, appeals relevant to company business, charities in which a member of staff is involved. Sponsorship proposals to G J Ward, Divisional Manager, Product Management. Generally no support for circular appeals, purely denominational (religious) appeals, local appeals not in areas of company presence, overseas projects and appeals from individuals.

Please read page 6 — Alphabetical listing

Name/Address	Officers	Financial Information	Other Information

☐ Osborne & Little plc
Design & sale of wallpapers & furnishing fabrics

49 Temperley Road,
London SW12 8QE
081-675 2255

Ch: Peter Osborne
Contact: Mrs J L Wallace
Press Office Assistant

Year Ends: 31 Mar '92
Donations: £20,840
Profit: £855,000
Turnover: £19,108,000

UK employees: n/a
Total employees: 149

Donations Policy: Preference for local charities in areas where the company operates. The main charity supported has been Trinity Hospice in Clapham. Most of the donations were raised through the sale of fabrics and wallpapers.

☐ Otis plc
Lift & escalator manufacturer

43-59 Clapham Road,
London SW9 0JZ
071-735 9131

Ch: Jack Leingang
Contact: Richard Kingdon
Director of Sales & Marketing

Year Ends: 30 Nov '91
Donations: £23,606
Profit: £12,885,000
Turnover: £151,340,000

UK employees: n/a
Total employees: 2,804

Donations Policy: Preference for local charities in areas where the company operates and charities in which a member of company staff is involved. Preference for children and youth; enterprise/training and mobility related causes. Grants to local organisations from £90 to £200. No response to circular appeals. No grants for fundraising events; advertising in charity brochures; appeals from individuals; purely denominational (religious) appeals; large national appeals; overseas projects.

☐ Owners Abroad Group plc
Tour operators

1st Floor,
Astral Towers,
Betts Way,
Crawley RH10 2GX
0293-588520

Contact: H M Klein
Chairman

Year Ends: 31 Oct '91
Donations: £15,000
Profit: £31,634,000
Turnover: £643,628,000

UK employees: n/a
Total employees: 2,248

Donations Policy: The main charity supported is The Family Holiday Association. The company helps with staff fundraising. For smaller organisations there is a preference for local charities in areas where the company operates, Manchester, Gatwick, Glasgow, Dublin, Belfast.

☐ Oxford Instruments Group plc
Advanced instrumentation manufacturers

Old Station Way,
Eynsham,
Witney,
Oxfordshire OX8 1TL
0865-881437

Ch: P M Williams
Contact: Kate Naylor
Secretary

Year Ends: 26 Mar '91
Donations: £15,000
Profit: £7,100,000
Turnover: £103,000,000

UK employees: n/a
Total employees: 1,444

BitC

Donations Policy: Supports the local home for mentally disabled people and other charities in the Oxford area. Preference for children and youth; social welfare; medical; education; enterprise/training.
No response to circular appeals. No support for fundraising events; purely denominational appeals; local appeals not in areas of company presence; large national appeals; overseas projects; purely political appeals.

☐ P & O Steam Navigation Co
Transport, property & services

79 Pall Mall,
London SW1Y 5EJ
071-930 4343

Ch: Lord Sterling
MD: B D MacPhail
Contact: J M Crossman
Company Secretary

Year Ends: 31 Dec '91
Donations: £431,000
Profit: £217,400,000
Turnover: £4,897,200,000

UK employees: n/a
Total employees: 66,545

Donations Policy: P & O is a decentralised group of companies and support is given accordingly.

☐ P & P plc
Computer sales

Todd Hall Road,
Carrs Industrial Estate,
Haslingden,
Rossendale,
Lancashire BB4 5HU
0706-217744

Ch: Sir Roland Smith
MD: D R Southworth
Contact: Personnel Department

Year Ends: 30 Nov '91
Donations: £1,615
Profit: £711,000
Turnover: £228,324,000

UK employees: n/a
Total employees: 902

☐ PA Holdings Ltd
Consultancy services

123 Buckingham Palace Road,
London SW1W 9SR
071-730 9000

Ch: J Foden
Contact: Julie DaVerne
Corporate Communications

Year Ends: 31 Dec '91
Donations: n/a
Profit: £3,824,000
Turnover: £170,651,000

UK employees: n/a
Total employees: 2,666

BitC

☐ G W Padley (Holdings) Ltd
Poultry & vegetable processing, arable farming

Anwick,
Sleaford,
Lincolnshire NG34 9SL
0526-832661

Ch: D G Padley
Contact: Secretary to the Chairman

Year Ends: 28 Jul '90
Donations: £3,160
Profit: £4,826,000
Turnover: £123,372,000

UK employees: n/a
Total employees: 2,999

Donations Policy: Preference for local charities in areas of company presence and charities in which a member of company staff is involved. Preference for children and youth; social welfare; medical; education; recreation; environment/heritage; arts; enterprise/training.
No response to circular appeals. No grants for fundraising events; advertising in charity brochures; appeals from individuals; purely denominational (religious) appeals; local appeals not in areas of company presence; large national appeals; overseas projects.

● **Alphabetical listing**　　　　　　　　　　　　　　　　　　　　　　　　　　　　　　　　　　　　　　Please read page 6

Name/Address	Officers	Financial Information	Other Information

☐ Michael Page Group plc
　　　　　　　　　　　　　　　　　　　　　　　　　　　　　　　　　　　Recruitment & executive selection

Page House,　　　　　　　　　　　　*Ch:* Lord Ripon　　　　　　*Year Ends:* 31 Dec '91　　　　*UK employees:* n/a
39-41 Parker Street,　　　　　　　　*CE:* Michael Page　　　　　　*Donations:* £7,660　　　　　　*Total employees:* 384
London WC2B 5LH　　　　　　　　*Contact:* W McGregor　　　　　*Profit:* £3,524,000
071-831 2000　　　　　　　　　　　　　Chair of Charities Committee　*Turnover:* £40,918,000

Donations Policy: The company operates the Give As You Earn scheme and matches employee contributions to registered charities.

☐ Pall Europe Ltd
　　　Supply of filters

Havant Street,　　　　　　　　　　*Ch:* M G Hardy　　　　　　　*Year Ends:* 31 Jul '89　　　　　*UK employees:* n/a
Portsmouth,　　　　　　　　　　*Contact:* Mrs Pamela Moore　　　*Donations:* £32,625　　　　　　*Total employees:* 1,292
Hampshire PO1 3PD　　　　　　　　　Secretary to Managing Director　*Profit:* £23,140,000
0705-753545　　　　　　　　　　　　　　　　　　　　　　　　　　*Turnover:* £72,265,000

Donations Policy: The company prefers to make donations to medical charities or causes. Donations are generally £10 to £400. The company rarely sponsors people or events.

☐ Palmer & Harvey (Holdings) Ltd
　　　　　　　　　　　　　　　　　　　　　　　　　　　　　　　　Tobacco & confectionery distribution

Vale House,　　　　　　　　　　　*Ch:* J H Chedzoy　　　　　　　*Year Ends:* 31 Mar '90　　　　*UK employees:* n/a
Vale Road,　　　　　　　　　　　*MD:* P Hudson　　　　　　　*Donations:* n/a　　　　　　　*Total employees:* 3,073
Portslade,　　　　　　　　　　*Contact:* M Gauntlett　　　　　*Profit:* £13,329,000
East Sussex BN41 1HG　　　　　　　　Personnel Manager　　　　　*Turnover:* £1,076,108,000
0273-420042

☐ Pannell Kerr Forster
　　　Accountants

New Garden House,　　　　　　　　*Ch:* R J C Pearson　　　　　　*Year Ends:*　　　　　　　　　*UK employees:* 2,500
Hatton Garden,　　　　　　　　*Contact:* E B Middleton　　　　　*Donations:* n/a　　　　　　　*Total employees:* n/a
London EC1N 8JA　　　　　　　　　Partner　　　　　　　　　　*Profit:* n/a
071-831 7393　　　　　　　　　　　　　　　　　　　　　　　　　　*Turnover:* n/a　　　　　　　　　% Club, BitC

Donations Policy: Throughout the UK the firm contributes free professional advice and cash donations to a range of organisations and supports the arts through donations and sponsorship.
No grants for fundraising events; advertising in charity brochures; appeals from individuals; purely denominational (religious) appeals; local appeals not in areas of company presence; large national appeals; overseas projects. No response to circular appeals.

☐ A G Parfett Ltd
　　　　　　　　　　　　　　　　　　　　　　　　　　　　　　　　Food, wine, spirits & tobacco wholesale

Didsbury Road,　　　　　　　　　*MD:* S Parfett　　　　　　　　*Year Ends:* 30 Jun '91　　　　　*UK employees:* n/a
Stockport,　　　　　　　　　　*Contact:* R Parfett　　　　　　*Donations:* £14,277 (1992)　　*Total employees:* 399
Cheshire SK4 2JP　　　　　　　　　　　　　　　　　　　　　　*Profit:* £2,511,000
061-429 0429　　　　　　　　　　　　　　　　　　　　　　　　　*Turnover:* £121,260,000

Donations Policy: Donations are given to a range of charitable organisations with preference for local charities in areas where the company operates. Preferred areas of support are children and youth, social welfare and recreation. Donations are not always in cash, but may be goods suitable for eg. raffles. Grants to national and local organisations range from £10 to £2,500.
No support for state run schools.

☐ Park Food Group plc
　　　　　　　　　　　　　　　　　　　　　　　　　　　　　　　　　　Packaging & supply of hampers

Valley Road,　　　　　　　　　　*Ch:* P J Sherlock　　　　　　　*Year Ends:* 31 Mar '91　　　　*UK employees:* n/a
Birkenhead,　　　　　　　　　　*MD:* P R Johnstone　　　　　　*Donations:* £2,101　　　　　　*Total employees:* 642
Merseyside L41 7ED　　　　　　*Contact:* Mrs M Johnstone　　　*Profit:* £3,992,000
051-653 0566　　　　　　　　　　　Secretary to the Managing　　*Turnover:* £119,565,000
　　　　　　　　　　　　　　　　　Director

☐ Parker Pen UK Ltd
　　　　　　　　　　　　　　　　　　　　　　　　　　　　　　　Design & manufacture of writing instruments

Newhaven,　　　　　　　　　　　*MD:* J G Margry　　　　　　　*Year Ends:* 28 Feb '91　　　　*UK employees:* n/a
East Sussex BN9 0AU　　　　　　*Contact:* Sue Stevenson　　　　*Donations:* £6,668　　　　　　*Total employees:* 2,603
0273-513233　　　　　　　　　　　Secretary to the Director　　　*Profit:* £22,895,000
　　　　　　　　　　　　　　　　　　　　　　　　　　　　　　Turnover: £170,409,000

☐ Ralph M Parsons Co Ltd
　　　Engineering

Kew Bridge Road,　　　　　　　　*Ch:* I Robinson　　　　　　　*Year Ends:* 31 Dec '91　　　　*UK employees:* n/a
Brentford,　　　　　　　　　　　*MD:* M F Knapp　　　　　　　*Donations:* £1,500　　　　　　*Total employees:* n/a
Middlesex TW8 0EH　　　　　　*Contact:* Ms J Pearson　　　　　*Profit:* n/a
081-995 1322　　　　　　　　　　　Secretary to the Managing　　*Turnover:* n/a
　　　　　　　　　　　　　　　　　Director

Donations Policy: Preference for local charities in areas where the company operates. Preference for children and youth; social welfare; medical; recreation. Grants to local organisations from £50 to £100.
No support for advertising in charity brochures; appeals from individuals; political or religious appeals.

Please read page 6 — Alphabetical listing

Name/Address	Officers	Financial Information	Other Information

☐ Pasminco Europe Ltd
Non-ferrous metals production

1 Redcliff Street,
Bristol BS99 7EA
0272-215491

MD: C A Holroyd
Contact: Mrs Erica Ricks
Secretary to the Managing Director

Year Ends: 30 Jun '91
Donations: n/a
Profit: £5,849,000
Turnover: £191,854,000

UK employees: n/a
Total employees: 927

☐ Paterson Zochonis plc
Cosmetics & toiletries

Bridgewater House,
60 Whitworth Street,
Manchester M1 6LU
061-236 7111

Ch: J B Zochonis
MD: G A Loupos
Contact: Mrs Bacchus
Secretary to the Chairman

Year Ends: 31 May '91
Donations: £52,000
Profit: £25,367,000
Turnover: £215,166,000

UK employees: n/a
Total employees: 3,830

Donations Policy: Preference for local charities in areas of company presence, particularly projects involving children and youth, social welfare, medical, education, recreation and disabled people.
Generally no support for circular appeals, fundraising events, advertising in charity brochures, individuals, denominational appeals or overseas projects.

☐ Pauls plc
Maltsters & manufacturers of animal foods

PO Box 39,
47 Key Street,
Ipswich,
Suffolk IP4 1BX
0473-232222

Ch: G W Paul
MD: P G W Simmonds
Contact: Miss Rose
Secretary to the Managing Director

Year Ends: 31 Dec '88
Donations: £20,967
Profit: £19,335,000
Turnover: n/a

UK employees: 2,023
Total employees: 2,164

Donations Policy: Preference for local charities in areas where the company operates and charities in which a member of company staff is involved. This company is part of the Harrisons & Crosfield Group (See separate entry).

☐ Pearce Signs Ltd
Illuminated Signs Manufacturer

New Cross Road,
London SE14 6AB
081-692 6611

Contact: George Garrett
Company Secretary

Year Ends: 31 Dec '91
Donations: £17,653
Profit: £825,000
Turnover: £29,500,000

UK employees: 750
Total employees: n/a

% Club, BitC

Donations Policy: Preference for medical, education and enterprise/training.
No grants for fundraising events; advertising in charity brochures; appeals from individuals; purely denominational (religious) appeals; local appeals not in areas of company presence; large national appeals; overseas projects. No response to circular appeals.

☐ Pearl Group plc
Life & general insurance

The Pearl Centre,
Lynch Wood,
Peterborough,
Cambridgeshire PE2 6FY
0733-470470

Ch: E Lyall
MD: Godfrey Bowles
Contact: Keith Goldsmith
Assistant Company Secretary

Year Ends: 31 Dec '91
Donations: £310,942
Profit: £59,600,000
Turnover: £1,039,600,000

UK employees: 9,600
Total employees: 9,600

% Club, BitC

Donations Policy: Support is concentrated in the areas of medical research and care for people with disabilities. The company is very selective about making grants, and has a policy of making long-term, usually three year, commitments to a small number of charities for sums of about £20,000 a year. The aim is to work with the charity so that both sides benefit from the involvement and from public relations opportunities.
No response to circular appeals. No support or sponsorship for individuals, and no support for fundraising events; advertising in charity brochures; purely denominational (religious) appeals; overseas projects.

☐ Pearson plc
News information & entertainment

Millbank Tower,
Millbank,
London SW1P 4QZ
071-411 2000

Ch: Viscount Blakenham
MD: F Barlow
Contact: Anette Lawless
Company Secretary

Year Ends: 31 Dec '91
Donations: £917,000
Profit: £173,800,000
Turnover: £1,600,400,000

UK employees: 17,927
Total employees: 28,492

% Club, ABSA

Donations Policy: National charities are supported centrally, and trade and local causes are normally supported by the operating subsidiaries. Nationally, the company makes a small number of substantial donations in chosen sectors. Preference is given where there is a business connection and where there is a possibility of monitoring the benefits and where staff can be involved. Local appeals should be addressed to the relevant local company.
No support for advertising in brochures or programmes.

☐ Pechiney World Trade (Holdings) Ltd
Metals & chemicals merchants

Pechiney House,
The Grove,
Slough,
Berkshire SL1 1QF
0753-522800

Contact: Susie Neall
Secretary to the Managing Director

Year Ends: 31 Dec '90
Donations: n/a
Profit: £5,765,000
Turnover: £331,620,000

UK employees: n/a
Total employees: 150

● **Alphabetical listing**   Please read page 6

Name/Address	Officers	Financial Information	Other Information

☐ Peek plc
Traffic & field data systems

207 Radley Road,
Abingdon,
Oxon OX14 3XA
0235-528271

Ch: Viscount Slim
CE: K E Maud
Contact: M A Jenkins
Company Secretary

Year Ends: 27 Dec '91
Donations: nil
Profit: £6,061,000
Turnover: £84,157,000

UK employees: n/a
Total employees: 1,190

Donations Policy: The company make no donations to charities, but supports employee fundraising.

☐ Pendragon plc
New & used vehicle dealers

Pendragon House,
Sir Frank Whittle Road,
Derby DE21 4EE
0332-292777

Ch: A N R Rudd
Contact: T G Finn
Chief Executive

Year Ends: 31 Dec '91
Donations: £1,227
Profit: £4,731,000
Turnover: £168,254,000

UK employees: n/a
Total employees: 1,072

☐ Pentland Group plc
General trading & service

The Pentland Centre,
Lakeside Squires Lane,
Finchley,
London N3 2QL
081-346 2600

Contact: Mrs J D Robertson
Personal Assistant to the Chairman

Year Ends: 31 Dec '91
Donations: £61,000
Profit: £19,553,000
Turnover: £340,132,000

UK employees: n/a
Total employees: 2,070

% Club, BitC

Donations Policy: Support for the scout movement, the arts (specifically the Philharmonia and the National Theatre), educational charities and the environment/heritage. Preference for local charities in areas where the company operates.
No response to circular appeals. No grants for appeals from individuals; purely denominational (religious) appeals; local appeals not in areas of company presence.

☐ Pentos plc
Books, posters & office supplies

9 Clifford Street,
London W1X 1RB
071-499 3484

Ch: T A Maher
Contact: M R M Jenner
Company Secretary

Year Ends: 31 Dec '91
Donations: £17,332
Profit: £15,200,000
Turnover: £204,300,000

UK employees: n/a
Total employees: 4,079

% Club

Donations Policy: Preference for appeals relevant to company business and local causes in areas of company presence. Preference for children and youth; education; recreation; arts. Where possible the company seeks to offer employee's time, together with stock and equipment rather than just a straight cash donation. Grants to national organisations from £50 to £500. Grants to local organisations from £50 to £1,000.
No grants for advertising in charity brochures; appeals from individuals; purely denominational (religious) appeals; local appeals not in areas of company presence; overseas projects.

☐ Pepe Group plc
Jeans manufacturers

Pepe House,
449-451 High Road,
London NW10 2JJ
081-459 8883

Ch: A K Shah
CE: J Sinyor
Contact: Financial Controller

Year Ends: 31 Mar '91
Donations: £2,407
Profit: £4,803,000
Turnover: £158,847,000

UK employees: n/a
Total employees: 1,021

☐ Perkins Foods plc
Frozen foods manufacture

Trinity Court,
Trinity Street,
Peterborough,
Cambridgeshire PE1 1DA
0733-555706

Ch: M Davies
CE: H G Phillips
Contact: Mrs Walker
Secretary to the Chief Executive

Year Ends: 31 Dec '91
Donations: £23,000
Profit: £24,253,000
Turnover: £260,131,000

UK employees: n/a
Total employees: 1,382

Donations Policy: The main donations go to the MacMillan Nurses Fund and the Injured Riders Fund. Small donations of £50 to £100 are given to other charities for example for fundraising and sponsored events.

☐ Perry Group plc
Motor vehicle dealers

Cambridge House,
Bluecoats Avenue,
Hertford,
Hertfordshire SG14 1PB
0992-554188

Ch: R R Allan
Contact: M Hickman-Ashby
Company Secretary

Year Ends: 31 Dec '91
Donations: £11,525
Profit: £20,454,000
Turnover: £300,104,000

UK employees: n/a
Total employees: 6,582

Donations Policy: 80% of company giving is to BEN (Motor Trades Benevolent Fund) and the balance distributed to other charities in October. Preference for local charities in the areas of company presence and appeals relevant to company business.
Generally no support for circular appeals, fundraising events, advertising in charity brochures, appeals from individuals, purely denominational (religious) appeals, local appeals not in areas of company presence, large national appeals or overseas projects.

☐ Persimmon plc
Residential building & development

Persimmon House,
Fulford,
York YO1 4RE
0904-642199

Ch: D Davidson
Contact: G Grewer
Company Secretary

Year Ends: 31 Dec '91
Donations: £55,000
Profit: £22,265,000
Turnover: £143,831,000

UK employees: n/a
Total employees: 701

% Club

Donations Policy: The company supports a large number of national and local charities throughout the UK from its 14 regional offices. Most donations go direct to registered charities rather than to individuals or for advertising in charity brochures.

Please read page 6 — Alphabetical listing

Name/Address	Officers	Financial Information	Other Information

PET (UK) Ltd
East Walls,
Chichester,
West Sussex PO19 1PQ
0243-788373

Contact: C N G Shipham
Managing Director

Year Ends: 30 Nov '90
Donations: £10,108
Profit: £4,015,000
Turnover: £120,979,000

Food manufacturing
UK employees: n/a
Total employees: 1,864

Michael Peters Group plc
49 Princes Place,
London W11 4QA
071-229 3424

Ch: M H B Peters
Contact: Margery Rayfield
Secretary to the Chairman

Year Ends: 30 Jun '89
Donations: £7,921
Profit: £2,340,000
Turnover: £45,818,000

Designers
UK employees: n/a
Total employees: 711

Peugeot Talbot Motor Co Ltd
Aldermoor House,
PO Box 227,
Aldermoor Lane,
Coventry CV3 1LT
0203-884000

Ch: J C P Bollot
MD: G H Whalen
Contact: S T E Fenn
Secretary to the Charitable Trust

Year Ends: 31 Dec '91
Donations: £181,000
Profit: £50,000,000
Turnover: £1,444,400,000

Motor vehicle manufacturers
UK employees: 6,969
Total employees: n/a

% Club

Donations Policy: The company only supports charities local to Coventry or associated with the motor industry. Grants range from £25 to £20,000. In kind support is given to many local organisations, offering long and short term vehicle loans, raffle prizes and other assistance. No support for brochure advertising, purely denominational appeals, overseas projects or anything political. The company will not support large national appeals such as Children in Need or Telethon.

Pfizer Group Ltd
Ramsgate Road,
Sandwich,
Kent CT13 9NJ
0304-616161

Ch: W J Wilson
Contact: Ms M Kitney
Public Affairs Officer

Year Ends: 30 Nov '90
Donations: £41,000
Profit: £4,788,000
Turnover: £161,578,000

Pharmaceuticals
UK employees: n/a
Total employees: 2,386

BitC

Donations Policy: No particular preferences, but support is not given to overseas projects.

PHH Europe plc
PHH Centre,
Windmill Hill,
Whitehill Way,
Swindon,
Wiltshire SN5 6PE
0793-887000

Contact: Sharon White
Executive Administrator

Year Ends: 30 Apr '91
Donations: n/a
Profit: £206,000
Turnover: £1,070,887,000

Vehicle leasing, relocation management services
UK employees: n/a
Total employees: 856

Philips Electronics UK Ltd
Philips House,
1-19 Torrington Place,
London WC1E 7HD
071-436 4044

Ch: A Poot
MD: C A M Busch
Contact: N Rigler
Public Relations Manager

Year Ends: 31 Dec '90
Donations: £50,000
Profit: £38,600,000
Turnover: £1,096,800,000

Manufacture & supply of electrical equipment
UK employees: n/a
Total employees: 12,152

Donations Policy: Each division of the company has it's own charity policy and budget, they will probably support local charities in areas of company operation and appeals that have staff support. Nationally the company is formulating a corporate donations policy.

Phillips Petroleum Co UK Ltd
Phillips Quadrant,
35 Guildford Road,
Woking,
Surrey GU22 7QT
0483-756666

Ch: K L Hedrick
Contact: Public Affairs Manager

Year Ends: 31 Dec '90
Donations: n/a
Profit: £75,694,000
Turnover: £525,100,000

Oil & gas
UK employees: n/a
Total employees: 714

Photo-Me International plc
Church Road,
Bookham,
Surrey KT23 3EU
0372-453399

Ch: P Payen
MD: D W Miller
Contact: P D Berridge
Company Secretary

Year Ends: 30 Apr '92
Donations: n/a
Profit: £16,410,000
Turnover: £100,819,000

Photo booths, ID systems, express print services
UK employees: n/a
Total employees: 1,993

Pickwick Group plc
The Hyde Industrial Estate,
The Hyde,
London NW9 6JU
081-200 7000

Ch: Ivor Schlosberg
Contact: Mrs Bobby Coofer
Personal Assistant to Managing Director

Year Ends: 31 Dec '90
Donations: £3,718
Profit: £6,923,000
Turnover: £74,510,000

Manufacturer of audio & visual products
UK employees: n/a
Total employees: 296

• **Alphabetical listing**   Please read page 6

Name/Address   *Officers*   *Financial Information*   *Other Information*

☐ Pifco Holdings plc
                                                                                       Electrical appliances

Princess Street,   *Ch:* Michael Webber   *Year Ends:* 30 Apr '89   *UK employees:* n/a
Failsworth,   *Contact:* Andrew Streets   *Donations:* £38,000 (1990)   *Total employees:* 280
Manchester   M35 0HS   Company Secretary   *Profit:* £2,854,000
061-681 8321   *Turnover:* £20,679,000   % Club

Donations Policy: Support for "charities which are involved in helping the less fortunate in our society and the relief of pain and suffering". The company also supports charitable events within the locality of each of its operating sites. Preference for children and youth; social welfare; medical.
No grants for appeals from individuals or local appeals not in areas of company presence.

☐ Pilkington plc
                                                                             Glass manufacturing & processing

Prescot Road,   *Ch:* Sir Anthony Pilkington   *Year Ends:* 31 Mar '92   *UK employees:* 10,000
St Helens,   *CE:* R Leverton   *Donations:* £281,000   *Total employees:* 43,800
Merseyside WA10 3TT   *Contact:* Miss J Hutchin   *Profit:* £77,000,000
0744-28882   Secretary of the Grants Committee *Turnover:* £2,611,000,000   % Club, BitC

Donations Policy: The company supports the community where it operates especially St Helens, with particular preference for the arts, social welfare, health and medical care, education, scientific research and enterprise projects.
In addition to UK donations £631,000 was given in donations overseas.

☐ Pillar Electrical Ltd
                                                                    Manufacturers of electrical plugs & sockets

279-281 Fore Street,   *Ch:* G H Sage   *Year Ends:* 31 Dec '88   *UK employees:* n/a
Edmonton,   *Contact:* B Edwards   *Donations:* £2,667   *Total employees:* 21
London N9 0PJ   Director of Personnel   *Profit:* £18,037,000
081-807 5151   *Turnover:* n/a

Donations Policy: Preference for local charities in areas where the company operates especially charities involved with children and youth, medical, and education. Generally donations are between £10 and £100.
No grants for advertising in charity brochures or purely denominational (religious) appeals.

☐ Pioneer Concrete (Holdings) Ltd
                                                                                       Concrete manufacturers

56-60 Northolt Road,   *Ch:* Rt Hon Lord Rawlinson of Ewell *Year Ends:* 30 Jun '91   *UK employees:* n/a
South Harrow,   *MD:* N J Nolan   *Donations:* £23,808   *Total employees:* 1,245
Middlesex HA2 0EY   *Contact:* A L J Thomas   *Profit:* £3,812,000
081-423 3066   Company Secretary   *Turnover:* £188,040,000

Donations Policy: The company chooses one charity each year to support and most donations are made to it. The company may also make small donations to local charities in areas of company presence.

☐ Pirelli UK plc
                                                                    Electrical wire & cable & tyre manufacture

40 Chancery Lane,   *Ch:* Earl of Limerick   *Year Ends:* 31 Dec '90   *UK employees:* n/a
London WC2A 1JH   *Contact:* D J Piper   *Donations:* £39,836   *Total employees:* 6,738
071-242 8881   Group Secretary   *Profit:* £15,800,000
                                                             Turnover: £514,000,000   % Club

Donations Policy: Preference for local charities in areas where the company operates and for appeals relevant to company business. Preference for children and youth; medical; arts. Grants range from £10 to £500.
No grants for fundraising events; advertising in charity brochures; appeals from individuals; purely denominational (religious) appeals; local appeals not in areas of company presence; overseas projects.

☐ Pitney Bowes plc
                                                                         Mailing, machines & office equipment

The Pinnacles,   *Ch:* D C MacDonald   *Year Ends:* 31 Dec '91   *UK employees:* n/a
Elizabeth Way,   *MD:* J N D Moody   *Donations:* £27,125   *Total employees:* 2,462
Harlow,   *Contact:* Paul Slater   *Profit:* £10,195,000
Essex CM19 5BD   Marketing & Communications   *Turnover:* £91,345,000
0279-426731   Co-ordinator

Donations Policy: Charitable giving is determined by an employee/management committee through Pitney Bowes Charity Chest. Donations raised by employees are matched pound for pound by the company.
Generally no support for fundraising events, brochure advertising, purely denominational (religious) appeals. The arts and overseas work are given low priority.

☐ Pittard Garner plc
                                                                                         Leather manufacturers

Sherborne Road,   *Ch:* J W W Pittard   *Year Ends:* 31 Dec '91   *UK employees:* n/a
Yeovil,   *MD:* A G Marriot   *Donations:* £15,544   *Total employees:* 1,596
Somerset BA21 5BA   *Contact:* R B Williams   *Profit:* £2,100,000
0935-74321   Finance Director   *Turnover:* £97,995,000

Donations Policy: Support only for local charities in areas of company presence, charities in which a member of staff is involved and leather related appeals (eg. Leather & Hides Trade Benevolent Fund).

Please read page 6 | Alphabetical listing ●

Name/Address	Officers	Financial Information	Other Information

☐ **Plysu plc** — Manufacture of polythylene containers

120 Station Road,
Woburn Sands,
Milton Keynes,
Buckinghamshire MK17 8SE
0908-582311

Contact: J Hartup
Secretary to the Chairman

Year Ends: 31 Mar '92
Donations: £3,000
Profit: £6,047,000
Turnover: £66,030,000

UK employees: n/a
Total employees: 1375

☐ **PMG Investments Ltd** — Motor distributors & engineers

Patrick House,
180 Lifford Lane,
Birmingham B30 3NT
021-459 4471

Ch: J A Patrick
Contact: Mrs P Giles
Secretary to Chairman

Year Ends: 31 Jul '90
Donations: £212,000 (1991)
Profit: £158,000
Turnover: £26,251,000

UK employees: n/a
Total employees: 288

Donations Policy: The company supports charities allied to the PMG group.

☐ **Pochin's plc** — Building & civil engineering contracting

Brooks Lane,
Middlewich,
Cheshire CW10 0JQ
0606-833333

Ch: N J Pochin
Contact: J H Woodcock
Marketing Director

Year Ends: 31 Aug '91
Donations: £16,344
Profit: £2,429,000
Turnover: £38,929,000

UK employees: n/a
Total employees: 718

☐ **Polaroid UK Ltd** — Photographic & optical equipment

Ashley Road,
St Albans,
Hertfordshire AL1 5PR
0727-59191

Ch: Lee Brewer
Contact: Eve Tate
Publicity Manager

Year Ends: 31 Dec '91
Donations: £28,303
Profit: £4,081,000
Turnover: £172,973,000

UK employees: 115
Total employees: n/a

Donations Policy: The entire budget for charities is committed annually to the Hertfordshire Community Trust. This trust distributes funds to several organisations in the area. Total community contributions in 1991 were £55,022, including the charitable donations.

☐ **Polygram Record Operations Ltd** — Record, cassette, compact disc & video distribution

1 Sussex Place,
London W6 9RS
081-846 8515

MD: M Howle
Contact: Anthea Joseph
Public Relations Officer

Year Ends: 31 Dec '90
Donations: £12,141
Profit: £15,949,000
Turnover: £160,453,000

UK employees: n/a
Total employees: 748

☐ **Polypipe plc** — Plastic pipes, profiles & fittings

Edlington,
Doncaster,
South Yorkshire DN12 1ES
0709-770000

Ch: Kevin McDonald
Contact: Vic Roberts
Marketing Director

Year Ends: 30 Jun '90
Donations: £83,331
Profit: £13,432,000
Turnover: £70,832,000

UK employees: n/a
Total employees: 849

Donations Policy: It is thought that the company make most of their donations to organisations local to areas of company presence.

☐ **Porsche Cars Great Britain Ltd** — Distributor of Porsche cars

Bath Road,
Calcot,
Reading,
Berkshire RG3 7SE
0734-303666

MD: P T Bulbeck
Contact: John Edwards
Manager of Marketing & Public Relations

Year Ends: 31 Jul '90
Donations: n/a
Profit: £7,266,000
Turnover: £121,329,000

UK employees: n/a
Total employees: 195

☐ **Portals Group plc** — Papermaking & engineering

Mill House,
Laverstoke,
Whitchurch,
Hampshire RG28 7NR
0256-892360

Ch: J L Sheffield
MD: J Lloyd
Contact: R L Lee
Company Secretary

Year Ends: 31 Dec '91
Donations: £66,000
Profit: £27,582,000
Turnover: £194,316,000

UK employees: n/a
Total employees: 3,139

Donations Policy: Preference for local charities in areas of company presence, appeals relevant to the business and charities in which a member of staff is involved. Preferred projects are those involving children and youth, medicine, education, environment and heritage, overseas development and enterprise/training. Grants to national organisations from £500 to £5,000. Grants to local organisations from £500 to £1,000.
Generally no support for circular appeals, advertising in charity brochures, individuals, purely denominational appeals, local appeals not in areas of company presence or large national appeals.

☐ **Porter Chadburn plc** — Sports clothing & toys distribution, furnishing fabrics

117 George Street,
London W1H 1TB
071-724 8584

Ch: R J Dinkin
Contact: Ms S Williams
Company Secretary

Year Ends: 29 Mar '91
Donations: £4,281
Profit: £7,016,000
Turnover: £111,672,000

UK employees: n/a
Total employees: 1,132

● **Alphabetical listing**   Please read page 6

Name/Address	Officers	Financial Information	Other Information

☐ Portsmouth & Sunderland Newspapers plc

Newspaper proprietors

37 Abingdon Road,
London W8 6AH
071-937 9741

Ch: Sir Richard Storey
MD: C D Brims
Contact: T F Lake
Company Secretary

Year Ends: 31 Mar '92
Donations: £56,046
Profit: £5,860,000
Turnover: £81,198,000

UK employees: 1,972
Total employees: n/a

% Club

Donations Policy: Supports charities within the circulation area of the company's newspapers or those connected with the newspaper industry. The company encourages staff to help charities and sponsors appeals for local communities in company newspapers. Grants to national organisations ranged from £250 to £1,000, and to local organisations from £50 to £250.
Generally no support for appeals from individuals, local appeals not in areas of company presence or overseas projects.
Total community contributions in 1991/92 were £550,000.

☐ Post Office Group

Postal services

30 St James' Square,
London SW1Y 4PY
071-490 2888

Ch: Sir Bryan Nicholson
MD: K M Young
Contact: R G Osmond
Head of Community Affairs

Year Ends: 31 Mar '92
Donations: £1,200,000
Profit: £247,000,000
Turnover: £5,149,000,000

UK employees: 201,937
Total employees: 201,937

BitC, ABSA

Donations Policy: Main areas of support are job creation and enterprise, inner city and rural regeneration schemes and industry/education links. Support is also given for disaster appeals and to arts organisations for special concerts and educational work. Grants to national organisations from £500 to £10,000; grants to local organisations from £250 to £1,000. Preference for appeals relevant to company business and charities in which a member of company staff is involved. Local appeals should be sent to local offices, but budgets for meeting such appeals is limited.
Total community contributions in 1991/92 were £1.8 million.
No support for purely denominational (religious) appeals, appeals from individuals, political appeals or overseas projects.

☐ Powell Duffryn plc

Engineering, fuel distribution, shipping

Powell Duffryn House,
London Road,
Bracknell,
Berkshire RG12 2AQ
0344-53101

Contact: R D C Hubbard
Chairman

Year Ends: 31 Mar '91
Donations: £34,000
Profit: £28,856,000
Turnover: £681,956,000

UK employees: n/a
Total employees: 9,668

% Club

Donations Policy: Preference for local charities, charities in Wales and those connected with the company business.

☐ PowerGen plc

Electricity supply

53 New Broad Street,
London EC2M 1JJ
071-826 2826

Ch: Sir Graham Day
CE: E A Wallis
Contact: Dianne Long
Head of Corporate
Communications

Year Ends: 31 Mar '92
Donations: £191,825
Profit: £359,000,000
Turnover: £3,009,000,000

UK employees: n/a
Total employees: 6,081

BitC, ABSA

Donations Policy: Community support is focussed on science, education and the environment, with particular emphasis on areas local to PowerGen sites.
No grants for appeals from individuals; purely denominational (religious) appeals; local appeals not in areas of company presence; overseas projects.

☐ Prebon Yamane (UK) Ltd

Financial & technical services

34-40 Ludgate Hill,
London EC4M 7JT
071-522 2222

Ch: M J Warren
CE: E A Teraskiewicz
Contact: Mrs Jacqueline Casson
Personnel & Administration
Manager

Year Ends: 31 Jul '89
Donations: £4,500
Profit: £429,000
Turnover: £88,293,000

UK employees: n/a
Total employees: 1,290

☐ Premier Consolidated Oilfields plc

Oil & gas exploration & production

23 Lower Belgrave Street,
London SW1W 0NR
071-730 1111

Contact: R Lascelles
Company Secretary

Year Ends: 31 Dec '91
Donations: £8,484
Profit: £13,628,000
Turnover: £32,019,000

UK employees: n/a
Total employees: 122

Donations Policy: The financial details above are for the previous 9 months.

☐ Pressac Holdings plc

Electromechanical component manufacturers

Park House,
104 Derby Road,
Long Eaton,
Nottingham NG10 4LS
0602-462525

Ch: J B Wagstaff
MD: E A Greasley
Contact: G C White
Group Chief Executive

Year Ends: 31 Mar '91
Donations: £7,384
Profit: £1,820,000
Turnover: £34,471,000

UK employees: n/a
Total employees: 9,597

Please read page 6 — Alphabetical listing

Name/Address	Officers	Financial Information	Other Information

☐ Price Waterhouse - United Kingdom
Chartered accountants

Southwark Towers,
32 London Bridge Street,
London SE1 9SY
071-939 3000

Contact: J Barrett
Secretary to the Charities Committee

Year Ends: 30 Jun '91
Donations: £150,000
Profit: n/a
Turnover: n/a

UK employees: n/a
Total employees: 6,750

% Club, BitC

Donations Policy: The donations figure is approximate. A variety of causes are supported in the areas of relief of suffering, the arts, education and science, environment and heritage, children and youth, and social welfare. Preference for smaller charities in areas of company presence rather than major charities, and to charities in which a member of staff is involved. Grants to national organisations from £100 to £5,000. Grants to local organisations from £100 to £500.
No response to circular appeals. No grants for fundraising events; advertising in charity brochures; appeals from individuals; purely denominational (religious) appeals; local appeals not in areas of company presence.

☐ Benjamin Priest Group plc
Engineering

Priest Street,
Cradley Heath,
Warley,
West Midlands B64 6JW
0384-66501

Ch: C J Walliker
MD: D F Abel Smith
Contact: Mrs P Ryder
Secretary to the Managing Director

Year Ends: 31 Mar '89
Donations: £4,614
Profit: £8,816,000
Turnover: £100,995,000

UK employees: n/a
Total employees: 1,882

Donations Policy: Preference for local charities in areas of company presence. Preference for charities involved with social welfare, medical and enterprise. The charity committee meets twice a year, in July/August and in January. There are about 20 payments of £70 each allocated at each meeting.
No support for advertising in charity brochures or purely denominational (religious) appeals.

☐ Primary Industries (UK) Ltd
Commodities & manufactured goods traders

Carrier House,
1-9 Warwick Row,
London SW1E 5ER
071-834 6767

MD: M Shaw
Contact: Personnel Officer

Year Ends: 30 Jun '91
Donations: n/a
Profit: £1,793,000
Turnover: £436,029,000

UK employees: n/a
Total employees: 66

☐ Princes Ltd
Distribution of food products to grocery trade

Royal Liver Building,
Pier Head,
Liverpool L3 1NX
051-236 9282

MD: T Akiyoshi
Contact: Steve Gamble
Personnel Manager

Year Ends: 31 Dec '90
Donations: £9,883
Profit: £1,468,000
Turnover: £184,897,000

UK employees: n/a
Total employees: 227

☐ Private Patients Plan Ltd
Medical insurance company

PPP House,
Vale Road,
Tunbridge Wells,
Kent TN1 1BJ
0892-512345

Ch: Sir Peter Gadsen
MD: R Forman
Contact: Mrs Anne Ainsley (address below) Projects Manager

Year Ends: 31 Dec '91
Donations: £270,000
Profit: £16,464,000
Turnover: £365,027,000

UK employees: n/a
Total employees: 1,633

Donations Policy: Of the donations figure above £220,000 is donated to the PPP Medical Trust Ltd. Grants from the trust are usually associated with care of the disabled and chronically ill, medical research and education and advances in the acute care of the elderly. The company also supports the arts particularly events and organisations near its head office in Tunbridge Wells. Preference for appeals relevant to company business and for charities in which a member of company staff is involved. Grants to national organisations from £700 to £60,000. Grants to local organisations from £75 to £1,600.
No grants for advertising in charity brochures; appeals from individuals; purely denominational (religious) appeals; large national appeals; overseas projects. No response to circular appeals.
Appeals to the company should be addressed to Mrs Anne Ainsley, Projects Manager, Strategic Communications Department, Private Patients Plan Ltd, Tavistock House South, Tavistock Square, London WC1H 9LJ (071-380 0967).
The correspondent of the trust is M E Kirkham, Appeals Secretary, PPP Medical Trust Ltd, at head office.

☐ Procter & Gamble Ltd
Detergents & allied products

PO Box 1EE,
Gosforth,
Newcastle-upon-Tyne
NE99 1EE
091-279 2000

Ch: E L Artzt
MD: M Clasper
Contact: Secretary to Charities Committee

Year Ends: 30 Jun '91
Donations: £52,000 (1990)
Profit: £71,357,000
Turnover: £1,043,979,000

UK employees: 5,000
Total employees: n/a

BitC

Donations Policy: Preference for local charities in areas of company presence, the North East, Manchester and Essex, across a wide range of causes including health, welfare, culture and the environment.
Generally no support for circulars, fundraising events, advertising in charity brochures, appeals from individuals, purely denominational (religious) appeals, local appeals not in areas of company presence or overseas projects.

☐ Alexander Proudfoot plc
Management consultants

Centenary House,
5 Hill Street,
Richmond,
Surrey TW9 1SP
081-948 7200

Ch: Lord Stevens of Ludgate
MD: John Prosser
Contact: Cathy Lasher
Company Secretary

Year Ends: 31 Dec '91
Donations: £6,200
Profit: £48,010,000
Turnover: £176,419,000

UK employees: n/a
Total employees: 1,569

Alphabetical listing

Name/Address — *Officers* — *Financial Information* — *Other Information*

☐ Provident Mutual Life Assurance Association
Insurance

Wedgewood Way,
Stevenage,
Hertfordshire SG1 4PU
0438-739000

Ch: Lord Farnham
Contact: Mrs Steadman
Company Secretary

Year Ends: 31 Dec '91
Donations: £69,795
Profit: n/a
Turnover: n/a

UK employees: n/a
Total employees: 1,477

BitC

Donations Policy: Appeals relevant to company business are preferred. Support mainly for children/youth, medical and enterprise. Direct support preferred.
No support for circular appeals, denominational appeals, appeals from individuals or overseas projects.

☐ Provincial Group plc
Insurance & finances

Stramongate,
Kendal,
Cumbria LA9 4BE
0539-723415

Ch: C F E Shakerly
Contact: J A Hogan
Marketing Communications Officer

Year Ends: 31 Dec '91
Donations: £108,073
Profit: (£22,900,000)
Turnover: n/a

UK employees: 2,153
Total employees: n/a

BitC

Donations Policy: Preference for projects in areas where company has a presence, especially north west England, and for projects involving a member of staff. Typical grants range from £100 to £1,000. Main donations are made through the Charities Aid Foundation, while local donations in Cumbria are channelled through the Provincial Trust for Kendal. This trust makes donations of £50 to £400 to various organisations and individuals in Cumbria.
No support for non-charities, circular appeals, fundraising events, advertising in charity brochures, appeals from individuals, purely denominational appeals or large national appeals.

☐ Prudential Corporation plc
Life & general insurance, financial services

1 Stephen Street,
London W1P 2AP
071-548 3709

Ch: Sir Brian Corby
MD: M Newmarch
Contact: Mrs J M Fowler
Community Affairs Manager

Year Ends: 31 Dec '91
Donations: £1,049,000 (UK)
Profit: £267,000,000
Turnover: n/a

UK employees: 25,886
Total employees: n/a

% Club, BitC, ABSA

Donations Policy: A recent review has identified two main areas of focus for the future programme. Support will be considered for organisations operating within the broad themes of "Caring in the Community" and "Safer Communities" who can illustrate that they provide a quality service and meet a clearly identified need.
No support will be given for circulars, fundraising events, brochure advertising or appeals from individuals.
In addition to UK donations, the secondment programme represented a further £251,000 and overseas donations totalled £218,000.

☐ Psion plc
Portable computer development

Alexander House,
85 Frampton Street,
London NW8 8NQ
071-262 5580

Contact: S McGowen
Secretary to Managing Director

Year Ends: 31 Dec '91
Donations: nil
Profit: (£2,197,000)
Turnover: £21,333,000

UK employees: n/a
Total employees: 270

% Club

Donations Policy: Support for education for children in developing countries and primary healthcare and preventative medicine. In the previous two years the company gave donations of about £30,000.

☐ QS Holdings plc
Clothing retail

58-59 Boundary Road,
Hove,
Sussex BN3 5TD
0273-430051

Ch: Mark Walters
Contact: Mrs C Esplin
Customer Services Manager

Year Ends: 31 Jan '92
Donations: £10,535
Profit: £7,790,000
Turnover: £45,553,000

UK employees: 750
Total employees: 750

Donations Policy: Preference for children and youth, social welfare, medical.

☐ Quaker Oats Ltd
Grocery products, chemicals & toys

Bridge Road,
Southall,
Middlesex UB2 4AG
081-574 2388

Ch: R G Lagden
MD: R S Thomason
Contact: Florence Thomas (See Below)
Secretary to the Director of Legal Affairs

Year Ends: 30 Jun '90
Donations: £5,434
Profit: £7,699,000
Turnover: £189,333,000

UK employees: 1,841
Total employees: 28,000

Donations Policy: Quaker gives exclusively to local charities and/or those involving company personnel or their close relatives. Some donations in kind are also made. Grants from £25 to £100.
Registered charities should contact Florence Thomas above, unregistered charities should contact Libby Newcombe, Consumer Promotions & Relations Manager.
Generally no support for circular appeals, advertising in charity brochures, appeals from individuals, purely denominational (religious) appeals, large national appeals, overseas projects.

☐ Queens Moat Houses plc
Hoteliers, restauranteurs

Queens Court,
9-17 Eastern Road,
Romford,
Essex RM1 3NG
0708-730522

Ch: J Bairstow
MD: M A Marcus
Contact: Mrs S Lewis
Marketing Manager

Year Ends: 31 Dec '91
Donations: £57,146
Profit: £90,400,000
Turnover: £543,300,000

UK employees: n/a
Total employees: 13,959

Donations Policy: Individual hotels may be involved with fundraising for local charities or may offer free weekend breaks, free meals etc. as prizes for draws/raffles.

Please read page 6   **Alphabetical listing** •

Name/Address	Officers	Financial Information	Other Information

☐ Quicks Group plc

Passenger & commercial vehicle dealers

Ashburton Road East,
Trafford Park,
Manchester M17 1QG
061-872 7788

Ch: N Quick
Contact: J A Quick
Executive Marketing Director

Year Ends: 31 Dec '91
Donations: £11,273
Profit: £2,982,000
Turnover: £208,737,000

UK employees: n/a
Total employees: 1,213

% Club

Donations Policy: All big and local appeals are considered on their merits. Support for education, medical and the arts.
No support for circular appeals, advertising in charity brochures, appeals from individuals, purely denominational (religious) appeals, overseas projects.

☐ Raab Karcher UK Ltd

Oil distributors & timber merchants

South Langworthy Road,
Salford,
Greater Manchester M5 2PX
061-737 0932

MD: W T Hughes
Contact: J G Walsh
Financial Manager

Year Ends: 31 Dec '91
Donations: £25,642
Profit: £410,000
Turnover: £195,438,000

UK employees: n/a
Total employees: 1,700

Donations Policy: Preference for local charities in areas where the company operates. Preference for children and youth; medical; environment/heritage; overseas aid/development.

☐ Racal Electronics plc

Radio communication, electronic equipment

Western Road,
Bracknell,
Berkshire RG12 1RG
0344-483244

Ch: Sir Ernest Harrison
Contact: Mrs S Butler
Secretary to the Racal Charitable Trust

Year Ends: 31 Mar '91
Donations: £213,000
Profit: £222,929,000
Turnover: £2,084,298,000

UK employees: n/a
Total employees: 38,461

Donations Policy: To relieve poor, needy, sick and disabled people, and to support those who are engaged in work, including research, to this end. Thus 70% of the budget is spent on health and medical care, 20% on social welfare and 5% on community services. Support is also given to organisations concerned with the environment and heritage.
About 300 national and 50 local grants are made annually. Grants to national organisations from £100 to £10,000; grants to local organisations from £25 to £50.
No support for circular appeals, appeals from individuals, expeditions, advertising in charity brochures, fundraising events, small purely local events in areas of company presence. Unless there are exceptional reasons the trustees prefer to deal directly with a charity rather than with intermediaries.

☐ Racal-Securities Ltd

Security systems

Racal Chubb House,
Staines Road West,
Sunbury-on-Thames,
Middlesex TW16 7AR
0932-785588

Ch: Sir Ernest Harrison
MD: P G Crossland
Contact: C Philips
Publicity Manager

Year Ends: 31 Mar '91
Donations: £15,496
Profit: £35,468,000
Turnover: £356,243,000

UK employees: n/a
Total employees: 12,562

Donations Policy: Preference for local charities in areas where the company operates.
A small number of advertisements are placed in brochures of charities not supported by the company's charitable donations. The contact for advertising is Roger Jones (0734-669969).

☐ Raine Industries plc

Contracting & housebuilding

Raine House
Ashbourne Road,
Mackworth,
Derby DE22 4NB
0332-824000

Ch: A N R Rudd
Contact: P W Parkin
Chief Executive

Year Ends: 30 Jun '91
Donations: £25,202
Profit: £20,271,000
Turnover: £352,064,000

UK employees: n/a
Total employees: 3,993

Donations Policy: The subsidiaries have different policies, but there would usually be a preference towards local charities in areas of company operation.

☐ Raine's Dairy Foods Ltd

Manufacture & sale of dairy produce

Raine House,
Crown Road,
Enfield,
Middlesex EN1 1TX
081-804 8151

MD: Mrs Jacobs
Contact: Mrs H Field
Secretary to the Chairman

Year Ends: 1 Oct '88
Donations: £23,145
Profit: £2,841,000
Turnover: £58,739,000

UK employees: n/a
Total employees: 900

Donations Policy: No set policy. Each appeal is looked at and judged on merit.

☐ Raleigh Industries Ltd

Bicycle manufacture & sale

Triumph Road,
Nottingham NG7 2DD
0602-420202

Ch: A Finden-Crofts
MD: R A L Roberts
Contact: Janet Burnett
Public Relations Manager

Year Ends: 31 Dec '90
Donations: £3,000
Profit: £13,860,000
Turnover: £100,158,000

UK employees: n/a
Total employees: 2,008

Donations Policy: The company receive about 2,000 applications each year asking for donations. The company do support some local charities but it is not company policy to make public their donations or their charitable policy.

● **Alphabetical listing**   Please read page 6

Name/Address	Officers	Financial Information	Other Information

☐ Rank Organisation plc
                                                                                                                                                            Leisure

6 Connaught Place,   *Ch:* Sir Leslie Fletcher   *Year Ends:* 31 Oct '91   *UK employees:* 37,000
London W2 2EZ   *MD:* M B Gifford   *Donations:* £199,988   *Total employees:* 44,993
071-706 1111   *Contact:* Brian C Owers   *Profit:* £250,500,000
                                       Company Secretary   *Turnover:* £2,114,200,000   BitC

Donations Policy: To support a broad range of charities in the categories of: children and youth; social welfare; medical; education; environment/heritage; arts. Grants to national organisations from £500 to £15,000. Grants to local organisations from £100 to £500. No response to circular appeals. No grants for fundraising events; advertising in charity brochures; appeals from individuals; local appeals not in areas of company presence; overseas projects.
Total community contributions in 1991 were £315,000.

☐ Rank Xerox (UK) Ltd
                                                                                                               Copiers & office systems

Bridge House,   *Ch:* D A Thompson   *Year Ends:* 31 Oct '91   *UK employees:* n/a
Oxford Road,   *MD:* V A Zelmer   *Donations:* £400,000   *Total employees:* 25,331
Uxbridge,   *Contact:* R Grimes   *Profit:* £206,100,000
Middlesex UB8 1HS   Marketing Communications   *Turnover:* £2,571,000,000   % Club, BitC
0895-251133   Manager

Donations Policy: Priority for educational projects, with particular emphasis on projects connected with information technology, its application and use. Some support also for social welfare and community projects. Grants to national organisations from £500 to £25,000. Grants to local organisations from £25 to £500.
No support for purely denominational (religious) appeals, appeals from individuals, fundraising events, advertising in charity brochures. Local appeals should be addressed to the appropriate local plant.

☐ Ranks Hovis McDougall plc
                                                                  Food manufacturers & distributors

RHM Centre,   *Ch:* S G Metcalfe   *Year Ends:* 31 Aug '91   *UK employees:* n/a
Alma Road,   *MD:* P Coker   *Donations:* £252,000   *Total employees:* 30,340
Windsor,   *Contact:* R Stag   *Profit:* £150,200,000
Berkshire SL4 3ST   Secretary of the Appeals   *Turnover:* £1,531,400,000   % Club, BitC
0753-857123   Committee

Donations Policy: Preference for local charities in areas of company presence, national charities centrally and appeals relevant to business, especially projects involving social welfare, community services, health and medical care, education and enterprise projects. Grants to national organisations ranged from £500 to £2,000, and to local organisations from £50 to £250.
No support for appeals from individuals, educational/explorational expeditions, local appeals not in areas of company presence and overseas projects. No sponsorship is undertaken.

☐ Ransomes, Sims & Jeffries Ltd
                                                Machinery manufacturers & property developers

Ransome Way,   *Ch:* H A Whittall   *Year Ends:* 31 Dec '91   *UK employees:* 1,294
Nacton Works,   *Contact:* T M Millar   *Donations:* £19,000   *Total employees:* 2,169
Ipswich,   Operations Director & Chairman *Profit:* £4,578,000
Suffolk IP3 9QG   of the Charities Committee   *Turnover:* £146,744,000
0473-270000

Donations Policy: The charity committee meets 2-3 times a year. Preference for local charities in areas where the company operates and charities with a member of company staff involved. Preference for children and youth; medical. Support for registered charities only.
No support for fundraising events; advertising in charity brochures, local charities not in areas of company presence, animal charities.

☐ Ratners Group plc
                                                                                                 Jewellery retailing

15 Stratton Street,   *Ch:* J McAdam   *Year Ends:* 3 Feb '92   *UK employees:* n/a
London W1X 5FD   *CE:* G I Ratner   *Donations:* £455,000   *Total employees:* 20,352
071-499 1000   *Profit:* (£122,328,000)
                                                                               Turnover: £1,128,634,000   BitC

Donations Policy: The company is currently making no donations to charity.
The figure for donations includes £350,000 made under deed of covenant in favour of the Charities Aid Foundation.

☐ Raychem UK Ltd
                                                                       Plastics, wire & cable manufacturers

Faraday Road,   *Ch:* P M Cook   *Year Ends:* 30 Jun '91   *UK employees:* n/a
South Dorcan,   *Contact:* Mandy Archer   *Donations:* £25,774   *Total employees:* 1,240
Swindon,   Secretary to the Personnel Officer *Profit:* £23,958,000
Wiltshire SN3 5HH   *Turnover:* £125,879,000
0793-528171

Donations Policy: All the company's giving is exclusively to local charities in areas of company presence; no other appeals are considered.

☐ Raytheon Europe Ltd
                                                                                 Electronic equipment

College Road,   *Ch:* Sir Clifford Carnford   *Year Ends:* 30 Nov '90   *UK employees:* n/a
Harrow,   *Contact:* M Wood   *Donations:* £7,000   *Total employees:* 2,386
Middlesex HA1 1YR   Company Secretary   *Profit:* £2,874,000
081-861 2525   *Turnover:* £103,287,000

Please read page 6 — Alphabetical listing

Name/Address	Officers	Financial Information	Other Information

☐ Rea Brothers Ltd — Banking

Aldermans House,
Aldermans Walk,
London EC2M 3XR
071-623 1155

Contact: Caroline Griffin
Company Secretary

Year Ends: 31 Dec '92
Donations: £3,743
Profit: (£1,500,000)
Turnover: n/a

UK employees: 72
Total employees: 72

% Club

Donations Policy: Preference for children and youth; social welfare and enterprise/training. An annual contribution of £1,850 is given to Young Enterprise. Grants to national organisations from £50 to £2,000. Grants to local organisations from £50 to £2,000.
No grants for fundraising events; advertising in charity brochures; appeals from individuals; purely denominational (religious) appeals; local appeals not in areas of company presence; large national appeals; overseas projects. No response to circular appeals.

☐ Reader's Digest Association Ltd — Publishers

Berkeley Square House,
Berkeley Square,
London W1X 6AB
071-629 8144

MD: S N McRae
Contact: Mrs Pamela Rowden
Charities Administrator

Year Ends: 30 Jun '91
Donations: £106,000
Profit: £10,702,000
Turnover: £160,744,000

UK employees: n/a
Total employees: 929

% Club

Donations Policy: Preference for donating to specific projects rather than general funds. Preference for organisations who (a) foster a spirit of enterprise and self-help, particularly in the fields of education, the arts/culture, environment or health education; (b) are involved in problem solving in the area of communication (eg. dyslexia, adult literacy, sub-titling, deafness, blindness, speech and learning difficulties).
Local appeals are not usually supported unless in Swindon, where the company has a presence. Projects in which members of staff are involved are more likely to be supported. Grants to national organisations range from £500 to £15,000. Grants to local organisations range from £250 to £2,500.
No grants for fundraising events; appeals from individuals; particular charities year after year; charities with primarily sectarian aims; overseas projects; maintenance and purchase of vehicles; expeditions; exchanges and study tours; state funded organisations such as schools and hospitals.

☐ Readicut International plc — Manufacturers of specialist textile products

PO Box 15,
Clifton Mills,
Brighouse,
West Yorkshire HD6 4ET
0484-721223

Ch: Sir Roland Smith
MD: C M Shaw
Contact: Mrs J Pickard
Secretary to Managing Director

Year Ends: 31 Mar '92
Donations: £21,000
Profit: £13,512,000
Turnover: £219,563,000

UK employees: n/a
Total employees: 4,055

Donations Policy: Preference for local charities in areas where the company operates and appeals relevant to company business.

☐ Really Useful Group Ltd — Development & exploitation of copyright

22 Tower Street,
London WC2H 9NS
071-240 0880

Ch: John Whitney
Contact: Brigadier Adam Gurdon

Year Ends: 30 Jun '89
Donations: £63,025
Profit: £7,399,000
Turnover: £28,607,000

UK employees: n/a
Total employees: 146

Donations Policy: The charities budget is about £60,000 a year. Almost all donations are to registered charities. The company also holds a monthly draw, giving free theatre tickets to charitable causes.

☐ Reckitt & Colman plc — Food & household products, pharmaceuticals

One Burlington Lane,
London W4 2RW
081-994 6464

Ch: Sir Michael J Colman
CE: V L Sankey
Contact: P D Saltmarsh
Company Secretary

Year Ends: 30 Dec '91
Donations: £308,000
Profit: £252,300,000
Turnover: £1,986,890,000

UK employees: n/a
Total employees: 23,000

Donations Policy: Recipient organisations should be registered charities. Main areas of support are appeals of national interest, appeals in areas where the company operates and appeals with relevance to the business of the company. The company's main divisions, in Hull and Norwich, deal with local charities.

☐ P L M Redfearn Ltd — Glass & plastic container manufacturers

Monk Bretton,
Barnsley,
South Yorkshire S71 2QG
0226-710211

Ch: U K Laurin
MD: A E Church
Contact: A Haycock
Personnel Manager

Year Ends: 1 Oct '88
Donations: £5,265
Profit: £5,263,000
Turnover: £110,249,000

UK employees: n/a
Total employees: 1,854

Donations Policy: No set policy. All appeals are looked at and judged on merit

☐ Rediffusion Simulation Ltd — Simulation equipment

Sussex Manor Business Park,
Gatwick Road,
Crawley,
West Sussex RH10 2YD
0293-562822

Ch: J Sandiford
Contact: Paul Spence
Corporate Communications Manager

Year Ends: 31 Dec '90
Donations: n/a
Profit: £4,265,000
Turnover: £211,716,000

UK employees: n/a
Total employees: 2,783

● **Alphabetical listing**   **Please read page 6**

Name/Address	Officers	Financial Information	Other Information

☐ Redland plc — Construction materials

Redland House,
Reigate,
Surrey RH2 0SJ
0737-242488

Ch: Sir Colin Corness
MD: R S Napier
Contact: S R O'Brien
Company Secretary

Year Ends: 31 Dec '91
Donations: £129,000
Profit: £186,000,000
Turnover: £1,503,600,000

UK employees: 8,500
Total employees: 30,000

BitC

Donations Policy: Preference for appeals closely related to the company's business and local appeals in areas where many employees live or work. In particular the company supports education, urban regeneration, community architecture and hospice projects.
Most local appeals should be addressed to the managing director of the relevant subsidiary; appeals local to Reigate/Redhill and most non-local appeals should be addressed to the contact above. No support for non-charities, campaigning work by charities, advertising in charity brochures, appeals from individuals, purely denominational (religious) appeals, local appeals not in areas of company presence, large national appeals or overseas projects.
World-wide donations totalled £325,000.

☐ Redrow Group plc — Contracting & civil engineering

Redrow House,
St David's Park,
Ewloe,
Clwyd CH5 3PW
0244-520044

Ch: S P Morgan
Contact: Debby Goodband
Public Relations & Marketing
Manager

Year Ends: 30 Jun '91
Donations: £7,490
Profit: £12,621,000
Turnover: £109,001,000

UK employees: n/a
Total employees: 534

BitC

Donations Policy: Each year one local and one national charity are nominated for support on a regional basis. These organisations are chosen at the discretion of the acting managing director in the region.
No support for advertising in charity brochures, purely denominational (religious) appeals, large national appeals, overseas projects. No sponsorship.

☐ Reed Executive plc — Employment agents

114 Peascod Street,
Windsor,
Berkshire SL4 1DN
0753-850441

Ch: A E Reed
Contact: Mrs E V Marks
Secretary to the Reed Charity

Year Ends: 31 Dec '91
Donations: £20,000
Profit: (£4,274,000)
Turnover: £63,940,000

UK employees: n/a
Total employees: 842

% Club, BitC

Donations Policy: The company concentrates its charitable support on helping women in the third world. It also supports organisations which help women in need in the UK. Grants to local organisations from £50 to £500.
No support for appeals from non-charities, campaigning work by charities, appeals from individuals, advertising in charity brochures, fundraising events, circular appeals and local appeals not in areas of company presence.

☐ Reed International plc — Publishing

Reed House,
6 Chesterfield Gardens,
London W1A 1EJ
071-499 4020

Ch: P J Davis
Contact: Jan Shawe
Chairman of the Charity
Committee

Year Ends: 31 Mar '92
Donations: £417,000
Profit: £231,600,000
Turnover: £1,630,500,000

UK employees: 10,100
Total employees: 18,300

% Club, BitC, ABSA

Donations Policy: Head office's main areas of support are: major national charities, publishing and literacy charities; charities focussing on community enterprise and education; charities based in Westminster; charities in which senior management have a direct interest.
At regional level, preference for local organisations in areas of company activity. Local appeals should be sent to the relevant local office. Grants to national organisations from £1,000 to £3,000. Grants to local organisations from £400 to £1,500.
Total community contributions in 1992 were over £2,000,000.
No support for appeals from individuals, purely denominational (religious) appeals, political appeals, sports appeals or local appeals not in areas of company presence.

☐ Regalian Properties plc — Property development

44 Grosvenor Hill,
London W1X 9JE
071-493 9613

Contact: David Goldstone
Chairman

Year Ends: 31 Mar '92
Donations: £6,575
Profit: (£26,804,000)
Turnover: £104,687,000

UK employees: n/a
Total employees: n/a

% Club, BitC

Donations Policy: Preference for children, youth and social welfare. Preference for charities in which a member of company staff is involved.
No grants for fundraising events; advertising in charity brochures; appeals from individuals; purely denominational (religious) appeals; local appeals not in areas of company presence; large national appeals; overseas projects.
No response to circular appeals.

☐ Remploy Ltd — Furniture, packing, assembly, health-care products

Remploy House,
415 Edgware Road,
Cricklewood,
London NW2 6LR
081-452 8020

Ch: I H Cohen
CE: A G H Withey
Contact: Ms Morag Wood
Public Relations Officer

Year Ends: 31 Mar '92
Donations: n/a
Profit: n/a
Turnover: £120,200,000

UK employees: n/a
Total employees: 10,643

Donations Policy: "Support is given to charities very rarely and only if they are concerned with disability or local charities in areas of company presence. There is no budget for charity donations as we concentrate on the wages of our employees - 8,500 of who are severely disabled." No response to circular appeals.

Please read page 6   Alphabetical listing •

Name/Address	Officers	Financial Information	Other Information

☐ Renishaw plc
Precision instruments

New Mills,
Wooton Under Edge,
Gloucestershire GL12 8JR
0453-842533

Ch: D R McMurty
Contact: D Champion
Project Buyer

Year Ends: 30 Jun '91
Donations: £16,875
Profit: £11,103,000
Turnover: £45,662,000

UK employees: n/a
Total employees: 765

Donations Policy: Priority to local appeals involving young people and national charities for children/youth. Appeals from individuals are occasionally supported.
No support for general appeals, brochure advertising, purely denominational (religious) appeals, fundraising events.

☐ Renold plc
Power transmission products machinery

Styal Road,
Wythenshawe,
Manchester M22 5WL
061-437 5221

Ch: J P Frost
Contact: David Catterill
Chief Executive

Year Ends: 31 Mar '92
Donations: £250
Profit: £3,000,000
Turnover: £121,500,000

UK employees: 1,638
Total employees: 3,063

Donations Policy: The company does not welcome unsolicited appeals at present in view of the small size of its charitable budget.

☐ Rentokil Group plc
Environmental & property care services

Felcourt,
East Grinstead,
West Sussex RH19 2JY
0342-833022

Ch: D K Newbigging
MD: C M Thompson
Contact: Brian Porter
General Manager

Year Ends: 31 Dec '91
Donations: £22,000
Profit: £94,606,000
Turnover: £388,972,000

UK employees: 6,590
Total employees: 13,972

Donations Policy: The charity budget is reviewed annually and is largely committed to existing covenants. The balance is given to charities which have some connection with the company's activities. Preference for local charities in areas where the company operates and charities in which a member of company staff is involved. Preferred areas of support are social welfare, medical, environment and heritage.
No support for circular appeals, individuals, purely denominational (religious) appeals, or local appeals not in areas of company presence.

☐ Reuters Holdings plc
International news organisation

85 Fleet Street,
London EC4P 4AJ
071-250 1122

Ch: Sir Christopher Hogg
MD: Peter Job
Contact: Sara Waterer
Reuter Foundation

Year Ends: 31 Dec '91
Donations: £600,000
Profit: £340,300,000
Turnover: £1,466,600,000

UK employees: n/a
Total employees: 10,640

% Club, BitC, ABSA

Donations Policy: Support mainly given in the form of university fellowships to journalists and photo-journalists from developing countries, at the universities of Oxford, Stanford, Bordeaux and Missouri. The foundation also gives to education, community, medical and environmental causes and the arts in various countries. Preference for local charities in areas where the company operates, appeals relevant to company business and charities in which a member of company staff is involved.
No grants for purely denominational (religious) appeals; local appeals not in areas of company presence; political causes; sports sponsorship.

☐ Rhone-Poulenc Rorer
Health care products

RPR House,
52 St Leonards,
Eastbourne,
East Sussex BM21 3YG
081-592 3060

MD: A I M Seth
Contact: Bill Gilmore
Manager

Year Ends: 31 Dec '90
Donations: n/a
Profit: £225,000
Turnover: £94,783,000

UK employees: n/a
Total employees: 1,413

☐ RHP Industrial Bearings
Manufacture of precision bearings

PO Box 18,
Northern Road,
Newark,
Notts NG24 2JF
0636-605123

Ch: Toshio Arata
CE: A J Bowkett
Contact: Richard Knowler
Company Secretary

Year Ends: 31 Dec '90
Donations: £802
Profit: £12,442,000
Turnover: £179,800,000

UK employees: n/a
Total employees: 3,987

☐ Marc Rich & Co Ltd
Traders in minerals & ores

49 Wigmore Street,
London W1H 9LE
071-935 4455

Ch: M Rich
Contact: Mrs A E Garneys
Personnel & Office Manager

Year Ends: 31 Dec '90
Donations: £170,000 (1991)
Profit: £7,843,000
Turnover: £806,833,000

UK employees: n/a
Total employees: 233

% Club

Donations Policy: Preference for children and youth; medical; education; arts.
No support for circular appeals; fundraising events; individuals; purely denominational (religious) appeals or political donations.

☐ Richard Ellis
Chartered Surveyors

Berkley Square House,
Berkley Square,
London W1X 6AN
071-629 6290

Contact: Peter Allanson
Deputy Partnership

Year Ends:
Donations: n/a
Profit: n/a
Turnover: n/a

UK employees: 620
Total employees: 1500

% Club

Donations Policy: Preference for youth, enterprise/training.
No grants for fundraising events; advertising in charity brochures; appeals from individuals; purely denominational (religious) appeals; local appeals not in areas of company presence; large national appeals; overseas projects. No response to circular appeals.

● **Alphabetical listing** Please read page 6

Name/Address	Officers	Financial Information	Other Information

☐ **Richer Sounds plc** — Electrical retail

20-30 Wilds Rents,
London SE1 4QG
071-407 5525

Ch: Julian Richer
MD: David Robinson
Contact: Liam O'Brian
Marketing Department

Year Ends: 1 Feb '92
Donations: £28,860
Profit: £4,339,000
Turnover: £15,960,000

UK employees: n/a
Total employees: 96

% Club

Donations Policy: Preference for social welfare and environment/heritage.
No response to circular appeals. No grants for fundraising events; advertising in charity brochures; appeals from individuals; purely denominational (religious) appeals; local appeals not in areas of company presence; large national appeals; overseas projects.

☐ **Rionda (London) Ltd** — Sugar dealers

58 Borough High Street,
London SE1 1XF
071-407 6421

Ch: L Vazquez
Contact: Company Secretary

Year Ends: 31 Dec '89
Donations: £4,711 (1986)
Profit: £1,479,000
Turnover: £82,684,000

UK employees: n/a
Total employees: 24

☐ **RMC Group plc** — Building materials suppliers

RMC House,
Coldharbour Lane,
Thorpe,
Egham,
Surrey TW20 8TD
0932-568833

Ch: J Camden
Contact: P J Owen

Year Ends: 31 Dec '91
Donations: £136,000
Profit: £167,400,000
Turnover: £2,797,700,000

UK employees: n/a
Total employees: 26,031

Donations Policy: No support for circular appeals, advertising in charity brochures, fundraising events or local appeals not in areas of company presence.

☐ **Thomas Roberts (Westminster) Ltd** — Timber, road materials

Brettenham House,
Lancaster Place,
London WC2E 7HX
071-836 5801

Ch: J Roberts
Contact: Mrs Beattie
Assistant to the Chairman

Year Ends: 31 Mar '89
Donations: £9,430
Profit: £3,354,000
Turnover: £62,258,000

UK employees: n/a
Total employees: 955

☐ **Robinson & Sons Ltd** — Health care product manufacturers

Chesterfield,
Derbyshire S40 1YE
0246-220022

Ch: A K Slipper
Contact: Karen McMahon
Personal Assistant to the Chief Executive

Year Ends: 3 Jan '88
Donations: £2,666 (1991)
Profit: £2,350,000
Turnover: £68,029,000

UK employees: n/a
Total employees: 1,400

Donations Policy: Preference for local appeals in areas of company presence and appeals relevant to the business. Preference for children and youth, education, medical, enterprise/training. Grants to local organisations from £10 to £1,000.
No support for circulars, large national appeals, appeals from individuals, purely denominational (religious) appeals or overseas projects

☐ **Robinson Brothers (Ryders Green) Ltd** — General chemicals

Phoenix Street,
West Bromwich,
West Midlands B70 0AH
021-553 2451

Contact: F D Robinson
Chairman

Year Ends: 31 Dec '91
Donations: £15,625
Profit: £1,268,000
Turnover: £23,598,000

UK employees: n/a
Total employees: 420

% Club

Donations Policy: Priority to local (black country) charities or national charities operating in areas of company presence. Preference for appeals relevant to the company's business and those where a member of staff is involved. Preferred areas of support: children and youth, social welfare, education and enterprise/training. Grants to national organisations from £50 to £300; grants to local organisations from £25 to £300.
No support for circular appeals, purely denominational (religious) appeals, local appeals not in areas of company presence, large national appeals or overseas projects.

☐ **Roche Products Ltd** — Chemical manufacturers

40 Broadwater Road,
Welwyn Garden City,
Hertfordshire AL7 3AY
0707-328128

MD: Dr K M Taylor
Contact: Dr Paul Hooper
Public Relations Manager

Year Ends: 31 Dec '90
Donations: £73,915
Profit: £2,871,000
Turnover: £190,521,000

UK employees: n/a
Total employees: 1,892

Donations Policy: Preference for medical/pharmaceutical charities or local charities in Hertfordshire.

☐ **Rockwell International Ltd** — Component manufacturers

Central House,
3 Lampton Road,
Hounslow TW3 1HY
081-577 2800

Contact: D L Williams
Area Manager Europe

Year Ends: 30 Sep '90
Donations: £60,000 (1992)
Profit: £1,785,000
Turnover: £256,157,000

UK employees: n/a
Total employees: 2,450

Donations Policy: 60% of donations are allocated by Rockwell UK Country Council, a committee of Rockwell UK business managers. Support is given to educational establishments. The remaining 40% is allocated locally by individual businesses. Grants to national organisations from £10,000 to £30,000. Grants to local organisations from £300 to £5,000.
Total community contributions in 1992 were £80,000.

Please read page 6 — Alphabetical listing

Name/Address	Officers	Financial Information	Other Information

☐ Rohm & Haas (UK) Ltd
Speciality chemicals

Lennig House,
2 Masons Avenue,
Croydon,
Surrey CR9 3NB
081-686 8844

MD: J M Fitzpatrick
Contact: Personnel Department

Year Ends: 31 Dec '91
Donations: £7,500
Profit: £37,228,000
Turnover: £215,547,000

UK employees: 550
Total employees: n/a

Donations Policy: The company states "we support one local charity each year which serves the local community in which we operate". Preference for children and youth; social welfare; medical; education.
No grants for purely denominational (religious) appeals; local appeals not in areas of company presence; large national appeals; overseas projects.

☐ Rolls Royce plc
Aero engine manufacturers

65 Buckingham Gate,
London SW1E 6AT
071-222 9020

Ch: Lord Tombs
MD: Sir Ralph Robins
Contact: R W Henchley
Company Secretary

Year Ends: 31 Dec '91
Donations: £307,000
Profit: £51,000,000
Turnover: £3,515,000,000

UK employees: n/a
Total employees: 61,400

BitC

Donations Policy: Appeals usually satisfy one of the following criteria: (a) relate to the armed services or education; (b) public relations and other activities recognised as directly or indirectly helpful to the company.
National charities with a connection with the company's business are supported at head office level. Grants to national organisations range from £500 to £5,000.
Local charities are supported by regional site committees. Grants to local organisations from £50 to £1,000.

☐ Ropner plc
Shipowners, insurance brokers

140 Coniscliffe Road,
Darlington,
County Durham DL3 7RP
0325-462811

Ch: J V Ropner
Contact: A P Theakston
Company Secretary

Year Ends: 31 Dec '91
Donations: £5,000
Profit: £5,267,000
Turnover: £14,613,000

UK employees: n/a
Total employees: 400

Donations Policy: Medical, children and youth and maritime causes are supported by the company and through the Ropner Centenary Trust, which generally donates around £20,000 to registered charities. Preference for local charities in the areas of company presence, appeals relevant to company business, charities in which a member of staff is involved. Grants to national organisations from £100 to £300; grants to local organisations from £100 to £250. Community contributions totalled £20,000.
Generally no support for advertising in charity brochures, purely denominational (religious) appeals, local appeals not in areas of company presence.

☐ Rosehaugh plc
Property development

9 Marylebone Lane,
London W1M 5FB
071-486 7100

Ch: Godfrey Bradman
Contact: Chris Forshaw
Secretary, Rosehaugh Charitable Trust

Year Ends: 30 Jun '91
Donations: £204,000
Profit: (£226,637,000)
Turnover: £159,776,000

UK employees: n/a
Total employees: 253

% Club, BitC

Donations Policy: Donations made to local charities in the areas where the company operates, appeals relevant to the business and to charities where the work relates to the built and natural environment. Grants to national organisations from £250 to £15,000; grants to local organisations from £100 to £2,000.
Generally no support for appeals from individuals, local appeals not in areas of company presence, overseas projects or school development and bursary funds.

☐ Rothmans International plc
Tobacco, luxury consumer products

15 Hill Street,
London W1X 7FB
071-491 4366

Ch: Lord Swaythling
MD: W P Ryan
Contact: M H Richards
Charities Committee (see address below)

Year Ends: 31 Mar '92
Donations: £385,163
Profit: £565,200,000
Turnover: £6,252,900,000

UK employees: n/a
Total employees: 20,972

% Club

Donations Policy: Support for national rather than local charities, though support is given to charities in areas of company presence. Preference for social welfare; education; environment/heritage; arts; overseas aid/development; enterprise/training. Grants to national organisations from £1,000 to £40,000. Grants to local organisations from £100 to £1,000.
No response to circular appeals. No grants for fundraising events; advertising in charity brochures; appeals from individuals; purely denominational (religious) appeals; local appeals not in areas of company presence. No support for sponsorship events.
Address for donations; Oxford Road, Aylesbury, Bucks HP21 8SZ.

☐ N M Rothschild & Sons Ltd
Merchant banking

New Court,
St Swithin's Lane,
London EC4P 4DU
071-280 5000

Ch: Sir Evelyn de Rothschild
Contact: Secretary to the Charities Committee

Year Ends: 31 Mar '92
Donations: £510,000
Profit: n/a
Turnover: n/a

UK employees: 629
Total employees: n/a

% Club, BitC

Donations Policy: Preference for social welfare causes. Support also given to children and youth, health and medical care, education, scientific research, environment and heritage, enterprise/training and the arts. Grants to national organisations from £250 to £1,000.
Donations are not normally made to local groups. No response to circular appeals. No grants for fundraising events; advertising in charity brochures; appeals from individuals; purely denominational (religious) appeals; local appeals not in areas of company presence; large national appeals; overseas projects.
Sponsorship proposals should be addressed to the company secretary.

● **Alphabetical listing**   Please read page 6

Name/Address	Officers	Financial Information	Other Information

☐ **Rotork plc**

Engineering

Rotork House,
Brassmill Lane,
Bath,
Avon BA1 3JQ
0225-428451

Ch: J Lancaster
MD: T W Eassie
Contact: Mrs Sue Hazell
Chairman of the Charity Committee

Year Ends: 31 Dec '91
Donations: £8,724
Profit: £9,501,000
Turnover: £51,462,000

UK employees: n/a
Total employees: 571

Donations Policy: Preference for local charities in areas of company presence and charities in which a member of staff is involved. Preference for children and youth; social welfare; medical; education; recreation; environment/heritage. There is a payroll deduction scheme for the Save the Children Fund. Grants to local organisations from £100 to £1,000.
Further community contributions totalled £7,000.
No grants for local appeals not in areas of company presence; large national appeals; overseas projects.

☐ **Roussel Laboratories Ltd**

Pharmaceutical & chemical products

Broadwater Park,
North Orbital Road,
Denham,
Uxbridge,
Middlesex UB9 5HP
0895-834343

Ch: E Sakiz
MD: G E Powderham
Contact: A Eaton
General Manager Corporate Communications

Year Ends: 31 Dec '89
Donations: £32,693
Profit: £6,173,000
Turnover: £39,002,000

UK employees: n/a
Total employees: 1,287

Donations Policy: In the last edition the company policy was: Preference for local patient-care and health-care appeals. The company now state, "It is not our company policy to make corporate charitable donations".

☐ **Royal Bank of Scotland Group plc**

Banking

42 St Andrew's Square,
Edinburgh EH2 2YE
031-556 8555

Ch: Lord Younger
CE: Dr G Mathewson
Contact: G P Fenton
Community Affairs Manager

Year Ends: 30 Sep '91
Donations: £1,059,644
Profit: £57,700,000
Turnover: n/a

UK employees: 23,896
Total employees: n/a

% Club, BitC, ABSA

Donations Policy: The bank supports a wide spectrum of causes in the areas where it operates. It prefers to support the national headquarters of a charity and not become involved in local branches fundraising activities. There are no special categories of activity that the bank supports; approaches from any category will be given consideration. Grants to national organisations from £250; grants to local organisations from £25 to £250.
Total community contributions in 1990/91 totalled £1,466,723.
No response to circular appeals. The bank does not as a rule give to individuals, university departments, third party approaches involving fundraising activities, advertising in charity brochures, overseas projects.

☐ **Royal Insurance Holdings plc**

Insurance

1 Cornhill,
London EC3V 3QR
071-283 4300

Ch: Sir John Cuckney
CE: Richard Gamble
Contact: Betty E Hicks
Assistant Manager, Corporate Relations

Year Ends: 31 Dec '91
Donations: £498,312
Profit: (£373,000,000)
Turnover: n/a

UK employees: 15,100
Total employees: n/a

% Club, BitC, ABSA

Donations Policy: Grants are distributed by head office and by the major subsidiaries which have their own separate budgets and policies. National and local grants range upwards from £250. Preference for education and training for youth, job creation projects for young unemployed people, assistance for small businesses and inner city regeneration. Support is also given to the arts, cultural organisations, social welfare, community services, health and medicine. Preference for local organisations in areas where company has a presence.
No grants for fundraising events; advertising in charity brochures; appeals from individuals; purely denominational (religious) appeals; local appeals not in areas of company presence.

☐ **Royal London Mutual Insurance Society Ltd**

Life & general insurance, pensions

Royal London House,
Middleborough,
Colchester,
Essex CO1 1RA
0206-761761

Ch: M J Pickard
Contact: S D Farmer
Company Secretary

Year Ends: 31 Dec '91
Donations: £95,800
Profit: (£4,300,000)
Turnover: n/a

UK employees: 3,950
Total employees: n/a

BitC

Donations Policy: Donations are concentrated on aspects of medical research and funding a university chair of finance. On a smaller scale the company has supported the arts and heritage appeals.
No unsolicited appeals.

☐ **RTZ Corporation plc**

Mining & industrial-metals & fuel

6 St James's Square,
London SW1Y 4LD
071-930 2399

Ch: Sir Derek Birkin
CE: R P Wilson
Contact: J H G Senior
Community Affairs Manager

Year Ends: 31 Dec '91
Donations: £987,000
Profit: £562,000,000
Turnover: £3,552,000,000

UK employees: 13,187
Total employees: 47,556

% Club, BitC, ABSA

Donations Policy: The company's policy in Britain is to focus its main community support on a limited number of significant projects in four areas where it believes it can make a distinctive contribution. These are education, the arts, the environment and world affairs. Priority is given to specific projects and events rather than buildings and general running costs. Grants to national organisations from £500 to £50,000. Grants to local organisations from £250 to £1,000.
Total community contributions in 1991 were £2,542,000.
No support is given directly or indirectly, to any sectarian, religious or political activity. No support for advertising in charity brochures, appeals from individuals, or sports organisations.

Please read page 6 — Alphabetical listing

Name/Address	Officers	Financial Information	Other Information

☐ **Rubery Owen Holdings Ltd** — Manufacturers & merchants

Booth Street,
Darlaston,
Wednesbury,
West Midlands   WS10 8JD
021-526 3131

Ch: A D Owen
Contact: R J Owen
Secretary to the Charitable Trust

Year Ends: 26 Sep '86
Donations: £17,463
Profit: £631,000
Turnover: £67,850,000

UK employees: n/a
Total employees: 1,564

Donations Policy: The company will support any registered charity, but prefers to support West Midlands charities and international disaster appeals. Grants range from £50 to £2,500. Donations total about £20,000 a year.
The company is a subsidiary of Rockwell International (see separate entry).

☐ **Rubicon Group plc** — Shopfitting & engineering

Conrad House,
Birmingham Road,
Stratford-upon-Avon
CV37 0AA
0789-414881

MD: Tim Wightman
Contact: George Duncan
Chairman

Year Ends: 31 May '92
Donations: n/a
Profit: £822,000
Turnover: £14,989,000

UK employees: n/a
Total employees: 231

☐ **Rugby Group plc** — Building materials

Crown House,
Rugby,
Warwickshire   CV21 2DT
0788-542666

Ch: G A Higham
CE: C P Jackson
Contact: Dr Hill
Company Secretary

Year Ends: 31 Dec '91
Donations: £25,233
Profit: £55,830,000
Turnover: £532,552,000

UK employees: n/a
Total employees: 6,630

Donations Policy: We have not been able to obtain a donations policy for the company.

☐ **Alexander Russell plc** — Building suppliers

1 Park Gardens,
Glasgow   G3 7YS
041-332 9944

Ch: S R Nicolson
MD: G R Nicolson
Contact: Mrs Carol Lawrence
Secretary to the Managing
Director & Chairman

Year Ends: 31 Mar '91
Donations: £7,754
Profit: £1,664,000
Turnover: £37,675,000

UK employees: n/a
Total employees: 441

% Club

Donations Policy: Each application dealt with on its merits.

☐ **Rutland Trust plc** — Financial, professional & business services

Rutland House,
Rutland Gardens,
London   SW7 1BX
071-225 3391

Ch: Sir R D Lygo
CE: M R F Langdon
Contact: N A Moss
Assistant Financial Controller

Year Ends: 31 Dec '91
Donations: £26,200
Profit: £8,248,000
Turnover: £94,647,000

UK employees: 939
Total employees: 939

Donations Policy: The company has no particular preferences or exclusions; considering each appeal on its merits.

☐ **Ryder System Holdings (UK) Ltd** — Transport services, aircraft maintenance

Ryder House,
16 Bath Road,
Slough,
Berkshire   SL1 3SA
0753-821363

Contact: Carl Simmons
Managing Director

Year Ends: 31 Dec '90
Donations: £18,761
Profit: £1,306,000
Turnover: £166,012,000

UK employees: n/a
Total employees: 2,109

Donations Policy: At the start of the year, staff vote for nominated charities which receive a percentage of the previous years company profits. Grants range from £100 to £7,000. Charities receiving support usually have staff involvement and/or are local to areas of company presence.

☐ **Ryland Group Ltd** — Vehicle distributors

54 St James Road,
Edgbaston,
Birmingham   B15 1JL
021-454 5223

Contact: P W Whale
Chairman

Year Ends: 30 Apr '91
Donations: £9,000
Profit: £211,000
Turnover: £142,504,000

UK employees: n/a
Total employees: 948

☐ **Saab Great Britain Ltd** — Distributors of motor vehicles

Globe Park,
Marlow,
Buckinghamshire   SL7 1LY
0628-486977

Ch: S Wennlo
Contact: S Earl
Promotions Manager

Year Ends: 31 Dec '90
Donations: £6,432
Profit: £1,562,000
Turnover: £215,323,000

UK employees: n/a
Total employees: 443

Donations Policy: Preference for local appeals in areas of company presence, social welfare and medical. The company makes major donations to BEN, Thames Valley Hospice and Imperial Cancer Care; these account for most of the annual donations budget.
No support for circular appeals, advertising in charity brochures, appeals from individuals, purely denominational (religious) appeals or overseas projects.

● **Alphabetical listing**   Please read page 6

Name/Address	Officers	Financial Information	Other Information

☐ **Saatchi & Saatchi Company plc**   Advertising agency

S Group Charitable Trust,   *Ch:* M Saatchi   *Year Ends:* 31 Dec '91   *UK employees:* n/a
80 Charlotte Street,   *CE:* R M Louis-Dreyfus   *Donations:* £221,000   *Total employees:* 18,336
London W1A 1AQ   *Contact:* The S Group Charitable Trust   *Profit:* £63,600,000
071-636 5060   *Turnover:* £5,072,800,000   % Club, BitC

Donations Policy: Preference for community-based organisations, mainly in Greater London, and to charities for homeless people and those providing for children and young people. Preference may be given to projects in which a member of staff is involved. Grants range from £125 to £2,000.
No response to circular appeals. No support for individuals, purely denominational (religious) appeals, local appeals not in areas of company presence, large national appeals, animal organisations, bricks and mortar appeals, research organisations, overseas projects.

☐ **Saga Holidays Ltd**   Tour & hotel operators

Middleburg Square,   *Ch:* R M de Haan   *Year Ends:* 31 Jan '91   *UK employees:* n/a
Folkestone,   *Contact:* A Wilson   *Donations:* £25,000   *Total employees:* 688
Kent CT20 1AZ   Personnel Manager   *Profit:* £1,007,000
0303-857808   *Turnover:* £121,429,000   BitC

Donations Policy: Preference for children and youth; elderly people and education. Donations are usually of bottles of whisky for fundraising. Some short break holidays are offered and occasionally small cash donations, generally of less than £100.
No grants for local appeals not in areas of company presence.

☐ **J Sainsbury plc**   Retail distributors of food

Stamford House,   *Ch:* D J Sainsbury   *Year Ends:* 14 Mar '92   *UK employees:* n/a
Stamford Street,   *MD:* D A Quarmby, R T Vyner   *Donations:* £1,400,000   *Total employees:* 77,547
London SE1 9LL   *Contact:* Mrs S L Mercer   *Profit:* £628,000,000
071-921 6000   Community Investment   *Turnover:* £9,202,300,000   % Club, BitC, ABSA

Donations Policy: The Sainsbury Charitable Fund has a proactive approach and receives the major project-based appeals. These must involve women and work, health/nutrition/diet, urban/inner city regeneration and the training/employment of young people. Appeals from organisations working with disabled and elderly people, under-fives and youth will also be considered under the Good Neighbour Scheme. Grants to national organisations from £50 to £10,000. Grants to local organisations from £20 to £1,000.
No response to circular appeals. Restrictions include applications from individuals, restoration/fabric of buildings, sport sponsorship, National Health projects, overseas projects, local appeals not in areas of company presence and political or religious causes. A separate budget is available for small local donations to charities and voluntary groups.

☐ **St Ives plc**   Printing, book binding

St Ives House,   *Ch:* R Gavron   *Year Ends:* 2 Aug '91   *UK employees:*
Lavington Street,   *MD:* B C Edwards   *Donations:* £20,299   *Total employees:* 3,429
London SE1 0NX   *Contact:* Ms Brenda Pike   *Profit:* £20,151,000
071-928 8844   Personal Assistant to the   *Turnover:* £217,689,000   % Club
                                            Chairman

Donations Policy: The arts, literature, heritage and social welfare are the preferred areas of support.

☐ **St James Place Capital plc**   Investment

27 St James's Place,   *Ch:* Lord Rothschild, Sir Mark   *Year Ends:* 31 Mar '92   *UK employees:* 99
London SW1A 1NW   *Contact:* Ms Melanie G Siddle   *Donations:* £125,000   *Total employees:* 99
071-493 8111   Secretary, J Rothschild Group *Profit:* £23,900,000
                                            Charitable Trust   *Turnover:* n/a   % Club

Donations Policy: Grants are made through the J Rothschild Group Charitable Trust which establishes a policy with clearly defined areas for support at the start of each financial year. Funds are allocated to: local appeals for charities working in the West End of London (where the company is based); appeals by staff and shareholders; and a smaller grants programme. The trustees have a positive approach to finding appropriate charities to support rather than responding to appeals. In 1991/92, the two main areas selected were pump priming and homelessness. Grants range from £250 to £5,000.
No response to circular appeals or advertising in charity brochures.

☐ **St Martins Holdings Ltd**   Commodity trading & catering

Adelaide House,   *Ch:* F K Jaffar   *Year Ends:* 30 Jun '88   *UK employees:* n/a
London Bridge,   *Contact:* Financial Director   *Donations:* £103,837   *Total employees:* 3,125
London EC4R 9DT   *Profit:* £5,322,000
071-626 3411   *Turnover:* £405,386,000

Donations Policy: The company supports local charities and other good causes on an ongoing basis, which have been initiated through personal contact, other appeals are therefore very unlikely to be considered. Typical grants range from £200 to £500.
No support for appeals from non-charities, individuals, secondment, arts, sponsorship, small purely local appeals not in areas of company presence or overseas projects.

☐ **Sale Tilney plc**   Industrial plant manufacturers, food distributors

28 Queen Anne's Gate,   *Ch:* R A P King   *Year Ends:* 30 Nov '91   *UK employees:* n/a
London SW1H 9AB   *MD:* R T Allsop   *Donations:* nil   *Total employees:* 686
071-222 1771   *Contact:* P A R Greenstreet   *Profit:* £4,448,000
                                            Company Secretary   *Turnover:* £128,284,000

Please read page 6 | | | Alphabetical listing •

Name/Address | *Officers* | *Financial Information* | *Other Information*

☐ Christian Salvesen plc

Distribution, manufacturing, specialist hire

50 East Fettes Avenue,
Edinburgh EH4 1EQ
031-552 7101

Ch: Sir Alick Rankin
MD: Dr Chris Masters
Contact: Peter O'Malley
Public Relations Manager

Year Ends: 31 Mar '92
Donations: £55,000
Profit: £67,200,000
Turnover: £484,300,000

UK employees: 7,850
Total employees: 11,493

% Club, ABSA

Donations Policy: Support for education and youth activities; industrial training; community and environmental charities local to areas of company presence and to projects in which a member of staff is involved. Grants range from £50 to £2,500. The company is also a strong supporter of the arts, particularly in Scotland.
No support for circular appeals, fundraising events, advertising in charity brochures, appeals from individuals, purely denominational (religious) appeals, local appeals not in areas of company presence, large national appeals, overseas projects or medically related appeals.

☐ Sandoz Holdings Great Britain Ltd

Chemical manufacture

Calverley Lane,
Horsforth,
Leeds LS18 4RP
0532-584646

MD: D T Kemp
Contact: Personnel Department

Year Ends: 31 Dec '90
Donations: £8,575
Profit: £5,632,000
Turnover: £185,973,000

UK employees: n/a
Total employees: 1,628

☐ Sandvik Ltd

Tool manufacture

Manor Way,
Halesowen,
West Midlands B62 8QZ
021-550 4700

Contact: Alan Boulton
Personnel Manager

Year Ends: 31 Dec '90
Donations: n/a
Profit: £11,637,000
Turnover: £153,988,000

UK employees: n/a
Total employees: 1,872

☐ Sanyo UK Sales Ltd

Distribution of electrical consumer products

Otterspool Way,
Watford,
Hertfordshire WD2 8JX
0923-257130

Ch: M Ogira
MD: T Natume
Contact: Ms A Broughton
Public Relations Officer

Year Ends: 31 Mar '87
Donations: £8,278
Profit: £2,543,000
Turnover: £106,161,000

UK employees: n/a
Total employees: 295

BitC

Donations Policy: Support only to local charities in areas where the company operates, especially Watford charities and community groups. The company loans equipment as well as making donations.
The company's charities committee is unable to support all the local appeals. No grants for advertising in charity brochures or arts projects, overseas projects are unlikely to be supported.

☐ SAPA Holdings Ltd

Investment company

Joseph Pitt House,
Pitville Circus Road,
Cheltenham,
Gloucestershire GL52 2QE
0242-245333

Ch: I S Bergenhem
Contact: Mrs C Law
Secretary to the Managing
Director

Year Ends: 31 Dec '88
Donations: £9,278
Profit: £11,653,000
Turnover: £88,266,000

UK employees: n/a
Total employees: 1,108

☐ Saudi International Bank Ltd

Banking

99 Bishopsgate,
London EC2M 3TB
071-638 2323

Ch: H E Sheikh Abdul Aziz Al-Quarish
Contact: Miss Penelope Ralph
Company Secretary

Year Ends: 31 Dec '91
Donations: £29,642
Profit: £22,400,000
Turnover: £48,100,000

UK employees: 226
Total employees: 270

% Club, BitC

Donations Policy: Preference for activities with a business or geographical link with the bank or its staff, in particular, educational, medical or cultural projects.

☐ Savage Group plc

Home improvements accessories

Corvill Mill,
Park Street,
Nr St Albans,
Herts AL2 2PF
0727-873745

Ch: Dr D Rogers
CE: A R Philipson
Contact: Mrs Golder
Assistant Company Secretary

Year Ends: 30 Jun '91
Donations: nil
Profit: (£115,000)
Turnover: £123,874,000

UK employees: 870
Total employees: 2,084

☐ Save & Prosper Group Ltd

Financial consultants

1 Finsbury Avenue,
London EC2M 2QY
071-588 1717

Contact: John Shelley
Director

Year Ends:
Donations: n/a
Profit: n/a
Turnover: n/a

UK employees: n/a
Total employees: n/a

% Club, BitC, ABSA

Donations Policy: The company supports a large number of community and educational projects largely through the Save & Prosper Educational Trust. Particular emphasis on special needs education and education in the arts. The company is a subsidiary of Robert Flemings Holdings Ltd. The trust had an income of £1,436,000 in 1990 and made grants of £1,133,000. Grants to organisations up to £10,000.
No grants for fundraising events; advertising in charity brochures; appeals from individuals and large national appeals.

● **Alphabetical listing** Please read page 6

Name/Address	Officers	Financial Information	Other Information

☐ **J Saville Gordon Group plc** Metal merchants & engineers

4 Wharfdale Road, *Ch:* J D Saville *Year Ends:* 30 Apr '92 *UK employees:* n/a
Tyseley, *Contact:* T G Hutchinson *Donations:* £10,000 *Total employees:* 179
Birmingham B11 2SB Company Secretary *Profit:* £3,825,000
021-707 3530 *Turnover:* £57,215,000

☐ **Savills plc** Surveying consultancy

20 Grosvenor Hill, *Ch:* George Inge *Year Ends:* 30 Apr '92 *UK employees:* n/a
Berkeley Square, *MD:* Aubrey Adams *Donations:* £40,000 *Total employees:* 585
London W1X 0HQ *Profit:* (£2,863,000)
071-499 8644 *Turnover:* £23,715,000 % Club, BitC

Donations Policy: Preference for local charities in the areas of company presence, appeals relevant to company business and charities in which a member of staff is involved. Preferred areas of support are projects involving medicine, enterprise/training and overseas aid/development. Grants to national organisations from £100 to £500. Grants to local organisations from £50 to £200.
Generally no support for advertising in charity brochures, appeals from individuals, purely denominational (religious) appeals, local appeals not in areas of company presence. Unsolicited appeals are unwelcome.
Appeals should be addressed to the local Savills offices, not the head office.

☐ **Savoy Hotel plc** Hotels & restaurants

1 Savoy Hill, *Ch:* Sir Anthony Tuke *Year Ends:* 31 Dec '91 *UK employees:* n/a
London WC2R 0BP *Contact:* G R C Shepard *Donations:* £42,352 *Total employees:* 2,887
071-836 1533 Managing Director *Profit:* £2,271,000
 Turnover: £79,219,000

☐ **SCA** Paper & packaging, office supplies

New Hythe House, *Ch:* Sir Christopher Benson *Year Ends:* 1 Apr '90 *UK employees:* n/a
New Hythe Lane, *MD:* J P Williams *Donations:* £72,845 *Total employees:* 12,663
Aylesford, *Contact:* Roger Hart *Profit:* £35,400,000
Kent ME20 7AB Personnel Director *Turnover:* £842,000,000
0622-883000

Donations Policy: The donations figure includes £19,177 for educational purposes. The company states with the economic climate being so bad, the charity budget has been cut drastically. When the economy improves the company should be able to increase it's charitable budget. The company now supports only local charities in the Aylesford or Maidstone areas, there is a preference to medical charities especially the local hospice, cancer, leukaemia and homes for elderly people. Donations are generally £15 to £250.

☐ **Scandinavian Bank Group Holdings Ltd** Banking

Scandinavian House, *Ch:* G F Bolton *Year Ends:* 31 Dec '87 *UK employees:* 493
2-6 Cannon Street, *MD:* E G Greve *Donations:* £8,500 *Total employees:* 493
London EC4M 6XX *Contact:* Adrian Bennett *Profit:* £26,581,000
071-236 6090 Head of Personnel *Turnover:* n/a

☐ **Scania (Great Britain) Ltd** Sale & import of Scania trucks

Delaware Drive, *Ch:* A Astrom *Year Ends:* 31 Dec '90 *UK employees:* n/a
Tongwell, *Contact:* P Sampson *Donations:* £11,191 *Total employees:* 255
Milton Keynes, Public Relations Manager *Profit:* £43,000
Buckinghamshire MK15 8HB *Turnover:* £122,996,000
0908-210210

Donations Policy: The company states that they have "a clear and well defined policy with regards to donations" and they support the "industry, international, national and local causes," but would not give more detailed information.

☐ **Scantronic Holdings plc** Control & data communication manufacturers

Scan House, *Ch:* C Brookes *Year Ends:* 31 Mar '92 *UK employees:* n/a
Xerox Business Park, *Contact:* M Canty *Donations:* £23,000 *Total employees:* 730
Mitcheldean, Investor Relations Manager *Profit:* £2,537,000
Gloucs GL17 0SN *Turnover:* £36,053,000
0594-543343

☐ **Scapa Group plc** Manufacture engineered fabrics & technical products

Oakfield House, *Ch:* R W Goodall *Year Ends:* 31 Mar '92 *UK employees:* 2,914
93 Preston New Road, *MD:* H Tuley *Donations:* £51,139 *Total employees:* 6,205
Blackburn, *Contact:* R W Goodall *Profit:* £44,662,000
Lancashire BB2 6AY Chairman *Turnover:* £300,206,000
0254-580123

Donations Policy: Donations primarily to those organisations with a local, company or personnel appeal. Preference for children and youth, medical charities, the environment and heritage and the arts. No support for purely denominational appeals or local appeals not in areas of company presence. Grants to national organisations from £50 to £500. Grants to local organisations from £50 to £5,000.

Please read page 6 | | | Alphabetical listing •

Name/Address	Officers	Financial Information	Other Information

☐ **Schering Agrochemicals Ltd** — Agrochemicals & veterinary products

Mount Pleasant House,
Huntingdon Road,
Cambridge,
Cambridgeshire CB2 5HU
0223-870312

Ch: T James
Contact: Miss P L Meakins
Public Relations Officer

Year Ends: 31 Dec '90
Donations: £38,691
Profit: £10,860,000
Turnover: £122,822,000

UK employees: n/a
Total employees: 2,223

Donations Policy: The company are currently reorganising their donations policy.

☐ **Schlumberger plc** — Manufacture & sale of electronic equipment

124 Victoria Road,
Farnborough,
Hampshire GU14 7PW
0252-544433

Contact: Alan Plumpton
Chairman

Year Ends: 31 Dec '91
Donations: £11,558
Profit: £14,631,000
Turnover: £147,390,000

UK employees: n/a
Total employees: 2,551

Donations Policy: Preference for local charities in areas where the company operates. Preference for children and youth; social welfare; medical.
No response to circular appeals. No grants for appeals from individuals; purely denominational (religious) appeals; local appeals not in areas of company presence; overseas projects.

☐ **Scholes Group plc** — Electrical equipment

The Old Rectory,
Station Road,
Wilmslow,
Cheshire SK9 1BU
0625-536538

Contact: R J Thornton
Company Secretary

Year Ends: 30 Jun '92
Donations: £4,000 (1991)
Profit: £3,170,000
Turnover: £61,965,000

UK employees: n/a
Total employees: 1,526

Donations Policy: Preference for local charities, those associated with the business or those in which a member of staff is involved. Support for children and youth, medical charities and the environment/heritage. Grants from £500 to £1000.
Generally no support for circular appeals, appeals from individuals, purely denominational (religious) appeals or local appeals not in areas of company presence.

☐ **Scholl plc** — Footwear & skincare products

Scholl House,
2-4 Sheet Street,
Windsor,
Berkshire SL4 1BG
0753-833444

Ch: G K G Stevens
CE: N Franchino
Contact: Bill Skerrett
Personnel Director

Year Ends: 31 Dec '91
Donations: £4,765
Profit: £16,071,000
Turnover: £144,354,000

UK employees: n/a
Total employees: 1,798

☐ **Schroders plc** — Merchant banking & investment

120 Cheapside,
London EC2V 6DS
071-382 6000

Ch: G Mallinckrodt
CE: W F W Bischoff
Contact: B Tew
Secretary, Schroder Charity Trust

Year Ends: 31 Dec '91
Donations: £281,000
Profit: £54,405,000
Turnover: n/a

UK employees: 1,420
Total employees: n/a

% Club, BitC, ABSA

Donations Policy: Only registered charities are supported, with a tendency to support national appeals. Local branches of national charities may also receive help, but very little money is given to purely local charities. Typical beneficiaries include organisations concerned with elderly people, health care, social welfare, education, medical, environment, overseas and the arts. Donations are usually for £500 to £2,000, larger donations may be spread over four or five years.
No grants are made to individuals.

☐ **Scott Ltd** — Disposable paper products

Crete Hall Road,
Northfleet,
Kent DA11 9AD
0474-336000

MD: C Andes
Contact: G Chilvers
Services Manager

Year Ends: 26 Nov '90
Donations: £29,030
Profit: £30,048,000
Turnover: £307,130,000

UK employees: n/a
Total employees: 2,874

Donations Policy: After a survey of the local population 60% wanted the company to invest in education and the transition between youth and adulthood. The company prefers to support charities and community organisations working with the 10-20 years old age group, local charities in areas where the company operates (Northfleet, Barrow-in-Furness or East Grinstead), charities in which a member of company staff is involved and community support. Donations range from £50 to £2,000. Charities would receive the smaller donations with community groups receiving the larger.

☐ **Scottish Amicable Life Assurance Society** — Insurance

150 St Vincent Street,
Glasgow G2 5NQ
041-248 2323

Ch: W Brown
MD: R M Nicolson
Contact: I MacKintosh
Assistant Marketing Manager

Year Ends: 31 Dec '91
Donations: £140,685
Profit: n/a
Turnover: n/a

UK employees: 2,211
Total employees: n/a

Donations Policy: Donations are given on a local basis. Support mainly youth, the arts and enterprise.
No support for overseas projects, purely denominational (religious) appeals, appeals from individuals, circular appeals or advertising in charity brochures.

● **Alphabetical listing**   Please read page 6

Name/Address	Officers	Financial Information	Other Information

☐ Scottish & Newcastle plc
Brewing & leisure

Abbey Brewery,
Holyrood Road,
Edinburgh EH8 8YS
031-556 2591

Ch: Sir Alick Rankin
MD: G B Reed
Contact: Cameron G Walker
Public Relations Officer

Year Ends: 30 Apr '92
Donations: £343,000
Profit: £239,100,000
Turnover: £1,487,000,000

UK employees: n/a
Total employees: 30,411

ABSA

Donations Policy: Mainly supports projects in communities where the company operates (ie. Scotland and the North East). Preference for arts and culture, social welfare, community services, health and medicine, conservation and the environment, education, science and enterprise. Preference for projects in which a member of staff is involved and appeals relevant to company business. Grants range from £100 to £1,000.
No response to circular appeals. No grants for advertising in charity brochures; appeals from individuals; local appeals not in areas of company presence and rarely for large national appeals. Sponsorship of individuals, other than company employees, is not undertaken. Sponsorship requests should be addressed to Jim Merrington. Local appeals should be directed to the regional offices.

☐ Scottish Equitable Life Assurance Society
Insurance

28 St Andrew Square,
Edinburgh EH2 1YF
031-556 9101

Ch: C F Sleigh
CE: D A Berridge
Contact: Roy Patrick
Company Secretary

Year Ends: 30 Dec '91
Donations: £35,700
Profit: n/a
Turnover: n/a

UK employees: n/a
Total employees: 1,500

Donations Policy: Primarily support is aimed at local charities. Grants range from £30 to £10,000. Preference for children and youth, medical and health. Business related charities are also supported. Direct support rather than advertising or sponsorship is preferred. The company is also involved in education and enterprise initiatives and sponsors the arts.
Sponsorship proposals should be addressed to D A Henderson.

☐ Scottish Heritable Trust plc
Floorcovering, property, manufacturing

18-20 Skeldergate,
York YO1 1DH
0904-620021

Ch: A C Duncan
MD: R D Garland
Contact: J Whitehead
Company Secretary

Year Ends: 31 Dec '91
Donations: nil
Profit: £792,000
Turnover: £96,532,000

UK employees: 1,706
Total employees: 2,690

Donations Policy: The company states they are unable to provide charitable support at this moment in time. In the past the policy has been: preference for local charities. Recipients must be registered charities. Main areas of support are children and youth, education, medical, overseas. Grants to local organisations from £10 to £500.
No support for circular appeals, advertising in charity brochures, fundraising events, purely denominational (religious) appeals, appeals from individuals.

☐ Scottish Hydro-Electric plc
Electricity supply

16 Rothesay Terrace,
Edinburgh EH3 7SE
031-225 1361

Ch: Sir Michael Joughin
CE: R Young
Contact: Mike Keohane
Head of Corporate
Communications

Year Ends: 31 Mar '91
Donations: £6,933
Profit: £60,300,000
Turnover: £566,100,000

UK employees:
Total employees: 3,484

Donations Policy: Preference for local charities in areas where the company operates. Preference for children and youth; social welfare; education; recreation; environment/heritage; arts.
No grants for advertising in charity brochures; appeals from individuals; purely denominational (religious) appeals; local appeals not in areas of company presence; large national appeals; overseas projects or sponsorship of teams eg. football.

☐ Scottish Nuclear Ltd
Electricity generator

3 Redwood Crescent,
Peel Park,
East Kilbride G74 5PR
0355-262000

Ch: J Hann
CE: R M Yeomans
Contact: R Marshall
Public Relations Manager

Year Ends: 31 Mar '91
Donations: n/a
Profit: £32,500,000
Turnover: £422,500,000

UK employees: n/a
Total employees: 1,976

☐ Scottish Power plc
Electricity supply

Cathcart House,
Spean Street,
Glasgow G44 4BE
041-637 7177

Ch: Murray Stuart
CE: Dr I M H Preston
Contact: Tom James
Director of Public Affairs

Year Ends: 31 Mar '92
Donations: £49,930
Profit: £259,900,000
Turnover: £1,384,600,000

UK employees: n/a
Total employees: 9,144

Donations Policy: The majority of donations are made locally with preference for charities in which a member of staff is involved. Preference for children and youth; environment/heritage; arts; enterprise/training. The company also undertakes arts and good cause sponsorship both nationally and locally.
No response to circular appeals. No grants for advertising in charity brochures; appeals from individuals (other than staff); purely denominational (religious) appeals; local appeals not in areas of company presence.

☐ Scottish Provident Institution
Insurance

PO Box 58,
6 St Andrew Square,
Edinburgh EH2 2YA
031-556 9181

Ch: D A Ross Stewart
MD: D E Woods
Contact: Colin Chifoln
Personal Services Manager

Year Ends: 31 Dec '91
Donations: £24,119
Profit: n/a
Turnover: n/a

UK employees: 1,134
Total employees: n/a

Donations Policy: "Due to the constitution of our company and the way that the law relates to us and other life insurance offices our freedom to make charitable donations is strictly limited. We are able to support appeals relevant to the business and operate a small community budget for this purpose."

Please read page 6 — Alphabetical listing

Name/Address	Officers	Financial Information	Other Information

☐ Scottish Television plc — Television programme contractor

Cowcaddens,
Glasgow G2 3PR
041-332 9999

Ch: Sir Campbell Fraser
MD: Gus Macdonald
Contact: Simon Forrest
Controller of Corporate Affairs

Year Ends: 31 Dec '91
Donations: £127,007
Profit: £8,618,000
Turnover: £114,157,000

UK employees: n/a
Total employees: 787

% Club

Donations Policy: The donations figure includes £124,675 to the arts and science and £2,332 to other charitable purposes. The company has a policy of only supporting groups and individuals concerned with media related arts in Scotland

☐ Scottish Widows' Fund & Life Assurance — Life insurance & pensions

PO Box 902,
15 Dalkeith Road,
Edinburgh EH16 5BU
031-655 6000

Ch: C H Black
MD: M D Ross
Contact: Fiona Tunstall
Public Relations Office

Year Ends: 31 Dec '91
Donations: £53,554
Profit: n/a
Turnover: n/a

UK employees: 2,995
Total employees: n/a

Donations Policy: The budget must be spent in furtherance of the interests of company members. Appeals with a medical aspect are more likely to get support. Geographically the company tries to be even handed, but generally it prefers to give locally in Scotland and avoid the South East where money is more readily available.

☐ Seagram Distillers plc — Distillers

111-113 Renfrew Road,
Paisley PA3 4DY
041-887 9131

Ch: I C Straker
Contact: I D Jackson
Company Secretary

Year Ends: 31 Jan '91
Donations: £1,483,000
Profit: £98,975,000
Turnover: £639,271,000

UK employees: n/a
Total employees: 3,627

Donations Policy: The company are in the process of setting up a charity committee to co-ordinate its charitable giving. Preference for Scottish charities and especially for organisations in the Renfrew area.

☐ Sealink Stena Line Holdings Ltd — Ship & harbour operators

Charter House,
Park Street,
Ashford TN24 8EX
0233-647022

Ch: R I J Agnew
MD: L E Ottosson
Contact: Chris Laming
Public Relations Manager

Year Ends: 31 Dec '90
Donations: £125,737
Profit: £18,200,000
Turnover: £309,000,000

UK employees: n/a
Total employees: 6,193

Donations Policy: The company states "we made a substantial loss in the financial year ending 31/12/91 and are no longer able to make charitable donations".

☐ G D Searle & Co Ltd — Ethical pharmaceutical manufacturers

PO Box 53,
Lane End Road,
High Wycombe HP12 4HL
0049-421124

Contact: J N Williams
Human Resources Director

Year Ends: 31 Dec '91
Donations: £25,000
Profit: £3,859,000
Turnover: £88,994,000

UK employees: 867
Total employees: 992

Donations Policy: Preference for charities concerned with medical relief, medical research and local charities in areas of company presence. Support also for children and youth, education, enterprise/training. Grants range from £10 to £500.
No response to circular appeals. No grants for advertising in charity brochures; purely denominational (religious) appeals; local appeals not in areas of company presence; large national appeals; overseas projects; animal charities.

☐ Sears plc — Footwear, stores

40 Duke Street,
London W1A 2HP
071-408 1180

Ch: G Maitland Smith
CE: L Strong
Contact: J D F Drum
Company Secretary

Year Ends: 31 Jan '92
Donations: £317,000
Profit: £81,200,000
Turnover: £1,979,100,000

UK employees: n/a
Total employees: 31,973

BitC

Donations Policy: Support for medical and health care charities and organisations related to the company business. Support also for enterprise initiatives and organisations devoted to tackling problems associated with inner city areas. Funds are currently fully committed.

☐ Securicor Group plc — Security services, parcels, mobile communications

Sutton Park House,
15 Carshalton Road,
Sutton SM1 4LD
081-770 7000

Ch: P A C Smith
MD: R S W Wiggs
Contact: Chairman, Securicor Charitable Trust

Year Ends: 30 Sep '91
Donations: £149,300
Profit: £33,026,000
Turnover: £565,101,000

UK employees: n/a
Total employees: 40,699

% Club

Donations Policy: Most support goes to the Multiple Sclerosis Society, however other one-off appeals of a general nature are occasionally considered. The Securicor Charitable Trust deals with other appeals from registered charities, favouring small specific appeals in the areas of children and youth, social welfare, medicine and health. Grants from £150 to £200.
Sponsorship proposals to the Group Marketing Manager.
Written applications only. No telephone calls. No educational grants, expeditions, advertising in charity brochures or publications, or purely denominational (religious) appeals.

☐ Securiguard Group plc — Security & cleaning services

168 Lavender Hill,
London SW11 5TG
071-924 1144

Ch: A P Baldwin
Contact: Richard Catt
Company Secretary

Year Ends: 5 Nov '91
Donations: nil
Profit: £5,025,000
Turnover: £161,578,000

UK employees: n/a
Total employees: 14,898

● **Alphabetical listing** Please read page 6

Name/Address	Officers	Financial Information	Other Information

☐ Sedgwick Group plc
International insurance & reinsurance broking

Sedgwick House,
The Sedgwick Centre,
London E1 8DX
071-377 3456

CE: S Riley
Contact: Ms Victoria Secretan
Community Programmes Manager

Year Ends: 31 Dec '91
Donations: £194,000
Profit: £82,400,000
Turnover: £685,100,000

UK employees: n/a
Total employees: 13,113

% Club, BitC

Donations Policy: Preference for local appeals in areas with a company presence and charities in which a member of staff is involved. Preferred areas of support: education/training for employment, homelessness, environmental issues, health, disability and race equality/equal opportunities. Grants to national organisations from £200 to £5,000. Grants to local organisations from £100.
No response to circular appeals. No support for fundraising events, advertising in charity brochures, appeals from individuals, purely denominational (religious) appeals or bricks and mortar appeals.
World-wide donations in 1991 were £963,000. A brochure on the company's community programmes is available.

☐ Seeboard plc
Electricity supply

Grand Avenue,
Hove,
East Sussex BN3 2LS
0273-724522

Ch: Sir Keith Stuart
CE: T J Ellis
Contact: S M Wide
Administration Director

Year Ends: 31 Mar '92
Donations: £107,000
Profit: £98,400,000
Turnover: £1,157,000,000

UK employees: n/a
Total employees: 6,340

ABSA

Donations Policy: Generally supports only organisations based in the Seeboard area. Preference also for appeals related to company business. Grants from £50 upwards. Total community contributions in 1991/92 were £300,000.
No grants for appeals from individuals; purely denominational (religious) appeals; local appeals not in areas of company presence.

☐ Seismograph Service (England) Ltd
Conductors of seismic surveys

Holwood,
Westerham Road,
Keston,
Kent BR2 6HD
0689-853355

Ch: I R Cheshire
Contact: M J Hughes
Assistant to Resident Director

Year Ends: 30 Sep '88
Donations: £2,020
Profit: £83,000
Turnover: £67,128,000

UK employees: n/a
Total employees: 1,167

Donations Policy: Preference is given to a small number of already defined national and local charities providing youth service or help to disabled people.
The company does not sponsor individuals and indirect donations through advertising agencies are not considered. Telephone, telex or fax appeals will not be considered.

☐ Self Serve Hygiene Ltd
Sanitary towel machines

Central Avenue,
West Molesey,
Surrey KT8 2HH
081-941 3033

Contact: Mrs Sheila Dann
Secretary to the Managing
Director

Year Ends: 31 Dec '91
Donations: £24,413
Profit: £258,000
Turnover: £5,225,000

UK employees: 122
Total employees: 122

% Club

Donations Policy: Donations are based on a percentage of company profits. Preference for local community causes in areas where the company operates and causes in which a member of company staff is involved. Preference for children and youth; social welfare; medical; education and recreation. Grants to national organisations from £50 to £250. Grants to local organisations from £50 to £2,500. Total community contributions in 1991 were £30,000.
No grants for advertising in charity brochures; purely denominational (religious) appeals and local appeals not in areas of company presence.

☐ SEMA Group plc
Information systems contractor

Legal House,
14 James Street,
London WC2E 8BT
071-831 6144

Ch: B J Gibbens
CE: M J Smith
Contact: Barbara Reid
Public Relations Manager

Year Ends: 31 Dec '91
Donations: £11,000
Profit: £14,015,000
Turnover: £412,501,000

UK employees: 7,450
Total employees: n/a

Donations Policy: Preference for charities in which a member of staff is involved, or is directly involved with a customer.

☐ Senior Engineering Group plc
Engineering

Senior House,
59-61 High Street,
Rickmansworth,
Herts WD3 1RH
0923-775547

Ch: D D McFarlane
CE: A J Bell
Contact: F H Fermor
Group Company Secretary

Year Ends: 31 Dec '91
Donations: £9,000
Profit: £18,266,000
Turnover: £297,580,000

UK employees: n/a
Total employees: 5,103

☐ Serco Group plc
Provision of technical services

Lincoln Way,
Windmill Road,
Sunbury-on-Thames,
Middlesex TW16 7HW
0932-785511

Ch: G G Gray
MD: R D White
Contact: A Robson
Company Secretary

Year Ends: 31 Dec '91
Donations: £11,000
Profit: £5,252,000
Turnover: £104,957,000

UK employees: n/a
Total employees: 4,196

Donations Policy: Preference for local appeals relevant to the business. Support given to children and youth, education, medical, overseas aid and development and forces charities.
No support for large national appeals, circular appeals, purely denominational (religious) appeals or appeals from individuals. Direct support preferred.

Please read page 6 — Alphabetical listing

Name/Address	Officers	Financial Information	Other Information

☐ Severn Trent plc
Water & sewerage services, waste management

2297 Coventry Road,
Birmingham   B26 3PU
021-722 4000

Ch: John Bellak
CE: Roderick Paul
Contact: Caroline Wilkinson
Assistant Company Secretary

Year Ends: 31 Mar '92
Donations: £145,853
Profit: £261,000,000
Turnover: £822,000,000

UK employees: 9,960
Total employees: 10,416

Donations Policy: Appeals from within the Severn Trent region are preferred. Preference for children and youth, medical and the arts.

☐ Shaftesbury plc
Restoration & refurbishment of commercial property

11 Waterloo Place,
London   SW17 4AU
071-839 4024

Contact: P L Levy
Chairman

Year Ends: 30 Sep '89
Donations: £1,930
Profit: £5,024,000
Turnover: n/a

UK employees: n/a
Total employees: 12

Donations Policy: Preferred areas of support: projects involving children and youth, social welfare, medicine, education and recreation. Typical grant range £100 to £500.
No support for circular appeals, fundraising events, advertising in charity brochures, appeals from individuals, purely denominational appeals, large national appeals, local appeals not in areas of company presence or overseas projects.

☐ Shandwick plc
Public relations consultants

61 Grosvenor Street,
London   W1X 9DA
071-408 2232

Ch: Peter Gummer
Contact: Lord Chalfont

Year Ends: 31 Oct '91
Donations: £141,000
Profit: £1,435,000
Turnover: £197,752,000

UK employees: n/a
Total employees: 2,034

Donations Policy: Preference for children and youth, medical, education, environment and heritage, and the arts.
Generally no support for circular appeals, appeals from individuals or purely denominational appeals.

☐ Shanks & McEwan Group plc
Construction & waste handling

22 Woodside Place,
Glasgow   G3 7QY
041-331 2614

Contact: H L I Runciman
Chairman

Year Ends: 25 Mar '92
Donations: £31,155
Profit: £31,127,000
Turnover: £145,780,000

UK employees: n/a
Total employees: 1,608

Donations Policy: We have been unable to obtain a donations policy.

☐ Sharp Electronics (UK) Ltd
Electrical & electronic equipment

Sharp House,
Thorp Road,
Manchester   M10 9BE
061-205 2333

Ch: S Mikuni
Contact: D R Wakefield
Personnel Manager

Year Ends: 31 Mar '91
Donations: n/a
Profit: £9,965,000
Turnover: £251,241,000

UK employees: n/a
Total employees: 1,413

Donations Policy: Preference for local charities in areas where the company operates. Preference for children and youth; medical and environment/heritage. The company prefers to donate products for fundraising purposes or for use within the receiving organisation. The policy is to donate 1% of pre-tax profits each year (ie. about £50,000 in 1990/91).
No grants for advertising in charity brochures; appeals from individuals; purely denominational (religious) appeals; local appeals not in areas of company presence; large national appeals; overseas projects.

☐ Sharpe & Fisher plc
Builders merchants, DIY

Gloucester Road,
Cheltenham,
Gloucestershire   GL51 8PT
0242-521477

Ch: R Stringer
Contact: T Williams
Development Director

Year Ends: 31 Dec '89
Donations: £4,984
Profit: £2,916,000
Turnover: £49,389,000

UK employees: n/a
Total employees: 651
% Club

☐ Sheerness Steel Co plc
Steel production

Sheerness,
Kent   ME12 1TH
0795-663333

Ch: W J Shields
Contact: Mrs L Brotherstone
Personnel Assistant

Year Ends: 31 Dec '91
Donations: £17,012
Profit: £16,630,00
Turnover: £181,419,000

UK employees: n/a
Total employees: 903
% Club

Donations Policy: Preference for local charities in the areas of company presence and charities in which a member of company staff is involved. Preferred areas of support: children and youth, social welfare, education, recreation, environment and heritage, the arts and enterprise/training. Grants to national organisations from £25 to £250. Grants to local organisations from £25 to £5,000.
Generally no support for circular appeals, advertising in charity brochures, appeals from individuals, purely denominational (religious) appeals, large national appeals or overseas projects.

☐ Sheffield Forgemasters Ltd
Steel forgings & castings

The Old Rectory,
School Hill,
Whiston,
Rotherham,
South Yorkshire   S60 1QR
0709-828233

Ch: D Secker Walker
CE: P M Wright
Contact: M A Brand
Finance Director

Year Ends: 31 Mar '91
Donations: £7,420
Profit: £17,585,000
Turnover: £142,670,000

UK employees: n/a
Total employees: 2,415

● **Alphabetical listing**　　　　　　　　　　　　　　　　　　　　　　　　　　　　　　　　　　　　　　　Please read page 6

Name/Address　　　　　　　　　　*Officers*　　　　　　　　　*Financial Information*　　　　　*Other Information*

☐ Sheffield Insulations Group plc　　　　　　　　　　　　　　　　　　　　　　　　　　　Insulation contractors

 Hillsborough Works,   *Ch:* W N Adsetts   *Year Ends:* 31 Dec '91 *UK employees:* n/a
 Langsett Road,   *Contact:* Michelle Case *Donations:* £16,000   *Total employees:* 857
 Sheffield,   Assistant to the Chairman *Profit:* £1,507,000
 South Yorkshire S6 2LW   *Turnover:* £132,132,000
 0742-852852

 Donations Policy: Preference for local charities in areas where the company operates and charities in which a member of company staff is
 involved. Preference for children and youth; environment/heritage. The company makes donations of cash and gifts in kind.
 No grants for local appeals not in areas of company presence and overseas projects.

☐ Shell UK Ltd　　　　　　　　　　　　　　　　　　　　　　　　　　　　　　　　　　　　　Oil industry

 Shell-Mex House,   *CE:* J A Collins   *Year Ends:* 31 Dec '91 *UK employees:* n/a
 Strand,   *Contact:* K W Guthrie   *Donations:* £2,090,000 *Total employees:* 12,349
 London WC2R 0DX   Grants Committee Secretary *Profit:* £128,000,000
 071-257 3000   *Turnover:* £6,688,000,000   BitC, ABSA

 Donations Policy: Support for a cross section of charitable organisations including those with a UK remit, or near a Shell location, or where a
 member of staff is involved. The furtherance of voluntary endeavour and projects of potential national significance are also favoured. Central
 resources usually benefit national concerns, while local ones aid organisations active within vicinity of major installations. Grants to
 national organisations from £500 to £10,000. Grants to local organisations from £25 to £500.
 No response to circular appeals. No grants for fundraising events; advertising in charity brochures; appeals from individuals; purely
 denominational (religious) appeals; local appeals not in areas of company presence; overseas projects; organisations of a sectarian nature;
 bricks and mortar appeals.
 Total community contributions in 1991 were £6,352,000 including support for various educational, enterprise and environmental
 initiatives. The company also sponsors the arts.

☐ Shepherd Building Group Ltd　　　　　　　　　　　　　　　　　　　　　　　Building & ancillary activities

 Blue Bridge Lane,   *Ch:* C S Shepherd *Year Ends:* 30 Jun '91 *UK employees:* n/a
 York,   *Contact:* W James   *Donations:* £140,000 *Total employees:* 3,923
 North Yorkshire YO1 4AS   Group Secretary *Profit:* £27,300,000
 0904-653040   *Turnover:* £387,300,000

 Donations Policy: Company support is concentrated in York and Yorkshire and avoids contributing to more than one charity or organisation
 operating in the same field. The main areas of support are children and youth, social welfare, education, medical, and enterprise/training.
 Generally no support for circular appeals, fundraising events, advertising in charity brochures, appeals from individuals, purely
 denominational (religious) appeals, local appeals not in areas of company presence, large national appeals or overseas projects.

☐ Sheppard Group Ltd　　　　　　　　　　　　　　　　　　　　　　　　　　　　　　　Scrap metal dealers

 Alexandra Buildings, *Contact:* C D Iles   *Year Ends:* 31 May '90 *UK employees:* n/a
 Branch Dock No 1,   Financial Director *Donations:* n/a   *Total employees:* 296
 Bootle,   *Profit:* £1,977,000
 Liverpool L20 1BX   *Turnover:* £110,662,000
 051-933 6440

☐ Sherwood Group plc　　　　　　　　　　　　　　　　　　　　　　　　　　　　　　　Lingerie manufacturers

 52-56 Nottingham Road, *Contact:* P Newbold   *Year Ends:* 31 Dec '91 *UK employees:* n/a
 Long Eaton,   Financial Director *Donations:* £17,021   *Total employees:* 2,703
 Nottinghamshire NG10 2BQ   *Profit:* £14,507,000
 0602-461070   *Turnover:* £118,180,000

 Donations Policy: We have been unable to obtain a donations policy.

☐ Short Brothers plc　　　　　　　　　　　　　　　　　　　　　　　　　　　　Aircraft & missile manufacturers

 PO Box 241,   *Ch:* Laurent Beaudoin *Year Ends:* 31 Jan '92 *UK employees:* n/a
 Airport Road,   *MD:* Roy McNulty *Donations:* £28,494   *Total employees:* 8,982
 Belfast BT3 9DZ   *Contact:* R Gordan   *Profit:* £28,548,000
 0232-458444   Head of Public Affairs *Turnover:* £392,449,000

 Donations Policy: Preference for appeals relevant to company business and services charities. Once the company starts to make a profit it
 will probably start supporting local charities and community organisations.

☐ Shotton Paper Co plc　　　　　　　　　　　　　　　　　　　　　　　　　　　　Pulp & paper mill operators

 Weighbridge Road,   *Ch:* P J Arvela   *Year Ends:* 31 Dec '91 *UK employees:* n/a
 Shotton,   *MD:* J K Lyden   *Donations:* £9,619   *Total employees:* 466
 Deeside CH5 2LL   *Contact:* Company Secretary *Profit:* £8,310,000
 0244-280000   *Turnover:* £121,463,000

 Donations Policy: Preference for local charities in areas of company presence.

Please read page 6 — Alphabetical listing

Name/Address	Officers	Financial Information	Other Information

☐ Sidlaw Group plc
North Sea oil & jute spinners

Nethergate Centre,
Dundee DD1 4BR
0382-23161

Ch: Sir R Smith
MD: M G N Walker
Contact: C M Nicol
Company Secretary

Year Ends: 30 Sep '91
Donations: £4,339
Profit: £8,270,000
Turnover: £84,567,000

UK employees: n/a
Total employees: 1,592

Donations Policy: Geared to local appeals (including local or Scottish branch of national charities, eg. the Salvation Army) plus major disaster or famine relief appeals. Preference for children and youth, medical and the arts.

☐ Siebe plc
Control devices, compressed air equipment

Saxon House,
2-4 Victoria Street,
Windsor,
Berkshire SL4 1EN
0753-855411

Ch: W M Pybus
CE: E B Stephens
Contact: R P A Coles
Company Secretary

Year Ends: 1 Apr '91
Donations: £39,000
Profit: £159,100,000
Turnover: £1,480,600,000

UK employees: n/a
Total employees: 30,548

Donations Policy: Preference for medical charities especially Red Cross, leukaemia and cancer related charities.

☐ Siemens plc
Electronics

Windmill Road,
Sunbury-on-Thames,
Middlesex TW16 7HS
0932-752310

Ch: Sir Jock Taylor
CE: J C Gehrels
Contact: Alister MacDonald
Marketing & Communications Manager

Year Ends: 30 Sep '90
Donations: £29,000
Profit: £21,477,000
Turnover: £359,857,000

UK employees: n/a
Total employees: 3,183

ABSA

Donations Policy: The different subsidiaries have different policies though most would be receptive to local charities in areas of company presence.

☐ Silentnight Holdings plc
Bedding upholstery manufacturers

Salterforth,
Colne,
Lancashire BB8 5UE
0282-812711

Ch: W M Davies
Contact: B McKenzie
Group Finance Director

Year Ends: 1 Feb '92
Donations: £70,381
Profit: £12,412,000
Turnover: £137,556,000

UK employees: n/a
Total employees: 3,071

Donations Policy: The company consider all applications on merit from local and national charities. Preference for children and youth; elderly people; education; medical. Donations are usually between £200 and £2,000.

☐ Simon Engineering plc
Engineering, contracting

PO Box 31,
Birdhall Lane,
Cheadle Heath,
Stockport,
Cheshire SK3 0RT
061-428 3600

Ch: R E J Roberts
MD: B R C Kemp
Contact: Fiona Watson
Secretary to the Director of Pensions

Year Ends: 31 Dec '91
Donations: £23,000
Profit: £18,305,000
Turnover: £514,508,000

UK employees: n/a
Total employees: 7,690

Donations Policy: Donations are only given to registered charities in the North West or to those connected with engineering. Preference to charities with company staff involvement and charities involved with local education or medical causes. The company may make one-off donations to emergency overseas causes. Grants to national organisations from £100 to £500. Grants to local organisations from £50 to £500.

☐ Simons Group Ltd
Construction, property, design

Monks Road,
Lincoln LN3 7JP
0522-510000

Ch: Paul Simon
Contact: Sue Goodacre
Publicity Department

Year Ends: 31 Dec '91
Donations: £105,782
Profit: £2,794,000
Turnover: £113,097,000

UK employees: n/a
Total employees: n/a

BitC

Donations Policy: The company has a long term commitment to some local charities in areas where it operates and donates small raffle prizes to local charities. The company has recently been involved with local sport sponsorship.
No grants will be given for national charities or for overseas projects.

☐ Sims Food Group plc
Fresh meat & poultry sales

Sims House, Sims Food Park,
Sherbourne Drive,
Tilbrook,
Milton Keynes MK7 8BS
0908-270061

Ch: J M Stone
Contact: B P Ford
Chief Executive

Year Ends: 30 Mar '91
Donations: £11,997
Profit: £16,027,000
Turnover: £227,602,000

UK employees: n/a
Total employees: 3,806

☐ William Sindall plc
Building & civil engineering contractors

Babraham Road,
Sawston,
Cambridge CB2 4LJ
0223-836611

Ch: J C S Mott
MD: M Grieve
Contact: C Everett
Marketing Manager

Year Ends: 31 Dec '91
Donations: £4,900
Profit: (£4,185,913)
Turnover: £63,887,490

UK employees: n/a
Total employees: 935

● **Alphabetical listing** Please read page 6

| Name/Address | Officers | Financial Information | Other Information |

☐ Singer & Friedlander Group plc
Merchant banking, investment management

21 New Street,
Bishopsgate,
London EC2M 4HR
071-623 3000

Ch: A N Solomons
Contact: J Hodson
Chief Executive

Year Ends: 31 Dec '91
Donations: £57,873
Profit: £15,470,000
Turnover: n/a

UK employees: n/a
Total employees: 244

Donations Policy: There is no set policy, each charity is considered on merit. Preference towards children and youth charities, local charities in areas of company presence and charities where company staff are involved. The company tends to support the less well known charities and also supports some charities outside their areas of operation. Some overseas projects are considered.

☐ Sirdar plc
Knitting wool manufacturers

Flanshaw Lane,
Alverthorpe,
Wakefield,
West Yorkshire WF2 9ND
0924-371501

Ch: J M Tyrrell
MD: F G Lumb
Contact: K F Henry
Director/Company Secretary

Year Ends: 30 Jun '92
Donations: £2,100
Profit: £5,051,000
Turnover: £52,034,000

UK employees: n/a
Total employees: 1,212

Donations Policy: Preference for local charities in areas of company presence, particularly social welfare and medical, and appeals relevant to company presence. Direct support preferred. Grants to local organisations from £50 to £250.
No support for circular appeals, appeals from individuals, overseas projects or purely denominational appeals.

☐ 600 Group plc
Machine tool manufacturers, engineers

Hythe End House,
Chertsey Lane,
Staines,
Middlesex TW18 3EL
0784-461545

Ch: Sir Jeffrey Benson
MD: B A Carter
Contact: H E Ashton
Company Secretary

Year Ends: 31 Mar '92
Donations: £5,369
Profit: £534,000
Turnover: £98,470,000

UK employees: n/a
Total employees: 2,692

Donations Policy: The company supports a pre-determined group of national charities, certain industrial charities, some national and international disaster appeals when they occur.
No support for circular appeals, brochure advertising, appeals from individuals or purely denominational (religious) appeals. The arts are a low priority.

☐ Sketchley plc
Workwear rental & dry cleaning

Rugby Road,
Hinckley,
Leicestershire LE10 2NE
0455-238133

Ch: J R Gillum
MD: A J Jones
Contact: Miss D Harris
Secretary to Sketchley Charitable Trust

Year Ends: 27 Mar '92
Donations: £1,394
Profit: £6,015,000
Turnover: £107,081,000

UK employees: n/a
Total employees: 4,648

Donations Policy: Preference given to charities in which a member of staff is involved.
No brochure advertising or support for overseas projects. The Sketchley Charitable Trust is not currently operative.

☐ SKF UK Ltd
Ball & roller bearing manufacturers

Bradbourne Drive,
Tilbrook,
Milton Keynes MK7 8BJ
0908-838305

Ch: Lord King of Wartnaby
MD: N S McCracken
Contact: C Haywood
Public Relations & Communications Manager

Year Ends: 31 Dec '90
Donations: £3,317
Profit: £5,854,000
Turnover: £169,293,000

UK employees: n/a
Total employees: 1,124

☐ Skipton Building Society
Building society

High Street,
Skipton,
North Yorkshire BD23 1DN
0756-700500

Ch: J B Haggas
CE: T Adams
Contact: Jo Watson
Assistant Marketing Manager

Year Ends: 31 Dec '89
Donations: n/a
Profit: £24,800,000
Turnover: n/a

UK employees: n/a
Total employees: 545

Donations Policy: Preference for local charities in the areas of company presence, and projects concerned with children and youth, social welfare, education, recreation, environment and heritage, the arts and enterprise/training.
Generally no support for appeals from individuals, purely denominational (religious) appeals, local appeals not in areas of company presence, large national appeals or overseas projects.

☐ Slough Estates plc
Industrial & commercial property development

234 Bath Road,
Slough,
Berkshire SL1 4EE
0753-37171

Ch: Sir Nigel Mobbs
MD: R W Carey, D R Wilson
Contact: Brigadier N M White
Manager External Affairs

Year Ends: 31 Dec '91
Donations: £222,200
Profit: £31,600,000
Turnover: £109,200,000

UK employees: n/a
Total employees: 397
% Club, BitC

Donations Policy: Support for a wide range of causes in the fields of art, music and culture; health research and care; youth; old age; education; relief of unemployment; the environment and conservation; welfare and the relief of poverty. Preference for local appeals in areas of company presence, principally Berkshire and Buckinghamshire. Typical grants range from £25 to £5,000.
No grants for non-charities; circular appeals; local appeals not in areas of company presence; overseas projects.

Please read page 6 | Alphabetical listing •

Name/Address	Officers	Financial Information	Other Information

☐ J Smart & Co (Contractors) plc
Building contractors

28 Crammond Road South,
Edinburgh EH4 6AB
031-336 2181

Ch: J Smart
Contact: A D McClure
Company Secretary

Year Ends: 31 Jul '91
Donations: £44,034
Profit: £4,439,000
Turnover: £14,784,000

UK employees: n/a
Total employees: 390

Donations Policy: Each appeal is looked at individually on its merits. Preference for charities in areas of company operation and/or with a Scottish base or office.

☐ Smith & Nephew plc
Healthcare products

2 Temple Place,
Victoria Embankment,
London WC2R 3BP
071-836 7922

Ch: Eric Kinder
CE: J H Robinson
Contact: Mrs B Bash (see below)

Year Ends: 31 Dec '91
Donations: £467,000
Profit: £132,400,000
Turnover: £791,700,000

UK employees: 4,894
Total employees: 13,864

Donations Policy: Most of the company's UK donations (£440,000) are channelled through the Smith & Nephew Foundation which supports education and research for individuals in the medical and nursing professions. The foundation also supports medical students undertaking intercalated BSc degrees. Financial support is given to the Wound Healing Research Unit at the University Hospital of Wales, Cardiff.
World-wide donations in 1991 were £969,000.
All awards are advertised in relevant medical or nursing journals. Further information from Mrs B Bash, Secretary to the Trustees, Smith & Nephew Foundation, address as above.

☐ David S Smith Holdings plc
Manufacture of paper & packaging services

16 Great Peter Street,
London SW1P 2BX
071-222 8855

Ch: D S Smith
MD: R D Brewster
Contact: Linda Courtney
Secretary to Chief Executive

Year Ends: 30 Apr '91
Donations: £37,863
Profit: £23,938,000
Turnover: £363,474,000

UK employees: n/a
Total employees: 4,896

Donations Policy: The company have no set policy. A lot of support has been given to the RNIB.

☐ Smith New Court plc
Securities

Smith New Court House,
20 Farringdon Road,
London EC1M 3NH
071-772 1000

Ch: Sir Michael Richardson
CE: M J P Marks
Contact: M Heath
Managing Director

Year Ends: 24 Apr '92
Donations: £37,000
Profit: £18,400,000
Turnover: n/a

UK employees: n/a
Total employees: 1,168

☐ W H Smith Group plc
Retail & distribution group

Strand House,
7 Holbein Place,
London SW1W 8NR
071-730 1200

Ch: Sir Simon Hornby
MD: Sir Malcolm Field
Contact: Valerie Evans
Donations Secretary

Year Ends: 30 May '92
Donations: £285,000
Profit: £112,700,000
Turnover: £2,127,500,000

UK employees: n/a
Total employees: 29,318

% Club, BitC, ABSA

Donations Policy: Support is concentrated on: trade and allied charities, product related, disadvantaged youth, the environment, care of sick and elderly people, education particularly literacy. Preference for local charities in areas where the company operates and charities in which a member of company staff is involved. Support is given to specific projects rather than general funds. Grants to national organisations from £500 to £5,000. Grants to local organisations from £20 to £500.
No grants for fundraising events; advertising in charity brochures; appeals from individuals; purely denominational (religious) appeals; medical research in general; political organisations; overseas projects; large national appeals (usually).
Total community contributions in 1991/92 were £1,300,000. Other support is given to enterprise and education initiatives and in the form of arts sponsorship, particularly organisations seeking to introduce the arts to young people. Sponsorship proposals to Michael Mackensie.

☐ SmithKline Beecham plc
Pharmaceutical & consumer products

New Horizons Court,
Brentford,
Middlesex TW8 9EP
081-975 2000

Ch: H Wendt
CE: R P Bauman
Contact: Miss Margaret Bailey
Contributions Co-ordinator

Year Ends: 31 Dec '91
Donations: £1,247,000
Profit: £1,002,000,000
Turnover: £4,685,000,000

UK employees: 10,100
Total employees: 54,000

BitC, ABSA

Donations Policy: Main areas of support are health and medical care, social welfare, elderly people, disabled people, education, and overseas aid/development (by product donation). Preference for local charities in areas of company presence, appeals relevant to company business and charities in which a member of staff is involved. Grants to national organisations from £100 to over £50,000. Grants to local organisations from £50 to over £10,000.
No support for circular appeals, fundraising events, appeals from individuals, purely denominational (religious) appeals, local appeals not in areas of company presence, large national appeals, political appeals, expeditions.
Worldwide donations in 1991 totalled £5,314,000.

☐ Smiths Crisps Ltd
Snack manufacture

1600 Arlington Business Park,
Theale,
Reading,
Berkshire RG7 4SA
0734-306666

Contact: P Warren
Marketing Department

Year Ends: 30 Jun '90
Donations: nil
Profit: £13,892,000
Turnover: £161,263,000

UK employees: n/a
Total employees: 3,434

● **Alphabetical listing** Please read page 6

Name/Address	Officers	Financial Information	Other Information

☐ Smiths Industries plc
Aerospace, marine & medical equipment

765 Finchley Road,
Childs Hill,
London NW11 8DS
081-458 3232

Ch: F R Hum
Contact: N Burdett
Assistant Company Secretary

Year Ends: 5 Aug '91
Donations: £288,000
Profit: £120,300,000
Turnover: £655,500,000

UK employees: n/a
Total employees: 12,109

% Club, BitC

Donations Policy: Wide ranging support for local and national causes, particularly those related to the company's business (ie. medical, industrial and defence) and in areas of company presence.

☐ Sock Shop Holdings Ltd
Socks

20 Nelson Way,
Yorktown,
Camberley GU15 3DW
0276-63000

CE: Juan Olaso
Contact: Sarah Cole
Marketing & Communications
Department

Year Ends: 28 Feb '89
Donations: £25,000
Profit: £4,319,000
Turnover: £44,375,000

UK employees: n/a
Total employees: 5,050

Donations Policy: The company has recently been taken over, and as yet a new donations policy has not been formulated.

☐ Solaglas International UK
Flat glass distribution & glazing

Waterside Drive,
Langley Business Park,
Langley,
Berkshire SL3 6EZ
0734-774900

Contact: I Eaton
Director

Year Ends: 31 Dec '90
Donations: £4,333
Profit: £11,839,000
Turnover: £132,536,000

UK employees: n/a
Total employees: 3,500

☐ Sony Broadcast & Communications Ltd
Video & audio equipment suppliers

Jays Close,
Viables,
Basingstoke RG22 4SB
0256-55011

Ch: K H Barratt
Contact: Ms C Walters
Product, Literature &
Demonstration Co-ordinator

Year Ends: 31 Mar '91
Donations: £150
Profit: £5,298,000
Turnover: £185,552,000

UK employees: n/a
Total employees: 527

☐ Sony Music Entertainment (UK) Ltd
Records & music

17-19 Soho Square,
London W1V 6HE
071-734 8181

MD: P Russell
Contact: Rhona Levene
Corporate Relations Executive

Year Ends: 31 Jan '91
Donations: £12,529 (1989)
Profit: £13,819,000
Turnover: £226,558,000

UK employees: n/a
Total employees: 923

Donations Policy: Preference for appeals relevant to the business, charities in which a member of staff is involved, and the arts.

☐ Sony (UK) Ltd
Manufacture & distribution of electronic goods

Sony House,
South Street,
Staines TW18 4PF
0784-467000

MD: N Watanabe
Contact: Brenda Jones
Communications Manager

Year Ends: 31 Mar '91
Donations: £39,000
Profit: £36,658,000
Turnover: £875,411,000

UK employees: 2,878
Total employees: n/a

% Club, BitC

Donations Policy: Preference for arts, education, community, youth and welfare charities.

☐ Sotheby's
Fine art auctioneers

34-35 New Bond Street,
London W1A 2AA
071-408 5423

Ch: The Rt Hon The Earl of Gowrie
MD: Roger Faxon
Contact: G D Llewellyn
Director

Year Ends: 31 Dec '92
Donations: £25,000
Profit: n/a
Turnover: n/a

UK employees: n/a
Total employees: n/a

% Club, BitC, ABSA

Donations Policy: The company tries to spread its resources as widely as the charity and sponsorship budgets allow. In addition to donations, Sotheby's provides help and sponsorship for charity auctions and makes its premises available for charity exhibitions.
Generally no support for appeals from individuals, purely denominational (religious) appeals, large national appeals or overseas projects.

☐ J Soufflet (UK) Ltd
Cereals, pulses & agricultural products

Cereals House,
21 Station Road,
Westcliff-on-Sea,
Essex SS0 7RA
0702-354433

MD: C F Haycroft
Contact: Company Secretary

Year Ends: 30 Jun '90
Donations: n/a
Profit: £780,000
Turnover: £272,520,000

UK employees: n/a
Total employees: 30

☐ South Wales Electricity plc
Electricity supply

St Mellons,
Cardiff CF3 9XW
0222-792111

Ch: J W Evans
MD: D H Jones
Contact: Mrs Jackie Roe
Public Relations Officer

Year Ends: 31 Mar '92
Donations: £20,400
Profit: £72,500,000
Turnover: £590,200,000

UK employees: n/a
Total employees: n/a

BitC, ABSA

Donations Policy: The company supports Age Concern Wales and groups working with disabled and disadvantaged people. It also sponsors the arts.

Please read page 6 — Alphabetical listing

Name/Address	Officers	Financial Information	Other Information

☐ South West Water plc
Water & sewerage services

Peninsula House,
Rydon Lane,
Exeter   EX2 7HR
0392-219666

Ch: Keith Court
Contact: H Wetherley
　　　　　Corporate Affairs Manager

Year Ends: 31 Mar '92
Donations: £36,000
Profit: £90,000,000
Turnover: £166,500,000

UK employees: n/a
Total employees: 2,072

Donations Policy: Preference for local charities in areas of company presence. Preferred areas of support: social welfare, education, environment and heritage, the arts. Grants generally in the range £500 to £1,000.
No support for circular appeals, advertising in charity brochures, appeals from individuals, purely denominational appeals, local appeals not in areas of company presence, overseas projects.

☐ South Western Electricity plc
Electricity supply

800 Park Avenue,
Aztec West,
Almondsbury,
Bristol   BS12 4SE
0454-201101

Ch: A W Nicol
MD: J J Seed
Contact: Michael Harman
　　　　　Public Relations Manager

Year Ends: 31 Mar '92
Donations: £67,000
Profit: £83,000,000
Turnover: £847,100,000

UK employees: n/a
Total employees: 5,676

Donations Policy: To give support to a variety of local organisations in the areas of company presence. The company also supports education and enterprise initiatives and sponsors arts and sports events particularly directed at young people.
No grants for appeals from individuals; purely denominational (religious) appeals; overseas projects.

☐ Southend Property Holdings plc
Property investment development & dealing

1 Dancastle Arcadia Avenue,
London   N3 2JU
081-458 8833

Ch: M Dagul
Contact: Margaret Barkwith
　　　　　Personal Assistant to the
　　　　　Chairman

Year Ends: 31 Mar '92
Donations: £5,790
Profit: £3,710,000
Turnover: £81,078,000

UK employees: 64
Total employees: n/a

☐ Southern Electric plc
Electricity supply

Littlewick Green,
Maidenhead,
Berkshire   SL6 3QB
0628-822166

Ch: D A Ross
MD: H R Casley
Contact: Julian Reeves
　　　　　Corporate Relations Department

Year Ends: 31 Mar '92
Donations: £21,518
Profit: £166,300,000
Turnover: £1,750,600,000

UK employees: n/a
Total employees: 8,340

BitC

Donations Policy: Preference for local charities in areas where the company operates and appeals relevant to company business. Particular attention to: projects to promote environmental care and conservation, particularly in rural areas; schemes promoting the welfare of elderly people, particularly related to energy matters; schemes promoting safety at work, in the home and in public places; vocational preparation
No response to circular appeals. No grants for advertising in charity brochures; purely denominational (religious) appeals; local appeals not in areas of company presence; large national appeals; overseas projects and media events.

☐ Southern Newspapers plc
Newspaper printers & publishers

45 Above Bar Street,
Southampton   SO9 7BA
0703-634134

Ch: J G Salkeld
MD: James Sexton
Contact: Chief Executive

Year Ends: 30 Jun '91
Donations: £5,379
Profit: £2,707,000
Turnover: £71,442,000

UK employees: n/a
Total employees: 1,763

Donations Policy: Support only local charities in areas where the company operates. Preference for medical; arts. Grants to local organisations from £100 to £500.
No support for circulars, purely denominational (religious) appeals; local appeals not in areas of company presence and overseas projects.

☐ Southern Water plc
Water & waste water treatment services

Southern House,
Yeoman Road,
Worthing,
West Sussex   BN13 3NX
0903-264444

Ch: William Courtney
MD: Martyn Webster
Contact: Graham Nicholson
　　　　　Company Secretary

Year Ends: 31 Mar '92
Donations: £26,000
Profit: £115,100,000
Turnover: £290,700,000

UK employees: n/a
Total employees: 3,103

Donations Policy: Preference for local charities in areas where the company operates and appeals relevant to company business. Within that policy the company has no particular exclusions or preferences.

☐ SP Tyres UK Ltd
Tyres & related products

Fort Dunlop,
Birmingham   B24 9QT
021-384 4444

Ch: G D Radford

Year Ends: 31 Dec '90
Donations: £515
Profit: £7,368,000
Turnover: £213,285,000

UK employees: n/a
Total employees: 3,685

Donations Policy: The company state "We do not make charitable donations".

☐ Spandex plc
Sign making & display, computers

1600 Park Avenue,
Aztec West,
Almondsbury,
Bristol   BS12 4UA
0454-616444

Contact: C E Dobson
　　　　　Managing Director & Chairman

Year Ends: 31 Dec '91
Donations: £950
Profit: £4,195,000
Turnover: £51,954,000

UK employees: n/a
Total employees: 217

• **Alphabetical listing**   Please read page 6

Name/Address	Officers	Financial Information	Other Information

☐ **Spencer Stuart Ltd**   Management consultants

16 Connaught Place,   Ch: C D Power   Year Ends: 30 Sep '91   UK employees: 50
London W2 2ES   MD: D H S Kimbell   Donations: £6,000   Total employees: 50
071-493 1238   Contact: Briony Marriott   Profit: £45,000
                                Office Manager   Turnover: £6,000,000   % Club, BitC

Donations Policy: To support organisations devoted to the training and rehabilitation of the disadvantaged, especially young people, particularly where this can help business regeneration either directly or indirectly. Preference for youth and enterprise/training. Grants to national organisations from £50 to £1,000. Grants to local organisations from £25 to £100.
No grants for fundraising events; advertising in charity brochures; appeals from individuals; purely denominational (religious) appeals; local appeals not in areas of company presence; large national appeals outside our specific policy and overseas projects.

☐ **Speyhawk plc**   Property development & construction

37 Queen Anne's Street,   Ch: T Osborne   Year Ends: 30 Sep '91   UK employees: n/a
London W1   Contact: S Langsford   Donations: £23,000   Total employees: 437
071-637 7653   Personal Assistant to the Profit: (£216,778)
                                Chairman   Turnover: £76,437,000   % Club

Donations Policy: Preference for local charities and appeals relevant to the business. Preference for social welfare, education and the arts.
No support for circular appeals, appeals from individuals or denominational appeals.

☐ **Sphere Drake Underwriting Management Ltd**   Insurance

52-54 Leadenhall Street   Contact: Ms Heather Williams   Year Ends: 31 Dec '91   UK employees: n/a
London EC3A 2BJ   Charities Committee Secretary   Donations: £4,704   Total employees: n/a
071-480 7340   Profit: n/a
                                                                Turnover: n/a

Donations Policy: The charity committee meets approximately four times a year. Only written requests for donations can normally be considered. No telephone calls.
Preference for children and youth; social welfare; medical and education. Preference for local charities in areas where the company operates, appeals relevant to company business and for charities in which a member of company staff is involved. Grants to national and local organisations from £100 to £500. Total Group donations in 1991 were £10,000.
No grants for advertising in charity brochures and local appeals not in areas of company presence. No response to circular appeals.

☐ **Spirax-Sarco Engineering plc**   Specialists in fluid control equipment

Charlton House,   Ch: C J Tappin   Year Ends: 31 Dec '91   UK employees: 1,256
Cirencester Road,   Contact: T B Fortune   Donations: £30,462   Total employees: 3,430
Cheltenham,   Managing Director   Profit: £22,481,000
Gloucestershire GL53 8ER   Turnover: £158,291,000
0242-521361

Donations Policy: Mainly support for local charities in areas where the company operates. Also preference for appeals relevant to company business and charities in which a member of company staff is involved, in particular for child welfare and medical research, education. Grants to national organisations from £50 to £400. Grants to local organisations from £20 to £1,000.
No response to circular appeals. No grants for advertising in charity brochures; purely denominational (religious) appeals; local appeals not in areas of company presence; large national appeals.

☐ **Spring Ram Corporation plc**   Home improvement products

PO Box 24,   Ch: W T Rooney   Year Ends: 3 Jan '92   UK employees: n/a
Spring Bank Business Park,   Contact: Secretary to the Chairman Donations: n/a   Total employees: 2,082
Gelderd Road,   Profit: £37,569,000
Birstall,   Turnover: £194,173,000
West Yorkshire WF17 9XG
0924-441142

Donations Policy: No charitable donations figure is given in the company annual report.

☐ **Stag Furniture Holdings plc**   Furniture manufacturers

Haydn Road,   Ch: P H Ryan   Year Ends: 31 Dec '91   UK employees: n/a
Nottingham NG5 1DU   CE: G H Ella   Donations: £13,000   Total employees: 813
0602-605007   Contact: J M Hornsby   Profit: £2,044,000
                                Personnel Manager   Turnover: £26,806,000   % Club

---

☐ **Stakis plc**   Hoteliers & gaming proprietors

3 Atlantic Quay,   Ch: Sir Lewis Robertson   Year Ends: 29 Sep '91   UK employees: 7,200
York Street,   CE: D M C Michels   Donations: £26,000   Total employees: 7,200
Glasgow G2 8JH   Contact: Alex Pagett   Profit: (£47,423,000)
041-804 4321   Director of Corporate Affairs   Turnover: £171,455,000

Donations Policy: The company has suspended donations for the time being. At present a single charity is nominated each year and staff efforts are directed towards that charity. In 1992, the target was to raise £75,000 for Alzheimer's Disease Society.

Please read page 6 — Alphabetical listing

Name/Address	Officers	Financial Information	Other Information

☐ Standard Chartered plc
Banking

1 Aldermanbury Square,
London   EC2V 7SB
071-280 7007

Ch: R D Galpin
Contact: Secretary to the Donations Committee, Chairman's Office

Year Ends: 31 Dec '91
Donations: £234,583
Profit: £205,300,000
Turnover: n/a

UK employees: 3,500
Total employees: n/a

BitC, ABSA

Donations Policy: In general, priority is given to charities in some way connected with the group's business and its countries of operation. The donations committee identifies a small number of charities each year to support usually for up to three years. Preference for social welfare, medical and overseas aid/development. Grants to national organisations from £100 to £27,500. Grants to local organisations from £100 to £500.
Generally no support for education, advertising in charity brochures, appeals from individuals, purely denominational (religious) appeals or local appeals not in areas of company presence.
Sponsorship proposals to Head of Group Communications Department.

☐ Standard Life Assurance Company plc
Life assurance

3 George Street,
Edinburgh   EH2 2XZ
031-225 2552

Ch: Norman Lessels
MD: A S Bell
Contact: R McCall, Sponsorship Manager

Year Ends: 15 Nov '91
Donations: £37,000
Profit: £2,401,600,000
Turnover: £4,734,900,000

UK employees: 6,067
Total employees: n/a

☐ Stanhope Properties plc
Property development

Lansdown House,
Berkeley Street,
London   W1X 6BP
071-495 7575

Ch: Sir Eric Sharp
MD: S Lipton
Contact: Company Secretary

Year Ends: 30 Jun '91
Donations: £48,859
Profit: (£77,399,000)
Turnover: £42,917,000

UK employees: 22
Total employees: n/a

% Club

Donations Policy: Preference for appeals local to the company's developments or relevant to the business. The company supports arts, training/employment projects and local charities.
No support for circular appeals, overseas projects, purely denominational appeals.

☐ Stanley Leisure Organisation plc
Betting office & casino operators

Stanley House,
4-12 Marybone,
Liverpool   L3 2BY
051-236 4291

Contact: L Steinberg, Chairman

Year Ends: 30 Apr '91
Donations: £24,865
Profit: £7,127,000
Turnover: £187,562,000

UK employees: n/a
Total employees: 3,171

% Club

Donations Policy: Preference for local charities, especially children and youth, social welfare, medical, education and recreation.
No support for circulars, fundraising events, advertising in charity brochures, appeals from individuals, purely denominational (religious) appeals, local appeals not in areas of company presence, large national appeals, overseas projects.

☐ Stanley Tools Europe
Hand tool manufacturers

Cory House,
The Ring,
Bracknell,
Berkshire   RG12 1AX
0344-51813

Contact: P Mollett, Personnel Officer

Year Ends: 31 Dec '88
Donations: £3,085
Profit: £6,540,000
Turnover: £69,437,000

UK employees: n/a
Total employees: 1,034

☐ Stanton plc
Manufacture & supply of pipeline systems

PO Box 72,
Nottingham   NG10 5AA
0602-300681

Ch: B Navel
Contact: D Slaytor, Employer Relations Manager

Year Ends: 31 Dec '91
Donations: £3,986
Profit: £9,916,000
Turnover: £123,583,000

UK employees: n/a
Total employees: 2,137

☐ Staveley Industries plc
Manufacturing & minerals

11 Dingwall Road,
Croydon,
Surrey   CR9 3DB
081-688 4404

Ch: B H Kent
Contact: Frank Blurton, Assistant Company Secretary

Year Ends: 31 Mar '91
Donations: £22,500
Profit: £28,000,000
Turnover: £329,500,000

UK employees: n/a
Total employees: 5,566

Donations Policy: Preference for local charities in the areas of company presence and appeals relevant to company business. Support for children and youth, education, environment and heritage, enterprise/training and the arts. Grants to national organisations from £250 to £1,000. Grants to local organisations from £50 to £250.

☐ Stemcor Ltd
Steel, chemicals & plant suppliers

Walker House,
87 Queen Victoria Street,
London   EC4V 4AL
071-236 1505

Ch: R D Oppenheimer
Contact: A D Kaizer, Company Secretary

Year Ends: 31 Dec '90
Donations: £16,667
Profit: £489,000
Turnover: £437,841,000

UK employees: n/a
Total employees: 1,483

Donations Policy: Preference for local charities in areas where the company operates, appeals relevant to company business and charities in which a member of company staff is involved. Preferred areas of support: children and youth, social welfare and medical. Grants to national and local organisations from £20 to £500.
No response to circular appeals. No grants for fundraising events; advertising in charity brochures; appeals from individuals; purely denominational (religious) appeals; overseas projects.

• **Alphabetical listing**   Please read page 6

Name/Address	Officers	Financial Information	Other Information

☐ Stephenson Harwood
Solicitors

One St Paul's Churchyard,
London EC4 M 8SH
071-329 4422

Contact: Christopher Stoakes
Marketing Partner

Year Ends:
Donations: n/a
Profit: n/a
Turnover: n/a

UK employees: n/a
Total employees: n/a

% Club

Donations Policy: Supports charitable projects connected with the law or London. Preference for local charities in areas where the company operates. Grants to national and local organisations from £50 to £10,000.
No grants for fundraising events; advertising in charity brochures; appeals from individuals; purely denominational (religious) appeals; local appeals not in areas of company presence; large national appeals and overseas projects. No response to circular appeals.

☐ Sterling Winthrop Group Ltd
Chemicals, pharmaceuticals

Onslow Street,
Guildford,
Surrey GU1 4YS
0483-505515

Ch: G D Proctor
Contact: S Lloyd
Director of Human Resources

Year Ends: 31 Dec '90
Donations: £81,924
Profit: £16,626,000
Turnover: £218,700,000

UK employees: n/a
Total employees: 2,789

Donations Policy: Preference for children and youth, social welfare, medical, education, recreation, environment and heritage. Grants range from £100 to £1,000.
Generally no support for circular appeals, advertising in charity brochures, appeals from individuals, purely denominational (religious) appeals or local appeals not in areas of company presence.
Sponsorship proposals to N Yeo, Chief Executive, Prescription Health; or C Herbert, Chief Executive, Sterling Health.

☐ William Steward (Holdings) Ltd
Electrical & mechanical manufacturers

Nash House,
Old Oak Lane,
London NW10 6DH
081-965 9888

Contact: Mrs Abbey Kharia
Marketing Department

Year Ends: 31 Mar '91
Donations: n/a
Profit: £1,058,000
Turnover: £93,457,000

UK employees: n/a
Total employees: 1,928

☐ Storehouse plc
Retail stores, household goods

Marylebone House,
129-137 Marylebone Road,
London NW1 5QD
071-262 3456

Ch: I H Davison
CE: D Dworkin
Contact: Lucinda Davies
Group Public Relations Department

Year Ends: 31 Mar '92
Donations: £313,000
Profit: £15,800,000
Turnover: £1,179,800,000

UK employees: 12,812
Total employees: 14,550

Donations Policy: The company concentrates its support on a variety of major charities, with preference for children and youth and charities relevant to company business. Unsolicited appeals are therefore unlikely to be successful and no response to circular appeals. Individual companies within the group have their own charitable budgets.

☐ Stormgard plc
Stationery & fashion wear

26 Broad Street,
Wokingham,
Berkshire RG11 1AB

Ch: W H Holmes
MD: D W Dunn
Contact: G Moyse
Commercial Director

Year Ends: 31 Mar '90
Donations: £6,357
Profit: £16,376,000
Turnover: £53,390,000

UK employees: n/a
Total employees: 1,150

Donations Policy: Preference for local charities in the areas of company presence, especially children and youth, medical, education and recreation. Generally no support for advertising in charity brochures, appeals from individuals or purely denominational (religious) appeals.

☐ Stormont Ltd
Ford & motor cycle distributors

3 Mount Ephraim,
Tunbridge Wells,
Kent TN4 8AG
0892-515666

Ch: J H Cleland
Contact: B Jenner
Marketing Manager

Year Ends: 31 Dec '89
Donations: £11,568 (1988)
Profit: £4,315,000
Turnover: £111,902,000

UK employees: n/a
Total employees: 556

☐ Strand VCI plc
Entertainment & leisure

Strand VCI House,
Caxton Way,
Watford,
Hertfordshire WD1 8UF
0923-255558

Ch: A I Phillips
Contact: Pauline Clerk
Personnel Manager

Year Ends: 31 Dec '91
Donations: nil
Profit: (£9,441,000)
Turnover: £70,196,000

UK employees: n/a
Total employees: 501

☐ Strong & Fisher (Holdings) plc
Clothing & fashion leather tanners

100 Irchester Road,
Rushden,
Northamptonshire NN10 9XQ
0933-410300

Ch: M Buswell
Contact: P F Morgan
Company Secretary

Year Ends: 31 Dec '91
Donations: £4,792
Profit: £1,717,000
Turnover: £114,591,000

UK employees: n/a
Total employees: 1,313

Donations Policy: Preference for local charities in the areas of company presence, especially projects involving children and youth or recreation. Grants to national organisations from £10 to £100. Grants to local organisations from £10 to £1,000.
Generally no support for circular appeals, fundraising events, brochure advertising, appeals from individuals, purely denominational appeals, local appeals not in areas of company presence, large national appeals or overseas projects.

Please read page 6 — Alphabetical listing

Name/Address	Officers	Financial Information	Other Information

☐ Sturge Holdings plc
Management services

9 Devonshire Square,
London EC2M 4YL
071-617 2000

Ch: D Coleridge
MD: P Rawlins
Contact: A J Brown
Company Secretary

Year Ends: 30 Sep '89
Donations: £24,777
Profit: £31,158,000
Turnover: £43,294,000

UK employees: n/a
Total employees: 1,111

Donations Policy: Preference for local charities in areas where the company operates and for charities in which a member of company staff is involved. Preference for children and youth; sick and elderly; medical. The company supports staff sponsorship and has made a donation to the Great Ormond Street Hospital Appeal. Donations are generally between £50 and £200.
No support for advertising in charity brochures.

☐ Stylo plc
Footwear retailers & wholesalers

Harrogate Road,
Apperley Bridge,
Bradford,
West Yorkshire BD10 0NW
0274-617761

Ch: I A Ziff
Contact: Alwin Ziff
Director

Year Ends: 31 Jan '92
Donations: £1,700
Profit: (£9,060,000)
Turnover: £91,888,000

UK employees: n/a
Total employees: 2,994

☐ Sulzer UK Holdings Ltd
General engineering

Westmead,
Farnborough,
Hampshire GU14 7LP
0252-544311

Contact: O H Peltzer
Finance Director

Year Ends: 31 Dec '90
Donations: £4,000
Profit: £880,000
Turnover: £129,782,000

UK employees: 1,271
Total employees: n/a

☐ Sumitomo Bank (UK) plc
Banking

Temple Court,
11 Queen Victoria Street,
London EC4N 4TA
071-971 1000

Contact: Personnel Department

Year Ends: 31 Mar '91
Donations: n/a
Profit: £8,573,000
Turnover: 7,542,767,000

UK employees: n/a
Total employees: 137

BitC

Donations Policy: As a member of the Per Cent Club, the company probably gave at least £43,600 in charitable donations in 1990. The American branch of the Bank made a donation of £1,000,000 to Eton College for a Japan programme.

☐ Sumitomo Corporation (UK) plc
Metals, oils, chemicals & textiles etc. traders

107 Cheapside,
London EC2V 6DQ
071-726 6262

Contact: John McCready
Senior Research & Information
Executive

Year Ends: 31 Mar '91
Donations: n/a
Profit: £8,573,000
Turnover: 7,542,767,000

UK employees: n/a
Total employees: 137

Donations Policy: The company states "we have a charity committee that allocates the budget pro-actively so we do not respond to appeals".

☐ Sun Alliance Group plc
Insurance

1 Bartholomew Lane,
London EC2N 2AB
071-588 2345

Ch: H U A Lambert
CE: R A G Neville
Contact: Mrs Stephanie Clarke
Charities Administration Officer

Year Ends: 31 Dec '91
Donations: £299,000
Profit: (£466,200,000)
Turnover: n/a

UK employees: 19,497
Total employees: n/a

BitC

Donations Policy: Main areas of support are medical research charities and social welfare organisations. Preference for national charities.

☐ Sun Life Association Society
Insurance

107 Cheapside,
London EC2V 6DU
071-606 7788

Ch: P J Grant
MD: J Reeve
Contact: T R Hegarty (see address below)
Administrator, Charitable
Appeals Committee

Year Ends: 31 Dec '91
Donations: £299,741
Profit: £41,700,000
Turnover: n/a

UK employees: n/a
Total employees: 3,418

% Club, BitC

Donations Policy: A list of priority charities is established at the beginning of each year. Preference for social welfare, medical and enterprise/training, although good appeals from other categories will be considered. Preference is given to appeals from organisations which are active in London and Bristol. Grants to national organisations from £1,000 to £10,000; grants to local organisations from £50 to £5,000.
Generally no support for non-charities, campaigning work by charities, circular appeals, fundraising events, advertising in charity brochures, appeals from individuals, purely denominational (religious) appeals or local appeals not in areas of company presence.
Contact T R Hegarty, Administrator of the Charitable Appeals Committee, Sun Life Court, St James Barton, Bristol BS99 7SL.

☐ Sun Microsystems Ltd
Computer equipment dealers

Sun House,
31-41 Pembroke Broadway,
Camberley,
Surrey GU15 3XD
0276-62111

MD: W W Passmore
Contact: Clare Brindell
Administrator, Human Resources

Year Ends: 30 Jun '90
Donations: n/a
Profit: £3,820,000
Turnover: £120,650,000

UK employees: n/a
Total employees: 443

Alphabetical listing

Please read page 6

Name/Address	Officers	Financial Information	Other Information

☐ Sunley Holdings Ltd

Building contractors

105 Park Street,
London W1Y 3FB
071-499 8842

Contact: J B Sunley

Year Ends:
Donations: n/a
Profit: n/a
Turnover: n/a

UK employees: n/a
Total employees: n/a

% Club

Donations Policy: The company's donations appear to be separate from those made by the Bernard Sunley Charity Foundation which makes annual donations of over £2,500,000 each year (for further details see A Guide To The Major Trusts).

☐ Surridge Dawson (Holdings) Ltd

Newspaper & magazine wholesalers

6th Floor (South Wing),
AMP House,
Dingwall Road,
Croydon CR0 9XA
081-680 9500

Ch: P M Brown
MD: J W Reddington
Contact: W D Clark
Company Secretary

Year Ends: 27 Jan '91
Donations: n/a
Profit: £3,879,000
Turnover: £167,133,000

UK employees: n/a
Total employees: 1,273

☐ Suter plc

Refrigeration contracting & equipment

St Vincents,
Grantham,
Lincolnshire NG31 9EJ
0476-76767

Ch: J D Abell
Contact: Mrs R Wright
Secretary to the Chairman

Year Ends: 31 Dec '91
Donations: £10,493
Profit: £17,800,000
Turnover: £205,700,000

UK employees: n/a
Total employees: 2,912

Donations Policy: Preference for local charities in the areas of company presence or appeals relevant to company business.

☐ Swan Hunter Shipbuilders Ltd

Shipbuilders

Wallsend Shipyard,
Wallsend,
Tyne & Wear NE28 6EQ

Contact: G R Woosey

Year Ends: 5 Oct '90
Donations: £6,287 (1991)
Profit: £5,083,000
Turnover: £115,412,000

UK employees: n/a
Total employees: 2,948

Donations Policy: The charitable budget is very limited and the company therefore confines its support to local charities with a connection with shipbuilding. Support also for medical, educational, environmental and enterprise/training charities. Grants to national organisations from £10 to £25. Grants to local organisations from £10 to £5,000.
Generally no support for circular appeals, fundraising events, advertising in charity brochures, appeals from individuals, purely denominational (religious) appeals, large national appeals or overseas projects.

☐ Swan Steel

Steel merchants

Barlow Road,
Broadheath,
Altrincham WA14 5HG
061-929 1909

Ch: W C Shaw
Contact: John MacDonald
Chief Executive

Year Ends: 31 Dec '90
Donations: n/a
Profit: £6,022,000
Turnover: £128,735,000

UK employees: n/a
Total employees: 465

☐ John Swire & Sons Ltd

Shipowners, road transport

Swire House,
59 Buckingham Gate,
London SW1E 6AJ
071-834 7717

Ch: Sir Adrian Swire
Contact: Mrs J Slade
Secretary

Year Ends: 31 Dec '91
Donations: £1,625,000
Profit: £430,000,000
Turnover: £2,591,000,000

UK employees: n/a
Total employees: 32,617

Donations Policy: The donations figure given is for world-wide donations. Main interests are the arts, medicine and education.

☐ T & N plc

Construction & engineering manufacture, plastic

Bowden House,
Ashburton Road West,
Trafford Park,
Manchester M17 1RA
061-872 0155

Ch: C F N Hope
Contact: Mrs S L Miller
Corporate Communications
Manager

Year Ends: 31 Dec '91
Donations: £104,522
Profit: £84,000,000
Turnover: £1,188,000,000

UK employees: n/a
Total employees: 40,280

Donations Policy: Preference for local charities in the areas of company presence, appeals related to company business and charities in which a member of staff is involved. Preference for education and medical. Grants range from £100 to £2,500.

☐ T & S Stores plc

Tobacco & confectionery retailers

Apex Road,
Brownhills,
Walsall WS8 7HU
0543-371977

Ch: K P Threlfall
MD: D Lockett-Smith
Contact: Kath Allen, Secretary to
the Retail Operational Director

Year Ends: 31 Dec '91
Donations: £2,000
Profit: £13,358,000
Turnover: £314,227,000

UK employees: n/a
Total employees: 2,841

☐ Tandem Computers Ltd

Computer systems

7 Roundwood Avenue,
Stockley Park,
Uxbridge UB11 1AU
081-569 1290

Ch: J Chapman
MD: D Everett
Contact: C Brodie
Financial Director

Year Ends: 30 Sep '90
Donations: £13,377
Profit: £1,503,000
Turnover: £97,607,000

UK employees: n/a
Total employees: 372

Please read page 6 — Alphabetical listing

Name/Address	Officers	Financial Information	Other Information

☐ Tarmac plc — Road stone & civil engineering

Hilton Hall,
Essington,
Wolverhampton,
West Midlands WV11 2BQ
0902-307407

Ch: Sir Eric Pountain
MD: B W Baker
Contact: A C Smith
Group Secretary

Year Ends: 31 Dec '91
Donations: £271,000
Profit: £21,000,000
Turnover: £3,225,100,000

UK employees: n/a
Total employees: 31,734

% Club, BitC

Donations Policy: The company is especially committed to the communities in which it is based. It gives to a wide range of projects and charities, from small business development to medical research and care, and including youth, religious and environmental enterprises. Grants to national organisations from £250 to £5,000; grants to local organisations from £50 to £5,000. Subsidiary companies sponsor the arts in their localities.
No support for circular appeals, appeals from individuals and local appeals not in areas of company presence.
As donations are made out of company profits the current economic recession has inevitably affected Tarmac's ability to respond to any appeals.

☐ Tate & Lyle plc — Sugar refiners, commodity traders

Sugar Quay,
Lower Thames Street,
London EC3R 6DQ
071-626 6525

Ch: N M Shaw
CE: S R Brown
Contact: G D Down
Assistant Secretary

Year Ends: 28 Sep '91
Donations: £260,000
Profit: £234,600,000
Turnover: £3,221,100,000

UK employees: 3,870
Total employees: 17,500

% Club, BitC

Donations Policy: Main areas of support are education, causes close to where the company operates, appeals relevant to company business and those with employee involvement. National charities are also supported, with preference for health and welfare. Children and youth, environment, arts and enterprise/training have also been supported. Grants to national and local organisations from £250 to £10,000.
No response to circular appeals. Generally no support for fundraising events, advertising in charity brochures, appeals from individuals, purely denominational (religious) appeals, local appeals not in areas of company presence or large national appeals.
Total community contributions in 1991 were £315,000. Sponsorship proposals should be addressed to D M Dale.

☐ Taunton Cider Co Ltd — Cider manufacturers

Norton Fitzwarren,
Taunton,
Somerset TA2 6RD
0823-332211

Ch: C F M Roberts
MD: J C G Stocks
Contact: Ms Jeanette Keech
Public Relations Manager

Year Ends: 6 May '91
Donations: £14,020
Profit: £10,264,000
Turnover: £100,760,000

UK employees: n/a
Total employees: 425

Donations Policy: Most of the companies donations are made through sponsorship proposals with the voluntary sector. The sponsorship committee meets every month. All sponsorship proposals, except those involving motor sponsorship, are considered on merit. The company are also careful when considering child related sponsorship.

☐ Tay Homes plc — Residential estate designers

Tay House,
55 Call Lane,
Leeds LS1 7BT
0532-426262

Ch: D T Spencer
MD: N A Stubbs
Contact: S Evans
Company Secretary

Year Ends: 30 Jun '91
Donations: £4,027
Profit: £8,257,000
Turnover: £70,583,000

UK employees: n/a
Total employees: 332

☐ Taylor Woodrow plc — Builders & civil engineering contractors

World Trade Centre,
St Katharines Way,
London E1 8TU
071-499 8871

Ch: C J Parsons
CE: H A Palmer
Contact: Ruth Barber
Trustee, Taylor Woodrow
Charitable Trust

Year Ends: 31 Dec '91
Donations: £126,911
Profit: (£2,700,000)
Turnover: £1,394,500,000

UK employees: n/a
Total employees: 8,884

% Club

Donations Policy: The company has the Taylor Woodrow Charity Trust. No particular preferences, but continues to support a wide range of charitable organisations and maintains an active interest in promoting relevant education. Each application is considered on its merits.

☐ Tektronix UK Ltd — Oscilloscope manufacturers

Fourth Avenue,
Globe Park,
Marlow,
Buckinghamshire SL7 1YD
0628 486000

Ch: F Doyle
MD: G J Kersels
Contact: K Gilbert
Secretary to the Managing Director

Year Ends: 27 May '89
Donations: £3,373
Profit: £2,839,000
Turnover: £53,298,000

UK employees: n/a
Total employees: 514

Donations Policy: The company do not support political organisations or purely denominational appeals. The company do support interdenominational charities; organisations local to company operations and charities with staff involvement. Some national charities are supported, these will be considered on merit.

☐ Telegraph plc — Newspaper proprietors

1 Canada Square,
Canary Wharf,
London E14 5DT
071-538 5000

Ch: C M Black
MD: P J D Cooke
Contact: Mrs Rosemary Millar
Chairman of the Appeals Committee

Year Ends: 31 Dec '91
Donations: £202,720
Profit: £40,544,000
Turnover: £219,120,000

UK employees: n/a
Total employees: 1,019

ABSA

Donations Policy: To support health related charities including research, emergency medical supplies and hospices; education with emphasis on rehabilitation, deprivation and disability; charities connected with company business. Generally no support for circular appeals, fundraising events, advertising in charity brochures, appeals from individuals or purely denominational (religious) appeals.

● **Alphabetical listing** Please read page 6

Name/Address	Officers	Financial Information	Other Information

☐ Tennants Consolidated Ltd
Chemical manufacturers

69 Grosvenor Street,
London W1X 0BP
071-493 5451

Contact: K A Alexander
Chairman

Year Ends: 31 Dec '90
Donations: £24,000
Profit: £11,892,000
Turnover: £144,998,000

UK employees: n/a
Total employees: 1,147

Donations Policy: The company make all their charitable donations through the Charities Aid Foundation.

☐ Tenneco Europe Ltd
Manufacturing

Leconfield House,
Curzon Street,
London W1Y 8JR
071-409 3900

Ch: Ken Carr
Contact: R Cecil
Vice President

Year Ends:
Donations: n/a
Profit: n/a
Turnover: n/a

UK employees: n/a
Total employees: n/a

Donations Policy: Appeals in writing only. Preference for local charities in the areas of company presence and charities in which a member of staff is involved. Preferred areas of support: children and youth, social welfare, enterprise/training and the arts.
No advertising in charity brochures, appeals from individuals or purely denominational (religious) appeals.

☐ Tesco plc
Multiple retailing

Tesco House,
Delamare Road,
Cheshunt,
Hertfordshire EN8 9SL
0992-32222

Ch: Sir Ian MacLaurin
MD: A D Malpas
Contact: Linda Marsh
Secretary to the Charitable Trust

Year Ends: 29 Feb '92
Donations: £260,000
Profit: £545,500,000
Turnover: £7,097,400,000

UK employees: n/a
Total employees: 87,033

% Club, BitC

Donations Policy: Preference for local charities in areas of company presence, especially in the fields of children and youth, social welfare, education, medicine, the environment and the arts. Grants to national organisations are £100 and over; grants to local organisations from £10 to £500.
No support for circular appeals, fundraising, individuals, purely denominational appeals, overseas or building projects.
Total community contributions in 1989/90 totalled £4,600,000.

☐ Tetra Pak Ltd
Packaging materials & machines

31-35 High Street,
Kingston-upon-Thames,
Surrey KT1 1LF
081-546 2188

Contact: Peter Wiggs
Manager of Communications
Department

Year Ends: 31 Dec '91
Donations: £67,000
Profit: £9,031,000
Turnover: £137,552,000

UK employees: n/a
Total employees: 233

Donations Policy: The company has no set policy; all applications are considered on merit.

☐ Texaco Ltd
Oil Industry

1 Knightsbridge Green,
London SW1X 7QJ
071-584 5000

Ch: G F Tilton
Contact: June Parham
Co-ordinator, Community Affairs

Year Ends: 31 Dec '90
Donations: £63,771
Profit: £148,394,000
Turnover: £4,135,223,000

UK employees: n/a
Total employees: 3,358

BitC, ABSA

Donations Policy: The company usually selects a particular area to support each year. Preference for local charities in areas where the company operates. Preference for children and youth; medical; education; environment/heritage; arts. Total UK community contributions in 1991 were £351,500.
No response to circular appeals. No grants for fundraising events; advertising in charity brochures; appeals from individuals; purely denominational (religious) appeals; local appeals not in areas of company presence; overseas projects; parliamentary appeals.

☐ Texas Instruments Ltd
Electronic component manufacturers

Manton Lane,
Bedford MK41 7PA
0234-270111

Ch: J B Butcher MP
MD: K J Sanders
Contact: Penny Fattori
Donations & Sponsorship
Secretary

Year Ends: 31 Dec '90
Donations: £28,087
Profit: £2,193,000
Turnover: £140,814,000

UK employees: 800
Total employees: 60,000

Donations Policy: Support is only given to organisations based in Bedford postal area, with preference for charities in which a member of company staff is involved. Preferred areas of support; children and youth; social welfare; medical; education; environment/heritage; enterprise/training; elderly and disabled people.
No grants for purely denominational (religious) appeals; large national appeals; overseas projects; appeals from outside the Bedford area.

☐ Thames Water plc
Water & sewerage services

Nugent House,
Vastern Road,
Reading,
Berkshire RG1 8DM
071-636 8686

Ch: Sir Roy Watts
CE: Mike Hoffman
Contact: Julian Le Patourel

Year Ends: 31 Mar '92
Donations: £106,000
Profit: £236,300,000
Turnover: £899,300,000

UK employees: n/a
Total employees: 9,015

BitC

Donations Policy: Preference for appeals relevant to company business. Preferred areas of support: social welfare, medical, education, environment and heritage. There is a staff payroll giving scheme which supports WaterAid, and this is likely to remain the only overseas charity supported by the company.
No support for brochure advertising, purely denominational appeals, local appeals not in areas of company presence, overseas projects.

Please read page 6 — Alphabetical listing

Name/Address	Officers	Financial Information	Other Information

☐ Thomson Corporation
Oil, travel, printing, publishing

The Quadrangle,
PO Box 4YG,
180 Wardour Street,
London W1A 4YG
071-437 9787

Ch: Lord Thomson of Fleet
Contact: Hilary Bateson
Information Manager

Year Ends: 31 Dec '90
Donations: £200,000
Profit: £17,400,000
Turnover: £1,530,200,000

UK employees: n/a
Total employees: 19,242

Donations Policy: The company supports major national charities connected with medical research, disability and social welfare. Recipient organisations must be registered charities and audited accounts should be supplied with any application. It gives 40 to 50 donations a year ranging from £200 to £5,000.
Generally no support for fundraising events, appeals from individuals, purely denominational (religious) appeals, local appeals not in areas of company presence. No sponsorships or advertising.

☐ D C Thomson & Co Ltd
Printer

Albert Square,
Dundee DD1 9QJ
0382-23131

Ch: B H Thomson
Contact: A McDougall
Company Secretary

Year Ends: 31 Mar '89
Donations: £6,483
Profit: n/a
Turnover: n/a

UK employees: n/a
Total employees: 2,761

Donations Policy: The company only considers appeals related to the publishing industry or from local charities.

☐ Thorn EMI plc
Electrical & electronic engineering, music

4 Tenterden Street,
Hanover Square,
London W1A 2AY
071-355 4848

Ch: Sir Colin Southgate
Contact: Claire Baker
Public Relations Manager

Year Ends: 31 Mar '92
Donations: £1,052,000
Profit: £255,100,000
Turnover: £3,954,400,000

UK employees: 31,200
Total employees: 53,757

% Club, BitC, ABSA

Donations Policy: Particular emphasis on the performing arts. The company has a wide programme of support encompassing disabled people and community welfare, education, environment and health, enterprise and training, in the UK and overseas. Preference for local charities in areas where the company operates, appeals relevant to company business and charities in which a member of company staff is involved. Grants to national organisations from £200 to £25,000. Grants to local organisations from £50 to £5,000. Total community contributions in 1991/92 were £4 million.
No grants for appeals from individuals; purely denominational (religious) appeals; political organisations.

☐ Thorntons plc
Confectionery manufacturers

Thornton Park,
Somercote,
Derby DE55 4XJ
0773-824181

Ch: C J Thornton
Contact: Mrs Liz Cooke
Secretary to the Deputy Chairman

Year Ends: 29 Jun '91
Donations: £62,000
Profit: £11,880,000
Turnover: £79,911,000

UK employees: n/a
Total employees: 2,000

% Club

Donations Policy: The company helps to finance schools/industry initiatives and sponsor events and organisations which are mainly local to its principal areas of operation. "We donate annually quantities of confectionery mainly in small amounts in support of a wide variety of charitable events. Our budget for straight financial gifting is limited and we prefer to restrict this to children's charities, to local causes and to charities with which our employees are involved." Preference for children and youth, social welfare, and environment and heritage. Grants to local organisations from £50 to £2,000.
No support for circulars, advertising in charity brochures, individuals, purely denominational (religious) appeals, or overseas projects.

☐ 3i Group plc
Capital investment

91 Waterloo Road,
London SE1 8XP
071-928 3131

Ch: Sir John Cuckney
CE: D E Marlow
Contact: Mrs J A Bowden
Executive Assistant

Year Ends: 31 Mar '92
Donations: £250,000
Profit: £40,075,000
Turnover: n/a

UK employees: n/a
Total employees: 969

% Club, ABSA

Donations Policy: Preference for appeals in areas of company presence or with staff involvement. Some arts sponsorship and secondments to charities.
No support for non-charities, individuals, advertising in charity brochures or bricks and mortar appeals.

☐ 3M UK Holdings plc
Coated materials & related products

3M House,
PO Box 1,
Bracknell RG12 1JU
0344-858000

Ch: John W Benson
Contact: Francis Brawn
Community Relations Manager

Year Ends: 31 Oct '91
Donations: £219,000
Profit: £31,548,000
Turnover: £509,869,000

UK employees: n/a
Total employees: 5,009

% Club, ABSA

Donations Policy: Supports a range of national charitable initiatives from relief of suffering, education and the arts. Support also for local community causes in and around the company's UK sites. Preference for appeals relevant to company business and charities in which a member of company staff is involved. Grants to national organisations from £1,500 to £50,000. Grants to local organisations from £50 to £5,000.
No grants for advertising in charity brochures; appeals from individuals; purely denominational (religious) appeals; local appeals not in areas of company presence.

☐ Daniel Thwaites plc
Brewers

PO Box 50,
Star Brewery,
Blackburn,
Lancashire BB1 5BU
0254-54431

Ch: J M A Yerburgh
MD: J D Kay
Contact: Mike Law or P A Baker
Marketing Manager or Sales Director respectively

Year Ends: 31 Mar '92
Donations: £4,673
Profit: £4,176,000
Turnover: £72,741,000

UK employees: n/a
Total employees: 1,650

• **Alphabetical listing**   Please read page 6

Name/Address	Officers	Financial Information	Other Information

☐ TI Group plc
General engineers

Lambourn Court,
Abingdon Business Park,
Abingdon,
Oxon OX14 1UH
0235-555570

Ch: C Lewinton
Contact: D P Lillycrop
Group Secretary

Year Ends: 31 Dec '91
Donations: £173,500
Profit: £105,200,000
Turnover: £899,500,000

UK employees: n/a
Total employees: 17,100

% Club, BitC, ABSA

Donations Policy: Main areas of support are the arts and culture, social welfare, community services, health and medical, conservation and the environment, education, science and enterprise. Within these broad categories, particular support is given to organisations dealing with major social problems, young unemployed people, training and re-training initiatives, drug abuse and stress. Preference for local charities in areas where the company operates.
No grants for circular appeals; fundraising events; advertising in charity brochures; appeals from individuals; purely denominational (religious) appeals; local appeals not in areas of company presence.
The group also sponsors the arts. Proposals for sponsorship should be addressed to J B Hutchings at the Head Office: 50 Curzon Street, London W1N 9DF.

☐ Tibbett & Britten Group plc
Transportation & distribution services

Ross House,
1 Shirley Road,
Windmill Hill,
Enfield,
Middlesex EN2 6SB
081-366 9595

Ch: J A Harvey
Contact: M R Stalbow
Finance Director

Year Ends: 31 Dec '91
Donations: £22,888
Profit: £13,460,000
Turnover: £181,233,000

UK employees: n/a
Total employees: 6,186

Donations Policy: The company supports worthwhile charities and projects, both local and national. Donations are usually £100 to £300 and paid in Charities Aid Foundation vouchers.
The company will not support individuals.

☐ Tilbury Douglas plc
Construction & property

Tilbury House,
Ruscombe Park,
Twyford,
Reading,
Berkshire RG10 9JU
0734-320123

Ch: J R T Douglas
CE: M C Bottjer
Contact: L Richardson
Company Secretary

Year Ends: 31 Dec '91
Donations: £3,243
Profit: £15,034,000
Turnover: £239,582,000

UK employees: n/a
Total employees: 3,077

BitC

☐ Time Products plc
Horological & associated activities

23 Grosvenor Street,
London W1X 9FE
071-416 4160

Ch: R N D Langdon
MD: M J Margulies
Contact: Secretary to the Directors

Year Ends: 31 Jan '92
Donations: £320
Profit: £7,615,000
Turnover: £51,063,000

UK employees: n/a
Total employees: 1,099

☐ Tioxide Group Ltd
Titanium oxide & titanium compounds

Tioxide House,
137-143 Hammersmith Road,
London W14 0QL
071-602 7121

Ch: A E Pedder
Contact: See below

Year Ends: 31 Dec '90
Donations: £270,000
Profit: £607,000
Turnover: £203,459,000

UK employees: n/a
Total employees: n/a

Donations Policy: Support mainly in Teesside and Humberside where company has its factories. Grants to national organisations from £500 to £5,000. Grants to local organisations from £100 to £1,000.
No response to circular appeals. No support for non-charities, advertising in charity brochures or fundraising events.
Teesside charitable appeals to Mrs D Hunter, Tioxide Europe Ltd, Haverton Hill Road, Billingham, Cleveland TS23 1PS. Grimsby area appeals to M Hinnigan, Tioxide Europe Ltd, Moody Lane, Grimsby, South Humberside DN31 2SW. In addition to charitable donations, community contributions in 1990 totalled £100,000.

☐ TIP Europe plc
Rental & leasing of trailers

Hilltop,
Pontefract Road,
Nottingley,
West Yorkshire WF11 8SP
0296-395050

Contact: J Cleary
Chairman

Year Ends: 31 Jul '91
Donations: £945
Profit: £6,009,000
Turnover: £103,094,000

UK employees: n/a
Total employees: 294

☐ Tiphook plc
Container manufacturers & rental

26 St James's Square,
London SW1Y 4JH
071-930 2000

Ch: R J Montague
MD: C A Palmer
Contact: Susan Ville
Director of Corporate Communications

Year Ends: 30 Apr '92
Donations: £132,417
Profit: £86,400,000
Turnover: £322,400,000

UK employees: n/a
Total employees: 975

% Club, BitC

Donations Policy: The company has a programme of long-term commitment to a number of important social and medical organisations, such as the Prince's Youth Business Trust and the British Diabetes Association. It also supports appeals in the communities where it operates.

Please read page 6 — Alphabetical listing

Name/Address	Officers	Financial Information	Other Information

☐ TMD Advertising Holdings Ltd
Advertising

143 Long Acre,
London WC2E 9AD
071-836 3456

Ch: D S Reich
MD: Mark Craze
Contact: Paul Greenhalgh
Financial Director

Year Ends: 31 Aug '87
Donations: £355
Profit: £885,000
Turnover: £51,015,000

UK employees: n/a
Total employees: 59

☐ TNT (UK) Ltd
Transportation services

TNT Express House,
Ables Way,
Atherstone,
Warwickshire CV9 2YR
0827 303030

Contact: Alan Jones
Managing Director

Year Ends: 29 Jun '91
Donations: n/a
Profit: £2,457,000
Turnover: £406,509,000

UK employees: n/a
Total employees: 8,928

☐ Tomkins plc
Manufacture of light industrial goods

East Putney House,
84 Upper Richmond Road,
London SW15 2ST
081-871 4544

Ch: M R N Moore
CE: G F Hutchings
Contact: V Goold
Personal Assistant to the Chief Executive

Year Ends: 2 May '91
Donations: £106,157
Profit: £112,098,000
Turnover: £1,039,026,000

UK employees: n/a
Total employees: 16,865

Donations Policy: Company policy is to give little and often "thus enabling our funds to be spread over as wide a field as possible". The company makes donations of £369,236 in the USA.
No support for overseas projects.

☐ Tomkinsons plc
Yarn & carpet manufacturer

PO Box 11,
Duke Place,
Kidderminster DY10 2JR
0562-820006

Ch: L D Maclean
Contact: M A Hield
Managing Director

Year Ends: 30 Sep '91
Donations: £8,917
Profit: £1,284,000
Turnover: £21,257,000

UK employees: n/a
Total employees: 450

Donations Policy: Preference for local charities in areas where the company operates, particularly in the fields of children and youth and education.

☐ Toshiba Information Systems (UK) Ltd
Photocopier, facsimile machines, portable computers

Toshiba Court,
Weybridge Business Park,
Addlestone, Weybridge,
Surrey KT15 2UL
0932-841600

MD: T Sato
Contact: Penny Patman
Secretary to the Managing Director

Year Ends: 31 Mar '92
Donations: £30,000
Profit: n/a
Turnover: £100,000,000

UK employees: 220
Total employees: n/a

Donations Policy: Preference for charities in areas of company presence, working in the areas of: children and youth; elderly and infirm; social welfare; medical; education; the arts. Grants to local organisations from £50 to £5,000.
No response to circular appeals. The company does not support appeals from individuals; purely denominational appeals; large national appeals; overseas projects.

☐ Toshiba (UK) Ltd
Electrical equipment

Toshiba House,
Frimley Road,
Frimley,
Camberley GU16 5JJ
0276-62222

Contact: Lesley Haynes
Marketing Supervisor

Year Ends: 31 Mar '91
Donations: n/a
Profit: £234,000
Turnover: £266,646,000

UK employees: n/a
Total employees: 1,321

BitC

☐ Total Oil Marine plc
Crude oil refining, petroleum products distribution

16 Palace Street,
London SW1E 5BQ
071-416 4200

Ch: Sir Philip Jones
MD: C Bryce
Contact: Peter Gavan
Corporate Communications Manager

Year Ends: 31 Dec '91
Donations: £40,017
Profit: £98,857,000
Turnover: £262,092,000

UK employees: n/a
Total employees: 784

Donations Policy: Preference for local charities in areas where the company operates and for appeals relevant to company business or which have a member of company staff involved. Preference for children and youth, and environment.
No response to circular appeals.

☐ Touche Ross & Co
Accountants

Peterborough Court,
133 Fleet Street,
London EC4A 2TR
071-936 3000

Contact: P M Stafford
Chairman

Year Ends:
Donations: n/a
Profit: n/a
Turnover: n/a

UK employees: n/a
Total employees: n/a

% Club, BitC

Donations Policy: Preference for children, youth and medical.
No grants for fundraising events; advertising in charity brochures; appeals from individuals; purely denominational (religious) appeals; local appeals not in areas of company presence; large national appeals; overseas projects. No response to circular appeals.

● **Alphabetical listing**   Please read page 6

Name/Address   *Officers*   *Financial Information*   *Other Information*

☐ Toyota (GB) Ltd
Vehicle import & distribution

The Quadrangle,   *Contact:* Simon Small   *Year Ends:* 31 Dec '89   *UK employees:* 400
Redhill,   *Donations:* £48,600   *Total employees:* n/a
Surrey RH1 1PX   *Profit:* n/a
0737-768585   *Turnover:* n/a   ABSA

Donations Policy: Grants are made to registered charities only, through the Toyota (GB) Charitable Trust. Grants are usually to national charities or local charities in areas of company presence, and for specific projects. Preference is given to charities that have a connection with motoring or the motor industry. The company also supports environmental and conservation projects, local education initiatives and the arts.
Total community contributions in 1989 were £100,100, including donations, sponsorship and in kind support.
No support for political or religious organisations or to overseas aid. No response to circular appeals.

☐ Toys "R" Us
Toys & children related products retailers

Geoffrey House,   *Ch:* D Rurka   *Year Ends:* 2 Feb '91   *UK employees:* n/a
Vanwall Business Park, *Contact:* Andrea Bolley   *Donations:* n/a   *Total employees:* 1,701
Vanwall Road,   Secretary to the Managing *Profit:* £18,362,000
Maidenhead,   Director   *Turnover:* £162,624,000
Berkshire FL6 4UB
0628-414141

Donations Policy: Donations of toys and gifts for fundraising events. The company makes no cash donations.

☐ Tozer Kemsley & Millbourn (Holdings) plc
Automotive distribution, property, timeshare, leisure

40 Church Street,   *Ch:* P D Collins   *Year Ends:* 31 Dec '90   *UK employees:* n/a
Staines,   *MD:* Reginald F Heath   *Donations:* £113,000   *Total employees:* 6,786
Middlesex TW18 4EP   *Contact:* Mrs Leatherer   *Profit:* £64,144,000
0784-460000   Personal Assistant to the Chief *Turnover:* £1,143,600,000
                              Executive

Donations Policy: The company only gives to BEN (The Motor and Allied Trade Benevolent Fund).

☐ Trafalgar House plc
Contracting, civil engineering, shipping

1 Berkeley Street,   *Ch:* Sir Nigel Broackes   *Year Ends:* 30 Sep '91   *UK employees:* n/a
London W1A 1BY   *CE:* Sir Eric Parker   *Donations:* £108,000   *Total employees:* 32,133
071-499 9020   *Contact:* I Fowler   *Profit:* £122,400,000
                              Company Secretary   *Turnover:* £3,202,400,000   ABSA

Donations Policy: Preference for appeals related to company business or close to company locations. National appeals also supported. The company's charity committee is made up of senior executives who decide which of the charity applications they will support.
The company sponsors the arts both nationally and locally. Sponsorship proposals should be addressed to W T Halford.

☐ Transport Development Group plc
Road transport, warehousing

Windsor House,   *Ch:* Sir James Duncan   *Year Ends:* 31 Dec '91   *UK employees:* n/a
50 Victoria Street,   *Contact:* John Kinley   *Donations:* £15,040   *Total employees:* 13,114
London SW1H 0NR   Company Secretary   *Profit:* £38,904,000
071-222-7411   *Turnover:* £584,280,000

Donations Policy: The company has no set policy, but donations are usually made to charities local to the areas where the company operates.

☐ Travellers Exchange Corporation plc
Bureaux de change operators

3-16 Woburn Place,   *Contact:* Lloyd Dorfman   *Year Ends:* 30 Dec '90   *UK employees:* n/a
London WC1H 0LS   *Donations:* n/a   *Total employees:* 376
071-278 3272   *Profit:* £39,000
                                                       Turnover: £224,037,000

☐ Travis Perkins plc
Timber products

Lodgeway House,   *Ch:* E R A Travis   *Year Ends:* 31 Dec '91   *UK employees:* n/a
Harlesdon Road,   *CE:* Alan Burridge   *Donations:* £20,603   *Total employees:* 3,684
Northampton NN5 7UG   *Contact:* Tom Glover   *Profit:* £14,004,000
0604-752424   Public Relations Manager *Turnover:* £310,291,000

Donations Policy: The company has about 200 branches nationwide. Local branch managers tend to nominate charities in their own areas, usually local organisations or local branches of national organisations. Donations are occasionally made to overseas charities. Grants are usually from £100 to £200 (but have been up to £1,000), paid in Charities Aid Foundation vouchers. The company have also made donations of materials eg. timber or sheeting.
Richard Mizen is in charge of the companies sponsorship and advertising budget.
No grants for advertising in charity brochures; appeals from individuals; local appeals not in areas of company presence; large national appeals.

Please read page 6 | Alphabetical listing ●

Name/Address	Officers	Financial Information	Other Information

☐ Trimoco plc
Retail motor dealers

77 London Road
Dunstable,
Bedfordshire LU6 3DT
0582-662262

Ch: R J Smith
Contact: R G Lee
Company Secretary

Year Ends: 31 Mar '92
Donations: £9,000
Profit: n/a
Turnover: £218,949,000

UK employees: 1,382
Total employees: 1,382

Donations Policy: Preference for local charities in areas of company presence and appeals relevant to the business (eg. BEN, the motor trades charity). Grants to national organisations up to £10,000; grants to local organisations from £50 to £500.
No response to circular appeals. No grants for fundraising events; advertising in charity brochures; appeals from individuals; purely denominational (religious) appeals; local appeals not in areas of company presence; large national appeals; overseas projects.

☐ Trinity International Holdings plc
Newspaper printing & publishing

6 Heritage Court,
Lower Bridge Street,
Chester CH1 1RD
0244-350555

Ch: S J Mosley
MD: D K Snedden
Contact: M P Ryan
Company Secretary

Year Ends: 31 Dec '91
Donations: £35,000
Profit: £13,303,000
Turnover: £135,493,000

UK employees: 1,787
Total employees: 3,158

Donations Policy: Preference for local charities in the Merseyside and North Wales areas. The papers produced include the Liverpool Echo and Daily Post, Mersey Mart and Wirral Globe.

☐ Triplex Lloyd plc
Foundries, engineers

Cranford House,
Cranford Street,
Smethwick,
Warley,
West Midlands B66 2RJ
021-555 6565

Ch: L Robertson
Contact: Julie Hill
Senior Executive

Year Ends: 31 Mar '91
Donations: £24,129
Profit: £7,568,000
Turnover: £200,256,000

UK employees: n/a
Total employees: 4,905

Donations Policy: The policy is under review. Probably preference for charities local to Birmingham and areas of company presence.

☐ Triumph International Ltd
Corsetry & swimwear manufacturer

PO Box 98,
Arkwright Road,
Groundwell,
Swindon,
Wiltshire SN2 5BE
0793-722200

Contact: Paul Santer
Personnel Manager

Year Ends:
Donations: n/a
Profit: n/a
Turnover: n/a

UK employees: n/a
Total employees: n/a

% Club

Donations Policy: Supports local charities in Thamesdown.
No response to circular appeals. No grants for fundraising events; advertising in charity brochures; appeals from individuals; purely denominational (religious) appeals; local appeals not in areas of company presence; large national appeals; overseas projects.

☐ TRW UK Ltd
Component manufacturers

Woden Road West,
Wednesbury,
West Midlands WS10 7SY
021-556 1212

MD: J Shaw
Contact: C Benefer
Personnel Manager

Year Ends: 31 Dec '90
Donations: £1,900
Profit: £2,341,000
Turnover: £142,216,000

UK employees: n/a
Total employees: 2,590

☐ Try Group plc
Contracting & construction

Cowley Business Park,
High Street,
Cowley,
Uxbridge UB8 2AL
0895-251222

Ch: H W Try
MD: P R Howell
Contact: H W Try
Chairman

Year Ends: 31 Dec '91
Donations: £3,005
Profit: £2,211,000
Turnover: £114,262,000

UK employees: n/a
Total employees: 515

Donations Policy: Preference for local charities in areas where the company operates and appeals relevant to company business.
No grants for local appeals not in areas of company presence or overseas projects.

☐ TSB Group plc
Banking

PO Box 33,
25 Milk Street,
London EC2V 8LU
071-606 7070

Ch: Sir Nicholas Goodison
MD: D McCrickard
Contact: Mrs K N Duncan
Director General, TSB Foundation
for England & Wales

Year Ends: 31 Oct '91
Donations: £3,352,000
Profit: (£47,000,000)
Turnover: n/a

UK employees: 39,773
Total employees: n/a

% Club, BitC, ABSA

Donations Policy: To support underfunded voluntary organisations, with an emphasis on helping disadvantaged and disabled people play their part in the community. Efforts are concentrated in two areas: social and community projects, and education and training. Grants to national organisations from £500 to £20,000; grants to local organisations from £50 to £5,000. Donations are made through the four TSB Foundations and applications should be made to the relevant one:
England & Wales: see above; Scotland: Mrs Margaret Robertson, Secretary, Henry Duncan House, 120 George Street, Edinburgh EH2 4TS; Northern Ireland: T A T Thompson, Secretary, 4 Queens Square, Belfast BT1 3DJ; Channel Islands: L P Bechelet, Assistant Secretary, 25 New Street, St Helier, Jersey.
Generally no support for circular appeals, fundraising events, advertising in charity brochures, appeals from individuals, purely denominational (religious) appeals, local appeals not in areas of company presence, large national appeals, overseas projects, animal welfare, geographic/scenic appeals.
Total community contributions in 1991 were £5,519,000. Sponsorship proposals to Mrs G Murkin, Sponsorship Manager.

● **Alphabetical listing** Please read page 6

Name/Address *Officers* *Financial Information* *Other Information*

☐ TSW - Television South West Holdings plc

Television programmes production

Derry's Cross,
Plymouth PL1 2SP
0752-663322

Ch: Sir Brian Bailey
MD: H Turner
Contact: David Sunderland
Director of Presentation & Public Relations

Year Ends: 31 Jul '90
Donations: £90,545
Profit: £4,702,000
Turnover: £44,003,000

UK employees: n/a
Total employees: 285

Donations Policy: Only groups operating within the TSW transmission area will be considered, with particular emphasis on the arts. Typical grants range from £10 to £2,000.
Generally no support for circular appeals, appeals from individuals, local appeals not in areas of company presence, large national appeals, overseas projects or commercial enterprises.
Arts sponsorship proposals to Jonathan Harvey at ACME, 15 Robinson Way, London E2 9LX.

☐ TT Group plc

Management services, industrial fasteners, packaging

Fernside Place,
12-13 Queens Road,
Weybridge,
Surrey KT13 9XB
0932-841 310

Contact: M G Leigh
Group Company Secretary

Year Ends: 30 Dec '91
Donations: £30,000
Profit: £14,638,000
Turnover: £158,315,000

UK employees: n/a
Total employees: 4,107

Donations Policy: The company has no set policy. Each application is considered on merit. Donations are generally under £1,000.

☐ Tulip International (UK)

Bacon processors

Caxton Way,
Thetford,
Norfolk IP24 3SB
0842-754521

Ch: B H Knudson
MD: S A Bernsen
Contact: Penny Meredith
Secretary to the Financial Director

Year Ends: 1 Oct '88
Donations: £3,213
Profit: £2,541,000
Turnover: £99,641,000

UK employees: n/a
Total employees: 1,217

☐ Tullett & Tokyo Forex International Ltd

International finance & investment company

Cable House,
54-62 New Broad Street,
London EC2M 1JJ
071-895 9595

MD: T J R Sanders
Contact: The President

Year Ends: 31 Dec '90
Donations: £21,115
Profit: £16,724,000
Turnover: £148,234,000

UK employees: n/a
Total employees: 1,615

Donations Policy: The company make donations to children's charities only.

☐ Tullis Russell & Co Ltd

Paper manufacturers

Markinch,
Glenrothes,
Fife KY7 6PB
0592-753311

Ch: D E Erdal
MD: J F S Daglish
Contact: Mrs C Croal
Tullis Russell Charities Committee

Year Ends: 31 Mar '92
Donations: £50,000
Profit: £889,000
Turnover: £95,962,000

UK employees: n/a
Total employees: 1,317

% Club

Donations Policy: Only supports local appeals in areas of company presence. Preference for children and youth; medical; education; environment/heritage; arts; enterprise/training. Grants to local organisations from £50 to £5,000.
No grants for fundraising events; advertising in charity brochures; purely denominational (religious) appeals; local appeals not in areas of company presence; large national appeals.

☐ Tunstall Group plc

Emergency communication equipment manufacture

Whitley Lodge,
Whitley Bridge,
South Yorkshire DN14 0HR
0977-661234

Ch: M J Dawson
MD: A J Stradling
Contact: Sharon Carroll
Personal Assistant to the Chairman

Year Ends: 30 Sep '91
Donations: £36,200
Profit: £4,370,000
Turnover: £37,139,000

UK employees: n/a
Total employees: 892

Donations Policy: Supports charities concerned with elderly people, especially Help the Aged. Trustees meet quarterly.

☐ TV AM plc

Breakfast TV contractor

Hawley Crescent,
London NW1 8EF
071-267 4300

Ch: I A N Irvine
Contact: B Gyngell
Managing Director

Year Ends: 31 Jan '90
Donations: £125,000
Profit: £24,037,000
Turnover: £80,827,000

UK employees: n/a
Total employees: 734

☐ Twil Ltd

Wire manufacturers

PO Box 119,
Shepcote Lane,
Sheffield S9 1TY
0742-561561

Ch: D W Ford
MD: D Young
Contact: R E Farris
Company Secretary

Year Ends: 31 Dec '90
Donations: £24,000
Profit: £9,085,000
Turnover: £285,250,000

UK employees: n/a
Total employees: 3,389

Donations Policy: The company supports youth and education, medical (especially research), welfare and benevolent charities, heritage, the environment and the arts. Preference also for local charities in the areas of company presence and appeals relevant to company business. Grants generally £25 to £500.
Generally no support for fundraising events, advertising in charity brochures, purely denominational (religious) appeals, local appeals not in areas of company presence.

Please read page 6 — Alphabetical listing

Name/Address	Officers	Financial Information	Other Information

☐ TWO (UK) Ltd
Petroleum products traders

Bishopstone,
36 Crescent Road,
Worthing,
West Sussex
071-930 3177

MD: Mrs J M Hale
CE: Miss M E Deuss
Contact: Company Secretary

Year Ends: 31 Dec '90
Donations: n/a
Profit: £2,066,000
Turnover: £1,428,738,000

UK employees: n/a
Total employees: n/a

Donations Policy: The office for donations may be Berkeley Street, London W1X 5AE.

☐ TWR Group Ltd
Motorsport, engineering, garage proprietors

Broadstone Grange,
Broadstone Hill,
Chipping Norton,
Oxon OX7 5QL
0608-678763

MD: T D T Wilkinshaw
Contact: Fiona Miller
Public Relations Manager

Year Ends: 31 Dec '90
Donations: n/a
Profit: £2,735,000
Turnover: £108,614,000

UK employees: n/a
Total employees: 664

Donations Policy: Preference for local charities in areas of company presence; appeals relevant to the business and projects/charities that have a member of staff involved.
The company does not support circular appeals.
For sponsorship proposals contact A King, Marketing Manager.

☐ Tyndall Holdings plc
Investment holding company

11th Floor,
Knightsbridge House,
197 Knightsbridge,
London SW7 1RB
071-412 0703

MD: K Kenny
Contact: Ms P G Edwards
Company Secretary

Year Ends: 31 Dec '91
Donations: £7,757
Profit: £209,000
Turnover: n/a

UK employees: n/a
Total employees: 369

Donations Policy: Preferred areas of support: children and youth, social welfare, medical, education.
Generally no support for circular appeals, appeals from individuals, purely denominational (religious) appeals, overseas projects.

☐ Tyne Tees Television Holdings plc
IBA TV programme contractors

The Television Centre,
City Road,
Newcastle-upon-Tyne NE1 2AL
091-261 0181

Ch: Sir Ralph Carr-Ellison
MD: I R Ritchie
Contact: Kathryn Cooper
Secretary to the Chairman

Year Ends: 31 Dec '91
Donations: £118,000
Profit: £213,000
Turnover: £58,283,000

UK employees: n/a
Total employees: 308

% Club, BitC, ABSA

Donations Policy: With the exception of grants made centrally to the television industry, the company aims to support regional community interests in industry, the arts, sport and charitable foundations. Grants to national organisations from £1,000 to £5,000. Grants to local organisations from £100 to £5,000. Total community contributions in 1991 were £192,000.
No response to circular appeals. No support for appeals from individuals, purely denominational (religious) appeals, local appeals not in areas of company presence, large national appeals, overseas projects, political appeals.
Sponsorship proposals to Peter Moth, Controller of Public Affairs.

☐ UCB Investments Ltd
Holding company

Star House,
69 Clarendon Road,
Watford WD1 1DJ
0923-248011

Contact: Financial Director

Year Ends: 31 Dec '90
Donations: n/a
Profit: £1,170,000
Turnover: £94,465,000

UK employees: n/a
Total employees: 1,269

☐ UGC Ltd
Automotive parts & accessories distribution

Unipart House,
Cowley,
Oxford OX4 2PG
0865-778966

Ch: R W Perry
CE: J M Neill
Contact: Patrick FitzGibbon
Public Relations Manager

Year Ends: 31 Dec '92
Donations: £35,000
Profit: £13,613,000
Turnover: £582,032,000

UK employees: n/a
Total employees: 4,590

Donations Policy: Preference for local charities in areas where the company operates, appeals relevant to company business and for charities in which a member of company staff is involved. Preference for children and youth; social welfare; medical; education; recreation; enterprise/training.
No grants for purely denominational (religious) appeals; overseas projects or animal charities.

☐ UK Corrugated
Corrugated container manufacturer

Starhouse,
69-71 Clarenden Road,
Watford WD1 1SB
0923-242306

Contact: P A Barrett
Chief Executive

Year Ends: 31 Dec '90
Donations: £5,432
Profit: £337,000
Turnover: £120,965,000

UK employees: n/a
Total employees: 1,794

☐ UK Paper plc
Paper products manufacture & merchanting

UK Paper House,
Kemsley,
Sittingbourne,
Kent ME10 2SG
0795-424488

Ch: T H Wilding
Contact: A Jeffs
Personnel Director

Year Ends: 30 Jun '91
Donations: £2,000
Profit: £600,000
Turnover: £217,900,000

UK employees: n/a
Total employees: 1,837

● **Alphabetical listing**   Please read page 6

Name/Address	Officers	Financial Information	Other Information

☐ **Ulster Television plc**   *Independent TV programme contractors*

Havelock House,
Ormeau Road,
Belfast BT7 1EB
0232-328122

Ch: R B Henderson
MD: J D Smyth
Contact: Mrs Linda Stirling

Year Ends: 31 Dec '91
Donations: £1,400
Profit: £1,946,000
Turnover: £25,145,000

UK employees: 299
Total employees: n/a

ABSA

Donations Policy: Priority to organisations concerned with the arts, sciences and television industry. Donations are only made to local charities.

☐ **UniChem plc**   *Pharmaceutical distribution services*

UniChem House,
Cox Lane,
Chessington,
Surrey KT9 1SN
081-391 2323

Ch: Lord Rippon of Hexham
CE: J F Harris
Contact: A J Goodenough
Company Secretary

Year Ends: 31 Dec '91
Donations: £10,000
Profit: £21,397,000
Turnover: £920,105,000

UK employees: 2,852
Total employees: 2,852

Donations Policy: "A fixed annual sum is paid to the Charities Aid Foundation, the distribution of this sum is reviewed annually." Grants to both national and local charities range between £500 and £3,000. The company does not support: fundraising events; advertising in charity brochures; appeals from individuals; purely denominational appeals; local appeals not in areas of company presence; large national appeals; overseas projects.

☐ **Unigate plc**   *Dairymen & food manufacturers*

Unigate House,
Wood Lane,
London W12 7RP
081-749 8888

Ch: Sir Brian Kellett
CE: R Buckland
Contact: P N Heriz-Jones
Company Secretary

Year Ends: 31 Mar '92
Donations: £158,000
Profit: £92,200,000
Turnover: £1,894,000,000

UK employees: n/a
Total employees: 26,000

Donations Policy: Supports a limited range of charitable causes on a highly selective basis and does not wish to encourage unsolicited appeals. Most donations are committed on a long-term basis.

☐ **Unilever**   *Food products, detergents, personal care products*

Unilever House,
Blackfriars,
London EC4P 4BQ
071-822 6921

Ch: M S Perry
Contact: Dr Tulip
Secretary to Appeals Committee

Year Ends: 31 Dec '91
Donations: £3,000,000
Profit: £1,792,000,000
Turnover: £23,163,000,000

UK employees: 33,098
Total employees: 298,000

% Club, BitC, ABSA

Donations Policy: Profit and turnover are of the worldwide business but donations are for the UK only.
Priorities are social welfare, particularly of the young and elderly, education and the environment. Preference is given to national charities and charities in areas where the company has factories and offices. Donations range from £500 to £50,000. The company also assists education, enterprise and environmental initiatives by means other than financial contribution and sponsors the arts. Total community contributions in 1991 were £5 million.
No grants for fundraising events; advertising in charity brochures; appeals from individuals; purely denominational (religious) appeals; local appeals not in areas of company presence.

☐ **Union Discount Co of London plc**   *Banking*

39 Cornhill,
London EC3V 3NU
071-623 1020

Ch: R A E Herbert
CE: G E Gilchrist
Contact: R J Vardy
Group Secretary

Year Ends: 31 Dec '90
Donations: £25,000
Profit: (£23,564,000)
Turnover: n/a

UK employees: 403
Total employees: n/a

BitC

Donations Policy: The company are at present reducing the amount donated to charities. Preference for charities in which a member of company staff is involved. Donations are about £200.
No donations for advertising in charity brochures.

☐ **Union International plc**   *Foodstuffs & by-products*

13-16 West Smithfield,
London EC1A 9JN
071-248 1212

Ch: H M Synge
Contact: J R Cuthbert
Company Secretary

Year Ends: 31 Dec '91
Donations: £57,000
Profit: £12,565,000
Turnover: £1,386,700,000

UK employees: n/a
Total employees: 22,479

Donations Policy: Support to charities connected with the business or which are in areas of company operation.

☐ **Union Texas Petroleum Ltd**   *Oil & gas exploration & production*

68-114 Knightsbridge,
London SW1X 7LR
071-581 5122

Contact: Charities Committee

Year Ends: 31 Dec '90
Donations: £55,778
Profit: £55,393,000
Turnover: £103,967,000

UK employees: n/a
Total employees: 32

Donations Policy: The staff committee decides the companies contributions. Preference for charities in which a member of company staff is involved and national charities or charities based in the London area. Preference also for charities involved with homelessness, children and youth; social welfare; medical; education and the environment. Some cancer charities, RNLI, Save the Children Fund and the Salvation Army receive regular donations from the company. The company matches staff fundraising £ for £ through the Give As You Earn Scheme and staff sponsorship.
The company will not support political, religious or military organisations.

Please read page 6 | Alphabetical listing

Unisys Ltd
Business machines, farm equipment

31 Brentfield,
Stonebridge Park,
London NW10 8LS
081-965 0511

Ch: J W Perry
Contact: Martin Sexton
Director of Company
Communications

Year Ends: 31 Dec '91
Donations: £85,552
Profit: £11,198,000
Turnover: £311,146,000

UK employees: n/a
Total employees: 2,538

BitC, ABSA

Donations Policy: Support tends to be given to local charities in areas of company presence such as hospitals and educational appeals. Preference for charities in which a member of company staff is involved and appeals relevant to company presence. Grants to national organisations from £50 to £20,000. Grants to local organisations from £50 to £10,000. One national charity is supported, currently Help the Aged. The company also supports enterprise initiatives and sponsors the arts.
Rarely respond to circular appeals. No grants for advertising in charity brochures; purely denominational (religious) appeals; local appeals not in areas of company presence; large national appeals; overseas projects.

Unitech plc
Electronic components manufacture

Apex Plaza,
Forbury Road,
Reading,
Berkshire RG1 1AX
0734-507075

Contact: P A M Curry
Chairman

Year Ends: 31 May '92
Donations: n/a
Profit: £12,046,000
Turnover: £251,831,000

UK employees: n/a
Total employees: 6,076

Donations Policy: No donations figure is given in the company annual report.

United Bank of Kuwait plc
Banking

3 Lombard Street
London EC3V 9DT
071-626 3422

Ch: Fahad Maziad Al-Rajaan
Contact: Miss D Perry
Secretary to the Manager

Year Ends: 31 Dec '91
Donations: £345,237
Profit: £16,100,000
Turnover: n/a

UK employees: 280
Total employees: n/a

Donations Policy: Of the total donations figure, £333,333 was donated to the The Gulf Trust Charity.

United Biscuits (Holdings) plc
Manu. of biscuits, cakes, crisps, chocolates, frozen foods

Church Road,
West Drayton,
Middlesex UB7 7PR
0895-432142

Ch: R C Clarke
CE: E L Nicoli
Contact: Graham Parker
Secretary to the Appeals Committee

Year Ends: 28 Dec '91
Donations: £631,000
Profit: £211,300,000
Turnover: £2,660,500,000

UK employees: n/a
Total employees: 40,226

% Club, BitC, ABSA

Donations Policy: The company supports educational and social welfare causes, especially charities caring for children, youth and elderly people. In addition, support is given to the environment, heritage and enterprise and training activities in inner city areas. Preference is given to charities where the business is located throughout the UK and in particular where a member of staff is involved. Grants to national organisations from £250 to £1,000; grants to local organisations from £250 to £500.
No response to circular appeals. No grants for advertising in charity brochures; appeals from individuals; local appeals not in areas of company presence.
Total community contributions in 1991 were £1,470,000.

United Engineering Steels Ltd
Steel manufacturing

PO Box 29,
Sheffield Road,
Rotherham S60 1DQ
0709-371234

Ch: Ian F Donald
CE: John S Pennington
Contact: Peter Brindley
Property & Administration Manager

Year Ends: 31 Dec '89
Donations: £14,575
Profit: £67,300,000
Turnover: £814,000,000

UK employees: n/a
Total employees: 10,900

ABSA

Donations Policy: The company make most of their donations through the Julian Melchett Trust (see entry for British Steel plc), which supports a wide range of charities. The committee meets twice each year and all applications are considered on merit. There is a strong preference to charities in areas of company presence eg. West Midlands, Sheffield/Rotherham, North Wales (Wrexham area). Preference for sick, poor, elderly or disabled people; social welfare; medical; education; recreation; environment/heritage and the arts.

United Friendly Insurance plc
Insurance

42 Southwark Bridge Road,
London SE1 9HE
071-928 5644

Ch: J R Rampe
MD: R E Balding
Contact: Ms Lesley Ohlson
Advertising & Promotions Co-ordinator

Year Ends: 31 Dec '91
Donations: £24,293
Profit: £13,392,000
Turnover: n/a

UK employees: n/a
Total employees: 4,087

United Glass Ltd
Manufacture of steel & plastic containers

Valley Road Industrial Estate,
Porters Wood,
St Albans,
Hertfordshire AL3 6NY
0727-59261

MD: J R Griffin
Contact: Miss Sue Fretwell
Secretary to the Managing Director

Year Ends: 3 Dec '91
Donations: £9,014
Profit: £5,707,000
Turnover: £159,856,000

UK employees: 2,237
Total employees: n/a

Donations Policy: Preference for appeals relevant to company business, local charities in the areas of company presence and charities in which a member of staff is involved.
No support for national appeals, purely denominational (religious) appeals, appeals from individuals or overseas projects. Direct support preferred.
In addition to direct donations, community sponsorship totalled about £2,000.

• **Alphabetical listing**   Please read page 6

Name/Address	Officers	Financial Information	Other Information

☐ United International Pictures
Motion picture distribution

Mortimer House,
37-41 Mortimer Street,
London W1A 2JL
071-636 1655

MD: Christopher Hedges
Contact: S B Patel
Chief Accountant

Year Ends: 29 Dec '90
Donations: n/a
Profit: £3,868,000
Turnover: £309,473,000

UK employees: n/a
Total employees: 190

Donations Policy: In general the company only supports film related charities.

☐ United Kingdom Atomic Energy Authority
Support for nuclear utilities

AEA Technology,
Harwell,
Oxon OX11 0RA
0235-821111

Ch: J N Maltby
CE: Dr B L Eyre
Contact: Mrs Denise Lewis
Personnel Officer

Year Ends: 31 Mar '91
Donations: n/a
Profit: £50,200,000
Turnover: £452,600,000

UK employees: n/a
Total employees: 10,752

☐ United Newspapers plc
Newspaper proprietors

Ludgate House,
245 Blackfriars Road,
London SE1 9UY
071-921 5000

Ch: Lord Stevens of Ludgate
MD: G J S Wilson
Contact: David Barron
Chairman, Charities Committee

Year Ends: 31 Dec '91
Donations: £1,168,000
Profit: £85,172,000
Turnover: £812,598,000

UK employees: 9,864
Total employees: 12,015

% Club, BitC

Donations Policy: The donations figure includes US support. The group centrally offers planned but limited support to national charities/appeals and newspaper industry charities. Preference for medical; education; environment/heritage; arts; enterprise/training. Grants to national organisations from £500 to £5,000. Local companies support their own local/regional and trade/professional charities/appeals. Grants to local organisations from £150 to £3,000.
Centrally, no response to circular appeals, and no grants for fundraising events, purely denominational (religious) appeals, local appeals not in areas of company presence, overseas projects.

☐ United Scientific Holdings plc
Armoured vehicles, optical equipment

United Scientific House,
215 Vauxhall Bridge Road,
London SW1V 1EN
071-821 8080

Ch: J Robertshaw
CE: N Prest
Contact: John Matthews
Company Secretary

Year Ends: 30 Sep '91
Donations: £26,000
Profit: £6,028,000
Turnover: £114,152,000

UK employees: n/a
Total employees: 3,136

Donations Policy: Preference for appeals relevant to company business, defence or services charities and the bigger national charities like Oxfam. The company's donations for 1992 are expected to total about £15,000, individual donations are generally about £250.
No grants for fundraising events; advertising in charity brochures; local appeals not in areas of company presence or drug related causes.

☐ United Technologies Holdings plc
Lifts, air conditioning, electronic & vehicle parts

The Otis Building,
43-59 Clapham Road,
London SW9 0JZ
071-735 9131

Contact: Felicity Stonehill
Communications Manager

Year Ends: 30 Nov '90
Donations: £41,716
Profit: £19,662,000
Turnover: £281,553,000

UK employees: n/a
Total employees: 4,276

Donations Policy: The company aims to support one national charity. Small donations may be made to local charities in areas of company presence.

☐ Universal Office Supplies plc
Stationery & office furniture

Units 3-4,
Hazlehurst Road,
Worsley,
Manchester M28 4SX
071-371 6423

Ch: M A Abrahamson
MD: P Smith
Contact: Terry Branigan
Marketing & Advertising
Department

Year Ends: 31 Dec '85
Donations: £14,018
Profit: £904,000
Turnover: £8,893,000

UK employees: n/a
Total employees: 132

Donations Policy: Mainly Jewish charities.

☐ Unwins Wine Group Ltd
Off-licence chain

Birchwood House,
Victoria Road,
Dartford,
Kent DA1 5AJ
0322-272711

MD: M A Wetz, R J A Rotter
CE: J M Charman
Contact: Peter Hunter
Promotions Director

Year Ends: 28 Feb '91
Donations: n/a
Profit: £970,000
Turnover: £95,897,000

UK employees: n/a
Total employees: 1,253

☐ Usborne plc
Agricultural services, property, motor products

Daisy Hill,
Burstwick,
Hull HU12 9HE
0964-671144

Ch: D W Sawyer
MD: D W Frame
Contact: P Harrison
Company Secretary

Year Ends: 31 Dec '91
Donations: £1,250
Profit: £4,120,000
Turnover: £210,024,000

UK employees: 246
Total employees: n/a

Please read page 6 — Alphabetical listing

Name/Address	Officers	Financial Information	Other Information

☐ USM Texon Ltd

Shoe & press cutting machinery

PO Box 88,
Ross Walk,
Belgrave,
Leicester LE4 5BX
0533-610111

Ch: Sir John Collyear
MD: D Gamble
Contact: J Siddons
Company Secretary

Year Ends: 31 Dec '90
Donations: £3,000
Profit: £5,617,000
Turnover: £164,101,000

UK employees: n/a
Total employees: 2,632

☐ Van Leer (UK) Ltd

Packaging manufacturers

78 Portsmouth Road,
Cobham,
Surrey KT11 1LB
0932-867363

Ch: W Rast
MD: S F Merritt
Contact: T Haw
Financial Director

Year Ends: 31 Dec '91
Donations: £1,300,000
Profit: (£2,258,000)
Turnover: £143,000,000

UK employees: 1,781
Total employees: 1,874

Donations Policy: Charitable donations are made mainly through the Dutch-based Bernard van Leer Foundation, which supports charities relating to children both able and disabled or socially deprived (see Guide to the Major Trusts). The UK donations budget is limited, but small donations are made to local appeals in areas of company presence. Grants to national organisations from £150 to £1,000. Grants to local organisations from £50 to £100.
No grants for fundraising events; appeals from individuals; purely denominational (religious) appeals; local appeals not in areas of company presence; overseas projects; the arts.

☐ Vanol (UK) Holdings Ltd

Trade in petroleum products

5 Prince's Gate,
London SW7 1QJ
071-823 9595

Contact: Patsi Shannon
Office Administrator

Year Ends: 31 Dec '90
Donations: n/a
Profit: £1,094,000
Turnover: £699,230,000

UK employees: n/a
Total employees: 3,241

Donations Policy: Support is given to the World Wide Fund for Nature and Guy's Hospital. A few small donations may also be given to local London charities.

☐ Reg Vardy plc

Motor vehicle dealers

Houghton House,
Wessington Way,
Sunderland SR5 3RT
091-584 2842

Ch: P Vardy
MD: G J Potts
Contact: D Williams
Group Public Relations Manager

Year Ends: 30 Apr '92
Donations: £18,900
Profit: £4,107,000
Turnover: £177,509,000

UK employees: n/a
Total employees: 1,000

Donations Policy: Reg Vardy plc is a major sponsor of the new Tyneside City Technology College and will be contributing £125,000 to this project over the next four years. In general the company aims to assist education and the arts and make a positive contribution to the communities where it operates. No support for circular appeals or local appeals not in areas of company presence. The company has a policy of limited sports sponsorship.

☐ Varity Holdings Ltd

Industrial management company

9 Upper Belgrave Street,
London SW1X 8BD
071-465 0610

Contact: A Don
Acting Chairman

Year Ends: 31 Jan '91
Donations: £23,784
Profit: £27,081,000
Turnover: £1,080,848,000

UK employees: 10,349
Total employees: n/a

Donations Policy: The company states "until the fortunes of the company have been restored to a level where we are able to pay dividends, we are not in a position to respond to appeals, no matter how worthy the cause."

☐ Vaux Group plc

Brewers & hoteliers

The Brewery,
Sunderland SR1 3AN
091-567 6277

Ch: Paul Nicholson
MD: Frank Nicholson, W P Catesby
Contact: H Florek
Group Public Relations Manager

Year Ends: 30 Sep '91
Donations: £143,000
Profit: £34,343,000
Turnover: £267,200,000

UK employees: n/a
Total employees: 6,554

% Club, BitC

Donations Policy: Most of the companies donations of over £500 are made through the Vaux Foundation, which meets every three months. Donations of less than £500 can be made regularly. Preference for groups operating in north-east of England, especially on Wearside, the North West and Yorkshire. Areas local to the companies Swallow hotels may also be supported. Three employees have been seconded to the Sunderland Enterprise Centre for two years each. The company prefers to make donations to specific projects rather than to fundraising events or to large national appeals. The company will not support individuals.

☐ Vauxhall Motors Ltd

Motor vehicle manufacturers

Griffin House,
PO Box No 3,
Osbourne Road,
Luton,
Bedfordshire LU1 3YT
0582-21122

Ch: W A Ebbert
Contact: Elaine Cowley
Charities Committee

Year Ends: 31 Dec '91
Donations: £446,582 (1990)
Profit: £132,600,000
Turnover: £2,572,600,000

UK employees: n/a
Total employees: 11,248

BitC

Donations Policy: The company concentrates its support on activities directly associated with the industry and its employees' interests, and in areas of its plants (Luton and Ellesmere Port). It supports a wide range of organisations including local schools and colleges, the arts, local sport and community events, local business enterprises, as well as local charities through sponsorships.
Most of the companies donations are made to the hospices local to Luton and Ellesmere Port and to the NSPCC. In 1992 the company supported the Children's Royal Variety Performance.
No grants for circular appeals; appeals from individuals; local appeals not in areas of company presence; overseas projects; political, religious or sectarian organisations.

● **Alphabetical listing**   Please read page 6

Name/Address   *Officers*   *Financial Information*   *Other Information*

☐ **Vickers plc**   Cars, engineering, defence & aerospace, medical

Millbank Tower,   *Ch:* Sir Richard Lloyd   *Year Ends:* 31 Dec '91   UK employees: 9,475
Millbank,   *MD:* Sir Colin Chandler   *Donations:* £160,941   Total employees: 11,831
London SW1P 4RA   *Contact:* David Bristow   *Profit:* (£12,400,000)
071-828 7777   Assistant Company Secretary   *Turnover:* £652,200,000   % Club, BitC

Donations Policy: Over half the charity allocation is disbursed by the company's local operating units. Head office supports organisations in the fields of medical and social welfare, education and training (including enterprise schemes), youth and sports, and service charities. Head office welcomes appeals from national charities and community organisations, particularly having a presence in areas of a company operating unit; approaches are also welcome when made direct to the operating unit. Grants to national organisations from £25 to £15,000. Grants to local organisations from £10 to £10,000.
No grants for advertising in charity brochures; appeals from individuals; purely denominational (religious) appeals; local appeals not in areas of company presence; circular appeals; matching funds schemes or sponsorship of students for overseas expeditions. Fundraising events and arts sponsorship are rarely supported.

☐ **Victaulic plc**   Manufacture & supply of pipeline products

Matrix House,   *Ch:* D C B Winch   *Year Ends:* 31 Dec '91   UK employees: n/a
2 North Forth Street,   *MD:* D C Stewart   *Donations:* £31,000   Total employees: 1,411
Central Milton Keynes   *Contact:* Miss Fiona Barrett   *Profit:* £14,323,000
MK9 1NW   Personnel & Office Administrator *Turnover:* £114,801,000
0908-691000

☐ **Vinten Group plc**   Film equipment manufacturers

Western Way,   *Ch:* J H A Wood   *Year Ends:* 31 Dec '91   UK employees: n/a
Bury St Edmunds,   *MD:* M A W Baggott   *Donations:* £4,267   Total employees: 818
Suffolk IP33 3TB   *Contact:* Gill Gorrod   *Profit:* £9,178,000
0284-752121   Group Secretary   *Turnover:* £63,311,000

Donations Policy: Preference for local charities in areas of company presence or charities in which a member of staff is involved. Grants from £100 to £250.
No response to circular appeals. No support for fundraising events, appeals from individuals, purely denominational appeals, local appeals not in areas of company presence, large national appeals, overseas projects or advertisements in charity brochures.

☐ **Virgin Music Group Ltd**   Recording industry

120 Campden Hill Road,   *Ch:* R C N Branson   *Year Ends:* 31 Jul '90   UK employees: n/a
London W8 7AR   *MD:* D G Cruickshank   *Donations:* n/a   Total employees: 881
071-229 1282   *Contact:* W Whitehorn   *Profit:* £15,607,000
                             Corporate Public Relations   *Turnover:* £308,598,000   % Club, BitC

Donations Policy: The Virgin Group in 1991 received about 100,000 requests for donations, as they support 35 major charities they do not make one-off donations. The charities supported include; the Disaster and Emergencies Committee; the Health Care Foundation; Parents Against Tobacco. The company also funds HELP, a youth advisory service. Voluntary organisations in the Notting Hill/North Kensington area are also supported.

☐ **Vodafone Group plc**   Mobile telecommunication services

Courtyard,   *Ch:* G A Whent   *Year Ends:* 31 Mar '91   UK employees: n/a
2-4 London Road,   *MD:* C Gent   *Donations:* £70,420   Total employees: 2,434
Newbury,   *Contact:* Terry Barwick   *Profit:* £244,658,000
Berkshire RG13 1JL   Corporate Affairs Manager   *Turnover:* £536,838,000
0635-33251

Donations Policy: Preference for charities local to Newbury, especially those involved with children and youth or disabled people. The company has sponsored classical music events and brass bands. No support for anything involved with motor racing.
Phil Williams is the contact for national charities.

☐ **Volex Group plc**   Manufacturers of cables, electrical systems

Dornock House,   *Ch:* J P Frost   *Year Ends:* 31 Mar '92   UK employees: n/a
Kelvin Close,   *MD:* H Poulson   *Donations:* £8,202   Total employees: 2,902
Birchwood Science Park,   *Contact:* A Dawber   *Profit:* £4,082,000
Warrington,   Group Secretarial Assistant   *Turnover:* £81,629,000
Cheshire WA3 7JX
0925-830101

Donations Policy: Preference for local charities in areas of company presence. The company prefers to make direct donations rather than advertising in charity brochures, prize donating, etc.. Grants range from £75 to £125.

☐ **Volvo Trucks (Great Britain) Ltd**   Volvo commercial vehicles & parts sales

Kilwinning Road,   *Contact:* Charles Quinn   *Year Ends:* 31 Dec '90   UK employees: n/a
Irvine,   Human Resources Manager   *Donations:* £14,340   Total employees: 581
Ayrshire KA12 8TB   *Profit:* £5,479,000
0294-74120   *Turnover:* £192,108,000

Donations Policy: Most charities and causes in the Ayrshire area are supported by the company. Preference for charities in which a member of company staff is involved. Donations are usually under £200, but a few larger donations are also made. The company gives a lot of support to it's local hospices. The company receive about five applications a week and cannot support them all.
The company will not support advertising in charity brochures; local appeals not in areas of company presence; large national appeals.

Please read page 6 — Alphabetical listing

Name/Address	Officers	Financial Information	Other Information

☐ Vosper Thornycroft Holdings plc
Shipbuilding

Victoria Road,
Woolston,
Southampton SO9 5GR
0703-445144

Ch: R J Withers
MD: M Jay
Contact: Stuart Shears
Company Secretary

Year Ends: 31 Mar '92
Donations: £13,155
Profit: £16,045,000
Turnover: £156,832,000

UK employees: n/a
Total employees: 2,030

Donations Policy: Preference for local charities in areas of company presence and appeals relevant to company business. Preferred areas of support: children and youth, social welfare, medical, education, enterprise/training. Grants to local organisations from £50 to £500.
No response to circular appeals. No grants for advertising in charity brochures, appeals from individuals, purely denominational (religious) appeals, local appeals not in areas of company presence, large national appeals, overseas projects.

☐ Voyager Group Ltd
Charter airlines, clubs, hotel management

120 Campden Hill Road,
London W8 7AR
071-221 5200

Contact: Michael Herriot
Managing Director

Year Ends: 31 Jul '90
Donations: n/a
Profit: £5,408,000
Turnover: £221,589,000

UK employees: n/a
Total employees: 2,089

☐ VSEL Consortium plc
Marine, offshore oil & gas engineers

Barrow-in-Furness,
Cumbria LA14 1AF
0229-823366

Ch: Lord Chalfont
CE: C N Davies
Contact: M Day
Company Secretary

Year Ends: 31 Mar '92
Donations: £116,210
Profit: £47,900,000
Turnover: £519,900,000

UK employees: n/a
Total employees: 13,028

Donations Policy: Preference for local charities in areas where the company operates and appeals relevant to company business. The company states that with policy change "almost all charitable and sponsorship requests are being turned down". Grants to local organisations from £30 to £50,000. Grants to national organisations from £50 to £500.
No grants for local appeals not in areas of company presence; large national appeals; overseas projects.

☐ Wace Group plc
Printers

Wace House,
Shepherdess Walk,
London N1 7LH
071-250 3055

Ch: F H ten Bos
MD: B Dudley
Contact: Marketing Manager

Year Ends: 31 Dec '91
Donations: £24,000
Profit: £18,281,000
Turnover: £305,345,000

UK employees: n/a
Total employees: 5,316

BitC

Donations Policy: Priority to charities related to company business. The main charity supported is NABS. Preference also for children's charities.

☐ John Waddington plc
Packaging & printing of games

40 Wakefield Road,
Leeds LS10 1DU
0532-770202

Ch: V H Watson
MD: M Buckley, D G Perry
Contact: Mrs S Shaw
Secretary to the Chairman

Year Ends: 1 Apr '91
Donations: £11,997
Profit: £16,027,000
Turnover: £227,602,000

UK employees: 3,522
Total employees: 3,806

Donations Policy: Support for local and trade charities. In addition to cash donations the company donates products for tombolas, etc.. It also does a lot of free printing. Some preference to charities where a member of staff is involved.
No support for circular appeals, large national appeals, overseas projects, fundraising events, denominational appeals, individuals.

☐ Wagon Industrial Holdings plc
Material handling, office equipment, engineering

Halesdane House,
Halesfield,
Telford TF7 4PB
0952-680111

Ch: P D Taylor
CE: J L Hudson
Contact: Mrs Sandra Revill
Secretary to the Chief Executive

Year Ends: 31 Mar '92
Donations: £17,000
Profit: £21,516,000
Turnover: £255,984,000

UK employees: n/a
Total employees: 4,446

Donations Policy: Most donations are by CAF vouchers, unless the cause is not a registered charity. Preference for "people-related" causes rather than eg. environment. Also prefer to make direct donations rather than sponsorship. Preference for children and youth; social welfare; medical. Grants to national and local organisations range from £25 to £250. Total community contributions up to 1992 were £20,871.
No grants for purely denominational appeals.

☐ Walkers Crisps Ltd
Manufacturers of potato products

Feature Road,
Thurmaston,
Leicester LE4 8BS
0533-691691

Ch: A C Mitchell Innes
MD: T Charlesworth
Contact: Paul Parrhenter
Marketing Manager (Crisps brands)

Year Ends: 30 Nov '91
Donations: £5,088
Profit: £37,011,000
Turnover: £146,303,000

UK employees: n/a
Total employees: 1,598

Donations Policy: To give direct assistance to local branches of national charities and charities especially helping the young, aged, sick and disadvantaged where a member of staff is involved.
No support for circulars, large national appeals, unsolicited appeals, denominational appeals or individuals.

☐ Wang (UK) Ltd
Computer distribution

Wang House,
1000 Great West Road,
Brentford TW8 9HL
081-568 9200

MD: A P Davis
Contact: Mrs Caroline Atkinson
Marketing Executive

Year Ends: 30 Jun '90
Donations: n/a
Profit: £7,838,000
Turnover: £129,722,000

UK employees: n/a
Total employees: 1,200

BitC

● **Alphabetical listing** Please read page 6

Name/Address	Officers	Financial Information	Other Information

☐ S G Warburg Group plc
Banking

1 Finsbury Avenue,
London EC2M 2PA
071-606 1066

Ch: Sir David Scholey
Contact: I B Marshall
Company Secretary

Year Ends: 31 Mar '92
Donations: £685,000
Profit: £166,300,000
Turnover: n/a

UK employees: 3,057
Total employees: 5,000

% Club, BitC, ABSA

Donations Policy: The company has an associated charitable trust but no information is available on the trust's donations. The company supports inner-city projects in areas of company presence.

☐ Warburtons Ltd
Bakers, manufacturing & wholesale

Hereford Street,
Bolton BL1 8JB
0204-23551

Ch: J P Speak
Contact: Mrs Lesley Wallwork
Marketing Manager

Year Ends: 24 Sep '90
Donations: £19,769
Profit: £8,320,000
Turnover: £115,114,000

UK employees: n/a
Total employees: 5,374

% Club, BitC

Donations Policy: Preference for appeals relevant to the business, local charities in areas of company presence, projects involving children and youth, social welfare, education, the environment and enterprise/training. The company has strong links with Wythenshawe New Heart Start Appeal.
No support for circular appeals, purely denominational (religious) appeals, local appeals not in areas of company presence, large national appeals or political appeals.

☐ Wardle Storeys plc
Manufacture of plastic sheeting

Brantham Works,
Brantham,
Nr Manningtree,
Essex CO11 1NJ
0206-392401

Ch: C T Clague
MD: B R Taylor
Contact: D Wilman
Company Secretary & Financial Director

Year Ends: 31 Aug '91
Donations: £4,810
Profit: £8,189,000
Turnover: £78,249,000

UK employees: n/a
Total employees: 2,028

☐ Warner-Lambert
Manufacturing chemists

Chestnut Avenue,
Eastleigh,
Hampshire SO5 3ZQ
0703-620500

Contact: Public Relations Manager

Year Ends: 30 Nov '90
Donations: £48,552
Profit: £1,703,000
Turnover: £141,085,000

UK employees: n/a
Total employees: 2,014

Donations Policy: Primarily the company gives substantial support to one or two local charities each year.
Generally no support for circular appeals, fundraising events, advertising in charity brochures, appeals from individuals, purely denominational (religious) appeals, local appeals not in areas of company presence, large national appeals, overseas projects. No sponsorship is undertaken.

☐ Wassall plc
Sealants, adhesives, bottle closures, packaging

39 Victoria Street,
London SW1H 0EE
071-333 0303

Ch: J D Miller
Contact: Mrs S Andrew
Finance Officer

Year Ends: 31 Dec '91
Donations: nil
Profit: £10,285,000
Turnover: £165,249,000

UK employees: n/a
Total employees: 3,265

Donations Policy: The company made no charitable donations in 1991.

☐ Waste Management International plc
Solid & hazardous waste management services

Windsor House,
55-56 St James's Street,
London SW1A 1LA
071-493 2554

Contact: Charles Powell
Director of Administration

Year Ends: 31 Dec '91
Donations: n/a
Profit: £96,367,000
Turnover: £606,870,000

UK employees: n/a
Total employees: 14,141

☐ Waterford Wedgwood UK plc
Fine bone china & earthenware

Barlaston,
Stoke-on-Trent,
Staffordshire ST12 9ES
0782-204141

Ch: K H Ashwell
Contact: Mrs Margaret Michell
Public Relations Executive

Year Ends: 31 Dec '91
Donations: £43,000
Profit: £828,000
Turnover: £252,719,000

UK employees: 7,348
Total employees: 9,564

Donations Policy: At present the company is not in a position to consider unsolicited charitable donations. They hope to reinstate the company's charitable budget within the next couple of years.

☐ Wates Building Group Ltd
Building contractors

1260 London Road,
Norbury,
London SW16 4EG
081-764 5000

Ch: M Wates
Contact: Doug Gillan
Personnel Manager

Year Ends: 31 Dec '88
Donations: £18,749
Profit: £22,884,000
Turnover: £236,942,000

UK employees: n/a
Total employees: 2,095

BitC

Donations Policy: The company supports charities local to areas of company operation. The main support goes to children and youth charities, this ranges from the scouts groups to the Little Sisters of the Poor, a local nuns group. The company have loaned a minibus and made a cash donation to the local police for their involvement with local deprived children.

Please read page 6 — Alphabetical listing

Name/Address	Officers	Financial Information	Other Information

Watmough (Holdings) plc
Colour supplements, catalogues, cartons, polythene

Jason House,
Hillam Road,
Bradford BD2 1QN
0274-735663

Contact: P G Walker
Chairman

Year Ends: 31 Dec '91
Donations: £16,678
Profit: £8,103,000
Turnover: £107,438,000

UK employees: n/a
Total employees: 1,729

Donations Policy: The company has a limited donations budget, and prefers to support local or client based charities. Preference for children and youth; social welfare; medical; recreation or the arts. Grants to charities and organisations from £10 to £500. Some charities are given help with printing. Total community contributions in 1991 were £50,000. The company sponsored part of the Harrogate International Festival by helping to bring over the Budapest Festival Orchestra.
Generally no grants for circular appeals; fundraising events; appeals from individuals; purely denominational (religious) appeals; local appeals not in areas of company presence or large national appeals.

Watson & Philip plc
Distribution of foodstuffs

PO Box 89,
Blackness Road,
Dundee DD1 9PU
0382-27501

Ch: Ian McPherson
MD: Simon Kirkpatrick
Contact: Margaret Speed
Secretary to the Director

Year Ends: 27 Oct '91
Donations: £14,557
Profit: £11,800,000
Turnover: £461,789,000

UK employees: n/a
Total employees: 2,804

Donations Policy: All grants are given through the Watson & Philip Charitable Trust. The company does not welcome unsolicited applications.

Watts Blake Bearne & Co plc
Clay processors

Park House,
Courtenay Park,
Newton Abbot,
Devon TQ12 4PS
0626-332345

Ch: Dr A I Lenton
MD: J D Pike
Contact: W J C Watts
Company Secretary

Year Ends: 31 Dec '91
Donations: £25,280
Profit: £3,728,000
Turnover: £61,446,000

UK employees: 625
Total employees: 1,065

Donations Policy: The company generally supports local charities in areas of company presence, appeals relevant to the business, charities in which a member of staff is involved or causes indicating self-help. Preference for children and youth; social welfare; medical; education; recreation; environment/heritage; enterprise/training. Grants from £20 to £250.
No response to circular appeals. No support for local appeals not in areas of company presence, large national appeals, overseas projects.

Wavebest Ltd
Food machines, dishwashers & commercial fridges

Hobart House,
51 The Bourne,
Southgate,
London N14 6RT
081-882 6141

Contact: J Gallaher
Company Secretary

Year Ends: 31 Dec '90
Donations: £5,770
Profit: £3,429,000
Turnover: £98,125,000

UK employees: n/a
Total employees: 1,745

Waverley Cameron plc
Stationery retailing, distribution of office equipment

344 Kensington High Street,
London W14 8NS
071-371 6423

Ch: James Gulliver
MD: Martin Abramson
Contact: Jane Dwyer
Personal Assistant to the Director

Year Ends: 31 Mar '90
Donations: £5,000
Profit: £1,431,000
Turnover: £51,419,000

UK employees: n/a
Total employees: 775

Wavin Plastics Ltd
Manufacture & marketing of plastic building products

Parsonage Way,
Chippenham,
Wiltshire SN15 5PN
0249-654121

Ch: A J Driessen
MD: B P Doe
Contact: J A Higgins
Financial Director

Year Ends: 31 Dec '91
Donations: £5,572
Profit: £4,858,000
Turnover: £91,844,000

UK employees: 918
Total employees: 918

Donations Policy: An annual contribution is made to the Wiltshire Community Trust to whom all individual applicants are referred unless there is special relevance to the business.
No response to circular appeals. No support for appeals from individuals.
In addition to charitable donations, other community contributions totalled £2,000. Sponsorship proposals to T Jones, Marketing Director.

Weetabix Ltd
Manufacturer of cereal foods

Burton Latimer,
Kettering,
Northants NN15 5JR
0536-722181

Ch: R W George
Contact: P Davidson
Media Research Officer

Year Ends: 31 Jul '91
Donations: £325,000
Profit: £19,711,000
Turnover: £184,426,000

UK employees: n/a
Total employees: 2,500

Donations Policy: The company supports all kinds of appeals in the Northamptonshire area.

Barry Wehmiller International plc
Container packaging supplies

PO Box 95,
Atlantic Street,
Altrincham,
Cheshire WA14 5EW
061-928 6344

Ch: N H McClean
MD: S M Brown
Contact: Anne-Marie Grimshaw
Personal Assistant to Chief Executive

Year Ends: 31 Jul '91
Donations: £10,000
Profit: £5,029,000
Turnover: £75,358,000

UK employees: n/a
Total employees: 944

• **Alphabetical listing** Please read page 6

Name/Address	Officers	Financial Information	Other Information

☐ Andrew Weir & Co Ltd
Shipping, insurance

Dexter House,
2 Royal Mint Court,
London EC3 4XX
071-265 0808

Ch: Lord Runciman
CE: Antony Cooke
Contact: J A Cove
Company Secretary

Year Ends: 31 Dec '90
Donations: £30,000
Profit: £1,288,000
Turnover: £194,489,000

UK employees: n/a
Total employees: 1,265

Donations Policy: The company states that they no longer make donations to charities and no applications will be considered.

☐ Weir Group plc
Engineers

149 Newlands Road,
Cathcart,
Glasgow G44 4EX
041-637 7111

Ch: Viscount Weir
MD: R Garrick
Contact: W Harkness
Company Secretary

Year Ends: 29 Dec '91
Donations: £50,858
Profit: £34,241,000
Turnover: £424,105,000

UK employees: n/a
Total employees: 6,223

Donations Policy: Of the total donations figure, £35,000 was given to the Weir Educational Trust and £15,858 was donated for general charitable purposes. The company tends to support sea charities, and general charities such as cancer charities and hospices. Preference for local charities in areas where the company operates. Grants range from £100 to £5,000.

☐ Wellcome plc
Research, production & sale of pharmaceuticals

Unicorn House,
PO Box 129,
160 Euston Road,
London NW1 2BP
071-387 4477

Ch: Sir Alistair Frame
CE: J W Robb
Contact: R V Sutton
Corporate Donations Executive

Year Ends: 31 Aug '91
Donations: £719,000
Profit: £402,900,000
Turnover: £1,606,300,000

UK employees: 6,176
Total employees: 18,711

% Club, BitC, ABSA

Donations Policy: Primarily directed towards medical and healthcare, sick and disabled people, further and higher education (primarily in medicine, science and technology), and charities/voluntary organisations near to main company sites. Typical grants to national organisations from £3,000 to £10,000; grants to local organisations from £25 to £1,000. Recurring grants for up to three years may be given.
No response to circular appeals. No support for political causes, denominational organisations which do not benefit the community as a whole, appeals from individuals, brochure advertising, fundraising events, large national appeals (from the major fundraising charities), funds for expeditions (although medicines may be given), medical research (such appeals are dealt with by the Wellcome Trust see Guide to the Major Trusts). The company does not undertake any form of commercial sponsorship arguing that it is inappropriate for an ethical pharmaceuticals manufacturer.
Community projects in education partnership, training and enterprise, equal opportunities and environmental improvement are funded from a separate charitable trust, the Operation Help Trust Fund, for which the contact is E J Romanowska, Community Relations Manager. Total community contributions in 1991 were £867,000.

☐ Welsh Water plc
Water & sewerage services

Plas y Ffynnon,
Cambrian Way,
Brecon,
Powys LD3 7HP
0874-623181

Ch: John Elfed Jones
MD: David Jeffrey
Contact: Mike Finn
Promotions Co-ordinator

Year Ends: 31 Mar '92
Donations: £35,000
Profit: £138,200,000
Turnover: £341,900,000

UK employees: n/a
Total employees: 4,133

BitC

Donations Policy: In October 1989, the company established the Welsh Water Elan Trust giving a £100,000 one-off donation and a further £90,000 spread over three years to the trust. 43,000 acres of land in the Elan Valley has also been leased to the trust to develop for public benefit. The donations figure quoted above is for sponsorship only; there is no separate figure for charitable donations available. Preferred areas of sponsorship are the arts, sport and projects promoting the Welsh language. There are no stated exclusions from charitable support.

☐ Wembley plc
Greyhound racing organisers

Wembley Stadium,
Empire Way,
Wembley HA9 0DW
081-902 8833

Ch: Sir Brian Wolfson
MD: Alan Coppin
Contact: Mrs S Ellis
Social Secretary

Year Ends: 31 Dec '91
Donations: £41,000
Profit: £8,369,000
Turnover: £169,903,000

UK employees: n/a
Total employees: 3,980

% Club, BitC

Donations Policy: Preference for charities in the Borough of Brent or involved in sport. Donations for raffle and tombola prizes are usually of Wembley merchandising or tickets for a tour of the stadium. Occasionally promoters of an event donate unsold tickets for Wembley to local organisations. Sid Franks is the Community Relations Manager.

☐ Wessex Water plc
Water & sewerage services

Wessex House,
Passage Street,
Bristol BS2 0JQ
0272-290611

Ch: Nicholas Hood
MD: Colin Skellett
Contact: Alan Crofts
Company Secretary

Year Ends: 31 Mar '92
Donations: £43,000
Profit: £76,900,000
Turnover: £190,800,000

UK employees: n/a
Total employees: 1,869

BitC

Donations Policy: Grants to registered charities operating in the area administered by Wessex Water plc only. The charities committee meets quarterly. In addition to direct donations, £35,000 was given by way of sponsorship to local, environmental and water related activities. This includes support for nature conservation trusts, Business in the Community, education, swimming clubs, water sports the disabled people and a variety of charities providing benefits for the local community.

☐ West Midland Farmers' Association Ltd
Animal feeds, seeds, fertilisers & agrichemicals

Llanthony Mills,
Merchants Road,
Gloucester GL1 5RJ
0452-521751

Ch: P A M Murray
Contact: M A McCausland
Managing Director

Year Ends: 31 May '91
Donations: n/a
Profit: £137,000
Turnover: £103,423,000

UK employees: n/a
Total employees: 480

Please read page 6 — Alphabetical listing

Name/Address	Officers	Financial Information	Other Information

☐ Westbury Homes (Holdings) Ltd

Housebuilding

Westbury House,
Lansdown Road,
Cheltenham,
Gloucestershire GL50 2JA
0242-236191

CE: R L K Fraser
Contact: Mrs C Hipkiss
Group Personnel Services
Manager

Year Ends: 28 Feb '92
Donations: £476
Profit: £15,120,000
Turnover: £131,751,000

UK employees: n/a
Total employees: 423

Donations Policy: The company states that they no longer make donations to charities and no applications will be considered.

☐ Western United Investment Co Ltd

Foodstuffs production

24-30 West Smithfield,
London EC1A 9DL
071-248 1212

MD: E H Vestey
Contact: Appeals Committee Secretary

Year Ends: 31 Dec '90
Donations: £122,000
Profit: £6,600,000
Turnover: £1,566,400,000

UK employees: n/a
Total employees: 25,007

Donations Policy: Donations are made through the Vestey Foundation. Preference for charities local to the company's main offices. Preferred areas of support are environment and heritage, children and elderly people, service, and organisations such as the RNLI and Operation Raleigh.

☐ Westland Group plc

Manufacturers of helicopters, hovercrafts

Westland Works,
Yeovil,
Somerset BA20 2YB
0935-75222

Ch: Sir Leslie Fletcher
CE: A W Jones
Contact: M Stewart
Appeals Secretary

Year Ends: 27 Sep '91
Donations: £83,294
Profit: £23,700,000
Turnover: £467,400,000

UK employees: n/a
Total employees: 9,240

Donations Policy: Support for the armed service charities; those of the company's main customers; activities in the areas of specific operation, particularly involving employees; educational establishments where there is a close affinity with employees or the company. No grants for running costs; annual appeals; appeals from individuals; purely denominational (religious) appeals; political appeals or appeals to support the arts.

☐ Whatman plc

Filtration & purification manufacturers

Whatman House,
St Leonards Road,
20/20 Maidstone,
Kent ME16 0LS
0622-676670

Ch: A R W Smithers
CE: Dr C Knight
Contact: A Brunger
External Relations Executive

Year Ends: 31 Dec '91
Donations: £18,800
Profit: £9,206,000
Turnover: £49,580,000

UK employees: 510
Total employees: 840

% Club

Donations Policy: About half the total donations are given as covenants. Preference for local charities in areas where the company operates, appeals relevant to company business and charities in which a member of company staff is involved. Preference for children and youth; social welfare; medical; education; enterprise/training. Grants to national organisations from £100 to £500. Grants to local organisations from £50 to £250.
No response to circular appeals. No grants for fundraising events (except locally); advertising in charity brochures; appeals from individuals (except locally); purely denominational (religious) appeals; local appeals not in areas of company presence; overseas projects.

☐ Whessoe plc

Engineers

Brinkburn Road,
Darlington,
Co Durham DL3 6DS
0325-381818

Ch: G Duncan
MD: C J Fleetwood
Contact: C W H Green
Group Human Resources Manager

Year Ends: 30 Sep '91
Donations: £11,135
Profit: £7,357,000
Turnover: £57,860,000

UK employees: n/a
Total employees: 1,162

Donations Policy: The company supports: local charities; certain national charities having a local impact; charities associated either with the company's industry or with diseases or illnesses suffered by employees/ex-employees. Preferred areas of support: children and youth, medical. Grants generally from £100 to £1,000.
Generally no support for fundraising events, advertising in charity brochures, local appeals not in areas of company presence.

☐ Wheway plc

Air filtration & conditioning systems

214 Hagley Road,
Edgbaston,
Birmingham B16 9PH
021-456 3634

Ch: John P McGowan
Contact: Mrs Jackie Howell
Personal Assistant to the Chairman

Year Ends: 31 Dec '91
Donations: £1,694
Profit: £2,805,000
Turnover: £89,332,000

UK employees: n/a
Total employees: 1,261

☐ Whitbread plc

Brewers

The Brewery,
Chiswell Street,
London EC1Y 4SD
071-606 4455

Ch: S C Whitbread
MD: P J Jarvis
Contact: P D Patten
Charities Secretary

Year Ends: 29 Feb '92
Donations: £640,613
Profit: £222,100,000
Turnover: £2,378,300,000

UK employees: n/a
Total employees: 36,269

% Club, BitC, ABSA

Donations Policy: The company supports a wide range of charities, through its charitable trust, under six broad headings: medical and health, welfare, education, humanities, environmental resources, and the arts. Each year the company highlights a number of priority areas to support, which may vary slightly from year to year. Priority is given to charities where staff members or pensioners are involved and to local appeals in areas of company presence. All appeals should be sent to the Head Office and local appeals will then be forwarded to the relevant local site. The company only sponsors individuals who work full-time for the company, sponsorships can be for a maximum of £250. Grants to local organisations range from £50 to £500. Grants to national organisations from £100 to £5,000. Most major sites actively encourage employee volunteering.
The company is also involved in local education initiatives.
No support for advertising in charity brochures, appeals from individuals, purely denominational (religious) appeals.

● **Alphabetical listing**   Please read page 6

Name/Address	Officers	Financial Information	Other Information

☐ **Whitecroft plc**   Textiles, building & engineering

Water Lane,   Ch: P A Goold   Year Ends: 31 Mar '92   UK employees: n/a
Wilmslow,   MD: M J C Derbyshire   Donations: £13,117   Total employees: 2,910
Cheshire SK9 5BX   Contact: A W Rippon   Profit: £4,491,000
0625-524677   Group Secretary   Turnover: £129,193,000

Donations Policy: The company prefers not to make a specific statement of policy, stating "We should prefer intending applicants to draw their own conclusions from the level of our donations".

☐ **Whitworths Holdings Ltd**   Food products

Victoria Mills,   Ch: R W George   Year Ends: 31 Mar '91   UK employees: n/a
London Road,   Contact: H Reynolds   Donations: n/a   Total employees: 1,821
Wellingborough,   Managing Director   Profit: £6,090,000
Northamptonshire NN8 2DT   Turnover: £117,386,000
0933-443444

☐ **Wickes plc**   DIY retailers

19-21 Mortimer Street,   Ch: H A Sweetbaum   Year Ends: 31 Dec '91   UK employees: n/a
London W1N 7RJ   MD: R E T Clark   Donations: £134,000   Total employees: 4,784
071-631 1018   Contact: M R Corner   Profit: £6,722,000
                               Administration Director   Turnover: £526,840,000   % Club

Donations Policy: Preference for local charities in the areas of company presence. Grants to national organisations from £100 to £20,000; grants to local organisations from £100 to £2,500.

☐ **Wiggins Group plc**   Property developers

Admirals Way,   Ch: S P Hayklan   Year Ends: 31 Mar '89   UK employees: n/a
South Quay,   Contact: D Hatton   Donations: £9,972   Total employees: 377
London E14 9RN   Company Secretary   Profit: n/a
071-538 1431   Turnover: £83,558,000   % Club

Donations Policy: Grants to organisations in areas of company operation only.

☐ **James Wilkes plc**   Manufacture of engineering products

Penistone Road,   Contact: Arthur Watt   Year Ends: 31 Dec '91   UK employees: n/a
Sheffield S6 2FN   Chairman   Donations: £9,923   Total employees: 538
0742-855000   Profit: £4,656,000
                                                             Turnover: £54,302,000

☐ **Wilkinson Group of Companies**   Domestic hardware sales

PO Box 20,   Ch: A H Wilkinson   Year Ends: 1 Feb '91   UK employees: n/a
Lawn Road,   MD: B K Fairhurst   Donations: £6,401   Total employees: 3,075
Carlton in Lindrick,   Contact: Mrs Linda Sanderberg Profit: £4,519,000
Worksop B15 3AQ   Secretary to the Chairman   Turnover: £105,507,000
021-503 0742

☐ **Wilkinson Sword Group Ltd**   Manufacture of tools & razors

Sword House,   Ch: Gordon Ross   Year Ends: 28 Dec '86   UK employees: n/a
Totteridge Road,   Contact: Louisa Bennett   Donations: £27,000   Total employees: 3,799
High Wycombe HP13 6EJ   Personnel Manager   Profit: £11,466,000
0494-533300   Turnover: £127,879,000

Donations Policy: The company make small and very occasional donations of products and cash up to £100.

☐ **Williams Holdings plc**   Engineering specialists

Pentagon House,   Ch: A N R Rudd   Year Ends: 31 Dec '91   UK employees: n/a
Sir Frank Whittle Road,   CE: B D McGowan   Donations: £136,000   Total employees: 14,917
Derby DE2 4EE   Contact: P Whitehouse   Profit: £168,300,000
0332-364257   Secretary to Managing Director Turnover: £1,001,743,000

Donations Policy: The company concentrates all its support into a single substantial donation, as a result of which the charitable budget is already allocated until 1994. Therefore the company will not respond to any requests it may receive.

☐ **Willis Corroon plc**   Insurance brokers

10 Trinity Square,   Ch: R J Elliott   Year Ends: 31 Dec '91   UK employees: n/a
London EC3P 3AX   CE: R M Miller   Donations: £481,000   Total employees: 11,369
071-488 8111   Contact: Christine Bevan   Profit: £96,100,000
                               Secretary, Charities Committee Turnover: £585,300,000   % Club

Donations Policy: Preference for job creation and training schemes, and local development and regeneration. Support is also given to the arts and national heritage, youth, education and medicine. The company's donations in the USA totalled £691,000.

Please read page 6 | Alphabetical listing •

Name/Address	Officers	Financial Information	Other Information

☐ Willmott Dixon Ltd

Building & maintenance contractors

34 Upper Brook Street,
London W1Y 1PE
071-409 2716

Contact: I Dixon
Chairman

Year Ends: 31 Mar '91
Donations: £49,000
Profit: £2,640,000
Turnover: £157,774,000

UK employees: n/a
Total employees: 1,100

% Club

Donations Policy: Preference for local charities in areas of operation or where a member of staff is involved. Grants mainly for education and enterprise/training.
No unsolicited or general appeals. No grants for advertising in charity brochures; purely denominational (religious) appeals; local appeals not in areas of company presence; overseas projects.

☐ Wilson Bowden plc

Property development & housebuilding

207 Leicester Road,
Ibstock,
Leicestershire LE67 6HP
0530-60777

CE: D C Wilson
Contact: K McEwan
Corporate Director

Year Ends: 31 Dec '91
Donations: £14,000
Profit: £27,800,000
Turnover: £135,900,000

UK employees: n/a
Total employees: 691

Donations Policy: The company has no set policy, both national and local are appeals are considered.

☐ Wilson (Connolly) Holdings plc

Housing estate builders

Tenter Road,
Moulton Park,
Northampton NN3 1QJ
0604-769171

Ch: L A Wilson
Contact: Brian Woods
Marketing Manager

Year Ends: 31 Dec '91
Donations: £53,701
Profit: £27,115,000
Turnover: £197,938,000

UK employees: n/a
Total employees: 799

BitC

Donations Policy: The company states that its funds are already fully allocated.

☐ Wiltshier plc

Builders

High Street,
Harmondsworth,
Middlesex UB7 0AQ
081-759 3331

Ch: M Davies
Contact: D Barratt
Marketing Director

Year Ends: 31 Dec '91
Donations: £4,410
Profit: £2,233,000
Turnover: £230,489,000

UK employees: n/a
Total employees: 1,586

☐ George Wimpey plc

Construction engineers

27 Hammersmith Grove,
London W6 7EN
081-748 2000

Ch: Sir Clifford Chetwood
CE: J A Dwyer
Contact: M P K Luchmun
Secretary to Charitable Trust

Year Ends: 31 Dec '91
Donations: £100,000
Profit: £16,100,000
Turnover: £1,689,900,000

UK employees: n/a
Total employees: 14,400

Donations Policy: Donations are made through the George Wimpey Charitable Trust. All requests from registered charities are considered, with preference for specific local charities in areas of company presence rather than national organisations, and for charities in which a member of staff is involved. Preference for children and youth; social welfare; education; training; and organisations concerned with disabled and underprivileged people. Grants from £50 to £5,000.
Total grants given by the trust were £546,324 in 1991.
No response to circular appeals. No grants for advertising in charity brochures; local appeals not in areas of company presence.
Sponsorship proposals should be addressed to Ms C Mascall.

☐ Winerite Ltd

Wine shippers & agents

Leeds No 4 Bond,
Gelderd Road,
Leeds LS12 6HJ
0532-837676

Ch: G Atkinson
Contact: Assistant Managing Director

Year Ends: 30 Jun '90
Donations: n/a
Profit: £2,748,000
Turnover: £157,728,000

UK employees: n/a
Total employees: 213

☐ Wintershall (UK) Ltd

Exploration & development of crude oil

c/o Bishop & Sewell Solicitors,
90 Great Russell Street,
London WC1B 3RJ
071-631 4141

Ch: B Rigby

Year Ends: 31 Dec '90
Donations: n/a
Profit: £1,365,000
Turnover: £402,669,000

UK employees: n/a
Total employees: n/a

Donations Policy: The company is German owned and makes no charitable donations in the UK.

☐ Witan Investment Company plc

Investment trust

3 Finsbury Avenue,
London EC2M 2PA
071-638 5757

Ch: Lord Faringdon
MD: Hugh Priestly
Contact: G Dawson
Company Secretary

Year Ends: 30 Apr '91
Donations: £26,190
Profit: £26,266,000
Turnover: n/a

UK employees: n/a
Total employees: n/a

Donations Policy: The company gives modest help annually to leading national charities with a proven management record. Occasionally it supports special appeals. Support goes mainly to children/youth, social welfare, medical and the arts.
Unsolicited appeals of all types (including large national appeals and brochure advertising) are not welcome.

• **Alphabetical listing** Please read page 6

Name/Address	Officers	Financial Information	Other Information

☐ Rudolf Wolff & Co Ltd

Commodity brokers

Plantation House,
31 Fenchurch Street,
London EC3M 3DX
071-626 8765

Contact: F Halford
Chairman & Trustee

Year Ends: 31 Dec '91
Donations: £122,448
Profit: n/a
Turnover: n/a

UK employees: 130
Total employees: 180

% Club, ABSA

Donations Policy: One per cent of pre-tax profits are donated to charitable causes, selected by a committee taken from all levels of staff. Preference for children and youth; medical; education; arts; overseas aid/development and enterprise/training. Preference for local charities in areas where the company operates and for charities in which a member of company staff is involved. Grants to national organisations from £250 to £1,500.
No grants for appeals from individuals or for local appeals not in areas of company presence. No response to circular appeals.

☐ Wolseley plc

Distribution of plumbing materials

Vines Lane,
Droitwich,
Hereford & Worcester WR9 8ND
0905-794444

Ch: J Lancaster
Contact: The Wolseley Charitable Trust

Year Ends: 31 Jul '91
Donations: £32,460
Profit: £80,283,000
Turnover: £1,737,581,000

UK employees: n/a
Total employees: 14,806

Donations Policy: Preference for local charities in areas where the company operates and charities in which a member of company staff is involved. Preference for children and youth; social welfare; medical; environment/heritage; arts. Grants to national organisations from £50 to £100. Grants to local organisations from £50 to £1,000.
No response to circular appeals. No grants for advertising in charity brochures; appeals from individuals; purely denominational (religious) appeals; local appeals not in areas of company presence; overseas projects.

☐ Wolstenholme Rink plc

Metal manufacturers

Springfield House,
Lower Eccleshill Road,
Darwen,
Lancashire BB3 0RX
0254-873888

Ch: S H Wright
MD: P J E Rink
Contact: J D Ackroyd
Company Secretary

Year Ends: 31 Dec '91
Donations: £6,441
Profit: £2,322,000
Turnover: £53,423,000

UK employees: n/a
Total employees: 519

% Club

Donations Policy: Preference for local charities in the areas of company presence. Unsolicited appeals outside this policy are unlikely to be supported and are not welcomed.

☐ Wolverhampton & Dudley Breweries plc

Brewers

Park Brewery,
Bath Road,
Wolverhampton,
West Midlands WV1 4NY
0902-711811

Ch: D Miller
MD: D G Thompson
Contact: H L Porter
Company Secretary

Year Ends: 1 Oct '91
Donations: £10,430
Profit: £33,047,000
Turnover: £187,638,000

UK employees: n/a
Total employees: 5,253

Donations Policy: Support only to local charities in areas where the company operates and preference for appeals relevant to company business. Preference for education; recreation; enterprise/training.
No response to circular appeals. No grants for advertising in charity brochures; purely denominational (religious) appeals; local appeals not in areas of company presence; large national appeals; overseas projects.
Sponsorship proposals should be addressed to D M Austin, Director of Marketing.

☐ John Wood Group plc

Engineering, oilfield logistics & supplies

John Wood House,
Greenwell Road,
East Tullos,
Aberdeen AB1 4AX
0224-875464

Ch: I C Wood
Contact: Victoria Wilson
Head of Public Affairs

Year Ends: 31 May '90
Donations: £60,442 (1991)
Profit: £9,510,000
Turnover: £120,838,000

UK employees: n/a
Total employees: 2,170

% Club

Donations Policy: Emphasis is on local community projects in areas of company presence and projects in which employees are directly involved. Preference for children and youth; social welfare; medical; education; environment/heritage; arts; enterprise/training. Grants range from £1,000 to £10,000. Total community contributions in 1991 were £75,000. Sponsorship favours arts programmes with an educational bias, particularly involving youth groups.
No grants for advertising in charity brochures; purely denominational (religious) appeals; local appeals not in areas of company presence; large national appeals; overseas projects.

☐ Woolwich Building Society

Building society

Watling Street,
Bexleyheath,
Kent DA6 7RR
081-298 5000

Ch: C A McLintock
CE: D H Kirkham
Contact: David Blake
Group Head of Corporate Affairs

Year Ends: 31 Dec '91
Donations: £300,000
Profit: £87,800,000
Turnover: £521,200,000

UK employees: n/a
Total employees: 8,300

% Club, BitC, ABSA

Donations Policy: Preference for local charities in the areas of company presence. The major community affairs programme covers enterprise and the built environment, education and the national curriculum, and training for unemployed people. Specific donations to charitable and voluntary bodies cover wide interests: help for disadvantaged and disabled people, medical projects and appeals of national importance, building, housing and conservation concerns. It prefers to support specified projects rather than core funding. Grants to national organisations up to £20,000, and to local organisations up to £5,000.
No support for fundraising events, brochure advertising, appeals from individuals, purely denominational (religious) appeals, overseas projects, political groups or animal charities.
Total community contributions in 1991 were £1.5 million.

Please read page 6 | Alphabetical listing

Name/Address	Officers	Financial Information	Other Information

WPP Group plc
Marketing services

27 Farm Street,
London W1X 6RD
071-408 2204

Ch: G Stevens
Contact: Charity Committee

Year Ends: 31 Dec '91
Donations: £167,000
Profit: £56,105,000
Turnover: £1,204,418,000

UK employees: n/a
Total employees: 21,218

Donations Policy: Preference for appeals relevant to company business. Preference for children and youth; medical; education. Grants to national organisations from £100 to £10,000. Grants to local organisations from £100 to £5,000.

John Wyeth & Brother Ltd
Pharmaceutical products, fine chemicals, baby foods

Huntercombe Lane South,
Taplow,
Maidenhead SL6 0PH
0628-604377

MD: P A Reacher
Contact: Director of Corporate Affairs

Year Ends: 30 Nov '90
Donations: £4,003
Profit: £16,473,000
Turnover: £107,457,000

UK employees: n/a
Total employees: 1,173

Yamaichi Bank (UK) plc
Banking

Guildhall House,
81-87 Gresham Street,
London EC2V 7NQ
071-600 1188

Contact: Don Rogers
General Manager

Year Ends: 31 Mar '92
Donations: £4,213
Profit: £4,033,000
Turnover: n/a

UK employees: 48
Total employees: 60

Donations Policy: Preference for children and youth, medical and the arts. Preference for appeals relevant to company business. Grants to national organisations from £100 to £500.
No grants for advertising in charity brochures; appeals from individuals; purely denominational (religious) appeals; circular appeals.

Yattendon Investment Trust plc
Newspaper publishing

Harbourne Court,
67 Harbourne Road,
Edgbaston,
Birmingham B15 3BU
021-456 4004

Ch: R P R Liffe
Contact: Andrew Peet
Promotions Manager

Year Ends: 2 Jul '88
Donations: £11,640
Profit: £8,304,000
Turnover: £42,404,000

UK employees: n/a
Total employees: 1,577

Yorkshire Bank plc
Banking

20 Merrion Way,
Leeds LS2 8NZ
0532-472000

Ch: Lord Clitheroe
CE: David Knight
Contact: The Secretary
Yorkshire Bank Charitable Trust

Year Ends: 30 Sep '91
Donations: £106,000
Profit: £107,030,000
Turnover: n/a

UK employees: n/a
Total employees: 6,187

ABSA

Donations Policy: Donations are made through the Yorkshire Bank Charitable Trust. Recipients must be registered charities and within the area covered by branches of the bank ie. in England from north of the Thames Valley to Newcastle-upon-Tyne. Charities considered for support include those engaged in youth work, facilities for less able-bodied and mentally disabled people, counselling and community work in depressed areas, with some support also being given for church extensions and the arts. The trustees would be unlikely to make more than one donation within any 12 month period. Grants are usually one-off for a specific project or part of a project, ranging from £100 to £1,000. Applications from individuals, including students, are ineligible. No grants to general appeals from national organisations.

Yorkshire Building Society
Building society

Yorkshire House,
Westgate,
Bradford BD1 2AU
0274-734822

Ch: R W Suddards
CE: D F Roberts
Contact: Dan Cargill
Assistant General Manager
Marketing Services

Year Ends: 31 Dec '91
Donations: n/a
Profit: £55,613,000
Turnover: £116,990,000

UK employees: n/a
Total employees: 1,461

Yorkshire Chemicals plc
Manufacturers of dyestuffs

Kirkstall Road,
Leeds LS3 1LL
0532-443111

MD: P A Lowe
Contact: Secretary, Consultative Committee

Year Ends: 31 Dec '91
Donations: £12,500
Profit: £11,005,000
Turnover: £92,794,000

UK employees: n/a
Total employees: 7,735

Donations Policy: Charities supported should be primarily concerned with poor, sick or needy people in the 'local' area and be people orientated. Preference for children and youth; social welfare; medical; recreation. Grants from £500 to £1,000.
No grants for fundraising events; advertising in charity brochures; appeals from individuals; purely denominational (religious) appeals; large national appeals; overseas projects.

Yorkshire Electricity Group plc
Electricity supply

Wetherby Road,
Scarcroft,
Leeds LS14 3HS
0532-892123

Ch: J S Tysoe
MD: J M Chatwin
Contact: Roger Dickinson
Group Company Secretary

Year Ends: 31 Mar '92
Donations: £114,791
Profit: £141,900,000
Turnover: £1,342,600,000

UK employees: n/a
Total employees: 7,126

BitC, ABSA

Donations Policy: Preference for local charities in areas of company presence and appeals relevant to company business. Preferred areas of support: children and youth, social welfare, medical, education, recreation, environment and heritage, and the arts.
No response to circular appeals. No support for appeals from individuals, purely denominational appeals, local appeals not in areas of company presence, large national appeals and overseas projects.

● **Alphabetical listing** Please read page 6

Name/Address	Officers	Financial Information	Other Information

☐ Yorkshire Television Holdings plc
Independent TV programme contractor

The Television Centre,
Leeds LS3 1JS
0532-438283

Ch: Sir Derek Palmer
MD: C Leach
Contact: Dr G Brownlee
Controller of Corporate Affairs

Year Ends: 30 Sep '91
Donations: £108,000
Profit: £13,091,000
Turnover: £191,414,000

UK employees: n/a
Total employees: 1,310

ABSA

Donations Policy: Support only to local organisations in the franchise area with a strong interest in the arts. Support also to medical and welfare charities and to local education and enterprise initiatives. Typical grants from £50 to £40,000.
Generally no support for circular appeals, fundraising events, advertising in charity brochures, appeals from individuals, purely denominational (religious) appeals, local appeals not in areas of company presence, large national appeals and overseas projects.

☐ Yorkshire Water plc
Water & sewerage services

2 The Embankment,
Sovereign Street,
Leeds LS1 4BG
0532-343234

Ch: Sir Gordon Jones
MD: Trevor Newton
Contact: Ken Auty (see address below)

Year Ends: 31 Mar '92
Donations: £79,200
Profit: £123,900,000
Turnover: £441,200,000

UK employees: n/a
Total employees: 4,900

Donations Policy: The annual budget is divided between charitable giving and sponsorship. Support is given to appeals from within the counties of Yorkshire and North Humberside, the only exception to this being support for WaterAid. Preference for charities in which a member of company staff is involved. Preference for children and youth; social welfare; medical; environment; arts; water based sport. Grants to local organisations from £10 to £12,600. Appeals should be addressed to K I Auty, Community Support Programmes Officer, Yorkshire Water Services Ltd, West Riding House, 67 Albion Street, Leeds LS1 5AA (0532-448201).
No grants for purely denominational (religious) appeals; local appeals not in areas of company presence; overseas projects; political appeals.

☐ Young & Co's Brewery plc
Brewers

Ram Brewery,
Wandsworth,
London SW18 4JD
081-870 0141

Contact: J A Young
Chairman

Year Ends: 31 Mar '91
Donations: £30,093
Profit: £5,035,000
Turnover: £58,524,000

UK employees: n/a
Total employees: 1,425

Donations Policy: In addition to cash donations, goods to the value of £2,205 were donated. Preference for local charities in areas of company presence, charities where a member of staff is involved and appeals relevant to the business. Support for most areas of work, apart from the arts and overseas aid/development.
No support for circular appeals, advertising in charity brochures, local appeals not in areas of company presence, large national appeals.

☐ Young & Rubicam Holdings Ltd
Advertising & public relations

Greater London House,
Hampstead Road,
London NW1 7QP
071-387 9366

Ch: J E de Deo
Contact: E McLachlan
Finance Director

Year Ends: 31 Dec '90
Donations: £16,190
Profit: £61,000
Turnover: £224,678,000

UK employees: n/a
Total employees: 979

% Club, BitC

Donations Policy: Preference for children and youth, medical care, and the arts.
No response to circular appeals. No grants for appeals from individuals; purely denominational (religious) appeals; local appeals not in areas of company presence; large national appeals; overseas projects.

☐ YRM plc
Building design, civil engineering

24 Britton Street,
London EC1M 5NQ
071-253 4311

Ch: Brian Henderson
CE: Timothy Poulson
Contact: Stephen Slater
Financial Director

Year Ends: 30 Apr '92
Donations: £8,762
Profit: £1,375,000
Turnover: £19,645,000

UK employees: n/a
Total employees: 397

☐ Yule Catto & Co plc
Speciality building products, chemicals

Central Road,
Temple Fields,
Harlow CM20 2BH
0279-442791

Ch: Lord Catto
MD: A Walker
Contact: K P F Bird
Company Secretary

Year Ends: 31 Dec '91
Donations: £29,000
Profit: £21,808,000
Turnover: £225,541,000

UK employees: n/a
Total employees: 2,795

Donations Policy: Support for an established list of charities approved by the company, mainly in the fields of children, youth, education, social welfare and medical. Unsolicited appeals are a waste of time.

☐ ZAL Holdings Ltd
Consultancy services, shipping line & travel agents

Zimco House,
16-28 Tabernacle Street,
London EC2A 4BN
071-638 6464

Contact: General Manager

Year Ends: 31 Mar '90
Donations: n/a
Profit: £1,933,000
Turnover: £104,832,000

UK employees: n/a
Total employees: 1,961

Donations Policy: The company is Zambian and only supports charities in Zambia working with hospitals, schools and orphanages.

☐ Zetters Group plc
Pools promoters

86-88 Clarkenwell Road,
London EC1P 1ZS
071-253 5376

Ch: Paul Zetter
MD: J D H Clarke
Contact: A Gibbs
Company Secretary

Year Ends: 31 Mar '92
Donations: £6,540
Profit: £1,036,000
Turnover: £22,945,000

UK employees: n/a
Total employees: 610

% Club

Radio stations

This section lists 145 BBC and Independent radio stations. They are listed in alphabetical order. This means that most of the BBC stations come first as they are filed under "BBC Radio ***". The exceptions are stations now known by their initials (eg. GMR, the BBC station for Greater Manchester). The Independent stations are also listed in alphabetical order.

Support by radio stations falls into the following broad categories:

- **Cash.** A few radio stations give to charity from their own resources. More have set up an associated charitable trust which gives grants in the franchise area (eg. BBC Radio Cornwall). The station raises money for its trust by on-air appeals and auctions, involving reporters and the public in fundraising events or setting them challenges etc.. The income of these trusts, therefore, can fluctuate from year to year, but can be considerable (eg. the Hereward Radio, CN.FM & KL.FM Appeal raised £160,000 in 1991).

- **Publicity/on-air appeals.** More commonly, radio stations serve as excellent vehicles through which charities can campaign, publicise an event, recruit volunteers, fundraise, ask for gifts in kind etc.. A proven ability to get the charity on local radio is a valuable adjunct to any sponsorship proposal you might send to a company in the Alphabetical listing section of this Guide.

As you read through the entries in this section, you will be struck by the potential for publicity local radio offers your charity. Many have a "What's On" diary broadcast either once a day or, more commonly, at intervals throughout the day. Charities often run excellent, attractive events; why not publicise them to a wide audience over the airwaves?

- **Features about charities.** Many stations also said that they are happy to undertake information broadcasts by and/or on behalf of charities. Again, not only is this general campaigning work important because it communicates the needs of your clients in exactly the way you want to put them across, it can also have unexpected advantages in fundraising terms. Some stations are also happy to run outside broadcasts from charity events if the event warrants it. This adds prestige and coverage.

Many charities have items which are newsworthy in themselves. It is not always a question of pleading "It's for charity" as a means of getting airtime, rather it may well be a story that the radio will want to cover anyway.

Finally, radio is a specialised, technical medium. To get the best from it, you should plan carefully. Here is a basic outline:

- Listen to your local station and familiarise yourself with its broadcasts. Get to know producers to approach with ideas or a press release.

- If you get a feature, talk it over with the producer. Explain to him or her what it is that you most want to get across to the listeners.

- Some stations have a community programmes producer or a helpline team who will help you make the broadcast. These are the best starting point, especially if you are planning a longer feature.

- There are various bodies offering training for voluntary groups in using the media. The addresses of the Directory of Social Change and Community Service Volunteers (CSV) are in the Useful contacts section at the back of this Guide. CSV have a very useful audio service which helps voluntary and community organisations send appropriate press releases and tapes to appropriate people in national and local radio. They also train groups in writing press releases and making the tapes.

The Radio Authority

The Radio Authority licenses and regulates all Independent Radio services. These comprise national, local, cable, national FM subcarrier, satellite and restricted services. The latter includes all short-term, freely radiating services (eg. special event radio) and highly localised permanent services such as hospital and student radio.

There is a constant process of advertising or re-advertising ILR licenses, so during the lifetime of this Guide there will be new stations in operation and current ones may lose their licence.

The Radio Authority also regulates programming and advertising, and has codes on each.

It publishes a very useful **Radio Authority Pocket Book** which gives basic details on all ILR stations. It is available from the Press & Information section of:

The Radio Authority, Holbrook House, 14 Great Queen Street, Holborn, London WC2B 5DG (071-430 2724).

Radio stations in this section

This is a list of the radio stations in this section. It is broken down into national stations and then local stations by order of county:

National

BBC Radio 1 FM
BBC Radio 2
BBC Radio 3
BBC Radio 4
BBC Radio 5
BBC Radio Scotland
BBC Radio Ulster & Radio Foyle
BBC Radio Wales
Downtown Radio (Northern Ireland)

Radio stations

England

Avon
BBC Radio Bristol
Brunel Classic Gold
Galaxy Radio
GWR Radio

Bedfordshire
BBC Radio Beds, Herts & Bucks
Chiltern Radio

Berkshire
210 Classic Gold Radio

Buckinghamshire
BBC Radio Beds, Herts & Bucks
CRMK

Cambridgeshire
BBC Radio Cambridgeshire
CN.FM
Hereward Radio
1332 The World's Greatest Music Station

Channel Islands
BBC Radio Guernsey
BBC Radio Jersey

Cheshire
Signal Cheshire

Cleveland
BBC Radio Cleveland
TFM

Cornwall
BBC Radio Cornwall
Pirate FM

Cumbria
BBC Radio Cumbria
BBC Radio Furness

Derbyshire
BBC Radio Derby
Trent FM

Devon
BBC Radio Devon
DevonAir Radio
Plymouth Sound
Radio in Tavistock

Dorset
2CR Classic Gold & 2CR FM

Essex
BBC Radio Essex
Breeze AM
Essex Radio
Mellow 1557

Gloucestershire
BBC Radio Gloucestershire
CD 603
Severn Sound & Severn Sound Supergold

Greater Manchester
GMR
Piccadilly Gold & Piccadilly Key 103
Sunset Radio

Hampshire
BBC Radio Solent
Ocean Sound Classic Hits & Power FM
South Coast Radio
210 Classic Gold Radio

Hereford & Worcester
BBC Radio Hereford & Worcester
Radio Wyvern

Hertfordshire
BBC Radio Beds, Herts & Bucks

Humberside
BBC Radio Humberside
Lincs FM
Viking FM

Isle of Wight
Isle of Wight Radio

Kent
BBC Radio Kent
Invicta Radio
RTM

Lancashire
BBC Radio Lancashire
RadioWave
Red Rose Gold & Red Rose Rock FM

Leicestershire
BBC Radio Leicester
Leicester Sound FM

Lincolnshire
BBC Radio Lincolnshire
Great Yorkshire Radio
Lincs FM

London
Capital Radio
Choice FM
GLR
London Broadcasting Company
London Greek Radio
London Talkback Radio
Melody Radio
Radio Kiss FM
RTM
Spectrum International Radio
Sunrise Radio
WNK Radio

Merseyside
BBC Radio Merseyside
Radio City

Norfolk
BBC Radio Norfolk
Broadland FM
KL.FM
SGR-FM

North Yorkshire
BBC Radio York
Great Yorkshire Radio
Minster FM

Northamptonshire
BBC Radio Northampton
KCBC
Northants Radio

Nottinghamshire
BBC Radio Nottingham
Trent FM

Oxfordshire
BBC Radio Oxford
Fox FM

Shropshire
BBC Radio Shropshire
Beacon Radio
Sunshine 855
WABC

Somerset
Orchard FM
Somerset Sound

South Yorkshire
BBC Radio Sheffield
Great Yorkshire Radio
Hallam FM

Staffordshire
BBC Radio Stoke
Signal Radio

Suffolk
CN.FM
SGR-FM

Surrey
County Sound Radio AM

Sussex
BBC Radio Sussex
County Sound Radio AM
Radio Mercury

Tyne & Wear
BBC Radio Newcastle
Great North Radio
Metro FM
Wear FM

West Midlands

BBC Radio CWR
BBC Radio WM
Beacon Radio
BRMB FM
Buzz FM
Mercia Sound
WABC

West Yorkshire

BBC Radio Leeds
Great Yorkshire Radio
Magic 828
The Pulse
Radio Aire
Sunrise FM

Wiltshire

BBC Wiltshire Sound
Brunel Classic Gold
GWR Radio
Spire FM

Northern Ireland

Classic Tracks BCR
Cool FM

Scotland

Borders

Radio Borders

Central

Central FM

Dumfries & Galloway

West Sound Radio

Grampian

North East Community Radio
NorthSound Radio
SLR BBC Radio Aberdeen

Highlands

Moray Firth Radio
SLR BBC Radio Highland

Lothian

Forth RFM
Max AM

Shetland Islands

SIBC

Strathclyde

Q96
Radio Clyde

Tayside

Heartland FM
Radio Tay

Wales

Clwyd

BBC Radio Clwyd
Marcher Sound

Dyfed

Radio Ceredigion

Gwent

Red Dragon FM
Touch AM

Powys

Radio Maldwyn

South Glamorgan

Red Dragon FM
Touch AM

West Glamorgan

Swansea Sound

● **Radio stations**

Name/Address	Contact	Donations/Support

☐ **BBC Radio 1 FM**

BBC Radio,
Broadcasting House,
London W1A 1AA
071-580 4468

Contact: Chris Burns
Chief Producer

The station broadcasts five or six social action broadcasts each year, usually with continuous air play for a full week. Programmes in 1992 included Which Way Now? (alongside Radio 5 with advice for 13/14 year olds choosing their examination subjects); Tell It Like It Is (offering support to young people feeling depressed and suicidal through a special Samaritans Linkline); Race Thro' The 90's (advice and information to help those experiencing racial discrimination, supported by a helpline and print material); Drug Alert (for drug users, with a helpline and leaflets), and Euro Action (information for unemployed people wanting advice on jobs, education, training and opportunities in the UK and Europe).
Research is underway for 1993 on teenage pregnancy and homelessness.
Occasionally there may be Wednesday evening broadcasts for charities between 8.30 and 9.00 pm or a one hour documentary (eg. broadcasts on Yugoslavia, National Aids Awareness, Keeping Mrs Dawson, and Banged Up, a phone-in from Dorchester Prison).

☐ **BBC Radio 2**

BBC White City,
Wood Lane,
London W12 7TS
071-580 4468

Contact: John Gurnett
Chief Producer

The station produces four or five projects each year. 1992 projects included Caring For Carers (supported by a free helpline and print material); People Need People (a joint project with the Volunteer Centre UK on volunteering opportunities with a telephone information line and a free leaflet); The Money Maze (information and advice on financial matters); Fair Play (advice on consumer redress, supported by a leaflet and helpline).
Research is underway for 1993 on health and fitness, loneliness and relationships, and financial investment.
Eileen Mullen is the Head of Viewer Relations.

☐ **BBC Radio 3**

BBC Radio,
Broadcasting House,
London W1A 1AA
071-580 4468

Contact: Nicholas Kenyon
Controller of Radio 3

The station concentrates its charitable broadcasts on Aids and Arts charities. In 1992, the station broadcast the St Cecilias Day Royal Concert at the Barbican in aid of the Musicians Benevolent Fund. In 1993, the Royal Festival Concert will be by the Royal Liverpool Philharmonic Orchestra. Scores are donated by composers and publishers; these are auctioned on air and the money raised is donated to Crusaid.
Adrian Thomas is the Head of Radio 3.

☐ **BBC Radio 4**

BBC Radio,
Broadcasting House,
London W1A 1AA
071-927 4806

Contact: Michael Green
Controller of Radio 4

The Week's Good Cause is the longest continuously running programme on air. The programme allows a five minute broadcast by a different charity each Sunday morning.
Social action projects on Radio 4 are produced by programmes like Woman's Hour and You & Yours. In 1992, Woman's Hour launched a project on breast cancer and You & Yours produced its second community care project alongside Radio 2.
Hahini Patel is the Producer of The Week's Good Cause (071-580 5213). Chris Langley is the Editor of Social Action Broadcasts.

☐ **BBC Radio 5**

BBC Radio,
Broadcasting House,
London W1A 1AA
071-580 5879

Contact: Pat Ewing
Controller of Radio 5

There are two or three projects broadcast on Radio 5. Some complement those on Radio One (eg. Which Way Now?). Student Choice, a post exam survival guide for students receiving their GCSE, A' level or Higher results, is supported by a helpline.
BBC Radio 5 is a relatively new station; it is expected that more charity broadcasts will be made over the coming years.

☐ **BBC Radio Beds, Herts & Bucks**

PO Box 476,
Luton LU1 5BA
0582-459111

Contact: Pam Spriggs
Presenter/Producer

The station has a Notice Board show giving information on local fundraising events, fun days etc.. There is also the Three Counties Morning Helpline which opens at 9.30 am and makes appeals on behalf of (and maybe with) local charities and community organisations for goods, items and services (including appeals for volunteers). There are monthly broadcasts/updates from many charities such as Macmillan Nurses, NSPCC, RSPCA, RNIB and the citizen's advice bureau. The station welcomes approaches from charities with ideas for programmes/features.

Radio stations

Name/Address	Contact	Donations/Support

☐ BBC Radio Bristol

PO Box 194,
Bristol BS99 7QT
0272-741111

Contact: John Boyes
Action Line Manager

The total pledged to Children in Need in 1991 was £67,640.
Each year the station runs five or six, week-long campaigns about a particular cause or charity. Some of the most successful appeals of recent times have been the Romanian orphans appeals run in association with Mencap. The station helped to send a 30 tonne lorry filled with everything from non-perishable foods to toys and specialist equipment. The station has also been actively involved in other Eastern European causes. Staff involvement with the main campaigns is encouraged.
Action Line is the main on air broadcast for charity and community organisations, run jointly with Community Service Volunteers. There are five charity/community broadcasts each day. There is a short bulletin by the radio station in the morning, followed by a 5-minute broadcast by the charity. In the afternoon there are three 3-4 minute broadcasts by the charity and radio staff. Short bulletins are also repeated on Sunday evenings. The Action Line telephone number is 0272-467467.
Malcolm Brammer is the Programmes Editor.

☐ BBC Radio Cambridgeshire

Broadcasting House,
Hills Road,
Cambridge CB2 1LD
0223-315970

Contact: Programme Organiser

The station has a 36-hour Christmas auction in early December. The money raised goes to the station's Trustline Charity. This charity makes grants to local groups helping elderly, young and disabled people. The station has helped to raise money/support for charities through on air appeals, outside broadcasts, and information broadcasts by and on behalf of charities.
The station welcomes approaches from charities with ideas for programmes/features.
There is a Careline that broadcasts throughout the day. It allows charity and community organisations to make appeals for equipment and volunteers and publicise fundraising events. On Sunday afternoon there is a 2 hour show in which local people, companies, charities and community organisations are interviewed and local causes and issues are discussed.

☐ BBC Radio Cleveland

95 FM,
Broadcasting House,
Newport Road,
Middlesbrough TS1 5DG
0642-225211

Contact: Mick Wormald
Programme Organiser

The total pledged to Children in Need in 1991 was £107,456.
The BBC Children in Need is always very successful in this area. Other charity broadcasts should be made as newsworthy as possible. Information on community and charity events is broadcast on an on-going basis throughout the station's mainstream programmes, especially during the Saturday morning show. Oxfam's Ethiopia appeals, local hospital fundraising and convoys of aid to Romania and Poland have been amongst the most popular broadcast appeals. Staff and volunteers from the station are actively involved in many of the station's causes.
John Watson is the Station Manager.

☐ BBC Radio Clwyd

The Old School House,
Glanrafon Road,
Mold,
Clwyd CH7 1PA
0352-700367

Contact: Tony Todd
Senior Producer

The total pledged to Children In Need in 1991 was £115,981.
Children in Need is the station's big charity campaign, for which they put on extra shows. Help the Aged is the next large charity the station supports.
The station has helped to raise money/support for charities through outside broadcasts and information broadcasts by and on behalf of charities. No support for advertising in charity brochures and purely denominational (religious) appeals.
What's On and Actionline are the two shows that broadcast local charity events and publicise local voluntary organisations when in need of donations of goods/gifts in kind. The station also gives volunteer information.

☐ BBC Radio Cornwall

Phoenix Wharf,
Truro,
Cornwall TR1 1UA
0872-75421

Contact: Julie Stanton
Programmes Organiser

The total pledged to Children in Need in 1991 was £45,000.
Cornwall Cares is a charitable trust, run in association with the station. It raises funds for named causes within Cornwall. Fundraising starts on May 1st and runs for 12 months.
The station's Helpline runs daily appeals asking for practical or physical help, support or specific items. The station welcomes approaches from charities with ideas for programmes/features.
The Helpline number is Truro 76222 or Liskeard 348503. It is run by Jill Needham.

● Radio stations

Name/Address   *Contact*   *Donations/Support*

☐ BBC Radio Cumbria

Hilltop Heights,
London Road,
Carlisle,
Cumbria CA1 2NA
0228-31661

Contact: Mike Marsh
Station Manager

The total pledged to Children in Need in 1991 was £105,000.
The What's On Diary, broadcast between 9-11.30 am each weekday, publicises local events and local voluntary organisations. The programme presenter, Alan Smith, reads out charity information sent in. On the show voluntary organisations ask for equipment to be donated or offer to buy at low prices. There are also one or two large campaigns/appeals each year for particular causes.
The station's Advisory Council must approve the station's support for any particular charities. Recently the major appeals have been for the Cumbria WRVS Christmas Appeal to collect non-perishable foodstuffs, clothing and gifts for children, young and elderly people.
The station also has a Lamb Bank which runs each day through the Spring for local farmers to match up lambless ewes with eweless lambs and vice versa.
Phil Ashworth is the Programmes Editor.

☐ BBC Radio CWR

25 Warwick Road,
Coventry CV1 2NA
0228-31661

Contact: Charles Hodkinson
Programmes Organiser

The total pledged to Children in Need in 1991 was over £100,000.
The station wants to involve a wide range of charities in its shows and welcomes suggestions from charities for programmes/features. All local charitable appeals are considered by the station's Local Advisory Council.
The station has helped to raise money/support for charities through outside broadcasts and information broadcasts on behalf of charities. It will not support advertising in charity brochures.

☐ BBC Radio Derby

PO Box 269,
Derby DE1 3HL
0332-361111

Contact: Jo Bucklow
Action Desk Manager

The total pledged to Children in Need in 1991 was £110,000.
The Radio Derby Money Mountain has been running since 1983 and has raised about £400,000 in total for local charities. In the Spring, the radio station appeals for charities to apply to become one of the charities supported by the Money Mountain. The Local Radio Regional Advisory Council decides which of the charities they will support. The appeal starts in October. In 1991, the Money Mountain raised £52,000 for Derbyshire Royal Infimary (50%), Burton-on-Trent Red Cross (25%) and Phab Club (25%).
The station also broadcasts four 2-6 minute appeals each weekday and three appeals over the weekend for charity/community organisations. It will provide training for the organisation to present themselves and their case on air. The station will also make broadcasts on behalf of charities.
Social Action Broadcasting involves "anything to do with the community, is alternative, issue based, non-political or profit making". Most of the funding for the Social Action Broadcasting comes from local companies sponsoring the cause. One of the biggest campaigns will be the Midland-wide campaign for homeless people. This campaign will have substantial air time on Midland radio and television; this sponsorship cost British Telecom very little and does not include a donation towards charities working with homeless people.
The Action Desk telephone number is 0332-369394.
Alex Trelinski is the Programmes Organiser.

☐ BBC Radio Devon

PO Box 100,
Walnut Gardens,
St Davids,
Exeter EX4 4DB
0392-215651

Contact: Helen Hughes
Programmes Editor

The total pledged to Children in Need in 1991 was £54,630.
The station's social action broadcasts are run by the Community Service Volunteers based in Plymouth. The Ian Brass show broadcasts appeals, through the Helpline, between 11am-12.00, on behalf of charities/community organisations. The afternoon show between 3pm-5pm acts as a volunteer bureau appealing for all kinds of volunteers for a wide range of charities. What's On broadcasts about 12 pages of charity/community events each day, throughout the day.
The Local Opt Out on medium wave for Plymouth has more charity broadcasts.

☐ BBC Radio Essex

PO Box 765,
Chelmsford,
Essex CM2 9XB
0245-262393

Contact: Alison Hartley
Community Helpline
Co-ordinator

The total pledged to Children in Need in 1991 was £300,000.
The station has a weekend auction of donated gifts to raise money for hearing aids for deaf children in Essex. The station has helped to raise money/support for charities through on air appeals, outside broadcasts and information broadcasts by and on behalf of charities. Each presenter reads out a full list of charity events during their show.
The Community Helpline runs from 10.15-10.30 am each weekday, during the John Hayes Show. The presenter broadcasts appeals from six or seven charities, making appeals for goods/gifts in kind, voluntary workers etc. and gives out phone numbers and addresses. Specialists from local voluntary groups often come in to talk about particular issues.
People can phone on 0245-495050, between 9.30 and 10.00 am. After 10 am this number is used for other programmes.

Radio stations

Name/Address	Contact	Donations/Support

☐ BBC Radio Furness

Broadcasting House,
Hartington Street,
Barrow-in-Furness
Cumbria LA14 5FH
0229-836767

Contact: Mark Jones
Senior Producer

This is an opt-out from BBC Radio Cumbria (see separate entry). This station broadcasts to Furness and South Lakeland between 6.00-8.00 am and between 2.30-4.30 pm.
The AM Show concentrates on news broadcasts, adoption of children from Eastern Europe, Help the Aged campaigns, job centre and employment initiatives. Presenters read out information sent to them by voluntary groups. Some of this information is turned into tapes that are then played by the presenters. "Even if a group are just having a coffee morning to raise money for a cause we will still try to use it."
The station has helped to raise money/support for charities through outside broadcasts and information broadcasts on behalf of charities.

☐ BBC Radio Gloucestershire

London Road,
Gloucester GL1 1SW
0452-308585

Contact: Mark Hurrell
Programmes Organiser

The total pledged to Children in Need in 1991 was £95,000.
The station welcomes approaches from charities with ideas for programmes/features. It has helped to raise money/support for charities through on air appeals and information broadcasts by and on behalf of charities. The station will not support advertising in charity brochures or purely denominational appeals.
Anna Kingston runs the Helpline (0452-307555).

☐ BBC Radio Guernsey

Commerce House,
Les Banques,
St Peter Port,
Guernsey
0481-728977

Contact: Bob Bufton
Station Manager

The total pledged to Children in Need by Jersey and Guernsey in 1991 was £45,066.
BBC Radios Guernsey and Jersey do a joint charities Christmas Appeal to raise money for needy members of the islands' communities. In 1991, the two stations raised over £60,000. £15,000 was raised during a six hour on air auction. The money was used to help unemployed families, elderly people on the islands, and local charities, usually through fuel or gift vouchers.
For the station's 10th anniversary they held a "Challenge Anneka" type appeal. Local charities were asked to send in challenges for the stations' reporters. The challenge taken on was to take a group of 12 people from the Cheshire Homes for lunch and a day out to Alderney. Social action broadcasts feature appeals during many of the stations' shows. Presenters read out information sent in by charities and the community. The station's What's On show includes in-studio interviews, outside broadcasts and details of events on the islands.

☐ BBC Radio Hereford & Worcester

Hylton Road,
Worcester WR2 5WW
0905-748485

Contact: Denzil Dudley
Programmes Organiser

The total pledged to Children in Need in 1991 was £125,000.
The station does not broadcast appeals for money but features the work of fundraisers in the daily Charity Check feature at 2.45 pm. Other charity/community broadcasts are made during normal programmes mainly between 9.00-4.00 pm.
The station has helped to raise money/support for charities through outside broadcasts. It broadcasts information on behalf of charities, and welcomes approaches from charities with ideas for programmes/features. There is no support for advertising in charity brochures.
James Coghill is the News Editor.

☐ BBC Radio Humberside

9 Chapel Street,
Hull HU1 3NU
0482-23232

Contact: Katy Noone
Producer of the Countywide show

The total pledged to Children in Need in 1991 was £91,155.
The Judy Murden Programme, 9.00-11.00 am, concentrates on community issues, often involving charities. Recently this centred on a local MP who wanted to move mentally disabled people away from a home because their neighbours did not like them being there. The station gave the issue plenty of air time, involving many local and national charities in discussions about Care in the Community. The show also gives details of charity events, volunteer information etc. which are repeated in other shows four times each day.
The station also links up occasionally with national charities for national campaign weeks eg. asthma, arthritis, multiple sclerosis.

☐ BBC Radio Jersey

Broadcasting House,
Rouge Bouillon,
St Hellier,
Jersey
0534-70000

Contact: Mike Vibert
News Editor

See entry for BBC Radio Guernsey.

● Radio stations

Name/Address   *Contact*   *Donations/Support*

☐ BBC Radio Kent

Sun Pier,
Chatham,
Kent ME4 4EZ
0634-830505

Contact: Clive Lawrence
Programmes Organiser

The total pledged to Children in Need in 1991 was £380,000.
The station has helped to raise money/support for charities through on air appeals and outside broadcasts. It welcomes approaches from charities with ideas for programmes/features. Social action broadcasts are made throughout the programming.

☐ BBC Radio Lancashire

Darwen Street,
Blackburn BB2 2EA
0254-262411

Contact: Mark Thomas
Programme Editor

The total pledged to Children in Need in 1991 was £114,228.
Other than Children in Need the station has not recently undertaken any major campaigns for a particular cause or charity. It gives charities access to the airwaves through outside broadcasts and studio interviews.
The station tries to cover as wide a range of causes as possible including charity events and activities. Stories should be made as newsworthy as possible and ideally cover the whole of Lancashire.
The Andy Peebles show, broadcast between 9.30-1.00 pm. covers many charity issues.

☐ BBC Radio Leeds

Broadcasting House,
Woodhouse Lane,
Leeds LS2 9PX
0532-442131

Contact: Helen Wheeler
Promotions Assistant

The total pledged to Children in Need in 1991 was £325,997.
The station will donate sweatshirts for charity raffles and occasionally old records and CDs. At Easter there is an Easter egg collection and collected eggs are donated to the charities working with local children. At Christmas the station also organises a "Toys and Tins" collection for charities working with children and elderly people.
The What's On programme announces details of charity events in the area. To guarantee more publicity, charities should try to do something unusual to grab people's attention. The station welcomes approaches from charities with ideas for programmes/features.
Some of the recent successful appeals through the Helpline have been "Wheels Across Yorkshire" to raise money to buy a minibus for disabled groups, and the appeal for Romanian orphans. For the latter, the station appealed for lorries, skilled volunteers (plumbers, electricians etc.), food, milk powder and specialist equipment. A West Yorkshire group then transported the people and items to Romania.
In 1993, there will be some large charity appeals/campaigns. Leeds celebrates its centenary and BBC Radio Leeds' 25th birthday.
Roger Whittaker is the Programmes Organiser.

☐ BBC Radio Leicester

Epic House,
Charles Street,
Leicester LE1 3SH
0533-516688

Contact: Steven Butt
Senior Programme Producer

The total pledged to Children in Need in 1991 was £86,000.
The station helped to set up the Radio Leicester Charitable Trust which has been raising large sums of money for local charities for 14 years. Mr Merrick is the Chairman of the trust. Money is raised during a weekend in October. Most money is raised during the on air auction of gifts donated by local companies and people. Willie Thorn has donated his time to coach people in frames of snooker; local flying organisations have donated hot air balloon trips; the local MP has taken people for the day to the House Of Commons; the local cinema has donated a screen for the special showing of films; the local brewery has brewed a special beer. All proceeds and collections go to the trust.
There are two social action broadcasts each day, 10.30 and 4.30, lasting 4-5 minutes each. They help to promote local voluntary organisations and causes. These broadcasts take the form most suitable for the particular charity or organisation.
Occasionally the station is involved in week-long campaigns which would form a major part of the station's news, interviews, reports and air time.

☐ BBC Radio Lincolnshire

PO Box 219,
Newport,
Lincoln LN1 3XY
0522-511411

Contact: Malcolm Swire
Programme Organiser

The total pledged to Children in Need 1991 was £106,372.
Go For Gold is the nation's 6th largest local radio charity. It started in 1988. Each year the station looks for a cause that will benefit a large part of the community. People holding fundraising events are sent an organisers pack containing posters, lapel badges and paying-in slips for their local bank. The campaign is launched at Easter and runs until the end of September.
In 1988, the fund raised £72,000 and provided 16 defibrillators for front line ambulances. In 1989, £90,000 was raised to buy over 300 nebulisers and flow meters for all the county's doctors and equipment for the hospitals was also purchased. In 1990, £59,000 was raised towards three ambulances for the St John Ambulance Brigade. In 1991, £85,000 was raised to provide the Lincolnshire Integrated Voluntary Emergency Service (LIVES) with 40 pulse-oximeters and 40 oxygen resuscitation kits. In 1992, the fund raised £40,000 which bought a mobile eye-screening facility comprising of a specialist camera and film and a vehicle to house and transport it.
The station also runs a What's On Diary giving details of charity/community events.

Radio stations

Name/Address	Contact	Donations/Support

☐ BBC Radio Merseyside

55 Paradise Street,
Liverpool L1 3BP
051-708 5500

Contact: Barbara Taylor
Programmes Organiser

The total pledged to Children in Need in 1991 was £129,899.
The station has its own Merseyside Charitable Trust, which raised £12,500 for the Christmas 1991 Toy Appeal. Most money is raised through concerts and by asking listeners to raise and donate funds. All charities in the franchise area can apply for a donation or grant from the trust. The trust has recently bought a specially adapted car to enable disabled people to learn to drive.
The station has a toys collection at Christmas to provide gifts to children from deprived backgrounds and works in association with local rotary clubs. The station often runs its own charity appeals/campaigns. Recently there was a successful Croatia Food Appeal in association with ASDA. Reporters were actively involved.
Presenters give details of charity events and make appeals for volunteers etc.. The station has helped to raise money/support for charities through on air appeals and information broadcasts by and on behalf of charities. The station welcomes approaches from charities with ideas for programmes/features.
The station will not support advertising in charity brochures, purely denominational appeals, large national appeals and overseas projects.

☐ BBC Radio Newcastle

Broadcasting Centre,
Barrack Road,
Newcastle-Upon-Tyne
NE99 2NE
091-232 1313

Contact: Derm Tanner
Programme Organiser

The total pledged to Children in Need in 1991 was £181,872.
The weekly Contact programme (Sundays 3.30-4.00 pm) is aimed at disability groups. The show gives details on fundraising, volunteering, information, legislation etc.. Contact works closely with the Dean Centre.
Bridge The Gap (Sundays 4.00-6.00 pm) is an Asian programme, presented by Sameena Bashley in English, and includes specialist information and advice for Asian listeners. It is followed by an Asian programme in Hindi-Urdu.
The Chinese Connection (Sundays 6.30-7.00 pm) is a weekly programme for Chinese listeners presented by Sow Fong Cole in Cantonese.
The station's What's On broadcasts information every day throughout the day as and when needed. The station would like people to contact them with information of what is happening in the community, but stresses people should make the stories as interesting as possible; try to catch the eye. In-studio interviews are always possible, as are outside broadcasts. The station sometimes dedicates a half hour programme to a cause and brings in specialists from charity/community organisations (eg. the recent Charity in a Time of Recession show). Occasionally the station may have a series of stories and interviews as a part of a week-long campaign on a particular cause.

☐ BBC Radio Norfolk

Norfolk Tower,
Surrey Street,
Norwich NR1 3PA
0603-617411

Contact: David Clayton
Programmes Organiser

Donations: £10,000
Total Raised: £15,000

The total pledged to Children in Need in 1991 was £100,000.
The station also has its own Radio Helpline Charitable Trust which makes donations of about £10,000 a year. Fundraising takes place throughout the year. The trust's contact is Wally Webb who runs the station's main social action broadcasts on Sundays between 12.00 and 2.00 pm. The station has helped to raise money/support for charities through on air appeals, outside broadcasts and information broadcasts by and on behalf of charities. A recent appeal for old Green Shield Stamps expected to raise £1,000; it in fact raised over £10,000.
The station prefers to support children and youth; social welfare; medical; education; environment/heritage. The station does not support advertising in charity brochures; large national appeals or overseas projects.
Most shows broadcast What's On, giving details of fundraising events and other things of interest happening in the community.

☐ BBC Radio Northampton

Broadcasting House,
Abington Street,
Northampton NN1 2BH
0604-239100

Contact: Nigel Dyson
Programmes Organiser

The station supports occasional charity appeals. In 1992/93, the station will support three local charities: Headway, Multiple Sclerosis, and the Northamptonshire Association for the Blind. A series of on air appeals and charity days are organised. The choice of charities was made by the station's Advisory Council.
The station's daily In Company programme, 1.10-4.00 pm, regularly features information about local and national charities.

☐ BBC Radio Nottingham

York House,
Mansfield Road,
Nottingham NG1 3HZ
0602-415161

Contact: Ken Warburton/Nic Brunger
Station Managers

Including BBC local television, the total pledged to Children in Need in 1991 was £300,000.
Money Spinner is the station's annual charity appeal. Launched in 1987, it has raised tens of thousands of pounds for local charities. The cash has bought equipment for the baby unit at the Queen's Medical Centre, the British Heart Foundation and two local organisations working with disabled people. The 1991 appeal raised over £52,000 to help the Spastics Society bring the Peto method of Conductive Education to Nottingham. During 1992, Money Spinner supported the work of ChildLine in the East Midlands. Each year the station is involved with the BBC Children in Need Appeal, publicising local fundraising events and inviting local charities to apply for grants from the fund.
The Action Line is committed to working with groups who are facing discrimination, under-representation or disadvantage, and giving them publicity. The station has helped to raise awareness/support for charities and community groups through on air appeals, outside broadcasts and information broadcasts by and on behalf of charities. The station provides telephone back-up to broadcasts and runs a daily helpline putting people in touch with the help and advice agencies they need. The Action Line Organiser is Anne Freeman.

● Radio stations

Name/Address   *Contact*   *Donations/Support*

☐ BBC Radio Oxford

269 Banbury Road,   *Contact:* Stewart Woodcock   *Donations:* £20,000
Oxford OX2 7DW   Programme Organiser   *Total Raised:* £19,000

The total pledged to Children in Need in 1991 was £210,000.
Each year the station runs highly successful charity auctions with local businesses and organisations donating prizes which are then auctioned on air. The money raised has paid for minibuses for Mencap and for elderly people and special equipment for the Special Care Baby Unit at the John Radcliffe Hospital. The largest venture has been the design and commissioning of the Radio Oxford Narrowboat for use by disabled and disadvantaged children.
The station has helped to raise money/support for charities through on air appeals and information broadcasts by and on behalf of charities. It welcomes approaches from charities with ideas for programmes/features. Preference for children and youth; social welfare; medical. Generally no support for advertising in charity brochures; appeals from individuals; purely denominational (religious) appeals; local appeals not in areas of company presence; large national appeals; overseas projects.
The Bill Heine programme (weekdays 10.00-1.00 pm) has a mixture of studio guests and phone-ins. It is the focal point for discussion of social affairs and the promotion of voluntary organisations and activities.

☐ BBC Radio Scotland

BBC Broadcasting House,   *Contact:* Joyce Snell
Queen Margaret Drive,   Appeals Organiser
Glasgow G12 8DG
041-330 2345

All registered Scottish charities can apply to have appeals broadcast free of charge. These appeals are usually to inform people of the charity, the work they are doing and to ask for support, volunteers, donations or gifts in kind, usually for particular projects. The station decides if the appeal will be on television or radio. The radio station runs one such appeal each month; there are four such television appeals each year. The charity must nominate its own speaker and write its own script, but the production staff will help. The appeals are broadcast on Sundays at 8.55 am lasting 5 minutes. Additional coverage is given in the Radio Times and on Ceefax. Charities can apply for broadcasts every two years.
Each day Radio Scotland gives way to Scottish Local Radio Stations for 2-4 half hour broadcasts. See separate entry for addresses of Scottish Local Radio Stations (SLR).

☐ BBC Radio Sheffield

60 Westbourne Road,   *Contact:* Everard Davy
Sheffield S10 2QU   Programmes Organiser
0742-686185

The total pledged to Children in Need in 1991 was £182,505.
Between 1987 and 1990, the station ran some very successful fundraising events for the Chris Fund, a children's hospital in Sheffield. The station feels that in the present economic climate it is unfair to ask people to continue contributing to a NHS hospital, especially when so many charities are also competing for the same limited amount of money.
The station runs a What's On Diary which gives details of events happening in the community; these are read out by all presenters and may form the basis for future features.

☐ BBC Radio Shropshire

PO Box 397,   *Contact:* Eric Smith
Shrewsbury SY1 3TT   Programme Organiser
0743-248484

The total pledged to Children in Need in 1991 was £60,000.
In 1990, the station mobilised listeners to raise £68,000 for a CT scanner for the local hospital. For 1991 and 1992, the station decided the economic climate was not suitable for them to be trying to raise money for any particular NHS hospital or charity.
The What's On Diary is read out by most of the presenters. The Helpline goes on air at 9.55 am and 11.55 am. Broadcasts promote the work of charities and ask for support and volunteers. The station prefers to make in-studio interviews but will occasionally make simple outside broadcasts about specific projects.

☐ BBC Radio Solent

Broadcasting House,   *Contact:* Steve Panton
Havlock Road,   Station Manager
Southampton SO1 0XR
0703-631311

The station has a half hour AM Helpline programme, once a week, which helps with debt counselling, welfare rights etc.. In the winter this is also a Coldline which gives help with keeping warm in winter and Snowline. The What's On Diary is read out by each presenter each day, giving details of charity events. The station must be given two weeks' notice.
The station interviews people from charities/community organisations that are involved with specific community topics/issues. It employs, part-time, a religious leader to make broadcasts and tapes for the community on a Sunday morning; many of these would cover charity/community issues.

☐ BBC Radio Stoke

Cheapside,   *Contact:* Mervin Gamage
Hanley,   Programme Organiser
Stoke-on-Trent ST1 1JJ
0782-208080

The total pledged to Children in Need in 1991 was £150,000.
The station has raised over £500,000 over the last three years for the BBC Children in Need and the station's own Rascal charity appeal. Its social action broadcasts make small appeals and give information on local fundraising events for 10-15 minutes each morning.
Interviews and outside broadcasts are considered. The station also organises some charity fundraising events eg. the local golf classic.

Radio stations

Name/Address   *Contact*   *Donations/Support*

☐ BBC Radio Sussex

Marlborough Place,
Brighton,
East Sussex BN1 1TU
0273-680231

Contact: Jim Beaman
Programmes Editor

The station's Two Wheel Appeal is held on the Sunday before Christmas to raise money for people in need over Christmas. Listeners phone-in pledges; motorcycle riders call the same day to collect the donations which are banked and distributed within days. £14,000 was raised in this way in 1991.
What's On, including fundraising events and appeals for volunteers or goods, is featured daily along with interviews with people from local charities. There are regular advice phone-ins with experts, covering issues from medical matters to self-help groups. A series on Aids, which made use of reactions from listening groups around the county, won a national award. The station welcomes approaches from charities with ideas for programmes/features.

☐ BBC Radio Ulster & Radio Foyle

Broadcasting House,
Ormeau Avenue,
Belfast BT2 8HQ
0232-338000

Contact: Paul Evans
Managing Editor of General Programmes

The station has helped to raise money/support for charities through on air appeals, outside broadcasts and information broadcasts by and on behalf of charities. The station welcomes approaches from charities with ideas for programmes/features. All registered charities can apply to have appeals broadcast. Applications are considered by the Northern Ireland Appeals Advisory Committee. There are 12 appeals each year (10 on radio and 2 on TV), transmitted on Sundays. Charities can apply for broadcasts every two years. Radio Ulster and Radio Foyle are both actively involved in the BBC Children in Need Appeal.
Both stations incorporate social action broadcasts into general programming. Insight, a programme for the blind, is the main social action broadcast, but the station works in connection with current events eg. Aids Week, Disability Awareness Week etc.. Christmas toy appeals are run annually to help provide toys and presents for needy children through the social services and the Salvation Army.
Rosemary Kelly is the Head of Corporate Affairs and Pat Loughrey is the Programmes Organiser.

☐ BBC Radio Wales

Broadcasting House,
Llandaff,
Cardiff CF5 2YQ
0222-572888

Contact: Roy Noble
General Manager

Roy Noble is actively involved with Lepra and charities working with disabled people. The station publicises charities and events during many shows. On Sunday morning Chris Stewart and Jenny Lewis are involved with the Sunday morning Events Slot, which includes details of charities and events throughout Wales.

☐ BBC Radio WM

PO Box 206,
Pebble Mill Road,
Birmingham B5 7SD
021-414 8484

Contact: Tony Wadsworth
Programmes Organiser

Along with BBC local television, the total pledged to Children in Need in 1991 was £1,500,000.
The station is more interested in news stories involving charities rather than just charity stories. The Bangladesh floods in 1991 inspired major campaigns with many local people having family, friends and connections over there. £10,000 was raised. Other week-long campaigns have included domestic violence, child abuse, gambling and addiction. There are usually six such campaigns each year. The station uses studio guests and sends out information packs. It has also helped raise money for the Birmingham Children's Hospital.
Most presenters read out the What's On information giving details of local events and organisations needing support of some kind.

☐ BBC Radio York

20 Bootham Row,
York YO3 7BR
0904-641351

Contact: Bill Jenkyns
Community Affairs Producer

The total pledged to Children in Need in 1991 was £111,429.
The station has recently run week-long campaigns for many charity issues such as child safety and homelessness. During such campaigns interviews and broadcasts are usually 3-5 minutes long and there may be up to five such broadcasts each day. Outside broadcasts are made if the event is interesting or unusual (eg. the Sick Children's Trust Teaparty). The station is trying to provide charity/community organisations with a back-up service to send out leaflets, information and counselling.
What's On information is regularly given on air. The station runs a Helpline for charities appealing for items and volunteers. Last minute appeals for venues for events have been known! The Helpline number is 0904-610606.
There is also a Grapevine line for listeners to tell of problems they are having in the community. The number is 0904-633899.

☐ BBC Wiltshire Sound

PO Box 1234,
Swindon SN1 3RW
0793-513626

Contact: Mike Gray
Programmes Editor

The total pledged to Children in Need in 1991 was £151,559.
The station has helped to raise money/support for charities through outside broadcasts at fundraising events and information broadcasts by charities. The station welcomes approaches from charities with ideas for programmes/features. It will be running an appeal for the Wiltshire Air Ambulance.
The Mark Seaman morning programme broadcasts regular 30 second trails and public service announcements by local community groups and organisations Monday-Friday; more are broadcast on Saturday mornings at 8.55 am.
Di Harris is in charge of the Careline.

● Radio stations

Name/Address	Contact	Donations/Support

☐ Beacon Radio

267 Tettenhall Road,
Wolverhampton   WV6 0PQ
0902-757211

Contact: Pete Wagstaff
Programme Director

Total Raised: £20,000

The station runs two annual appeals, one for the Rainbow Hospice and another for an Air Ambulance. The station makes no specific social action broadcasts/programmes, but does broadcast on-air appeals and information on behalf of charities, and has made outside broadcasts at charity events. It prefers to work with children and youth, social welfare, medical, environment/heritage and overseas aid/development. No response to circular appeals. Support is given only to local charities within Beacon Radio's franchise area. Beacon Radio's sister station is WABC.
Broadcast Area: Wolverhampton, Black Country, Shrewsbury and Telford.

☐ Breeze AM

PO Box 300,
Southend-on-Sea   SS1 1SY
0702-430966

Contact: Peter Kerridge
Community Affairs Manager

The station's social action broadcasting is dealt with by the Community Affairs Department shared with its sister station Essex Radio. There are hourly bulletins detailing community related events. There are two annual appeals, one of which (Cash for Kids at Christmas) raised nearly £30,000 in 1991. With Essex Radio, the station administers the Helping Hands Trust (see entry for Essex Radio).
Broadcast Area: Southend & Chelmsford.

☐ BRMB FM

Radio House,
PO Box 555,
Aston Road North,
Birmingham   B6 4BX
021-359 4481

Contact: D L Bagley
Group Head of Marketing

BRMB will publicise information about local charitable events and activities at intervals throughout programming. Details should be sent (giving one week's notice) to the Deputy Programmer.
Broadcast Area: Birmingham.

☐ Broadland FM 102.4

47/49 St George's Plain,
Colegate,
Norwich   NR3 1DB
0603-630621

Contact: Bob Norman

Total Raised: £35,000

Broadland FM runs Operation Santa Claus, which takes place over one weekend close to Christmas. This involves an on-air auction of items donated largely by businesses and listeners. There is also a record sale and other fundraising events arranged by local people. The proceeds are distributed to local charities. The station only gives to charities in its franchise area and prefers to work with children/youth, social welfare and medical charities. It does not respond to requests for advertising in charity brochures; appeals from individuals; purely denominational (religious) appeals; large national appeals; overseas projects.
A regular What's On diary publicises charitable and community events. Contact Dick Hutchinson, Head of Features.
Broadcast Area: Norwich and Great Yarmouth.

☐ Brunel Classic Gold

PO Box 2000,
Bristol   BS99 7SN
0272-279911

Contact: Trevor Fry
Programme Controller

Broadcast Area: Bristol, Swindon and West Wiltshire. See also entry for GWR Radio.

☐ Buzz FM

The Spencers,
20 Augusta Street,
Jewellery Quarter,
Birmingham   B18 6JA
021-236 4888

Contact: Suzanne Virdee

Broadcast Area: Birmingham.

☐ Capital Radio

Euston Tower,
Euston Road,
London   NW1 3DR
071-608 6080

Contact: Richard Eyre
Managing Director

Donations: £81,000
Total Raised: £1,150,000

The station prefers to support children's charities in the London area. Each year at Easter the station runs Help a London Child which is an on-air radiothon for London children. In 1990/91, £750,000 was raised. There is a Christmas Toy and Food Appeal which raised £250,000 worth of goods in kind in same year. A further £150,000 worth of goods in kind is raised annually for other causes. Every year the station also commits itself to spending a certain amount on advertising in charity publications.
The station is a member of ABSA. It gives donations towards the arts in London and sponsors various music events in and around London. Applications for donations and charity advertising should be directed to Richard Eyre, Managing Director. Tasmin Wheeler is the Administrator for Help a London Child. For sponsorship contact Peter Turner, Head of Community Affairs.
Broadcast Area: Greater London.

Radio stations

Name/Address	Contact	Donations/Support

☐ CD 603

PO Box 2,
Cheltenham GL53 7YA
0242-255023

Contact: Carmal Bharma
Information

Broadcast Area: Cheltenham.

☐ Central FM

Central Action, Block 6,
Springkerse Industrial Estate,
Munroe Road,
Stirling FK7 YUU
0786-51188

Contact: Stephen Daly
Central Action

The station broadcasts appeals from local voluntary groups for equipment, volunteers or to publicise activities. Welfare rights, public information and health campaigns are also aired. It will consider ideas for programmes/features. The station does not support purely denominational (religious) and political appeals.
Broadcast Area: Stirling.

☐ Chiltern Radio

Chiltern Road,
Dunstable LU6 1HQ
0582-666001

Contact: Lee Finan
Station Organiser

The station broadcasts a Billboard of announcements at 20 and 40 minutes past each hour during normal programming. Details should be sent at least 10 days beforehand.
Broadcast Area: Luton and Bedfordshire.

☐ Choice FM

16-18 Trinity Gardens,
London SW9 8DP
071-738 7969

Contact: Martin Sims
News Programmer

The station has a Community Billboard broadcasting community announcements. Groups should write or fax details to the station who will try to slot announcements into normal programming.
Broadcast Area: Brixton.

☐ Classic Tracks BCR

Russell Court Building,
Claremont Street,
Lisburn Road,
Belfast BT9 6JX
0232-438500

Contact: Mike Gaston
Programme Controller

Total Raised: £2,103

The station has a policy of access to both daytime and evening programmes. Currently the station produces 37 hours per week of access and community broadcasting. This includes information broadcasts by and on behalf of charities and roadshows.
No support for advertising in charity brochures; appeals from individuals; purely denominational (religious) appeals; large national appeals. The station will be involved with telethon in the future, but prefers to work with charities within its franchise area.
Programming/social action broadcasts information from Brian Latewood.
Broadcast Area: Belfast.

☐ CN.FM 103

PO Box 1000,
Vision Park, Chivers Way,
Histon,
Cambridge CB4 4WW
0223-235255

Contact: What's on Diary

Broadcast Area: Cambridge & Newmarket. CN.FM's sister station is Hereward Radio. See separate entry for details.

☐ Cool FM

Newtownards,
County Down BT23 4ES
0247-815555

Contact: Janet McCraken

What's On items can be included throughout programming. Cool FM is a subsidiary of Downtown Radio.
Broadcast Area: Greater Belfast.

☐ County Sound Radio AM

Broadfield House,
Brighton Road,
Crawley RH11 9TT
0293-519161

Contact: Philippa Head
What's On Desk

Total Raised: £50,000

Annual on-air auction in November. Also two annual on-air appeals for gifts in kind.
Broadcast Area: Guildford, Haslemere, Reigate and Crawley.

● Radio stations

Name/Address   *Contact*   *Donations/Support*

☐ CRMK (Community Radio Milton Keynes)

14 Vincent Avenue,
Crownhill,
Milton Keynes   MK8 0AB
0908-265266

Contact: Station Manager

CRMK is a voluntary organisation and works closely with other local charitable groups. There are regular community information/what's happening features, jobspots etc.. Community information is at least one minute per hour. The station broadcasts on air appeals and information broadcasts by and on behalf of charities. It does not support purely denominational (religious) appeals.
Contact the Programme Controller for information regarding programming or social action broadcasts.
Broadcast Area: Milton Keynes.

☐ DevonAir Radio

35-37 St David's Hill,
Exeter   EX4 4DA
0392-430703

Contact: Programme Controller

The station broadcasts a What's On Diary throughout normal programming. Write to the station with details.
Broadcast Area: Exeter, East Devon and Torbay.

☐ Downtown Radio

Newtownards,
County Down   BT23 4ES
0247-815555

Contact: Florence Ambrose
Grapevine

The station has a What's On diary with regular bulletins about local charity events. It also features interviews with representatives from voluntary groups. Downtown joined with Ulster Television in Telethon in 1988, 1990 and 1992, involving joint programme production and the presenters appearing on both media. The 1992 total raised was the highest per head in the UK and the only area to exceed the 1990 figure.
Broadcast Area: Northern Ireland.

☐ Essex Radio

Radio House,
Clifftown Road,
Southend-on-Sea   SS1 1SX
0702-333711

Contact: Community Action Department

Every year Essex Radio runs a charitable appeal to coincide with its own birthday on 12th September. Separate in-kind appeals are also sometimes run.
The station broadcasts public service announcements at intervals throughout normal programming publicising the needs of local and voluntary organisations. Apply in writing to the address above.
The station also administers the Essex Radio Helping Hands Charitable Trust, whose criteria in selecting charities are as follows: that any group must be essentially community based; its work should be wide-reaching across the community; it can make effective use of the money or items awarded, and its work is innovative and interesting.
Broadcast Area: Southend and Chelmsford.

☐ Forth RFM

Forth House,
Forth Street,
Edinburgh   EH1 3LF
031-556 9255

Contact: Mark McKenzie
What's On

Radio Forth Ltd operates two stations, Forth RFM and Max AM (see separate entry). Both have their own charity appeals and broadcasts. RFM held a weekend on-air auction of rock memorabilia in July 1992. The station was given gold, silver and platinum discs, tickets for the Edinburgh Playhouse for 1 year etc.. The auction raised over £6,000 for the Milestone House, the only Aids Hospital in Scotland. The station also gives information on charity/community events through the What's On Diary.
Voluntary organisations should send interesting news information to the News Department. David Johnstone is the News Editor.
Broadcast Area: Edinburgh, Fife and the Lothians.

☐ Fox FM

Brush House,
Pony Road,
Oxford   OX4 2XR
0865-748787

Contact: Anna Hall
Community Liaison Officer

The station broadcasts Fox Report, a daily news programme between 6pm and 7pm, which often includes information and news from community based groups. There are also regular What's On broadcasts (contact the What's On desk to publicise events). Newsworthy items should be directed to the Action Desk. Ideas for programmes/features should be sent to the Promotions Department or Anna Hall.
Broadcast Area: Oxford and Banbury.

☐ Galaxy Radio

Broadcast Centre,
25 Portland Square,
Bristol   BS2 8RZ
0272-240111

Contact: Lisa Tandy
Head of Sponsorship

Broadcast Area: Bristol.

Radio stations

Name/Address	Contact	Donations/Support

☐ GLR (BBC Greater London Radio)

35c Marlybone High Street,
London W1A 4LG
071-224 2424

Contact: Gloria Abramoff
Editor

Other than the Children in Need campaign, GLR does not involve itself with charity appeals, campaigns or broadcasts, except for large charity events, concerts, cabarets and comedy nights. However if charity events are large enough they may get onto Friday's What's On slot. Interviews with charities are usually only made if the cause or item is particularly newsworthy or interesting.
Social action broadcasts at Christmas usually concentrate on loneliness, crime and crime prevention. Air time is given to ethnic minorities.

☐ GMR (BBC Greater Manchester Radio)

New Broadcasting House,
PO Box 951,
Oxford Road,
Manchester M60 1SJ
061-200 2000

Contact: Debbie Kelly
Promotions Manager

The total pledged to Children in Need in 1991 was £237,312.
The station's main focus for charitable support has been the GMR Victoria House Appeal, raising over £350,000 in two years. The money raised will help build an accommodation block in the Christie Hospital for the parents of children being treated for cancer. It was raised through raffles, auctions and special events such as the Norman Wisdom Charity Golf Classic.
Though most of the station's fundraising has been focused on the above appeal, the station will help other charities by giving them on air publicity or sending along a presenter to make a personal appearance. It broadcasts information on charities and fundraising events and makes outside broadcasts. Presenters make speeches, opens fetes, events and charity shops and offices.
There are Dare Devil Days which raise money and awareness for the Spastics Society, and the Who Cares slot (broadcast on Mondays between 6.30-7.00 pm) which makes appeals for and with charities.

☐ Great North Radio

Newcastle-upon-Tyne
NE99 1BB
091-496 0377

Contact: Steve Parkinson
Programme Controller

The station runs a number of awareness projects to highlight community and charitable initiatives throughout the year. The station considers all appeals carefully and a wide range of community concerns are broadcast (eg. Crimestoppers newsdesk, personal safety and security week, environment week, the Yellow Brick Road Hospital fundraising campaign). It also responds whenever possible to community and individual needs through its Happy Endings programme. The presenter is set a number of challenges by listeners and the local community and the audience are asked to help solve the problems with advice or physical help.
Daily community appeals, updates, events etc. are publicised within normal programming. Plans are in progress for adopting certain charities to increase awareness. The station will consider ideas for programmes/features from charities.
Broadcast Area: Tyne & Wear and Teesside.

☐ Great Yorkshire Radio

PO Box 777,
Sheffield
0742-582121

Contact: Dean Papall
Programme Controller

Broadcast Area: Yorkshire, Lincolnshire.

☐ GWR Radio

PO Box 2000,
Bristol BS99 7SN
0272-279900

Contact: Steve Orchard
Programmes Organiser

The station is setting up a Community Trust Newspot sponsored by local companies; some of this money will be donated to local charities.
The station's annual Christmas Auction Appeal raises between £100,000-£200,000 each year. Prizes donated included the use of a Concorde Simulator (raising about £1,200), several luxury holidays eg. Caribbean (£3,000 each), one or two cars, a complete wedding package etc..
From the money raised the station makes about 700 donations of £50-£75,000 to local charities.
The station's Classic Gold AM broadcasts appeals in May, along with many other south west stations, raising over £44,000 for the Spastics Society.
The Promotions Department were involved with the CAFOD and Christian Aid 500th anniversary campaign of Columbus setting out for America.
The station allows 15 minutes each day for charity broadcasts, divided between editorials, interviews and advertising. 10 days' notice has to be given for the daily What's On Diary.
Sally Ogden is the Station Director (0272-294881).
Broadcast Area: Bristol, Bath, Marlborough, Swindon, West Wiltshire.

☐ Hallam FM

900 Herries Road,
Sheffield S6 1RH
0742-853333

Contact: Steve King
Programmes Organiser

Total Raised: £42,000

Radio Hallam publicises special events and broadcasts appeals for help on behalf of organisations throughout normal programming. It will consider ideas from charities for programmes/features. Organisations can also write with details to the What's On Diary.
The station has its own charitable trust which distributes all monies raised in its year-long Help a Hallam Child appeal to local children's charities. This appeal climaxes annually in September.
The station only supports local charities within its franchise area. Preference for children and youth; education and the arts. No support for advertising in charity brochures, purely denominational (religious) appeals or large national appeals.
Broadcast Area: Sheffield, Rotherham, Barnsley and Doncaster.

● Radio stations

Name/Address	*Contact*	*Donations/Support*

☐ Heartland FM

Lower Oakfield,
Pitlochry,
Perthshire PH16 2DS
0796-474040

Contact: Sarah Bull
Administration

Heartland FM is a community radio station.
Broadcast Area: Pitlochry and Aberfeldy.

☐ Hereward Radio 102.7 FM

PO Box 225,
Queensgate Centre,
Peterborough PE1 1XJ
0733-346225

Contact: Appeal Director

Total Raised: £159,919

Hereward Radio, CNFM 103 (Cambridge) and KL.FM (Kings Lynn) are sister stations. They do not give to charity directly from station reserves, but support the Hereward Radio, CNFM and KLFM Appeal (itself a registered charity). For this they have a year round appeal for disabled people, with the main fundraising drive from Autumn until Christmas.
The stations are always open to ideas for programme/features from charities. They have on air appeals, information broadcasts by charities and outside broadcasts at charity events. No support for advertising in charity brochures; appeals from individuals; purely denominational (religious) appeals; local appeals not in the franchise area. CNFM and KL.FM have separate entries.
Broadcast Area: Peterborough.

☐ Invicta Radio

Radio House,
PO Box 100,
Whitstable,
Kent CT5 3YR
0227-772004

Contact: Johnny Lewis
Programmes Organiser

Total Raised: £35,000

The station has set up the Invicta Appeal for the Disabled, which gives grants to disabled individuals, social services and charities working for disabled people. All beneficiaries must be based in Kent. Applicants should write in with details of their needs to George Stewart, Chairman, c/o the above address.
Broadcast Area: Maidstone & Medway, East Kent.

☐ Isle of Wight Radio

Dodnor Park,
Newport,
Isle of Wight PO30 5XE
0983-822557

Contact: Linda Couch
Station Manager

Broadcast Area: Isle of Wight.

☐ KCBC

PO Box 1530,
Kettering NN16 8PU
0536-412413

Contact: Jean Bennett
Head of Sales

Broadcast Area: Kettering & Corby.

☐ KL.FM 96.7

PO Box 77,
18 Blackfriars Street,
Kings Lynn PE30 1NN
0553-772777

Contact: What's On Diary

Broadcast Area: Kings Lynn. KL.FM's sister station is Hereward Radio. Please see separate entry for details.

☐ Leicester Sound FM

Granville House,
Granville Road,
Leicester LE1 7RW
0533-551616

Contact: Stewart Linnell
Programmes Controller

The station runs Leicester Sound Careline which broadcasts appeals from voluntary and statutory organisations for equipment and volunteers and publicises their activities. Tim Dickens, Operations Manager can also be contacted regarding social action broadcasts.
Broadcast Area: Leicestershire.

☐ Lincs FM

Witham Park,
Waterside South,
Lincoln LN5 7JN
0522-549900

Contact: David Lloyd
Programmes Manager

The station will broadcast information on behalf of charities which must be sent at least seven days beforehand.
Broadcast Area: Lincolnshire and South Humberside.

Radio stations

Name/Address	Contact	Donations/Support

☐ London Broadcasting Company

72 Hammersmith Road,
London W14 8YE
071-371 2000

Contact: Anna Hamilton
Director of Marketing

Total Raised: £1,100,000

The station associates itself with a number of "carefully selected charitable organisations to boost their fundraising efforts for specific projects". In 1991, the station raised £100,000 for the Hammer Cancer Appeal and £10,000 for the RNIB through an on-air charity auction.
Broadcast area: London.

☐ London Greek Radio

Florentina Village,
Vale Road,
London N4 1TD
081-800 8001

Contact: G Gregoriuo
Programme Controller

Broadcast Area: Haringey, London.

☐ London Talkback Radio

72 Hammersmith Road,
London W14 8YE
071-333 0003

Contact: Robin Malcolm
Programme Controller

Broadcast Area: London.

☐ Magic 828

PO Box 2000,
Leeds LS3 1LR
0532-421830

Contact: What's On Diary

Magic 828's sister station is Radio Aire FM. Please see separate entry for details.
Broadcast Area: Leeds.

☐ Marcher Sound (Clwyd)

The Studios,
Mold Road,
Gwersyllt,
Wrexham LL11 4AF
0978-752202

Contact: Phil Roberts
Programme Controller

The station tries to accommodate charity appeals and causes. It ran a very successful Sponsor a Christmas Child in Romania appeal. The station has a What's On diary broadcast nine times a day. Contact Jason Fox, What's On Manager, ext. 232.
Broadcast Area: Wrexham and Deeside.

☐ Max AM

Forth House,
Forth Street,
Edinburgh EH1 3LF
031-558 3277

Contact: Tom Steele
Director of Programmes

Total Raised: £30,000

The station organises the Max AM Help a Child Appeal annually in November. After a series of fundraising events this culminates in an auction of items given by individuals, retailers and manufacturers. The funds are distributed to specific areas of need to help local children. The largest sum raised was £100,000 which built a holiday centre near Edinburgh for disabled and disadvantaged children. Max Action is broadcast daily for those seeking help. Preference for children and youth; social welfare; medical; education. No support for advertising in charity brochures. No response to circular appeals. Support is only given to charities in Max AM's franchise area.
Max AM's sister station is Forth RFM (see separate entry).
Broadcast Area: Edinburgh, Fife and the Lothians.

☐ Mellow 1557

21-23 Walton Road,
Frinton-on-Sea,
Essex CO13 0AA
0255-675303

Contact: J Farmer
Station Director

The station does not make donations to charity. However, it "offers and encourages" local charities to get involved with the station to raise funds through Action 1557 Charity Features. It has helped to raise money with on-air appeals and broadcasts information on behalf of charities.
Broadcast Area: Tendring.

☐ Melody Radio

180 Brompton Road,
London SW3 1HF
071-584 1049

Contact: Peter Black
Head of Presentation

Broadcast Area: Greater London.

● Radio stations

Name/Address	Contact	Donations/Support

☐ Mercia Sound

Hertford Place,
Coventry CV1 3TT
0203-633933

Contact: Jane Robinson c/o Chris Radley
Programmes Organiser

The station organises a Walkathon in June to which the public pledge money and raise sponsorship for local charities. Mercia Action gives community information and at 2.50 pm there is a What's On and Lost & Found.
When involved in a campaign, the station will make up to six broadcasts a day for a week. These include broadcasts by the station's staff, studio interviews and outside broadcasts. Recent campaigns have included Healthy Heart and a look at drug addiction/prevention.
In the run up to Christmas, the station promotes the Snowball Appeal, a big fundraising exercise for local children's charities. The appeal finishes with an on air auction a couple of days after Christmas. Some of the items auctioned have included rare Beatles memorabilia, donations from Coventry City FC and a trip to the Houses of Parliament with the local MP.
The station runs a Media and Publicity Skills course for up to 60 unemployed people lasting for 12 months.
Broadcast Area: Coventry.

☐ Metro FM

Newcastle-upon-Tyne
NE99 1BB
091-488 3131

Contact: Giles Squire
Programme Director

Total Raised: £38,000

The station raises money throughout the year to give to charities based within its franchise area.
Broadcast Area: Tyne & Wear.

☐ Minster FM

PO Box 123,
Dunnington,
York YO1 5ZX
0904-488888

Contact: Jon Darch
Station Manager

Broadcast Area: York.

☐ Moray Firth Radio

PO Box 271,
Inverness IV3 6SF
0463-224433

Contact: T Prag
Managing Director

Total Raised: £55,000

The station gives publicity to charity/community organisations through interviews and outside broadcasts (eg. the recent Somalia Appeal was with the Save the Children Fund). It includes interviews and features in its ordinary programmes and regularly broadcasts the pledgeline telephone number. The station has a special phone system in operation when running special charitable campaigns.
In February the station also raises money for the Moray Firth Radio Trust. Money is raised through an on-air auction (selling about 1,200 items) and involvement in many other fundraising events. The station raises about £50,000-£60,000 each year, the money being given to over 200 local charities and individuals. In 1992, donations ranged between £50 and £5,000. The largest ever donation was £10,000.
Broadcast Area: Inverness and Moray Firth area.

☐ North East Community Radio (NECR)

PO Box 303,
Aberdeen AB9 8XA
0651-891605

Contact: Margaret MacNaughton
Head of Sales & Public Relations

Broadcast Area: Aberdeen.

☐ Northants Radio

Broadcast Centre,
The Enterprise Park,
Boughton Green Road,
Northampton NN2 7AH
0604-792411

Contact: Colin Wilsher
Station & Programme Organiser

The station gives material rather than financial support. It has information broadcasts by and on behalf of charities and holds outside broadcasts at charity events. It also holds an annual Northants Radio Yellow Brick Road Appeal administered by the Children's Society to help children in the Northants area.
The station produces and broadcasts Comunicare which contains commercial messages and appeals for local organisations at no cost.
The station prefers to support children and youth; social welfare; medical causes. No support for advertising in charity brochures, appeals from individuals and purely denominational (religious) appeals. No response to circular appeals. The station will consider ideas for programmes/features from charities.
Broadcast Area: Northamptonshire.

☐ NorthSound Radio

45 King's Gate,
Aberdeen AB2 6BL
0224-632234

Contact: Jon Trowsdale
Programme Controller

Broadcast Area: Aberdeen.

Radio stations

Name/Address	Contact	Donations/Support

☐ Ocean Sound Classic Hits & Power FM

Radio House, Whittle Avenue,
Segensworth West,
Fareham,
Hants PO15 5PA
0489-589911

Contact: J Scott
Programme Director

Broadcast Area: Portsmouth, Southampton and Winchester.

☐ Orchard FM

Haygrove House,
Shoreditch,
Taunton,
Somerset TA3 7BT
0823-338448

Contact: David Rodgers
Controller

Broadcast Area: Yeovil and Taunton.

☐ Piccadilly Gold & Piccadilly Key 103

127-131 The Piazza,
Piccadilly Plaza,
Manchester M1 4AW
061-236 9913

Contact: John Chapman
Controller

Broadcast Area: Greater Manchester.

☐ Pirate FM

Carn Brea Studios,
Wilson Way,
Redruth,
Cornwall TR15 3XX
0209-314400

Contact: Joseph Swain
Marketing & Sales Director

Broadcast Area: Cornwall.

☐ Plymouth Sound

Earls Acre,
Plymouth,
Devon PL3 4HX
0752-227272

Contact: Louise Churchill
Station Director

Donations: £55,000
Total Raised: £55,000

The station runs an annual appeal called Operation Santa which is usually broadcast during the first week of December. There is an on-air auction, sponsored events and listener involvement. The station gives almost exclusively to children and youth related causes within its franchise area.
Its main social action broadcast is the Wednesday Walk-in between 2pm and 3pm on the first Wednesday of each month. The programme involves listeners talking live on-air about social issues or their community-related projects.
No support is given for advertising in charity brochures; appeals from individuals; purely denominational (religious) appeals; appeals outside the franchise area; large national appeals and overseas projects.
Plymouth Sound is a sister station to Radio in Tavistock.
Broadcast Area: Plymouth.

☐ The Pulse

PO Box 3000,
Bradford BD1 5NE
0274-731521

Contact: Alan Ross
Programme Controller

Broadcast Area: Bradford, Huddersfield and Halifax.

☐ Q96

26 Lady Lane,
Paisley PA1 2LG
041-887 9630

Contact: Bob McWilliam
Programme Controller

Broadcast Area: Paisley.

☐ Radio Aire FM

PO Box 2000,
Leeds LS3 1LR
0532-452299

Contact: What's On Diary
Programme Controller

The station is purely musically orientated with no specialist community programming. However publicity is given to local charities and community groups throughout normal programming. Contact the What's On dairy at least seven days in advance of the proposed broadcast.
Radio Aires' sister station is Magic 828.
Broadcast Area: Leeds.

● Radio stations

Name/Address	Contact	Donations/Support

☐ Radio Borders

Tweedside Park,
Galashiels   TD1 3TD
0896-59444

Contact: Rod Webster
Board of Trustees

Total Raised: £20,000

The Radio Borders Charity Trust Fund distributes funds raised mainly through an annual charity auction. This is a live charity auction supported by local businesses and normally held each spring. Local charities and causes should write to the trustees for funds. The station also broadcasts Borders Action which has details of local events broadcast four times each day. The station only supports charities within its franchise area. It broadcasts appeals and has made outside broadcasts at charity events.
Broadcast Area: The Borders.

☐ Radio Ceredigion

Unit 6E,
Science Park,
Cefnllan,
Aberystwyth
0970-626626

Contact: Teleri Bevan
Programme Controller

Broadcast Area: Ceredigion. Radio Ceredigion is a community radio station.

☐ Radio City

PO Box 967,
Liverpool   L69 1TQ
051-227 5100

Contact: Lesley Marshall
What's On Desk

The station has a charitable trust called Give a Child a Chance which raises money "for the relief of poverty or deprivation or the promotion of the physical, mental or general welfare of children" who live in the Radio City franchise radio. There is also a What's on desk which deals with social action broadcasts.
Broadcast Area: Merseyside.

☐ Radio Clyde plc

Clydebank Business Park,
Clydebank   G81 2RX
041-306 2200

Contact: What's On Desk

There is an annual Cash for Kids at Christmas appeal held in conjunction with Clyde Action. Clyde Action also provides short community news bulletins. Contact Robert Caldwell at Clyde Action, 30 West Nile Street, Glasgow G1 2QH.
Broadcast Area: Glasgow.

☐ Radio Kiss FM

Kiss House,
80 Holloway Road,
London   N7 8JG
071-700 6100

Contact: Gordon McNamee
Managing Director

At present no policy has been developed, but individual directors or department heads choose organisations for the station to support. These tend to be larger well-known charities. Publicity is given to charities on a daily magazine programme called The Word. Contact Lisa L'Anson, Presenter or Lorna Clarke, Producer.

☐ Radio Maldwyn

c/o Davies Memorial Gallery,
Newtown,
Powys   SY16 2NZ
0686-626220

Contact: Dave Bowen
Station Manager.

Broadcast Area: Montgomeryshire. Radio Maldwyn is a community radio station. It will be on-air in March 1993.

☐ Radio Mercury

Broadfield House,
Brighton Road,
Crawley   RH11 9TT
0293-519161

Contact: John Wellington
Programme Controller

Total Raised: £45,000

The station organises Operation Santa Claus every Christmas. This a weekend of fundraising activities to help local charities for children or elderly people.
The station has a Radio Mercury Action Desk, enabling local groups to discuss a wide range of issues and to give advice during a five-minute live interview. Voluntary organisations wanting coverage should contact the Action Desk at the address above.
Broadcast Area: Reigate and Crawley.

☐ Radio in Tavistock

Earls Acre,
Plymouth   PL3 4HX
0752-227272

Contact: Helen Churchill
Station Director & Programme Controller

Radio in Tavistock is a sister station of Plymouth Sound Radio. Please see separate entry for details.
Broadcast Area: Tavistock.

Radio stations

Name/Address	Contact	Donations/Support

☐ Radio Tay

PO Box 123,
Dundee BD1 9UF
0382-200800

Contact: Ally Ballingall
Programmes Organiser

The station has a regular What's On and two slots each day for charity/community broadcasts. Week-long campaigns are sometimes run. People come in from various charities throughout the week to talk about the work they do, particular problems, causes etc.. The station has run campaigns on drug/alcohol abuse, crime, the third world, debt etc. and has involved charities such as Alcoholics Anonymous, Victim Support, citizen's advice bureau, Oxfam, Red Cross any many smaller local organisations. Live interviews are generally 3-5 minutes long; the station occasionally pre-records interviews. Angela Doran is the Actionline Manager (0382-200400).
The station launches its own fundraising appeal in August which continues until after Christmas to raise money for local children and youth charities. Money is raised by listeners holding car washes, discos etc., the main fundraiser being the station's charity auction. The station is usually given a new caravan and 2-4 two-day prizes at the Glenneagles Equestrian Centre. It raised about £100,000 for the appeal in 1991.
Broadcast Area: Dundee & Perth.

☐ Radio Wyvern

Barbourne Terrace,
Worcester WR1 3JZ
0905-612212

Contact: Mike Morgan
Head of Sales

Broadcast Area: Hereford and Worcester.

☐ RadioWave

965 Mowbray Drive,
Blackpool FY3 7JR
0253-304965

Contact: Simon Tate
Programme Controller

Broadcast Area: Blackpool.

☐ Red Dragon FM

West Canal Wharf,
Cardiff CF1 5XJ
0222-384041

Contact: John Dash
Head of Programmes

Broadcast Area: Cardiff and Newport.

☐ Red Rose Gold & Red Rose Rock FM

Red Rose Community Trust,
PO Box 301,
Preston PR1 1YE
0772-556301

Contact: John Myers
Programme Director

Donations: £500
Total Raised: £35,000

The station does not concentrate exclusively on registered charities, but donates on a basis of need. There is an annual on-air charity auction. Support is only given to charities within its franchise area. Preference for children and youth; medical; environment/heritage; arts; overseas aid/development. No support for circular appeals; purely denominational (religious) appeals; large national appeals; overseas projects.
The station will consider ideas for programmes/features from charities. It will also broadcast information on behalf of charities and has made outside broadcasts at charity events. It has an Action Desk with social action features.
Broadcast Area: Preston & Blackpool.

☐ RTM 103.8FM

Tavy Bridge,
London SE2 9UG
081-311 3112

Contact: Patrick Rudden
Programme Director

Total Raised: £50,000

The station runs a number of week-long campaigns on subjects such as the environment, education and training. There are one-off features on a daily basis. The station also supports local charity events with on-air and where appropriate outside broadcasts. It will consider ideas from charities for programmes/features. RTM is working with Orlando '93, raising money to take disabled children of Marlborough School in Sidcup to Disneyworld at Easter 1993. No support is given to local appeals not within the franchise area, large national appeals and overseas projects. No response to circular appeals.
Broadcast Area: South east London and north west Kent.

☐ Severn Sound & Severn Sound Supergold

Broadcast Centre,
67 Southgate Street,
Gloucester GL1 2DQ
0452-423791

Contact: Alan Thompson
Station & Programme Organiser

Broadcast Area: Gloucester and Cheltenham.

☐ SGR-FM

Electric House,
Lloyds Avenue,
Ipswich IP1 3HZ
0473-230350

Contact: Mike Stewart
Programme Director

Broadcast Area: Ipswich and Bury St Edmunds. The Bury St Edmunds telephone number is 0284-701511.

● Radio stations

Name/Address   *Contact*   *Donations/Support*

☐ SIBC

Market Street,
Lerwick,
Shetland ZE1 0JN
0595-5299

Contact: Inga R Walterson
Managing Director

Broadcast Area: Shetland Islands.

☐ Signal Cheshire

Regent House,
Heaton Lane,
Stockport SK4 1BX
061-480 5445

Contact: John Evington
Programme Director

Broadcast Area: Stockport and Congleton.

☐ Signal Radio

Studio 257,
Stoke Road,
Stoke-on-Trent ST4 2SR
0782-747047

Contact: John Evington
Programme Director

Broadcast Area: Stoke-on-Trent and Stafford.

☐ SLR BBC Radio Aberdeen

Broadcasting House,
Beechgrove Terrace,
Aberdeen AB9 2ZT
0224-625233

Contact: Jim Murray

One of the main recent broadcasts was the Christian Aid campaign to raise food, blankets, clothes etc. for Malawi as part of the Anneka Rice campaign.
The station's main What's On programme is during the 7.30-8.00 am show which can also include features and interviews.

☐ SLR BBC Radio Highland

Culduthel Road,
Inverness
0463-221711

Contact: Mike Walker
Programmes Organiser

This station opts out 3 times each day from BBC Radio Scotland. The 7.30-8.00 am slot gives the main What's On broadcasts. The afternoon slots have features and interviews; Friday afternoon is the main time for community/charity broadcasts. A recent community campaign was the neighbourhood watch scheme sponsored by the local council to encourage the community to care for their neighbours.

☐ Somerset Sound (BBC Radio)

14-16 Paul Street,
Taunton TA1 3PF
0823-252437

Contact: Richard Austin
Programmes Organiser

The total pledged for Children in Need in 1991 was £67,640 (together with Radio Bristol).
The station opts out from BBC Radio Bristol for a few hours each day and covers campaigns such as homelessness and car crime. The station's What's On slot covers community events twice daily, such as fashion shows for local hospitals. There is a weekly community slot for volunteer bureaux in Somerset looking for volunteers for specific projects.
Food and Toy Appeals are broadcast for disadvantaged families; items are then distributed by the Salvation Army and social services.
The Yeovil station's telephone number is 0935-32071.
Sheelagh Leigh-Ewers is the Actionline Manager.

☐ South Coast Radio

Radio House, Whittle Avenue,
Segensworth West,
Fareham,
Hants PO15 5PA
0489-589911

Contact: J Scott
Programme Director

Broadcast Area: Portsmouth, Southampton and Winchester.

☐ Spectrum International Radio

Endeavour House,
Brent Cross,
London NW2 1JT
081-905 5000

Contact: Wolfgang Bucci
Programme Controller

The station provides music, news and information for ethnic communities.
Broadcast Area: Greater London.

Radio stations

Name/Address — *Contact* — *Donations/Support*

☐ Spire FM

City Hall Studios,
Malthouse Lane,
Salisbury,
Wiltshire
0772-416644

Contact: Chris Carnegy
Managing Director

Broadcast Area: Salisbury.

☐ Sunrise FM

30 Chapel Street,
Little Germany,
Bradford BD1 5DN
0274-735043

Contact: Geeta Varma
Programme Controller

The station provides music, news and information for Asian and other ethnic communities.
Broadcast Area: Bradford.

☐ Sunrise Radio

Cross Lances Road,
Hounslow,
Middlesex TW3 2AD
081-569 6666

Contact: Geeta Kohli/Dr John Walshe

Donations: £12,000
Total Raised: £65,000

The station provides music, news and information for Asian and other ethnic communities. It broadcasts on-air appeals and information by and on behalf of charities. It aims through its social action broadcasting to raise social awareness and is willing to receive ideas for programmes/features from charities.
Preference for social welfare; medical; education and overseas aid/development.
For information on social action broadcasts contact Suman Komli.
Broadcast Area: Hounslow and Southall.

☐ Sunset Radio

23 New Mount Street,
Manchester M4 4DE
061-953 5353

Contact: Duncan Smith
Programme Controller

The station provides soul and dance music, news and information for ethnic communities.
Broadcast Area: Manchester.

☐ Sunshine 855

South Shropshire
Communications Ltd,
Highridge House, The Sheet,
Ludlow,
Shropshire SY8 4JT
0584-873795

Contact: Programme Director

The station's main social action broadcasting is given to job creation. Airtime is given to local organisations. There are also Helpline and What's On information bulletins. The station will consider ideas from charities for programmes/features.
Preference for children and youth; education; recreation; environment/heritage; arts. No support for advertising in charity brochures; appeals from individuals; purely denominational (religious) appeals; local appeals outside the franchise area; large national appeals; overseas projects. No response to circular appeals.
Contact Tony Paul for information regarding programming/social action broadcasts.
Broadcast Area: Ludlow (South Shropshire).

☐ Swansea Sound

Victoria Road,
Gowerton,
Swansea SA4 3AB
0792-893751

Contact: Andrew Armitage
Head of Programmes (News & Features)

Broadcast Area: Swansea.

☐ TFM

Yale Crescent,
Thornaby,
Stockton-on-Tees,
Cleveland TS17 6AA
0642-615111

Contact: Brian Lister
Programme Director

Broadcast Area: Teesside.

● **Radio stations**

Name/Address *Contact* *Donations/Support*

☐ **1332 The World's Greatest Music Station**

PO Box 225, *Contact:* Andy Gillies
Queensgate Centre, Director of Programmes
Peterborough PE1 1XJ
0733-34622

The station supports its own registered charity; it has no other charity involvement.
No support for fundraising events; advertising in charity brochures; appeals from individuals; purely denominational (religious) appeals; local appeals not in areas of company presence; large national appeals; overseas projects. No response to circular appeals.
Broadcast Area: Peterborough (mid-Anglia region).

☐ **Touch AM**

PO Box 99, *Contact:* John Dash
Cardiff CF1 5YJ Head of Programmes
0222-237878

Broadcast Area: Cardiff and Newport.

☐ **Trent FM**

c/o Nottingham CVS, *Contact:* Paul Martin
33 Mansfield Road, Trent FM Careline
Nottingham NG1 3FF
0602-413121

The station has the Trent FM Careline which is administered from Nottingham Council for Voluntary Service. The Careline's policy is a "commitment to working with groups who are facing discrimination, under-representation or disadvantage in some way". The Careline is involved in social action broadcasting giving community groups, campaigning organisations and charities the opportunity to publicise their views and/or organisation on air. There are three Careline bulletins broadcast each day. There are also regular live interviews, outside broadcasts and regular 30-second "adverts" broadcast at various times of the day to target different listeners. A Helpline enables listeners to be put in touch with relevant help and advice agencies.
Broadcast Area: Nottingham and Derby.

☐ **2CR Classic Gold & 2CR FM**

5 Southcote Road, *Contact:* Programme Controller
Bournemouth BH1 3LR (see below)
0202-294881

Trevor Fry is the Programme Controller for Classic Gold; Jean-Paul Hansford for FM.
Broadcast Area: Bournemouth.

☐ **210 Classic Gold Radio**

PO Box 2020, *Contact:* Graham Leader
Reading RG3 5RZ
0734-413131

210 Classic Gold is the sister station to 210 FM. Please see separate entry.
Broadcast Area: Reading, Basingstoke and Andover.

☐ **210 FM**

PO Box 210, *Contact:* Graham Ledger
Reading,
Berkshire RG3 5RZ
0734-413131

The station's Give a Child a Chance appeal was started in 1985 and has raised over £600,000 for children and children's organisations in Berkshire, north Hampshire and south Oxfordshire. The money is raised for able-bodied and disabled children up to the age of 18. The station also takes part in outside broadcasts at charity events. Preference for children, youth and social welfare. No grants for advertising in charity brochures or purely denominational (religious) appeals. The station only gives to charities within its franchise area.
The station will consider ideas for programmes/features which should be sent to the Careline Desk.
Charitable appeals should be sent to Debbie Edwards.
Broadcast Area: Reading, Basingstoke and Andover.

☐ **Viking FM**

Commercial Road, *Contact:* Roy Leonard
Hull HU1 2SG General Manager & Programme
0482-25141 Controller

Broadcast Area: Humberside.

☐ **WABC**

267 Tettenhall Road, *Contact:* Pete Wagstaff
Wolverhampton WV6 0DQ Programme Director
0902-757211

WABC is the sister station to Beacon Radio. Please see separate entry.
Broadcast Area: Wolverhampton, Black Country, Shrewsbury and Telford.

Radio stations

Name/Address	Contact	Donations/Support

☐ Wear FM

Forster Building,
Chester Road,
Sunderland SR1 3SD
091-515 2103

Contact: Margaret Banks
Administrator

Broadcast Area: Sunderland. Wear FM is a community radio station.

☐ West Sound Radio plc

Campbell House,
Bankend Road,
Dumfries DG1 4TH
0387-50999

Contact: Gordon McArthur
Programme Controller

Donations: £1,500
Total Raised: £80,000

The station has helped raise money by broadcasting on-air appeals and information and outside broadcasts on behalf of charities. There was also a Radiothon for Ayrshire Hospice and support for Scottish Television's Telethon appeal.
Preference for children and youth and medical appeals. No support for advertising in charity brochures and appeals from individuals. No response to circular appeals.
Broadcast Area: Ayrshire, Dumfries and Galloway.

☐ WNK Radio

185B High Road,
Wood Green,
London N22 6BA
081-889 1547

Contact: Pauline Clark
Head of Sales

Broadcast Area: Haringey, London.

Per cent giving and the Per Cent Club

The idea of a Per Cent Club is that individual companies tie their level of giving to a pre-determined percentage of the company's pre-tax profits or dividends. Companies that commit themselves to do this are then enrolled as members of the club. Membership gives them a certain level of recognition both through Per Cent Club annual reports and companies' own annual reports and publications. There is also usually a prestigious annual dinner or reception for the Chairmen or Chief Executive Officers of member companies.

The aim of Per Cent Clubs is to promote increased levels of support by the private sector both for charities generally, but also for the social issues which most concern businesses and the local communities in which the company operates.

Background

There are now four separate Per Cent Clubs in Britain: the Per Cent Club itself, which is nationwide and essentially for national or multinational companies, and three regional or local Per Cent Clubs in Scotland, Sheffield and the North East.

Per Cent Clubs originated in the United States, the first Five Per Cent Club being established in Minneapolis. There are now Per Cent Clubs in many major cities in the US. These Per Cent Clubs are largely Two Per Cent, Five Per Cent and even Ten Per Cent Clubs. The 2% minimum stems from the President's Task Force on Private Sector Initiatives in the early 1980's which recommended that companies give at least 2% of pre-tax net income (profits). The higher 10% level stems both from the Biblical practice of tithing (giving away 10% of one's income) and the upper level for deductibility in the US of company donations to non-profit tax-exempt bodies. There is currently only one Ten Per Cent Club in existence, in Birmingham, Alabama, which has two member companies. Over 750 companies in the US have now committed themselves to giving 2% or more of their profits to the community by joining a Per Cent Club.

The idea of bringing Per Cent Clubs to Britain was first mooted by the then Sir Hector Laing, Chairman of United Biscuits, in a speech to members of Business in the Community in 1983. It lay dormant for some years, but in 1986 it was revived under the leadership of Sir Mark Weinberg, then Chairman of the Allied Dunbar financial services company (a subsidiary of BAT Industries).

The original idea was to establish a One Per Cent Club with giving tied to 1% of pre-tax profits, but this was felt to be over-ambitious and was possibly too high to promote, at least for the time being. Therefore, an initial level of 0.5% was proposed with a commitment for members to achieve a full 1% subsequently. In recognition of these aims the club would be called the Per Cent Club.

The Per Cent Club was launched on 15th December 1986 by HRH The Prince of Wales at a reception hosted by Margaret Thatcher at 10 Downing Street. At the launch, 66 companies joined; by August 1992 this had risen to about 300 companies. These are listed at the end of this article. Most but not all of the main company donors are now members of the Per Cent Club.

Terms of membership

The initial publicity never mentioned a commitment greater than 0.5% of pre-tax profits or 1% of dividends. At the annual general meeting held in July 1990 the aim of encouraging members to give at least 1% of pre-tax profits was proposed for the first time. This higher rate has not been adopted by the Club and probably will not be in the near future.

The qualification for membership relates total contributions to UK generated pre-tax profits, or dividend payments arising from UK operations. As stated above, contributions should be equivalent to at least 0.5% of pre-tax profits or 1.0% of dividends.

"Contributions" needs some definition. In 1991, the Per Cent Club published a handbook to help companies define, quantify and report their community involvement entitled *Reporting Community Involvement: Guidelines for Companies*. The broad definition of community involvement is "business activities intended to address the social and economic needs of the community in which a company operates".

There are various forms of corporate community involvement. They include:

- **Financial assistance** including cash donations, sponsorship, loan guarantees or venture capital funds;
- **Staff time** through secondments and employee volunteering schemes;
- Access to **facilities or services**, ranging from office photocopiers and fax machines to technical laboratories;
- Loans or donations of **equipment**;
- **Managed workspace**;
- Other **in kind** contributions.

The different quantifiable elements may include:

- **Time** contributed by employees with professional expertise (eg. accountants, surveyors, lawyers, trainers);

Not a grant giver

Please note that neither the Per Cent Club nor any of the local Per Cent Clubs hold or administer funds themselves, so **no** applications should be made to them. Nor will they give addresses of member companies.

A list of members is published in the Per Cent Club annual report. The 1992 report (published in December 1992) includes for the first time a list of members of the Sheffield and North East Per Cent Clubs.

Per cent giving and the Per Cent Club

- **Direct employment costs** of secondees and staff administering community involvement activities;
- **Goods or equipment** which can be quantified as cost of production including overheads, cost of purchase or net realisable value, whichever is lowest;
- **Cash**;
- **Use of company facilities**.

Other activities are difficult or impossible to quantify in monetary terms because they are not straightforward cash transactions, or are part of a larger commercial venture. However, in certain cases where a company's quantifiable contribution may not be quite enough to meet the Per Cent Club's qualifying level, they may be deemed to be sufficient to tip the balance. These include:

- **On-the-job time** given by employees who are not part of the community affairs function and are not generally costed on an hourly basis;
- **Corporate fund-raising activities** in which employees participate;
- **Partnership sourcing** ie. buying goods or services from small local suppliers (rather than larger companies) to support their long-term growth;
- **Business activities in economically depressed areas** to stimulate local regeneration;
- **Administration and organisational costs** of employee payroll giving and special appeals.

And these contributions could be in relation to:

- Any **charity** or charitable organisation.
- A **charitable trust** or foundation set up by the company, which in turn would pass on these contributions to beneficiary charities or spend the money itself directly for charitable purposes.
- Any other **community or social responsibility activity** such as Business in the Community, employment/job-creating schemes, inner city development schemes, projects in deprived areas, business-education partnerships, support for schools etc.. Some of these payments would be charitable; many probably would not be charitable (although they would qualify for tax relief either if paid to an enterprise agency or where they were deemed to be a proper business expenditure).

This move by the Per Cent Club to encouraging its members to adopt a similar basis of reporting is very welcome. If adopted, it should help standardise the league tables of rankings of company donations and contributions in publications such as this.

Local Per Cent Clubs

There are also local Per Cent Clubs in Sheffield and the North East. Both have a current membership of about 100 companies. The Scottish Per Cent Club, with 30 founder members, was launched on 25 November 1991 by the Secretary of State for Scotland. Details of these Per Cent Clubs are given below. The same qualifying level for membership as the Per Cent Club itself has been adopted by each of the other Clubs in turn.

Per Cent Club addresses

The Per Cent Club is a club in only the widest sense of the word. There is no written constitution and its only formal activity is an annual meeting attended by the chairman or chief executive of each member company.

The development of the Club is in the hands of a steering committee (which meets occasionally) and of Business in the Community which provides administrative back-up.

Membership of the Per Cent Club as at August 1992 was as on the list below. The Chairman or Chief Executive Officer is the designated member of the Club, although most of the companies have a Community Affairs Manager or Department which deals with incoming appeals.

Further information on the Per Cent Club and the regional Per Cent Clubs is available from:

The Per Cent Club

5 Cleveland Place, London SW1Y 6JJ (071-925 2899).
Joint Chairmen: Lord Laing and Sir Mark Weinberg
Executive Director: Jeremy Lunn

The North East Per Cent Club

c/o Durham University Business School, Mill Hill Lane, Durham DH1 3LB (091-374 2246).
Chairman: Roger Spoor
Secretary: Albert Knight

The Sheffield Per Cent Club

Don Valley House, Savile Street East, Sheffield S4 7UQ (0742-765028).
Chairman: Hugh Sykes
Secretary: Arnold Johnson

The Scottish Per Cent Club

c/o Scottish Business in the Community, Romano House, 43 Station Road, Corstophine, Edinburgh EH12 7AF.

Important note: Many companies in the Per Cent Club have experienced a sudden increase in their appeal mail because of their membership. The assumption that all these companies have extra resources to give away is incorrect. Most that have joined will be already giving at or above the levels required for membership. Remember too that these levels relate to UK-earned profits and not to the total profits earned by the company, and a substantial proportion may be coming from overseas. Few companies want to allocate extra resources to support unsolicited applications received through the post. Indeed one could make a good case **not** to send an unsolicited application to a Per Cent Club member, because many have carefully thought through policies for community support and charitable giving. Equally, the fact that a company has not joined should not be taken to mean that it does not give substantially, or that it has not thought through what it is doing. We are listing the membership of the Club because it is of public interest, but (and this applies to any listings of company names) blind mailing of appeals without thought helps neither you the applicant, companies, or indeed charities generally.

● Per cent giving and the Per Cent Club

Members of the Per Cent Club

- Abbott Mead Vickers Ltd
- Acatos & Hutcheson plc
- Albright & Wilson Ltd
- Allied Dunbar Assurance plc
- Allied Irish Banks plc
- Allied London Properties plc
- Allied Partnership Group plc
- AMEC plc
- American Express Bank Ltd
- Amersham International plc
- Arthur Andersen & Co
- Anglia Television Group plc
- Armour Trust plc
- ASDA Group plc
- Laura Ashley Holdings plc
- Associated British Foods plc
- Associated Newspapers Holdings plc
- Attwoods plc
- Avon Cosmetics Ltd

- Bank of Scotland
- Barclays Bank plc
- Barings plc
- BAT Industries plc
- Bayer UK Ltd
- J E Beale plc
- Bentalls plc
- S & W Berisford plc
- Bernstein Group plc
- Bestway Cash & Carry Ltd
- BET plc
- Blue Circle Industries plc
- BMP DDB Needham Worldwide Ltd
- BOC Group plc
- Bodycote International plc
- C T Bowring & Co Ltd
- Bridon plc
- Brintons Ltd
- British Aerospace plc
- British Gas plc
- British Land Company plc
- British Nuclear Fuels plc
- British Railways Board
- British Telecom plc
- Brown Shipley Holdings plc
- Bryant Group plc
- Bucknall Austin plc
- Bunzl plc
- Burmah Castrol plc
- Burton Group plc

- Cable & Wireless plc
- Cadbury Schweppes plc
- CALA plc

- Campbell Grocery Products Ltd
- Canon (UK) Ltd
- Cantors plc
- Caparo Industries plc
- James Capel & Co
- Cargill UK Ltd
- Carlton Communications plc
- Central Independent Television plc
- Century Ltd
- Charnos plc
- Christies International plc
- Ciba-Geigy plc
- Citibank NA
- Clifford Foods plc
- Coats Viyella plc
- Conder Group plc
- Control Securities plc
- Coopers & Lybrand Deloitte
- Cresvale Ltd
- James Cropper plc

- DAKS Simpson Group plc
- DHL International (UK) Ltd
- Digital Equipment Co Ltd
- Dixons Group plc
- DMB & B Holdings Ltd
- Dow Chemical Co Ltd
- Du Pont (UK) Ltd
- Duchy of Cornwall
- Dunhill Holdings plc
- Dwyer plc

- The Economist Newspaper Ltd
- Elders IXL Ltd
- J A Elliot (Holdings) Ltd
- Richard Ellis
- Ernst & Young
- Espree Leisure Ltd
- Eurotherm International plc
- Eurotunnel

- Farmington Trust
- Ferguson Industrial Holdings plc
- Ferranti International plc
- FI Group plc
- Fine Art Developments plc
- Fisons plc
- FOCUS Ltd
- Forbes Trust
- Foster Wheeler Ltd
- Frizzell Group Ltd

- Geest Holdings plc
- S R Gent plc

- Gerrard & National Holdings plc
- Michael Gerson Ltd
- Gillette Industries Ltd
- Girobank plc
- GKN plc
- Glaxo Holdings plc
- Glynwed International plc
- Grampian Holdings plc
- Grand Metropolitan plc
- Grant Thornton
- Greycoat Group plc
- Guardian Royal Exchange plc
- Guinness plc

- Harris Ventures Ltd
- Hawthornes Colour Printers
- Healey & Baker
- Heidelberg Graphic Equipment Ltd
- Heron International plc
- Hewden Stuart plc
- Heygate & Sons Ltd
- Hi-Lo Manufacturing Ltd
- Highland Distilleries Co plc
- Hillier Parker May & Rowden
- Hillsdown Holdings plc
- Hunting plc
- Charles Hurst Holdings Ltd

- IBM (UK) Ltd
- Iceland Frozen Foods Holdings plc
- Indespension Ltd

- Jaguar Cars Ltd
- S C Johnson Ltd
- Jones Lang Wootton

- Kalamazoo plc
- Kellogg Company of Great Britain Ltd
- Kleinwort Benson Ltd
- Knight Frank & Rutley
- KPMG Peat Marwick

- Ladbroke Group plc
- John Laing plc
- Lamont Holdings plc
- Legal & General Group plc
- Leigh Interests plc
- Lex Service plc
- Linklaters & Paines
- Littlewoods Organisation plc
- Lloyds Bank plc
- London & Edinburgh Trust plc
- London & Manchester Group plc

Per cent giving and the Per Cent Club

- Louis Newmark plc
- Low & Bonar plc
- LWT Holdings plc

- McDonalds Restaurants Ltd
- Macfarlane Group plc
- ED & F Man Ltd
- R Mansell Ltd
- Manweb plc
- Marks & Spencer plc
- Martini & Rossi Ltd
- MCL Group Ltd
- Mecca Leisure Group plc
- Medical & Media Communications
- John Menzies plc
- Merck Sharp & Dohme Ltd
- Mercury Asset Management Group plc
- Merrill Lynch Europe Ltd
- Meyer International plc
- Midland Group
- Miller Group Ltd
- Mitsubishi Group Ltd
- Mobil Holdings plc
- Morgan Grenfell Group plc
- J Murphy & Sons Ltd

- National Westminster Bank plc
- Nestle UK Ltd
- Neville Russell
- NFC plc
- Nissan UK Ltd
- Northern Electric plc
- Northern Engineering Industries plc
- Norwich Union Insurance Group

- Ocean Group plc

- Pafra Ltd
- Pannell Kerr Forster
- Pearce Signs Group
- Pearl Assurance Group plc
- Pearson plc
- Pentland Group plc
- Pentos plc
- Persimmon plc
- Peugeot Talbot Motor Company Ltd
- Pifco Holdings plc
- Pilkington plc
- Pirelli UK plc
- Portsmouth & Sunderland Newspapers plc
- Powell Duffryn plc

- Price Waterhouse & Co
- Prudential Corporation plc
- Psion plc

- Quicks Group plc

- Rank Xerox Ltd
- Ranks Hovis McDougall plc
- Rea Brothers plc
- Reader's Digest Association Ltd
- Reed Executive plc
- Reed International plc
- Regalian Properties plc
- Reuters Holdings plc
- Marc Rich & Co Ltd
- Richer Sounds plc
- Robertson & Baxter Ltd
- Robinson Brothers Ltd
- Rosehaugh plc
- Rothmans International plc
- N M Rothschild & Sons Ltd
- Royal Bank of Scotland plc
- Royal Insurance Holdings plc
- RTZ Corporation plc
- Alexander Russell plc

- Saatchi & Saatchi Advertising Ltd
- J Sainsbury plc
- St Ives Group plc
- St James's Place Capital plc
- Christian Salvesen plc
- Saudi International Bank
- Save & Prosper Group Ltd
- Savills plc
- J Henry Schroder Wagg & Co Ltd
- Scottish Television plc
- Securicor Group
- Sedgwick Group plc
- Self Serve Hygiene Ltd
- Sharpe & Fisher plc
- Sheerness Steel Co plc
- Slough Estates plc
- W H Smith Group plc
- Smiths Industries plc
- Sony (UK) Ltd
- Sotheby's
- Spencer Stuart Associates Ltd
- Speyhawk plc
- Stag Furniture Holdings plc
- Stanhope Properties
- Stanley Leisure Organisation plc
- Stephenson Harwood
- Sun Life Assurance Society plc
- Sunley Holdings Ltd

- Tarmac plc
- Tate & Lyle plc
- Taylor Woodrow Construction Ltd
- Tesco plc
- Thames Television plc
- Thorn EMI plc
- Thorntons plc
- 3i plc
- 3M UK plc
- TI Group plc
- Tiphook plc
- Top Technology Ltd
- Touche Ross & Co
- Trebor Group Ltd
- Triumph International Ltd
- TSB Group plc
- Tullis Russell & Co Ltd
- TVS plc
- Tyne Tees Television Ltd

- Ultramar plc
- Unilever plc
- United Biscuits (Holdings) plc
- United Newspapers plc

- Vaux Group plc
- Vickers plc
- Virgin Holdings plc

- S G Warburg Group plc
- Warburtons Ltd
- Wellcome Foundation Ltd
- Wembley plc
- Whatman plc
- Whitbread & Co plc
- Wickes plc
- Wiggins Group plc
- Willis Corroon Group plc
- Willmott Dixon Holdings Ltd
- Winterthur Insurance Company Ltd
- Wise Group
- Rudolf Wolff & Company Ltd
- Wolstenholme Rink plc
- John Wood Group plc
- Woolwich Building Society

- Young & Rubicam Ltd

- Zetters Group plc

Company trusts

What are company trusts?

Until April 1986 if a company wished to obtain the tax advantages available on charitable giving it had to make its donations in one of three ways: make a covenant directly to a charity; use the Charities Aid Foundation; or the company could set up its own charitable trust through which to make its payments.

The 1986 Finance Act introduced a single payment procedure for charitable donations for Open Companies. This was extended in 1990 to Close Companies, so any company can now make single payments direct to a charity without losing any tax benefits, provided such payments are made under deduction of tax (and for a Close Company the donation should be at least £400, the current minimum payment under the Gift Aid scheme).

If charitable donations are paid direct to individual charities, income tax must be deducted and reclaimed **each time** a payment is made. Therefore, it is more convenient to make a single payment for the **whole** of the donations budget either to the Charities Aid Foundation or to a company trust, deducting and reclaiming just one income tax payment. Indeed, at its simplest a company charitable trust is no more than a book-keeping device. It is basically a charitable bank account to pay money into, reclaim the tax and pay the money out to the recipient charities. The **IBM UK Trust** operates on this basis. It is the administrative vehicle through which the Community Affairs Department pays out its cheques. The trust will also purchase gifts in kind from the company for donation to charities.

A company trust can also be a catalyst in the process of forming a donations policy. Once a trust is formed, trustees (usually mainly senior directors) have a legal responsibility to ensure that the trust acts within its charitable objects. Also, the company trust usually works with a fixed annual budget, with funds coming from the company plus any interest earned on undistributed balances. These two factors should help the company form a clearer donations policy. The trustees are serviced by a charities department, a trust administrator or the company secretary.

Occasionally a company will establish a trust in addition to its donations committee to distribute part of its charitable contributions (eg. the **BP General Educational Trust** for BP's educational contributions).

Company trusts' income comes from one of the following sources:

- a transfer of cash from the company to the trust;
- a transfer of assets from the company to the trust (the trust then spends the income generated from these assets, which are often company shares);
- a simple accumulation of income over a number of years.

1. A grant-making trust supported by income

Sometimes this means that the trust is simply the channel through which the company makes its donations to charity. In other words, there is still the expectation that the donation will improve the company's PR. However, the trust can assume a life independent of the company. The emphasis begins to shift from serving the needs of the company towards meeting certain charitable objectives. The trust is still supported by payments from the company, but it operates much more as a professional grant-making body with trustees drawn from outside the company's staff, perhaps supplemented by professional advisers. Examples of this include the **Allied Dunbar Charitable Trust** (see *The Major Companies Guide*) and the **Bernard van Leer Foundation UK Trust** which supports experimental work in the field of education and disadvantaged children (see *A Guide to the Major Trusts*).

2. A grant-making trust with its own capital resources

Alternatively, the company trust may have its own capital. For example, the original promoters of the company may have set up a charitable trust, transferred a part of their shareholding to the trust, and have the income from this investment available for distribution to charity. Here it is not the company's pre-tax profits that are being distributed, but the dividends received by the trust on its shareholding.

Such a trust will initially own only shares in its parent company. This could be quite a considerable shareholding, even 100% as was the case with the **Wellcome Trust** (which owned the whole of the pharmaceutical firm The Wellcome Foundation before it began selling off the shareholding). If the holding represents a major stake in the company, the trustees may be in a position of great influence over the affairs of the company. For example, **Baron Davenport's Charity** in the Midlands had trustees from the then Davenport's Brewing Company and Birmingham City Council, when the company was faced with a hostile take-over from Wolverhampton & Dudley Breweries. The trust owned 20% of the company and eventually decided to accept the take-over offer. In many instances the shareholding will be relatively small, as with the **Laura Ashley Foundation**, where the trust was established at the time of the public flotation of the company.

Another method of setting up a company trust is for the company itself to transfer a capital sum out of its own resources. This is usually done in one of two ways. Firstly, the company could create new shares and transfer these to the trust. Secondly, the company could transfer a sum out of its accumulated reserves (as when the **Yorkshire Bank Trust** received a cash transfer of £250,000 from Yorkshire Bank plc).

Finally, a trust may accumulate some resources of its own over a period of

Company trusts

time in the form of undistributed money. Capital generated this way is usually only small scale.

Once a trust is established with its own resources, it exists as an institution in its own right, separate from the company and with its own continuing source of income. The income distributed by the trust is not the company's income (although it will usually consist of dividends received from shares in the company held by the trust); nor will the charitable donations made by the trust be included in the total of the charitable donations which must be declared by the company. However, the trustees of the trust and the senior directors of the company may well be the same people and the trust may share its offices with the company. To all intents and purposes the trust can be considered a creature of the company. Charities sending their appeal to the company may even find that the donation they receive is paid by the trust, not by the company.

The question then arises of how to establish whether a trust is simply a tax-effective means of company giving or whether it is additional money on top of the company's own charitable donations.

There is a real problem of definition. The trust may have been set up alongside the company, but legally it is a separate body controlled by its own trustees. Although such a trust may originally have been closely connected with the company, over time the two paths may begin to diverge. Those who control the trust's money may no longer be so closely connected with the company. Or the trust may be so large that it begins to assume a momentum of its own with a donations policy quite different from that of the company with which it is (or was) associated.

For example, the **Nuffield Foundation** was set up by Lord Nuffield and endowed with shares in his motor car company. That company, through a series of take-overs, eventually became the British Motor Corporation, which was then itself taken over by Leyland Motors to form British Leyland. Since then it has become Leyland DAF; this was taken over by the Rover Group who were in turn taken over by British Aerospace. While this has been going on the Nuffield Foundation has sold off its original shareholding and diversified its investments. Its trustees now consist of several peers, knights and professors, none of whom have ever made a motor car. The policies of the trust are very specifically confined to medical, scientific and social research, education and the care of old people. It is doubtful whether the Nuffield Foundation could ever have been considered a company trust, but it certainly is not one now.

But what about the **Wolfson Foundation** which shares offices with Great Universal Stores, the company run by Sir Isaac Wolfson? Or the very much smaller **Weinstock Fund** which is administered from the headquarters of GEC, the company run by Lord Weinstock? Both are closely connected with companies or with their founders, but the companies also undertake their own charitable donations programmes. Are they company trusts? Probably not, but the dividing lines are certainly not very clearly drawn.

Some company trusts have been established as the vehicle to undertake the whole of the company's donations programme. The company itself will then be giving nothing to charity directly as a matter of policy. These would certainly be considered company trusts. So too would those trusts which are part endowed and part funded by covenanted income from the parent company. But for many other trusts it is a matter of subjective judgement as to whether they should be considered company trusts or not.

Most trusts which could be considered to be company trusts would meet the following criteria:

- The trust is run from the head office of the company.
- The trustees include the founder of the company and/or consists of directors of the company (and others).
- The trust is named after the company with which it is associated.
- The trust's donations policy is co-ordinated with the company's own donations policy.
- The trust secretary is in close contact with the company's own charitable donations committee.

A further point to note is that the situation is changing all the time. New trusts are being established by newly successful entrepreneurs. Long-established trusts may sever their links with the company, either by gradually deciding to go their own ways or through a take-over of the parent company after which the trust has no links at all with the company. This was the case with the **William Leech Property Trust** when the William Leech building firm was taken over by housebuilders CH Beazer.

One important point to note is that if you receive a donation from a company trust, you cannot reclaim any tax on this donation. Similarly, if a company gives you a Charities Aid Foundation voucher, you cannot reclaim the tax there. This is because the company has already made a tax-effective payment to the company trust (or the Charities Aid Foundation) and the whole of the tax due on this amount has already been reclaimed by the company trust (or the Charities Aid Foundation). Tax cannot be reclaimed twice!

There is no comprehensive listing of company trusts. Where we know that a company makes some of its donations through an associated trust, we have stated this in the entry. Otherwise, the Charities Aid Foundation's *Directory of Grant-Making Trusts* is the closest, but they are not listed in a separate section (largely because it is hard to define when a company trust stops being a creature of the company and becomes an independent trust).

If you apply to trusts using the CAF *Directory of Grant-Making Trusts* (and, to a lesser extent, our own *Guide to the Major Trusts*) and to companies using this Guide then there will be some overlap. You will be in danger of approaching twice those company trusts funded by companies' income and those which work in tandem or close co-operation with the company's own donations programme. You have to decide whether to approach the trust as part of your corporate fundraising or as part of your efforts to raise money from trusts. The general rule is that the larger the trust, the more likely it is to operate as a grant-making trust in its own right. You need to avoid sending out a duplicated mail shot so that the company receives two or several identical appeals simultaneously, addressed both to the company and to the charitable trust it is associated with.

Further information

The Directory of Grant-Making Trusts from the Charities Aid Foundation, 48 Pembury Road, Tonbridge, Kent TN9 2JD. This gives details on about 2,500 grant-making trusts in the UK with incomes of £1,500 or more. Cost of 1993 edition will be about £55.

A Guide to the Major Trusts from the Directory of Social Change, Radius Works, Back Lane, London NW3 1HL. This gives detailed information on the grant-making of 300 large trusts the vast majority of whom make grants of £150,000 or more annually. Cost of 1993 edition: **£14.95** (plus £1.50 postage).

Secondment of staff

Secondments are an important part of company support for charity. The total value of secondments in salary terms is about £25 million a year. A large proportion are in areas of finance, administration, marketing and market research. Many are linked to fundraising; some are involved with the contract culture (a KPMG Peat Marwick accountant was recently seconded for three weeks to report on the implications of contracting for voluntary groups in Leicester covering issues of legal and charitable status and how to draw up business plans, tender bids and service agreements).

Since 1983, secondments have been a deductible expense when the company calculates its Corporation Tax liability as long as the secondment **is on a basis which is expressed and intended to be of a temporary nature.**

Types of secondment

Secondments come in many forms. They can be full-time or part-time, used at any stage of the secondee's career (from management trainee to pre-retirement) and last anything from a dozen hours to one or more years.

Recently there has been a move away from long-term, full-time secondments towards **short-term or "mission" secondments** (also called development assignments), where the secondee aims to undertake a particular task within a limited time-span. These are typically done part-time over three months to a total of 100 hours.

Development assignments were pioneered by Marks & Spencer with the Action Resource Centre (ARC) in 1988. The 500th assignment was completed in mid-1992 by a cashier at TSB who reviewed the accounting systems and methods of promotion of the Nest Playcentre in Birmingham. The secondee felt: "it has been very useful in developing my skills, and being able to work more independently has given me more confidence in my job at TSB". The playcentre thought it "has helped us take on new ideas from a fresh and business perspective".

A newer concept is the transition secondments scheme pioneered by British Coal Enterprise and ARC. In 1992, after further pit closures and reorganisation in British Coal, a pilot scheme was run with ARC Nottinghamshire whereby surplus British Coal staff were seconded to local voluntary organisations. The placements lasted up to 40 days over a period of three to four months and were part of a careers counselling and job search package.

Managing the secondment

For a secondment to work there must be a match between the skills of the secondee and the needs of the recipient organisation. ARC advises: "Careful matching is crucial, preceded by needs assessment on both sides. Arrangements for induction, monitoring and evaluation should be made at the outset, along with agreement of the practical details such as insurance and expenses. The objectives and responsibilities of each party must be clear throughout." ARC have their own development assignments management procedures (see chart below).

Therefore a secondment can only normally be arranged (a) if the company has sufficient resources (b) if there is a suitable person available with the required skills, and (c) if the proposed secondee actually wants to be seconded.

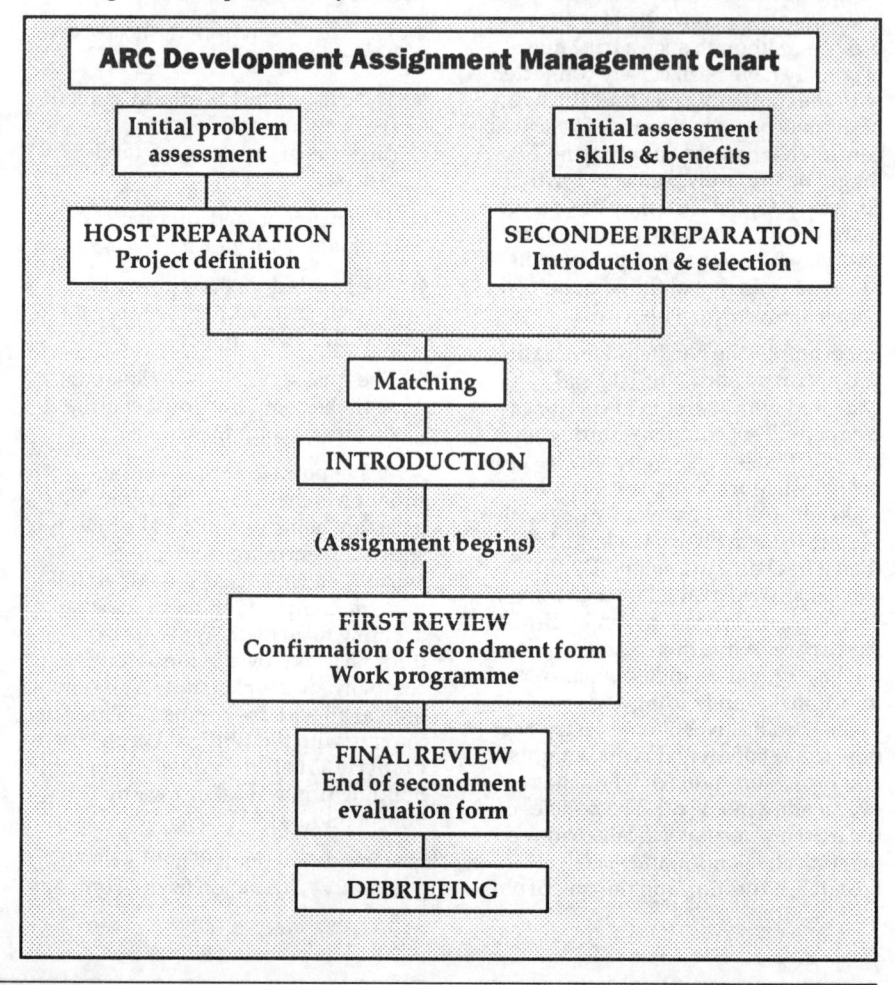

ARC Development Assignment Management Chart

- Initial problem assessment → HOST PREPARATION: Project definition
- Initial assessment skills & benefits → SECONDEE PREPARATION: Introduction & selection
- Matching
- INTRODUCTION
- (Assignment begins)
- FIRST REVIEW: Confirmation of secondment form / Work programme
- FINAL REVIEW: End of secondment evaluation form
- DEBRIEFING

Secondment of staff

Much secondment is to enterprise, training, local regeneration initiatives, local education compacts, environmental improvement initiatives or other concerns of particular interest to business. Even so, most seconding companies are also prepared to consider making secondments to charitable organisations.

Other forms of company staff involvement

Other ways in which professional staff can be put at the disposal of the community which cannot strictly be called secondment include:

- **Retired volunteers** working full-time or part-time for a charity. Here the 'secondee' is no longer the responsibility of the company, and is supported through a pension rather than a salary. But a company can encourage their executives to volunteer after retirement either by making their own arrangements or via the scheme operated by the Retired Executives Action Clearing House (REACH), an initiative supported largely by companies.

The REACH service keeps a register both of charities requiring a retired executive and retired executives wanting a placement with a charity, and tries to match skills to needs. There also needs to be a geographical match. At present REACH makes 500-600 placements a year. Another scheme is RSVP supported by Community Service Volunteers.

- **Professional help** given in-house by the company. Here the charity comes to the company rather than vice versa to be given some form of free help. This could either be a permanent arrangement or something to meet a particular need (such as a centenary fundraising appeal or an initiative to coincide with the International Year of whatever). Help with promotion or advertising is commonly sought.

- **Volunteering** where the company supports and encourages its staff who wish to help a charity in their own time. Some companies make donations to charities in which members of staff are involved, or will match pound for pound (up to a specified limit) any money raised by members of staff. Many more companies give preference to requests for support made via a member of staff or for those causes that the member of staff is involved with (*for more information see article on Employee volunteering*).

- **Training**. Most companies run training and management development courses for their own staff. Such training can be very useful for charity employees (eg. a museum shop manager given training in retailing, shop display or security). Companies have given places to charity staff on their training courses; IBM even runs a special and extremely successful creative management training course for charities they are in contact with.

Secondment in the charity world is usually thought of as the loan of a company employee to the voluntary organisation, but it can extend beyond this. Successful secondments have been obtained from central government or even from a local authority.

Who benefits?

IBM have defined the following benefits of the arrangements:

For the employee

- An opportunity to practise and test business skill in an alternative environment.
- The development of previously unused skills.
- The development of a lasting interest in social problems.
- Encountering different concepts, ideals, priorities, values, cultures and ways of life.

For the receiving organisation

- Expertise and experience it could not otherwise afford to buy in.
- A fresh approach to a problem.
- A contact in a different field of work which may be helpful in the future.

For the seconding company

- The increased experience and broadened approach of its secondees.
- The easing of promotional log jams and staff imbalances.
- An opportunity to influence realistic community planning.
- General approval that employees give to such enlightened company initiatives.
- Keeping its goals and values in step with those of the rest of the community.

The recipient charity should be aware that a number of conditions must be met to get any real value out of the arrangement:

- There should be a match **between skills and needs**.

- The secondee should be **happy with the arrangement**. If it is an alternative to redundancy late in the person's career this may not always be the case. Equally the secondee must support the charity's aims and objectives and be prepared to put real effort into the assignment.

- The secondee should **be on the same wavelength** as his/her co-workers in the charity. This has two aspects. Firstly there are his/her attitudes towards the charity beneficiaries and the problems being tackled. Secondly there is the ability to adapt to working in a voluntary organisation which can be very different from the corporate environment. Back-up services may not be available and cost may be much more of a factor in deciding how to get something done.

So a secondment may not necessarily be a golden egg laid by a corporate goose. The recipient charity should try to select the secondee in the same way as it selects any other member of staff. The fact that the secondee comes free should not influence the importance of getting the right person for the job. It is easier for a charity to raise money to pay a person it wants to employ than it is to compensate for the problems that arise with a secondee who is not right for the job.

However, where the secondment works well it is an extremely valuable source of help to the charity, and an arrangement which benefits all three parties involved: the corporate donor, the recipient charity and the secondee.

Action Resource Centre

Action Resource Centre is an independent charity, which was set up in 1973. It is a bridge between the voluntary and business sectors. ARC is at the focal point of the secondment process. It pioneered community secondments for company staff more than a decade ago. Now it promotes secondment by companies and acts as a clearing house for secondments and business volunteer placements.

The addresses of ARC, REACH and Community Service Volunteers can be found in the Useful contacts section at the end of the book.

This article has been compiled with the help of David Hemsworth of Action Resource Centre.

Employee volunteering

The involvement of employees in community initiatives is not a new phenomenon. Surveys show that 66% of all volunteers are in employment, and that 22% of volunteers get involved through contacts at the workplace. In a recent survey of senior executives from 100 of the UK's top 500 companies, 84% said companies should support their employees' involvement in the community, and over 70% saw the key benefits as enhancing community relations, improving public image and increasing employee morale.

Working on their own or in groups, staff have raised literally millions through charity events of all kinds. Although fundraising is by far the most popular activity, ever increasing numbers are getting involved as volunteers. What is new is the emergence of positive company support for such activities as an integral part of a company community investment policy. A few companies, such as Allied Dunbar, Whitbread, IBM and Grand Metropolitan, have been involved in employee volunteering for some time. Recently, these and other companies got together with the Action Resource Centre, the Volunteer Centre and Business in the Community to promote a national campaign to promote and establish employee community involvement in companies across the UK. The campaign was timely and is already bearing fruit. Employee volunteering seems set to become a permanent feature of company giving throughout the decade, and not just in large companies. There are many examples of smaller enterprises (eg. Video Arts) running innovative and successful programmes.

There a number of reasons for this:

- In times of recession, companies are looking for ways to enhance, but hopefully not replace, declining or static cash donations to meet ever increasing demands for support.

- As patterns of work change, employees are increasingly taking an interest in establishing a more balanced working life, one where their outside interests can be fostered, accommodated and valued by their employer.

- Companies are giving more attention to the potential benefits of successfully meeting some of the "extra mural" expectations staff have.

- A number of charities and intermediary agencies such as volunteer bureaux have developed attractive tailor made schemes for individual or groups of companies.

The Employees in the Community Campaign has focused on and exploited these elements. Launched in June 1990 with an initial two-year remit, the objective by December 1992 was to have 50 active and formulated company programmes up and running, and a further 200 companies committed to the concept and in the process of planning programmes. These targets look likely to be met.

The campaign has been built around three linked areas of activity:

Promotional events and schemes

These included the annual National Challenge where teams of company volunteers take on specific tasks set by charities and community groups to be completed within a fixed timescale; a National Action Day, sponsored by Allied Dunbar and American Express, which provided a focus for all the campaign's activities, and allowed new companies to see employee volunteering in action; and the UK Award for Employee Volunteering, sponsored by Whitbread, and now attracting 50 nominations annually.

Publications

These support both companies and voluntary agencies looking to run programmes. Particularly useful to volunteer seekers is *Making the Most of Employee Community Involvement* sponsored by BT, and to company managers wanting to set up schemes there is *Employees in the Community - Handbook for Action*, sponsored by Allied Dunbar. The quarterly magazine *Working Out* covers on company employee volunteering schemes and successes. These and other useful titles are available from Business in the Community or the Volunteer Centre UK (addresses below).

Building networks

Arguably the most important outcome of the campaign so far has been the networking of contacts and the pooling of information and ideas for improving and developing schemes. A group of 40 company staff responsible for employee volunteering in their companies now meets quarterly at a well attended forum whose role is "to be a source of inspiration and innovation" for people working in the field. A similar network for voluntary organisations is running equally effectively. In addition, regionally coordinated initiatives in Leeds, Leicester, Birmingham, Liverpool and Edinburgh are giving impetus to the campaign at local level, and more are likely to be set up in the coming year. Finally, visits are organised to successful company programmes both in the UK and further afield, an invaluable opportunity to "see for yourself".

It is not simply a question of winning the commitment of employers. Organisations which involve volunteers and intermediary bodies which act as brokers in local areas are both crucial to the success of the campaign. Indeed, a priority for the next phase of the campaign will be to concentrate on introducing employee volunteering both to the volunteers involvers and to employers in chosen localities, alongside giving support and resources to the important but often overstretched local brokers.

What is the future for employee volunteering? One scenario is that it could grow dramatically over the next few years, particularly as the economy picks up. The recession has been a constraint on many companies who have bought into the ideas but want better trading conditions before they implement schemes. On the other hand,

Employee volunteering

the traditionally cautious private sector may be slow to take on and develop new activities in this field. However, there are good grounds to believe that employee community volunteering will become a significant and permanent component of corporate community involvement in the UK. If charities find creative ways to attract and retain the interest of volunteers from the workplace they will both secure a new and valuable form of support in the short term and lay the foundations for more productive relationships in the longer term.

Useful contacts

Jo Paton, Development Officer Employee Volunteering, The Volunteer Centre UK, 29 Lower King's Road, Berkhamsted HP4 2AB (0442-873311).

Amanda Bowman, Manager, Employees in the Community Programme, Business in the Community, 5 Cleveland Place, London SW1Y 6JJ (071-925 2899).

David Hemsworth, Director of Communications, Action Resource Centre, 102 Park Village East, London NW1 3SP (071-383 2200).

Publications

Employees in the Community: A Handbook for Action is indispensable for any staff member responsible for establishing and running an employee involvement programme. Gives details on all types of programmes from fundraising through hands on volunteering to secondment. Includes comprehensive how-to information on all aspects of running a programme from set-up to evaluation, plus sample company materials. Updating service available. Available from Business in the Community and the Volunteer Centre UK.

Lessons from America is an introduction to corporate volunteerism in the USA and the practical lessons for UK companies. Available from Business in the Community.

Making the Most of Employee Community Involvement is a handbook for non-profit organisations. Available from the Volunteer Centre UK.

Understanding Employee Volunteering is a 12 page introductory pamphlet on employee volunteering, with case studies. Available from the Volunteer Centre UK.

This article has been written by Jerry Marston, Community Affairs Manager, Allied Dunbar Assurance plc, winners of the 1992 UK award for employee volunteering.

Case studies

Allied Dunbar

Every year, Swindon-based Allied Dunbar stages a Challenge event where staff volunteer teams are recruited to take on challenges set by Wiltshire charities, schools, hospitals, and other welfare organisations. In July 1992 over 1,000 staff (40%), their family and friends took on and successfully completed over 100 different projects, "donating" about 7,000 hours of work in the process. They included:

- Organising outings and sporting events for children with special needs.
- Designing and producing publicity material for a 25th anniversary appeal.
- Refurbishing and redecorating charity premises.
- Building raised gardens in residential homes.
- Canal restoration and cleaning.

The Allied Dunbar Challenge, which was the inspiration for the National Challenge, is the major focus of Allied Dunbar's comprehensive community involvement programme, in which staff have also raised over £1 million for local and third world charities.

For further information, contact Krista Potts, Staff Charity Co-ordinator (0793-514514).

GEC

Every year since 1987, GEC's Development Training Unit has organised an overseas expedition as a staff training project for the Group's companies. Previous teams have worked in Morocco, Pakistan and Nepal, and the 1992 team were in rural Kenya building a dormitory at an orphanage.

Staff at all levels can apply. The age range is typically 18-25. In the 9 month build up to the field trip, the 20 people (from around 70 applicants) spend a weekend a month planning, team building and training. They usually spend 5 weeks abroad completing the project, and at the end of the exercise give a senior level presentation and submit a written report of their experience. The theme of each expedition is "personal development through adventure, service and teamwork". A high degree of commitment is required to succeed. Participants must contribute 2 weeks net wages towards costs and fundraise for rest of the budget, including air fares. Their company generally allows matching paid leave, and contributes to the fundraising.

The annual expedition is one of a series of community-orientated training projects run by the GEC Management College. This includes organising a 12-day children's camp for disadvantaged children from Coventry's schools.

Contact Barry Roberts, Development Training Co-ordinator (0788-810656).

W H Smith

To mark its bicentenary in 1992, staff of W H Smith Group decided to raise money for the Samaritans LinkLine project, following presentations by four charities to staff representatives.

The LinkLine Appeal will establish the setting up of one national telephone number which will put callers through the nearest available free Samaritan line for the cost of a local telephone call. It will mean that a desperate, possibly suicidal person will always get through and it will use vital Samaritan volunteer time to the best possible effect.

Communication of the project was essential, so a video featuring W H Smith staff explaining the project was distributed to all branches of the W H Smith Group. The staff set themselves a target of £500,000 (achieved by the middle of October) which the Group matched by a further £500,000. Each part of the business set its own target and a hugely diverse programme of local fundraising activities took place all over the country. Centrally organised initiatives included a celebrity golf day and the Blue Balloon Badge Campaign when all the Group retail outlets (W H Smith Retail, Our Price and Waterstones) sold enamel brooches in the shape of a balloon on behalf of the Samaritans for a minimum donation of £1.

This will also help a secondary aim, the setting up of a W H Smith Charitable Trust. This trust will be administered by a staff committee and will become the focal point of a new employee volunteering initiative, enabling staff to support charities of their own choosing.

Contact Tim Prideaux, Community Affairs Manager (071-730 1200).

Sponsorship

Sponsorship is a term which is used very loosely. It is often a disguise for a request for cash. "Will you sponsor me in the Great North Run" is actually a request for a donation; "will you sponsor a page in our programme" is usually a request for advertising. Sponsorship must not to be confused with company charitable giving, rather it is the payment of money by a business to promote the business name, products or services. Looked at cynically, it is mutual exploitation for mutual benefit. It is normally viewed a part of a business's general promotional expenditure and as such is normally allowable for tax purposes.

Why do businesses sponsor?

These are some of the usual reasons:
- Name awareness.
- Enhancement of a corporate image.
- Opportunities to entertain customers, clients and VIPs.
- Improved investor relations.
- Services or facilities which benefit staff.
- Involvement with the community.
- Improved staff relations/morale.
- Recruitment incentives.
- Association with a high-quality event.
- Access to a specific market.
- Product or service promotion.

Companies also sponsor as part of their corporate or social responsibility. This is where sponsorship approaches charitable donations. Many larger sponsors make little or no distinction between sponsorship and giving as part of their corporate responsibility programmes, and often such companies have established trusts through which such payments are made.

Timing can be crucial. The company may want to sponsor to tie in with an anniversary; it may want to overcome a particular PR problem; it may have a special need to advertise (eg. to coincide with a product launch, the opening of a branch or factory, the award of a major contract etc.).

What are companies looking for?

Charities should be able to offer at least some of the following:
- A respectable partner (with the right image).
- A proven track record (preferably in securing and delivering sponsorships).
- An interesting project (at least to the company management and possibly also company staff).
- Genuine value for money.
- Visibility (company name will be high profile).
- Appropriateness (eg. not asking one motor manufacturer to provide a vehicle produced by a rival, an all too common occurrence).
- Targeted audience (possibly leading to direct marketing eg. providing the company's wine at the charity's gala dinner).
- Other tangible benefits (eg. good publicity; media coverage; link with brand advertising [eg. Cornhill Test Cricket]; entertainment opportunities for company directors and staff; access to VIPs, royalty, TV or sports people; involvement of company employees or retirees; training or experience for employees etc. etc..

Nevertheless, if your organisation can offer a sponsorship package (ie. a project which offers sufficient benefits to a business to warrant proposing it as a promotional opportunity and not just as an appeal for funds) you should go through the process outlined below. The money available through sponsorship budgets can be much greater than through charitable budgets, so you must plan accordingly.

How to develop a sponsorship package

A successful sponsorship has three basic elements:
- It matches the image of the company and the work of the charity.
- It has the correct target audience or target area for the company.
- It sells the benefits of the sponsorship to the company (including how the sponsorship would meet the company's commercial objectives).

1. Self analysis

You must determine what you do, why you do it, why it is important, and why what you would like to do in the future is important. Are you successful? Are your services fully used or your events fully subscribed? (If not you would do better to improve your marketing than look for sponsorship, as it is easier to increase your income this way; businesses want to associate themselves with successful organisations.) Do you know who your supporters are? A survey can be a useful tool in persuading companies that by supporting you they will reach precisely their target market. The more you analyse your own operations, the better armed you will be to seek sponsorship. Can you back up your claims with statistics?

How good is your management? It can be helpful to create a development or fundraising sub-committee consisting of business people who are sympathetic to your aims and prepared to work to raise sponsorship for you.

2. Packaging the project

You may well want both to develop your educational work and put on a huge royal gala, but it is unlikely that the same sponsor will want to support both projects. By separating these projects you can approach those businesses with a track record in supporting educational work or with an obvious interest in the youth market with one package, and those with a desire for high-profile, prestigious events with the other.

3. Research

Researching the companies you are going to approach is vital. Read the financial pages of the newspapers, the marketing and PR magazines, the Kompass Guides, Key British Enterprises etc.. These should be available in a public library. Keep an eye on the local press to find out companies moving into the area (both in the features pages and see who is advertising for jobs). Write and ask a company for their annual report - most will willingly send you one. By this process - a slow but necessary one - you will build up a picture of potential sponsors, what their interests and plans are, where they operate, where they will soon be opening a new plant. When you have found a business that you think fits in with your plans, you are ready to make an approach.

How to approach a sponsor

1. Companies tend to plan one year or even two years ahead. To have a good chance, you must approach a business well in advance of the event. Six months is the absolute minimum.

2. Write a succinct, neat and comprehensive resume of the proposal covering who you are, what the project is, where it will be taking place, the dates, the likely audience, the publicity you will be generating, the cost or range of costs, and the benefits to the sponsor.

3. The benefits to the sponsor must be clearly outlined. Will you incorporate the sponsor's name into the title of the project eg. the ABSA/W H Smith Sponsorship Manual, or will you acknowledge their support on posters, programmes, leaflets and advertisements? Are there good facilities for entertainment of clients? Will you offer a free page of publicity in your brochure? Be as flexible as you can.

4. Write a brief covering letter which is addressed by name to the person in the company who deals with sponsorship. If you do not know who it is, telephone and ask. If they do not know, write to the head of the PR department or, for smaller companies, to the chief executive. It is often appropriate to have such a letter signed by the chairman of your development sub-committee, particularly if he/she is a fairly well-known in business. This lends credibility to your work.

5. Since you will only be approaching those companies whose profile suits your project, you should tailor your proposal specifically to each company. Duplicated proposals tend not even to be read.

6. If the company has a local branch near you, try to persuade the local manager of your project's worth and enlist his or her help in approaching head office.

7. Try to ensure that you and not the potential sponsor have to make the next move. Finish your letter with a sentence such as: "I would very much appreciate the opportunity to discuss this proposal with you in greater depth. May I ring your office in a few days' time to arrange a mutually convenient date to meet?" If you get an immediate answer no, you will at least stop wasting your time. If you hear nothing, you have at least a tacit agreement to meet.

8. Many arts groups hold "cultivation evenings" whereby you invite potential sponsors to come and see your work. They enjoy a drink with you and your development sub-committee members in the interval and hear something about your plans. You may even enthuse someone sufficiently to want to support you. You must follow up those who came to such an evening; for a short while they will feel in your debt if you gave them a good time.

The meeting

When you get a meeting with a potential sponsor to discuss your proposals further, dress according to their conventions, not yours, and go prepared to be flexible. Whoever represents you on such occasions should be able to make immediate decisions about what your organisation can or cannot do and must be familiar with all your activities. Ensure that everyone knows what the next step is - it is worth writing to confirm your understanding of the next moves. Will he/she be presenting your proposal to their committee? Do they want further information? Do they want to see further examples of your publicity material?

Management of the sponsorship

Many organisations seem to think that taking the cheque and running is all that is necessary. It is not. A good sponsorship deal is a true partnership, and you will need to meet regularly to discuss how the project is developing. Fundamentally, the more you keep your sponsor in touch, the better your relationship will be, and the more likely you will be to retain the sponsorship for another year. If you are sensible, you will have exchanged letters of agreement or contracts setting out exactly what each party will do. In this way there will be no confusion over who organises the press launch or the catering, for example. Your sponsor will be as keen as you are to ensure that the project is a success so ask for advice. Do not offer to do things that your sponsor would do better and more efficiently.

Also, make sure that you begin negotiations for a renewed sponsorship well before the current one expires. It may be that the sponsorship has served its purpose for the current company (eg. they have achieved maximum publicity from it) and they do not want to renew it. However, it may still be very attractive to another company. Don't leave it until the day before the sponsorship expires to begin negotiations. Write it into the sponsorship agreement that if the current company has not renewed the sponsorship by, say, six months before the expiry date, you are then free to seek an alternative sponsor.

How to find a sponsor

Who sponsors?

The charitable giving statistics in this book relate to larger companies. A much wider range of companies get involved in sponsorship. Smaller and quite local companies (for the sponsorship of a local event) or even brands or subsidiaries of larger companies may all be interested if there is a proposal that takes their fancy.

Finding a sponsor

There are thousands of businesses in Britain. You must narrow down the field to the companies which you think are most likely to have an interest in sponsoring your particular organisation or the activity it is running.

You may be able to offer specific and valuable benefits to a company such as entertainment facilities, access to celebrities or some sort of benefit to be enjoyed by the company staff. There may be larger companies with well-developed sponsorship programmes which might be interested in supporting just the sort of activity for which you are looking for sponsorship because it is a good proposal which interests them. On the other hand, there may be a particular reason why the company might want to undertake a sponsorship. For example:

- To celebrate an anniversary by sponsoring something special.

- To overcome a particular PR problem. The company may be seen

Sponsorship

as noisy, dirty, smelly or be trying to improve its image locally as part of an effort to secure planning or other approval for something it wishes to do.

- To coincide with a product launch, the opening of a branch or factory, or the award of a major contract at home or overseas.
- To be identified with the qualities your organisation represents (such as innovation or community concern) as part of a wider PR strategy.
- To link in with brand advertising (such as the **Mars** London Marathon).

A number of these opportunities arise not just because of the *nature* of the sponsorship, but also because the *timing* is appropriate. To identify the most likely companies you need information, facts and figures, but also news of events. There are quite a lot of resources available to you whether your activity is national, regional or local in scope:

1. National

- **Directories** or reference works which are available in most libraries:

    Hollis Press & Publications Annual

    Key British Enterprises (20,000 firms)

    Kompass (available in regional editions)

    The Sponsorship Yearbook

    A Guide to Company Giving

    ABSA Yearbook (which lists all members and arts sponsorships undertaken by some of them and Business Sponsorship Incentive Scheme awards).

- **The media:** Specialist magazines such as *Campaign, Marketing, Marketing Week* and *PR Week* carry sponsorship information and features. There are also periodicals devoted entirely to sponsorship called *Sponsorship News* and *Sponsorship Insights*. These all provide valuable advance information on new product launches, marketing campaigns and which advertising and PR agencies are involved in which activities.

National press events listings give an indication of who is doing what currently. The financial pages also give valuable snippets of information. Business adverts in the national press highlight companies which attach particular importance to communicating with the public, and also something of their style and the image they wish to project.

2. Regional and local

- **The media:** Look through the regional and local press (as for the national press).

- **Development corporations and associations:** These exist to bring new business into the area and new business often needs to raise its public profile. They produce directories of firms in the area and also a bulletin or newsletter which can help identify potential sponsors.

- **PR firms and advertising agencies:** These are often looking for ideas to sell to their clients. Contact can be established via the professional body or through a direct approach. You might be able to open a dialogue or establish a relationship which will bear fruit in the longer term. They can provide useful guidelines or other information on their client's needs.

- **Development units of local authorities:** They perform a similar role to Development Corporations, but on a district rather than a regional level.

- **Local industry bodies** such as Chambers of Commerce, or places where local company directors meet eg. Rotary and Round Table.

- **Direct personal contact:** You will have a network of business contacts that you and your organisation might utilise. These can help you find your way through to an appropriate local company and even open the door for you.

- **Yellow Pages/Thomson's directories:** A last resort!

Sponsorship and donations

Sponsorship is a term which is very loosely used. It often means little more than a donation which is publicly acknowledged and which might therefore generate some good publicity for the donor. Applicants sometimes feel that if they suggest what they are looking for is "sponsorship", they are more likely to be successful than if they were to request a donation; and companies may also think of their support as sponsorship because this sounds more impressive. But true sponsorship is more than a donation; it is a partnership between the donor and recipient.

In tax terms, a sponsorship would normally be classed as a business expense incurred "wholly and exclusively" for the purpose of the business of the company, and it would also be subject to VAT as the provision of a service to the sponsor. In practical terms, it is also a business expense, with the company laying out its money in the expectation of some sort of return.

That return may be **good publicity, media and press coverage**, or PR for the company or its brands. There may also be other benefits, such as **entertainment** opportunities for staff and senior directors; **access** to people such as TV personalities, royalty, politicians or other VIPs who may be already associated with or happy to do something for a good cause; opportunities for **involvement of employees** or retirees.

Sponsorship can mean that a charity incurs a VAT liability. If the charity's total sponsorship income in a year exceeds £36,600 (the VAT threshold for 1992/93) the charity will have to register for VAT. Similarly, if the sponsorship income when added to the charity's other standard-rated income exceeds £36,600, the charity will have to register for VAT.

Generally speaking as part of the sponsorship proposal, the applicant will list the tangible benefits which it hopes will accrue to the company. Because of the reciprocal benefits for both parties, sponsorship is a two-sided rather than a one-sided relationship and the support given is likely to be more substantial. Because of the closer involvement and also because of the larger sums of money involved, the company will adopt very different criteria in deciding which sponsorship proposals to proceed with than for its charitable donations programme. It will be looking at its own needs and for the proposal that matches these needs. It will ensure that the organisation it is sponsoring has objects at least compatible with its own and that it has the professional expertise to carry out the sponsorship as set out in the proposal.

The difference between sponsorship and donations is well illustrated by the different guidelines adopted by a large company in assessing sponsorship proposals and grant applications. The guidelines here are those used by **Shell UK**; the annotations are our own:

1. Shell's sponsorship criteria

Appropriateness: Is the activity/event appropriate to the sponsor (having regard to the nature of the sponsor's business and the work of the organisation seeking sponsorship)?

Partnership: Is there scope for partnership, or is the applicant simply seeking money?

Real involvement: What involvement is being looked for from the sponsor, and how well does this meet the needs of the sponsor?

Continuity: Is there scope for a continuing relationship (over the next few years), or is the activity/event just a one-off?

Initiative: Does the sponsorship represent a new initiative, something that would not happen without the company's support? Is it interesting and lively? It is much more attractive to back an interesting proposal and an interesting organisation.

'Professional' approach: Has the applicant approached the business of getting sponsorship in a professional way, and can he/she demonstrate a similar professionalism in the running of his/her organisation?

Visibility: How 'visible' will the event be, and what specific publicity and PR benefits will accrue to the sponsor?

Value for money: Does the deal represent value for money? What are the benefits and how much money is being asked from the sponsor? How does this rate as compared with other possible sponsorships that the company might consider? The relationship of cost to return and the importance of the return to the company are the dominant factors affecting the decision to sponsor or not to sponsor.

2. National grants criteria

Grants from head office are made to national organisations, not to local branches or affiliates of national organisations or to purely local organisations.

Non-political: Charitable grants are not made for political purposes or to organisations which are deemed to be to political.

Not 'bricks and mortar': 'Bricks and mortar' building appeals are not supported; the company prefers to give its money for people and activities (other companies do support bricks and mortar appeals).

Close to major company locations: Local charities close to the company's major employment centres are supported. Such charities benefit employees, their families and the local community generally and their support can provide good local publicity. Normally local grant decisions will involve the local management. Applications may be dealt with locally at the discretion of the local manager/director or be processed centrally.

Employee involvement: The involvement of the company's employees with the applicant organisation is a very significant factor for deciding who the company should support. Employees can be involved in an official capacity (as trustees), as volunteers, or in helping raise money for the charity. Wherever there is some employee involvement, this should be mentioned in the application.

Pilot initiatives of potential national significance: The support of a pilot project (which works) will bring credit to the company, and will be seen as particularly cost-effective in view of the further developments arising from its success. Traditionally grant-making trusts have favoured innovation whilst companies have tended to play safe.

However some of the larger and more thoughtful company givers are now happy to promote innovation.

Business links (education): Educational projects which link schools to business are a current priority concern for many companies, particularly those concerned with science and technology.

Good chance project will develop concerted efforts: If the donation encourages the recipient to encourage and draw upon the voluntary efforts of its supporters, this makes the appeal a more attractive prospect for the donor.

This is one company's list of guidelines. Some factors not included here which are important to many companies are: (a) support for enterprise, employment and training projects, which many large companies give priority to; (b) leverage, where a smallish donation can be used to have a more substantial effect. Leverage can be defined in many different ways, but if there is a leverage factor then it does no harm to stress it. Every company knows that the individual grants or donations it makes are relatively small in size, but likes to feel that the money is being well spent and effectively used.

Arts sponsorship

Arts sponsorship has grown substantially in recent years. In 1976, the total spent was estimated at £600,000; in 1982, £12.5 million; in 1986, £25 million. The most recent ABSA survey (1990/91) showed business support for the arts at £57 million. Of this, £44.7 million was sponsorship; the remainder was corporate membership of arts groups.

Not all this money goes to traditionally 'safe' art (opera, ballet, exhibitions, classical music). Increasingly, companies which enter the sponsorship field are looking for different projects and different art forms with which to associate their names. Similarly, local, community-based sponsorships are proving popular with the business which wishes to show itself to advantage within a particular town or area.

In 1990/91, ABSA analysed over 1,350 arts sponsorships undertaken by member companies in the year. In terms of the number of sponsorships awarded, by far the greatest support was for music with over 450 sponsorships. Festivals and drama had 150-200 each, visual arts, education and awards over 100 each, dance over 50, and capital, literature, film and other under 50 each. Over 300 were awarded in Greater London, about 200 in Scotland and 170 were national. The remaining 643 were spread unevenly throughout the rest of England, Wales and Northern Ireland (a further 20 were international). 892 sponsorships were in the £1,000 - £10,000 range; 274 in the £11,000 - £50,000 range; 43 in the £51,000 - £100,000 range, and 59 over £100,000.

The Business Sponsorship Incentive Scheme (BSIS)

The BSIS is administered by the Association for Business Sponsorship of the Arts (ABSA) on behalf of the government. It is a valuable adjunct to any sponsorship proposal.

The scheme is designed as an incentive to businesses either to sponsor the arts for the first time or to increase their commitment to the arts. It offers both government endorsement and financial awards.

Sponsorship money from a business that has never sponsored before may be matched £1 for £1. The minimum sponsorship eligible is £1,000.

Sponsorship from a business that has sponsored the arts before but is increasing its budget may be matched, but at reduced ratios (ie. £1 of government money for every £2 of increased sponsorship for a company's second sponsorship; £1 for every £4 thereafter). The maximum BSIS award is £25,000.

BSIS was launched in 1984. It has grown rapidly. By April 1989, 356 awards had been made which represented new or increased sponsorship of £6.14 million matched by £2.91 million of government money. By May 1992, 2,142 awards had been made representing new or increased sponsorship of £32.6 million matched by £16.5 million of government money. The budget for the BSIS in 1992/93 was £4.5 million.

The financial award is made to the arts organisation, but the money must be used to improve the existing sponsorship (perhaps by way of extra marketing or the extension of a tour to other venues), thereby increasing the benefit to the sponsor. In addition, winning sponsors are invited to meet the Minister for the Arts and receive a commemorative certificate, usually with a photographer on hand to record the presentation, and the Office of Arts and Libraries puts out official press releases. These extras can be a major incentive to a business to consider sponsoring the arts, and you should use them when making your approach. Full details of the BSIS (including the official application form) are available from ABSA - see address below.

Before submitting an application for a BSIS award, organisations should ensure that the sponsorship is eligible (ie. that it involves an arts or museum activity and that it is either a first-time sponsorship or that it represents new sponsorship money). An organisation may receive up to two awards in each fiscal year, up to a maximum of £25,000. A completed application must be submitted at least 8 weeks in advance of the event. Since there is no guarantee of an award and the award is for extra work, schemes should be viable whether or not an award is granted. The application must be filled in both by the sponsor and the arts organisation and must therefore be discussed with the sponsor to see how the award should be spent if granted. Any queries should be raised with ABSA before an application is submitted.

The applications are assessed according to some or all of the following criteria:

- The business support must be in the form of commercial sponsorship not a donation (patronage).
- The sponsor must obtain a return (credits, publicity, facilities) appropriate to the money involved.
- The organisation seeking sponsorship must be bona fide.
- The existence of the BSIS scheme should be a factor in attracting the sponsor. The scheme is intended to encourage businesses to sponsor.
- The proposed use of the award should be to provide greater benefits for the sponsor than would otherwise be possible.
- The sponsor should indicate an interest in developing or continuing an arts sponsorship programme in the future.
- The arts organisation should (where feasible) have retained the support of any sponsors whose sponsorship won awards in previous years.

The scheme is cash-limited. Awards are discretionary and cannot be guaranteed, although 90% of applications are successful.

Arts sponsorship

Business in the Arts

Business in the Arts is an ABSA initiative. It aims to improve the quality of management in the arts through the involvement of business. The initiative is supported by twelve companies (Arthur Andersen, BP, British Gas, Conoco, English Estates, ICI, IBM, Marks and Spencer, NatWest, The Post Office, Prudential and W H Smith) and a grant from the Office of Arts and Libraries. There are three main areas of activity:

The Business Skills Placement Scheme

This places business people on secondment with arts organisations to act as management advisers. The secondments are for a few hours a week spread over two or three months. They may be voluntary (ie. in the secondee's spare time) or during work hours, depending on the company. The scheme operates in London and Scotland as well as through affiliated offices in several areas of England.

The Enterprise Advisory Service

This aims to provide advice on the management of smaller arts organisations. It is run in conjunction with Business in the Community, enterprise agencies and similar organisations.

The Arts Management Training Initiative

This develops management training packages at universities and colleges for potential and existing arts managers. It also encourages businesses to open up their own in-house training courses to arts managers.

In addition, Business in the Arts Bursaries, sponsored by English Estates, will be available in 1993. They offer senior arts managers a unique opportunity to attend short management courses run by leading business schools and colleges.

All enquiries relating to Business in the Arts should be made to the Director, Tim Stockil.

The Association for Business Sponsorship of the Arts (ABSA)

ABSA was established by the business community in 1976 as the independent national trade association for sponsors of the arts. Its priority is to provide a service for its members (see the list below) but a number of its services are of value to arts organisations as well. The **ABSA/W H Smith Sponsorship Manual** gives a step by step approach to raising sponsorship. The latest edition was published in 1986.

A second publication, **The Sponsor's Guide**, which costs £11.50 plus £1 postage, covers the use of sponsorship, setting a policy, making a choice, selecting activities, exploiting extra opportunities, achieving objectives working with an arts organisation, budgeting, getting value for money, tax and VAT, the Business Sponsorship Incentive Scheme, sample contracts and letters of agreement. Although aimed principally at sponsors, the publication will also be of interest to those seeking sponsorship.

ABSA's latest publication is aimed at business and the arts and sets out guidelines for carrying out arts sponsorship. Called **Principles for Good Practice in Arts Sponsorship** it is a useful reference for all those involved in managing arts sponsorship.

Arts organisations can join ABSA's mailing list at a cost of £25 a year. Amongst the publications sent to those on the mailing list is ABSA's Annual Report which details all the sponsorships undertaken by its members in the previous year. ABSA also employs regional administrators to co-ordinate the BSIS, to encourage business sponsorship and to advise arts organisations. This advice tends to take the form of seminars, often organised in conjunction with Regional Arts Boards or the Arts Council, although regular contact is maintained with many arts organisations throughout the country. ABSA publishes a **Tax Guide** to sponsorship in association with Arthur Andersen & Co.

Further information

For further information, contact:
ABSA, Nutmeg House, 60 Gainsford Street, Butlers Wharf, London SE1 2NY (071-378 8143).
Director General: Colin Tweedy.

There are also ABSA offices in:

Scotland
ABSA, Room 316, Scottish Post Office Board, West Port House, 102 West Port, Edinburgh EH3 9HS (031-228 4262).
Director: Helen Petrie.

Northern Ireland
ABSA, 181a Stramillis Road, Belfast BT9 5DU (0232-381591).
Director: Andrew McIlroy.

Wales
ABSA, c/o Welsh Arts Council, 9 Museum Place, Cardiff CF1 3NX (0222-221382).
Director: Guy Silk.

North
ABSA North, Dean Clough Office Park, Dean Clough, Halifax, West Yorkshire HX3 5AX (0422-345631).
Director: Christopher Pulleine.

ABSA publishes a quarterly **Business and Arts Bulletin** on arts sponsorship which gives news, case histories and company profiles. This is sent to everyone on the mailing list.

The ABSA awards

Each year ABSA offers awards for the best sponsorship during the previous year.

In 1991, 11 ABSA/Daily Telegraph awards were offered in 10 categories. The winners each receive £5,000 and a work of art. The following were the winners:

(a) **Arts & urban regeneration:** Citibank, partly for its Community Music project which "brings music to young people in badly deprived areas. The project has given the opportunity for a young offender to compose and record to professional standards, for 12 teenagers, some with disabilities, to attend a music weekend in the country, and for a group from a Newham estate to compose music on computers."

(b) **Arts & disabled people:** Purolite International. "Taciton, the act of touching" was a "touring hands-on exhibition of contemporary craft work for visually impaired and blind people with the emphasis on tactile stimulation".

(c) **British art overseas:** United Distillers. The company employs 500 people in Japan and sponsored Scottish Ballet's first Japanese tour.

(d) **Commission of new art in any medium:** Barclays Bank. "Barclays New Stages has so far enable 21 new works to be performed by fringe theatre companies nationwide and the Royal Court to stage its first alternative theatre festival in 20 years."

(e) **Corporate programme:** British Gas for "making arts available in all their variety and vitality to the widest possible audience". This included support for London Festival Orchestra's concerts in churches and cathedrals, the British Gas Ballet Central brought dance to schools and the community centres, and Youth & Music's Stage Pass enables young people (including British Gas's employees) to experience different art forms.

(f) **First-time sponsor:** Silhouette fashion frames. This Austrian-owned company sponsored the "Egon Schiele & His Contemporaries" exhibition at the Royal Academy. The exhibition had previously been postponed for two years through lack of sponsorship.

(g) **Long term commitment:** Digital Equipment Company. "Since 1986, the

• **Arts sponsorship**

Partners in Dance Programme, including the Digital Dance Awards, has created 50 new works with over £2 million going directly to dance."

(h) **Single project:** Prudential Corporation. The Prudential Awards for Arts "have provided much needed cash for companies as diverse as Theatre Royal at Stratford East, the Liverpool Philharmonic and the Grizedale Society in Cumbria, which resulted in sculpture in the middle of a forest".

(i) **Sponsorship by a small business:** Bryant & Tucker and Banbury Plastics. Bryant & Tucker makes machine-embroidered badges. It commissioned the "Concerto for Embroidery Machine & Percussion" for the Warwick Festival. "The aim was to make the machine perform its proper function, producing a finished embroidery whilst making an interesting range of sounds which Matthew Griffiths incorporated into a percussion piece." The concert took place in the Bryant & Tucker factory. "Every member of the audience was given a piece of embroidery to commemorate the performance."

Banbury Plastics supported the Banbury Museum "Coming of the M40" project which showed "that industry can be a stimulus for artwork. Among the resulting works were two sculptures of construction workers - Bert and Fred - a dance performance complete with motorway lights and a composition centred on motorway sounds all created by young people."

(j) **Youth sponsorship:** Woolwich Building Society sponsors a national competition to find new playwriting talent amongst people aged 15 to 21.

The BP Arts Award is made to the arts organisation which has made the most effective use of sponsorship to maintain and develop its activities. It was awarded to the National Jazz Youth Orchestra which has used sponsorship to commission new music, buy and maintain transport and equipment and pay a previously unpaid employee. The prize money (£5,000) will be used for travel bursaries for members of the orchestra living outside London. The winner also receives a sculpture.

There are also ABSA Scottish awards and ABSA Northern Ireland awards which are awarded in broadly similar categories to the above. Further details are in the ABSA annual report.

ABSA membership (1992)

- Abbey National plc
- Acanthus Associated
- AIB Bank
- American Airlines
- American Express
- Amersham International plc
- Arthur Andersen & Co
- Gavin Anderson & Co
- Arts Council of Great Britain
- Arts & Industry Ltd
- ASW Holdings plc
- AT & T (UK) Ltd

- BAA plc
- Baillie Gifford & Co
- Bang & Olufsen Ltd
- Bank of Scotland
- Bankers Trust Company
- Barclays Bank plc
- Charles Barker
- BASF plc
- Bass Brewers
- Bass Ireland Ltd
- BAT Industries plc
- BBC Enterprises Ltd
- Belfast Telegraph Newspapers Ltd
- BET plc
- BMW (GB) Ltd
- BOC Group
- Booker plc
- C T Bowring (Charities Fund) Ltd
- BP Oil UK Ltd
- British Council
- British Film Institute
- British Gas plc
- British Petroleum
- British Petroleum Co plc (Scotland)
- British Railways Board
- British Steel plc
- British Telecom
- British Telecom Northern Ireland
- Broadway Malyan
- Burmah Castrol plc
- James Burrough Ltd
- Burton Group
- Business in the Community

- Cable & Wireless plc
- Cadogen Management
- Cameron & Co
- Carlton Communications plc
- Carroll, Dempsey & Thirkell
- Causeway Communications Ltd
- Central Independent Television plc
- Champagne Piper-Heidsieck SA
- Channel 4 Television
- Chemical Industries Association
- Chevron UK Ltd

- Christian Salvesen plc
- Christie's International plc
- Ciba-Geigy plc
- Citibank
- Citigate Corporate Ltd
- City Acre Property Investment Trust Ltd
- C & J Clark Ltd
- Clerical Medical Investment Group
- Clydeside Bank
- Coats Viyella plc
- Coca-Cola Bottlers (Ulster) Ltd
- Collyer-Bristow
- Commercial Union
- Confederation of British Industry
- Coopers & Lybrand Deloitte
- Coopers & Lybrand Deloitte (NI)
- Countrywide Communications Ltd
- Creative Pencil Ltd
- Crowcroft Gourley
- Crown Brewery plc

- Daily Telegraph
- Dawson International plc
- Dean Clough Industrial Park Ltd
- Dentsu UK Ltd
- Derwent Valley Foods Group Ltd
- Digital Equipment Co Ltd
- Digital Equipment Co Ltd (NI)
- Dixons Group plc
- Drivers Jonas
- Durrington Corporation Ltd

- East Midlands Electricity plc
- Eastern Electricity
- Edinburgh Solicitors Property Centre
- Elf UK plc
- English Estates
- English Heritage
- Ernst & Young
- Esso UK plc
- European Marketing Services
- Eurotunnel UK

- Faloon Decorative
- Anthony Fawcett Consultants
- Ferguson Industrial Holdings plc
- Fiat UK Ltd
- Fina plc
- Friends Provident
- Future Image Ltd

- Gallaher Ltd
- Gallaher Ltd (NI)
- General Electric Company plc
- Glaxo Holdings plc
- Glenbank Holdings Ltd
- John Good Holbrook Ltd

Arts sponsorship

- Granada Television Ltd
- Grand Metropolitan plc
- Groupe Chez Gerard
- Guardian Royal Exchange UK Ltd
- Guinness & Co (NI) Ltd
- Guinness Brewing Worldwide
- Guinness plc

- Hammerson Group plc
- Hammond Suddards Solicitors
- Hanson plc
- Herring Baker & Harris
- Hill & Knowlton
- Hillsdown Holdings plc
- Hoechst UK Ltd
- Honeywell Control Systems Ltd
- HTV Ltd
- Hydro-Electric

- IBM UK Ltd
- Identity Creation for Business
- IMG
- Imperial Chemical Industries
- Imperial Tobacco Ltd
- IMS - International Media Sponsorship
- Inchcape plc
- Inspiration Ltd
- Institute of Directors
- InterCity

- J T Group Ltd
- Jaguar Cars Ltd
- S C Johnson

- Kallaway Ltd
- Kleinwort Benson Ltd
- Kodak Ltd
- KPMG Peat Marwick

- Labatt Brewing UK
- Ladbroke Group plc
- John Laing plc
- Legal & General Group plc
- Lehman Brothers International
- Life Association of Scotland
- Lloyds Abbey Life plc
- Lloyds Bank plc
- Logica plc
- London Docklands Development Corporation
- London Electricity plc
- London Weekend Television

- McGrigor Donald
- Mail on Sunday
- Manweb plc
- Marketing Action
- Marks & Spencer plc
- Marks & Spencer (NI)
- Mars GB Ltd
- Marsh Christian Trust
- Maxwell Stamp plc

- Mercury Communications Ltd
- Midland Bank plc
- Milton Keynes Borough Council
- Milton Keynes Marketing
- Mobil North Sea Ltd
- Mobil Oil Co Ltd
- Montblanc
- Motorola Communications Services

- National Grid Co plc
- National Power
- National Westminster Bank
- NCC Property plc
- NCR Ltd
- Neste (UK) Ltd
- Nestle (UK) Ltd
- Nicholson & Bass Ltd
- Nikon UK Ltd
- Northern Electric plc
- Northern Ireland Bankers' Association
- Northern Ireland Electricity plc
- Northern Ireland Transport Holding Co
- Northumbrian Water Group
- Norwich Union Insurance Group

- Old Bushmills Distillery Co Ltd
- Olivetti UK Ltd
- OMV UK Ltd

- David Patton & Sons NI
- Pearson plc
- Performers Alliance
- Perrier (UK) Ltd
- Phillips Fine Art Auctioneers
- Post Office
- PowerGen UK plc
- PPP
- PR Consultants Scotland
- Project Planning
- Prudential Corporation

- Radio Clyde plc
- Reed International plc
- Reuters Ltd
- Royal Bank of Scotland plc
- Royal Insurance Holdings plc
- Royal Insurance UK Ltd
- Royle Group
- RTZ Corporation plc

- S4C
- J Sainsbury plc
- Save & Prosper Educational Trust
- J Henry Schroder Wagg & Co
- Scottish & Newcastle Breweries plc
- Seeboard plc
- Shell Northern Ireland
- Shell UK Ltd
- Siemens plc
- W H Smith Group plc

- SmithKline Beecham
- Sotheby's
- South Wales Electricity
- Spero Communications
- Spirit Design Ltd
- Sponsorship Workshop Ltd
- Standard Chartered Bank
- Statoil (UK) Ltd
- Sundridge Park Management Centre

- Texaco Ltd
- Thorn EMI plc
- 3i plc
- 3M UK plc
- TI Group plc
- Times Supplements Ltd
- Total Oil Marine plc
- Toyota (GB) Ltd
- Trafalgar House plc
- Trotman & Co Ltd
- TSB Bank Northern Ireland plc
- TSB Bank plc
- TSB Group plc
- Tyne Tees Television Ltd

- Ulster Carpet Mills Holdings Ltd
- Ulster Pension Trustees Ltd
- Ulster Television plc
- Unilever
- Union Bank of Switzerland
- Unisys Ltd
- United Biscuits (UK) Ltd
- United Distillers
- United Engineering Steels Ltd

- VAG (UK) Ltd
- Visa International

- S G Warburg Group plc
- Water Services Association
- Welbeck Golin Harris
- Wellcome Foundation Ltd
- Whitbread plc
- Whyte & Mackay Group
- Wincanton Distribution
- Wolff Olins
- Rudolf Wolff & Co Ltd
- Woolwich Building Society

- Yorkshire Bank plc
- Yorkshire Electricity Group plc
- Yorkshire Television Ltd

Note: *Members include local authorities, professional and other institutions, marketing/sponsorship consultants and sponsoring companies.*

Social sponsorship

Sponsorship is increasingly spilling over from the arts into other areas of charitable activity. There is now a well-established market for sponsorship of environmental and wildlife conservation schemes, with a number of agencies offering industry sponsorship opportunities in this area (especially the **World Wide Fund**, the **Groundwork Foundation** and UK 2000).

Charities in other fields are looking hard at the possibilities of sponsorship. It is established practice in many large organisations where resources of staff and time are more readily available (although still at a premium!). Finding sponsorship has become a specific role within the organisation.

However, social sponsorship need not and does not only work for large voluntary organisations. It is not just charity events (such as entertainments and other fundraising activities) or publications (where the donor's name can be prominently mentioned) which attract such money. The potential is much wider than this, both at national and local level.

Large national companies are not interested in sponsoring only major charities with a nationwide coverage. However, there must be a reason why sponsorship of a particular project will make sense to that company. They may, for example, be interested in raising their profile within the area where their manufacturing is carried out. Body Shop, well known for its involvement in wider community and environmental issues, felt it very worthwhile to sponsor (by agreeing to offer funds to be matched 50/50) a newly converted, fully accessible coach for Link Line, a local charity which provides transport and organises holidays for disabled people. Link Line happens to be based at Littlehampton as are Body Shop's headquarters. The matching funds were supplied by Store Properties, a local company.

Yorkshire Electricity have combined an interest in supporting the arts with an interest in wider community issues by installing an audio description system at the West Yorkshire Playhouse in Leeds. This allows the visually impaired theatre goer to enjoy the visit to the full. The project fitted in well with Yorkshire Electricity's current Community Events programme "Building on Ability". It should also be noted that Yorkshire Electricity were able to release the money for this sponsorship from ABSA's Business Sponsorship Incentive Scheme (see article on Arts sponsorship). A similar scheme operates for sports sponsorship. If this were extended to social sponsorship it would be a major incentive and would demonstrate government support in a practical way for one of the few additional sources of funding available to the voluntary sector.

Some organisations may be small but have a national remit. This geographical spread combined with a possibly smaller scale, highly targeted sponsorship may appeal to some companies. Lander Urban Renewal sponsored the publications of one such organisation - the National Tower Blocks network which deals with all aspects of tower block living and works with tenants, local authorities, housing associations and architects. Despite the relatively small distribution (2,500) the publication was closely targeted and read by far more than the figure indicates. The fact that Lander were able to offer some free design consultancy and training services emphasises that the value of a sponsorship may well not be in cash alone. Getting to know the companies you are approaching, letting them get to know you and get a feel for the work you are doing can lead to additional support that neither side may have foreseen as useful at the outset.

On a larger scale, Nationwide Building Society have recently taken on a three year sponsorship supporting the Citizen's Advice Bureau Money Advice Unit in its debt counselling work. The unit acts as researcher, trainer and policy maker for the face to face bureaux. Unfortunately in the current financial climate the bureaux and the building societies share many of the same clients and both sides feel that by working together and learning from each other, they can alleviate some of the distress and causes of multiple debt and homes repossession.

The above examples are varied and do not follow a pattern, except that you are unlikely to forge a sponsorship arrangement for running or revenue costs alone. Sponsorship relies on the sponsor being enthused by a particular project or time limited piece of work with an identity they can clearly associate with. It is a **business** arrangement from which they will be expecting a return in the form of recognition, publicity, raised public awareness etc.. Whilst you should include running costs for the project in the sponsorship proposal, they are not your selling point.

Charities have begun to think in terms of sponsorship, to design schemes that are attractive and affordable to companies, and to make their requests known. Consequently they are tapping into this kind of company support. However, the recession cannot be ignored. It is having an impact on the sponsorship budgets which have been frozen or reduced in some cases. Alongside this, in times of financial difficulties the workload of the voluntary sector increases. The encouraging aspect is that more companies see social sponsorship as a better use of their marketing budget and better for their public image than lavish corporate hospitality, major sports sponsorship and - to some extent - sponsorship of the arts.

However, it is not necessarily that simple. Asking for sponsorship does not automatically mean that you will get more money; the company requires a respectable partner with a proven track record to collaborate with. The scheme must capture the company's interest and the benefits you offer should be carefully considered and specified in your proposal. Even if you are a well-run organisation approaching the right company with an attractive scheme, there may still be problems. The company might not be geared up to giving in this way; or it may misunderstand the request simply because it has come from a charity and send you a donation instead.

But whatever the difficulties of getting it, good cause or social sponsorship is an important potential area of support, and something that an alert charity fund-raiser should at least be thinking about. This chapter discusses the essential differences between sponsorship and donations and gives practical advice on setting about finding a sponsor.

Community Links: a case study in social sponsorship

Charity is not enough

Community Links is a social action centre in Newham, East London. Founded by local volunteers in 1977, we work in a variety of ways on projects with children and teenagers, families, people with disabilities, the elderly and the isolated. Many of our most significant developments over the last 10 years have been financed by companies.

"Community Links is clearly moving towards a position when no self-respecting local enterprise can afford not to be seen sponsoring some part of its work." This was the opinion expressed by Duncan Scott and Paul Wilding of Manchester University in their book *Sponsoring Voluntary Action - Rhetoric or Reality*. They were investigating the role of commercial sponsorship in the voluntary sector and they concluded that "Community Links is fast in danger of being held up as the model ... it is a very rare bird indeed".

It is true that over the last decade as much as half our income has been derived from what we prefer to call social sponsorship. It began in 1977 when we had ideas and energy but no track record and no money. We found that the statutory authorities were sceptical or openly critical, the trusts distant and cautious. We didn't know any individual with money, so we approached local businesses. Some, perhaps identifying with the entrepreneurial spirit, supported us with small donations. We became increasingly dependent on these gifts. It was a perilous form of funding; there was no contractual relationship and no security. Yet unlike statutory funding, it seemed that the potential was limited only by the extent of our energy. We looked around and saw how sport and the arts had discovered the same potential. They had recognised, as we were recognising, that charity is not enough, and so set about establishing a business relationship. We looked at what we could offer in return and we discovered social sponsorship.

Social sponsorship is when a company underwrites the cost of an event, a building or a piece of work in return for publicly and prominently associating their name with the name of the charity. It is a mutually beneficial arrangement. Essentially it is this characteristic which distinguishes social sponsorship from a grant or a donation. The term is very often used inaccurately to describe a grant or an act of philanthropy. It isn't either of these. It is a straightforward business deal.

Sponsorship differs from a donation at every stage in the process. A request for a donation may be a generalised appeal to the heart. It will be addressed to the company secretary or manager of the charities budget, and will offer little in return. A sponsorship request will be a specific proposal designed for the business brain, not heart. It will be addressed to the marketing director, and will offer specific benefits at a clear price.

A donation might be given or refused without any face-to-face contact. If there is a meeting it will focus on the work of the charity, not the potential for working together. A successful sponsorship deal, on the other hand, is dependent upon co-operation, so a meeting to discuss all possible areas of mutual benefit will be the first step.

If the company decides to make a donation there is unlikely to be any further commitment on either side. The company won't want anything from the charity beyond, perhaps, an annual report. Equally the charity cannot ask for any commitment to future funding. If a sponsorship deal is struck, however, there are likely to be clear contractual commitments on both sides. The charity might guarantee media coverage in house magazines and trade press as well as the mass media. They may agree to stage an event, an opening or a presentation to provide the focus for publicity. They may guarantee celebrity connections. They might offer to use this opportunity, and charity's unique capacity for crossing boundaries, to introduce the company to politicians or other opinion formers. They could agree to provide practical services for customers or workers, or they might be working together on a particular promotional campaign. In return for some or all of this, the company will make agreed, guaranteed payments, possibly over a period of several years.

From the outset we have been berated by critics and sceptics in both the business and voluntary sectors who say that social sponsorship cannot and indeed perhaps should not work. We say, "Look at our record and see that it can; consider the wider context and recognise that it must and that, one day, it will!"

It was barely 20 years ago that Shelter and Oxfam and a handful of national charities were leading the voluntary sector into serious commercial advertising. Campaigns such as Shelter's *Christmas - you can stuff it* were similarly criticised. Some charities protested about the ethics of such publicity and preferred to persevere with their own genteel amateurism, but in time the results began to make the case. Few now doubt the need for professional advertising skills when mounting a fundraising campaign. It is hardly surprising that a sector which took so long to understand advertising should now be so wary of what Victor Head calls "the newest marketing skill".

The figures indicate that the local voluntary sector ignores the potential of social sponsorship at its peril. Sponsorship of sport grew from £50 million in 1981 to over £250 million in 1991, and arts sponsorship has increased 1,000% over the last decade. Commercial giving to charity, on the other hand, has, allowing for inflation, take-overs and the increasingly creative presentation of company accounts, remained fairly static in recent years. It is especially important to note that, contrary to popular belief, the vast majority of this sponsorship money has been spent on individual deals worth £10,000 or less. In other words, the high-prestige snooker championship is not a typical sponsorship deal; a long-term association with a local football team is a much more typical example.

We concluded long ago that the limits on charitable giving is attributable as

Social sponsorship

much to myopia as meanness. Relatively few companies operate well-considered grants policies. Donations are inconsequential and largely determined by the personal whim of individual directors. Sponsorship budgets, in contrast, are handled by thrusting marketing executives promoting their own reputations as fast as the product. Little wonder they corner any spare resource. Local agencies have been slow to spot the trend, and persist in rattling the box under the wrong nose. Partly because of the voluntary sector's preoccupation with traditional funding sources and partly because of its ambivalence towards the commercial world, the potential for sponsorship of social endeavours has been almost wholly ignored.

Our local experience indicates that social sponsorship works. Sensitively arranged and properly presented, the association of a company with a worthwhile social project can be less an act of philanthropy and more one of enlightened self-interest.

Over the last decade, Community Links rooms, events, vehicles, projects and publications have been sponsored by a wide range of companies including Morgan Bank, Trebor, Kia Ora, Asda and Cadbury Schweppes. Perhaps more importantly we have devoted an increasing amount of time to helping other agencies develop their fundraising in this way. In recent years we have worked with groups across the UK helping to develop social sponsorship for a wide variety of projects. We have undertaken a consultation exercise sharing our social sponsorship thinking with business people, advertising and media executives, politicians, academics and colleagues in the voluntary sector. The results serve as a guide to any agency in the business or voluntary sector contemplating social sponsorship.

Disadvantages for the voluntary sector

Some voluntary agencies were afraid that companies would want to present them, or the community they serve, in an unacceptable way. We understand the reservation but if the initial contract is clear and detailed the problem need never arise. Other agencies said that there were companies from whom they would accept a donation but would not want a high profile public association. Again, we accept this limitation, but would argue that unequivocal guidelines can simplify the choice of partners without ruling out everybody. The fact that marketing executives are not accustomed to social sponsorship was the disadvantage most consistently mentioned by voluntary sector colleagues. Companies have to be "sold" the idea of social sponsorship before they can be "sold" the idea of partnering a particular charity. This makes sponsorship twice as hard to get as a commercial donation. We agree, and believe that educating marketing executives on a national level about the potential of social sponsorship is a high priority.

Disadvantages for the company

If social sponsorship is going to generate new money the initial costs will have to be found from somewhere - profit margins, marketing budgets, etc.. Obviously a good social sponsorship deal is good business just like a good advertising campaign, but talk of new money initially worried some business people. Others were concerned that some charities would be amateurish, incompetent or unacceptably radical. They would therefore be unable to deliver the kind of image the company sought. We argue that this may be true of some but given proper support it need not be true of the vast majority.

Advantages for the voluntary sector

Domestic comparisons with sport and the arts, or international comparison with comparable agencies in other countries, clearly demonstrate the biggest advantage for the voluntary sector. More and more agencies are beginning to realise the potential for new money in social sponsorship. Furthermore it is a form of funding that can, as we have proved, snowball rapidly. Some agencies felt that the degree of security involved in a sponsorship deal was the major advantage over donations, whilst many pointed out that good sponsorship gives the agency a higher profile. This can have a range of knock-on benefits for fundraising and for other agency activities.

Advantages for the company

Almost all the business respondents acknowledged that social sponsorship enhances the corporate image. There is more obvious goodwill and far fewer negative impressions associated with voluntary agencies than with sport or the arts. Furthermore the voluntary sector offers a range of practical benefits for customers and workers, and potential for creative product promotions. Many voluntary agencies have good contacts with the media and plenty of 'human interest' stories to offer them. Associating the company name with a voluntary agency can be a cheap way of getting extensive and sympathetic publicity. The good contacts often extend to celebrities, local and national politicians and other opinion formers. Charity crosses boundaries and a good sponsorship deal can give the business friendly access to a wide range of contacts. However, many business people are not aware of the tax advantages, enhanced by the 1986 Budget. This was consistently true of small to medium businesses but also remarkably common amongst very large ones. Sponsorship is something they have never considered. They have consequently never investigated the implications for their tax bill.

We put together the results of the consultation and our own practical experience and we concluded that social sponsorship is not easy money. It demands time, care, imagination and persistence to construct a deal that is profitable for both partners and true to the ideals of the agency. However, the experience of sport and the arts and international comparisons demonstrate unequivocally that the local voluntary sector is not getting nearly as much as it could out of the British commercial sector, largely because it appears to offer so little in direct return. We have glimpsed the potential and are determined to spread the word to the rest of the voluntary sector: **take care of business and business can take care of you!**

Ten practical tips

1. Be sure to identify the right person in the company before making the first contact. Remember you're looking for the marketing director not the manager of the charity budget. The person on the switchboard can usually give you the name.

2. Remember the size of the payment will be dependent upon the value of the sponsorship to the sponsor, not the cost of the work for you. The payment may be more or less than the cost of the project. For instance you may persuade a company to give you £5,000 for associating their name with a publication that will be widely distributed, but which will only cost you £1,000 to print. Alternatively, you may only be able to charge £1,000 for association with a low profile project which will actually cost £10,000.

3. Help companies use their own resources to make the sponsorship work. Suggest, for instance, that they might like a picture story in their house magazine or in the trade

Social sponsorship

press. Most are very keen to impress their colleagues and their rivals, but few think of this without prompting.

4. Sponsorship, especially long-term deals, is all about working together. Promise only what you know you can deliver, and always try to deliver a little bit more than you promised.

5. When you first start talking about social sponsorship, your "friends" will equate your local project with the Embassy Snooker Championship and suggest you take a good long holiday. Tell them that most sponsorship money comes in sums of under £10,000 and that we're talking horses for courses. You do not intend to compete with international championships but you have got at least as much to offer as the local football team.

6. Get into the habit of reading adverts. Look particularly at local papers and trade press. Who has got money to spend on promotion, what kind of image are they trying to promote, who are they trying to reach and how can you help them?

7. Name drop! One satisfied sponsor can help you get another.

8. Before you begin think about an ethical code. Are there some companies you wouldn't wish to be associated with? What are the issues that matter to you - investment policies, environmental policies, employment policies? It may take time to think these things through, but remember you are going to be committing yourself to a high profile association. Time spent on this now could prevent acute embarrassment in the future.

9. Don't be put off by narrow-minded people who tell you that social sponsorship just lets the government off the hook. Sponsorship is an addition to state funding not an alternative. All voluntary agencies worthy of the name must do everything they can to maximise their income from every source that is ethically sound and practically viable.

10. Keep at it! Its harder to get sponsorship than it is to get a donation, but its worth much more in the long run. After every negative letter remind yourself there's another post tomorrow. Good luck!

This article has been written by Community Links.

Profile of Community Links

Community Links was formed by local volunteers in 1977 to work practically on the problems that concerned them. Our first home was a tiny lock up shop in Newham, East London. Today we own a multi-purpose centre just down the road from that first base. A strong local presence was established over a period of years. The growth of our activities meant that the search for new premises became a priority again during 1991.

Community Links is a social action charity. We work in a variety of ways on projects with children and teenagers, families, people with disabilities, the elderly and the isolated. Links is a warm and welcoming agency run by local people. Our wide range of activities gives everyone an opportunity to help others and to help themselves.

Our local success has led to a national role. Much of our work is unique and we have been increasingly recognised as innovators, developing and promoting new ideas for the relief of problems in our inner cities. For instance our programme for delinquent teenagers and younger children at risk has pioneered new solutions to familiar difficulties, and our work on improving the quality of life for tower block tenants has also attracted extensive national interest. Most of the pioneering work has been financed by commercial sponsors and we have been increasingly asked to advise others on this form of funding.

Statutory grants from local and central government will account this year for less than half of Community Links' total revenue budget; the balance must be found from commercial sponsors, fundraising events, trusts and other voluntary supporters. Community Links is also currently undertaking a major capital project.

They have agreed with Newham Council a 125-year peppercorn lease on a 1,300 square metre building in Canning Town in the East End of London. We plan to make this a self-financing community building with income generated by lettings, a cafe and shop, training and larger meeting facilities. These will be run alongside the community-based activities.

At commercial prices, the total development has been costed at £895,000. However, all professional services (eg. chartered surveyors and solicitors) have been donated, as have a number of materials (eg. soft furnishings and catering equipment).

The cash target is £600,000. Tate & Lyle, a major local employer and long-standing supporter of Community Links, has sponsored the project to help regenerate the second most deprived area in the UK. Texaco Ltd's sponsorship has so far comprised £45,000 in cash, office equipment made available through relocation and the offer of future employee involvement. Community Links believe this represent the UK's biggest ever local charity sponsorship. The Henderson Administration Group have hosted two appeal receptions in their city offices, to which influential business people have been invited to come and hear about the work of Community Links.

What does Community Links offer in return for these sponsorships? "The Centre will offer sponsors the opportunity to support particular rooms or areas of activity, permanent acknowledgement being displayed on a 'roll of history makers' to be unveiled at an opening ceremony alongside some of the important figures in the 100-year history of the building; a book about the development has been commissioned (supported by the Gulbenkian Foundation) and is due to be published in 1993; press interest is high and acknowledgement will be provided in all published materials including press releases. It is hoped that this development will act as a model for similar initiatives in other areas of the UK; the need has never been greater."

Community Links is based at Canning Town Public Hall, 105 Barking Road, London E16 4HQ (071-473 2270).

Joint promotions

Joint promotions are a relatively new way of raising money. Like sponsorship they involve a partnership between a commercial company and a good cause. But in a sense they are the converse of a sponsorship. Sponsorship involves a company providing money towards an activity undertaken by a charity in return for publicity or other benefits. In a joint promotion the charity becomes involved in the promotion of a company product or brand in return for a cash payment of some sort.

Most joint promotions are conducted at a national level with national charities linking themselves to national brands. Some charities derive a considerable income from this source - for example the **World Wide Fund, National Children's Home** and **Save the Children Fund**. It is clear from those that are involved that only certain types of charity will appeal to the commercial companies and their marketing consultants. Anything that is too distressing or which would only have the support of a minority is not likely to succeed in this area of fundraising. Anything that is of only local interest will not be right for a national promotion. But there is no reason why this method of raising money cannot be adopted to work at a local level, for example to promote the opening of a local supermarket or shopping centre.

There are no hard figures as to the amount of money charities receive from joint promotions. It is small compared with donations or sponsorship. But some promotions do involve quite substantial sums - a **British Heart Foundation** promotion with Flora margarine raised about £250,000. This section looks firstly at how joint promotions work and secondly at how to raise money from this source.

How joint promotions work

Sales promotion is a marketing tool used to communicate with a selected audience, be it consumers, retailers, wholesalers or the sales force. As with advertising, it is used to support the manufacturer's brand. The main media for sales promotions are owned by the manufacturers and include their packs and point of sale material. However, the main media for advertising are owned and controlled by a second party - press, radio, TV, posters.

Where a manufacturer undertakes a joint promotion, whether it is with a charity or otherwise, it is purely a business arrangement conducted on strictly commercial terms. The money available for promotions comes from the company's marketing budget and is handled by its marketing management. The primary objective of using this money is to promote the company's brands. The money is not there to support a charity, however worthy the cause. If the joint promotion is with a charity, the charity will receive some financial benefit from the arrangement but this is a payment for services rendered and not a charitable donation. It is entirely different from where a charity obtains money in the form of a grant from the company's charity donations budget.

A company will undertake a joint promotion with a charity only if it can see a benefit from the arrangement. The charity therefore not only has to have a scheme or an idea which is good, but also one which is appropriate to the particular product the company wishes to promote. However, the charity should realise that its proposed scheme or idea will be competing with many other promotional ideas.

To give some idea of how a joint promotion is in competition with other forms of marketing, let us take as an example a packet of breakfast cereal. The manufacturer might:

- Print something on the pack which can be cut out and used, played with or collected;
- Put something inside the pack which can be played with or collected;
- Arrange a competition on the pack;
- Make a free offer of cash or some desirable item in return for proof of purchase of one or more packs;
- Offer the product at a special price;
- Arrange a special promotion in conjunction with a commercial concern, such as free rail tickets or Post Office first-day covers;
- Enter into a joint promotion with a charity.

Clearly a joint promotion with a charity is just one of the many possible options open to the manufacturer. The manufacturer starts with a pack and its contents. Something must be printed on the pack, at least saying what it contains and giving the product a brand identity. Some promotions, such as the printing of children's games or recipes, can be easily included in the pack design and incur virtually no additional cost. Some promotions with special offers can be self-liquidating, ie. the cost of the offer is met entirely by the proceeds of sales that arise from it. A manufacturer may also decide to use some or all of the marketing budget to cut prices and thereby increase sales. At a time of low demand, this is something many manufacturers might do in an attempt to boost sales.

The selection of a particular type of promotion depends on the budget available to meet the objectives for the brand and the most cost-effective method of communicating the promotion to its audience. If a charity wishes to involve itself in joint promotions, it has to create a saleable proposition for itself which can compete with these options.

Charities interested in joint promotions should remember that sales promotion not only involves packs and window displays; it is a multi-level activity involving the distributive trade (both wholesalers and retailers) and the company's own sales force. The joint promotion has to appeal and be relevant to whoever handles the products, be they the grocers, the chemists, the sales representatives who sell it out from the factory, or the general public.

It is important to understand the process that occurs when a manufacturer decides to mount a promotion if you are to be successful in participating in it. A manufacturer will normally start with a marketing plan. This plan will detail the activity for the brand and may include a promotion or a number of promotions for that brand during the year. Therefore, the first point to note is the time lag involved. Many companies work six, 12 or 18 months ahead. So if there is something you want to raise money for which is suitable for a joint promotion, you have to approach companies in good time.

The manufacturer will next produce a brief which will give details of the market, the promotional objectives, the strategy to meet these objectives for the brand and of course the timing of the campaign. This brief will then be implemented either by the company's marketing department or by a promotional consultant. If the strategy calls for a solution which is appropriate for a joint promotion with a charity, the company or its consultants will then look around for a suitable charity. However, business people often react like consumers, especially when looking at an area where they have little experience. Firstly they will probably explore the charities they already know about. Some charities are nationally known; some have built a "presence"; some have a track record of past success.

Although in the main the company will approach the charity, charities likewise can approach a company with suggestions for schemes. For small schemes there may be some surplus promotion money floating around and the scheme might be implemented; for larger schemes it may be that you do not fit into their plans at that moment. Nothing has been lost; when they next consider a promotion at least they know that you exist.

The give and take of joint promotions

What can a charity offer a commercial concern? Here are seven of the major attractions:

- **Respectability:** Companies may believe that their image is not as good as it might be, and that by linking up with a charity they can raise the level of their respectability in the eyes of the market place.
- **Corporate responsibility:** The company is seen to be contributing to a charity of some kind and this can only benefit its corporate image.

- **Publicity:** An opportunity to get wider publicity than may be available through the normal trade channels. Very often the media will respond to a charity promotion in a way that they would not respond to a normal trade promotion.
- **Public sympathy:** An opportunity to play upon the sympathy of the market; very often individuals will buy a product if they feel that part of the proceeds at least are going to a charitable cause.
- **Access to markets:** The joint promotion offers access to markets which otherwise would be difficult for the company to get into, particularly schools. Another important area is the membership of the charity where it is well-defined and a segment of the market that the company wishes to reach.
- **Access to VIPs to promote the company's products:** Industrial companies find it difficult to get hold of popular celebrities, and they feel, rightly or wrongly, that charities do have this ability. It is obviously to the advantage of a company to be linked with people who are respectable household names.
- **Industrial property:** Most large charities have a logo or a name which is recognised across the country. This is a valuable industrial property, and many companies feel that by linking themselves with that logo they can expand their markets.

Before getting involved in a joint promotion, it is very important to know what you the charity can give to the company that they themselves cannot buy or get in some other way. For example, the **World Wide Fund** obviously offers an association with animals; it also has a logo which is well known; it offers a possibility that the companies will reach a wider market than they could do otherwise; it can offer a proof of scientific accuracy for material being put out as part of the promotion book that is being published (the sculpture or drawing of an animal, or whatever).

Every charity should look at itself to establish its strengths and what it could offer a company in a joint promotion. Try also to discern why the promoter wants to associate with you. Very often charities are approached by companies seeking, say, respectability. Does the charity want to associate its good name with that organisation simply to raise their level of respectability? This is something that should be investigated very thoroughly if the charity does not want to end up feeling exploited or

Joint promotions •

with its good name in ruins, whatever the level of financial return it is seeking from the arrangement.

The charity should ascertain what it is going to gain from the promotion. Normally it will be doing it solely or mainly for the financial return, and unlike the company it has no real interest in increasing the sales of the particular brand. The factors which will guide the charity as to the financial return it should expect from a joint promotion are: firstly, the scale of the promotion; secondly, an estimate of the value of the endorsement of the company; and thirdly, the amount of work that the charity has to undertake. The **World Wide Fund**, for example, normally looks for a return of at least ten times the cost and effort put into a promotion (although a lot does depend on what is being promoted) and it also likes to see a minimum guaranteed return wherever possible.

Recent award-winning promotions involve some links that are obvious and some not so obvious. "Anneka's Andrex Appeal" linked Andrex to the Guide Dogs for the Blind Association through Andrex's television advertising. The link between Bostik and the RSPCA was less obvious until the graphics used for the Bostik "Seal Appeal" linked the sealing properties of Bostik products to an appeal for seals being run by the RSPCA. Other successful joint promotions have linked Johnson Wax Shoe Shine with the Boy Scouts and Bovril with the Lions Clubs (both being used for sampling for the manufacturer and fundraising for the organisations); and Timotei Shampoo to the charity Plant Life (for the Meadow Project) and BP with Save the Children Fund.

Finally, the 1992 Charities Act requires companies, as commercial participators in a joint promotion, to make a clear and accurate statement in their promotions stating:

- The name (or names) of the benefiting institution(s).
- If the promotion will benefit more than one institution, the proportions in which the institutions are respectively to benefit.
- The method by which this is to be determined. This only needs to be stated in general terms (ie. the proportion of the price of the goods sold which is to be given to the charity/charities, or the amount of the lump sum payment[s] to the charity).

Failure to do this will be an offence.

This section was written by Keith Bantick, Chairman of Promotional Campaigns Ltd.

Business in the community

The business of business is business. Or, as Milton Friedman once wrote, "There is one and only one social responsibility of business - to use its resources and engage in activities designed to increase its profits". If business fails this will help nobody. This view could be used to justify a company **not** giving to charity. At the other extreme lies the notion that an important concern of business is the well-being of the community in which it operates. A company should be a responsible institution within society, both contributing to the needs and helping nurture the well-being of the society. For if society fails, then business will fail too. Business has a corporate responsibility which means that it should be involved in the community.

Connecting these two seemingly incompatible views is the concept of business in the community. Business cannot insulate itself from the economic and social well-being of the community. High unemployment, inadequate training and job opportunities for young people, high costs of essential services and lack of local sub-contractors all affect the success of business itself. By helping solve the problems of society, a company will also be contributing to is own success, albeit indirectly. Self-interest and philanthropy can therefore coincide.

This is the underlying principle behind the organisation **Business in the Community (BitC)**. Founded in 1982, "Business in the Community aims to make community involvement a natural part of successful business practice, and to increase the quality and extent of business activity in the community". Its membership has grown from 30 to 500 major UK businesses. BitC argues that the growth of corporate community involvement "is not because business leaders have become more altruistic; nor is community involvement a temporary fad which will disappear during economically adverse conditions such as recession. It is the result of a fundamental change in British corporate culture. It stems from a growing recognition that companies can benefit from meeting the needs of the community at large."

Directions for the Nineties

In 1991, BitC undertook a campaign to establish a national agenda for long-term business action in the community. The resulting report, *Directions for the Nineties*, recommended that "businesses should deepen community involvement to include more employees across a wider range of company functions; widen community involvement to encompass more companies; and encourage partners in the community (government, local authorities, voluntary, not-for-profit and community organisations) to work with companies to make business involvement more effective". A Leadership Team for **Promoting the business case for community involvement**, chaired by Eric Nicoli, Group Chief Executive of United Biscuits, is developing the programme. Currently, BitC is encouraging companies to adopt an A.C.T.I.O.N model in which they:

- **ASSESS existing community involvement**, determining how long-term business needs can be met through such involvement and adopting a board policy;

- **COMMIT the company at all levels** through senior management leadership, employee involvement and integration of community involvement into management development and appraisal;

- **TELL stakeholders** (including shareholders, employees, customers and the wider community) about the company's community involvement activities;

- **INTEGRATE community involvement with mainstream business functions** such as marketing, purchasing and personnel;

- **ORGANISE programmes professionally with measurable targets** against which progress can be regularly monitored and reviewed;

- **NURTURE long-term partnerships** with organisations in the community.

Two recent initiatives were undertaken to support this general promotional work:

- **Seeing is believing:** "Strong commitment from top management is essential to the success of corporate programmes." To encourage more business leaders to support community involvement, BitC established a Seeing is Believing programme. Business leaders are invited personally by the Prince of Wales to visit projects illustrating business involvement with local communities and attend a "report back" seminar at the end of the year. By the end of 1992, over 300 business leaders had participated in the scheme.

- **Involving employees in the community** was launched in June 1990 in partnership with Action Resource Centre and the Volunteer Centre UK. For more information, see the article on Employee volunteering.

Directions for the Nineties identified three other priority areas: education, environment, and economic development and enterprise.

Education

A recent survey by the Department of Education and Science revealed that although 90% of schools had established links with industry only 10% of companies were involved with education. BitC aims to redress this imbalance by encouraging businesses to support over 150 Education Business Partnerships and 61 inner city Compacts. This should create a countrywide network through which employers can become involved with local education authorities and schools. It is being promoted by a BitC Education Unit.

Business in the community

Environment

The Business in the Environment Target Team was established in 1989. Its initiatives have included:

- A survey of company environment policies.
- Launching *Your Business and the Environment - An Executive Guide* plus a training video for employees *Grime Goes Green* featuring John Cleese.
- Publication of *Your Business and the Environment - A DIY Review for Companies* for smaller companies.
- 17 regional roadshows staged in partnership with the Department of Trade and Industry and attended by 3,500 senior business people.

Current initiatives include a regional networking programme to promote environmental policies; establishing environmental performance indicators; developing an environmental education package, and promoting partnerships through community environmental initiatives.

Economic Development and Enterprise

A BitC Leadership Team is working to identify key opportunities for business involvement with economic development and enterprise. Various other initiatives include:

- **Support for community economic development** through the Community Development Unit.
- **Investing in Community Enterprise** is a short-term initiative aimed at identifying and expanding private-sector capital fiance for community development.
- The **Customised Training** initiative encourages employers and Training and Enterprise Councils to work with communities to develop the skills and employment prospects of the local workforce.
- **Building business support organisations** through local enterprise agencies, TECs, local business partnerships and chambers of commerce. BitC provides information, training and quality development programmes to and about such agencies.

Other Business in the Community Initiatives

Business Leadership Teams

These were developed from the Calderdale inner city regeneration partnership of 1987. Senior leaders from the private and public sectors develop and implement plans for tackling local issues through practical action. There are **Rural Partnerships** in Cumbria, the North East and Shropshire.

The Professional Firms Group

This can be approached through the BitC Community Development Unit. Member firms pledge free-of-charge professional services to community projects. Participating companies cover a wide range of expertise including engineering, law, accountancy, quantity surveying and architecture and have helped with feasibility studies, development plans and technical services.

Opportunity 2000

This aims to increase the quality and quantity of women's participation in the workforce. 61 top companies have pledged themselves to specific action targets after an initial operations assessment.

The Per Cent Club

This is administered by Business in the Community (see separate article).

Regional network

BitC now has 11 regional offices staffed by over 40 secondees. "As part of Business in the Community's *Directions for the Nineties* strategy, regional offices are working with member companies and representatives of voluntary and public sector organisations to help businesses widen and deepen their involvement in the communities where they operate."

Advice and further information

Advice and further information about Business in the Community's various schemes, initiatives and services can be obtained from either the head office or any of the regional offices.

Contacts

Business in the Community
227a City Road, London EC1V 1LX (071-253 3716).

Chairman: Neil Shaw, Chairman, Tate & Lyle plc.
Chief Executive: Julia Cleverdon.

Regional offices

There are regional offices of Business in the Community as follows (contact the Business in the Community Regional Director):

Northern Ireland: Belfast Enterprise Centre, 103/107 York Street, Belfast BT15 1DB (0232-438300).

Wales: Cymru BITC Wales, 2nd Floor, Arcade Chambers, Duke Street, Duke Street, Cardiff CF1 2BA (0222-221711).

North East: c/o Durham University Business School, Mill Hill Lane, Durham DH1 3LB (091-374 2246).

Yorkshire & Humberside: c/o Asda Stores, Britannia House, Britannia Road, Morley, Leeds LS27 0BT (0532-539141).

North West: c/o British Aerospace plc, Civil Aircraft Division, Chester Road, Woodford, Stockport, Cheshire SK7 1QR (061-439 5050 ext. 3060).

West Midlands: Northfield School, Tinkers Farm Road, Northfield, Birmingham B31 1RR (021-411 1252).

East Midlands: c/o Nationwide Building Society, 44 Oxford Street, Wellingborough, Northamptonshire NN8 4JH (0933-226224).

Eastern: Business in the Community, 227a City Road, London EC1V 1LX (071-253 3716).

Southern: British Telecom, Telephone House, 16 Paradise Street, Oxford OX1 1BA (0865-795608).

South West: Office 58, Small Business Centre, Wylds Road, Bridgwater TA6 4BH (0278-445851).

London: Business in the Community, 227a City Road, London EC1V 1LX (071-253 3716).

Scottish Business in the Community

In Scotland there is the independent but associated **Scottish Business in the Community**. "Our mission is to be evangelists of Corporate Social Responsibility ... we encourage, advise and persuade businesses to adopt a pro-active role in the communities in which they live and work and to become actively involved in partnerships to address the critical needs of our society." Programmes include enterprise trusts, business support groups, business and the environment, business-education compacts and secondments (through Action Resource Centre).

For further information contact:
Scottish Business in the Community, Romano House, 43 Station Road, Corstorphine, Edinburgh EH12 7AF (031-334 9876).

Chairman: Tom Farmer, Kwik-Fit Holdings plc
Director: John Moorhouse.

• Business in the community

Member companies of Business in the Community

- AB Electronic Products Group plc
- Abbey National plc
- Allied Dunbar Assurance plc
- Allied London Properties plc
- Allied-Lyons plc
- AMEC plc
- Amerada Hess Ltd
- American Express Bank Ltd
- Amersham International plc
- Amstrad plc
- Arthur Andersen & Co
- ARCO British Ltd
- ARCO Chemical Europe Inc
- Arjo Wiggins Appleton plc
- ASDA Stores Ltd
- Ashurst Morris Crisp
- Associated British Foods plc
- ASW Holdings plc
- Attwoods plc
- Automobile Association
- Avon Cosmetics Ltd

- B & Q plc
- BAT Industies plc
- Bain United Kingdom Inc
- Bamford Hall Holdings Ltd
- Banca della Svizzera Italiana
- Bank of England
- Bank of Japan
- Bank of Tokyo
- Bankers Trust International Co
- Barclays Bank plc
- Barings plc
- Barratt Developments plc
- Bass plc
- Bellway Urban Renewals Ltd
- BET plc
- BICC plc
- Blue Circle Industries plc
- BOC Group plc
- Boots Co plc
- Bovis Construction Ltd
- BPCC Ltd
- Bradford & Bingley Building Society
- BREL Ltd
- Bristol & West Building Society
- British Aerospace plc
- British Airways plc
- British Alcan Aluminium plc
- British Coal Enterprise
- British Gas plc

- British Land Co plc
- British Nuclear Fuels plc
- British Petroleum Co plc
- British Railways Board
- British Steel (Industry) Ltd
- British Telecom plc
- Broadgate Builders (Spalding) Ltd
- Bryant & May Ltd
- Bunzl plc
- Burmah Oil plc
- Burson-Marsteller Ltd
- Burton Group plc

- Cable & Wireless plc
- Cadbury Schweppes plc
- Calor Gas plc
- Candover Investments plc
- Canon (UK) Ltd
- Caparo Industries plc
- Capital Radio plc
- Carlton Communications plc
- Central Independant Television plc
- Charter Consolidated plc
- Chartered Trust plc
- Charterhouse plc
- Chemical Bank
- Ciba-Geigy plc
- Citibank NA
- City Acre Property Investment Trust
- Clayhithe plc
- Clerical Medical & Life Assurance
- Clifford Chance
- Co-operative Bank plc
- Coats Viyella plc
- Coca-Cola Northern Europe
- Colonial Mutual Group
- Commercial Union Assurance Co plc
- Conoco UK Ltd
- Coopers & Lybrand Deloitte
- Corange London Ltd
- Corporation of Lloyds
- Corporation of London
- Costain Group plc
- Courage Ltd
- Coutts & Co
- Credit Suisse First Boston
- Crown Communications Group plc
- Crown Estate

- Daiwa Europe Ltd
- DHL International (UK) Ltd
- Digital Equipment Co Ltd
- Dixons Group plc
- Drivers Jonas
- Duchy of Cornwall
- Dun & Bradstreet Ltd
- Dyke & Dryden Ltd

- East Midlands Electricity plc
- Eastern Electricity plc
- Electra Investment Trust plc
- B Elliott plc
- Richard Ellis
- Equity & Law plc
- Ernst & Young
- Esso UK plc
- Eurotunnel
- Evered Bardon plc

- FI Group plc
- Fidelity Investment Services Ltd
- Albert Fisher Group plc
- Fishmongers Co
- Fisons plc
- Ford Motor Company Ltd
- Forte plc
- Freshfields

- Gallaher Ltd
- Gardner & Theobold
- Gateway Foodmarkets Ltd
- GE Capital Financial Services
- General Electric Co plc
- Gerrard & National Holdings plc
- Sir Alexander Gibb & Partners Ltd
- Gillette Industries Ltd
- Girobank plc
- GKN plc
- Glaxo Holdings plc
- Frank Graham & Partners
- Grand Metropoliton plc
- Greaves Joseph & Co
- Grimley J R Eve
- Grosvenor Estate
- Guardian Royal Exchange plc
- Guinness plc

- Halifax Building Society
- Hambros plc
- Hanson plc
- Harrisons & Crosfield plc

Business in the community

- ☐ E C Harris
- ☐ Healey & Baker
- ☐ H J Heinz Co Ltd
- ☐ Heron Corporation plc
- ☐ High Point plc
- ☐ Hillier Parker & May Rowden
- ☐ Honda UK Manufacturing Ltd
- ☐ Honeywell Ltd
- ☐ Hongkong & Shanghai Banking Corporation
- ☐ House of Fraser Holdings plc
- ☐ Hunt Thompson Associates

- ☐ IBM UK Ltd
- ☐ Iceland Frozen Foods plc
- ☐ ICI plc
- ☐ Inchcape plc
- ☐ C Itoh (UK) plc

- ☐ JT Group Ltd
- ☐ Jaguar Cars Ltd
- ☐ Jaques & Lewis
- ☐ Johnson Wax Ltd
- ☐ Jones Lang Wootton

- ☐ Kellogg Co of Great Britain
- ☐ Kingfisher plc
- ☐ Kleinwort Benson Ltd
- ☐ Knight Frank & Rutley
- ☐ KPMG Peat Marwick

- ☐ Ladbroke Group plc
- ☐ John Laing plc
- ☐ Legal & General Group plc
- ☐ Lehman Brothers International
- ☐ Levi Strauss & Co Europe SA
- ☐ Lex Service plc
- ☐ Litttlewoods Organisation plc
- ☐ Lloyds Bank plc
- ☐ London Electricity plc
- ☐ London Electricity Board
- ☐ Lowe Bell Communications Ltd
- ☐ Lucas Industries plc

- ☐ Mailcom plc
- ☐ E D & F Man
- ☐ Manpower plc
- ☐ Manweb plc
- ☐ Market Access International
- ☐ Marks & Spencer plc
- ☐ Alfred McAlpine plc
- ☐ McDonalds Hamburgers Ltd
- ☐ McKenna & Co
- ☐ McKinsey & Co Inc UK
- ☐ MEPC plc

- ☐ Merck Sharp & Dohme Ltd
- ☐ Mercury Asset Management Group plc
- ☐ Meyer International plc
- ☐ Midland Bank plc
- ☐ Midlands Electicty plc
- ☐ Thomas Miller & Co
- ☐ Mitsubishi Group
- ☐ Mitsui & Co Europe Ltd
- ☐ Morgan Grenfell Group plc
- ☐ Mountleigh Group plc

- ☐ Nabarro Nathanson
- ☐ Nash Broad Wesson
- ☐ National Grid Company plc
- ☐ National Home Loans Corporation plc
- ☐ National Power plc
- ☐ National Westminster Bank plc
- ☐ Nationwide Building Society
- ☐ NEC (UK) Ltd
- ☐ Nestle Holdings (UK) plc
- ☐ Neville Russell
- ☐ Newcastle Breweries Ltd
- ☐ Newspace Risk Management Services
- ☐ NFC plc
- ☐ Normura International plc
- ☐ Northern Electric plc
- ☐ Northern Foods plc
- ☐ NORWEB plc
- ☐ Norwich Union Insurance Group
- ☐ Nuclear Electric plc

- ☐ Ocean Group plc
- ☐ Oxford Instruments Group plc

- ☐ P-E International plc
- ☐ PA Consulting Group
- ☐ Pannell Kerr Forster
- ☐ Pearce Signs Ltd
- ☐ Pearl Assurance Company Ltd
- ☐ Pentland Industries plc
- ☐ Pfizer Ltd
- ☐ Pilkington plc
- ☐ Post Office
- ☐ PowerGen plc
- ☐ Price Waterhouse
- ☐ Principality Building Society
- ☐ Procter & Gamble Ltd
- ☐ Provident Mutual Life Assurance
- ☐ Provincial Group plc
- ☐ Prudential Corporation plc

- ☐ Rank Organisation plc
- ☐ Rank Xerox UK Ltd

- ☐ Ranks Hovis McDougall plc
- ☐ Ratners Group plc
- ☐ Redland plc
- ☐ Redrow Group Ltd
- ☐ Reed Executive plc
- ☐ Reed International plc
- ☐ Regalian Properties plc
- ☐ Reuters Holdings plc
- ☐ Rexel Engineering Ltd
- ☐ Rexel Ltd
- ☐ Robson Rhodes
- ☐ Rockware Group plc
- ☐ Rolls-Royce plc
- ☐ Rosehaugh plc
- ☐ N M Rothschild & Sons Ltd
- ☐ Royal Bank of Scotland
- ☐ Royal Institute Chartered Surveyors
- ☐ Royal Insurance Holdings plc
- ☐ Royal London Mutual Insurance
- ☐ RTZ Corporation plc
- ☐ Russell Reynolds Association Inc

- ☐ Saatchi & Saatchi Advertising
- ☐ Safeway plc
- ☐ Saga Group plc
- ☐ J Sainsbury plc
- ☐ St George plc
- ☐ Samuel Montagu & Co Ltd
- ☐ Sanyo UK Sales Ltd
- ☐ Saudi International Bank
- ☐ Richard Saunders & Partners
- ☐ Save & Prosper Group Ltd
- ☐ Savills plc
- ☐ Schroders plc
- ☐ Sears plc
- ☐ Sedgwick Group plc
- ☐ Shell UK Ltd
- ☐ Simons Group Ltd
- ☐ Slaughter & May
- ☐ Slough Estates plc
- ☐ Herbert Smith & Co
- ☐ W H Smith Ltd
- ☐ SmithKline Beecham
- ☐ Smiths Industries plc
- ☐ Sony (UK) Ltd
- ☐ Sotheby's
- ☐ South Wales Electricity plc
- ☐ Southern Electric plc
- ☐ Spencer Stuart Ltd
- ☐ Speyhawk plc
- ☐ Standard Chartered Bank Ltd
- ☐ Stoy Hayward
- ☐ Sumitomo Bank Ltd
- ☐ Sumitomo Finance International plc

Business in the community

- Sun Alliance Group
- Sun Life Assurance Society
- Swiss Bank Corporation

- Tarmac plc
- Tate & Lyle plc
- Tesco plc
- Texaco Ltd
- Thames Television plc
- Thames Water plc
- J Walter Thompson Co Ltd
- Thorn EMI plc
- TI Group plc
- Tilbury Douglas
- Tiphook plc
- Top Technology Ltd
- Toshiba Corporation
- Touche Ross & Co
- TSB Group plc
- TVS plc
- Trusthouse Forte
- Geoffrey Tucker Ltd
- Tyne Tees Television Ltd

- Unilever (UK) Holdings Ltd
- Union Discount Co of London plc
- Unipart Group of Companies Ltd
- Unisys Ltd
- United Biscuits (Holdings) plc
- United Newspapers plc
- Unity Trust Bank plc

- Vaux Group plc
- Vauxhall Motors Ltd
- Vickers plc
- Virgin Holdings plc

- Wace Group plc
- Wang UK Ltd
- S G Warburg Group plc
- Warburtons Ltd
- Wates Building Group Ltd
- Wellcome Foundation Ltd
- Welsh Water plc
- Wembley plc
- Wessex Water plc
- Whitbread & Co plc
- Williams Lea Group Limited
- Wilmott Dixon Holdings Ltd
- Wilson (Connolly) Holdings plc
- Winward Fearon & Co
- Woolwich Building Society

- Xios Systems UK Ltd

- Yorkshire Electricity Group
- Young & Rubicam Ltd
- Young Enterprise

This list excludes enterprise agencies, governmental bodies, charities and similar organisations in membership with Business in the Community.

Members of Scottish Business in the Community

- Alexander Russell plc
- Arthur Anderson & Co
- Argyll Group plc
- Arjo Wiggins Fine Papers Ltd

- Bank of England
- Bank of Scotland plc
- Barclays Bank plc
- Barratt Northern Ltd
- Ben Line Group Ltd
- Boots Company plc
- British Airways Scotland
- British Alcan Aluminium plc
- British Coal Enterprise Ltd
- British Gas plc (Scotland)
- British Steel Ltd
- British Telecom
- Burton Group plc

- Christian Salvesen plc
- Clydesdale Bank plc
- Coats Viyella plc
- Colonial Mutual Ltd

- Dawson International plc

- Eagle Star Insurance Company
- Ernst & Young
- Esso Petroleum Company
- Ethicon Ltd

- James Finlay plc
- Ford Motor Company Ltd
- Forte plc

- General Accident plc
- Grampian Holdings plc
- Grand Metropolitan plc

- D M Hall & Son
- Harper Collins Publishers

- Highland Distilleries Co plc

- ICI plc
- ICL UK

- Johnston Press plc

- Kingfisher plc
- KPMG Peat Marwick
- Kwik-Fit Holdings plc

- Laing Scotland
- Levi Strauss & Co

- Marks & Spencer plc
- John Menzies plc

- NFC plc

- George Outram & Co Ltd

- Pilkington Brothers plc
- Price Waterhouse
- PRM Marketing Ltd
- Prudential Assurance Co Ltd

- Robertson & Baxter Ltd
- Royal Bank of Scotland plc

- ScotRail
- Scotsman Publications Ltd
- Scottish Amicable Life Assurance Society
- Scottish Brewers Ltd
- Scottish Homes
- Scottish Life Assurance Company
- Scottish Mutual Assurance plc
- Scottish Post Office Board
- Scottish Power
- Scottish Widows' Fund & Life Assurance Society
- Shell UK Ltd
- Sun Microsystems Scotland Ltd

- Tarmac Construction Scotland
- Thorburn plc
- Tilbury Douglas plc
- TSB Scotland plc

- United Biscuits plc
- United Distillers plc

- Weir Group plc
- Willis Corroon Scotland
- Work Wise Ltd

Business in the community

Location of Local Enterprise Agencies in the UK

Aberared
Aberdeen
Accrington
Aldershot
Alloa
Alton
Ammanford
Armagh
Ashford
Ashton-under-Lyne
Ayr

Ballyclare
Ballymena
Banbridge
Banbury
Bangor
Barnard Castle
Barnsley
Barnstaple
Barrow-in-Furness
Basildon
Basingstoke
Bath
Bathgate
Batley
Bedale
Bedlington
Belfast
Birkenhead
Birmingham
Bishop Aukland
Blackburn
Blackpool
Bolsover
Bolton
Bradford
Bradford on Avon
Braintree
Brentwood
Bridgend
Brigg
Brighton
Bristol
Bromley
Burnley
Burton-on-Trent
Bury
Bury St Edmunds

Cambourne
Cambridge
Camden
Campbeltown
Cannock
Canterbury
Cardiff
Carlisle
Carrickfergus
Castlederg
Chelmsford
Chester
Chester-le-Street
Chesterfield
Chichester
Chippenham
Chorley
Clacton-on-Sea
Clitheroe
Clydebank
Coalisland
Coatbridge

Colchester
Coleraine
Congleton
Consett
Corby
Coventry
Crewe
Crossgates
Croydon
Cumbernauld
Cumnock
Cupar

Dalkeith
Darlington
Dartford
Deal
Deeside
Deptford
Derby
Derry
Doncaster
Down
Downpatrick
Dudley
Dumbarton
Dundee
Dungannon
Dungiven
Dunmurry

East Barnet
East Kilbride
Eastbourne
Edinburgh
Ellesmere Port
Enniskillen
Exeter
Exmouth

Fleetwood
Folkestone
Frome

Gateshead
Gillingham
Glasgow
Glenrothes
Gloucester
Grangemouth
Grantham
Gravesend
Grays
Great Yarmouth
Greenock
Grimsby
Guildford

Halifax
Hamilton
Harlow
Harrogate
Harrow
Hartcliffe
Hartlepool
Hastings
Hatfield
Haverfordwest
Hemel Hempstead
Hillingdon
Hinckley
Holywell

Hull
Huntingdon

Inverness
Ipswich

Jersey

Keady
Kendal
Kettering
Kilbirnie
Kilmarnock
Kings Lynn
Kirkby

Lanark
Lancaster
Larne
Launceston
Leeds
Leith
Letchworth
Leven
Leyland
Lincoln
Liverpool
Llanelli
London
Loughton
Lowestoft
Luton

Macclesfield
Maidstone
Manchester
Mansfield
Margate
Middlesbrough
Milton Keynes
Minehead
Moray
Modren
Morpeth
Motherwell

Neath
Nelson
Newcastle
Newport
Newry
Newton Abbot
Newtownards
Northampton
Norwich
Nottingham

Oldham
Omagh
Ormskirk
Oxford

Paington
Paisley
Penrhyndeudraeth
Pentrebach
Perth
Peterborough
Peterlee
Pitlochry
Plymouth
Poole

Portadown
Portsmouth
Preston

Rawtenstall
Reading
Redditch
Rhondda
Rhostyllen
Rochdale
Romford
Rotherham
Runcorn
Ruthin

St Albans
St Austell
St Helens
St Peterport
Sale
Salford
Salisbury
Scarborough
Selby
Sheffield
Shildon
Sittingbourne
Skipton
Solihull
South Shields
Southampton
Southport
Stafford
Stevenage
Stevenston
Stewart
Stirling
Stockport
Stoke-on-Trent
Strabane
Sutton
Swansea
Swindon

Taunton
Telford
Tiverton
Tonbridge
Twickenham

Uttoxeter

Walsall
Warrington
Warwick
Waterside
Watford
West Bromwich
Westcliff
Weston Super Mare
Whitby
Wigan
Winsford
Wisbech
Wolverhampton
Worcester
Workington
Worksop
Worthing

Yeovil
York

For further information contact Business in the Community.

Payroll giving

Tax-free giving to charity by employees at the workplace through payroll deduction was introduced in the *1986 Finance Act*. The scheme came into effect from 6th April 1987.

Payroll giving is **not** company giving; it is giving by individual employees (and retirees) receiving their pay (or pensions) by PAYE. Employers may be in the private sector (companies and other businesses), public sector (civil service, armed forces, local government, health service, police, nationalised industries, etc.) or even the non-profit sector (charities, trade unions, churches etc.). However, the larger companies in this Guide employ a significant proportion of the workforce and companies have a vital role to play both in introducing schemes into workplaces and encouraging employees to participate by facilitating effective promotion. However, it is important to emphasize that payroll giving is voluntary for the company as well as for the employee.

Payroll giving is an important opportunity for charities to generate regular tax-efficient giving for their work. Estimates as to how much it will raise have varied greatly, but if a relatively small proportion of the working population were to give generously in this way, the annual total raised for charity could exceed £100 million. This may not happen for a decade or more. At present it is raising over £10 million a year and the agencies operating it are convinced that, with the mechanism in place, employers and charities will encourage large numbers of charity supporters to give in this way.

The basics of the scheme

The scheme has the following features:

- First, the **employer must agree** to offer a scheme or schemes to the employees. This is done by entering into a contract with an agency charity. The employer is responsible for making the deductions (and therefore automatically ensures that any tax benefit is only obtained by taxpayers, although the non taxpayer in employment can give to charity through payroll giving). Where an employer does not wish to operate a scheme, the employee cannot give to charity by payroll deduction.

- Each employee can to give **up to £600 a year** to charity by regular deductions from pay. Such deductions are made out of gross pay before tax (but not before National Insurance contributions) are deducted. The effect of this is that for every £1 donated it has cost a basic rate tax payer only 75 pence. Unlike a covenanted donation, which is also tax-effective, the recipient charity receives the donation gross and does not have to reclaim any tax. The scheme is available to everyone paid by PAYE, including pensioners.

- The employee must be able to choose **any charity in the UK**. The scheme cannot be restricted to particular named charities, although individual charities can promote the scheme using literature and forms which ask the donors to give to their own charity.

- In the first instance the **deductions are passed to an approved Agency Charity** for onward distribution to the charities selected by the employee-donor. This reduces the work that the employer has to do. The agency charity must also ensure that the beneficiary organisations chosen by the employee are bona fide charities. If they are not, the payment cannot be made to the indicated organisation and the employee has to find another charity to benefit.

- Schemes must **meet guidelines** for operation laid down by the Inland Revenue, and each scheme and the agency charity operating it have to be approved by the Inland Revenue. The guidelines lay down stringent requirements for the time scale for passing the money from the employer to the agency charity and for recording and reporting on the donations made by the agency charity on the employee's behalf. The published guidelines are available from HMSO (Statutory Instrument 1986, No 2211).

- The costs of administering the scheme may be met by a **small charge** levied by the Agency Charity. This ranges up to 7.5% depending on the agency and the amount deducted. In some voucher schemes the interest earned by the donations pending distribution will cover costs and no charges will be levied. The employer must bear any costs of making deductions and passing these on to the Agency Charity as well as any other costs incurred in offering and publicising a payroll giving scheme at the workplace.

Making the payroll giving scheme work

Before the payroll legislation came into effect there was a great deal of concern among charities that they might miss out on a golden opportunity. Now the scheme is in place charities feel that it is more difficult to influence employers and employees than they realised. The success of payroll giving does not depend on having schemes available to employees, but persuading individual employees to use this new tax-free opportunity to support a good cause. Part of this encouragement will come from the charities hoping to benefit. They should include information about payroll giving on literature and circulate appropriate forms to their supporters.

But charities must rely principally upon the track record they have established over a period of many years. One of a charity's strengths is the advocacy of its supporters, not least in their place of work.

It has become increasingly clear during the first six years of tax-effective payroll giving that the employer, who was cautiously interested when the legislation came into effect in 1987, has an absolutely crucial role to play in the promotion of the scheme. Payroll giving has really taken off where employers have supported and encouraged its effective promotion and because they have identified the benefits it offers, not only to charity but also to the employer's relations with the local community, their pensioners, and their own employees.

Payroll giving

Payroll giving: the experience so far

The scheme was launched on the 6th April 1987. By 6th April 1992, the Charities Aid Foundation's *Give As You Earn* had achieved the following:

- 2,558 employers covering over 7 million employees plus an undisclosed number of pensioners had entered into an agreement to operate the *Give as You Earn* Scheme.
- 138,207 employees had signed deduction forms for *Give as You Earn*. This was up from 48,000 two years earlier.
- The average monthly donation was £6.06 a month (initial research had suggested a figure of £2.50).
- The average donor gave to **1.4 charities**. The local/national breakdown of donations was as follows: **20% to local** charities; **40% to major national** 'brand name' charities and **40% to smaller national** charities. About half were not existing regular supporters of the charity.
- The take-up by employees varied from company to company from virtually no immediate response to around a 40% response. At some locations a 100% sign up was reported. Much depends on the promotion given by the company and any preparatory work put in by charities and consortia at a local level. It is likely that the average will end up somewhere in the **5-10%** range, but it could be a great deal higher.
- Charities received over **£8.5 million** in the year to April 1992, and money was coming in at an annual rate of **£10 million** as at April 1992.
- In addition, the other main national payroll agencies, Barnardos and the Charities Trust, together received over £2.66 million in the year to 5th April 1992. 145,000 employees contributed, but with a smaller monthly donation (£1.60 for Barnardos and £2.25 for the Charities Trust).

These figures offer a glimpse of how the scheme is going. The important thing is that payroll giving has got off the ground and money is flowing and will continue to flow to charities. It will take time to develop and some years before it approaches anything like the suggested target of £100 million a year to charity. However, there is a reasonable chance that it can become a really successful and effective way for people to contribute to charity.

Broadly speaking, effective promotion of payroll giving is undertaken by one of the following methods:

- If you are a charity, identify and train an appropriate person who as a volunteer or an employee negotiates entry into places of employment and presents the case for the charity to employees. A few larger charities (eg. Barnardos) do this with teams of people. Barnardos have done it for years, long before tax-effective payroll giving in 1987. Groups of charities, generic and non generic (there were different arguments for each), have joined together to promote payroll giving in this way.
- Charities, particularly consortia, have employed semi-commercial organisations (eg. Social Services Advertising and Bell Marketing) to negotiate entry to places of employment and to promote payroll giving face to face to employees on their behalf.
- The Charities Aid Foundation particularly has encouraged employers to facilitate the creation of employee teams of charity enthusiasts representative of the company or the location to organise a Give As You Earn payroll giving campaign on a particular day or week. Sometimes such a campaign is focused on a particular charitable cause or the raising of funds for a charity committee, but essentially employees can choose their own charities. In February 1992, the Charities Aid Foundation Give As You Earn payroll giving scheme launched a National Campaign based upon employer involvement spearheaded by the Reader's Digest.

Below are a few specific hints for charities wishing to build on the above to get support via payroll giving.

- If you are a local charity, find out who are the major employers in your area. There may be a list of these produced by the Economic Development or Rating Department of the local council. This provides a good 'hit list' of workplaces. Remember the statutory employers as well as the private sector employers.
- Find out from the main agency charities which companies and employers have agreed to introduce schemes, and when they plan to do so. It is at this stage that forms will be available at the workplace for employees to sign, and that the best opportunity exists to sign up a donor.
- Get hold of information packs and sample documents from the main agency charities.
- Unless you have a close contact with a company, it is worth concentrating on those companies which have already agreed to introduce a payroll scheme rather than going out to persuade other companies to do so. You will have more than enough work to do and opportunities to raise money with those companies that have agreed to go ahead.
- Your existing supporters are usually the most effective starting point. Inform them of the scheme. Ask them to promote your cause at their workplace when the forms are around to be signed. For the more committed, you could even set targets (sign up a certain number of their colleagues) and run a training session to explain the scheme, show them the forms and how they have to be filled in, and encourage them to go out and get support.
- Produce a simple promotional brochure. Design your own payroll deduction form or coupon for donors to sign on the dotted line and fill in the amount they wish to give (guidelines about such forms are available from Give As You Earn). Suggest an amount. You could highlight an aspect of your work which you are raising money for, and show what a particular size of donation will achieve. Showing prospective donors why you need the money, how you will use it and what benefits this will achieve can be very successful in encouraging people to give. You can then give this leaflet to your supporters to circulate to their friends and at their workplace. You can mail it to supporters or even use it in a direct mail fundraising drive.

You can do much more but the above ideas should get you started. Your charity may well receive some support even if you do nothing, simply because people have heard of you and want to support you. But if you put in the work to develop the idea of payroll and encourage people to want to give to you, you may achieve a great deal more than this.

Remember, if you are a charity with employees it looks pretty poor if you ask employees to offer payroll giving to their employees and don't offer it to your own.

What a company can do

A company is at the centre of payroll giving. It must agree to offer a scheme. It can do this passively, simply announcing the opportunity and circulating deduction forms for

Payroll giving

Some developments in the payroll giving scheme

Payroll giving limit increased to £600 a year

The Chancellor in the 1990 Finance Act increased the tax-free payroll giving limit to £600 per year with effect from 6th April 1990. The limit has risen progressively from the original limit of £120 per year in the first year of the Scheme (although charities are still lobbying for the removal of the upper limit). This means that a payroll donor over a full year can give up to £50 per month or just over £11 per week tax free.

Payroll giving simplified: a breakthrough for charities

Charities have always wanted to promote payroll giving using the charity's own form which only features their charity, and does not offer the donor any choice. Such a form would be ideal for direct mail, for example. It could be produced like any other mailing, highlighting particular projects, areas where money is being spent, or any other details the charity wishes to emphasise.

The initial restrictions requiring promoters to give donors a free choice of charity on the charity choice form have been removed by the Inland Revenue. This is a great opportunity to make the payroll giving scheme user-friendly.

Charities can now:

1. Produce their own form in their own style.

2. Advertise their charity by name anywhere on the form.

3. Not offer a choice of other charities (although you can't say that other charities can't benefit from the payroll giving scheme).

4. Suggest donations of a particular size by offering tick boxes (anything from £1 per week to £50 per month).

Charities should obtain from the donor all the information necessary for the agency charity to process the coupon. This includes: the donor's name; the donor's address; the name of the donor's employer or pension fund; the donor's workplace location or pension fund address, and the donor's employee/personnel staff reference number and department. All this information and the donation amount must be included on the completed coupon. If the charity is printing its own coupons then these should conform to the specifications laid down by the Payroll Agencies Association (*see end of article*).

Charities should instruct their supporters to return the completed coupon to the charity (not to employer) for processing. The information can be transferred onto a standard coupon (if it does not meet the PAA specifications) to facilitate efficient processing and sent to the appropriate agency. If it is sent to the wrong agency, it will be passed on to the agency that the supporter's employer is contracted with. Because of the administration involved, up to four months can elapse between completing the form and the first deduction being made.

Where donors are employed by non-contracted employers (ie. who do not offer a payroll scheme to their employees), these employers will then be asked to participate in the payroll giving scheme. If any employer/pension fund refuses to take part in payroll deduction, the charity choice form will be returned to the charity, who can then ask the donor to give by bankers order or Deed of Covenant.

Consortia

Some charities have grouped together to establish consortia for payroll giving. Guidelines have now been issued by the Inland Revenue on how such consortia should be constituted to be acceptable to the Inland Revenue.

The payroll agent may only pass money to charities. A consortium is not a charity (unless it has established itself as one). However a consortium may receive payroll donations with the Inland Revenue's approval, where the following conditions are satisfied:

1. There is a Memorandum of Understanding regarding the members of the consortium and their respective shares of the donations.

2. Each member is a recognised charity in its own right.

3. The consortium applies for and obtains approval from the Charity Division of the Inland Revenue (approved consortia will be notified to each payroll agent).

4. Donations held by payroll agents for the consortium will be given to the members of the consortium in the proportion specified in the Memorandum at (a) above.

5. No donations will be given by the payroll agent to any person or charity other than the consortium members.

signature; or it can actively promote the scheme and encourage its employees to sign up. Here are some simple things a company might be persuaded to do by those promoting payroll giving (not all at nil cost it must be said):

- Actively promote the scheme at plant level. Don't just make forms available; explain the scheme, what it is, how it works, why it is a good idea. If possible, use existing networks within the company.

- Work together with a staff committee to plan a promotion at the workplace. Don't forget union representatives, the staff, charity or welfare committee members, and try and make the committee representative of the workplace (ie. not just personnel or payroll staff but people from sales and marketing as well - they are most likely to understand the significance of a "selling" campaign face to face).

- Where possible identify a group of charities or a charity, probably local, who will help you spearhead the campaign. This will encourage employees to promote other causes in which they believe. Agree to match £ for £ (or on some other basis) employees' donations. A number of leading companies are thinking of doing this. It means that a £10 a month contribution costs a basic rate tax payer at 25% only £7.50 and makes £20 available to charity! In addition, matched funds are tax free for the employer.

- Agree to pay the administrative costs which are deducted by the agency charity before money is send to the recipient charities. In this way every £ donated by the employee will go to charity. Together with matching employees' donations, this package makes an important psychological point **and** allows the employer to mirror the employees' pattern of giving.

- Offer the facilities and resources which will lead to the establishment of staff charities. In this way the staff charity committee can build up a fund of money and respond to charity appeals on behalf of employees. There are now many examples throughout the UK. The prototype (pre-dating tax-effective payroll giving in 1987) is the Allied Dunbar Charity Fund (for details contact Des Palmer, Allied Dunbar Centre, Swindon SN1 1EL, who has various reports on the Allied Dunbar staff charities).

Payroll giving

The main agencies

This a list of payroll agencies approved by the Inland Revenue as at August 1992:

Give As You Earn (Charities Aid Foundation)

Foundation House, Coach and Horses Passage, The Pantiles, Tunbridge Wells TN2 5TS (0892-512244)

Give As You Earn is the leading agency. It offers a comprehensive service to employers. The first scheme includes the facility for individuals to choose up to four pre-selected charities and/or give together with other employees into a pre-nominated group account. Or any donor giving £10 a month or more can use CAF vouchers ("Charity Cheques" without face value which are completed in favour of a chosen charity, the amount entered and signed and used just like cheques) and doesn't have to pre select the charities to be supported. CAF makes an administrative charge of 5% with a minimum of 25p per deduction processed and a maximum of £2. There is no minimum where employers report by magnetic tape.

Give As You Earn's second scheme (which can work in parallel with the first scheme) attracts no administrative charge and involves the employer creating a single group account into which any employee can pay. All group accounts are distributed to charity by the decision of a committee made up of the donors or their representatives.

The Give As You Earn service is being actively promoted by CAF to national and local employers in England and Wales. Elsewhere in Britain the same service is offered to local employers by the following further members of the Give As You Earn consortium:

Scottish Council for Voluntary Organisations, 18-19 Claremont Crescent, Edinburgh EH7 4QD (031-556 3882).

Northern Ireland Council for Voluntary Action, 127 Ormeau Road, Belfast BT7 1SH (0232-321224).

United Way of Merseyside (North West England), PO Box 14, 8 Nelson Road, Edge Hill, Liverpool L69 7AA (051-709 8232).

Barnardos Agency Charity

Tanners Lane, Barkingside, Ilford, Essex IG6 1QG (081-550 8822)

This agency was established to appeal, at least initially, mainly to the many employers who are already making payroll deductions for the benefit of Barnardos and to develop the work of Barnardos in fundraising by its members. However, the agency, like all agencies, must allow contributors to direct their deductions to any charities they like.

Charities Trust

PO Box 15, Kershaw Avenue, Crosby, Liverpool L23 0UU (051-928 6611 Ext. 245)

This is the first agency set up by a commercial company. It was established jointly by the Littlewoods Organisation (the stores and pools company), and the Moores Family Charity Trust (the Moores family founded Littlewoods) to market payroll nationally. Like all the other payroll agencies it is itself a charity and not a commercial enterprise. Their strategy to develop payroll is one of friendly involvement with employers and employees, with managers available to talk to Payroll Managers and company staff. The agency has attempted to provide maximum communication with employees and maximum publicity at the workplace to encourage a good take-up.

Other payroll agencies include:

Birmingham Voluntary Service Council (Charity at Pay Day)
Chest Heart and Stroke Association (Scottish Branch)
Royal Society for Mentally Handicapped Children and Adults
South-West Charitable Giving
Motor and Cycle Trades Benevolent Fund (BEN)

The following agencies were established by individual companies to help their own employees to give:

Bristar Foundation
Minet Employees Charitable Trust
Lankro Employee Charity Fund
S Group Charitable Trust (Saatchi & Saatchi)
Lloyd's Charities Trust

The Payroll Agencies Association

In 1989 a Payroll Giving Association was established to represent the interests of and provide a coordinating forum for the payroll giving agencies. It also has the specifications for charities wishing to produce their own payroll giving coupons. It can be contacted through the Charities Trust (see above).

This article has been written by the Charities Aid Foundation.

Useful contacts

In this section we list some national agencies which may be helpful in the context of company giving.

1. Secondment

Action Resource Centre

1st Floor, 102 Park Village East, London NW1 3SP (071-383 2200)

Chief Executive: Andy Powell
Communications Director: David Hemsworth

To assist local communities by involving business and professional people in the work of community organisations. Through its national network ARC provides brokerage and consultancy for all types of secondment: full-time or part-time, from 50 hours to one or more years; early career, mid-career, pre-retirement; as a tool for management development, staff planning and community investment.

ARC's secondment service includes matching secondees to placements and a programme of induction, monitoring, evaluation and publicity.

ARC are also involved in providing business volunteering schemes to companies, and support to voluntary organisations through management education and training courses, community trading advice and the recycling of surplus office furniture and equipment.

ARC area offices:

ARC Avon c/o the Bristol Initiative (0272-394040)
ARC Bradford (0274-721635)
ARC Derby (0332-364784)
ARC Greater London (071-383 2200)
ARC Greater Manchester (061-236 3391)
ARC Leeds (0532-370777)
ARC Leicestershire (0533-543398)
ARC Merseyside c/o Premier Brands UK (051-678 8888)
ARC Nottinghamshire (0602-470749)
ARC Tower Hamlets (071-375 0259)
ARC West Midlands (021-643 9998)
ARC Scotland c/o Scottish Business in the Community (031-334 9876)

Community Service Volunteers

237 Pentonville Road, London N1 9NJ (071-278 6601)

Executive Director: Elizabeth Hoodless

CSV promotes volunteering by arranging short-term placements for young people. It has a separate scheme called **RSVP** which provides opportunities for volunteering in the community for retirees.

National Association of Volunteer Bureaux (NAVB)

St Peter's College, College Road, Saltley, Birmingham B8 3TE (021-327 0265)

Contact: Helen Reeve

The NAVB represents a national network of 300 local volunteer bureaux. They provide an information service on matters relating to volunteering. Its publications include a directory of volunteer bureaux. It also provides general advice and support to volunteer bureaux.

REACH

89 Southwark Street, London SE1 0HD (071-928 0452)

Director: Jill Munday

REACH finds part-time expenses-only jobs for retired business or other professional men and women who want to use their skills to help voluntary organisations with charitable aims. This service is free and available for jobs throughout Britain. (REACH produces a biannual newsletter called *Reach Forward*, available on request.)

The Volunteer Centre UK

29 Lower Kings Road, Berkhamsted, Herts HP4 2AB (0442-873311)

Director: Mrs Andrea Kelmanson
Contact: Jo Paton, Development Officer, Employee Volunteering

The Volunteer Centre UK is the national resource agency promoting volunteering. It has a particular interest in encouraging company employees and retirees to get involved in the community. A free catalogue giving details of publications, training and consultancy services is available on request.

The Volunteer Centre UK and Action Resource Centre jointly publish a quarterly magazine **Working Out (Employees in the Community)**, which is available free on request.

Besides using any of the above agencies or schemes, any charity seeking a secondment or voluntary help can approach a company direct and ask for help.

2. Sponsorship

Action Match (a project of Community Links)

Canning Town Public Hall, 105 Barking Road, London E16 4HQ (071-473 2270)

Action Match is a specialist voluntary agency promoting business sponsorship of social causes. It provides training, advice and consultancy on social sponsorship for voluntary and community groups.

Useful contacts

Community Links, the parent organisation of Action Match, is moving into and refurbishing the Canning Town Public Hall. Owing to this major project Action Match will be scaling down its work with the voluntary sector from October 1992 for 10 months.

During this period the Action Match Business Consultancy will continue to develop. Through the consultancy, services will be offered to companies interested in undertaking social sponsorship. Publicity materials and information about the consultancy services will be available from Spring 1993.

Action Match will forward previously published materials about social sponsorships on request; these act as an introduction to this form of fundraising.

A series of events relating to sponsorship within the voluntary sector are planned from mid 1993.

Association for Business Sponsorship of the Arts

Nutmeg House, 60 Gainsford Street, Butlers Wharf, London SE1 2NY (071-378 8143)

Director: Colin Tweedy
Contact: Caroline Kay, Head of External Affairs

ABSA promotes business sponsorship of the arts. It was set up and is funded by companies already involved in sponsorship. It advises both businesses and arts organisations on good practice in sponsorship and how to go about it. Business in the Arts, an ABSA initiative, aims to help arts managers develop their managerial capabilities and improve the organisation's effectiveness. The main work includes a placement scheme which matches business advisors to arts organisations. Companies in-house training courses have been opened up to arts managers.

Area offices: *North:* Dean Clough, Halifax, West Yorkshire HX3 5AX (0422-345631).

Northern Ireland: 181a Stramillis Road, Belfast BT9 5DU (0232-664736).

Scotland: Room 206, West Port House, 102 West Port, Edinburgh EH3 9HS (031-228 4262).

Wales: 9 Strydyr Amgueddfa, Caerdydd CF1 3NX; 9 Museum Place, Cardiff CF1 3NX (0222-221382).

Groundwork Foundation

85-87 Cornwall Street, Birmingham B3 3BY (021-236 8565)

Contact: Cynthia de Souza, Communications Manager, or Ken Davies, Director of External Relations

Groundwork is a network of local charitable trusts operating in 30 areas of Britain (set to grow to 50 within 2 years). It works in partnership with business, public agencies and voluntary bodies on environmental improvement projects in and around urban areas. The Foundation coordinates the work of the local trusts and promotes business sponsorship of environmental projects. It produces a quarterly newspaper, *Groundwork Today.*

3. Enterprise and training

Common Purpose

c/o Coopers, Lybrand & Deloitte, 128 Queen Victoria Street, London EC4P 4JX (021-625 0550)

Contact: Julia Middleton, Chief Executive

Common Purpose develops programmes of education and training designed to bring together leading representatives of private, public and voluntary sector organisations in particular cities.

Community Development Foundation (CDF)

60 Highbury Grove, London N5 2AG (071-226 5375)

Chief Executive: David N Thomas
Contact: Sukhvinder Stubbs, Director of Corporate Affairs

CDF is a Home Office sponsored agency. It works in partnership with local authorities, government departments, businesses and the community in influencing policy makers, promoting best practice and supporting community initiatives. It offers consultancy and training on a range of issues involving community activity. It launched a Community Investment Charter in Spring 1991 with the support of 85 leading companies, development agencies and TECs. CDF works with Charter signatories on neighbourhood regeneration and health and social care issues. It produces an annual report on key trends within the community and produces the signatories handbook which contains case studies of community investment programmes.

Local Enterprise Agencies

There are now over 300 local enterprise agencies all over the country which provide advice and training to small businesses and to people setting up in business. Some go further than this and get involved in community action schemes which bring the resources of the local business community to work in partnership with statutory agencies, whilst mobilising public and private sector resources to help this process. Enterprise agencies can be a useful source of financial advice and help with business planning and funding, although the quality of enterprise agencies will inevitably vary considerably from one agency to another. **Business in the Community** *(see above)* publishes a **Directory of Enterprise Agencies,** which gives the names, addresses and contacts of each agency plus a list of corporate supporters providing donations, secondments or in-kind help to the agency. A full list of the locations of enterprise agencies is given at the end of the article on Business in the Community.

4. Education

Confederation of British Industry

Centre Point, 103 New Oxford Street, London WC1A 1DU (071-379 7400)

Contact: Margaret Murray

The CBI promotes the involvement of companies in economic and social regeneration as well as encouraging industry links with education. It has published several reports on education and training in recent years. The first, in 1988, entitled "Building a stronger partnership between business and secondary education" set out employers' expectations of the education system, and promoted business/education partnership activities. The second, "Towards a skills revolution" published in 1989, has been influential with 28 of its 40 key recommendations having been implemented to date. These were followed by "World Class Targets" published in 1991 which sets out the targets which need to be achieved if Britain is to be competitive in world terms. It outlines the action plans of the supporting groups which include governments, national organisations, TECs and local enterprise agencies.

Council for Industry and Higher Education (CIHE)

100 Park Village East, London NW1 3SR (071-387 2171)

Contact: Patrick Coldstream, Director

CIHE is an independent body made up of the heads of major companies, universities, polytechnics and higher education colleges. It aims to promote partnership with higher education and represent their joint thinking to government.

• **Useful contacts**

Industrial Society

Quadrant Court, 49 Calthorpe Road, Edgbaston, Birmingham (021-454 6769)

Contact: Roger Opie, Head of Education Department

The Society seeks to build closer links between industry and schools, particularly by working with local education authorities. It runs courses and conferences and produces publications for charities.

5. Donations

Charities Aid Foundation

48 Pembury Road, Tonbridge, Kent TN9 2JD (0732-771333)

Director: Michael Brophy

The main function of CAF is to act as a vehicle for tax-effective giving by companies and individuals. Charity accounts can be opened to simplify and co-ordinate companies charitable giving. It is the largest agency operating a payroll giving scheme, **Give As You Earn**. A list of companies and other employers contracted with CAF to operate a **Give As You Earn** scheme at the workplace is available from the Payroll Officer of CAF at Foundation House, Coach and Horses Passage, Tunbridge Wells TN2 5TS (0892-512244).

CAF promotes company giving in a number of ways. It publishes an annual **Charity Trends** which lists the donations of the top 400 companies. It co-ordinates the **Council for Charitable Support**, a committee of senior business people committed to increasing the contribution of the business community to charity. The council has published an 8-page booklet on **Guidelines for Charitable Giving** outlining some of the reasons and ways in which companies might give.

CAF also publishes a monthly magazine **Charity** covering all aspects of charitable giving.

6. Promoting good practice

Business in the Community

227A City Road, London EC1V 1LX (071-253 3716)

Chief Executive: Julia Cleverdon
Executive Vice Chairman: Stephen O'Brien
Chief Executive of International Business in the Community: Robert Davies

Business in the Community aims to involve business and industry more widely with the economic, training, social and environmental needs of the local communities in which they operate and in society generally. It is supported by nearly 500 leading companies. Its members also include representatives of government departments, voluntary agencies and trade unions.

BitC is the coordinating body for the national network of enterprise agencies; it oversees the development of Business Leadership Teams, partnerships between local business leaders and public sector and community agencies; it coordinates the national and local Per Cent Clubs, which aim to encourage higher levels of community contributions by business; and it promotes various other initiatives including education business partnerships, environmental involvement and rural and urban community regeneration.

In Scotland there is the independent but associated **Scottish Business in the Community**: Romano House, 43 Station Road, Corstorphine, Edinburgh EH12 7AF (031-334 9876).
Director: John Moorhouse.

The Corporate Responsibility Group

Priory House, 8 Battersea Park Road, London SW8 4BG (071-498 3716)

Contact: Asifa Vanderman

The group comprises executives who administer corporate social responsibility programmes. It aims to promote best practice through workshops, seminars and the exchange of information, focusing on practical ways of managing corporate giving programmes effectively.

It has a membership of 30 leading companies: Allied Dunbar, Barclays Bank, British Gas, British Nuclear Fuels, British Petroleum Company, British Railways Board, British Telecom, Coopers & Lybrand Deloitte, Esso UK, Grand Metropolitan, IBM UK, Kellogg Co of Great Britain, Kingfisher, Lloyds Bank, Marks & Spencer, Midland Bank, National Westminster Bank, Nestle UK, Pearson, Philips Electronics & Associated Industries, Pilkington, Post Office, Prudential Corporation, Shell UK, W H Smith, SmithKline Beecham, Tesco, TSB Group, United Biscuits, Whitbread & Co.

Directory of Social Change

Radius Works, Back Lane, London NW3 1HL (071-435 8171)
Federation House, Hope Street, Liverpool L1 9BW (051-708 0117)

Directors: Michael Norton and Luke FitzHerbert

The Directory of Social Change is an independent charity which works to promote company giving in a variety of ways. It runs many courses for charities including how to raise money from industry, how to use the media and produces a range of publications *see Useful publications.*

EIRIS Services

504 Bondway Business Centre, 71 Bondway, London SW8 1SQ (071-735 1351)

Contact: Cathy Debenham, Marketing & Publications

To research company groups on the FTA All Share Index on a number of ethical and environmental criteria to enable investors and potential partners to make ethical decisions. Applicants fill in questionnaires and they are sent the relevant information or fact sheet. There is a charge for this service.

New Consumer

52 Elswick Road, Newcastle-upon-Tyne NE4 6JH (091-272 1148)

Director: Richard Adams

New Consumer is an independent, not-for-profit organisation mobilising consumer power for positive economic, social and environmental change. It publishes a quarterly magazine, **New Consumer**. It also published **Changing Corporate Values** in 1991, an analysis of Britain's biggest consumer companies from a social perspective and, in 1992, published **Britain's Best Employers?** looking at companies social and ethical background and **The Shareholders Action Handbook.**

The Per Cent Club

c/o Business in the Community, 227a City Road, London EC1V 1LX (071-253 3716)

Contact: Jeremy Lunn, Executive Director

The Per Cent Club is a group of more than 300 leading companies which have committed themselves to contribute at least a half per cent of their pre-tax profits to the community in cash and in-kind. A publicity pack on how the Club works

Useful contacts

and conditions for membership is available from Business in the Community, which provides the secretariat for the Club.

Regional Per Cent Clubs for locally based companies were launched in Sheffield in May 1989 and the North East of England in December 1989 and Scotland in 1991. These clubs share the same aims and objectives but are otherwise administratively separate from the Per Cent Club itself.

Sheffield: Don Valley House, Savile Street East, Sheffield S4 7UQ (0742- 765028)

North East: c/o Durham University Business School, Mill Hill Lane, Durham DH1 3LB (091-374 2246)

Scotland: c/o Scottish Business in the Community, Romano House, 43 Station Road, Corstorphine, Edinburgh EH12 7AF (031-334 9876).

Useful publications

The Directory of Social Change publishes a wide range of books on different aspects of company giving and other matters affecting charities. These can all be ordered from the Publications Department, The Directory of Social Change, Radius Works, Back Lane, London NW3 1HL (071-284 4364).

Please send payment with your order if possible. Cheques should be made payable to **The Directory of Social Change**. There is a postage and packing charge of £1.50 per order (**not** per book) and an additional handling charge of £1.00 for orders sent without payment.

Orders can also be made by fax (071-284 3445) or by Access, Visa, Mastercard and Eurocard (071-284 4364).

Grants guides

The Major Companies Guide
A detailed survey of the company giving policies of the leading 400 companies with information on each company's structure (including subsidiaries and principal locations), its directors, donations staff, donations policies, involvement in the arts, education, environment and community economic development programmes. It also gives information on application procedures and advice to applicants. *1991 edition, £14.95*

The Arts Funding Guide
The only comprehensive UK guide for arts fundraisers, covering over 180 trusts and 200 companies, details of funding from official sources, Europe, the US and trade unions. Also includes fundraising advice and case studies. *1992 edition, £14.95*

Environmental Grants
Information on sources of funds for environmental work. Includes charitable trusts, major companies, grant aid schemes by government departments and statutory agencies, and funding programmes run by environmental organisations themselves. *1993 edition, £14.95*

Also available:

A Guide to the Major Trusts
1993 edition, £14.95

The West Midlands Grants Guide
1991 edition, £9.95

The London Grants Guide
1992 edition, £12.50

The Educational Grants Directory
1992 edition, £14.95

A Guide to Grants for Individuals in Need
1992 edition, £14.95

Handbooks

Raising Money from Industry
A practical guide to successful fundraising from companies. It provides a background to company giving, its scale, why companies give support, how they make support available, the kinds of project or organisation companies prefer to support. It shows how to approach companies, gives advice on writing a better application letter and has case studies of individual companies' community involvement programmes. *1989 edition, £5.95*

The Corporate Donor's Handbook
A comprehensive guide to all aspects of a successful corporate community support programme with practical information, case studies and advice for the grant-maker on how to deal with applicants. It will also be of interest to grant-seekers as it gives a thorough insight into how companies devise their policies, what they are likely to be interested in, and how they manage this activity. Published with the support of a number of leading UK companies. *1991 edition, £12.50*

High Street Giving
A guide to the local giving policies of national companies with a presence in the "high street" including retailers, hotels, restaurants and other local outlets. *1990 edition, £7.95*

Community Award Schemes
A guide to award schemes and competitions mostly sponsored by business where the scheme involves projects or activities of community benefit. *1990 edition, £7.95*

Company Giving in Europe
A survey of company giving in 11 member states in the European Community with over 20 case studies. *1991 edition, £12.50*

Useful publications

Sponsorship

Finding Sponsors for Community Projects
All you need to know about getting sponsorship. It shows how to develop a sponsorship idea, how to cost it, how to sell it to a potential sponsor, how to develop a good working relationship with a sponsor, where to go for professional advice (if you need it). It is aimed particularly at smaller and local organisations seeking sponsorship support for the first time. It is published jointly with Friends of the Earth. *1990 edition, £7.95*

Social Sponsorship
An introductory 8-page leaflet to getting sponsorship for local community projects. Published in association with Action Match. *£0.95*

The Arts Sponsorship Handbook
A practical guide on every aspect of arts sponsorship. *1993 edition, £7.95*

Tax-effective company giving

Tax-effective Giving: A Practical Guide for Charities
A guide to covenants, payroll giving, single gifts, gifts of capital and in-kind giving. *Sixth edition, 1992, £9.95*

A Guide to Gift Aid
A comprehensive review of the Gift Aid scheme which enables single tax-deductible donations by Close Companies. It gives advice on how this scheme operates and how to use it to encourage support. *1992 edition, £7.95*

VAT: A Practical Guide for Charities
Everything you need to know about VAT, how it works, what reliefs are available and what problems you are likely to encounter. *1992 edition, £9.95*

Tax & Giving subscription service
A subscription service on all aspects of tax-effective giving which includes background briefings for charities, guidance notes for donors and sample documents and letters for obtaining donations. Subscribers receive updates covering any changes in the law and practice. *1992/93 subscription rate: £25 a year*

Fundraising generally

The Complete Fundraising Handbook
Everything you need to know about fundraising, from basic principles and sources of income to skills and techniques. *1992 edition, £9.95*

How to Write Better Fundraising Applications
A unique practical guide, with worked examples, exercises and guidance notes. *1992 edition, £9.95*

Organising Local Fundraising Events
A very practical guide to running a successful local event, from planning and publicity, through financial and legal issues, to what to do if things go wrong. *1993 edition, £7.95*

Other titles

In addition to the above, the Directory of Social Change supplied the following books as at Autumn 1992 (a full list of publications is available on request):

Grants guides & directories
HIV & AIDS: A Funding Guide @ £7.95
Voluntary Agencies Directory @ £10.95
Third World Directory @ £9.95

Fundraising
Corporate Citizen (see next page) @ £30/£55 a year
Raising Money from Trusts @ £7.95
Trust Monitor @ £20 a year
Fundraising for Your School @ £7.95
Researching Local Charities @ £3.95
Sell Space to Make Money @ £2.95
Business & Environmental Groups @ £9.95
Set of fundraising notes @ £7.50

Europe
US Foundation Support in Europe @ £12.50
Tax & Giving in Europe @ £5.95
VAT in Europe @ £4.95
Community Partnerships @ £12.95
Grants from Europe @ £7.95
Networking in Europe @ £10.95
Changing Europe @ £7.95
Meeting People's Needs in Germany @ £8.95

Charity contracts
Contracts in Practice @ £8.95
From Grants to Contracts @ £8.95
Quality of Service @ £8.95
Costing for Contracts @ £8.95
Purchase of Service @ £9.50
Contracts for Social Care @ £10.00
Quality & Contracts @ £12.75

Promotion & PR
Advertising by Charities @ £7.95
Charity Annual Reports @ £4.95
Charity Newsletters @ £9.95
Basic PR Guide @ £7.95
Design for Desktop Publishing @ £14.95
Marketing: A Guide for Charities @ £7.95

Finance & law
Charities: The New Law @ £19.95
Investment of Charity Funds @ £7.95
The Complete Trustee part 1 @ £7.95
A Practical Guide to Company Law @ £7.95
Charitable Status: A Practical Handbook @ £7.95
Accounting & Financial Management @ £7.95
Socially Responsible Investment @ £7.95

Action & research
Lobbying @ £9.95
Campaigning Handbook @ £9.95
Charitable Status of Schools @ £12.95
State Schools: A Suitable Case for Charity? @ £9.95
Funding Black Groups @ £6.95
Charity & NHS Reform @ £20/£40

Organisation & management
Charity Franchising @ £9.95
Voluntary but not Amateur @ £7.95
Just About Managing @ £10.95
Starting & Running a Voluntary Group @ £3.95
Getting Organised @ £5.95
Working Effectively @ £4.95
Planning Together @ £11.95

Corporate Citizen

Opportunities & challenges

More and more companies are widening their vision, seeing their role not just in business terms but in the context of the wider community. This presents opportunities and challenges for the voluntary sector. New and very different relationships are forming. As well as more direct financial support there are more partnerships, more commercial tie-ups, more secondments and more gifts in kind.

Developing insight

To ensure your organisation doesn't miss out you'll need to start looking at:

- What individual companies do and how they do it.
- What other areas of community involvement you could be in competition and co-operation with.
- How your organisation can benefit or suffer from any or all of these changes in the long term.

To develop a successful campaign which takes advantage of all aspects of corporate community involvement, it is essential not only to have all the relevant information at your fingertips but also to appreciate corporate needs and perspectives. You need to help companies look beyond their immediate business concerns to see the advantages of working with you.

CORPORATE CITIZEN is a new quarterly magazine, unique in its appeal to both corporate and voluntary sectors. In a mix of original research, guest reviews and opinions, and news, it covers:

Information

- Who are the top corporate donors in the UK?
- Who are their intermediaries?
- What are their priorities?
- Who benefits?
- What forms can community involvement take?
- What are the new initiatives?

On-going issues

- What issues does company involvement raise for charities?
- For the voluntary sector?
- For the communities themselves?

CORPORATE CITIZEN, through a problem page and regular feedback, offers a platform for debate and a problem-solving forum.

Strategic background

- How does community involvement fit in with overall company policy?
- Why do companies get involved?
- What community involvement trends can be identified?
- What's happening in Europe?
- In America?

Recent issues have examined the impact of employee volunteering and the potential of tapping into companies' communication strategies. Future issues are scheduled to look at community development, answering social need, education and training, as well as regional and local giving.

Corporate Citizen

Published in partnership with The Directory of Social Change.

Edited by Laura Irvine.

Published in January, April, July and October.

Available on subscription only from The Directory of Social Change, Radius Works, Back Lane, London NW3 1HL (071-284 4364).

Price: £55 for companies and statutory bodies; £30 for voluntary organisations. (Add £10 for overseas subscriptions; details of multiple subscriptions on request.)

Corporate Citizen *at the heart of company involvement in the community.*